MODERN HOSPITAL
INTERNATIONAL PLANNING PRACTICES

MODERN HOSPITAL

INTERNATIONAL PLANNING PRACTICES

ERVIN PÜTSEP

INTRODUCTION BY JOHN WEEKS

LLOYD-LUKE LTD 49 NEWMAN STREET LONDON

FIRST PUBLISHED 1979
SECOND PRINTING 1981

ISBN 0 85324 141 4
PRINTED IN SWEDEN

INTRODUCTION

In addition to the sheer size and complexity of its technical planning problems, hospital design presents architects with some contradictory design issues. The contradiction is one of scale — two different scales of perception by its users affect the design. A hospital really is like a house, with private and shared rooms. But while a hospital is a house, it is far too big to be understood in detail, by everyone in it; individuals relate more closely to their own working groups than to the hospital as a whole. The image of the whole hospital, shared by each group, is seen differently from different geographical starting points.

The architect has the task of designing a highly complex structure for a very complex organisation, but his design has to have sufficient clarity of form to be understood by all who use it. In addition, he has to design individual territories — the departments — for each of the groups whose successful interaction is the basis of the work of the hospital. Two different scales of perception are present throughout the building; the intimate, group based departmental environments, and the less intimate but no less important image of the whole.

A family house is small in scale. Every part of it, including the contents of the cupboards and the drawers, and the positions of the light switches are familiar to everyone in the family. Individual rights to privacy are understood without the need for territorial defence, yet everyone identifies with the whole. On the scale of a hospital the individuals in a family are replaced by groups and within the whole, the roles of groups are recognised. At the departmental level, the group territory, indeed the cupboards and the drawer contents will be known, yet the whole hospital is at the same time the house for all the groups and, although much more patchily, it also is familiar. One group, the patients, are twenty-four hour inhabitants. They have their own world with which they become completely familiar, recognising the nurses, noting the relationships between them, knowing which is the linen cupboard and where the medicines are kept. They know the difference between operating theatre and laboratory attendants and each patient knows exactly what is in his or her locker and where it is. But they may have little knowledge of the shape of the hospital as a whole, and only a very hazy impression of where their ward is in relation to where they entered the building.

It is of course the administrative corps of the hospital that has to take the lion's share of responsibility for making a community out of these different groups. However, the architect has a duty too. It is his task to design the complex so that it is possible for the two scales of identity to be realised in harmony, so that communications are eased rather than made difficult, and so that the place of individual group territories can be recognised within the whole. The image of the enormous house is one which is relevant to the architect's problem, and it is one to which reference should be made during the design process.

A solution to the resolution of these two scales of perception can be seen in the design — or non-design — of villages. A village is made up of different kinds of buildings, private houses, shops, public buildings, church, offices and places of public assembly; each one of these has an individual front door and a facade which is quite different from its neighbours, and thus every functioning element in a village has an identifiable presence. In the development and growth of a village many buildings will have followed natural market forces and changes in the social and demographic make-up of the village. However, despite the changes the shape of the village, based on the line of the High Street, is usually unchanged, and still, in order to find directions, reference is always made to the High Street. Even under the pressures of modern traffic it maintains its function as the main communication artery, and stamps the shape of the village in the minds of all who use it. No matter how frequently individual buildings in the village may change, the shape remains the same.

The different scales of perception which I have referred to as being present in the minds of the users of hospitals, are present in villages. While individual group territories are understood intimately, there is as well a shared perception of the whole. The perception of the whole binds a community together, and the presence of private territories does not interfere with the communal, shared image.

No matter how complex a hospital, its map must be easy to understand by all its users. If the major means of communication is used by everyone at some part of the day, giving access to the public areas — the restaurant, library, shops etc., as well as to the front doors of each of the departments, this will be a wonderfully useful reference, and the key, in everyone's mind, to the shape of the hospital.

But each separate department needs its own identity and within it, its own map, its own private and public spaces as well as its own front door. The hospital must be designed so as to allow the identity of the many 'families' which form its work force to be identifiable, physically, from inside the complex. Thus, it is better designed, not as a single block, in which the identity of the various parts are submerged in the mass of the whole, but a complex with separate parts, just as a village is constructed of separate, identifiable buildings.

This model has particular value in hospital design since a continuous process of change occurs throughout its life, which causes modification to be made to each of the individual departments. A village, with its separate buildings can absorb this process of change without destruction: A hospital needs to absorb change in the same way.

In a monolithic block change is difficult to absorb easily, indeed one department may only be expanded at the expense of another and communication paths become very complex. When the departments are separated many can be designed with an open end and can be extended as required, so that each department can be changed independantly. This reflects the reality of the hospital as an institution — it is not static, it is altering all the time.

Thus the physical form of the hospital will change over a period of time as it responds to internal and external forces and will acquire complexity as it ages. But these complexities are organic, that is to say they grow 'naturally'; they are not predictable by the architect.

In this shifting, changing situation, what is the design task for the architect? The importance of a simple street communication is clear. Around it, many changes will occur, but the street itself is the unchanging core and continues to be the reference point for all the people who use the hospital. It is the common key to the shared, communal map of the whole and it remains the main physical linkage between all the parts.

The architect must bring order to the process of change by designing the building round a binding centre; if the centre fails to bind, a chaotic environment will result and the image of the whole will disappear in the minds of the users of the hospital and the communal image will gradually disappear. Hospitals do not need, and cannot use a simple external form, but the internal communication map must be simple. The architect must design a street system, locate the front doors and allow the inhabitants of each of the departments to effect the changes required to serve changing functions without distorting the image of the whole.

Ervin Pütsep's book covers the design problems of hospitals more thoroughly, and with deeper insight than any other in the literature of hospital design now. To encompass the great depth of technical knowledge required for the design of hospitals, it is necessary also for architects to comprehend the real nature of their design problem. I suggest that the image of the enormous house, which I have attempted to develop in this introduction, is highly relevant, and may act as a focusing image. It enables the complexities of the technical requirements to be brought together invisibly into a whole concept which respects the fundamental requirement, to build a community. A hospital is not a factory, in which the assembly line dictates all aspects of the design but a community in which the interaction of individuals is fundamental to the successful working of the whole. A hospital is an enormous house.

22nd January 1979
John Weeks

PREFACE

The concern of hospital planning is the quality of medical care and the improvement of its standards. There is no place for perpetuation of the *status quo* as well as for astounding innovations.

Continuing advances in medicine and society impose great demands on the planning team. The planners must be aware of the ideology of the community. Attitudes and aspirations must be clearly understood. At the same time they have to be generalists with a good grounding in the basic disciplines of their specialization.

A sound general design can always be modified in detail: a perfect detail does not guarantee a perfect whole. Unless the basic nature of a problem is understood, there is a danger that time will be spent in obtaining knowledge of relatively unimportant details.

The role of the hospital architect and planner in an ever-more intricate interweaving of factors that form the framework of the society has become very complicated.

Although the planner cannot define all the problems in an increasing complexity of life, as one of the key generators of design information, he has to acquire wide knowledge of all aspects of the hospital — no doubt, an extremely complicated task — and convey facts to the administrative group responsible for decision making.

He also has to ensure that all the vital requirements are coordinated and integrated in the architectural end product.

It is important to point out that a design can be only as good as the experience and research upon which it has been based. There is no substitute for competence.

Today much is decided by many. Already Aristotle had observed that not necessarily nor inevitably, it is arrived at the truth by majority vote. True then. True now[1].

---

1 Herzog Raymond H: Management and Leadership. 1973, World Hospitals 9:141-142.

The need of spreading information on planning issues in wide circles is bigger than ever before. There should be no overdesigned, in excess built hospitals only because there is no understanding what makes a design optimal.

In several countries the author has consulted surgeons, anaesthesiologists, radiologists, planners, bacteriologists and other learned sources, all of them distinguished for their work. Their help has been valuable.

The assistance of Enno Abel, Gothenburg, Peep Algvere, Stockholm, Jon Gjessing, Sundsvall, Peter Heimann, Bergen, Gunnar Högberg, Stockholm, Jan Kjellander, Örebro, K A Klannemark, Ronnebyhamn, Argo Kõvamees, Torbjörn Lundman, Stockholm, Sten Meurling, Sundsvall, Tiit Rähn and Ingemar Sjölander, Stockholm, Herbert Sunzel, Varberg, Allan Tamm, Boden, Jan Thorp, Stockholm and particularly of Gunnar Laurell, Uppsala, Bo Norberg, Jaan Novek, Bertil Nyström, Ilmar Sulg and Per Erik Wiklund, Stockholm, has been of extreme importance.

I am indebted to the reviewers of my earlier books, particularly to William C Beck, William W Mushin and Carl W Walter.

Ernest Hemingway has said: There are some things which cannot be learned quickly, and time, which is all we have, must be paid heavily for their acquiring. They are the very simplest things, and because it takes a man's life to know them, the little new that each man gets from life is very costly and the only heritage he has to leave.

After several decades in the field of hospital planning, one has to agree.

15th January 1979

Ervin Pütsep

ELEMENTS OF HOSPITAL PLANNING

An efficient hospital requires a well-balanced organization for compassionate care within an adequate technical and environmental framework. This basis has remained vital throughout the centuries, although patterns of diagnostics and care have changed.

The wide public has maintained a very trustful and uncomplicated view on hospitals, which sometimes are seen as secular cathedrals that display the wonders of science and inspire awe in their believers or as modern shrines at — or in — which proper obeisance to technology will result in miraculous cures[1]. However, some have denounced the hospital as an unnatural environment that makes iatrogenic complications inevitable.

Health care fifty years hence cannot be visualized, but it will certainly be delivered also in facilities planned now. Tomorrow is born out of today.

For serious planners and designers already a medium-sized hospital is a very demanding task as the range of its complex functions and interests — medical, administrative, social, technical, cultural — in dynamic reciprocal reliance is great.*

The humans interact with three quite distinct worlds: world 1 — the ordinary physical world, world 2 — the mental world, and world 3 — the world of actual or possible objects of thought, the world of concepts, ideas, theories, arguments, and explanations. The world 3 undergoes a slow, secular evolutionary change[2]. This change is gradual, directional, and integrative in the sense that it builds anew upon whatever level may have been achieved beforehand[3]. In the field of hospital planning all the three worlds are clearly felt. There are many complications. The planning of a period is defined by the limits of the knowledge attained by that period.

The hospital as a whole works under the control of two distinct boundary systems: the higher one is the hospital organization, which harnesses the lower one, which in itself consists in several levels of functions and functional procedures on which the success of the hospital depends.

---

1   Twaddle Andrew C and Hessler Richard M: A sociology of health. The C V Mosby Company. St Louis 1977, p 234.

*   The complexity of a larger hospital could in a way be compared with the Fourth Symphony by America's greatest composer, the ancestor of avant-garde music Charles Ives (1874—1954).
    It takes an immense orchestra to perform this in 1916 composed work, supplemented by a brass band, a greatly expanded percussion section, and a chorus. So vast are the forces and so complicated is the musical texture that three conductors are needed for the performance. There is one section where twenty-seven different rhythms are played simultaneously (Ewen David: Composers of Tomorrow's Music. Dodd, Mead & Company. New York 1971, p 19).

2   Popper Karl: Objective Knowledge — an Evolutionary Approach. Clarendon Press. Oxford 1972.

3   Medawar Sir Peter: Technology and Evolution. in Technology and the Frontiers of Knowledge. Doubleday & Company Inc. Garden City New York 1975, p 106.

These boundary conditions recognize the hospital forming a *de facto* hierarchy. Each level is relying for its workings on the level above it*.

It has become increasingly difficult to weigh all the problems of the hierarchic system of a hospital in order to amalgamate these and other disciplines as a basis for the creating of a balanced threedimensional anticipatory form to be constructed at minimal cost and to please the general public.

Total project cost considerations are planning, financing, construction, and equipment. The equipment costs alone account for 25 to 30 per cent of the total. Proper equipment planning and selection are essential.

Planning ought to be thinking in the probable terms of tomorrow, but it is frequently thinking in the terms of to-day, if not in the terms of yesterday. Planning involves and requires understanding and evaluation of the current cultural mainstreams, the economic and technological conditions, and the goals of the community.

Frequently, the hospital planning process concentrates on the designing of buildings and their architectural appearance and devotes inadequate attention to the planning of organizations and equipment as well as accommodating them and generating spaces to meet policies. The long-term cost of operating a hospital can be greatly increased by the initial failure to plan proper systems and equipment.

The objectives should be fully understood. The implications of the planning ideas, data and designs, when they progress from the idea to a staffed and maintained hospital should be predictable[4].

---

* Michael Polonyi (Life's Irreducible Structure. 1968, Science 160:1308–1312) has illustrated the structure of such a hierarchy by showing the way how five levels make up a spoken literary composition.

The principles of each level operate under the control of the next-higher level. The voice is shaped into words by a vocabulary; a given vocabulary is shaped into sentences in accordance with a grammar; and the sentences are fitted into a style, which in turn is made to convey the ideas of the composition.

Each level is subject to dual control: control in accordance with the laws that apply to its elements in themselves, and control in accordance with the laws of the powers that control the comprehensive entity formed by these elements.

The principles governing the isolated particulars of a lower level leave indeterminate conditions to be controlled by a higher principle.

Voice production leaves largely open the combination of sounds into words, which is controlled by a vocabulary.

A vocabulary leaves largely open the combination of words to form sentences, which is controlled by grammar, and so on.

Consequently, the operations of a higher level cannot be accounted for by the laws governing its particulars on the next-lower level. A vocabulary cannot be derived from phonetics; a grammar from a vocabulary. A correct use of grammar does not account for good style; and a good style does not supply the content of a piece of prose.

4 see also Moss Raymond: The Planning Team & Planning Organization Machinery. Medical Architecture Research Unit. The Polytechnic of North London. Stencil. December 1975, p 24.

The pure passion to innovate can be hazardous if the hospital as a total philosophical and operational entity is poorly understood. Some of the fundamental humanitarian aspects may be neglected for technical innovations or even fads.

The perpetuation of some fallacies of planning which have often been the cause of poor hospital design, should likewise be avoided. Particularly the unmotivated belief in the inevitability of rapid obsolescence is a frequent cause of elaborate and costly adaptable buildings[5].

Readiness for immediate adaptability as a counterweight to early obsolescence is part of the philosophy of desirable perpetual contemporaneity with three built-in varables: time, place and content*.

A hospital emerges in three interdependent processes: analysis-planning-programming, designing, and construction.

Basically, the functions will be separated into two groups: those which can be defined with reasonable accuracy and those which remain relatively indeterminate and open to change[6]. Maximum efficiency should be sought for every precise function. For functions which cannot be pinned down, the design has to be anticipatory.

The procedure of analysis is becoming increasingly complex as the priorated and dominating aspects shift and alter.

The known depths of all involved factors have to be viewed at from a proper angle simultaneously and synthetically. The concurrent requirements of complex systems have to be assembled and balanced. This would be easier to achieve if the available information is broken down into manageable elements for analysis and regrouping. This technique cannot be separated from interpretation.

The opposite of the synthetic planning approach is the monoparametric planning mode, in which out of the complex field of problems one aspect haphazardly rises or is deliberately chosen and then is given dominance. The past fifty years have been a truly golden age of planning based on one or a few priorited elements, a circumstance that has lead mostly to disappointing results.

---

5   see also Briggs F R: Common fallacies of functional planning. 1974, Hospital Progress 55:2:90–95.

*   This problem has been ingeniously solved in music by John Cage in his composition for piano 4′ 33″. The pianist is directed to produce no sounds and to make any environmental sound to become the content of the performance (see also Roger Sutherland: John Cage and Indeterminancy. 1971, London Magazine 11:3:55–63). The basic philosophical approach of 4′ 33″ is akin to the thinking behind the glass houses of Mies van der Rohe, which reflect their environment (see also Hoogerwerf Frank W: Cage contra Stravinsky, or delineating the aleatory aesthetic. 1977, international review of the aesthetics and sociology of music 7:235–247).

6   Shadrach Woods cited by Erenurm Vello: Tidsberoende problemlösning och strukturalistisk metod. Stencil, Stockholm 1972, p 50.

The process for analysis and planning, which has to withstand competent public scrutiny, moves usually through four distinct stages without signalling abrupt changes[7].

A direct limited-structure search, constrained by the policy intentions starts the process. To secure a good facility, during the initial period of planning the main medical, ecologic, managerial, economic, social, demographic, and technological factors and possibilities have to be identified.

Planners and programmers must also take into account the forces that have developed and continue to shape the existing arrangements for the provision of health care.

The available technology can to a very large degree be speeded or slowed according to social and cultural demands of a situation or an era. Technologies can be created to satisfy recognized demands, but they can also be ignored or allowed to lie idle for years[8].

The basic decisions to be taken concern the character, the size and the siting of the hospital as well as the degree of the hospital's adaptability to future developments. In the whole chain of decisions during the hospital generation process errors up to 100 per cent can be found in the initial political or administrative statements and early declarative building programmes*.

The programme is a major document leading to design. It should include the facts, intentions, and assumptions about the organization stated so clearly that a facility can be drawn from it. E g a functional programme for a laboratory would include in narrative form what is proposed to be done in the space to be designed, the identi-

---

7   see also Beller Ronald E and White Jr Lowell E: Long-Range Planning for a Department of Surgery: A System Analysis Approach. 1972, Journal of Medical Education 47:855–861.

8   see also Kira Alexander: The Bathroom. The Viking Press. New York 1976, p 5.

*   During discussions on basic guidelines and early stages of the design, it has happened that thoughts have wandered to the Cheshire-Puss and Alice in Wonderland as well as to Mullah Nasrudin as judge.

   'Cheshire-Puss' she began, rather timidly . . .
   'Would you tell me, please, which way I ought to go from here?'
   'That depends a good deal on where you want to go to', said the Cat.
   'I don't much care where —' said Alice.
   'Then it doesn't matter which way you go', said the Cat.

Carroll Lewis: Alice's Adventures in Wonderland. Macmillan. London, Melbourne, Toronto. St. Martin's Press. New York 1968, p 81.

   Nasrudin was made a judge and listened to his first case.
   When the prosecution rested its argument, he stood up and said: 'I believe you are right!'
   When the defense had finished its summation, Nasrudin again stood up and said: 'I believe you are right!'
   The clerk of the court came in front of the judge: 'Your honour, they cannot both be right!'
   'I believe you are right!' said Nasrudin.

Shah Idries: The Sufles. Doubleday. New York 1971, p 67.

fication of all laboratory divisions and their descriptions as well as the list of each division's procedures and their number on monthly or annual basis. Personnel should be tabulated. Special techniques and other unusual circumstances should be pointed out.

One of the most essential duties of the hospital programmer is to dress the hierarchy of the requirements, necessities and solutions[9].

Other purposes of a functional programme can be comprehended[10]. It could be used to clarify terminology, common understanding, and agreement among the parties involved, being at the same time a device for group interaction and negotiation. In representing a concensus, the programme may serve political purposes.

The programme is a reference to original intent for years to come, when original staff change their minds or new personnel without commitment to earlier decisions appear.

The programme is an instrument to determine the staffing levels for selection of equipment and thus may serve as a means for organization of capital and labour. Attention has been drawn to the non-use of the time dimension in determining the amount of space allocated. Policies for the programmed use of spaces by the same or a variety of users are relatively undeveloped[11].

The programme could also be used as a reference manual for the implementation of a project and the orientation of employees.

The value of a brief should not be measured by its wealth of details, or by its precision, but mainly by how well the strategic lines along which the hospital can be designed are specified[12].

A collection of detailed data by no means guarantees a well functioning hospital.

It is always undesirable to make an effort to increase precision for its own sake, since this usually leads to loss of clarity. One should never try to be more precise than the problem demands[13]. A meaningful incompleteness must be maintained. The complexity of this aspect is mostly underestimated.

Programming should be heuristic, indicating directions and not algorithmic, mathematically precise.

9 also Aurousseau Paul at the IV UIA International Public Health Seminar. Prague. October 1972.

10 Selbst Paul L at the Conference on Health Facility Planning and Design in the Developing countries. The World Trade Institute New York. December 1975.

11 Moss Raymond: Boundless scope in space . . . 1978, Health and Social Service Journal 88:348–349.

12 see also Borup Axel: Hospital design today — Hospital design tomorrow. The National Health Service of Denmark. Copenhagen 1975, p 51.

13 Popper Karl: Unended Quest. Fontana/Collins. Glasgow 1976, p 24.

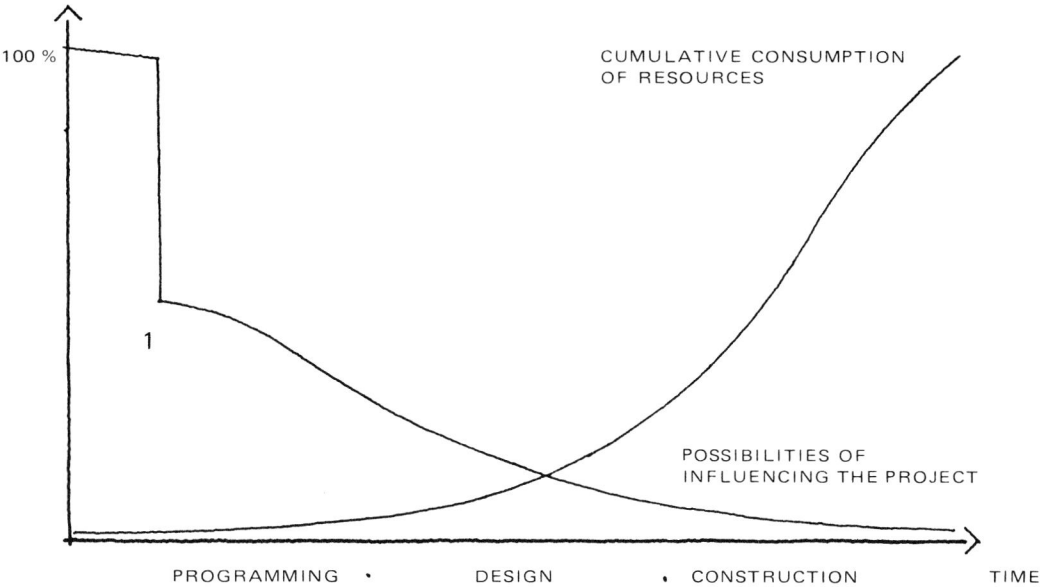

100 %

CUMULATIVE CONSUMPTION
OF RESOURCES

1

POSSIBILITIES OF
INFLUENCING THE PROJECT

PROGRAMMING · DESIGN · CONSTRUCTION TIME

The possibility to influence a project and its cost is reduced during the course of its development after the client has decided to establish the requirements of the user and started to investigate the problems. The largest reduction of possibilities to influence the design occurs at point 1, which marks the client's decision concerning implementation. The figure is based on a study by Stig Nordquist.

In a good and dynamic functional programme the criteria for the physical design and the qualitative requirements on the medical standard and other standards should represent a *range* of realistic variables, the assignment of priorities, and the phase mode if such is a value.

To involve variables in a hospital programme is difficult because frequently a precise and detailed description on the proposed hospital is required for the approval of funds.

Via subsequent approach to departmental endeavours in the second stage the object system is defined.

The third stage is for analyzing the scope of departmental operations. The final phase consists of an explicit description of the hospital at a chosen point in time.

27

As the primary purpose of hospitals is to take care of patients, the care needs of patients should directly dictate the character of every care function throughout the hospital. Otherwise, the mechanics become an end in themselves. Departmental, environmental, or organizational needs may siphon off the resources and energy to the detriment of the patient.

The complexity of the hospitals makes them differentiated, highly specialized. This very differentiation gives rise to the need for making a smoothly functioning whole of these specialized components. The hospital system cannot remain viable if the needs of the patients — the only rational reason for the existence of a hospital — do not serve as the basis for integration[15].

15 see also Kraegel Janet M, Mousseau Virginia Schmidt, Goldsmith Charles, Arora Rajeev: Patient Care Systems. J B Lippincott Company. Philadelphia, Toronto 1974, p 212.

SOME ASPECTS OF HEALTH CARE

Operative health care

Health is a social value. This is reflected in provision of services, which need to consider ethical and philosophical issues as well as medical-scientific and medical-behavioural issues[1].

In the realm of medicine controversies arise between individual and society, man and technique. At the same time medicine shows paradigmatically and vicariously the possibility of overcoming the drastic signs of the gulf between these spheres[2].

In the most general terms the practice of medicine could be defined as the utilization of clinical and experimental observations and acquired knowledge within the framework of a health philosophy and in the combat of disease.

At the risk of over-simplification the four major health problem groups are: handicapped by congenial defects or pre-natal damage; handicapped as a result of trauma; people with major degenerative diseases, such as coronary and cerebrovascular disease, degenerative conditions of the locomotor system, and malignant disease; people with chronic and disabling psycho-social illnesses.

These make an increasingly heavy claim on resources and are contrastad by other acute health problem groups which are extremely difficult to judge, define and measure in precise terms*.

The goal of medical research work has been to diminish diseases and enrich life, but it has produced tools which prolong diseased, diminished lives. The proportion of people who have a disabling or chronic disease has increased.

There is an unintended but major effect of many technical improvements stemming from health research and progress in health technology. The increasingly common chronic conditions represent the failures of success. The techniques used to-day to improve life expectation perpetuate sick lives more than they do to healthy lives[3].

Population screening diagnostic categories have been too vague and too subjective to permit clear distinction of the treatable and the abnormal from the very wide range of so called normal variations[4].

---

1   Williamson John D: Healthward Care. 1977, Social science & medicine 11:187–190.

2   Stoffels Hans: The Problem of Objectivity in Medicine: The Epistemological Position of Viktor von Weizsäcker's Anthropological Medicine. 1975, the human context 7:517–529.

*   E g high rate of appendectomy in Japan is believed to be secondary to the fee-for-service system in the medical insurance programmes, which often leads to unnecessary treatments (Yoshida Yoichi and Yoshida Katsumi: The High Rate of Appendectomy in Japan, 1976, Medical Care 14:950-957).

3   see also Gruenberg Ernest M: The Failures of Success. 1977, Milbank Memorial Fund Quarterly/Health and Society 55:3–24.

4   Miller Henry: Medicine and Society. Oxford University Press. London 1973, p 38.

Every disease entity has its own pathogenetic chain. Understanding this chain for a particular disease reveals the weak links that might be exploited for prevention or therapy. A technology to be fully effective needs to abolish only one link out of many, provided that the chosen link is sufficiently important to the pathogenetic process. In a multifactorial event, individual factors are by no means of equal weight. A disease with a strong social linkage can be completely controlled by a technology without change in the social factors to which it is linked[5].

Many writers assume that diseases of multifactorial origin cannot be cured by a specific technology unless the multifactors, or at least a number of them, are appropriately controlled. This is simply not the case[6].

There is no evidence that the origin of various diseases of heart and blood vessels and of cancer, about which so little is known, is any more multifactorial or environmentally induced than the microbial diseases which are under control[7].

There are major differences between the sexes in morbidity and mortality rates. At all ages males have higher death rates and are more frequently afflicted with the chronic diseases associated with considerable reductions in longevity. Trend data indicate that males have become relatively more disadvantaged during a period characterized by major advances in medicine and increased access to care[8].

In contrast: in all countries for which data are available, women report more acute illness than men and make greater use of health services. Total rates of hospitalization are higher for women than for men, even when these rates are age-standardized and exclude obstetrical conditions. Women are larger consumers of medicines than men, both in Great Britain and in the United States[9].

In the absence of information concerning the relative contribution of biological, psychological, and social processes to reported disease rates, it is difficult to know whether research in the area of sex differences should focus primarily on illness itself, on illness behaviour, or on the behaviour of medical practicioners[10].

According to *David Mechanic* * women seem to report many more subjective symptoms than men. Also, much of the excess chronic illness reported by women is in part a reflection of how they define and respond to illness and to their life situations.

---

5   McDermott Walsh: Medicine: the public good and one's own. 1978, Perspectives in Biology and Medicine 21:167–187.

6   ibid

7   ibid

8   Lewis Charles E and Lewis Mary Ann: The potential impact of sexual equality on health. 1977, The New England Journal of Medicine 297:863–869.

9   Nathanson Constance A: Sex, illness, and medical care. 1977, Social Science & Medicine 11:13–25.

10 ibid

*   Sex, illness behavior, and the use of health services. 1978, Social Science & Medicine 12:207–214.

It has been stated[11], that if the development is towards a nonsexist society, it would be better to seek increased opportunities for women in occupation, business and commercial affairs, and a reduction in the morbidity and mortality of men. Perhaps this proposal evades the fundamental question: What is the better measure of equality — for women to die like men, or for men to live (a little bit) like women?

Different patients have different needs, and different physicians have different methods of treating their patients. It is very strongly emphasized that this freedom of method choice must be preserved[12].

The charismatic authority of the doctor can constitute treatment in itself. Understanding between doctor and patient — that singularly personal relationship involving a complex mixture of the communications of often unfamiliar facts, emotions, hopes, fears and taboos — is continually confused by lay misconceptions, none of which may be declared, but many nevertheless deeply felt[13].

The key problem of medicine has been and is to establish firm scientific understanding. Advances in medicine have derived from basic discoveries in physics, chemistry and biology, which have been extended by application to specific problems.

There have been profound changes in medical science since World War II. Medicine of the recent decades has been faced with rapid emergence of biophysics, bioengineering and biomathematics and the integration of the skills of the biologist and the engineer*. The application of energy sources such as ultrasonics, laser light beam, radioactive energy and heat-sensitive crystals, is reflected in the automatic sampling and analysis of body fluids, monitoring for critical care, artificial organs, prosthetic devices, physical therapies and computer technology[14].

However, a graph depicting, as a function of time, the exponential increase in the number of scientific papers, journals of original publications, review articles, and thematic monographs paralleled by another depicting the rate of discovery of significant remedies that should be implemented immediately would not show such a rapidly rising curve[15].

The current technology of medicine is divided according to achievement into three groups: the low technology consisting of essentially supportive therapy; the halfway technology of the makeshifts employed to help a patient compensate for the inca-

11 Lewis Charles E and Lewis Mary Ann: The potential impact of sexual equality on health. 1977, The New England Journal of Medicine 297:863–869.

12 see also Crowe John K: Scanning and Planning. 1977, Mayo Clinic Proceedings 52:399–400.

13 Margaret Turner-Warwick in The Times, June 25, 1975.

* In the United States only some 5,000 companies with a gross annual product of $ 1,600,000,000 have been involved in biomedical engineering.

14 see also Technology and Health Care. 1976, The Medical Journal of Australia 1:376–377.

15 see also Meyer Thomas C: 1975, Bulletin of the New York Academy of Medicine 51:720.

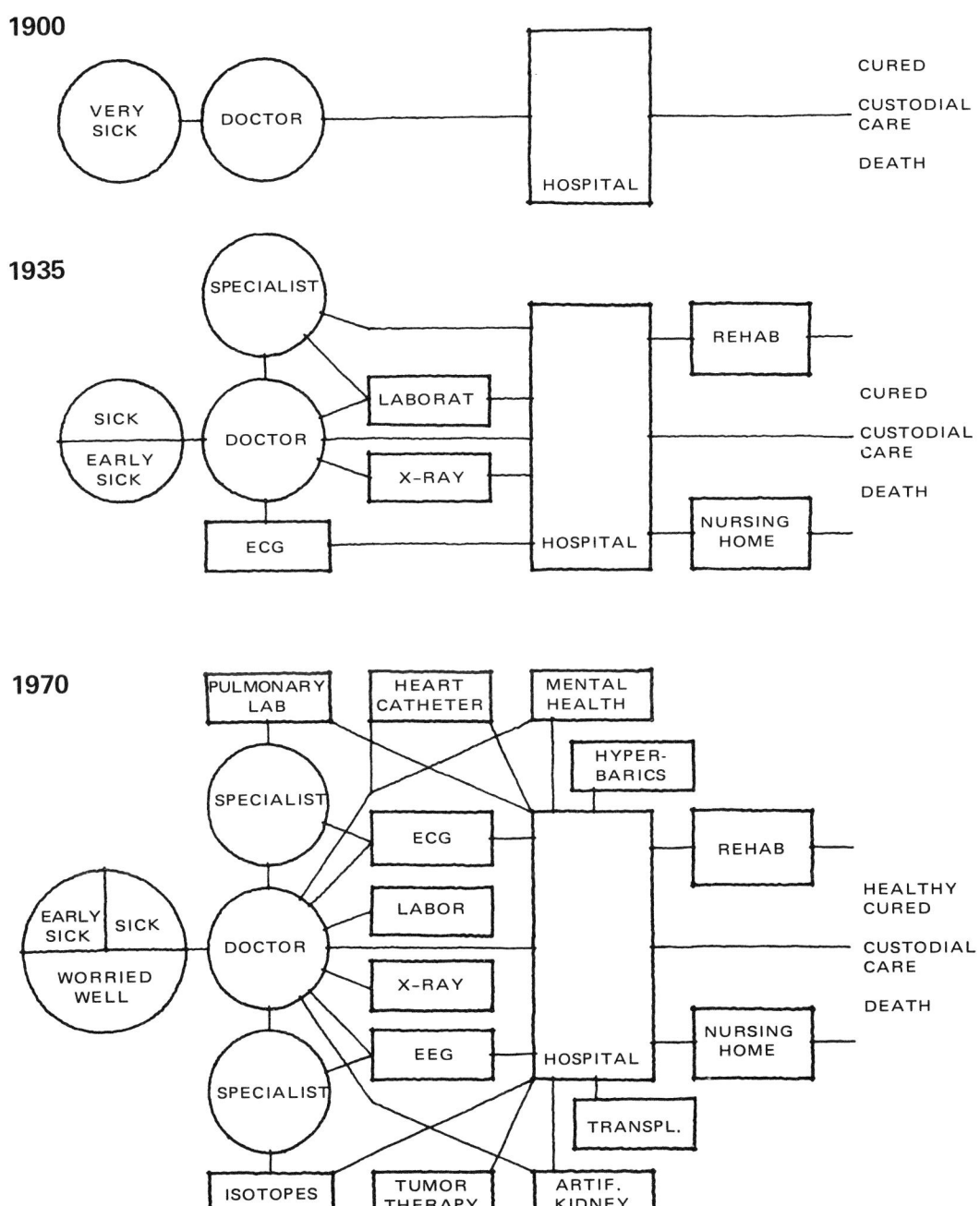

1900

1935

1970

This century medical care has become complex. The changes since World War II have been profound as the figures based on Sidney R Garfield's study The delivery of medical care (1970, Scientific American 222:4:15) indicate.

pacitating effects of incurable diseases; and the high technology including immuniza-
tions, the anti-infective agents, and hormones and vitamins for patients who lack
them; and some curative surgical procedures[16]. When properly performed, for the
right reasons and at the right time, surgery ranks as the uppermost echelon of effectiveness in medicine[17].

Complexity and a high degree of technical mechanization have often been mistaken
for qualitative superiority*, or even for symbols of the whole of medicine[18]. To iden-
ify technical development with medical development is as wrong as to identify building technology with architecture.

Many physicians feel that modern equipment is an obstacle in the communication
between them and the patient but also between them and the staff.

It is becoming increasingly apparent that modern medicine, with its emphasis on
technology and specialization, is threatening to dehumanize hospital care. In view of
this it is appropriate to consider *J Douglas Wright's* acronymical observation about
today's hospitals that SAVE — Science, Administration, Value, Efficiency — is taking
over from CARE — Compassion, Art, Reliability, Emphathy[19].

Increased specialization in hospitals has led to a form of alienation from the broader
aims of the health service: staff often regard themselves as workers on a mass-produc-
tion line. The automated organization has become the main driving force, directing
and controlling human beings instead of being controlled by them. Seventy-six per
cent of contacts between staff and patients last less than 30 seconds, and are of a
routine technical nature[20]. Hospital care must be rehumanized, as it was in the old
charity hospitals. Any factor which prevents ward staff engaging themselves in depth
with their patients must be removed.

Concern for the care of the human being as a whole in the hospital needs contribution of all the human sciences.

---

16 Thomas L: The technology of medicine. 1971, The New England Journal of Medicine 285:1366–1368.

17 Davies Hywel: Modern Medicine. Abelard. London. 1977, p 11.

* It is not quite unjustified to remind us of the little prince's meeting with the merchant.
  This was the merchant who sold pills that had been invented to quench thirst. "You need only swallow one
  pill a week, and you would feel no need of anything to drink".
  "Why are you selling those?" asked the little prince.
  "Because they save a tremendous amount of time", said the merchant.
  "Computations have been made by experts. With these pills, you save fifty-three minutes in every week".
  "And what do I do with those fifty-three minutes?"
  "Anything you like . . ."
  "As for me", said the little prince to himself, "if I had fifty-three minutes to spend as I liked, I should walk
  at my leisure towards a spring of fresh water."
  de Saint-Exupery Antoine: The little prince. Penguin Books. Middlesex. England 1971, p 86.

18 see also Thomas Lewis: The Technologies of Medicine. 1972, The Yale Journal of Biology & Medicine
   45:2:III–VIII.

19 cited by Sweetser Frank Loel: The Outsiders. 1977, The Guthrie Bulletin 46:135–140.

20 Gustafsson Rolf Å: Sjukhusets psykosociala arbetsmiljö: rutinmässiga tekniska moment hotar trivsel och
   vårdsamspel. 1977, Landstingens Tidskrift 64:10:33–34.

The medical need is a matter of judgement and not an absolute state. There is also a distinction between medical needs and wants. Today's wants may be the needs of tomorrow. The dividing line between physical fitness and medical need can be moved considerably.

Public opinion also can or even has to be led away in some situations from demand of health care.

The traditional distinct boundaries between health care and sick care as well as those between somatic and psychiatric care are less obvious than ever before the majority of people deviates from the norms which currently define health and normality[1]. Insomnia, worry and anxiety have become recognized medical problems.

Patients generally desire convenient access to immediate, considerate, and knowledgeable medical care, which should also be comprehensive, co-ordinated and continuous. They prefer that minimal bureaucracy, and the least number of people, either professional or nonprofessional, are interposed between themselves and their physicians[2].

In a particular country or an area three kinds of organized health and hospital care could be envisaged: what is theoretically possible, what is desired and planned, and what is currently achieved*. They have to be identified and established for the whole population or for some section thereof, selected for particular reasons.

The availability of medical personnel and economic resources has to be analyzed to make an efficient medical and social service possible. Trained personnel, material resources, and all other forms and measures of help to the sick and injured should be coordinated, so that the assistance could be delivered rapidly and competently.

The planning of any segment of the health service system should be determined by and shaped around the life patterns and value systems of the population to be served[3].

In the acute health care there are three co-ordinated health care elements: attention and care given by general practitioners on out-patient basis; attention and care given

1   see also v Nussbaum Henrich: Wer hier nicht krank wird, darf als trotzig gelten. in Die verordnete Krankheit. ed by Henrich v Nussbaum. S Fischer Verlag. Frankfurt (Main) 1977, p 15.

2   see also Ranney Brooks: Shadows or light? 1976, American Journal of Obstetrics and Gynecology 125:283–289.

*   Peter Safar has prepared (for developing nations) a seven grade health care list: 1 sanitation, inoculations, infectious disease prevention, 2 birth control to maintain zero population growth, 3 alleviation of pain and suffering, including anaesthesia for operative procedures, 4 emergency care, including transportation, life-saving operations and safe emergency anaesthesia, 5 primary medical care, 6 speciality care, 7 sophisticated intensive care (Safar Peter: Health Care Delivery Problems and Goals: A Personal Philosophic Appraisal. in Public Health Aspects of Critical Care Medicine and Anesthesiology. ed by Peter Safar, F A Davis Company. Philadelphia 1974, p 2–32).

3   also de Beer Johan: Brief review of changes in health policy, especially in the light of the Health Act of 1977. Second Southern African Hospital Symposium. Pretoria. November 1977.

by specialists on out-patient basis; and attention and care given by specialists on in-patient basis. In the care of chronic cases a fourth element is added: attention and care given by general practitioners on in-patient basis.

Currently there is an enthusiasm for the renaissance of primary care. It lies partly in the expectation that a widening of that sector will decrease utilization of other, more expensive sectors. The anticipated saving might be more a supposition than a fact[4].

At any rate a considerable amount of health care could be provided with heavier use of paraprofessionals. An in itself lower medical care level may need assistance from very advanced technology as in the case of some vaccinations.

Objective criteria are needed for establishing each patient's diagnosis and the status of his condition when he enters the health care system.

Although it is preferred every patient to have a single diagnosis, this is a restricted view of what disease is humanly about. *Lawson* has shown that the elderly average five to six diagnoses per person, and *Thomas C Meyer* that between 20 and 50 per cent of the patients of the doctors whose practices he studied could be categorized under no pathological entity or nosologic syndrome[5].

Every citizen should be able to enter the health care system within reasonable time at any time and, with the certainty that the appropriate level of care for him is available. This is not always the case.

In the sixties in the southern part of the German Federal Republic, 89.05 per cent of the patients needed only the treatment by general practitioners[6]. 9.34 per cent needed specialist treatment and only 1.61 per cent had to be hospitalized.

When the medical needs of out-patients were studied in Gothenburg, Sweden[7], in 1969, the percentage of general list cases was 49, specialist cases 48 and super-specialist cases 3.

In 1973 in the Netherlands about 76 per cent of the patients could have been treated by the general practitioners*, about 21 per cent by specialists as out-patients, and about 2 per cent had to be hospitalized[8].

In Estonia 10 to 20 per cent of those seeking medical advice of general practitioner were not qualified for a consultation[9].

The sickness certification 1975 among two mining or industrial practices centred on villages in Yorkshire, United Kingdom, indicates the following grading of certificates: medically essential,

4   see also Kane Robert L: Primary care: contradictions and questions. 1977, The New England Journal of Medicine 296: 1410–1411.

5   Freymann John Gordon: Medical audit. 1975, Bulletin of the New York Academy of Medicine 51:748.

6   Siegfried Häussler cited by Krüsi G: Sinnvolle Hospitalisation aus der Sicht des praktischen Arztes. in Krankenhausprobleme der Gegenwart. vol 7. ed by E Haefliger and V Elsasser. Verlag Hans Huber. Bern, Stuttgart, Wien 1974, p 161.

7   Modell för driftsplanering inom den öppna öron-, näs- och halssjukvården i Göteborg. Spri Rapport 11/72. Stockholm 1972, p 5.

*   in Sweden, 1972, the percentage was estimated to be from 38 to 46.

8   Festen H at the 8. internationales Krankenhaussymposion. TU Berlin. February 1976.

9   Ilmoja Vello: Polikliiniku registratuuri töö korraldus. 1977, Nõukogude Eesti Tervishoid 20:51–53.

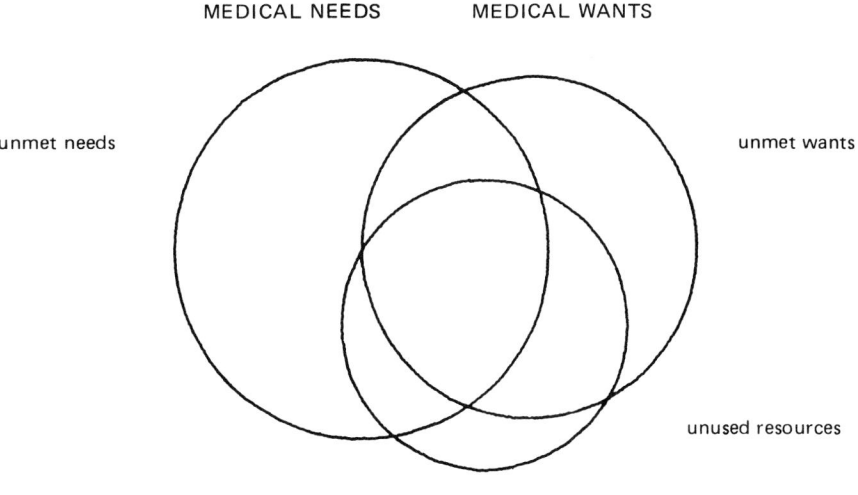

MEDICAL NEEDS   MEDICAL WANTS

unmet needs

unmet wants

unused resources

MEDICAL RESOURCES

Usually the medical resources are smaller than the medical wants, which in their turn are smaller than genuine medical needs. In Sweden 1974 it was assumed, that of the total population 34 per cent are healthy, and 25 per cent have their needs and wants met. 27 per cent of the population have unmet wants and needs.

medically desirable, socially reasonable, more expected than clinically justified, frankly injusti-fiable[10]. Almost all the sickness certificates issued by these general practitioners could be divided into a half that was medically essential and a half that was medically desirable. Only four per cent were thought to be reasonable on social more than on medical grounds, only one per cent gave the doctor cause for concern, and again only one per cent were thought by the doctor to be really unjustifiable[11].

Outside the groupings who seek primary care are the patient who take care of themselves without medical staff assistance. They may represent as many as 60 per cent of all sicknesses[12].

When needs for medical and social services of the age group 19 to 65 years in Sweden were investigated, it was found that 39 per cent of the population had met needs for medical services and 43 per cent had unmet needs[13].

---

10 Wilkes Eric: The trouble with patients. 1976, The Journal of The Royal College of General Practicioners 26:873–878.

11 ibid

12 Hall Paul in 1975, Läkartidningen 72:4367.

13 Bygren Lars Olov: Met and Unmet Needs for Medical and Social Services. The Almqvist & Wicksell Periodical Company. Stockholm 1974, p 111.

The hospitals should invariably be designed in support of the needs of the health centres and other units rendering primary health care at the peripheral level, and *not vice versa*[14].

The hospital with its specialized facilities and staff has to limit itself to the functions that cannot be performed elsewhere, channeling a number of functions to a closely associated, carefully planned, less expensive satellite facility network and not to divert scarce and costly resources to uses for which they are not needed.

Hospitalization ought to be reserved to the greatest extent for patients whose conditions require highly qualified staff and complicated apparatus, whereby the quality levels of hospitals and other health care facilities have to be made distinct. There is no need to provide all hospitals with a lavish technical equipment. *Virtuoso* medicine ought to be performed only in the facilities of the medical care top echelon.

In the effort to assign the patient to a service area according to the extent of care required, six elements have been introduced: critical care, inter-mediate care, self-care, long term care, house care, and outpatient care.

Although experiments in this line carried out in England and the US have been worthwhile, it is difficult to analyse how successful they were in terms of patient care as there is no exact unit of measurement that could be applied[15].

The in-patient care has at least three broad levels: critical or intensive, intermediate and minimal. E g in England and Wales in 1968 1 per cent of the patients received intensive care. 72 per cent intermediate care, and 27 per cent minimal care[16].

At least 10 per cent of the patient days have been judged inappropriate at a hospital level of care. This percentage may under some circumstances be considerably higher.

Anywhere between 10 and 30 per cent of US hospitalized patients may currently be in the wrong place. They could be in a nursing home, or receiving home care, but are hospitalized either because there is no alternative available or because the hospital is willing to keep them to help keep up the occupancy rate or because their insurance will cover them in the hospital but not elsewhere[17].

---

14 also de Beer Johan: Brief review of changes in health policy, especially in the light of the Health Act of 1977. Second Southern African Hospital Symposium. Pretoria. November 1977.

15 Walker W F: Current concepts of intensive care. in Intensive care. ed by W F Walker and D E M Taylor. Churchill Livingstone. Edinburgh, London & New York 1975, p 7.

16 Biddulph Constance at the 8. internationales Krankenhaussymposion. T U Berlin. February 1976.

17 see also Allen Rex Whitaker and von Károly Ilona: Hospital Planning Handbook. A Wiley-Interscience Publication. New York, London, Sydney, Toronto 1976, p 82.

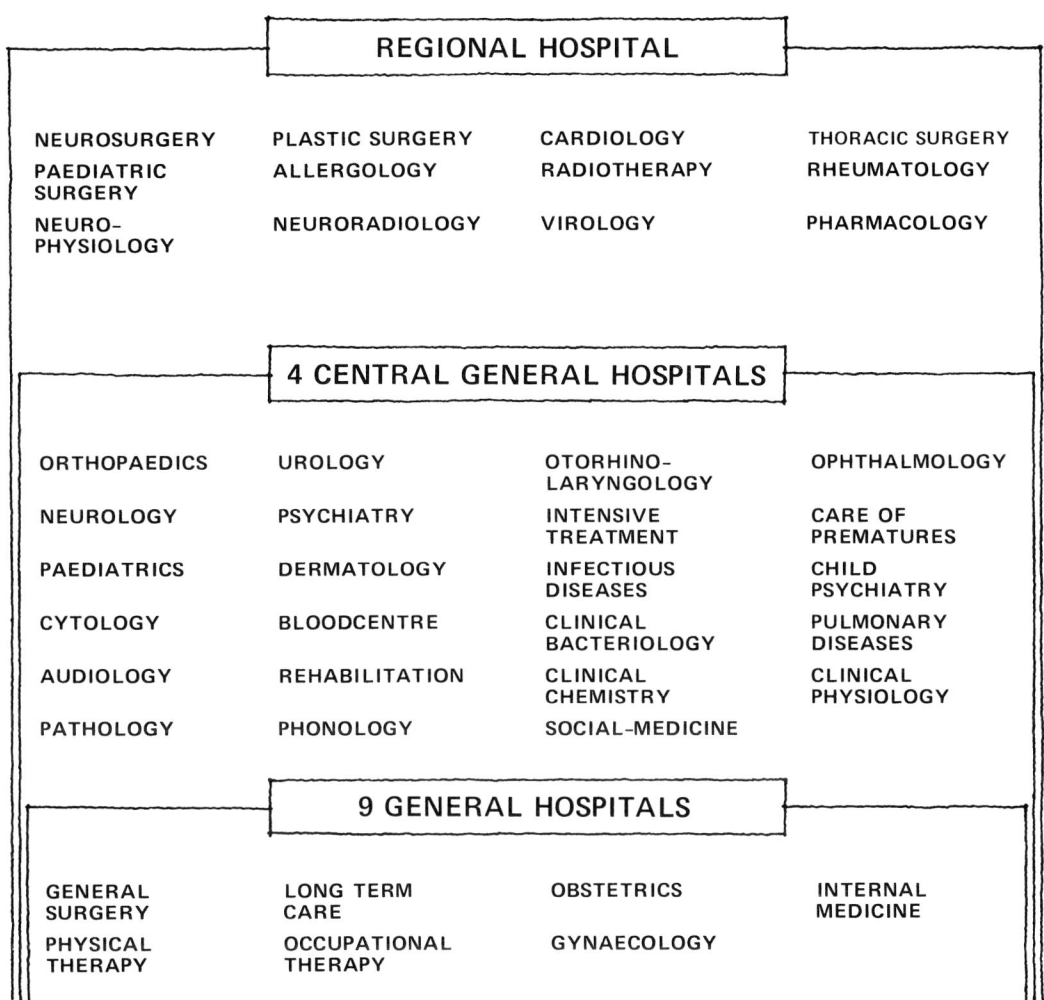

In Sweden, regional hospitals offer the most specialized care with more than 30 specialities.
Each county has at least one central general hospital, with 15 to 20 specialities, and a number
of general hospitals.

Nursing homes have their own care level categorizations*.

From the view-point of critical care, four categories of hospitals have been described.
Category 4 hospitals do not provide intensive care at all, category 3 hospitals provide

---

* In one Swedish county in 1977, 22 per cent of the nursing home patients were occupying beds on a wrong
level (Gefle Dagblad, November 12, 1977).

intensive nursing care, category 2 hospitals basic intensive medical care, and category 1 hospitals advanced intensive medical care[18].

A development to be expected is a regrouping within the system of clinical departments. The current specialities might give way to programme-orientated clinics such as a musculoskeletal clinic including orthopaedics and rheumatology or a clinic for human growth and development including obstetrics and gyneacology and paediatric

Some others visualize a changed system with 32 organ areas, still others five main organ blocks, including 20 specialities. E g the head-neck block would include seven units: brain, eye, ear, nose and nasal cavities, jaw, mouth and throat with the exception of spine, and dental[19].

Specialist hospitals promote high standards. The fact that the staff deal only with a small range of disease leads to their developing special skills.

The differentiation of health care demands that respect for knowledge and recognition of abilities of more outstanding colleagues has to be reinstated.

Many physicians believe that if they cannot manage a patient well with their own five senses and available equipment no one else can. Yet they will readily admit that there are superior and master pianists, figure-skaters, singers, dancers, composers and artists. They readily accept the fact that these people are trained to render masterful performances and productions, whereas others remain amateurs. But, they will not accept the fact that this is also true in their own specialities[20].

The categorization and differentiation of hospitals on the availability of medical expertise and proper use of facilities, will most likely become a major health care planning feature.

18 Safar Peter, Benson Don M, Esposito Gerald, Grenvik Åke and Sands Patricia A: Emergency and Critical Care Medicine: Local Implementation of National Recommendations. in Public Health Aspects of Critical Care Medicine and Anesthesiology. ed by Peter Safar. F A Davis Company. Philadelphia 1974, p 103.

19 Hackethal Julius: Nachoperation. Verlag Fritz Molden. Vienna, Munich, Zurich, Innsbruck 1977, p 209.

20 see also Burch George E: Technocrats or doctors? 1977, American Heart Journal 94:1–2.

Economics of health

Long immune from serious outside looks, medicine now has extramural critics by the score, who join forces or dispute with those medically trained, trying to convince the public that with increased medical costs increasing benefits in terms of health have not come.

The economics of health remain a nonsatisfactorily investigated field. The conquest of most of the acute and chronic infections in the industrialized world has left medicine preoccupied with diseases of multiple aetiology and long duration.

Each new advance in technology represents an increased cost in prolonging life for a relatively small number of patients and for relatively short periods[1].

Some costly developments* have created horrenduous problems of coping with life that will never retain functional viability, but will involve complex and agonizing decisions for health professionals and the families of patients. Reduction of mortality from degenerative disorders to less than 5 per cent is associated with a massive and perhaps unaffordable increase in hospital care cost[2].

In the past physicians could explicitly ignore the costs of what they did. This is one major reason why medical care costs so much[3].

Information on cost-effectiveness and cost benefit of medical care is scanty and unreliable[4]. The ultimate qualitative results of surgical or medical treatment do not lend themselves to easy quantification. Usually studies rely on effortlessly measured parameters, such as length of stay in hospital.

Optimum investment is always expected to result in optimum achievement. In the health care the cost raise for the quality increase is at the beginning low. Later, each degree of quality increase requires considerably growing costs. At the same time, the real value of increased quality rises rapidly at the beginning, but after having reached the point of balance further quality raises add little, if anything, to the use value.

To make a medico-technical or administrative reform or change meaningful, an evaluation-system must be at hand before any revision is put into operation. The operational evaluation of a change should be continuous.

---

1   see also Technology and Health care. 1976, The Medical Journal of Australia 1:376–377.

*   Survivors who have severely damaged central nervous systems may cost society as much as US $ 1 million per lifetime (Safar Peter and Grenvik Åke: Organization and Physician Education in Critical Care Medicine. 1977, The Journal of Anesthesiology 47:82-95).

2   Laver Myron B: A Time to Measure. 1976, The Journal of Anesthesiology 45:114-116.

3   see also Neuhauser D: Cost Effective Clinical Decision Making: Are Routine Pediatric Preoperative Chest X-rays worth it? 1978, annales de radiologie médecine nucléaire 21:80–83.

4   see also Miller Henry: Medicine and Society. Oxford University Press. London 1973, p 21.

In the health care cost and benefit ratio should be implied with afterthought. Cost benefit studies cannot be used as substitutes for clinical judgment[5].

The real benefits of quality improvements cannot be disregarded or discouraged only to stem rising costs. Neither can technology be withheld because it benefits too small a percentage of patients. However, expensive medical innovations should be adopted in larger scale only when justified after adequate studies.

There is also a humanitarian approach. A level of care and cure should be achieved that is appropriate for what is considered the existing level of civilization.

Hospital cost containment is not a panacea in the battle against the rising costs of medical care. Even if it were thoroughly successful, hospital cost containment would only address the inflation problem in one component of the medical care sector. Medical inflationary pressures might continue unabated outside of hospitals. Indeed, there is considerable concern that hospital cost containment will transfer inflation problems — and technology — to non-hospital settings, conceivably exacerbating overall inflation and making containment of costs within hospitals a Pyrrhic victory. In addition, of course, is the real possibility that a programme of hospital cost containment will not work[6].

5   see also Vayda Eugene: When Is Surgery Indicated? 1977, Milbank Memorial Fund Quarterly/Health and Society 55:495–504.

6   Warner Kenneth E: Effects of Hospital Cost Containment on the Development and Use of Medical Technology. 1978, Milbank Memorial Fund Quarterly/Health and Society 56:187–211.

Health and medical care cost

Although disease is a universal phenomenon, man's ills vary with his ethnic background, geographic location, causation, time, severity and outcome. Consequently, the build-up, character, management, use and cost of health care facilities varies from country to country, and even regionwise.

The human and economic conditions in the about 150 states of the world community are grossly inequite. Some 90 of them accounting for close to 60 per cent of the world's population, have an annual *per capita* income under US $ 500. 25 states accounting for 8 per cent of the world's population, have annual incomes of over US $ 500. 15 states — about 16 per cent of the world's population — have annual incomes of US $ 1,500. 15 states — approximately 13 per cent of the world's population — have *per capita* annual incomes over US $ 2,500. Only 5 states — 6 per cent of the world's total population — have *per capita* incomes of over US $ 5,000 per year.

Of the 65 primitive and developing countries for which data are available, in 17 countries governments make health outlays that are less than US $ 1 *per capita.* The average outlays for the very poor countries with a *per capita* income under US $ 100 is only 82 cents[2]. The average rises to US $ 1.42 for countries with *per capita* incomes between US $ 101 and 200 and to US $ 2.85 for countries where the *per capita* income is between US $ 201 and 300[3].

The labour-intensive operations of hospitals have for some time produced considerable cost increases. Health services have become one of the biggest employers. In most countries health care staffs are not less than 4 per cent of the working population[4]. The diffusion of technology in the health care system, and particularly in hospitals, is recognized as a primary element fueling the medical cost spiral[5].

Scientific and technical progress has not made old treatments cheaper, but rather developed a range of new diagnostic methods and treatments. More expenditures are directed towards the few, selected not so much by social class or wealth but by medical technology itself. This evolution is world-wide rather than peculiarly national[6].

Widening of the base of availability of medicine has not resulted in lowering of the peak or flattening of the health expenditure pyramid. The peak is still rising higher.

1   Brzezinski Zbigniew: Towards a new international order. 1976, Lugano Review LR 6:1–6.

2   Health. Sector Policy Paper. World Bank Headquarters. Washington DC, 1975, p 32.

3   Health. Sector Policy Paper. World Bank Headquarters. Washington DC, 1975, p 32.

4   Chester T E: Health Care in a Changing World. 1977, World Hospitals 13:91–93.

5   Iglehart John K: The Cost and Regulation of Medical Technology: Future Policy Directions. 1977, Milbank Memorial Fund Quarterly/Health and Society 55:25–59.

6   see also Mahler H: Health — a demystification of medical technology. 1975, The Lancet 2:829–833. Holman Halsted R: The 'Excellence' Deception in Medicine. 1976, Hospital Practice 11:4:11, 18, 21.

Between 1950 and 1974 the *per capita* expenditures in the United States and in the United Kingdom on all health services increased by 500 per cent or fivefold. In Sweden the increase was fully 2,500 per cent or 25 fold*.

The rapid increase of the share of health and medical care of the gross national product has become a major concern in many countries, as no amount of research appears capable of reducing health care cost[7].

In the North American macro-economy medicine is as big as agriculture. In the US its total outlay had increased in the fiscal year 1976 to 8.64 per cent of the gross national product[8]. In the Netherlands it was even higher — 8.9 per cent[9].

In Finland this share is about 8 per cent[10], in Canada 7.3 per cent[11], in Australia 6.8 per cent[12] and in the United Kingdom 6 per cent[13]. In Sweden the health care cost may increase to more than 10 per cent of Gross National Product[14].

Also in industrially developing countries, where a considerably smaller portion of the GNP — e g 1.4 per cent in Algeria, 1.7 per cent in Kenya and 2.5 per cent in Malaysia[15] — is spent on medical care, the costs are on the rise.

Every western country is facing the prospect of an ever-increasing share of its national wealth being spent on medical care. At present health planners are pinning their faith on increased emphasis on prevention: but a healthier population will still develo its illness, even if they are postponed for ten years or more.

An unanswered question is whether society can continue to attempt to provide the best that medicine can offer to the whole population. As more and more medical problems are found to have expensive solutions, spending may be forced to increase towards 10 per cent and even 20 per cent of the nation's wealth or some form of rationing by price, by age or some other criteria or merit has to be introduced**.

Is the share of cost for health care from cradle to grave basically unjust or unfair? In Sweden, as an example, to run the hospitals a year costs as much as the Swedes

* Anderson Odin W: The model health service — a search for Utopia. 1978, Nordisk Medicin 93:163–168.

7 see also Laver Myron B: A Time to Measure. 1976, The Journal of Anesthesiology 45:114-116.

8 Iglehart John K: The Cost and Regulation of Medical Technology: Future Policy Directions. 1977, Milbank Memorial Fund Quarterly/Health and Society 55:25–59.

9 1977, Krankenhaus Umschau 46:299.

10 Maurer H J and Soila P: Future of diagnostic radiology. 1975, Annals of Clinical Research 7:295–300.

11 Godber Sir George: An open-ended commitment. in The Health Care Cost Explosion: Which Way Now? ed by David Alan Ehrlich. Hans Huber Publishers. Bern, Stuttgart, Vienna 1975, p 1.

12 Kronborg Royce at the 20th International Hospital Congress. Tokyo. May 1977.

13 The Times, January 31, 1977.

14 Rexed Bror: How Sweden plans for the 1980s. in The Health Care Cost Explosion: Which Way Now? ed by David Alan Ehrlich. Hans Huber Publishers. Bern, Stuttgart, Vienna 1975, p 75.

15 Health. Sector Policy Paper. World Bank Headquarters. Washington DC 1975, p 74.

** Tony Smith in The Times, September 8, 1978.

spend on chocolate, alcohol and tobacco and the total health care cost equals with the combined expenditures for alcohol and soft drinks, chocolate and pastries, tobacco and cigarettes[16]. In the US the amount of money put into medical care is not even half of what is spent on booze, tobacco and entertainment[17].

The cost rise has been considerable, but a French study shows that the cost rise for tombstones, toys, cars, grammophone records, perfumes, TV sets, fruit juices and domestic fuel — just to mention a few items — has been much higher[18].

16 Reizenstein Peter and Bengmark Stig: Patienten i sjukvårdsorganisationen. Esselte Studium. Stockholm 1974, p 28.

17 Del Guerico Louis R M: Triage in cold blood. 1977, Critical Care Medicine 5:167–169.

18 Rosch Georges in The Health Care Cost Explosion: Which Way Now? ed by David Alan Ehrlich. Hans Huber Publishers. Bern, Stuttgart, Vienna 1975, p 199.

Doubt about some practices operative in health care

The mode of practice in acute medical situations has evolved slowly out of administrative and professional convenience. The current practices seem not to be the theoretically best possible as they rely on the standards which were valid and probably theoretically good or best at the time, when the majority of the now practising physicians received their basic professional training.

The health professions are notoriously conservative* and it would be odd if they were not so[1]. Also the responses to changes in population and morbidity have usually been slow and slight. Mostly these changes are limited to *disjointed increments* — small changes primarily within the existing structure[2].

Although the scope of contemporary medicine is immense, few accept the fact that the number of true cures available today, in spite of great advances in medical sciences, is very limited, although there are many treatments[3]. We remain very ignorant about some of the commonest symptoms, such as pain, fatigue, anorexia, obesity, weight loss, dyspnoea, cough and sputum, constipation and diarrhoea[4].

It is thought that currently only about a tenth is known about how the body works in comparison to that what will be known in a hundred years' time[5].

The accelerating rate at which the number of scientific workers is being doubled may well have nothing to do with the qualitative scientific development. The history of medical development is replete with examples of techniques, procedures, or medications that were theoretically attractive or anecdotally effective but, when subjected to carefully controlled study, showed to be ineffective or potentially dangerous[6]. Many studies of the practice of medicine have not been without its critics. Much of the criticism has been justified, much not[7].

Doubt about some of the current basic principles and models operative in health care is increasing. The public has shown awareness, concern and sophistication about

---

*   Already Sir Astley Cooper (1768—1841), surgeon to George IV, stated: If you are too fond of new remedies, first, you will not cure your patients; secondly, you will have no patients to cure.

1   see also Godber Sir George: An open-ended commitment. in The Health Care Cost Explosion: Which Way Now? ed by David Alan Ehrlich. Hans Huber Publishers. Bern, Stuttgart, Vienna 1975, p 3.

2   see also Bennett A E and Holland W W: Rational planning or muddling through? 1977, The Lancet 1:464–466

3   see also Sodick D H: Revascularization of the heart: Numerators in search of denominators. 1971, American Heart Journal 81:149–157.

    Morowitz Harold J: The Merck of Time. 1976, Hospital Practice 11:12:107–108.

    v Nussbaum Henrich: Wer hier nicht krank wird, darf als trotzig gelten. in Die verordnete Krankheit. ed by Henrich v Nussbaum. S Fischer Verlag. Frankfurt (Main) 1977, p 18.

4   Campbell E J M: Clinical science. in Research and Medical Practice: their interaction. Elsevier-Excerpta Medica-North-Holland. Amsterdam, Oxford, New York 1976, p 48.

5   Vane J R: The Place of Fundamental Research in the Discovery of New Drugs. 1977, Triangle 16:119–122.

6   see also Dixon Richard Erwin: The role of airborne bacteria in theatre-acquired surgical wound infection. 1973, Cleveland Clinic Quarterly 40:115–124.

7   Davis Hywel: Modern Medicine. Abelard. London 1977, p X.

Levels of progressiveness displayed by different physicians, as seen by Robert H Williams (To Live and To Die. When, Why, and How. ed. by R H Williams. Springer–Verlag 1973, p 183).

Top character represents smallest proportion of individuals, who, after carefully studying past developments, extrapolate probable course of future events. Second character gets less clear picture of future because of insufficient study of past. Third character has desire but not ability to visualize the future. Fourth subject represents largest proportion — those who are not sufficiently interested in past or future. Bottom subject dwells in patterns of past and not only fails to contribute to progress but also often actively opposes it.

the possibiliteis in modern health care of suboptimization. The public starts to realize the facts of hospital infection, the high percentage of mistakes in drug distribution to inpatients, the amount of normal tissue removed through surgery, the variance in accuracy of X-ray information or laboratory results used in diagnostic and therapeutic decision, the variance in outcomes for given diseases[8]. Poor quality of care is gradually being perceived as a constant threat.

Improving cultural standards have meant increasing scepticism towards the science of medicine[9]. Higher-education groups — at least in the US — tend to have many

8   see also Blanpain J E: Characteristics of the modern health service and hospital: a challenge for information systems. 1976, Acta Hospitalia 16:183–191.

9   see also Elštein Natan in 1975, Nõukogude Eesti Tervishoid 18:357.

fewer operations, a result consistent with previous findings of a strong positive relation between health and education[10].

Numerous medical innovations are presumedly beneficial, quite literally, on the otherwise repugnant basis of *res ipsa loquitur.* The clear logic of the concept simply justifies its use. Such innovations often do not lend themselves to prospective scientific analysis, blinded or otherwise[11].

Little of the current medical practice has ever been subjected to the rigorous testing all new pharmaceuticals get.

E g the coronary bypass procedure has been permitted to come to the public and become a billion-dollar industry without a proper protocol and with little if any hint of licensure, certification, restriction or restraint upon it. It has been done in institutions where there is no possibility for the accumulation of significant data about the procedure. As a result, the current opinions about bypass are based, after ten years, on only a fraction of the data which could be available[12]. In the absence of rigorous investigation another expensive procedure may be prematurely accepted only to be proven ineffective later[13].

Drawing on evidence presented in the assessment of surgical innovations *Weinstein, Pliskin,* and *Stason* remind that about half of the innovations considered were less satisfactory than existing treatments. It cannot be predicted, *ex ante*, in which instances experimental or control groups will fare better[14].

Every year considerable numbers of ineffective, sometimes harmful and dangerous substances and devices reach the market and eventually the unsuspecting public not only wastes money on useless products but may also expose itself to serious injury or additional health problems[15].

Many serious practices lack any firm foundation in scientific understanding[16]. The frequent lack of correlation between antemortem and postmortem diagnoses has been continuously and dramatically stressed by autopsy studies*.

---

10 Bombardier Claire, Fuchs Victor R, Lillard Lee A and Warner Kenneth E: Socioeconomic factors affecting the utilization of surgical operations. 1977, The New England Journal of Medicine 297:699–705.

11 Polk Jr Hiram C, Trunkey Donald and Curreri P William: Better Definition of the Usefulness of Burn Units. 1977, Journal of Surgical Research 23:6–7.

12 Rodgers David L: Bypass, Boeing and Billions. 1977, The Western Journal of Medicine 126:410–411.

13 Vayda Eugene: When Is Surgery Indicated? 1977, Milbank Memorial Fund Quarterly/Health and Society 55:495–504.

14 ibid

15 Brosseau B L P: Weeding out the charlatan. 1977, Dimensions in Health Service 54:8:6.

16 see also Cooper Michael H: Rationing health. 1974, New Society 28:602:131–132.
Kornberg Arthur: Research, the lifeline of medicine. 1976, The New England Journal of Medicine 294:1212–1216.
also Stolte J B at the 8. internationales Krankenhaussymposion. TU Berlin, February 1976.

* E g Richard Cabot, in 1912, analyzed 3,000 autopsies at Massachusetts General Hospital to determine clinical errors. A quarter of a century later, Dr. Edward Gall, at the same institution, found the same percentage of errors in 1,000 cases and, more recently, at the Cincinnati General Hospital, analyzing another 1,000 cases, discovered the same sizable percentage of error: more than 40 per cent (Prutting John: Autopsies — Benefits for Clinicians. 1978, American Journal of Clinical Pathology 69:2 (suppl):223–225.

There are procedures in vogue that are not well founded and represent unsubstantiated impressions and beliefs carried down through the years from textbook in scissor and glue pot fashion and from one practitioner to another[17].

The complications of modern medical treatment certainly loom large in textbooks of therapeutics, and occupy a sizeable fraction of beds in any medical ward[18].

Obviously it is not always easy to avoid falling victim of a medical fashion. On the other hand, there is a risk of paralysis when the scientists — also in medicine — are asked — there is already a strong tendency — to guarantee that nothing, anywhere, ever, will go wrong[19].

When all difficulties and complications are set against the progress particularly made during the last generations* in the ability to care for the sick, to understand the natural and man-made phenomena that produce disease and, the extraordinary benefits to the patients — relief of pain, disablement, and distress — they can be regarded only as an inevitable nuisance.

One of the reasons why it has been so difficult to see the effects of the medical successes of our time, is the suffering from an ailment of modern technological man, his fragmented specialization[20].

The views of the planners are necessarily negativistic as they have to emphasize how far short are the hospital and medical care goals rather extolling the considerable progress made in the recent times[21].

---

17 see also Hey E: Resuscitation at birth. 1977, British Journal of Anaesthesia 49:25–33.

18 Miller Henry: Medicine and Society. Oxford University Press. London 1973, p 6.

19 see also Culliton Barbara J: Science, Society and the Press. 1977, The New England Journal of Medicine 296:1450–1453.

* Until relatively recently the major impact of the physician was that of his person rather than of his medications.
   In 1770 general practice knew little besides the plague and the pox. In 1860 the ordinary citizen recognized the medical names of only a dozen diseases.
   In 1930 there was not much treatment to have any faith in: only insulin for the diabetic, liver for the anaemic and digitalis for the cardiac. X-rays were ghostly and the electrocardiograph a delicate toy. The doctor used mostly his own eyes, hands and ears.

20 see also Gruenberg Ernst M: The Failures of Success. 1977, Milbank Memorial Fund Quarterly/Health and Society 55:3–24.

21 see also Donabedian Avedis: Measuring and evaluating hospital and medical care. 1976, Bulletin of the New York Academy of Medicine 52:51–59.

Medical expectations

The pattern of science and consequently of medicine is a stepwise extension of what came before[1].

Some of the optimism of the great utopists of the renaissance period is still evident in the medical expectations and health care facility planning*.

There are evident expectations by many that medicine can improve also the quality of life — which stripped of its trappings emerges as a deeply personal matter — and that this goal is related somehow to access to a high quality of health care. But it is by no means clear just what is meant by quality of life or just how medicine and health care can bring about its improvement[2].

The experience of medical expectations and prognoses has up to now been of a very modest order as there are thousands of ways of being wrong for each opportunity of being correct[3].

Consequences of some developments have not always been immediately understood. E g already by 1940 it could have been predicted that some chronic diseases and disabilities would become more common because there were better techniques for thwarting killers which had been weeding out the chronically ill[4].

There have been rapid developments in medical sectors which were hardly mentioned in prognoses or even wholly neglected. This has particularly been the case with the medico-technical development**.

In surgery the prognoses have frequently been too optimistic.

---

1   see also Kornberg Arthur: Research, the lifeline of medicine. 1976, The New England Journal of Medicine 294:1212–1216.

*   Sir Thomas More (1478–1535) indicated in his Utopia, Book 2, that special care will be taken of the sick, who are looked after in public hospitals. These hospitals are so spaciously laid out as to be comparable to as many small towns. The intent of this design is twofold: first, that the sick, however variable their number, should never be crowded so close together as to cause discomfort and inconvenience; and second, that those who have a contagious disease may be isolated from the rest in order to prevent the spread of infection. These hospitals are very well appointed and equipped with everything conductive to health. Besides, such diligent treatment and constant attendance of expert physicians are given that, though no one is sent there against his will, hardly anybody in the whole city, when suffering from illness, would not rather be nursed there than at home.

Tommaso Campanella (1568–1639) believed in his La città del sole or Civitas solis that the citizens of the one future time sun state would live up to hundred or two hundred years as a result of a continuous control by the physicians.

2   Watts Malcolm S M: Medicine and the quality of life — A report of a forum. 1977, The Western Journal of Medicine 126:499–504.

3   see also Biörck Gunnar: Medicinska utvecklingslinjer och framtidens sjukvårdsorganisation. 1953, Svenska Läkartidningen 49:1057–1071.

Om tio år . . . 1965, Läkartidningen 62:21–31.

Framtiden devalverad? 1972, Läkartidningen 69:2033–2043.

4   see also Gruenberg Ernest M: The Failures of Success. 1977, Milbank Memorial Fund Quarterly/Health and Society 55:3–24.

**   Also the conspicious practical success of some major technological developments like radar and jet propulsion seem to have come almost unexpectedly.

Scientific endeavour has been focused on small areas of growth as new techniques are exploited, while those fields in which research was considered unprofitable have been neglected[5]. Incongruous, unlinked facts have tended to be excluded or underrated.

Quite often discoveries have been the result of serendiptious observations in disparate disciplines, seemingly unrelated or made by bright, independent, non-goal-oriented people[6].

It seems improbable, with the single exception of selfpoisoning, that the present pattern of illness can be so moulded in the immediate future as to reduce the number of acute admissions. In the long term patient education can be effective in diminishing demand[7].

The expectations of scientific experts with regard to technological progress have been reduced considerably over the last few years. The scientific base has become more static. Radical new ideas have tended to bog down in big-company or governmental bureaucracy[8]. Technical breakthroughts thought to be almost accomplished in early seventies have been delayed by 5 to 20 years[9].

The rate of development of scientific and technological advances necessitating added equipment and specialized personnel in medical performance areas has decelerated. One of the reasons is that a significant portion of one or two generations of young US investigators was not engaged in the biological arts, a circumstance called a tragedy of dimensions that may never be fully appreciated[10].

This decline is contrasted by the need to develop areas of study outside the traditional paths of the scientific and engineering disciplines[11] and to continue research in biomedical science and medical services, which will not be met by any means during the next decades.

Probably for some time the technological advances in all fields will be dominated by the refinements of already made discoveries and innovations and fewer devices will be developed and enter the marketplace[12].

Instead of increasing the technological sophistication of diagnosis, attention might be turned to developing of effective and for patients more pleasant methods of treating chronic diseases[13].

5   Kirk R M: Editorial. 1975, Annals of the Royal College of Surgeons of England 57:1–2.

6   see also Moser Robert H: An Anti-Intellectual Movement in Medicine. 1975, The Western Journal of Medicine 122:433–449.

7   see also Himsworth R L: Acute medical care in hospitals in the 1980s. 1976, British Journal of Hospital Medicine 16:605–611.

8   see also: The Breakdown of US Innovation. 1976, Business Week. Number 2419, p 56.

9   see also Greenwald Douglas: Technology: modest expectations. 1975, Modern Healthcare 4:6:EI–E4.

10 Editorial: An Anti-Intellectual Movement in Medicine? 1974, JAMA 227:432–434.

11 see also Hammond Georg S: The Scientific Aspects of Future Shock. 1973, Rehovot 7:2:22–26.

12 see also Joel J Nobel in 1976, Hospital Progress 57:10:55.

13 see also Chamberlain Jocelyn: Population screening. in Recent advances in medicine. 16th edition. ed by D N Baron, Nigel Compston and A M Dawson. Churchill Livingstone. Edinburgh and London 1973, p 333.

Many wonder whether not a moratorium should be declared on technological advances of the recent years in medicine and the situation reviewed in terms of health priorities and the need to apply fully the knowledge already existing. Studies need to be done for the entire range of hospital technologies, particularly for the patients' benefits[14].

In spite of the slowing down of the development speed, there is a danger that the discrepancy between medical realities and medico-technical possibilities would be increased.

The decline in the field of pharmacology has been considerable. The long road to application has stifled creativity. The golden age of drug discovery may be drawing to a close[15].

Genuinely new drugs have appeared in decreasing numbers, and many which temporarily glittered in Germany, England or France, where standards are less stringent than in the United States, Sweden, and Canada, were soon forgotten or are remembered with embarrassment[16].

According to *David Schwartzman** the US drug companies compete for sales by discovering, and then marketing, the new drugs that society needs. The financial backing must come from the profits from the sales of existing drugs. Nevertheless, the cost of drug development is now so great, and the financial returns so precarious, that pharmaceutical innovation is in danger of drying up.

Research into drugs for less common diseases is already at a standstill, and few companies find it economic to invest in pharmaceutical research for the developing world. Since the Second World War drug development has been the particular provenance of the pharmaceutical industry with a few notable exceptions. Academic pharmacologists and clinical pharmacologists have devoted their research to elucidating fundamental principles of drug action and drug handling[17].

And still there are pharmacological goals that would keep clinical pharmacologists very busy for a long time: to protect the great positive achievements in medicine and — since life cannot be lengthened — to pursue investigations to make life, as well as disease, more tolerable[18]. Drugs for the relief of symptoms rather than etiology is a goal truly worthy of intensive study and originally the only realistic goal of medicine. Better pain relievers, more effective drugs for anxiety, insomnia and

14 see also Technology and Health Care. 1976, The Medical Journal of Australia 1:376–377.

15 see also Goldberg Leon I: Creativity in new drug development: an academic challenge. 1978, Perspectives in Biology and Medicine 21:188–195.

16 Henry Simmons and Nicolas Wade cited by Illich Ivan: Limits to medicine. Marion Boyars. London 1976, p 7

* Innovation in the Pharmaceutical Industry. The Johns Hopkins University Press. Baltimore 1977.

17 Rawlins Michael D: No Utopia yet. 1977, British Medical Journal 2:1076–1077.

18 Modell Walter: Clinical Pharmacology: A Retrospective View of its Future. 1977, Triangle 16:123–127.

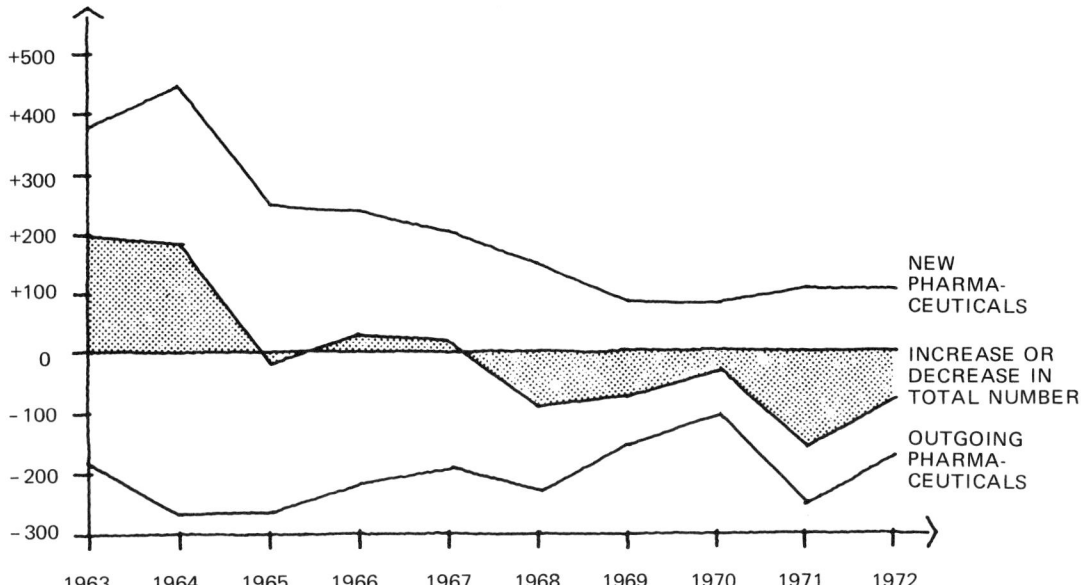

The number of available pharmaceuticals is being reduced. In Sweden the cost of producing a new pharmaceutical was increased four times between 1965 and 1970.

depression, as well as for less common discomforts of disease are needed as well as drugs for the very common as well as the rare causes of mental and physical suffering.

There should also be intensified study in the clinical pharmacology of the aging process, not only for its relief but also with the possibility in mind of staying what is now assumed to be an inevitable process of biologic deterioration. Without such progress a longer life would be biologically, medically and sociologically undesirable, even dangerous and an overwhelming economic burden to a burgeoning world[19].

Most significant changes may be expected in the manning of the health care pyramid. Many primary care functions may be assumed by other health professionals and many secondary and tertiary level physicians may become specialized technicians[20].

19 Modell Walter: Clinical Pharmacology: A Retrospective View of its Future. 1977, Triangle 16:123–127.

20 see also Watts Malcom S M: Medicine and the quality of life — A report of a forum. 1977, The Western Journal of Medicine 126:499–504.

The aspect of public knowledge of consumer expectations is most important. Information on outcomes as well as costs of medical care should be routinely formulated in a manner suitable for presentation to be public[21]. Critical attitudes on the part of physicians must be coupled with changes in consumer attitudes. Unrealistic expectations must be replaced by the knowledge of what medical treatments can and cannot do[22].

A special obligation is placed on mass media. It is the obligation to fairness in reporting all sides and all positions in health care and cure development. It means resisting the temptation to report the scary-story side more enthusiastically than the others. The radio, press and TV may create confused issues and desorientate public opinion about them[23].

Many of the newsbreaking methods are only half-way solutions, in many areas they fall far too short.

Commenting on the medical television programmes of BBC the chairman of the corporation Sir *Michael Swann* has suggested that the effect of these programmes has been modestly beneficial to most people. There has been not much evidence of increased anxiety among patients even after watching programmes about cancer. About one in 20 family doctors appear likely to be consulted by one or more patients seriously troubled by what they have seen[24].

These figures vary in different countries.

Finally, it should be pointed out that in many countries it is increasingly realized that the resources available, such as hospital beds, surgical specialists, and primary care physicians, affect the magnitude of demand and utilization and that there is an uncertain relationship between the use of more services and health status[25].

21 see also Costs, Risks and Benefits of Surgery. ed by John P Bunker, Benjamin A Barnes and Frederick Mosteller. Oxford University Press. New York 1977, p 394.

22 Vayda Eugene: When Is Surgery Indicated? 1977, Milbank Memorial Fund Quarterly/Health and Society 55:495–504.

23 see also Culliton Barbara: Science, Society and the Press. 1977, The New England Journal of Medicine 296:1450–1453.

24 The Times, May 13, 1978.

25 V R Fuchs cited by Mechanic David: Prospects and Problems in Health Services Research. 1978, Milbank Memorial Fund Quarterly/Health and Society 56:127–139.

Adoption of innovations

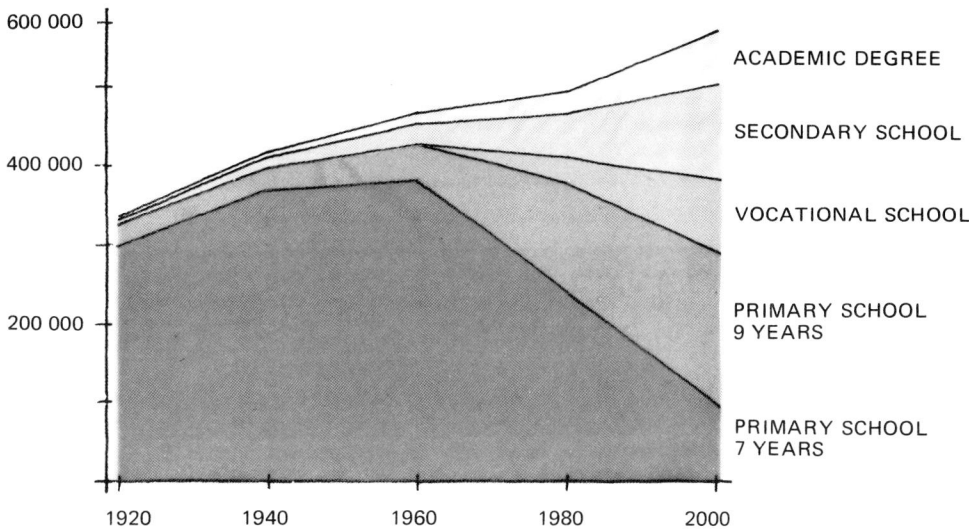

Although the educational standards of the health care staff are continuously improving — as a study by SPRI, Stockholm, confirms — for adoption of innovations regular post-graduate studies are essential.

A gap exists where large quantities of knowledge, experience and information are accumulated, but groups or individuals fail to incorporate it into their routines and lives. Obviously, they do not accept the change or they become confused by the results.

An understanding of the reasons for adoption of innovation in health care is essential for those making policies intended to either speed up or slow down diffusion. As a guide to action, the literature is disappointing[1].

It is mostly very demanding to introduce innovations and improvements in hospitals. Continuous training of staff and updating their abilities is an important part in the health care field in spite of the fact that mostly only minor improvements are achieved.

The advancements in medical practices are made mostly by gradual replacements[*]. These periods of adjustment in medical procedures and hospital routines are not only natural but also necessary.

---

1   Lennarson Greer Ann: Advances in the Study of Diffusion of Innovation in Health Care Organizations. 1977, Milbank Memorial Fund Quarterly/Health and Society 55:505.

*   Also the natural sciences have not advanced in virtue of the universal appeal of rationality. Their theological classicist and methaphysical opponents were not converted but displaced (Andreski Stanislaw: Social Sciences as Sorcery. Andre Deutsch. London 1972, p 92).

The conservatism appearing not least in the clinicians, makes it difficult to change the accustomed routines and tests, including the outdated ones[2].

A surgical operation with satisfactory results will be replaced only when much evidence shows that the change is a definite advance. The time scale of such alterations is much slower than when a totally new technique is introduced. The former may take five to ten years to be generally accepted, the latter less than five years[3].

In clinical medicine the time lapse between a method is invented and it becomes a clinical routine is mostly at least ten years[4].

When the Bureau of Research and Planning of the California Medical Association investigated the medical application of computers[5], it was stated that the process of training all the clinicians in the hospital, plus three shifts of nurses, book-keepers, ward secretaries, and all other personnel involved, in the fundamentally simple technique of computer usage, is prohibitively time-consuming and costly.

It seems that there must be a time gap of at least one educational generation before a major administrative change or installation of a major system in most hospitals can be considered feasible.

The differentiation of hospitals gains further importance, when new procedures are developed. First the application of a new procedure should be restricted to a few institutions which can generate a full range of hard data. Then, after five or ten years, when the procedure and its areas of usefulness are fully understood, it would be released for the general public application, along with a complete set of instructions[6].

Although this adoption and application scenario is currently not widely applied, the existence of time lapses between inventing methods and procedures and their becoming general routines should be profoundly appreciated as an important aspect in the process of generating a health care facility.

Although there is a need for continually expanding horizons, it has to be reminded constantly that replacement or other change is not necessarily progress and that not everything old is obsolete[7].

2   see also Astrup Poul: Clinical chemistry as a medical discipline. 1977, The Scandinavian Journal of Clinical & Laboratory Investigation 37:1–5.

3   Duthie H L: Surgeon's Decisions. Oliver & Boyd. Edinburgh 1971, p 105.

4   see also Hälso- och sjukvård inför 80-talet. Socialstyrelsen. Stockholm 1973, p 71.

5   Medicine and Computers. Engagement or Marriage? 1973, The Medical Journal of Australia 2:953–954.

6   see also Rodgers David L: Bypass, Boeing and Billions. 1977, The Western Journal of Medicine 126:410–411.

7   see also T(homison John B): On obsolescene. 1978, Southern Medical Journal 71:1322.

Attitudes to health, preventive health

Modern medicine holds to an essentially deterministic and mechanistic view of disease, in which the individual has no control over his disease and consequently must submit himself to the intervention of an external agent[1]. This approach has to be changed and is already being changed.

Health is a personal matter and in most cases a highly individual responsibility. The life situation of the individual within the structure of the whole society is decisive for his need for medical care and for satisfaction of these needs.

Neither the proportion of doctors in a population, nor the clinical tools at their disposal, nor the number of hospital beds is a causal factor in the changes in over-all panorama of diseases. There is a limit to the extent of collective action to reverse the ravages of time, ameliorate the human condition and forestall the ultimate death[2].

Health in community should not essentially be seen as a group of mass health activities, but as a person-to-person relationship, carried out on a large scale[3].

Prevention is being given an increasing part in the health care panorama. Primary prevention could be defined in terms of interventions designed to prevent the occurence of *disease* or *injuries* responsible for disability or death; and secondary prevention in terms of interventions aimed at changing the expected course of disease through early detection and treatment.

Preventive health care encompasses a vast array of programmes. Many of them compete for attention, some of them are of doubtful value. A society could not possibly afford the cost of all the programmes that might offer some potential of disease prevention[4].

Preventive programmes have different levels of effectiveness, and different factors affect the level of a particular programme's effectiveness both in theory and in practice. Some of these are implemented within the traditional medical care system — inoculations —, others have no close relationship with the system — seat belts —, some require no patient action or decisions — sewage disposal —, others need the patient's complete cooperation — management of asymptomatic hypertension.

1   see also Goldblatt David P: Modern medicine's short-comings: can we really conquer disease? 1977, Perspectives in Biology and Medicine 20:451–456.

2   see also White Kerr L: Life and Death and Medicine. 1973, Scientific American 229:23–33.

3   see also Martin Jean F: International Health Planning: Socioenvironmental Dimensions and Community Participation. 1975, American Journal of Public Health 65:175–177.

4   Lave Judith R and Lave Lester B: Measuring the Effectiveness of Prevention: I. 1977, The Milbank Memorial Fund Quarterly/Health and Society 55:273–289.

Improvement in health, drinking and smoking information, mental hygiene, occupational health, environmental care, and traffic policies is necessary. Motoring needs to be deglamourized.

Structured programmes are required to acquaint people with balanced diet, protection of the environment and the value of exercise. Greater support for physical fitness and sports programmes on a continuing and not intermittant basis is essential[5].

Through these and other means self-confidence might be restored in the ability to look after one's own health and people would come to avoid some behaviour patterns which make them liable to the disease.

By emphasizing personal responsibility in the prevention of illness rather than treatment, through a change in health habits a number of problems might be eliminated or caught at a less urgent stage.

The people's reporting systems to the medical staff could improve and people would not ask to be screened before the value of that particular screening has been proved[6]. Also an increased voluntary involvement in the care and understanding of handicapped and elderly people is probable.

It has been indicated that there is a known set of health habits which, if learned, taught, and practiced, would result in significantly longer and healthier lives. It is postulated that the group as a group would have longer and healthier lives. To what extent this would comfort the individual cannot be stated[7].

Except for the long-known obvious excesses, there is really no solid evidence that could identify one way of living as significantly different from another in terms of health. Indeed, such evidence would be very hard to come by for it would involve careful lifelong epidemiologic studies of people whose life habits could be periodically observed and recorded. Retrospective studies can at best be only suggestive[8].

It is also a big step to go from identifying the change areas in health habits to designing a programme for its resolution. Much work ought to go into innovative experimental programmes, and such programmes ought to be carefully evaluated before they are implemented on a large scale[9]. At the same time the authors state that unfortunately, effective preventive techniques are lacking and the adage *An*

5   see also Brosseau BLP: Our suicidal lifestyles. 1976, Dimensions in Health Service 53:9:5.

6   see also Chamberlain Jocelyn: Population screening. in Recent advances in medicine. 16th edition. ed by D N Baron, Nigel Compston and A M Dawson. Churchill Livingstone. Edinburgh and London 1973, p 333–362.

7   Mc Dermott Walsh: Medicine: the public good and one's own. 1978, Perspectives in Biology and Medicine 21:167–187.

8   Mc Dermott Walsh: Medicine: the public good and one's own. 1978, Perspectives in Biology and Medicine 21:167–187.

9   Lave Judith R and Lave Lester B: Measuring the Effectiveness of Prevention: I. 1977, The Milbank Memorial Fund Quarterly/Health and Society 55:273–289.

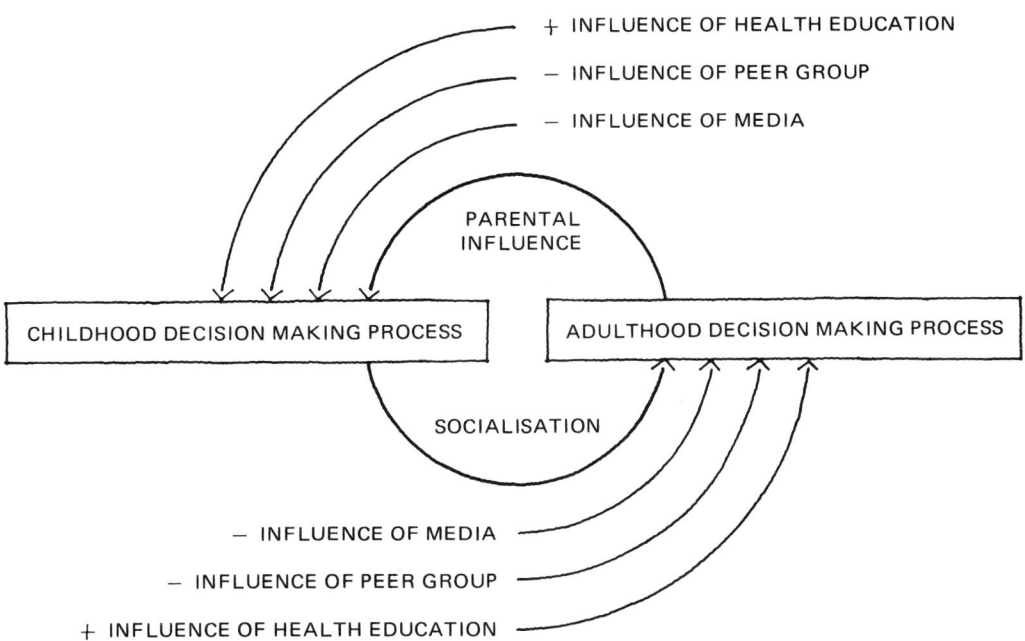

The success of health education is influenced primarily by childhood decisions which will be affected by parental and other adult influences, peer group pressure, the media. Some factors such as ignorance and poverty provide only a minus influence, whereas others such as health education itself usually provide only a plus influence (see also Dodds John: Taking a positive approach to society's negative attitudes. 1977, Health and Social Service Journal 37:1220-1221).

ounce of prevention is worth a pound of cure is misleading because it lumps into one category — prevention — a host of different kinds of programmes[10].

Also other experts[11] indicate that statements that more intensive application of currently known preventive and therapeutic measures could markedly reduce the toll of all major diseases, happen to be untrue. There are many diseases whose toll could not be markedly reduced: cancer and arteriosclerosis, to name but two.

10 Lave Judith R and Lave Lester B: Measuring the Effectiveness of Prevention: I. 1977, The Milbank Memorial Fund Quarterly/Health and Society 55:273-289.

11 see also Davies Hywel: Modern Medicine. Abelard. London 1977, p X.

Emerging social welfare and health care policies

Before the planning and designing of a major hospital is started, also the main lines in the ideologies and policies of the social welfare and health care of the society must be clearly comprehended.

As long as health resources in the society are finite, unlimited health care can not be considered a right[1]. The distributive justice or injustice of the health service's supply is established through political processes where ideologies* and cultural changes have a dominant role. They are constrained by the size of the health service' share in the gross national product.

For the establishment of long-range health care policies, there should be a system at hand which would indicate the stand of all medical specialities at any given moment, their application cost, the expected realistic improvements in the existing medico-technological organization and the range of sickness benefits.

Traditional competence and responsibility relative to health planning have been a prerogative of the medical profession. The growing size and complexity of hospitals introduced independent administrators and technologists into the staff structure. The requirements of individual care brought among others psychologists, physiotherapists, and social workers, as well as laboratory technicians into an influential position.

Still more competence was involved in the form of systems engineers, economy analysts and operational analysts. These new professions gradually emphasized the need for improved medico-statistical and epidemiological services. Finally, the sociologists and social psychologists appeared to plead the case of the recipients of medical care.

Most of the professional analysis of medical care operations is concerned with the framework of the institutions rather than with the essential processes of medical care, i e the decision-making concerning diagnosis and treatment, including the evaluation of these activities[2].

Increased pressure from organized groups of patients could be expected[3].

---

1   see also Chapman Walsh Diana and Bicknell William J: Forecasting The Need For Hospital Beds: A Quantitative Methodology. 1977, Public Health Reports 92:199–210.

*   An ideology is a comprehensive pattern of cognitive and moral beliefs about man and society. These beliefs, which are broad in scope, have an authoritative and explicit nature. They are highly systematized or integrated around central values and are accompanied by highly affective overtones that demand adherence (Shils Edward: The concept and function of ideology. in International Encyclopedia of Social Sciences 7. ed by David Sills. Macmillan Company. New York 1968, p 66).
    Ideologies are more distinct when discrepancies occur between what is real or what exists and what should be

2   Holst Erik: Professional health planning and the health professions. in Health, medicine, society. ed by Magdalena Sokolowska, Jacek Holówka and Antonina Ostrovska. D Reidel Publishing Company. Dordrecht-Holland/Boston-USA 1976, p 426.

3   Barley Simon in 1978, British Medical Journal 2:23.

Health services research is likewise expected to gain in importance, although it has faced considerable scepticism among public officials*.

The health services research has to focus on the production, organization, distribution, and impact of services on health status. Although the field shares some concerns with behavioural studies, such as the determinants of health status, reactions to illness, health promotive behaviour, and factors affecting adherence to medical advice, its main attention is on improving the distribution, quality, effectiveness, and efficiency of medical care.

As complete and lasting freedom from disease can never be achieved, one of the biggest faults in the present situation seems to be the circumstance, that the genuine role and intentions of health care in society are by no means clearly seen[4].

Being ignorant of the context of basic health care problems and the particularities of the country or region may mean to misunderstand and misjudge some of the sub-problems gravely.

Solutions of medical problems are inextricably interwoven with cultural, social and economic phenomena. Also population predictions, based on three sets of assumptions which concern fertility, mortality, and migration, are vital.

The assistance of the science of health, as distinct from the science of medicine, to deal with problems in man's psychosphere, sociosphere, and biosphere is necessary.

The health care system is not the only determinant of the total health of the population. Health is linked to the general level of development of the community and not to the structure of the health care system, how important this system may be.

An understanding of the causes for demand of medical care and hospital beds should lead the public health care authorities to influence the plans for residential, technical and social environments and to advocate higher spatial housing standards. The qualitative standard of housing has been developing in most countries and areas much more slowly than the health care standard and living standard. This must be regarded as one of the greatest developmental failures. Modern apartments are increasingly unfit for the sick. They do not invite and make possible for the family members to get involved in the direct care for their own sick.

Adjustments of external factors will in the long run mean more to the reduction of the total national expenditure for health care and hospital services than improvements in the hospital organization.

---

* see also Mechanic David: Prospects and Problems in Health Services Research. 1978, Milbank Memorial Fund Quarterly/Health and Society 56:127–139.

4 see also Berglund Kåre: Vägar mot mänskligare sjukvård. 1976, Landstingens tidskrift 63:2:38–42.

The basic predictions from involved professions should be taken critically. Myths, misconceptions, outdated concepts, cultural blind spots, and misrepresentations, should be avoided. And yet these are the obvious base of much of the health planning which has been proposed[5].

An overestimate of some need has costly long range implications and is far more serious an error than an underestimate.

Trying to survive at all costs is a basic human instinct. However, it is undeniable that the expenses incurring in view of the survival of a human being are limited by t expenses needed for the life of the others. Life in itself has an infinite price, yet this is a price which one has in fact to share with others[6].

Practically nowhere health services are matching up to the current public demands which very likely will be increased by the driving forces at ground level. Authorities will always be faced with an insatiable demand. There seems to be no limit to the amount of medical and health care an individual is capable of absorbing. The more health service available, the bigger seems to be the demand[7].

The definition of ill health has widened the scope of medical care; also the threshold of tolerance to disease has been on the decline for some time. Under unfortunate circumstances health care approaches could develop into a jungle[8].

Swedish findings[9] suggest that the growth of health-care consumption is to be mainly explained by the dramatic depressions of the out-of-pocket prices and by the improvements of sickness benefits. In Sweden the sickness benefits already amount nearly 100 per cent of ordinary money wage, while the average out-of-pocket price is very close to zero. Any future growth of health-care consumption within the present framework caused by these, in the past so important, factors cannot be expecte Instead, contrary to what has been true in the past, population changes are likely to constitute the main source of growth in health-care consumption.

The appropriate ground for the distribution of medical care is ill health, not social worth, individual merit, or lottery. Everybody is equal in the random susceptibility

5   see also Roth Russel Burton: Tenth Guthrie Memorial Lecture. 1972, The Guthrie Clinic Bulletin 41:108.

6   Piettre André: Aspects of Economics, Ethics and Civilisation. 1977, Intensive Care Medicine 3:253–256.

7   see also Nummi Pekka: Upplösning av en kirurgisk kö. 1973, Nordisk Medicin 88:14–15.
    Rexed Bror: Privilege in Health Provision. at the Conference: The limits to medicine. Davos, March 1975.

8   see also Health Care Costs — A Call for A M A Leadership, Editorial. 1977, The Western Journal of Medicine 126:493.

9   Dahlberg Lars: Empirical studies in public planning. Department of Economics. University of Gothenburg. Memorandum no 67. Gothenburg 1977, p 4:26.

to health crises. Therefore, a medical criterion should provide the initial basis of selection for any medical care resource. This medical criterion can be refined by considering such factors as the kind and severity of illness, the relationship of the disease to other organic impairments, and the degree of realibility of the prognosis, with the objective of helping all patients in some way, given the limited resources.

The principal issues in the debate about medical priorities are the relationship between medical aid and the ideal of positive health; the tension between individual freedom and the power of state, which is implicit in all theories of social justice; and the problem of establishing equity in a context of diverse and competing medical needs[11].

Motivated health care aims do not exist always. The basis for evaluation of various health care components is not uniform. Medical priorities are frequently settled on the arbitrary basis of habit and tradition. Some selected sophisticated health care approaches are inappropriate unless backed up by outreach and preventive services. The immediate relief may not be lasting if the person must return to low quality living conditions.

In planning for medical activities the not readily measurable human factors must make precedence over any mathematical or other calculations and speculations. Also in our era of space travel and electronic microscopes, of transplants and laser-rays, of computers and cyclotrons, a fundamental humanitarian philosophy has to play a decisive part.

Efforts to redistribution of health care resources will succeed only if reasons for the change are rational, and the underlying decisions open to public discussion[12]. There is hardly any other area than medicine in the highly technologic societies, where dilettanteism has so widely spread, it has been stated[13].

The pace of technical and medical advances has also brought with it a continually growing list of problems of choice for those involved in the building-up of health care systems. In each advent there are benefits and risks.

Judgements have to be made about the allocation of scarce human and economic resources. The philosophy of providing all desired and expected services to everyone may eventually eliminate the ability to finance basic primary care, while exotic, highly technological, highly expensive care is available[14]. One man's medical advance could become another man's health deprivation.

11 Campbell A V: Establishing Ethical Priorities. Mankind and Medicine In the Third Millenium Conference. Cape Town. September 1976.
12 see also Chapman Walsh Diana and Bicknell William J: Forecasting The Need For Hospital Beds: A Quantitative Methodology. 1977, Public Health Reports 92:199-210.
13 v Nussbaum Henrich: Wer hier nicht krank wird, darf als trotzig gelten. in Die verordnete Krankheit. ed by Henrich v Nussbaum. S Fischer Verlag. Frankfurt (Main) 1977, p 15.
14 see also TeKolste Elston: Health Care: The Clash Between Resources and Limitations. 1977, Hospital Progress 53:74-77, 94.

Over-eagerness and rush to adapt new methods, techniques and principles of the health sciences which have been introduced in one area or region, in other areas or regions without a close understanding of the local factors involved, has frequently slowed, not advanced public health efforts[15].

The development of new medical techniques and services must not increase the inadequate distribution of many well-established techniques in the health system of a nation.

Health planning is not a small undertaking. A minimum estimate of the annual cost of areawide health planning in the USA is $52,500,000[16]. The answer to the questio whether this planning is worth the price depends on the value of the long-run benefits of coordination and cooperation, which cannot be measured at all unless some common measures of benefit can be devised and agreed upon, and on a necessarily very subjective assessment of the likelihood of these benefits being realized.

Some of the health planning aims to ensure equality of care in all parts of the country. As has been pointed out by *Magdalena Sokolowska*, medical ethics are applicable only to the doctor/patient or nurse/patient relationship — not to health issues on a macro or societal level[17].

The diversion to actual health care of the millions paid in salaries to bureaucratic officials might do more to rise the standards than colourless committee-meetings and paper pushing[18].

15 see also Yoeli Meir: A century of advances in the health sciences: the global view. 1975, The American Journal of the Medical Sciences 270:503–513.

16 May Joel: Is planning worth the price? 1974, Hospitals 48:18:51–55.

17 cited by Holst Erik: Professional health planning and the health professions. in Health, medicine, society. ed by Magdalena Sokolowska, Jacek Hołówka and Antonina Ostrovska. D Reidel Publishing Company. Dordrecht-Holland/Boston-USA 1976, p 430.

18 May Joel: Is planning worth the price? 1974, Hospitals 48:18:51–55.

Objectives of hospital authority

The objectives of the authority governing a hospital involve the provision of medical diagnosis, prescription and treatment; nursing care and treatment; hospital rooms and hotel facilities; medical rooms and equipment; teaching and research facilities, facilities for discovering new needs and for modifying the services provided[1].

Bureaucratic organization is useful for the large-scale production and provision of goods and services. It is inimical on the other hand, to the free development of ideas and to the intimacy of the confidential doctor—patient relationship, which is delicate and often poignant, requiring great personal sensivity on the part of the physician[2].

In adaption of medical knowledge the expert has to be chosen and the length of his being in charge determined. Organizational structures for knowledge work must be both rigid and adaptable, have clear authority and remain task-focused. The difficulties in the specialist management may increase in the future[3].

The quality of the doctor—patient relationship is undermined if doctors are organized in manager subordinate relationships.

In the first place, confidentiality cannot be preserved if whoever is the doctor's 'manager' is to be accountable for he must be able to check upon what is being done. Once confidentiality is gone, the immediate doctor–patient relationship becomes more of an economic transaction, and loses the quality of being a complex social transaction.

These difficulties can be overcome by retaining clinical freedom, the judgement in diagnosis and treatment for hospital doctors, which in itself does not preclude so-called peer group reviews.

The rest of the services in a hospital can readily be bureaucratically organized[4]. They include nursing, administration, the various therapies and diagnostic and laboratory services.

These services, mostly highly professional, do not carry the accountability for *deciding* the diagnosis and the general programme of therapy, nor for confidential discussions of prognosis with the patient. They can be called upon by the accountable physician by prescription. They do not require the clinical authority carried by the physician[5].

---

1   Jaques Elliott: A General Theory of Bureaucracy. Heinemann London. Halsted Press, New York 1976, p 246.

2   ibid, p 344.

3   see also Vapaavuori M: Future Shock. 1973, Annales Chirurgiae et Gynaecologiae Fenniae 62:241.

4   Jacques Elliott: A General Theory of Bureaucracy. Helnemann London. Halsted Press. New York 1976, p 346.

5   ibid, p 347.

There is frequently a striking parallelism between hospitals and some non-profit organizations, which have been characterized as receptacles into which limitless funds can be poured. New uses are easily found, and still other uses with not yet provided financing will inevitably arise[6].

A contemporary health care building has become an expensive item of hardware already initially. The costs of running it are high and ever increasing. A room in a *de luxe* hotel will always be cheaper than a bed in a hospital[7].

An increased intensity of use of hospitals is assumed to decrease hospital costs in the same pace. As a matter of fact the cost reduction has been observed not to correspond to the reduction in the length of stay. Savings seems to occur only when patients can be given treatment on out-patient basis, without admission to hospital.

The analysis of the hospital as a management system and a microeconomy unit has not been profound.

In spite of the fact that salaries are nearing already the 80 per cent margin of the health care running cost in some supercomplex countries, e g in the Federal Republic of Germany[8], and Sweden, paradoxally enough, it is quite usual to meet uncomplete knowledge of the efficiency of the rapidly expanding personnel organization. The hospital as a total operation entity seems to be not too well understood by the vast majority of the hospital workers on all levels.

In early seventies there were already up to 75 staff categories in a hospital, most of them new to service[9]. At the same time studies of employment conditions show lack of flexibility between functions and lack of co-operation between sections[10].

This circumstance is a major obstacle in planning efficient hospitals. Even smaller adjustments in staffing and improvements in their efficiency would be considerably more rewarding in cost controlling than far bigger efforts in the physical planning and construction of a hospital.

The higher the quality level of the hospital, the more reason is there to be fully active seven days a week. It cannot be the objective reasons but the organizational aspects of the hospital, when towards the week-end a considerable number of patients have to leave the wards*.

6 see also Baumol W J and Bowen W G: On the performing arts: the anathomy of their economic problems. 1965, American Economic Review 55:497–498.

7 Biörck Gunnar: The Challenges of Emergency Care. 1974, Journal of the Royal College of Physicians of London 8:101–106.

8 see also Bauer W: 8. Deutscher Krankenhaustag. Eröffnungsansprache. 1975, Der Krankenhausarzt 48:509–51

9 see also Palmer H: Pasienten i sentrum. 1971, Norsk Sykehustidende 44:197–206, 208–210, 212.

10 see also Kruse F H A M: Intramurale zorg mist mankracht beheersing. 1977, Ziekenhuis 7:40–43.

* the care was ended for 25 per cent of patients released that week on Saturdays when a 6-day week was adapted, and 28 per cent on Fridays when a 5-day week (Elštein Natan: Arštiabi järgivuse küsimusi. 1977, Nõukogude Eesti Tervishold 20:48–50).

	UNIVERSITY HOSPITALS	250–500 BED HOSPITALS
PHYSICIANS		
NURSES		
STUDENT NURSES		
AUXILLIARIES		
PARAMEDICALS		
ADMINISTRATION		
SERVICES		
EXTERNALS		

Number of staff per 100 patient beds in Swiss university and medium sized hospitals in 1972 (Veska 36:631).

Hospitals must be permitted to adjust staffing ratios in the most economical and beneficial manner. Obviously, there are medical areas where mathematical analysis and time and motion studies do not help the hospital administration*.

Requirements for numbers of personnel and duties which are for the material benefit of some individuals must not be imposed upon the hospital. The assignment of personnel and duties must be the prerogative to the hospital and not dictated through injudicious labour contracts[11].

---

* A string-quartet by Ludwig van Beethoven or Gabriel Fauré is not more productively performed if it is executed in double speed, or if the second violine is eliminated.

11 see also Brosseau B L P: More health care with less. 1975, Dimensions in Health Service 52:12:6.

Nurses, paramedicals

A very central role in the hospital development is played by the nurses. Modern nursing practice has emerged as an oddly static, dependent, and exploited health care occupation[1].

The proper role of nurses is a longdebated question[2]. Nursing is a diverse collection of professionals, rather than a single occupational group. This amalgam of professionals receives highly varied training and conducts widely dissimilar functions. Basically, they can be divided into two groups: technical nurses who perform routine clinical activities and professional nurses who assume educational, administrative, and more complex clinical responsibilities.

The unique function of the nurse is to assist the individual sick or well, in the performance of those activities contributing to the health or its recovery or peaceful death that he would perform unaided if he had the necessary strength, will, or knowledge. And to do this in such a way as to help him gain independence as rapidly as possible[3].

Some of the nursing care is generated by the medical diagnosis and prescription, but most of the total care of the patient for the whole of the day is left to nurses: feeding, toiletting, teaching.

Good nursing in all hospitals requires above all things kindness, especially to sick people. The nurse must be accurate in observing and recording simple things. She must be prepared to hold hands, rub backs, carry bedpans, and listen with interest to the patient's stories — not only the medical ones but also the personal ones — the hopes, griefs, prides, doings of the kids and so on[4].

The nursing process involves assessing, planning, implementing, and evaluating patient care as its principal elements. The ward sister is involved also in functional management: planning, organizing, communicating, directing, controlling, and co-ordinating. The nurse has also a third role — the teacher's.

Her opportunies for teaching in the sense of imparting knowledge to patients and learners are likely to fall by the wayside, when the pressure from other sources is great. There is also social learning. In this case the ward sister may act as a role model for both learners and patients without any conscious effort on her part. Her presence is all that is required[5].

1   Twaddle Andrew C and Hessler Richard M: A sociology of health. The C V Mosby Company. St Louis 1977, p 201.

2   see also Rowbottom Ralph: Hospital Organization. Heinemann, London 1973, p 146.

3   V Henderson according to Sheahan John: Ward sister—manager, nurse, or teacher? 1978, Nursing Mirror

4. Davies Hywel: Modern Medicine. Abelard. London 1977, p 16.

5   Sheahan John: Ward sister — manager, nurse, or teacher? 1978, Nursing Mirror 146:20:18–21.

While nursing remains a strongly sex-typed profession, the ideal nurse in an American study* has been described not as stereotypically feminine but as someone capable of displaying both feminine characteristics i.e. warmth, understanding, gentleness, helpfulness, kindness and characteristics considered masculine i.e. independenc, competitiveness, selfconfidence, decision making. Obviously it is important for the nurses to be psychologically androgynous, to possess both masculine and feminine characteristics.

Both men and women may display either masculine or feminine behaviour, depending on which is more appropriate in a given situation. Since both masculine and feminine characteristics are important in nursing, rigid sex typing of the profession should end. Nursing does not need women; it needs qualified people of both genders**.

In the general health care panorama not all nursing — in the sense of patient-contact — is done by nurses. In the United Kingdom in 1975 about 90 per cent of nursing was given by the totally untrained[6].

The nursing profession is in the midst of an identity crisis[7]. Nursing is believed to be facing the most exiting and difficult era in its entire history[8].

Since a couple of decades ago promotion for the good nursing started to mean leaving the bedside and becoming an administrator. Since the best nurses are not the best administrators, false concepts of nursing began to be hatched[9].

Far too much time and effort have been spent on management, education and research into nursing and not enough on enabling nurses actually to care for patients. Money is being poured into developing a research-based profession, while more effort is needed to be put into what is happening where the patient is[10].

By the year 2000 the group of nursing nurses could have disappeared. With an ever-increasing list of non-nursing duties and with a greater proportion of managerial duties not always executed as effectively as they might be, the superstructure of nurses could disappear. There has been ample demonstration that auxiliaries and

---

* Minnigerode Fred A, Kayser-Jones Jeanie S, Garcia Gerard: Masculinity and Femininity in Nursing. 1978, Nursing Research 27:299–302.

** ibid

6 Nuttall Peggy: Nursing in the year AD 2000. 1976, Journal of Advanced Nursing 1:101–110.

7 see also Maxmen Jerrol S: The postaphysician era. John Wiley & Sons. New York, London, Sydney, Toronto 1976, p 148.

8 Twaddle Andrew C and Hessler Richard M: A sociology of health. The C V Mosby Company. St Louis 1977, p 200.

9 Davies Hywel: Modern Medicine. Abelard London 1977, p 17.

10 Eve Bendall cited by Kerrane Tom: Challenge of changing patterns in nursing. 1977, Health and Social Service Journal 37:1244--1245.

learners can at least "get by" with a minimum of supervision and that the undue reliance on the untrained worker has been accepted to a surprising extent[11]. On the other hand doctorally prepared nurses have appeared. There have been several societal and professional forces that have influenced the development of doctoral programmes for nurses. In the US they include the changing role of women in society; the declared crisis in health care delivery; the emergence of new types of health care facilities; the evident need for research to systematically examine nursing phenomena; the need to change nursing education programmes to fit societal imperatives, and the evident dissatisfaction of consumers with care, cure, and treatment modalities[12].

Also the quest for increased status of nursing has led to the proposal of degree courses in nursing, which are believed to make little sense, for nursing has insufficient content to merit it[13]. The course would inevitably become one in medicine, or much worse, in sociology and psychology[14].

Doctorally prepared nurses may challenge other nurses in terms of disciplined modes of thinking, scientific methods of inquiry, and research approaches to nursing education and practice problems. They have provided a skepticism about old premises and practices, as they formulate critical problems which need investigation. Having a critical mass of doctorally prepared nurse-scholars, researchers, and theoreticians in the nursing field would stimulate new goals and leadership directions.

The full and continuing impact of nurses with doctoral preparation is yet to be realized by the nursing profession and the public at large[15].

When a hierarchy of functional areas in US nursing, within which the need for nurses with doctoral preparation exists, was identified, the highest priority of need was assigned to academic settings. Ranking second were the service agencies which provide direct health care to the public. In sum, the need for highly prepared nurses is reflected in virtually every key policy and decision-making position in the profession[16].

There is also a question whether the acquisition of autonomy through new roles will serve in the best interests of the consumer[17]

11 Nuttall Peggy: Nursing in the year AD 2000. 1976, Journal of Advanced Nursing 1:101–110.

12 Leininger Madeleine: Doctoral programs for nurses: a survey of trends, issues, and projected developments. in The doctorally prepared nurse. DHEW Publication No (HRA) 76–18. Bethesda, Maryland 1976, p 4.

13 Davies Hywel: Modern Medicine. Abelard London. 1977, p 17.

14 ibid

15 Leininger Madeleine: Doctoral programs for nurses: a survey of trends, issues, and projected developments. in The doctorally prepared nurse. DHEW Publication No (HRA) 76–18. Bethesda, Maryland 1976, p 4.

16 Conference summary. in The doctorally prepared nurse. DHEW Publication No (HRA) 76–18. Bethesda, Maryland 1976, p 102, 103.

17 Twaddle Andrew C and Hessler Richard M: A sociology of health. The C V Mosby Company. St Louis 1977, p 201.

Also the paramedical professions have claimed, and have been granted, increasing independence.

The term paramedical refers to occupations whose work is both organized around tasks of healing and ultimately controlled by the authority of physicians. The tasks performed by paramedical workers have tended to assist, rather than directly replace, the focal tasks of diagnosis and treatment.

The medical profession has dominated or encompassed the paramedical profession by exercising control over the knowledge base of these professions. i e by controlling the knowledge and skills that these professions apply; and by controlling access to their services, i e only physicians can use these. Although medicine has created and dominated a series of auxiliary or paramedical occupations, the control of these occupations is shifting from the medical to the paramedical professions and the health care runs the risk of being fragmented into a series of independent and uncoordinated medical and paramedical services. The victim of such a process would be the patient[18].

There is a considerable potential for conflict in the interfacing of physicians and nurses and paramedicals, or management and physicians, of physicians and patients[19] even medical staff and the society. If balancing of the interests of different groups fails, the future of the traditional hospitals is put in doubt[20].

18 Alaszewski Andy: Doctor and paramedical workers — the changing pattern of interprofessional relations. 1977, Health and Social Service Journal 87:no 4562: B1–B4.

19 see also de Jonghe E: Zorgenfuncties en sociaal-economische functies: interesseconflict. 1975, Acta Hospitalia 15:214–230.

20 also Stolte J B at the 8. internationales Krankenhaussymposion. TU Berlin. February 1976.

HOSPITAL PATIENT

The patient is a member of the society under influence and care of a health organization. The word patient is derived from the Latin *patior* — to suffer. In many cases the character of the patient's demand for hospital care is both medical and socio-psychological.

The concept of the sick person is in the state of continuing evolution[1].

One of the most obvious facts about patients is their individuality. Each human is unique. The combination of circumstances that gave rise to her or him can never again be duplicated.

Also the ever present difficulties in communication between planners and architects and representatives of other human sciences converge on the same central situation: the diversity of man. The scientists exploring the human being trend to build up unitary models of man from an all too narrow factual base, which is the limited segment under their particular attention. One could speak of a *HOMO MEDCUS* as well as of a *HOMO PSYCHIATRICUS,* a *HOMO SOCIOLOGICUS* and a *HOMO ECONOMICUS*[2].

All these and other models reflect a circumscribed professional experience of a specialist group. They do not give material for good overall planning purposes.

The authorities have to provide and maintain all the measures as may be necessary to attain and support the patient's state of complete physical, mental, and social well-being.

Respect of dignity is one of the most basic rights and needs of the patient[3]. In spite of that most hospitals provide less than a minimum of normal privacy for the patient[4].

Entry into the hospital environment means entry into a system in which the patient generally has less control of daily events than in the home environment. It is assumed that already this experience produces stress which requires a coping or adaptation procedure on the part of patients[5].

In fact, the patient enters frequently the hospital in a vulnerable state, being to some degree incapacitated by disease and apprehensive about the outcome. The

---

1   see also The role of the patient. 1974, The Medical Journal of Australia 1:683.

2   see also Elias Norbert: Sociology and psychiatry. in Psychiatry in a changing society. ed by S H Foulks and G Stewart Prince. Tavistock Publications. London, New York, Sydney, Toronto, Wellington 1969, p 122

3   see also La Charte Du Malade Hospitalisé. Paris. Circulaire de 20 septembre 1974. Madame Simone Veil, Ministre de la Santé.
    Sweetser Frank Loel: The Outsiders. 1977, The Guthrie Bulletin 46:135–140.

4   see also Feldman Wulff: Sjukhuspsykologi, Natur och Kultur. Stockholm 1977, p 66.

5   Volicer Beverly J, Isenberg Marjorie A and Burns Mary W: Medical-surgical differences in hospital stress factors. 1977, Journal of Human Stress 3:2:3–13.

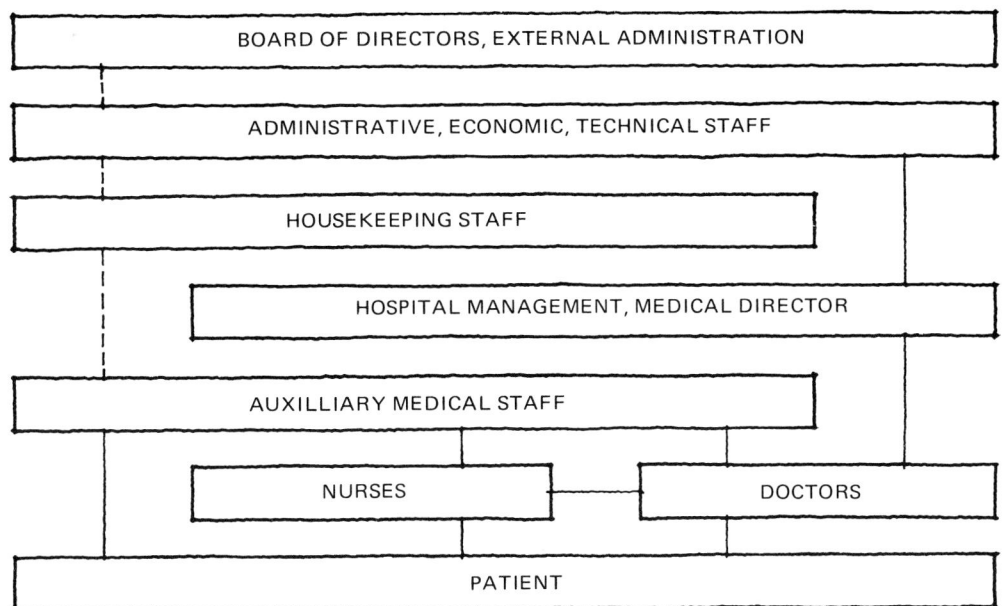

In hospital the patient has less control of daily events than in the home environment, as he is depending upon the activities of many staff groups and administrative decisions. In a medical or biological functional diagram the patient should be at the top with the physicians and nurses in the first row below.

hospital adds to this vulnerability by enforcing additional dependencies, intensifying the helplessness of patients and making them passive participants in a drama in which they have little to say about events that are for them more than usually consequential[6].

The psychosocial stresses experienced by hospital patients are mainly stresses brought about by the mere fact of hospitalization, regardless of the nature of the illness or reason for hospitalization[7].

Growing evidence suggests that these stresses are measurable and associated with observable physiologic changes*.

Many suffer in the hospital under unpleasance caused by three forms of contemporary social behaviour: togetherness, conformity and herd-mindedness. Each of

6   Twaddle Andrew C and Hessler Richard M: A sociology of health. The C V Mosby Company. St Louis 1977, p 255.

7   Volicer Beverly J, Isenberg Marjorie A and Burns Mary W: Medical-surgical differences in hospital stress factors. 1977, Journal of Human Stress 3:2:3–13.

*   Volicer Beverly J: Hospital Stress and Patient Reports of Pain and Physical Status. 1978, Journal of Human Stress 4:2:28–37.

these forms of behaviour operates in direct opposition to the autonomy that almost all psychologists feel is a precondition of self-actualization[8].

Much unhappiness results from promulgating the concept that all people are equal, and that in instances where they are unequal they can be equalized[9].

In a diversified society everybody is right in his own way. This means that any general hospital solution will be at best a compromise — satisfactory to some, inconvenient to others.

Even the requirements of disabled people differ. What may help one person may sometimes hinder another. No arrangement will be perfect for people of every size and with every kind of disability[10].

Although one of the objects of hospital care is to decause stress and anxiety, many hospitals inadvertently decrease the patient's psychic strength by depersonalizing him[11]. *T S Eliot*[12] has provided a deeply felt description of this aspect in act one of his play *The Cocktail Party:*

> You're suddenly reduced to the status of an object —
> A living object, but no longer a person.
> It's always happening, because one is an object
> As well as a person. But we forget about it
> As quickly as we can.

The main hospital stress factors are unfamiliarity of surroundings, loss of independence, separation from spouse, financial problems, isolation from other people, lack of information, threat of severe illness, separation from family, and problems with medications[13].

The effects of hospital stress on patients are not well understood, but there are thought to be both psychological and physical effects[14].

Higher stress scores for surgical patients compared with medical patients have been indicated[15].

---

8 Winthrop Henry: The group as a surrogate for the individual. 1974, Bulletin of the Menninger Clinic 38:239–249.

9 see also Williams Robert H: Prologue. in To Live and To Die. When, Why, and How. ed by Robert H Williams. Springer-Verlag. Berlin, Heidelberg, New York 1973, p 13.

10 Harkness Sarah P and Groom Jr James N: Building without Barriers for the Disabled. Whitney Library Design. New York 1976, p 13.

11 see also Taylor Carol: In Horizontal Orbit. Rinehart and Winston. New York, Chicago, San Francisco, Atlanta, Dallas, Montreal, Toronto, London, Sydney 1970, p 88.

12 Eliot T S: The Cocktail Party. Faber and Faber Ltd. London 1958, p 26.

13 Volicer Beverly J, Isenberg Marjorie A, and Burns Mary W: Medical-surgical differences in hospital stress factors. 1977, Journal of Human Stress 3:2:3–13.

14 ibid

15 ibid

Hospital personnel continue in their scientifically unsupported manner of perceiving patients behaving in an infantile way[16]. It should be mentioned, that not all patients feel this infantilisation as disturbing or offending[17].

There still are remnants from the one-time philantropic attitude of the medical body who received from the indigent nothing. In an extensive study of patient adjustment to hospitalization, *Hans Mauksch* [18] observed that in addition to getting well, most patients must also strive for psychological survival in a power system where the rules for behaviour are often ambiguous.

Patients, whom nurses dislike, are also discriminated by them. Most patients realize the power of the nurse and fear to anger her as they quickly learn that patients out of favour are ignored and hospital rules strictly enforced. They feel the need to show co-operation, trust and confidence, and not to be too demanding[19].

A study by a veteran British nurse, *Felicity Stockwell*[20], indicates that patients with physical defects such as deafness, obesity, or disfigurement, those of foreign nationality, and those whose hospitalization was longer than three months are significantly more unpopular among nurses.

Unpopular are also those that grumble, complain, and demand attention, and those the nurses think should not be in the hospital at all. A certain way to become an avoided patient was to have a terminal disease.

Age, sex, or illness — except for psychiatric and terminal illness — appear not to be important in influencing the nurses' attitudes. Some patients are neither popular nor unpopular. These have virtually no verbal communication with nurses: routine tasks are carried out without exchange of a word. Although patients may prefer not to talk, it is more likely they are afraid to take the initiative.

Patients nurses like best are those who know their nurse's name; are able to communicate readily with nurses; can joke and laugh with nurses, and co-operate in being helped to get well and express determination to do so.

Patients come to a hospital to be treated and not to be administred. Therefore the regularity with which hospital routine takes precedence over the rest requirements of the patient is amazing[21].

---

16 Bremer J: Psychologische kenmerken van de ziekenhuissituatie. 1974, Acta Hospitalia 14:220–240.

17 Feldman Wulff: Sjukhuspsykologi. Natur och Kultur. Stockholm 1977, p 49.

18 cited by Sweetser Frank Loel: The Outsiders. 1977, The Guthrie Bulletin 46:135–140.

19 see also Twaddle Andrew C and Hessler Richard M: A sociology of health. The C V Mosby Company. St Louis 1977, p 255.

20 Nelson Barbara Koval: Study Indicates Which Patients Nurses Don't Like: the Unpleasant, Long-Term, Mentally Ill, Hypochondriacs, and the Dying. 1973, Modern Hospital 121:8:70.

21 see also Cousins Norman: Anatomy of an illness. 1976, The New England Journal of Medicine 295:1458–1463.

The process that reduces a person to a patient, is only partly understood[22]. This includes also the losing of confidence in the knowledge, which the patient was so sure about before entering the hospital[23].

One of the factors may be the objectivist type of medicine now being widely practiced, in which the disease and not the patient is the object of care[24]. The other may be the paradoxal situation that the patient who outside the hospital had been overflooded with general health information, suddenly is deprived of all information concerning his own health[25].

Anxiety and fear are the inevitable consequences of poor communication between doctors and patients[26]. Frequently patients who complain about their doctors want two things: someone to give them a scientific explanation hedged with doubts and someone to do the magic and deal with the uncertainty[27].

The importance of the information factor should not be overestimated, as the average patient is generally ignorant in most of the health matters: anatomy, physiology, causes and symptoms of illness.

Some random examples illustrate the scope of medical ignorance: according to a study by *Korsch* and *Negrete*[28] only 50 per cent of the mothers understood the causes of the sickness of their children after a paediatric consultation and only 42 per cent of the mothers followed the medical advice. Several investigations indicate that a major portion of patients does not take their medicines as prescribed[29].

It has also been stated that the medical staff should not regard the patient as a passiv object who would be given all possible information[30]. Delivering and receiving medical information is a delicate procedure.

Hospitalization may represent a crisis for both the patient and his family.

Hospitalization is a period of strain for patients, whose emotional needs probably vary as much as their physical conditions. Hospitalization for them is an uncommon,

22 see also Dörner Klaus: Wie werde ich Patient oder: Sozialisation in fünf Stadien. in Die verordnete Krankheit. ed by Henrich v Nussbaum. S. Fischer Verlag. Frankfurt (Main) 1977, p 48.

23 Beels Christine: The Childbirth Book. Turnstone Books. London 1978, p 57.

24 Tange A: Une médicine pour l'homme: du malade — objet ou sujet malade. 1976, Hospitalia 20:177–183.

25 see also von Uexküll Thure: An den Grenzen der Medizin. in Die verordnete Krankheit. ed by Henrich v Nussbaum. S Fischer Verlag. Frankfurt (Main) 1977, p 106.

26 see also Reynolds Maureen: No news is bad news: patients' views about communication in hospital. 1978, British Medical Journal 1:1673–1676.

27 Muir Gray J A in 1978, British Medical Journal 2:23.

28 cited by von Uexküll Thure: An den Grenzen der Medizin. in Die verordnete Krankheit. ed by Henrich v Nussbaum. S Fischer Verlag. Frankfurt (Main) 1977, p 112.

29 Varför följs given ordination så dåligt? 1977, Folia CIBA/Geigy 1:2–6.

30 Patienten i sjukvården — kontakt och information. Rapport från en expertgrupp inom medicinalansvarskommittén. Statens offentliga utredningar 1977:66. Socialdepartementet. Stockholm 1977, p 10.

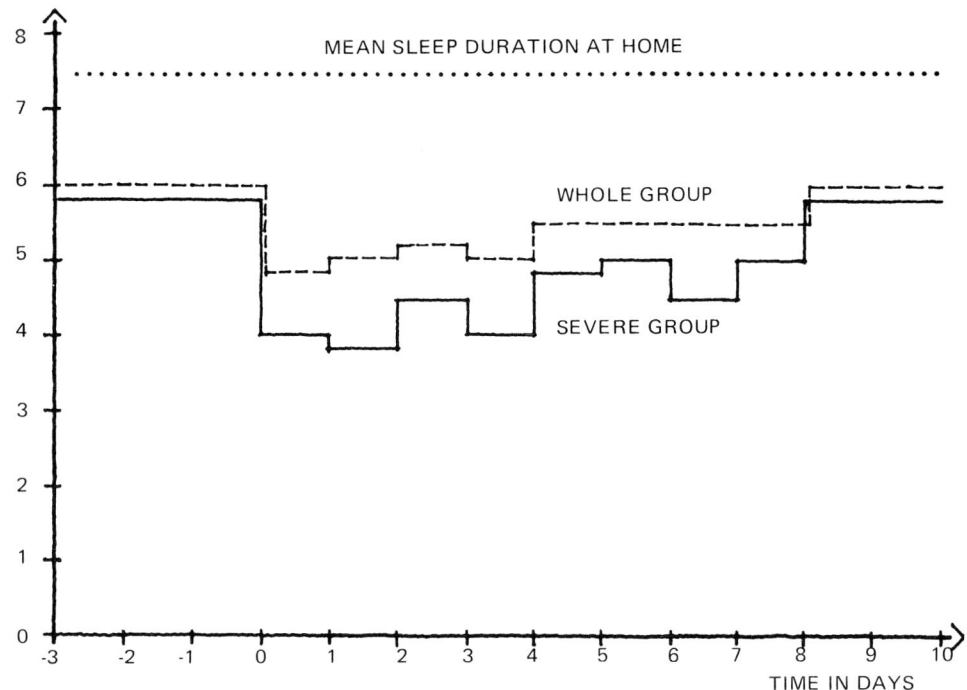

TIME IN HOURS

MEAN SLEEP DURATION AT HOME

WHOLE GROUP

SEVERE GROUP

TIME IN DAYS

Sleep duration in hospital before and after operation. F Murphy, S Bentley, B W Ellis, H Dudley have provided evidence to support anecdotes that acute hospitals with open wards are not places in which it is easy to obtain a sound night's sleep. The further decrease in sleep after injury may, because it is long lasting, represent a primary effect of surgery and anaesthesia on the brain.

often unpleasant, experience. The physical discomfort, environmental estrangement and forced isolation, together with the fears and anxieties associated with sickness, tend to threaten or weaken the patient's existing adaptive mechanisms and defences.

Some patients can be alert, but as in the case of endotracheal respiration utterly frustrated for being unable to communicate[31]. Apprehensions arise both from the patient's natural preoccupation with his own physical condition, and from his necessary dependence on the abilities of others to effect treatment. In order to deal effectively with the physical condition, the emotional factors involved must be recognized[32].

The patient may be affected by his pathophysiological status with its accompanying discomforts, mechanical apparatus, constant observation periods and therapies,

31 Sluiter H J: Intensive Care Medicine: A balance of skill and art. 1977, The Netherlands journal of medicine 20:137–141.

32 Turner Gerald P: Is science killing compassion? 1977, Hospital Administration in Canada 19:7:4.

lack of privacy, time disorientation, sensory monotony, sleep deprivation, as well as by his personal reactions to illness, life and family problems.

Vulnerable patients include those with high levels of anxiety and depression proneness, females under 40 years of age, those who have not been in hospital before, those admitted for a series of tests, and those with infective or undiagnosed illness[33].

Sleep* is more than rest, it is a state of unresponsiveness brought about by active nervous mechanisms, a form of rest that ensures that the whole body, including the nervous system**, can recuperate[34].

A study of hospital sleep patterns shows that the deficit is principally due to early awakening[35].

Sleep deprivation may actually improve some depressed and schizophrenic patients, at least briefly. This observation highlights general ignorance about the functions of sleep and the effects of sleep deprivation[36].

33 Wilson-Barnett Jenifer and Carrigy Ann: Factors influencing patients' emotional reactions to hospitalization. 1978, Journal of Advanced Nursing 3:221–229.

* Sleep is characterized by rhythms and cycles indicated by biological, behavioural, and elctroencephalografic alterations. The average normal night's sleep consists of 4 to 5 sleep cycles, with each of these being 90 to 120 minutes long. Four sleep stages and dream sleep generally occur within a cycle in a predictable pattern.

** It is the brain functions such as the power to sustain attention that are more obviously impaired by sleep deprivation. Although the mature brain no longer grows, it still needs synthetic activity. It rivals the liver in its high rate of turnover of proteins and nucleic acids, consistent with its role in information processing, storage and retrieval, which rely on synthetic activity over and above the protein synthesis required for enzymes and renewal of structural components.

34 Adam Kirstine and Oswald Ian: Sleep is for Tissue Restoration. 1977, Journal of the Royal College of Physicians of London 11:376–388.

35 Murphy F, Bentley S, Ellis B W and Dudley H: Sleep deprivation in patients undergoing operation: a factor in the stress of surgery. 1977, British Medical Journal 2:1521–1522.

36 Mendelson Wallace B, Gillian J Christian and Wyatt Richard Jed: Human Sleep and Its Disorders. Plenum Press. New York and London 1977, p 212.

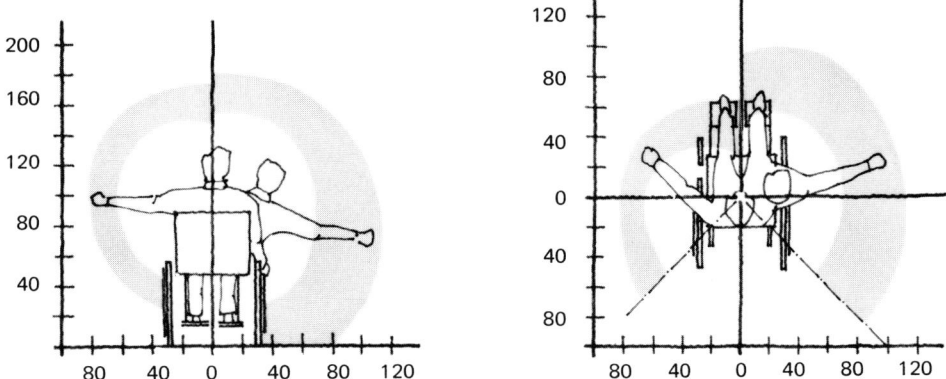

The upper area of reach of a chairbound person is within the low to middle range of a standing person.

Wheelchair users have capabilities as varied as those of the ambulant population. Accidents, illness-related disability, and congenital defects affect all parts of the body, leaving limbs in various stages of weakness, paralysis, or absence. The healing process is much longer in disabled than in able-bodied people.

The most common wheelchairs have a width of about 0.60 to 0.62 m, the seat being approximately 0.48 m above floor. A turn of 180 degrees should be possible in a 1.80 to 1.85 m diameter. A corridor width of 1.05 m is required to make also a turn into a 0.8 m clear door opening possible. Corridors with a width of 1.8 m allow wheelchairs to pass.

Reaching from a seated position is limited and depends on access to the location of the item being reached. If side approach to a telephone or vending machine is possible then the highest operable part of the equipment can be located 1.35 m above the floor. If approach from the front is the only means of access, then the highest operable part should not be higher than 1.2 m from the floor. In toilet rooms towel or tissue dispensers and other equipment must be located not higher than 1 m from the floor[1].

1   Jones Michael A and Catlin John H: Design for access. 1978, Progressive Architecture 59:4:65–71.

Intensive care unit patients

The most common patient problem in a burn unit is the pain; in the surgical intensive care unit, the delirium; in the respiratory intensive-care unit, the chronic depression; and in the cardiac-care unit, the anxiety*.

Particularly the psychological problems in intensive care and treatment units represent a complex issue.

Death is a constant presence and threat. Patients are bound to be aware of it, often despite the efforts of the staff to screen them from it. Death figures in the fantasies of the patients despite denial either of its presence or of the intensity of its emotional impact[1].

Numerous cases have been reported of acute emotional distress in intensive care and treatment of patients, whose life is threatened.

There have been many demonstrations of the relationship between psychological states and physiological changes which could have an adverse effect on the coronary intensive care patient.

Most of the patients will have delusional states in varying degrees while on the unit. There might be psychological implications in a patient who is continuously reminded of being so seriously ill as having to be nursed in the strange environment of the ICTU.The importance of recognizing psychiatric disorders in severely ill patients has been stressed[2]. The main psychosomatic aspects revolve around reactive psychic disorders and the states of delirium, clouding of consciousness, and confusion[3]. Serious psychological breakdowns are rare — less than 0.5 per cent — of all patients admitted to the ICTU[4].

Of course, even within the same country the various types of ICTU cannot be easily compared. Numerous factors — psychological climate, design, discharge procedures, nature of the organic conditions involved, personnel — determine the specific character of a unit and in this way exert a particular influence on the patient. If only for this reason it is difficult to give a general description of the psychiatric or psychological problems which can arise in various ICTUs. Moreover, interpretation of the various results is subject to limitations. One of these limitations lies in the fact that

* Farber Irving J: Hospitalized Cardiac Patient. 1978, New York State Journal of Medicine 78:2045–2049.

1 Nadelson Theodore: The Psychiatrist in the Surgical Intensive Care Unit. 1976, Archives of Surgery 111:113–117.

2 see also Brock-Utne J G, Cheetham R W S and Goodwin N M: Psychiatric problems in intensive care. 1976, Anaesthesia 31:380–384.

3 see also Freyberger Hellmuth: Psychosomatic aspects of an intensive care unit. in Modern Perspectives in the Psychiatric Aspects of Surgery. ed by John G Howells. Brunner/Mazel, Publishers. New York 1976, p 549

4 Tomlin P J: Psychological problems in intensive care. 1977, British Medical Journal 2:441–443.

the behaviour sciences deal with less factual, less sharply defined and more contro-versial events and acts than their practitioners would wish[5].

In spite of all obvious problems, intensive care and treatment units are tolerated well by practically all patients. No lasting psychic deviations have been found later[6].

The intensive-therapy patient is mostly conscious*, and is disturbed by the activ-ities, light and particularly by noise[7] in an open ICTU.

Homologous stimulation, solitude, confinement, isolation** and invariant input predispose to illusions and hallucinations***.

There is a deterioration in intellectual performance with an increased susceptibility to influence and stimulus seeking behaviour.

Patient stress is described in an account of the experience of Mr *Lawrie*[8], an analytical chemist, who was curarised and ventilated for nine days. He experienced discomfort related to lying in one position for any length of time and found himself looking forward to positional changes. He hallucinated when the effects of his drugs subsided. He suffered from double vision and large objects seemed to be nearer than they actually were: the ceiling appeared to be only about 0.5 m above him. Therefore he preferred not to be left on his back. His hearing was very acute: sounds were magnified and he heard most conversations in his vicinity, but his worst memories were when he could hear nothing.

5   see also Bazelmans J: Intensive care: virtue or vice? 1977, The Netherlands journal of medicine 20:220–226.

6   see also Freyberger H: Intensivbehandlungseinheit: Psychosomatische Aspekte, 1976, Der Krankenhaus-arzt 49:797–805.

*   75 to 85 per cent of patients have been substantially conscious for the whole or for the majority of their stay in the ICTU. see also Keep FPJ: Stimulus deprivation in windowless rooms. 1977, Anaesthesia 32:598–600.

7   see also La lutte contre le bruit. Collection du ministère des affaires sociales. Masson et Cie. Paris 1968, p 11, Pessi Teuvo T: Experiences gained in intensive care of surgical patients. 1973, Annales Chirurgiae et Gyne-cologiae Fenniae 62:suppl. 185, p 10.

**   In normal subjects, this kind of stress includes abnormal states of brain activity, and is used as part of the technique in dictatorships for including a state of suggestibility in political prisoners about to be cross-examined.

*** A perceptual disorder, e g an hallucination, emerges as the individual provides his own stimulus in a depriving environment in order to maintain his level of arousal.

8   cited by Melia Kath M: The Intensive Care Unit — a stress situation? 1977, Nursing Times 73:5:17–20

Elderly patients

The results of interdisciplinary research in gerontology in recent years — whether in the field of psychology or in medicine, psychiatry, sociology, or ecology — give added weight to the demand for a differential gerontology. It must be questioned whether psychological and physical aging processes conform to any universal laws[1].

In the aging process there are not only interindividual differences — i e persons born in the same year may show marked differences in their 'biological', 'functional', 'social' and 'psychological' ages — but that there are also differences with regard to the intraindividual aging process, that there are patterns of intraindividual development which vary interindividually.

Psychological research in gerontology during the past 20 years has been able to show that the 'deficit' model of aging, which is still widely entertained, is in need of revision or modification. There need not be an age-induced deterioration in the mental sphere. There is neither a general (i e affecting all fields) nor a universal (i e affecting all persons) aging deficit[2].

Elderly patients vary greatly in emotional stability and in mental acuity. The results of research point to the primary significance of a personality structure characterized by a generally higher level of activity, which usually goes with a more elevated mood and more marked ability to adapt to, or to cope with, any given life situation[3].

The over 65 years old patients are considered to have the highest degree of individuality[4], in spite of the fact that measurable mental deterioration* occurs in as many as 25 per cent of them[5]. Many elderly patients easily lose contact with reality when placed in new surroundings. Disorientation and hallucinations may occur due to darkness, or after a minimal dose of drugs[6].

---

1 Lehr U: Preparation for Old Age — More than just a Medical Problem. 1977, Triangle 16:93–103.

2 ibid

3 ibid

4 Feldman Wulff: Sjukhuspsykologi. Natur och Kultur. Stockholm 1977, p 141.

* The term senile has no scientific grounds and depression, anxiety and rigidity can be seen in all age groups. F.M. Carp in 1969, using a senility index, took 295 persons with an average age of 72 and 270 persons with an average age of 20 and scored them on the index. A high score meant 'senile'. He discovered that his group aged between 17 and 25 scored 31.2 whereas the 52 to 92 age group scored 14.9. On Carp's results the only conclusion is that people aged 17 to 25 are more senile than those in their seventies.
There is no clear relationship between the pathological anatomy of brains, i e volume size reduced by dead cells, and senile behaviour (Eastmar Mervyn: Medical noose that strangles the social work function. 1977, Health and Social Service Journal 86:1108--1109).

5 Titcher J, Zwerling I, Gottschalk L and Levine M: Psychological reactions of the aged in surgery. 1953, American Archives of Neurology and Psychiatry 79:63.

6 see also Stahl William M: Supportive Care of the Surgical Patient. Grune & Stratton. New York and London 1972, p 251.

The sensory perceptions of aged people suffer under sensory understimulation and disengagement. Because of sensory impairment and the loss of visual, tactile, aural levels of perception, the environment will be for the aged increasingly confusing and frustrating.

The visual acuity of the eye influences perceiving objects at a distance. The opacity of the lens determines the way light is transmitted and affects perception of colours and textures. Elderly see colours almost 20 per cent less keenly than those with normal vision, particularly in the cold end of the spectrum. Colours too often blend, and closely realted textures cannot be differentiated[7].

Glare is a major visual difficulty with the elderly. Direct and indirect glare caused by shiny walls and floors, make it difficult to distinguish between rooms and cupboard doors. Shiny floor areas can be mistaken for openings in the floor. The perception of subtly shaded mural paintings and signs on doors is rendered impossible[8]. Glare should not be confused with light level. The light level must be increased for the elderly[9].

The aural aspect should be mentioned. The elderly have trouble distinguishing meaningful sounds. The background hum of heating, ventilating and air conditioning systems, easy for younger people to adapt to along with television noises etc need to be modified for the elderly[10].

7   Leon Pastalan cited by Stephens Susanne: Hidden barriers. 1978, Progressive Architecture 59:4:94–97.

8   see also Welter Rudolf: Sinneswahrnehmungen von alten Menschen. 1975, Bauen + Wohnen 29:308–310.

9   Leon Pastalan cited by Stephens Susanne: Hidden barriers. 1978, Progressive Architecture 59:4:94–97.

10 ibid

Paediatric patients

Children should be admitted to hospital only if it is absolutely inevitable.

The sophistication of late twentieth century medical science and technology is not matched by a maximal awareness of advances in the field of child psychology as applied to hospitalization*. The infants must be treated as persons in their own right.

Children of all social groups suffer emotional stress when admitted to hospital[1]. Many children do not master it without symptom formation. In a random sample of American children admitted to a pediatric hospital 63.7 per cent of the children were in need of psychiatric consultation because of the incidence of psychopatholo[2]

Emergency hospitalization constitutes an even greater stress than elective admission for both children, parents and staff[3].

The most common cause of psychological disturbance in children in hospital is a sense of lost affection. Separation from the mother is felt most severely in the first three years of life, particularly between the sixth and fifteenth month[4]. Only a day' separation from the mother would mean practically nothing for the child[5].

It has been found that children under three years may stop in their mental development when hospitalized and their games and play may be carried out on a lower intellectual level than before hospitalization[6].

Toddlers and children under five years of age not only suffer from the separation from their parents and accustomed surroundings, but it is also difficult to explain to them the reasons for undergoing such unpleasant experiences as injections, intravenous therapy, gastric suction and operations[7]. Before the age of five, the concerns commonly held by children are abandonment, pain and mutilation, invasion of body orifices, and loss of control over their usual routines[8].

---

* see also Deasy P F: The Special Needs of Children in Hospital. 1978, Irish Medical Journal 71:521–522.

1 see also Dahlin-Widström Barbro: Sjuka barn — barn på sjukhus. 1971, Läkartidningen 68:49–52.

2 Stocking Myron, Rotheny William, Grossen George and Goodwin Rhoda: Psychopathology in the Pediatric Hospital — Implications for Community Health. 1972, American Journal of Public Health 62:551–555.

3 Roskies Ethel, Bedard Paul, Gauvreau-Guibault Helene and Lafortune Danielle: Emergency Hospitalization of Young Children: Some Neglected Psychological Considerations. 1975, Medical Care 13:570–581.

4 see also Foz F: Preparacion del nino para la hospitalizacion y la intervencion quirurgica. 1972, Labor Hospitalaria 4:179–190.

5 Anna Freud and D Burlingham cited by Feldman Wulff: Sjukhuspsykologi. Natur och Kultur. Stockholm 1977, p 122.

6 Tulva Taimi: Pedagoogiline töö lastehaiglas. 1974, Nõukogude Eesti Tervishoid 17:339–341.

7 Rickham P P: Pediatric Surgery and the Child in Hospital. in Synopsis of Pediatric Surgery. ed by P P Rickham, R T Soper and U G Stauffer. Scientia Bokförlag, Uppsala and George Thieme Publishers, Stuttgart 1975, p 3.

8 Petrillo Madeline and Sanger Sirgay: Emotional Care of Hospitalized. J B Lippincott Company. Philadelphia-Toronto 1972, p 119.

Eleven to sixteen-year-olds usually dread leaving the hospital in a dependent position, and worry about their occupation choice[9].

The majority of children who undergo surgical procedures are able to differentiate and integrate their fears and painful experiences, and psychopathology does not become a part of their clinical history[10]. In 20 per cent of the cases, children's fears of operation have resulted in severe postoperative reactions[11]. The extent of the surgery is not so important as the fact of interference with the child's body[12].

Children in hospitals appear to be less afraid than the grown-ups[13], perhaps they are more trusting or naive. However, the children are frequently more afraid of injections[14].

These observations have been based on children and infants living in Europe and North America and confirmed even in South Africa. Until the living standards of the entire non-White population group have been raised to that enjoyed by the average White, the anomaly will remain that a sick non-White child in hospital may be physically better off than he is at home. Hospital personnel need constantly to remind themselves that psychologically this is seldom the case[15].

All periods of illness, whatever their length, seem painfully long to children because they differ from adults in their concept of time and turn all periods of time into waiting times[16].

Time passes more slowly for the child than for the adult. *P LeComte Du Nouy*[17] has noted that time for a middle-aged of 50 years flows about ten times as fast as it does for a child of 5 years, and for a young man of 20 four times as fast as 5-year old. This intellectual aspect of the child must be considered as a factor not least in planning units where paediatric patients are waiting to be operated or in an other way medically treated.

9 Petrillo Madeline and Sanger Sirgay: Emotional Care of Hospitalized. J B Lippincott Company. Philadelphia-Toronto 1972, p 119.

10 Schwarzbeck Charles: The Surgical Experience: A Child's Inner World as Seen Through Psychological Testing. 1977, Clinical Proceedings 33:43–50.

11 Hughes Robert B: Children's fears of surgery. 1967, Hospital Topics 45:9:116–117.

12 Robertson B A: The Child in Hospital. 1977, South African Medical Journal 51:749–752.

13 Ramsay M A E: A survey of pre-operative fear. 1972, Anaesthesia 27:396–402.

14 see also Laan Ingrid: Lapse emotioonidele mõjuvatest teguritest halglas. 1973, Nõukogude Eesti Tervishold 16:54–56.

15 Leary P M: The South African Child in Hospital. 1973, South African Medical Journal 47:647–648.

16 T Bergman and Anna Freud cited by Robertson B A: The Child in Hospital. 1977, South African Medical Journal 51:749–752.

17 Wines Donald B: Architectural Aspects of Services for Children. in Red is the Color of Hurting. Planning for Children in the Hospital. ed by Milten F Shore. National Institute of Mental Health. Bethesda, Maryland 1967, p 77.

The child is more interested in activity involving people than in a distant view. Children in bed require something to hold their interest and compensate for their immobility[18]. The ward should be so planned that the sick child can always see an adult[19].

The children are sensitive to space and their response to it is strongly emotional, but any toys or other security objects seem to give the child more comfort than the environment.

Playrooms and outdoor play areas for children must be provided. The child in hospital has a need to play out the anxieties and problems of being in a strange and frightening environment, and the hostile feelings he may harbour towards parents who seem to have abandoned him and staff who cause him pain.

Charak Samhita recommended already in 600 BC that to please the child patient a variety of toys — coloured, light, musical, beautiful and not sharp-pointed — should be available*.

Play is essential for children who have not the capacity to understand the procedure or the verbal language to express their feelings about the procedures. Play gives a child the assurance that he can still use his body and limbs normally. By occupying himself in creative activities he is, in a sense, repairing those parts of himself which he feels have been broken or damaged. Play is also a means of socializing the children with each other[20].

A full-time child-life worker should be responsible for the playroom programme. The playrooms should be in the sunny area accommodating about 25 children. It should be furnished with low stationary tables and child-sized chairs.

One corner could be reserved for painting, another for child-sized playhouse furniture and the third for large construction trucks. Equipment which increases the mobility of already active children is disruptive and unsafe.

Puzzles of all types, tea sets, dolls, dishes, small blocks, and games all can be used in a superwised playroom. Hobby horses with springs and all forms of battery toys are impractical[21].

18 Field Hermann H: Environmental Design Implications of a Changing Health Care System. in Environment and Cognition. ed by William H Ittelson. Seminar Press. New York and London 1973, p 134.

19 see also Robertson B A: The Child in Hospital. 1977, South African Medical Journal 51:749–752.

* A E De Sá cited by Atwell J D: Changing patterns in pediatric surgical care. 1978, Annals of the Royal College of Surgeons of England 60:375–383.

20 see also Robertson B A: The Child in Hospital. 1977, South African Medical Journal 51:749–752.

21 Heagarty Margaret C and Bond Deborah H: Pediatric Patients Need Diversion. 1974, Hospitals 48:9:50.

Neonates

From the moment of birth, the newborn is acutely aware of his surroundings. Newborn infants, with their relatively sophisticated sensory systems, respond preferentially to stimuli that occur in human social interaction. The infant's contribution has been woefully underestimated until recently[1].

At birth the neonate can see, focus, follow, and exhibit visual preferences. Furthermore, recent evidence suggests that newborn infants are especially interested in facelike configurations. Within minutes after birth, babies visually follows a facelike pattern more than others of similar brightness, complexity, and symmetry. Neonates can also interact with adults by imitating visually presented behaviours[2].

Newborn infants do respond more to the female than to the male voice and will rapidly develop a preference for the mother's voice through her caregiving and interaction[3].

Auditory noise without signal value to the infant appears consistently to hamper development. Repeated encounters with meaningless sound serve to habituate the attention and arousal of the orienting response to such sounds[4].

Perinatal medical care was introduced with the purpose of further decreasing mortality and morbidity by preventing infection and managing physical problems. However maternity unit routines were established before research in paediatrics, anthropology, developmental psychology, ethology, and physiology created a new appreciation of the remarkable capacities of the neonate for social interaction and of the importance of the newborn period for a mutual parent—infant involvement.

In industrialized societies the previous pattern of frequent nursing and abundant physical interaction has been replaced by one of intermittent artificial feeding and minimal contact. Perinatal medical management has additionally imposed a pattern of early separation on mother and neonate.

Neonates may be upset by unusual maternal appearance or behaviour. When bottle-fed by their mothers wearing a mask, one-week-old infants become distressed, avoid their mothers physically and visually, feed poorly. and have disruptions in their sleep cycle. The social responses of healthy mothers and infants are also altered by hospital routines which involve separation.

1   see also Lozoff Betsy, Brittenham Gary M, Trause Mary Anne, Kennell John H, and Klaus Marshall H: The mother-newborn relationship: Limits of adaptability. 1977, The Journal of Pediatrics 91:1–12.

2   Goren C C, Sarty M, and Wu P Y K: Visual following and pattern discrimination of face-like stimuli by newborn infants. 1975, Pediatrics 56:544.

3   Condon W S and Sander L W cited by Lozoff Betsy et al: The mother-newborn relationship: Limits of adaptability. 1977, The Journal of Pediatrics 91:1.

4   McVicker Hunt J: Environmental programming to foster competence and prevent mental retardation in infancy. in Environments as therapy for brain dysfunction. ed by Roger N Walsh and William T Greenough. Plenum Press. New York and London 1976, p 231.

The infant more readily organizes his cycles of sleeping, waking, and crying if exposed to a single caregiver in the first ten days of life. Newborn infants who room-in cry distinctly less and establish a day-night rhythm more quickly than infants in a traditional nursery with multiple caregivers and four-hour feeding schedules.

It is inhuman to force on infants artificial schedules based on the convenience of hospitals shifts. In particular, sleep cycles can be disrupted for months after the baby has spent a longer time in a brightly lit nursery[5]. Equally cruel is the *neonatal exile,* the interrupted mother-child contact, caused by the assumption that the mothers are infection risks[6].

Current programmes encourage the presence of both parents, their participation in feeding where this is practical, and an openess to inform them fully concerning their infant's condition. This interaction between the infant and his family is believed to safeguard the child's emotional, social and physical development. However, there is still need for some clear guidelines by which to determine the optimal amount of tactile, visual, auditory, and other forms of stimulation necessary for the early development of the newborn, especially the immature infant[7].

There is no medical reason why healthy mothers and babies should not be together from the time of birth to the time of discharge from the hospital[8].

5   Petrillo Madeline and Sanger Sirgay: Emotional Care of Hospitalized Children. J B Lippincott Company. Philadelphia-Toronto 1972, p 137.

6   see also Halvorsen Sverre: Pediatriske aspekter ved sykehushygiene. 1977, Tidsskrift for den Norske laegeforening 97:707–709.

7   Segal Sydney: Perinatal intensive care: pediatric aspects. in Perinatal medicine. ed by James W Goodwin, John O Godden, and Graham W Chance. The Williams & Wilkins Co. Baltimore 1976, p 593.

8   Lozoff Betsy, Brittenham Gary M, Trause Mary Anne, Kennell John H, and Klaus Marshall H: The mother-newborn relationship: Limits of adaptability. 1977, The Journal of Pediatrics 91:1.

INFORMATION, PROGRAMMING, PLANNERS

Need for information

The need for accurate and technically correct planning information and the want to reduce uncertainty is overwhelming. Uncertainty in itself is the complement of knowledge. It is in the gap between what is known and what needs to be known to make a correct decision[1].

Written and graphic statements, drawings and sketches are the most usual means of information and communication for the parties involved in the process of planning.

Models, diagrams and words do not always convey meanings and ideas in the way intended. Worse still: they may convey a very conflicting meaning, which was not apparent to the originator of the communication, to others. This circumstance may pass undetected until the end result makes it all too evident[2].

The more information is generated, the bigger is the need to analyse and organize it to achieve a mutual understanding among the participants in the planning process.

Even the most dedicated planner is able to read only a limited fraction of the out-pouring of professional literature. In some sections the available studies are hardly used. E.g. it has been estimated that the average academic paper is read only by 1.3 people. Though some papers are read by several people and a few by hundreds, a large number are never seen save by the author and his editor*.

In recommendations on the sizing and the planning of facilities based on *status quo*, analysis is frequently crowded out as well as evaluation and creative imagination, both necessary for solving the genuine needs of medical science and technology. Instead of a maximum of vigilance in planning procedure, stagnated mediocrity can be found.

In the planning process the review of literature and reports will indicate what has previously been done, what planning methods have been employed, and what aspects should be stressed to develop knowledge.

Hospital planning based only on the strength of current practice is doubtful, particularly in hospital areas and practices, where environment and facilities have acted. as a constraint on function.

Whether one subscribes to the belief that built environment determines behavioural patterns, or that behaviour occurs in spite of the environment, there can be no

1   Mack Ruth P: Planning on uncertainty. Wiley-Interscience. A Division of John Wiley & Sons Inc. New York, London, Sydney, Toronto 1971, p 1.

2   see also Green John R B: Health service facilities planning and design. Part I. School of Health Administration, University of New South Wales, Kensington, Australia. Stencil 1974, p 9.

*   John Wilkinson cited by Cook Olive: The average academic paper is read by 1.3 people. 1971, Ark 48:28–29.

doubt that shortcomings in buildings are made up by behavioural adaption[3], a circumstance not to be overlooked.

The six honest serving-men of *Rudyard Kipling** from the turn of century still provide the most reliable assistance and deserve all respect and appreciation.

Handling the flood of available information requires a good basic training. With unlimited information and unrecognizable systems**, chaos is close.

For almost every item in a building programme there is the qualification that too much of a good thing is undesirable[4]. Only the tools and information needed have to be grasped and collected, everything else has to be disregarded and discarded***.

---

3   see also Aylward Graeme and Lapthorne Keith: Designing for stability in designing for change. University of Cambridge. Department of Architecture. June 1974, p 90.

*   I keep six honest serving-men
         (They taught me all I knew);
         Their names are What and Why and When
         And How and Where and Who.
     Kipling Rudyard: Just So Stories For Little Children. Macmillan & Co Ltd. London 1971, p 83.

**   It has happened that presented material has brought in mind "a certain Chinese encyclopaedia" in which animals are divided according to (a) those belonging to the Emperor, (b) stuffed, (c) tamed, (d) suckling-pigs, (e) mermaids, (f) fabulous, (g) stray dogs, (h) included in the present taxonomy, (i) that gambol madly . . . (n) which, seen from afar, look like flies.

4   Sommer Robert: Personal Space. Prentice-Hall, Inc. Englewood N J 1969, p 158.

***The attempts of overambitious, undisciplined and unlearned collecting of facts brings to mind the two elderly cranks from Gustave Flaubert's last novel, Bouvard and Pécuchet, who tried to investigate every branch of knowledge.

Obstacles in spreading and utilizing planning information

One of the obstacles in spreading of hospital planning information is confidentiality[1] A frank and detailed exposition of any errors and malfunctions encountered by an investigator may be treated by the involved instances as a confidential report and thus withdrawn the pool of experience.

Health care literature has also a sector — larger than most disciplines have — of informative papers with a very limited circulation[2]. This sector covers so called unpublished material, and refers to research reports, theses, dissertations, management engineering papers, modeling theories, experience brochures, and system analysis. There are also so-called invisible working parties, small groups of specialists who collaborate intimately without formal organizing.

To do a literature review for each facility, and to keep that review up-to-date, is a time-consuming, and staff-consuming process. To go beyond the published material to interviews with experienced people, occasional surveys, and other groups, planning groups, and community groups are too small to undertake the lesser job, let alone the greater one[3]. The need for intelligence officers, information brokers, information communicators and technological gatekeepers is on the increase[4].

Well-trained and specialized hospital planners, architects and advisors reduce the problem of information reviewing. Much of hospital planning and design information is both confusing and unnecessary. The official advice has a strong tendency to degenerate into often troublesome norms and standards, which quickly become obsolete.

A lot of available information — the motives behind these publications vary — is designed to stop people thinking. They may easily lead to a blind conformity.

Not all what is written is read and understood, let alone effectively utilized. Worse, there are planners and designers who are too happy to use available material without any critical thought.

This circumstance is a very definite threat towards professionalism of the planner and a definite risk to increase insensitivity towards the object involved[5]. Early-out-of-use solutions may be the result of this kind of negligence.

1   see also Pibouleau R F: Introduction to National and International Exchange of Knowledge and Experience. 1975, World Hospitals 11:63–64.

2   see also Weeks Lewis W: "Unpublished" Literature: A Valuable Source of Information on Hospital Financial Management. 1977, Hospital & Health Services Administration 22:1:57–71.

3   see also Russell Louise B: The diffusion of the new hospital technologies in the United States. 1976, International Journal of Health Services 6:557–580.

4   see also Laan Ilmar: Teadlane ja informatsioon. 1976, Nõukogude Eesti Tervishoid 19:36–39.

5   see also Thiberg Sven: människa närmiljö samhälle. Statens Råd för Byggnadsforskning. Stockholm 1975, p 2

The way in which planning documents are judged, arranged, and their suitability for checking, cross indexing and re-use on other projects are important factors in ensuring that maximum use is made of the cumulative and collective efforts of planning teams[6].

6   see also Green John R B: Health service facilities planning and design. Part I. School of Health Administration, University of New South Wales, Kensington, Australia. Stencil. 1974, p 25.

Temporary validity of knowledge

Temporary validity of some of the knowledge and relativity of truth in the planning process, obvious in the ever changing world, represent major obstacles in the process of hospital generation. Doubts are as changeable as answers[1].

Solutions are not eternal but merely suit the period.

All statements in ideologies, sciences, and creative planning, even in visualization, are interim. Stand-points and opinions respond continuously to outside impulses and pressure, and to given or taken opportunities to look at existing problems from changed vantage points.

Nobel laureate *Werner Heisenberg*[*] stated in his uncertainty principle that man alters truth in the very process of measuring it and that the act of observing a phenomenon may alter the behaviour being studied.

Over the long periods of time inevitably involved in the planning, design, and construction of large hospitals, people may come and go, alter their minds and even forget things and agreements. Technical, social, and political changes may require far-reaching modifications in policies and consequences from individuals and institutions.

This long time span makes the channels of communication very extended. A decision on how a particular service or department was meant to function may meet a completely changed situation by the time the department is ready to start.

Change is a constant factor in the course of life. Change, of course, is not necessarily a progress.

Genuine changes should be clearly distinguished from fashions. Being accustomed to rapid changes of styles in art, popular music, cinema, and literature, it is not surprising that also other creative activities, including sciences — which is the lifeline of medical development — try to follow fashions.

Change is initiated where strain and stress emerge. Even smallest perturbations are cumulative in their effect. Changes include growth, specialization, differentiation, and reintegration on higher or lower levels.

The science advances are jerky and erratic. The line of science progress is a zigzag line, not a curve approaching its asymptote[2].

1   Finch Roy: Questioning the Question. 1966, The Lugano Review V-VI: 90-95.

*   Werner Heisenberg (1902—1976) presented the first coherent formulation of quantum mechanics, which explains the structure of the atom.

2   Koestler Arthur: Drinkers of infinity. Hutchinson. London 1968, pp 260 and 267.

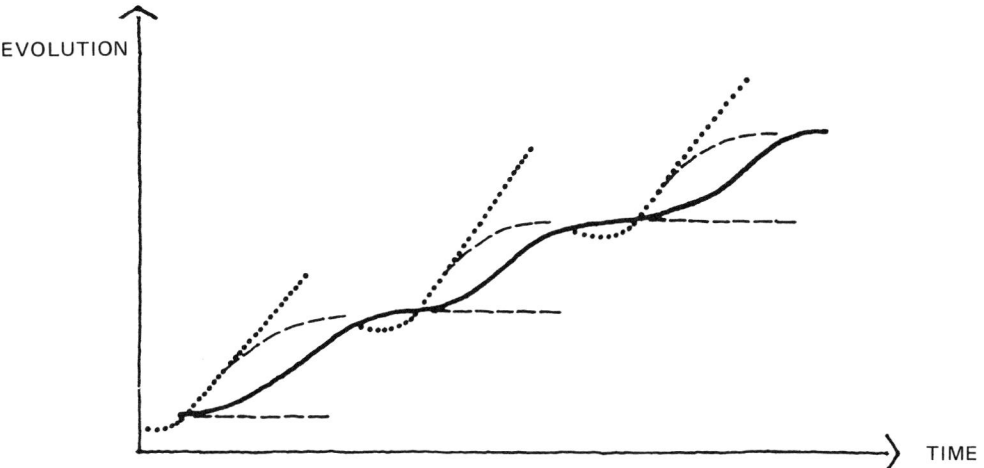

EVOLUTION

TIME

Nobel laureate Jonas Salk has revealed the pattern of perturbations that continually occur in the cultural evolutionary process, which proceeds dialectically. A period of rapid change is followed by a tranquil interval, which in its turn is disturbed by an innovation to give rise to a further step.

The organizational change has usually been dominated by the aspect of growth*, less by regrouping or qualitative improvements. Mostly, the exponential growth of an organization is made up by a number of smaller sigmoid curves under an envelope curve. An initial period of slow growth is followed by rise and expansion, which later, due to evoked latent reactions, gives way to a period of limited increase. The final phases are either the level of equilibrium or shrinkage or dissolution.

The growth of a hospital, or its departments, may be irregular and spasmodic. There are sectors of discontinuity. Growth in one sector may be paralleled by decay in another.

Although the speed of a development along the rising main S-curve is of interest, the overwhelming concern for the hospital planner is to detect its directional changes in time. If a major growth occurs unexpectedly or if the transformation to equilibrium or shrinkage does not occur in a predicted time — too soon or too late — the users of the hospital meet considerable complications.

The small sigmoid curves should not escape the attention of the planner. There are areas in which growth or decay can be forecasted and consequently programmed.

---

* Nobel laureate Dennis Gabor feels that the growth addiction has become the universal creed of our world
(Gabor Dennis: The Mature Society. Secker & Warburg. London 1972, p 2).

Some forces are always contributing to change and to move upward, some forces are horizontal and resist or counter change. At the side of a pressure for change, there is always the preference for continuity. Thus the problem is not continuity *versus* change, but continuity *and* change[3].

Resistance to advanced programme is often a function of the way change is introduced. Most planners have run into trouble when the planning was done without introducing first the new ideas to those who control resources and who will be affected.

Adaption to change, which requires learning as well as unlearning, is sometimes a painful procedure. Immediate acceptance of the new for the sake of novelty alone is condoned only by journalists whose interest lies in the sensational[4].

Because the long-term memory store of the elderly is full, there is a lot to forget and, because short-term memory weakens with age, there is less chance of new events getting into the long-term store[5]. This is why most of the changes in societies can only come about over a long period, the period of change being 15 to 30 years[6].

In evolutionary processes that which survives is not only the *fittest*, but that which *fits best* in the constantly changing circumstances[7].

3 see also Bakema Jacobe: Continuity versus change. 1975, Art & Architecture (Tehran) 6:25–26:9–10.

4 Lippard Lucy R: Changing. E P Dutton. New York 1971, p 28.

5 Abercrombie M L J: The difficulties of changing. in Health Care in a Changing Setting: the UK experience. Elsevier. Excerpta Medica. Amsterdam, Oxford, New York 1976, p 3–19.

6 see also Martino J P: The pace of technological change. 1972, The Futurist 6:70–72.

7 see also Salk Jonas: The survival of the wisest. Harper & Row, Publishers. New York, Evanston, San Francisco, London 1973, p 27.

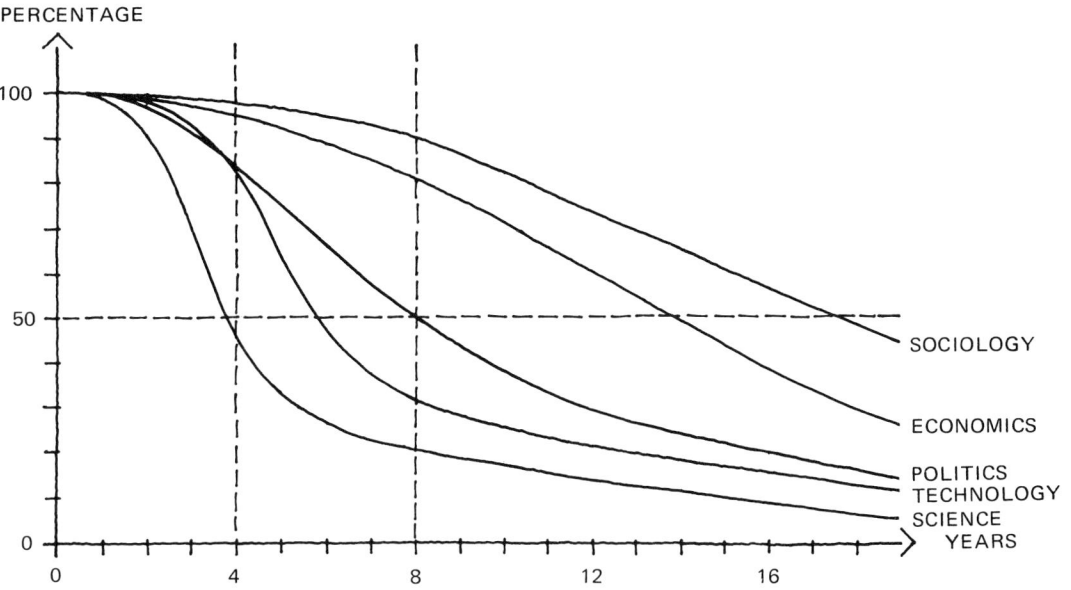

The reliability of forecasting varies in different areas of concern. Busch has indicated that most difficult is to predict development in sciences, easiest in sociology.

To predict is a very pronounced natural desire. *Abraham Lincoln* made a plaintive plea for more guidance in a changing world: "If we could first know where we are and whither we are tending, we could better judge what to do and how to do it."

This plea has an immense importance for planning of health care organizations and facilities. However, the attempts at predicting the future are accepted as a serious science only in our days.

Engagement in the future and overwhelming enthusiasm for predicting what might exist or be needed should not cause serious negligence concerning current situations and existing problem complexes, which remain the foundation of all planning work.

There are many limitations and difficulties in attempts at predicting the future. The notion of predicting *future* ideas or theories involves a logical selfcontradiction as it simply cannot be done[1].

1   Medawar Sir Peter B: The Cost/Benefit Analysis of Pure Research. 1973, Hospital Practice 8:9:11–12.

In many cases premises for predicting developments are not taken from the nature of man. Important factors are overlooked or deliberately ignored. Unimportant, even fictional, but easily measurable factors are manipulated instead.

One particularly risky class of predictions includes any prediction that certain advances in science or medicine will not or cannot take place. It deserves a special name but has not yet received it[2].

Increased attention should be given to forecasting, which is concerned with what ought to be — or with what is thought to be — desirable or preferable and with establishing policies which will guide events away from their current probable course towards a more desired state. The objections to this approach are that it is primarily élitist and that it will inevitably involve conflict[3].

At any rate, the scope of the society's future engagement in health care has to be prognosticated.

For a period of 20 years a vision is needed, the general terms have to be postulated and some expectations identified. A series of related schemes specialized with respect to function, finance, organization level, personnel, and the time periods should accompany the basic study.

The salient features of the basic document have to be developed in three over-all sub-scenarios: the over-all medical service plan for 10 to 15 years, the operation plan for 3 to 5 years, and the budget for 1 year.

Qualitative future estimates are obtained either through experts' opinions or through manipulating information about factors believed to be relevant. These often are probabilistic because events are very seldom related to each other in a simple deterministic way. Even a single process is rarely without variability in its output.

The accuracy of a forecast probably depends on the adequacy of model formulation. However, there is no criterion to determine the reliability of forecasting technique.

Frequently a simple linear extrapolation of the past-present against quantitative estimates is applied. Historial time series data are extended to carry the trend of the past-present into the future. When in such a prediction no account is taken into the possible influences of outside factors, most of the reliability* of the prediction is lost.

2   Medawar Sir Peter B: Some Follies of Prediction. 1975, Hospital Practice 10:4:73–74.

3   see also Nuttall Peggy: Nursing in the year AD 2000. 1976, Journal of Advanced Nursing 1:101–110.

*   Henry Miller has presented an illuminating anecdote: a projection based on trends in horse-drawn traffic in the 1870's would have predicted that by 1970 the surface of the globe would be covered by 1.8 m of manure (Medicine and Society. Oxford University Press. London 1973, p 14).

Inspired by the successes of natural scientists, many sociologists have made attempts at finding some natural laws ruling human societies and have tried — not very successfully — to extrapolate the future from them in very general terms. These attempts have often been used against sociologists by their critics[4].

In the *Delphi method* a number of information sources is approached individually, e g to determine the date of a turning point of a particular development. The delivered individual predictions are circularized without attribution. On basis of these predictions another set of individual forecasts is made. The new set is recircularized for a renewed individual prediction. Then the median date of predictions is taken as the consensus date. This way of forecasting — in many ways valuable — can be completely upset by the occurence of a single, discrete event.

Concerning high technologization in forecasting, it has been stated[5] that it is a sad fact that forecasts — particularly economic forecasts — despite their use of sophisticated mathematics and capacious computers, are by no means infallible. Indeed, the profession's recent history is littered with embarrassing examples of forecasts that differed from each other or from what actually happened.

4   Wiberg Håkan: Vision of the future. Stencil. Lund 1977, p 199.

5   see also Beardwood Roger: Economic forecasts: a waste of money? 1977–78, Profile 14:16–18.

Medical documentation

Good planning teams need to be well informed also about medical development.

The continuous expansion of scientific enterprises has generated a vast accumulation of facts, opinions, but also pseudo-scientific publications. It is easy to be overwhelmed by the size of the libraries and archieves and so disregard a fundamental ignorance in many subjects.

In 1973, using a broader criterion, there were 7,000 medical journals. This number has since then increased slightly. Of these probably only a fifth — in itself a very large number — make a real contribution to the advancement of medical science and practice[1]. Research on research on life saving advances in the treatment of cardiovascular and pulmonary diseases indicates that out of 4,000 scientific articles screened only about a tenth — 529 papers — were considered key papers and absolutely essential[2].

It has been stated that in research work about 60 to 80 per cent of investigations are doubled or repeated because of lacking co-ordination[3]. It has also been stated that the surgical literature today is replete with investigative studies that have little, if any value[4].

Frequently it is assumed that a high percentage of current medical knowledge will be obsolete in ten years. The difference between medico-technological and humanistic insights is phenomenal. Sophocles, Shakespeare and Strindberg represent 2,500 years of well playable theatre and at least ninety-five per cent of the average performing artist's repertory consists of music written between 1700 and 1920[5]. A medico-technological book is said to be out-of-date in five years.

This all complicates the search for adequate information.

1   Howard-Jones Norman: Our medical literature-then and now. 1973, British Journal of Medical Education 7:70–85.

2   Comroe Jr Julius H and Dripps Robert D: Scientific Basis for the Support of Biomedical Science. 1976, Science 192:4235:105–111.

3   Hussar Ülo and Murasev Eugen: Meditsiin tänapäeva teaduste süsteemis. 1974, Nõukogude Eesti Tervishoid 17:403–407.

4   Boyden Allen M: Surgical Education. 1974, The American Journal of Surgery 126:2.

5   Cooper Martin: Knowing by Heart. 1977, Encounter 49:2:30–33.

The need to rely upon hospital statistics is frequently heavy, but these are often inappropriate and could be a source of error in the planning process. Mostly they demonstrate a work load at a particular point in time and are of little value in contemplating future trends because policies and techniques change[1].

A frequent and grave danger is the illusion that datas that can be quantified and produced by a computer are more important than those which cannot.

It should not be persisted in the belief that each number appearing in statistics is equivalent to absolute truth as long as it is recorded accurately enough[2]. A definite demarcation line between secure knowledge and qualified opinion cannot be obtained. The loss of distinction between health and illness, which had been quite clear when the infectious diseases dominated, has complicated the situation of health statistics. The complications have increased since the predominance of chronic diseases started.

Neither does the ancillary science of statistics furnish a general comprehension of the subject matter in natural sciences and the humanities. Biostatisticians have tended to concentrate on the establishment of causality and have neglected the estimation of the quantitative association. Both parts are important and necessary for a complete evaluation[3].

Health statistics and judging quality of medical care in terms of outcomes achieved is considered the most direct way to assess quality. To date most attempts to evaluate quality of care have focused on the structure or process of medical care. These studies share the common assumption that adequate resources and technology — structure — contribute to adequate diagnostic workups and treatment — process — which in turn result in favorable health status — outcome[4].

A very serious limitation of the health statistical approach is associated with its emphasis and orientation. Life and death are reduced to bare percentages. The preoccupation is with death rates, instead of the problems of living, dependancy and disability. Information on the breadth of the outcome criteria is absent.

Mortality or return to function are heavily influenced by intervening factors such as genetic makeup and the physical and social environment that are beyond the control of the medical care system.

---

1   see also Neal F E: Chairman's summary. in The Planning of Radiotherapy Departments. ed by T J Deeley. British Journal of Radiology Special Report 12. London 1976, p 72.

2   see also Maier W: Statistik — ein Patentrezept? 1975, Geburtshilfe und Frauenheilkunde 33:366–369.

3   Lave Judith R and Lave Lester B: Measuring the Effectiveness of Prevention: I. 1977, The Milbank Memorial Fund Quarterly/Health and Society 55:273–289.

4   Brook Robert H, Davies-Avery Allyson, Greenfield Sheldon, Harris L Jeff, Lelan Tova, Solomon Nancy W, Ware Jr John E: Assessing the Quality of Medical Care Using Outcome Measures: An Overview of the Method. 1977, Supplement to Medical Care 15:9:1.

Information about many outcomes is not readily available or contained in the patient's medical record, requiring the use of follow-up patient interviews. These are expensive to conduct and may be difficult to complete. Death or incidence of major complications, may be so uncommon that detection of significant differences in these outcomes between patient groups requires a sample so large that the feasibility of the study is limited[5].

Deaths from particular conditions tell nothing about other, concurrent conditions which seldom cause death. E g deaths from stroke, lung cancer, and coronary disease say nothing about the prevalence of prolapse, varicose veins, and hernia[6]. Death or restoration of normal function often occur so late in the course of treatment that timely evaluation is impossible.

Autopsies are needed to have a clearer understanding of the true incidence of disease. Death certificates do not supply these facts, since so few of them are based on autopsy verification. As W *Farr* has observed: The clinician makes a guess on the death certificate that leaves everyone happy. He is happy because the chart is signed out. The medical librarian is happy because she can now report something specific like thrombus of the lenticulostriate artery. The collector of morbid and mortality rates is happy because he can tabulate this guesswork and call it 'vital statistics'. Standard review organizations are happy because all orders are signed, a note is made each day, and discharge diagnoses are carefully listed, often without really knowing whether diagnostic and therapeutic errors remain undisclosed and are buried with the dead. The autopsy provides facts and accurate, unbiased data upon which medical statistics should be founded[7].

Also planning which relies solely on institutional indicators — length of stay, cost per case, cost per day in hospital, and the incidence of hospitalization — may be a hazard of increasing inequalities in distribution of resources[8].

Health statistics indicate the amount of people who seek medical care but they do not show the real need for medical care in a society. In summing up his experience *John Fry,* a British general practitioner, concluded that medical care is sought for only about a fourth of all illnesses that occur in the community[9].

5   Brook Robert H, Davies-Avery Allyson, Greenfield Sheldon, Harris L Jeff, Lelan Tova, Solomon Nancy W, Ware Jr John E: Assessing the Quality of Medical Care Using Outcome Measures: An Overview of the Method. 1977, Supplement to Medical Care 15:9:1.

6   see also Bennett A E and Holland W W: Rational planning or muddling through? 1977, The Lancet 1:464–466.

7   Prutting John: Autopsies — Benefits for Clinicians. 1978, American Journal of Clinical Pathology 69:2 (supplement): 223–225.

8   see also Wennberg John E, Gittelsohn Alan and Shapiro Nancy: Health Care Delivery in Maine III: Evaluating the Level of Hospital Performance. 1975, The Journal of the Maine Medical Association 66:298.

9   Dingle John H: The Ills of Man. 1973, Scientific American 229:3:77–84.

Experience from Gothenburg, Sweden, indicates that the fourth of population that is least interested in health care, is in the greatest need for it[10]. Mostly the discomfort is accepted or the problems are approached by self-medication*.

It is believed that about 50 per cent of those who have a light illness, adapt self-treatment. When the illnesses are serious, the percentage of self-treatment is reduced to about 10 per cent[11].

10 Werkö Lars at the symposion Sjukvården och samhället. Gothenburg, October 1974.

*   In the US one third of medicaments are sold for self-medication (R M Coe cited by Dörner Klaus: Wie werde ich Patient oder Sozialisation in fünf Stadien. in Die verordnete Krankheit. ed by Henrich v Nussbaum. S Fischer Verlag. Frankfurt (Main) 1977, p 58).

11 Dörner Klaus: Wie werde ich Patient oder: Sozialisation in fünf Stadien. in Die verordnete Krankheit. ed by Henrich v Nussbaum. S Fischer Verlag. Frankfurt (Main) 1977, p 60.

Research into hospital function and design, hospital evaluati

It is unsafe to base planning models entirely, or even mainly, on historical models, relationships and data. To do so would be like steering the ship by watching its wake[1].

Research is the basis for progress into the future. There is a need to investigate and monitor various aspects of the design, space and cost requirements of hospitals continuously. In this context research must be regarded as a resource in much the same way as money, manpower, materials and energy[2].

As long as that literature has a tradition of overwhelming honesty, it is a prime tool of research.

However, hospital planning information based on scientific research is scarce, because research in medical services — as distinct from medical science — and as the basic determinant in the planning process has not been significant. With much regret it must be notified, that a good hospital research unit is an extremely rare phenomenon. Most of the countries lack university level health care facility research units.

The research into hospital function and design — as scarce as research into health service — should be the responsibility of an office or centre, run independently and with more freedom of action than a government department[3] or any other bureaucratic body. Good research results could also be expected from quality institutions of higher learning.

Data collected routinely in hospitals are often of suspect quality, principally because they are not used for any significant purpose. In the USA in 1972 an array of the distribution of net and gross building areas to function in 50 selected community hospitals was published*. In the last paragraph of his review *James J Souder* writes: Comprogram has relentlessly driven a computer through 41,000 bits of trivia The computer has won. It has spewed forth, in neat arrays, almost 450 pages of useless numbers. Whatever the basic intent of the Public Health Service study may have been, it could not have been this.

That American publication is not an isolated case**.

1   Hammond III John S: Do's & don'ts of computer models for planning. 1974, Harvard Business Review 52:2:110–123.

2   Webb T L: Rational buildings for health care. Mankind and Medicine in the Third Millenium Conference. Cape Town. September 1976.

3   see also Aurousseau Paul in the review of Principles of Hospital Planning. 1968, World Hospitals 4:1:35.

*   Comprogram: Hospital Space Allocation. Center for Environmental Research. Boston 1972.

4   1973, Hospitals, 47:10:50–52.

** following random publications could be mentioned as examples from Sweden: Måttrekommendationer för rum inom sjukvårdsanläggningar. Spri råd 5.16.Stockholm 1973.
    Sjukhusbyggnader 2. Spri rapport 6/75. Stockholm 1976.
    Sterilcentraler. Spri rapport 15/76. Stockholm 1976.

All surveys should add to the hospital knowledge in a sensible way*. A fancy free and unequivocal transference of expensive over-elaborated and over-detailed time and motion studies that take no account of any trend in possible developments or alternatives to routines, can only result in shortlived truths. The more definite and precise the instructions are, the more the proposed precise spatial solutions will be time and situation-bound and development-resistant.

It is dissatisfactory when the design has to be based on collection of automated aids, which are solely concerned with findings supposedly precise answers to tactical short term questions. Momentary perfectionism should in no situation be appreciated.

The first types of measurements to evaluate the effectiveness of a hospital were those involving such elements as floor space, staffing patterns and financial factors. The basic weakness of this method is the assumption that a proper structural environment automatically results in effective medical care.

Frequently attempts to measure and evaluate the general hospital lay-out tend to concentrate on the judgement of the main characteristics of the circulation aspect: frequency and type, urgency and bulk[1]. Circulation requirements, manifesting the relative proximity of activities have traditionally been taken as the function to be quantified and optimized.

The reduction of circulation factors within the departments to pure mathematical values can not be achieved. The obtainable circulation data should be used only as *one* component in the planning or evaluation process. They should be parallelled by other, possibly more vital aspects.

The traditional approaches and criteria used in evaluation of health facilities design are inadequate in terms of both contemporary expectations and availability of scientific knowledge, as the evaluation procedures have leant too heavily on the subjective reactions and intuitive judgement[2].

Any realistic attempt to evaluate the design of hospitals requires multi-disciplinary knowledge. The design-in-use evaluation processes should be both analytical and judgemental.

---

*
   There have been surveys similar to one by the Greater London Council, which disclosed that most people eat at midday and in the evenings and that expensive restaurants in London's theatre-land are fullest before and after theatre performances (Kayhan, July 8, 1975).

1 see also Lada Anastasia: Communication Patterns in General Hospitals. Medical Architecture Research Unit. The Polytechnic of North London. Stencil. London 1973, p 57.

2 see also Wheeler E Todd: Evaluating the existing hospital. A paper prepared for the IV Public Health Seminar, Prague, October 1972.

Professionals from the fields of medicine and architecture should consult behaviour scientists, professionals from the fields of public health and administrative science and industrial and human factors engineers[3]. A proper place has to be found for the user's comments and advice.

There is a danger that evaluation studies may become too theoretical.

The evaluation of single whole hospitals should be part of an interhospital assessment dealing with similar functions or cycles of activity.

If evaluation studies of existing hospitals are to be made a meaningful basis of design improvements, there should be a widely accepted method which puts the results of such studies in an immediately applicable shape[4].

Many design requirements may change greatly before the results of any evaluation can be adapted. Changes are easiest to emerge in the top echelon of the health care hierarchy.

In a situation where standards of amenity and service are difficult to define the conclusion would be implemented only if they promise financial improvements[5].

3   Field Hermann H, Hanson John A, Karlis Constantine J, Kennedy Donald A, Lippert Stanley and Ronco Paul G: Evaluation of Hospital Design. Tufts-New England Medical Center. Boston, Mass. 1971, p 27.

4   see also Green J R B: Evaluation of health service buildings. 1974, Hospital & Health Care Administration 4:4:6–8.

5   see also Hunter J K: Evaluating of New Hospital. 1972, World Hospitals 7:1:201–205.

Substitute devices for research

In many instances instead of solid research results substitute devices such as fragmentized prototype plans, list-of-room type programmes[1] and bubble-diagrams have been offered. The literally interpreted bubble diagrams have occasionally resulted in most amazing misinterpretations[2].

While a minimum amount of space per person is necessary, this figure is not sufficient as a basis for design decisions. Neither should rules-of-thumb form a basis for generating programmatic requirements.

Such indicators as departmental area per bed, workload per bed and cost per bed are severely abused providing in many instances a fictitious sense of reliable comparison and a faulty basis for formulating programme requirements and capital needs[3].

From a very thorough survey of floor-space data in a large number of hospitals in the USA, it was concluded that there is practically no correlation between hospitals[4]. Obviously not much importance can be placed on comparisons of this kind between hospitals.

Increasingly it is being understood that the approach of publishing specific m^2 requirements for various hospital sections is based on a fallacious concept[5]. E g the use of an average m^2 figure for laboratory design will often be misleading. The actual m^2 figure in existing laboratories which appear to be providing adequate service varies greatly[6].

What has just been said by no means is to discriminate the finding out how hospitals and their equipment are actually used and the role of feedback of experience from them. On the contrary, this feedback is badly needed instead of frequent efforts spent on collecting data and developing methods of prediction.

A purposeful accumulation of experiences can protect from the repetition of mistakes.

---

1 see also Lindheim Roslyn: Uncoupling the Radiology System. Hospital Research and Educational Trust. Chicago 1971, p 1.

2 personal communication: 1975, Raymond Moss, London.

3 see also Boyar Robert L: Functional and Space Programming. No publishing year. The Rourke Report 4:3:1–4.

4 AIA committee on Hospital Architecture: Hospital Department Area Studies. 1963, Journal of American Institute of Architects 48:83–89.

5 see also Manual for laboratory planning and design. College of American Pathologists. Skokie, Ill 1977, p 54.

6 ibid

Codes, norms, standards

In most countries the hospital is subjected to more demanding codes and design regulations than any other building type*. Considering the role of the hospital, its occupants, and the absolute necessity for safety and reliability, it is in principle difficult to object to this circumstance.

The main motivating factors for the introduction of national norms for hospital buildings have been summarized by those who introduce these norms as the need to determine health care needs and priorities more carefully within severe economic restraints; the need to ensure that what is built represents the best value for money; and the need for conformity and coordination[1].

Nobody, no matter how well informed, can develop standards that will prepare him for all events.

Data for planning are mostly compromises and the standards are embodied in legal rules, codes and regulations which lag generally behind the social consciousness and even more behind the expert scientific knowledge**.

The grade of thoroughness with which design recommendations were originally worked out is seldom evident[2]. Even an institution with good reputation may occasionally produce a *lapsus*. The planner cannot check the validity of all planning information he is to use. Most of it has to be accepted on trust.

The path of standards for bigger functional units has been insecure. In general, their *raison d'être* has been to provide, often without thought for the future, an immediate answer to a current pressure[3]. Building codes reflect and perpetuate the technology of some earlier period. They restrict the potential use of new ideas

---

* E g in the United States in February 1977, the General Accounting Office reported that the Department of Health, Education, and Welfare issued nearly 600 proposed or final health-related regulations during fiscal 1976. Since that time, almost twice as many regulations have been issued, a large portion of which govern the design and construction of health care facilities (Sprague Joseph G: Codes, regulations and compliance: a never-ending dilemma. 1978, Hospitals 52:4:90–92).

1 also D Cowan: National norms for hospitals. Second Southern African Hospital Symposium. Pretoria. November 1977.

** As an example: of about one hundred laws, regulations, standards, directives and recommendations of the German Federal Government, German Länder governments, The German Standards Institute and professional bodies concerned with the planning and construction of hospitals in force in December 1970, the majority was a hindrance rather than a help to hospital planners. Some lay down unimportant or outdated conditions — e g one Land directive stated that hospitals must have electric illumination (Novotny F: Brauchen wir Richtlinien und Verordnungen für Planung und Bau von kranken Krankenhäusern? 1974, Das Krankenhaus 66:8–12).

At a symposion 1975 in Tallinn, Estonia, when the work of some contemporary architects was studied, it was found that the current building legislations and codes of Soviet Union would not have allowed the execution of any of the designs of the last decades by Alvar Aalto, Eero Saarinen, Louis Kahn, Oscar Niemeyer, Felix Candela, Frei Otto, Marcel Breuer, Kenzo Tange and some others.

2 see also Thiberg Sven: Människa närmiljö samhälle. Statens Råd för Byggnadsforskning. Stockholm 1975, p 95.

3 see also Radford Robert: The Harness Hospitals Development Programme. 1974, Build International 7:43–56

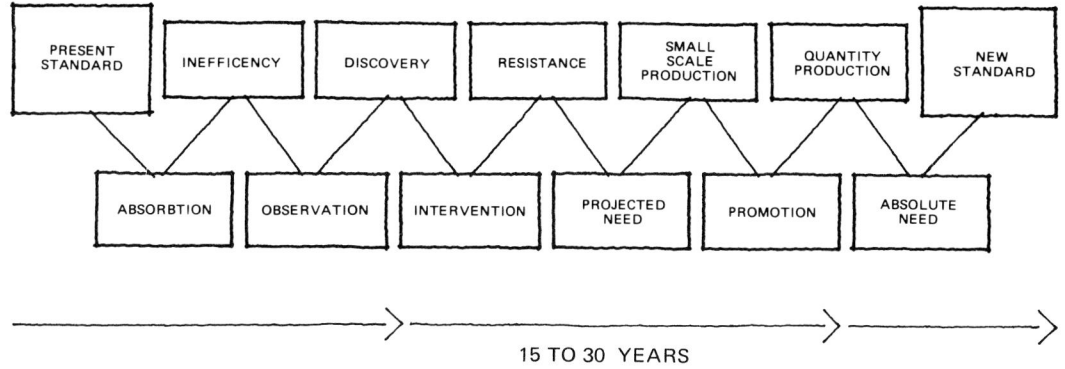

A minimum of twelve progressive stages can be detected in progression from one general standard to the next, has Frederick J Kiesler indicated. Every need has its own accents in the development movement.

and materials. Standardization must not result in making planning an affair of geometric ordering, a game of grids.

The norms are meaningless unless they are reasonable and realistic and not founded on averages borrowed from some foreign countries. Even within the boundaries of one single country the norms cannot be applied without making provisions for the environment, the climate, the specific needs for the project with its specialities in various departments.

The norms should not necessarily concentrate on providing a functional project at the lowest cost, since it often happens that by the provision of a small additional facility and small increased cost, the function of the building can be considerably superior with the accompanying long-term benefit to the taxpayer[4].

Frequently it is asserted that in a system's approach the classification, standardization, storage, retrieval and re-use of complex briefing and design data pays dividends in saving manpower, time and money[5]. In fact standardized solutions are rarely the most economic for non-standard situations[6].

Standardized hospital solutions are not designed with such an excellence that they justify a numerous copying. E g when the College of American Pathologists tried

4 also G Colyn: Briefing for hospital design and construction — the architect's viewpoint. Second Southern African Hospital Symposium. Pretoria, November 1977.

5 see also Moss Raymond: Boundless scope in space . . . 1978, Health and Social Service Journal 88:348–349.

6 Perez Sheriff Maria: Calculation, Tendering, Cost-Control and Organization of the Building Phase. 1975, World Hospitals 11:98–103.

to compose a list of laboratories which demonstrated excellent design, after nearly two years of effort, it appeared that such a list cannot be compiled[7].

The chief shortcomings of standard designs in general, and of standard designs of health facilities in particular, are that a standard design is quite time-worn already at the moment of its adaption for a concrete building site, and that a standard design never satisfies the local demands strictly[8]. Repetition has been the great enemy of art in general[9].

Under special circumstances a standard design of a minor unit can give quite satisfactory results, but mostly it is unprepossessing and functionally inadequate.

A slight improvement in using standardization could be expected when a so called standard consists of a number of variants and subvariants.

Although it has been strongly recommended that permanent, impartial, objective national organizations should be established to interpret, expand and update earlier accepted norms and regulations[10], lack of sound research frequently suppresses the developmental efforts. The standards are seldom revised after a five years interval, which is considered a maximum.

No wonder that opposition against centrally steered hospital planning *en-detail* is increasing. It has been required[11] in the US, that the regulatory agencies must switch from antiquated specification and cookbook approaches to writing regulations. The diverse groups that are involved in writing standards must set their special interests aside and work for safe facilities at reasonable costs.

Regarding design standardization the assumed advantages of a large, on-going programme of standardization in the hospital field have yet to be proven[12].

When planning is standardized, there is a great danger that the already restricted planning freedom is converted into bureaucratic rigidity. This development is undesirable and totally unnatural towards the evolvement of new thoughts and progress lines. Total standardization in planning means the freezing of development. The champions of standardization fail to mention such matters as job satisfaction, a fact causing considerable concern in the architectural profession.

7   Manual for laboratory planning and design. College of American Pathologists. Skokie, III 1977, p 54.

8   see also Jachowicz Ryszard L: Problems of Planning and Building of Health Care Facilities in Mongolia. Stencil. Warsaw 1975, p 6.

9   Marcel Duchamp cited in John Cage. ed by Richard Kostelannetz. Allen Lane. The Penguin Press. London 1971, p XVII.

10 Webb T L: Rational building for health care. Mankind and Medicine in the Third Millenium Conference. Cape Town, September 1976.

11 Sprague Joseph G: Codes, regulations and compliance: a never-ending dilemma. 1978, Hospitals 52:4:90–92.

12 Moss Raymond: Hospital design and the National Health System. Part two. MARU 1/75. The Polytechnic of North London 1975, p 55.

On any hospital design the statistical chances of a better solution and improvements are extremely high. It has been estimated that there are millions of possible combinations in a design for a major hospital[13]. While this argument is theoretically true, its weight is reduced by the fact that the number of experienced hospital architects is rather limited.

The suggested way out of bureaucracy is often to replace outdated solutions by a revolt rather than by a process of constant change[14].

The report on America's housing needs by the Joint Center for Urban Studies of the Massachusetts Institute of Technology and Harvard University[15] has indicated that there is such a wide variety of need and taste, in different places, for different people, that any generalized or centralized solution will not work. The recommendation — for specialized, local solutions of many kinds, on many levels — is highly applicable, also in the health care facility planning.

13 Louw W, Straub R and Kirkby P D: The design brief. Symposium Hospital function and design: a forward look. Pretoria, October 1971.

14 see also Zeidler Eberhard H: Planning for flexibility. 1975, national hospital and health care 1:8:10–19.

15 cited by Huxtable Ada Louise: Kicked a Building Lately? Quadrangle/The New York Times Book Co. New York 1976, p 33.

Semantics of planning process

Despite the immense impact of the audiovisual media, the written word still remains the most important single means of communicating knowledge and ideas[1].

The majority of the subject matter communicated among humans is in the form of natural language. The basis for this communication process lies in the complex concept known as language comprehension. In the broadest sense, the concept of language comprehension invokes the notion of understanding, that is, the perception of meaning of any piece of natural language by all of the human beings engaged in the communication process irrespective of whether their role is that of speaker, listener or correspondent[2].

The semantic aspect of the planning and designing process deserves attention as, unfortunately, the easy transmission of information from the client to the design team has not so often been achieved.

Perhaps the major complication occuring in the hospital field is the multidisciplinary nature of both the briefing and the design teams. Professions with an interest in the brief for a hospital include doctors, nurses, administrators, paramedical staff, technical staff, social workers, and so on. On the design team there will be architects, mechanical and electrical engineers, civil and structural engineers, surveyors, other technical specialists and a range of environmental scientists. The problem is the lack of a common technical language which is needed for an understanding of common objectives[3]. At the King's Fund, London, it has been found that some words commonly used in the hospital planning process are not capable of common interdisciplinary interpretation.

The words and language used by various participants in planning and design too often confuse and create misunderstandings*. Particularly the scientific language of the sociologists — if included in the team — does not ease the use of presented material as it is peculiar and changing — also between one writer and another — from day to day to accord with current fashions.

Unprecise and careless use of some words in fashion has not improved the semantic aspects. E g in the fifties when the word *flexibility* was first used in the planning context, in the minds of most people it meant the ability to move easily room partitions and to extend easily those departments which were expected to have a fast

---

1   Ten million books. Editorial. 1974, Endeavour 33:2.

2   see also Pratt Arnold W: On the matter of medical linguistics. in Medinfo 77. ed by David B Shires and Hermann Wolf. North-Holland Publishing Company. Amsterdam, New York, Oxford 1977, p 223.

3   also Goodman H: Current trends in the United Kingdom. Second Southern African Hospital Symposium. Pretoria. November 1977.

*   The situation is analogue to patients meeting doctors. Many patients have difficulty in discussing bodily functions with their doctor, either through ignorance or shyness, and a wide vocabulary of euphemisms and slang terms has risen. Joy Parkinson (A Manual of English for the Overseas Doctor. Churchill Livingstone. Edinburgh and London 1976) lists 34 ways to feel nervous and 53 ways to describe madness.

growth rate. Towards the end of the sixties *flexibility* without further definitions, meant either everything or nothing, depending upon one's own interpretation[4].

Misunderstanding is far worse than non-understanding. The latter is recognizable, the former is not — until it is too late. Then the damage done may be irreversible[5].

It is vital for programming to define what a particular activity is. Frequently there is a blurred distinction between spatial and activity components of the problem[6]. It is quite usual to find, as an example, *'laboratory'* and *'office'* as generic titles, a shorthand intended to describe spaces and imply activities. It would be more practical, useful and rewarding to replace the title *'laboratory'* e g with *'microbiological media preparation'*, *'plate pouring'*, *'storing'*, *'administration'*. The proposed replacement may reveal the potential for alternative functional groupings and resource allocations that would otherwise remain hidden[7].

The lure of the synonym to avoid repetition should be avoided in programming and briefing as meaning may be subtly altered. Adjectives and adverbs should have a very limited application.

4   see also First phase of an investigation into the education & training needs of health facility planners. MARU 5/73. The Polytechnic of North London. Stencil. June 1973, p 4.

5   see also Green J R B: Design for user needs. 1975, national hospital and health care 1:7:28–34.

6   see also Aylward Graeme and Lapthorne Keith: Designing for stability in designing for change. University of Cambridge. Department of Architecture. June 1974, p 79.

7   see also Aylward Graeme M: Towards a Theory for Describing and Designing Adaptability in the Built Environment. Transactions of the Bartlett Society 1968–69. School of Environmental Studies. University College. London 1969, p 127–148.

Planning organization, managers, architects, public participation

Administrative professionalism requires competence, at every point in the health care and cure organization from the top to the first line supervision. Moulding a collective resource takes knowledge of organizational dynamics, and proper methods.

Neither experience nor knowledge can be replaced by formalistic working parties or committees. Furthermore, there is a risk that a planning organization would grow steadily and become exceedingly complicated. This again may decrease the efficiency of those who participate. A rigid organizational build-up hampers the possibilities of gradually improving the committee work[1].

There is no evidence yet that computer based systems for both planning and detailed design of hospitals are the answer to everybody's problems[2]. Inspection of any quantity of planning data quickly reveals the requirement for the linguistic component as part of the intellectual basis for planning data processing. In the absence of a competent means of satisfying the language comprehension problem, modest hope exists that one can create sophisticated computer programmes that will recognize, register and represent planning data and in turn, process such data in a manner which faithfully mimics human intelligence[3].

Perhaps in the future man will actually attempt to synthesize linguistic intuition. The task of programming and computerizing intuition may appear fantastic, but with infinitely better computers the attainment of such a goal is not to be ruled out entirely[4].

In itself, the need for an interdisciplinary planning approach is profound. The sooner this is understood, the better for the quality of the hospital programme and basic building concept development.

Because planning is a multi-professional exercise, the so called gaps between professional knowledge may become as influential for the outcome as the professional knowledge itself[5].

The economist's role is to widen the hospital planners' information base, to take some account of the value-for-money implications of decisions. The economist cannot make the decisions nor eliminate the element of judgement from planning decisions[6]. The involvement of social and other scientists would be premature in the

1   see also Om Planering vid Statliga myndigheter. Liber Förlag/Allmänna förlaget. Stockholm 1977, p 223.

2   see also Green John R B: Health service facilities planning and design. Part I. School of Health Administration. University of New South Wales, Kensington, Australia. Stencil. 1974, p 3.

3   see also Pratt Arnold W: On the matter of medical linguistics. in Medinfo 77. ed by David B Shires and Hermann Wolf. North-Holland Publishing Company. Amsterdam, New York, Oxford 1977, p 223.

4   Mutt Oleg: Some problems of acceptability in language and the teaching of English. in Linguistica II. Tartu Riiklik Ülikool. Stencil. Tartu 1970, p 9.

5   see also Moss Raymond: The Planning Team & Planning Organization Machinery. Medical Architecture Research Unit. The Polytechnic of North London. Stencil. December 1975, p 9.

6   A Creese cited by Vayda Eugene: When Is Surgery Indicated? 1977, Milbank Memorial Fund Quarterly/ Health and Society 55:495–504.

design process unless they are thoroughly familiar with hospitals and their problems. Otherwise they can easily become mere sources of anecdote, myth, and analogy[7].

The expertise and commitment of the administrative staff, in planning activities are essential. Their activities include operational planning, developing the programmes to carry out the mission; administrative planning to divide responsibilities, and resource planning. Planning for facilities cannot be carried out rationally or well if the other kinds of planning are missing or just haphazard. Many poor structures are the result of ambiguity or indecision.

The share of the managerial aspect in the hospital and health care facility generation scheme is salient. The administrator's central role must be clearly understood.

The demands on a manager or hospital director are almost limitless: he must be a generalist capable of understanding and interpreting financial, economic, medical, aesthetical, and logistic matters and he must excel at personnel management[9]. He would take a great responsibility for the continuous programme budgeting which deals concurrently with the resources and costs entailed both for construction and running the hospital according to the evolving programme and design.

As the part of management is overwhelming in the hospital generation procedures, the quality of the managers has to be scrutinized. Managerial stardom as well as managerial obsolescence can be damaging to planning efforts. Managerial super-stars and even starlets may expand their interest and influence into architectural and technical matters, and into other areas where their knowledge may be limited or nonexisting.

Some managers have at one time performed satisfactorily but have lost much of their former effectiveness. Their obsolescence is caused by the failure to keep up with cultural advances and by retaining an old management idea[10]. Also economical, and interpersonal obsolescences have been observed.

In spite of the availability of statistical, economical and sociological data, standards, prototypes and diagrams, numerical, graphic and verbal material, the creative skills of the architect are paramount for solving the planning task[11].

Creativity is concerned with seeing critical casual elements or dimensions of problems and synthesising these elements into appropriate solution patterns. Creative imagination is also expressed by relating history, human and organizational elements, and environmental activities to personal experiences and values. The influ-

7 see also Sommer Robert: Personal Space. Prentice-Hall. Englewood Cliffs N J 1969, p 157–158.

9 see also Bandelier R: El director de hospital, decisior responsable. 1976, Estudios sobre Hospitales 78:31–33, 35–37, 39, 41–42.

10 see also Garas R H: Managerial obsolescence — a diagnostic and prognostic approach. 1975, Hospital Administration in Canada 17:9:17–20.

11 see also Kücker Wilhelm: Entwerfen mit Methode? 1976, Bauen + Wohnen 30:81–84.

ence of the creative process, which encompasses an integrated understanding of hospital work and problems, can be invaluable already throughout the programming process.

As the programme excerts the largest single influence on the conception of the project, the architect chosen for the hospital should always start his work in the briefing phase. He should participate from the start in the key programme review meetings together with other key members of the multi-disciplinary planning team.

The architects have been called the focal point between the groups of people concerned with planning, design, and provision[12] of health care facilities. The age of increasing technical, legal, economic, and particularly organizational complexities, has forced the architect to assume multiple roles as design expert, group leader, mediator and educator[13]. The architect can also be regarded as catalyst, advisor, enabler and advocate[14]. However, this architect has to be very different from the lonely, vulnerable and gentle figure of the past[15].

Of course, he should be very different also from the incompetent servile technocrat who has made the word *architect* disrespectful*.

At this point, some comments on the importance of documentation, both of the programming and the design. All discussions with the client, however informal, should be fully minuted. Often this very operation is neglected because in the course of the briefing process a personal and, in most cases, good relationship is built up between the client and the planners. The need for proper documentation then does not seem so essential. This, however, is where the biggest mistake could be made. Clients may change their personnel and policies may change and, if decisions were not properly documented, serious problems could arise. The same principles should be strictly adhered to regarding interdesign team decisions.

Whenever possible, documentation should be standardized, e g in the technical section standard drawings could be prepared to explain certain decisions. The details on these drawings should then apply throughout the project without having to rediscuss specific problems which may lead to inconsistency. Documentation consists, therefore, not only of the formal minutes but also letters, memoranda, drawings, sketches, etc[16].

---

12 Green John R B: Health service facilities planning and design. Part I. School of Health Administration, University of New South Wales, Kensington, Australia. Stencil, 1974, p 4.

13 Selbst Paul L: Criteria for Evaluating the Hospital Architect. 1976, Hospital Progress 57:2:62–64.

14 personal communication: 1978, G W Peck, Fredricton, N B, Canada.

15 see also Brett Lionel: Architecture in a Crowded World. Schocken books. New York 1972, p 130.

* When Nobel laureate Samuel Beckett was working on his play Waiting for Godot, of all suggested alternatives architect seemed to the rehearsers the worst insult that one could ever say (Bair Deirdra: Samuel Beckett. Harcourt, Brace, Iovanovich. New York 1978, p 426).

16 also Geyer C F: Briefing from the mechanical and electrical engineering viewpoint. Second Southern African Hospital Symposium. Pretoria. November 1977.

There are two points about possible interference in hospital generation process, which should be mentioned.

Firstly, various groups have been called upon to judge the merits of a design irrespective of qualification and background knowledge for doing so. Many good designs have been fouled or eliminated through the activities of these groups.

The idea that interested citizens would wish to have some say about policies of hospital development and planning is a logical extension of the public participation movement, which emerged in the sixties as a response to some social problems. In almost every occupation there is a growing demand among unskilled and semi-skilled for their voices to be heard in management and planning decisions. Medicine and hospitals are no exceptions[17].

An understanding, co-operative public is indeed a great stabilizing influence. On the other hand, it must be understood that plain spreading of planning information to achieve improvements in the finished building is valueless unless met by knowledge*.

Some results of the so called majority-decisions may be suspicious. A correct approach may be overthrown by two faulty ones.

The current participation phenomenon could be regarded in many ways as part of the growing triumph of mediocrity[18], which is a disturbing trend in many societies**. Too much participation by outsiders, too much talk in any endeavour, can be paralyzing[19]. The probability of innovative solutions remains extremely limited.

The number of those who are to have a hand in the decision has to be reduced to a minimum. This does not exclude the participation of experts in the examination of

---

17 see also Avery Jones Sir Francis: Getting the N H S back on course. 1978, British Medical Journal 2:5–9.

*   Four people were given a piece of money.
    The first was a Persian. He said: 'I will buy with this some angur.'
    The second was an Arab. He said: 'No, because I want inab.'
    The third was a Turk. He said: 'I do not want inab, I want uzüm.'
    The fourth was a Greek. He said: 'I want stafil.'

    Because they did not know what lay behind the names of things, these four started to fight.

    They had information but not knowledge. One man of wisdom could have reconciled them all knowing that each in his own language wanted the same thing, grapes.

    Rumi Jalalkdin: The Four Men and the Interpreter. in Shah Idries: The Way of the Sufi. Penguin Books. Harmondsworth, Middlesex, England 1975, p 111.

18 Davidson H Justin: The top of the world is flat. 1977, Harvard Business Review 55:2:89–99.

** In this connection parallels in experimental music can be found. To perform Frederic Rzewski's Free Soup the audience are asked to bring instruments and to play with the "performers", who are instructed to try to relate to each other and to people and act as naturally and free as possible, without the odious role-playing ceremony of traditional concerts. Rzewski's Sound Pool sets up an improvisation in which a wide variety of people may participate; its most explicit restriction is that imposed on the stronger players, who are required for the most part to do accompanying work, that is, help weaker players to sound better.

    The same composer's Les Moutons de Panurge is for any number of musicians playing melody instruments plus any number of non-musicians playing anything (Ballantine Christopher: Toward an aesthetic of experimental music. 1977, The Musical Quarterly 63:224–246).

19 see also Culliton Barbara J: Science, Society and the Press. 1977, The New England Journal of Medicine 296:1450–1453.

the question, but it limits them strictly to a consultative role. Time limits have to be put on both discussion and decision.

There would be a third, important rule for the public participators, but also for all those who make decisions, that they assume also responsibility for them, as a group no less than as individuals.

Secondly, it is not unusual to find repressive actions by larger organizations, when they feel that new for the public advantageous forms will affect the stability of the existing system[20].

20 see also Berglund Kåre: Vägar mot mänskligare sjukvård. 1976, Landstingens tidskrift 63:2:38–42.

DESIGN CONSIDERATIONS

Biological design approach

For hospital design biological and artistic approaches are used. Both of them lead to distinct solutions of departmental layouts, circulation problems and to characteristic general hospital patterns.

The *biological* approach bases the design on the functional needs and on the balance of the hospital organization with its environment. In this philosophy the lower boundaries of functions are represented by certified facts, the upper by pure, rationally manipulative concepts.

The hospital development model incorporates the elements of growth, aggregation, formation, differentiation, regrouping, and separation. The increasingly distinct functions, capabilities, and organizational clusters grow until a further differentiation into specialities and sub-specialities occurs which requires new units or departments. Aggregation of specialities produces cross-professional teams with their own requirements on hospital space and the consequent need of regrouping.

The hospital is certainly not a simple mechanical addition of different departments and functions.

To meet the future needs of functional balance and spatial growth after the initial period of equilibrium, the hospital design has to be above all *anticipatory.*

A hospital, which imposes a rigid pattern of work on its users, no matter how excellent that pattern might have been theoretically at the time of its conception, is in the long run far less appreciated that the one which may be used in a couple of ways and is extendable. A design anticipating change means a design for stability.

Already in 1855 *Isambard Kingdom Brunel** had found a sound basis: The several parts of the hospital must be capable of being united by covered passages into a whole and extendable by the addition of parts to any size[1].

The general requirements of the anticipatory planning, which could also be called the open-end planning[2] are:

each functional unit of the organization should be expandable at different rates, or replaceable

the circulation and transport patterns should enable extension without disturbing the basic connections

the structural systems should be coordinated.

---

* Isambard Kingdom Brunel (1806–1859), British civil and mechanical engineer of outstanding originality. Designed a complete prefabricated hospital building which was shipped in parts to the Crimea in 1855.

1 Rolt L T C: Isambard Kingdom Brunel. Longman. London 1972, p 226.

2 see also Weeks John: Hospital for the 1970's. Reprinted from the Journal of the Royal Institute of British Architects. December 1964, p 3.

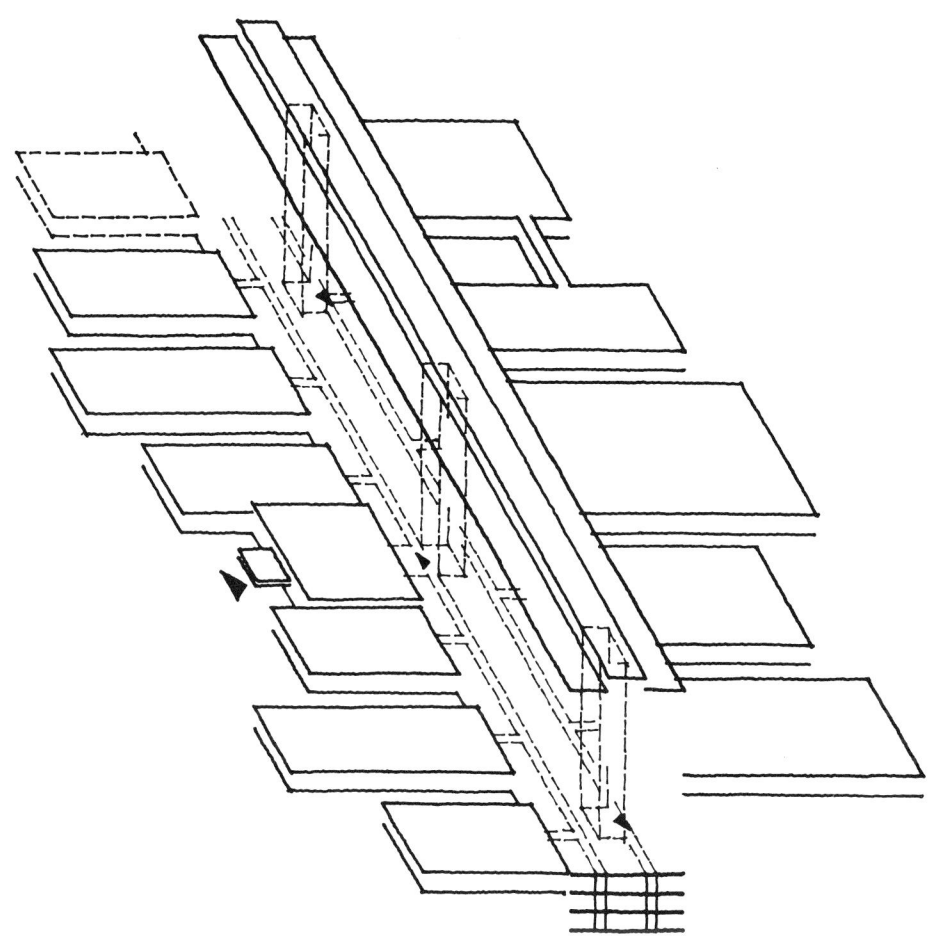

Principle for a linear 1000 bed hospital from 1968. On one side out-patient departments, on the other medical performance areas. Segregated elevator systems. Pütsep International.

A distinct plan must be provided. Every possible parameter and continuum has to be rigorously planned and systematized, so that a total system and order can be maintained. Somehow the greatness of a plan seems to be poised between absolute determinism and absolute freedom.

123 Linearity suggests itself immediately as an anticipatory form which exhibits a high degree of stability with reasonable adaptability.

In the linear spine system additive departments are entered from a central spine, which may have several levels. It steers the circulation and may house the mechanical service mains. The circulation and energy routes run past the departments and units they serve. There are no thoroughfare departments. This system takes the hospital growth easily, as the departments linked to the linear spine cannot strangle themselves. Labyrinthine paths, so common in large buildings, are avoided.

The linear spine system is a straight line arrangement, but it could be bent through 90° or in other geometrical configurations generated by the pecularities of a site. All deviations from the straight line cause restrictions in the freedom of planning.

The linear circulation core in a large hospital has similarities with the Main street of a small town. In this area the medical and paramedical activities meet other activities of the society. It is also the meeting area for the outer and inner hospital communities.

Diversity without diffusion can be assured by giving different segments of the main corridor some specific character. The higher density of visual elements along the spinal circulation system heightens its image quality and increases its memorability which is intensified by the awareness of time and weather, if natural light and outside views are available.

In the preconception of linear spines, the final configuration of the hospital is not the dominant criterion for design. The functional departmental volumes attached to the linear core are independent, non-permanent, expandable or interchangeable components.

This circumstance gains a particular importance during the preconstruction phase.

A basically linear communication system also simplifies the development of the site in stages.

The image of large hospitals designed linearly will be low, irregular and not monumental. Purposefully designed spaces and gardens around the hospital would contribute to the well-being of the people in the hospital.

The hospital's keeping up with the general development is eased when the independent circulation system and the individually designed departmental units are combined with the Ise Jingu* conception.

When an obsolete department has to be updated, its temporarily minimized functions are delegated to a temporary structure in the hospital complex, the department itself dismantled and an updated department erected. Since the circulation core is independent and separated from the departmental areas, the activities within the hospital are not interfered.

---

* At the most sacred shrine of Shinto — The ise Grand Shrine — the major shrine and its enclosure has since more than a thousand years been rebuilt every twenty years in a slightly modified form on an adjoining site to take advantage of the preserved basic situation and investments.

Artistic design approach

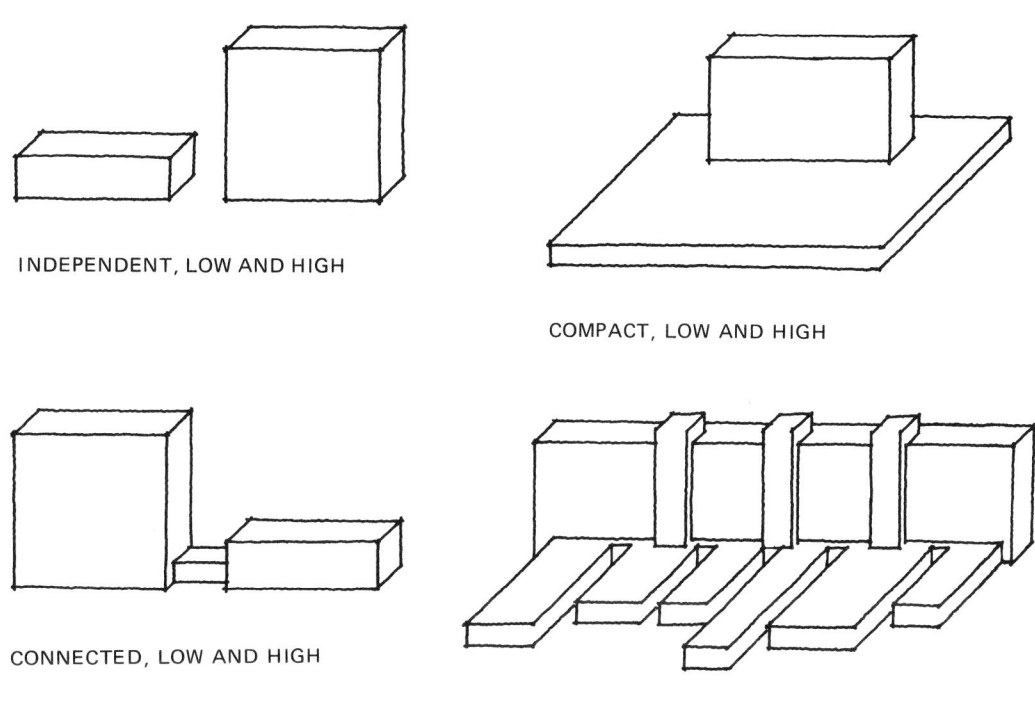

INDEPENDENT, LOW AND HIGH

COMPACT, LOW AND HIGH

CONNECTED, LOW AND HIGH

COHESIVE, LOW AND HIGH

Variations in existing hospital shapes are almost unlimited. Basically four groups could be identified, most of them belonging to the artistic approaches. The cohesive group includes the hospitals based on biologic design.

The creative impulse in the *artistic* approach is based primarily on forms, patterns, and predetermined spaces in the creation of a hospital building. Even in cases when it is emphasized that structural and mechanical modules have been developed to accommodate a variety of functions and to ease building rehabilitation, the buildings are meant to keep their shape, their original artistic totality and wholeness.

These overtly monumental and systematic hospital buildings are generally much more admirable as pieces of large-scale sculpture than the common, older hospitals, but also much less useful[1].

1   see also McLaughlin Herbert: The Monumental Headache. 1976, Architectural Record 160:1:118.

In a fashionable artistic approach conceived building — obviously it is not always easy to avoid falling victim of an elegant solution to an irrelevant problem — there is frequently a conflict between complex and fluid procedure systems and the rigidity of environmental structures and settings as there is always a gulf between the constantly changing scene of the imaginative life of the individual and the very fixed scene of the outer world.

In most cases, the changes are caused by upgrading the services. Only few are lowered. When alterations in departmental lay-outs are requested, they do not consist in redistributing functions in a given area, but in demanding additional space.

The transitory process meets great difficulties in structures conceived as geometrical straitjackets or as closed, compact and final architectural statements, which are *petrifications of an era or idea*[2].

Most of the so called artistic forms exhibit poor focus expansion values. No matter how efficiently they may expand their perimeters, their forms will build up internal stress, which results in either a reactionary self-limiting situation, or a high cost and functional disturbances when the central focus is to be renewed.

The principle of the qualified, functionally developed shape instead of the *a priori* determination of shape, the search for the essence of an architectural assignment have to loosen up the one-sided, overhasty, formal dogmatism that has formed like a rigid crust over architectural thinking[3].

To make independent growth of the various units and departments possible, the medical performance areas have to be at the ground level. The anticipatory approach requires generous sites.

Site limitations have been a frequent restraint. However, it has been shown clearly that, even assuming the purchase of a big hospital area at the highest imaginable property prices, this item would still constitute only a very small share of the total initial building cost[4].

When a limited site is the inevitable choice for a new hospital, also the hospital size has to be limited. Large hospitals containing all specialities should give way to some kind of programme-orientated clinics such as human growth and development clinic including paediatrics, obstetrics and gynaecology, and musculoskeletal clinic including rheumatology and orthopaedics. Separate specialized clinics need to be less anticipatory than large complex hospitals.

2   Rowan Ian C: Editorial. 1968, Progressive Architecture 11:93.

3   Joedicke Jürgen: Über Wesen und Gestalt. 1978, Bauen + Wohnen 32:137.

4   Borup Axel: Hospital design today — Hospital design tomorrow. The National Health Service of Denmark. Copenhagen 1975, p 294.

Architectural qualities

Architecture as the art and science of building the entire man-made environment, in terms of the way it works as much as the way it looks, is like everything else always in the state of metamorphosis[1]. Also a hospital expresses the period-bound requirements of a health cure and care organization, its management system, and the creative architectural ambitions of the same era*.

According to *Louis Henri Sullivan*** a building, being an embodiment of life, should be conceived as a living entity where form follows function. Sullivan saw the function as the sum of all material and spiritual, intellectual, and emotional activities within the building[2]. It could be added that a building without comfort, safety, and inviting quality, peace-silence, beauty and proper atmosphere has no significance as architecture[3].

In spite of the fact that UNESCO has reclassified architecture from art to social science, the essence of architectural design, its six pillars — so well formulated by *Eero Saarinen*** — respect for function, structural integrity, awareness of our time, integration with environment, expression of meaning, unity of design, remain.

In the light of critical analysis which has repeated over and over that the rejection of the cultural and architectural past and the inability to recognize and resolve conflicting interests are the main weakness of today's architecture[4], it would seem that in outstanding health care facility solutions global experience has to be merged with the local wisdom.

Hospital planning and architecture have a time-scale which makes them look ridiculous if they are pushed around like the rag trade by every breath of modishness. Like enormous ships, they need plenty of sea room, can only change course in great sweeps and take ages to lose momentum[5].

---

1   see also Huxtable Ada Louise: Kicked a Building Lately? Quadrangle/The New York Times Book Co. New York 1976, p 42.

*   Shortlived disposable hospitals are an exception. They come to use only in a very limited scale and under highly irregular conditions. The idea of using disposable hospitals widely is one of the extensions of the philosophies of disposable culture, in itself an outcome of a particularly wasteful system of thinking which has little regard for human perfection and quality of human life. Rightfully it has been said that objects planned and designed to be discarded, are designed with insufficient care. Also safety and disposability do not seem to be compatible.

** Louis Henri Sullivan (1856—1924), one of the American pioneers of the modern movement in architecture.

2   Zewi Bruno: Towards an organic architecture. Faber & Faber Limited. London 1950, p 84.

3   Komendant August E: 18 Years with Architect Louis I Kahn. Aloray Publisher. Englewood N J 1975, p 166.

*** Eero Saarinen (1910—1961), Finland-born American architect, whose imaginative solutions to problems of modern architecture have been widely acclaimed.

4   see also Mandell Betty: Alienation and Architecture. 1975, the human context 7:247–253.

5   see also Brett Lionel: The Sixties. 1969, London Magazine 9:425:179–182.

The art and science of medicine, concerned with man-as-man, requires — but seldom demands — an environment conceived *nobilimente**, that is pleasant and peaceful, an environment that will help to restore — as far as environment can — the dignity of a man who has lost his own on the bedpan or in the operation room[6].

Bricks and mortar alone do not make an outstanding hospital. To produce high creative work probably needs both time and waste. Good science emerges from dull science, and good literature from a mass of valueless stuff. Hospital development is no exception.

Much of the hospital architecture's strength must come out of the intense regard for the needs of patients, staff and visitors and not from the *architect's skill in squeeing drama out of a circulation diagram*[7].

Solutions derived by minds which are both trained and experienced in the specific discipline of hospital design could be expected to be logical and effective. Sensitive architects produce balanced, unconcerned architects dehumanizing buildings[8]. Therefore the choice of the designer is of great importance.

A faceless and impersonal style in designs may reflect the multicommittee system under which they were built and the set of regulations designed with the intention to ensure ease of maintenance. Unfortunately, there is little the architect can do about the committee system that also awards him a contract[9].

There are contemporary authors who wish to believe that a new or different architecture can be made to order for large and coherent groups. It only seems that there are few such audiences and no such methods for decreeing a new architecture. Socially responsive architecture, which hospital architecture has to be, by no means can be based on some kind of haphazard popular consensus.

The complex structure of society and the natural evolution of events should not be squeezed into artificially preconceived molds. The temptation toward quick solutions must be avoided.

Much of hospital architecture affects people from beyond the focus of awareness. They are not sure what it is about a building or room that affects them[10]. This may explain the use of expressions like *white purity of the hospital*[11].

---

*   nobilimente was used by Sir Edward Elgar to mark the andante introduction of his Symphony No 1 in A-flat. It may be well that he himself coined it. No exact translation is satisfactory. The word seems to contain overtones of seriousness, nobility and dignity.

6   Friedman Sigmund L: Medical Schools and Teaching Hospitals: Curriculum, Programming and Planning. 1965, Annals of New York Academy of Sciences 128:2:462.

7   Weeks John: Introduction. 1956, Architectural Design 26:1:2.

8   see also Hellman Louis: The myth of the machine aesthetic. 1973, Built Environment 2:1:29–32.

9   Sommer Robert: Tight Spaces. Prentice-Hall Inc. Englewood Cliffs N J 1974, p 106–107.

10 Sommer Robert: Personal Space. Prentice-Hall Inc. Englewood Cliffs N J 1969, p 160.

11 Jencks Charles A: The Language of Post-modern Architecture. Academy Editions. London 1977, p 31.

Architectural layout is one factor among many that affects communication and morale[12]. A building can make a good situation better or a bad situation worse. Thus a good hospital not only permits, but actually stimulates good hospital care. An inadequate creates direct and almost unsurmountable limitations on its personnel[13].

It should always be insisted on quality of the built environment. No opportunity to develop a design should be missed, nothing should be left to chance. Design quality cannot be added to a hospital, which is finished.

Material difficulties must not be allowed to impoverish the human spirit.

12 Sommer Robert: Tight Spaces. Prentice-Hall Inc. Englewood Cliffs N J 1974, p 145.

13 also Burgun J Armand at the Conference on Health Facility Planning and Design in the Developing Countries. New York, The World Trade Institute. December 1975.

Needs of people with disabilities, personal privacy

All the known functional needs of the hospital must be satisfied.

This is achieved by creating proper spaces in an adequate technological framework. Both recognized and emerging trends in environmental requirements and needs must be observed.

After the general design characteristics have been determined, the nature of functions to transpire in each individual space must be determined. Minute attention has to be directed to the fixed and major movable equipment, wall finishes, ceiling finishes, floor coverings, the placement and seing direction of doors, and the size and position of windows.

The order in which different requirements and components of the hospital are considered, determines very greatly the physical character of the finished facility.

Not only when mentally ill are involved, the designers and planners must restrain themselves from projecting their own perspectives and capabilities on others. To make such projections in health care facility designs is not only ignorant but arrogant, as the consequences of design are enormous[1].

The degrees of ability in motor development, comprehension, communication, hearing and vision vary widely. There are also temporary disabilities in form of illnesses, broken limbs, and strained backs.

In the US it is estimated that nearly 60 per cent of the population is mobility-impaired at any one point in time having problems with one or more elements of the built environment[2].

Most buildings, facilities, and equipment are traditionally designed for the average adult of average weight, height, stamina, agility, reaction time, eyesight, and hearing. The problems of wide variations in agility, stamina, and reaction time are not often seen and understood by the ablebodied population and even by the planners-designers. Consequently, the requirements of these people — they may have loco-motor, manipulatory or sensory disabilities, or a combination of these — are rarely considered during the design process. Lack of these considerations in the health care facility planning process is highly regrettable.

E g most blind people follow a memorized route. Protrusions and obstacles such as standing ashtrays and water fountains should be eliminated in passageways for the blind, as well as for the elderly and the nonambulatory. The main obstacles are unexpected hazards: movable or temporary objects, people moving across their path. The blind prefer narrow corridors and no large open spaces[3].

1   Izumi Kiyo: Perceptual Factors in the Design of Environments for the Mentally Ill. 1976, Hospital & Community Psychiatry 27:802–806.

2   Jones Michael A and Catlin John H: Design for access. 1978, Progressive Architecture 59:4:65–71.

3   Harkness Sarah P and Groom Jr James N: Building without Barriers for the Disabled. Whitney Library of Design. New York 1976, p 16.

Also nonpublic hospital areas such as offices and laboratories should be designed for use by all employees, including the handicapped.

It is a happy irony that architectural qualities owed to the disabled are essentially no different from what should be provided for *all* users[4].

Most of the hospital spatial arrangements were initially provided on some communal basis. The tighter the arrangements, the more profound is their influence on the individual.

If in the psychiatric hospitals, to guard against the occasional violent or suicidal patient, all must surrender their privacy, and sometimes their dignity, in the general hospitals this kind of reconsideration is invalid.

In itself, the current concepts of personal privacy are a relatively recent development, which explains the sometimes surprising lack of respect for basic sanitation. Degrees of privacy, either desired or possible, are also a function of family values and of socioeconomic or other status. In societies with resources on the increase, the respect for the patient's private life and the shift to more private and personal facilities is inevitable as well as the adaption of individualized care.

In groups, where crowded living conditions force a lack of privacy or where privacy has never been experienced, privacy norms are much less severe than they are in situations where they are realistic societal requirement[5]. High densities associated with choice present no problems, but crowding people against their will gives rise to endless difficulties[6].

As indicated the aspect of personal privacy is of a relatively recent development. It is a part in understanding the questions of personal territoriality.

Possession of territory helps the patient meet a need for security and identity, loss of it can upset psychological homeostasis[7].

Use of space, in its simplest terms could be regarded as a nonverbal communication. Where people sit and stand in relation to each other reflects how they feel about one another.

The predisposition towards personal territory determines how much intrusion by others a patient could accept.

Personal space is an invisible boundary around the body. *K B Little*[8] has said that it is the area immediately surrounding the individual in which the majority of his in-

4   Dixon John Morris: Accessible and perceivable. 1978, Progressive Architecture 59:4:6.

5   see also Kira Alexander: The Bathroom. The Viking Press. New York 1976, p 166.

6   Mead Margaret in 1970, Ecistics 30:308.

7   Stillman Margot J: Territoriality and Personal Space. 1978, American Journal of Nursing 78:1670–1672.

8   cited by Stillman Margot J: Territoriality and Personal Space. 1978, American Journal of Nursing 78:1670–1672.

teractions takes place. It has no fixed or geographic reference points, moves about with the individual, and expands and contracts under varying situations. It does not extend uniformly in all directions.

The human being is surrounded by four distance zones which differ in sensory input[9]. *Intimate* distance — to 45 cm — allows for the adults the most bodily contact for perception of breath and odour. Visual distortions are present. *Personal* distance - 45 to 120 cm — means that the self of the person is extended and surrounded by a small protective sphere. Voice is kept moderate, body odour is not apparent, and visual distortion is gone. *Social distance* — 120 to 360 cm — is for impersonal trans-actions. Perceptual information is not complete, as many details are lost. *Public* distance — more than 360 cm — means that individuals are not personally involved, only subtle facial expressions are lost, voices must be projected. It is common under certain conditions for one person to react to another as an object or part of the background[10].

The interpretation and the use of space are derived from past experiences and are influenced by both cultural and social expectations. People from different cultures not only inhabit different sensory worlds and structure space differently, they also experience it differently[11].

9 Hall Edward T: The Hidden Dimension. Doubleday & Company, Inc. Garden City, New York 1966, p 110–122.

10 Sommer Robert: Personal Space. Prentice-Hall, Inc. Englewood Cliffs, N J. 1969, p 37.

11 see also Stillman Margot J: Territoriality and Personal Space. 1978, American Journal of Nursing 78:1670–1672.

Basic hospital areas, zoning of components, room sizes

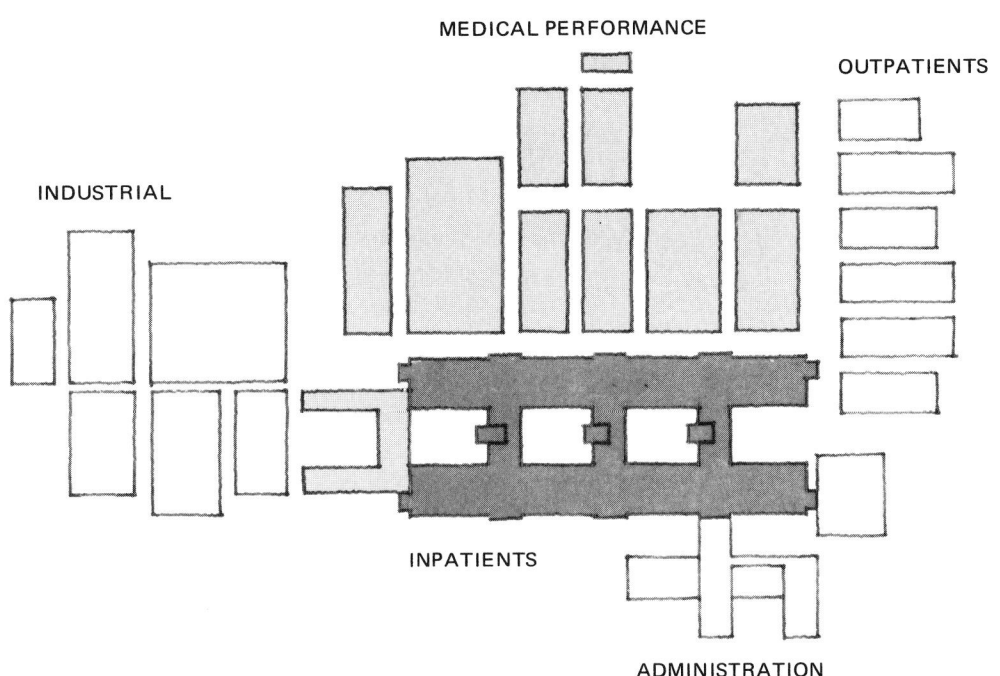

INDUSTRIAL

MEDICAL PERFORMANCE

OUTPATIENTS

INPATIENTS

ADMINISTRATION

Basic areas in a large hospital. Pütsep International.

In general hospital there are five rather characteristic and homogenous areas, which have to be arranged so that the interdepartmental circulation flow is kept reasonable.

The *in-patient area* houses the residential patients and here their medico-clinical routines are followed. The *medical performance* or *clinical service area* contains the surgical department, including the maternity section, diagnostic and therapeutical X-ray units, pathological laboratories, and the physio-therapy unit, used both by residential and non-residential patients. In the *out-patient area,* which includes the independent emergency department, non-residential patients are admitted for consultation, examination, diagnosis, and treatment.

These three areas are subdivided, articulated and organized to respond to the various requirements, patterns, and aspects of the medical work.

The *industrial* or *non-clinical service area* includes catering, house-keeping, maintenance, and central supply services, and the laundry. *Administration, public* and *staff* facilities form another group.

133

In large hospitals facilities for *research,* and in teaching hospitals units for *teaching* are added.

The main hospital component areas have different development and change rates.

The basic in-patient area — the nursing units — still dominate the hospital set-up. For some time transition from in-patient treatment to out-patient treatment with the intention to relieve the pressure on the in-patient beds has been observed.

The hospital attached out-patient areas anticipate fluctuations, even reductions, mainly because of the continuously and irregularly changing medical practice concepts — e g the introduction of health care centres — and community needs.

The changes in the relative size of the medical performance and industrial areas have been considerable. E g in the Netherlands the growth rates between 1960 and 1972 were for the in-patient area 20 per cent, for the medical performance area 40 per cent, for the out-patient areas 80 per cent and for the technical facilities 110 per cent[1].

More recently, in the most complex countries a slowing down of all growth rates has been observed.

There are other considerations to support the articulated and subdivided hospital. Certain economies of cost and energy conservation can be attained by separating hospitals into component buildings that have systems and construction suited to their use[2].

To zone the component areas may ease some of the technical problems. There are sub-areas with windows for long lasting activities and low dependency on service ducts; sub-areas with windows for long lasting acitvities and high dependency on service ducts; sub-areas without windows and high dependency on service ducts; sub-areas without windows and low dependency on service ducts; circulation areas; and service ducts.

A tight fit between the abstract space demands set out in a brief and the reality of the actual provision might mean an initially more economic building. This would be at the expense of some buffer space to hedge against changes[3].

A loose-fit strategy, which is based on the additional capacity concept, may well be harmful to the performance of the organcyte in terms of its total resources through its life span[4]. Being designed to meet unforeseen rates of changes, the extra capacities have a very small probability of meeting future requirements[5] and the

1   Kruisheer J E at the IV UIA International Public Health Seminar. Prague, October 1972.

2   see also Frye Jason W: The impact of energy conservation on hospital design. 1978, Hospitals 52:4:105–110.

3   see also Aylward Graeme and Lapthorne Keith: Designing for stability in designing for change. University of Cambridge. Department of Architecture. June 1974, p 62.

4   ibid, p 66.

5   ibid, p 94.

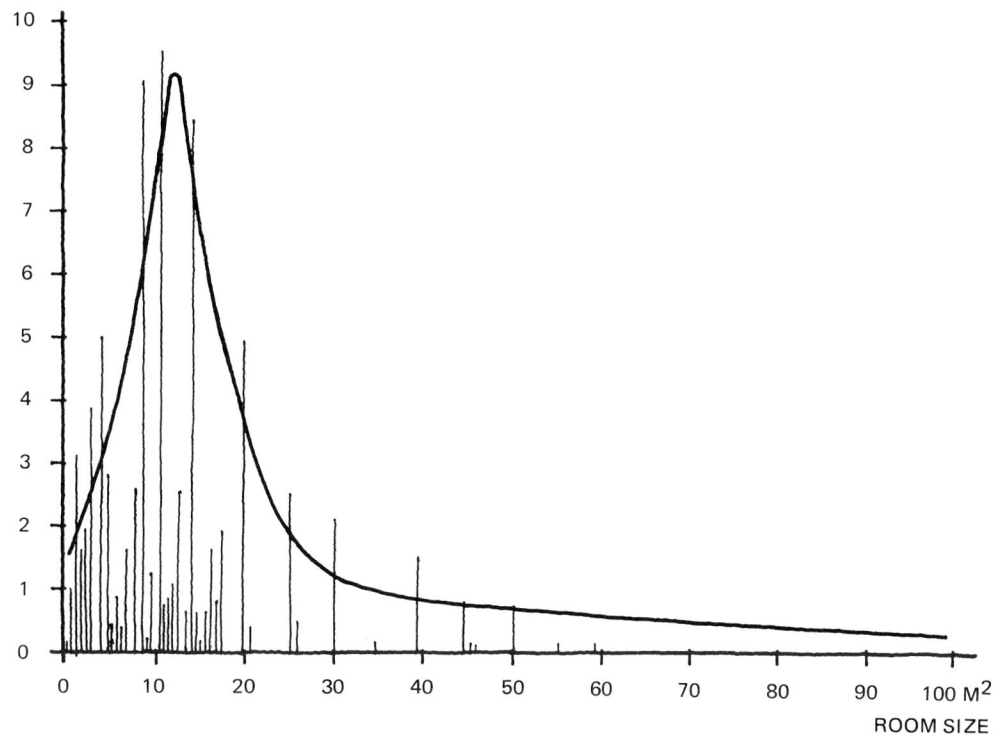

PERCENT OF ROOMS
15 M² OR LESS

ROOM SIZE

Room size distribution in UK hospitals in 1976 according to John Weeks, Gordon Best, James Cheyne, Ellen Leopold shown together with Peter Cowan's curve of theoretical room distribution from 1964.

building will become obsolete as any other. The extra built-in capacity is an added disadvantage as it speeds up the rate of decay.

Between one half and two-thirds of the rooms in most hospital buildings have been under 20 m² in area[6]. The largest single group of rooms was within the size range between 10 and 15 m².

Recent findings[7] on room sizes tend to support the conclusions drawn by *Peter Cowan*: for hospitals a small range of room sizes appears to accommodate the great majority of activities; the majority of these rooms — 70 per cent — are between 5 and 25 m²; not more than 15 per cent are larger than 20 m².

---

6   Cowan Peter: Studies in the growth, change and ageing of buildings. Transactions of the Bartlett Society 1962–63. Bartlett School of Architecture. University College. London 1964, p 55-62.

7   Weeks John, Best Gordon, Cheyne James and Leopold Ellen: Distribution of Room Sizes in Hospitals. 1976, Health Services Research 11:227–240.

This crude utilization index says nothing about room shape or location, available equipment, or services. Nothing about the usefulness of any room size can be said[8].

It is still quite reasonable to suppose that rooms of 15 m² will serve a very large proportion of hospital needs and would guarantee, if technically properly equipped and prepared, a good degree of interchangeability in use.

Jan Delrue indicated in 1972 that eight standard room sizes would guarantee 90 per cent of all functions of a hospital programme[9].

The designing of adjacent rooms as mirror images should be avoided, as only one of the designs is basically correct. The mirror image may upset the proper functioning of the room.

8   Weeks John, Best Gordon, Cheyne James and Leopold Ellen: Distribution of Room Sizes in Hospitals. 1976, Health Services Research 11:227–240.

9   cited by Mikho Emanuel: Hospital building for developing countries: A system approach. 1974, World Hospitals 10:150–162.

Construction basics, hospital life time

A cost-benefit based analysis should be undertaken as regards the polyvalence of the design and construction and the length of the building life. It would be a false economy to reduce construction costs, if it would result in increased operating costs. It may be worth spending an extra 40 per cent for the initial construction to save 10 per cent in annual operating costs, at least in the USA[1].

Present codes and regulations in many countries tend to require uniform construction throughout an entire building, in spite of the fact that the standards of construction applied to hospitals have evolved beyond functional or therapeutic needs.

The hospital construction must be adjusted to the functional needs, be simple, rapidly executable and economical. It should agree with the particular materials it is made of. The limits of these aims have to be controlled by the safety of the structure, the site conditions, and unusual local requirements[2].

Some structural arrangements, or kinds of engineering installations may be shown theoretically to facilitate specific operational and functional requirements. Often it is found that some other physical arrangements satisfy these requirements equally, if not better. Because of the uncertainty factor in the relationship between building forms and functional performance and costs, it would be misleading to attempt to measure the total cost or benefits of any particular feature of building design, without first defining the specific objectives sought[3].

The transport requirements play a considerable part in the hospital generation process.

The hospital transport system must be so simple to operate that it can be used by all groups. It must manage all loading conditions. There must be no disturbing noise. The system should not contribute towards spreading nosocomial infections.

An investigation from 1969 for an efficient hospital* shows that passanger transport — most of it taking place within very limited periods — accounts for 90 per cent of hospital transports. The remaining 10 per cent account for goods and food transport. Goods transport can be carried out during periods of minimum loading of the hospital's general — lift based — transport system, even at night.

1   Report to the Congress. Study of Health Facilities Construction Costs (B.160431(3)) by the Comptroller General of United States. November 20 1972. US Government Printing Office 1973, p 58.

2   see also Komendant August E: Contemporary concrete structures. McGraw-Hill Book Company. New York 1972, p XI.

3   see also Green J R B: Hospital building design — integration of structure and engineering service. 1974, Hospital & Health care administration 4:12:9–15.

*   cited by Borup Axel: Hospital Design Today — Hospital Design Tomorrow. The National Health Services of Denmark. Copenhagen 1975, p 258.

As a complement to the hospital lift systems automatic internal distribution systems in all sizes have been introduced. Their merits must be evaluated at an early stage, as their installation is not always justified.

The smallest scale systems relate to materials which would otherwise be transported by the human hand. The largest demand usually a mechanical lift to transport vertically or a cart or a wagon and sometimes special corridors. There are automatic cart inject-eject lifts, which have been in use for some time in spite of the fact that time is wasted waiting and nursing the cart on and off the lift. Electrically guided vehicles for food trays or supplies, rely on wire guided paths in the floor and can travel up a six per cent grade. They can follow paths which are generated in minutes by spraying on the carpet. These tracks remain invisible to the naked eye.

Large-scale pneumatic tubes are used to transport bags of soiled linen and trash.

Many of the ideas of building systems have suffered technological myopia and have led into a blind alley: the expected economies have shrunk or disappeared entirely, the tendency to monotonity and anonymity has increased, the adaptibility to the user's requirements has been reduced[4].

The design of all technical components and installations must be balanced. Examples of over-design in hospitals include refrigeration equipment covering twice the actual needs and lighting levels up to four times in excess of that necessary[5].

The hospital has shown a special knack for built-in obsolescence. This derives in part from the use and reuse of retrospective standards that have accumulated in agency and architects' files and in the minds of administrations.

Obsolescence can also be described as functions passing into disuse, either because a need no longer exists or because it is met currently by more acceptable means. The service system obsolescence occurs when mechanical equipment falls behind revised standards. In addition to the obsolescence in a health care facility, there is a depreciation due to changes either by physical deterioration or by wear and tear, which is proportional to use rather than age.

The life-length aspect of the hospital should be weighed in at the beginning of a planning process, when the economic life of the hospital and the implications of its change and growth are considered.

Various design concepts are being suggested to offset the energy crisis. They include using solar energy systems, using windmills, tapping underground geothermal and

4   see also Fesel Gerd: Bauen mit Systemen. 1978, Bauen + Wohnen 32:225–229.

5   Cowan D: National norms for hospitals. Second Southern African Hospital Symposium. Pretoria. November 1977.

aquifer streams, recycling heat generated by incineration of waste, and returning to use of natural resources such as wood and coal. Unfortunately, none of these approaches have proved feasible for application in large, high-rise buildings. Right now, hospitals are going to have to use existing systems for heating and air conditioning. However, through careful design, considerable savings can be achieved[6].

In a hospital building the depreciation rates vary for different components. Patterns for this process are complicated and still quite unclear.

The life time of a hospital building as a whole is frequently estimated to about 65 years. It may be convenient to assume that hospital buildings should be replaced after 60 to 90 years, but the chronological age can not be used to determine the functional suitability of hospital building[1]. Hospitals should be used until their usefulness has been truly exhausted. There is no society which can afford to replace hospitals every 50 or 60 years.

Generally the supporting physical structure of a building has a life-time of more than 100 years, the basic installations, such as wiring, and plumbing, last 20 to 30 years. The elevators last 15 to 25 years, oxygen, vacuum and compressed air plants 20 to 30 years. In the USA mechanical equipment is made obsolete within less than ten years[2].

The general domestic hospital equipment will last 5 to 20 years, the medico-technical equipment 7 to 12 years. E g the useful life of much of radio-therapeutical equipment is probably no more than about 10 years[3].

Usually, when the supporting physical structure is replaced massive investment is involved. Therefore supporting physical structures should not be integrated with other building elements.

Service systems should be easily replaceable, and accessible for new tappings throughout their whole length. It should be easy to accommodate installations and add new lines.

The current rate of medico-technical and domestic equipment obsolescence, even if this obsolescence in some cases may be artificial, indicates that these features should not be built into the structure.

6   Taylor William J: Careful planning can reduce cost problems in hospital construction. 1978, Hospitals 52:4:97–102.

1   see also Sears Dan and Auld Robin: Hospital Buildings: A Suitable Case for Treatments. 1974, World Hospitals 10:207–210.

2   Feldstein Martin S: Hospital Cost Inflation: Study of Non-profit Price Dynamics. 1971, American Economic Review 61:853–876.

3   see also Deeley T J: Considerations in the expansion of existing radiotherapy departments. in The Planning Radiotheraphy Departments. ed by T J Deeley. British Journal of Radiology. Special Report 12. London 1976, p 60.

Macroelements, universal envelopes

Functional and aesthetic design considerations have to respect well motivated requirements of production[1]. However, long-term determination of the shape of a hospital building by the short-term technical and economic conditions imposed by the construction process without understanding the basic needs of the hospital would amount to manufactoring cars without wheels[2].

Large scale attempts to systematize and standardize the building industry have neither artistically nor economically been successful in the past, because total standardization is unsuited for an industry where repetition is only a minor factor in the total needs[3].

Macroelements or universal envelopes causing the *tyranny of pre-determined closed spaces*[4], well illustrated by this fragment of a hospital description — the shape of the operation department floor is largely dictated by that of the ward under — have been a major fact counteracting the hospital development process. When judging this general concept, the temptation is great to cite *Eric Severeid* who has proclaimed that most problems are caused by solutions[5]. Also *Louis Kahn* could be cited: The right thing badly done is always greater than the wrong thing well done[6].

Construction should be the consequence and not the cause of planning[7]. Huge cube-shaped containers believed to be less expensive to design and build than buildings with identations still catch considerable attention in hospital production as they are believed to solve the problems of perpetual contemporaneity's three variables: time, content and place.

In the German Democratic Republic a macroelement of 1200m^2 — 5 by 7.2 m in one direction and 5 by 6 m in the other — has been made the basis of a whole hospital set up[8]. This area size was greatly determined by the that time fire regulations. The chosen macroelement was expected to house 54 to 60 regular beds *or* 16 to 22 intensive care beds *or* 36 to 38 obstetric beds *or* 60 paediatric beds *or* 40 beds for infectious patients *or* a maternity with 18 prepartum beds, 4 labour rooms and 7 delivery rooms *or* an operation unit of 4 operation rooms and 6 recovery beds *or* a

1   see also Rados F Marta: Méretegységesités, tipizálés, ciöregydrtás a kórházepitesbén. 1970, Magyar épitömusveszét 2:60–61.

2   see also Mühlestein Erwin: Was ist eigentlich nicht mobil? 1972, Bauen + Wohnen 26:159.

3   see also Zeidler Eberhard H: Planning for flexibility. 1975, national hospital and health care 1:8:10–19.

4   Gainsborough Hugh and Gainsborough John: Principles of hospital design. The Architectural Press. London 1964, p 158.

5   cited by Ranney Brooks: Shadows or light? 1976, American Journal of Obstetrics and Gynecology 125:283–289.

6   Komendant August E: 18 years with Architect Louis I Kahn. Aloray Publisher. Englewood N J 1975, p 23.

7   see also Makowski Robert J: Hospital Planning — Synthesis and Restatement. 1973, Hospital Progress 54:4:24–38.

8   Jaenisch R, Glomb J, Höckert M, Rautengarten H and Simon M: Entwicklungstendenzen in der Planung und Projektierung von Gesundheitseinrichtungen. in Das stationäre und ambulante Gesundheitswesen. vol 19. VEB Verlag Volk und Gesundheit. Berlin 1973, p 72–143.

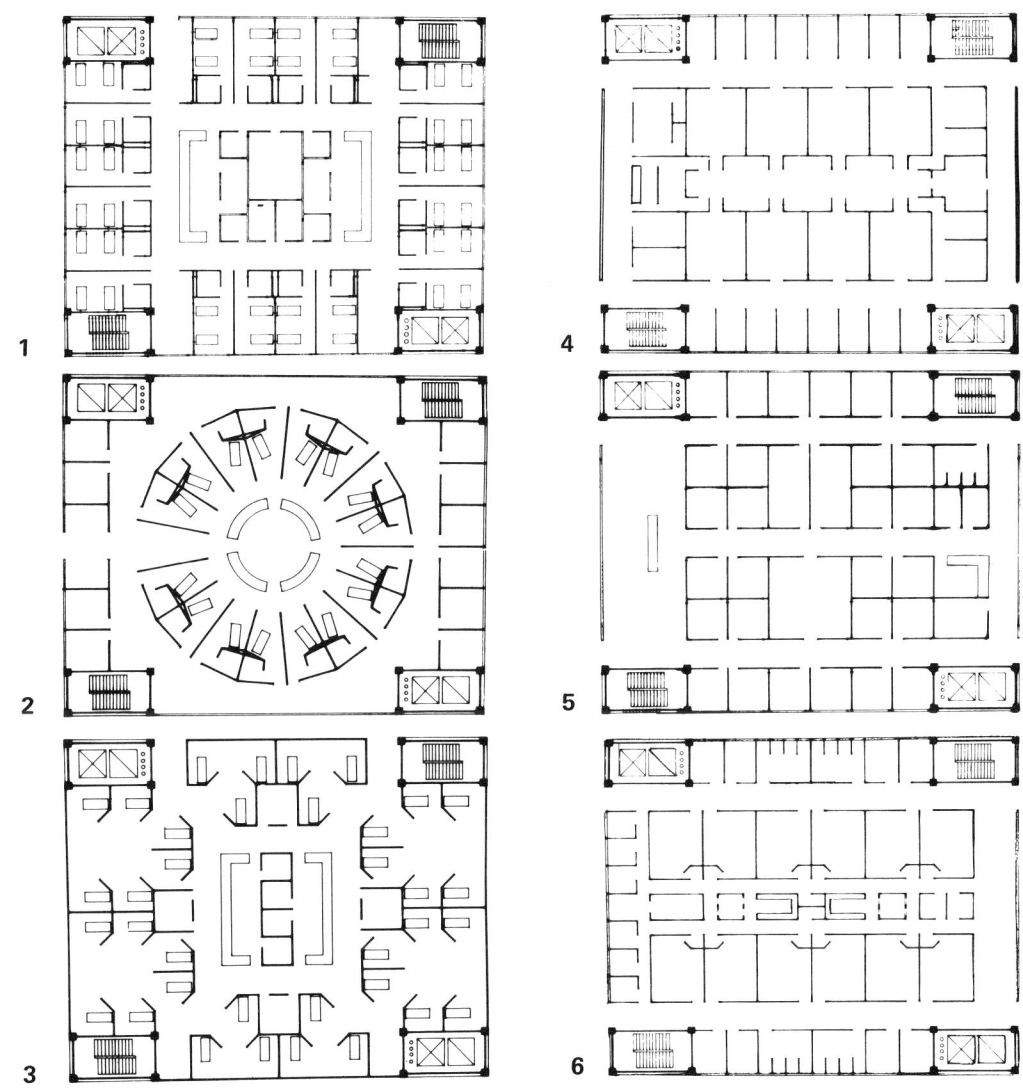

C F Murphy Associates, Chicago, believe that a uniform module of 813 m² (30.5 by 26.6 m) satisfies the spatial needs of various nursing units (1–3) as well as the needs in therapy and diagnostics (4–6).

six-room X-ray diagnostic unit including an angiography unit *or* an out-patient unit for 9 to 12 physicians *or* a unit for physio-therapy *or* a pathological laboratory *or* an emergency unit *or* a catering unit for 1500 people.

In the US a uniform module planning unit of 813 m² (30.5 by 26.6 m) has been proposed[9].

9   Jahn Helmut and Goettsch James, CF Murphy Associates: Entwicklung eines Bausystems für den Kranken-hausbau. 1975, Bauen + Wohnen 29:113–116.

In the German Federal Republic a basic unit of about 1,000 m² has been made a basis of various nursing units[10] and even for a whole hospital[11].

In Switzerland[12] a 22-floor hospital tower is based on an almost square shape containing 560 m² functional area, when elevators, stairs and waiting areas have been excluded. The floors house a cantonal pharmacy, an institution for clinical chemistry and haematology, ward units with 18 respective 28 beds, an ENT-clinic on three floors and an eye-clinic on three floors.

All super modular exercises are typical one-big-technical-idea solutions, which are vulnerable when future development is considered. *John Weeks*[13] holds that all *universal envelope* hospitals conceal enormous stresses as departments attempt to find their size without bursting the envelope.

The claims that deep plan hospitals save time and funds in the treatment of patients are not corroborated. The opposite is the truth.

In a study undertaken by the Department of Health and Social Security, London, on four different configurations, each of them having a gross floor area of 37,161 m it was shown that savings in building costs in the deep compact type block were negated by a steep rise in costs associated with the need for artificial lighting and air-conditioning[14].

In New Zealand deep-plans effect on the increase of hospital building cost begins to show at depths exceeding 17 m and reaches the full effect at the depth of 34 m[15]. The figures vary from country to country, but the indication is clear.

In South Africa, it has been estimated, that the running and maintenance costs for artificial lighting and air-conditioning could represent at least US $ 26/m² per year in addition to normal running expenses. The additional cost on a 350-bed deep plan hospital would be in the order of US $ 200,000 per year for the nursing units and administrative areas only[16].

Also high-rise buildings limit the scope of adaptability to functional changes and have a higher percentage of non-usable areas. In the Netherlands about 8.5 per cent of the areas in low-rise constructions, but 12 per cent in the high-rise constructions are needed for walls, columns and mains shafts[17].

---

10 Mayer Walter: Variable Pflegeeinheit. 1975, Bauen + Wohnen 29:202–203.

11 Joedicke Jürgen and Mayer Walter: Gegliederte und aufgelockerte Anlage. 1975, Bauen + Wohnen 29:193–19

12 Zehnder P: Das Hochhaus II des Kantonspitals St. Gallen. 1. Baubericht. 1976, Veska 40:60–64.

13 cited by Moss Raymond: Hospital design and the National Health Service. Part two. MARU 1/75. The Polytechnic of North London 1975, p 38.

14 Capital Projects Code (CAPRICODE). Comparative cost of different shaped blocks. Study 1. Department of Health and Social Security. Hospital Building Procedure Note 6, appendix 2. London, September 1972.

15 DeLiefde G Z: The hidden costs of the deep plan hospital buildings. 1972, New Zealand Hospital 24:2:25–27

16 P Power cited by Cowan D: National norms for hospitals. Second Southern African Hospital Symposium. Pretoria, November 1977.

17 de bouwkundige opzet van het laboratorium voor klinische chemie. National Ziekenhuisinstituut. Utrecht 1975, p 97.

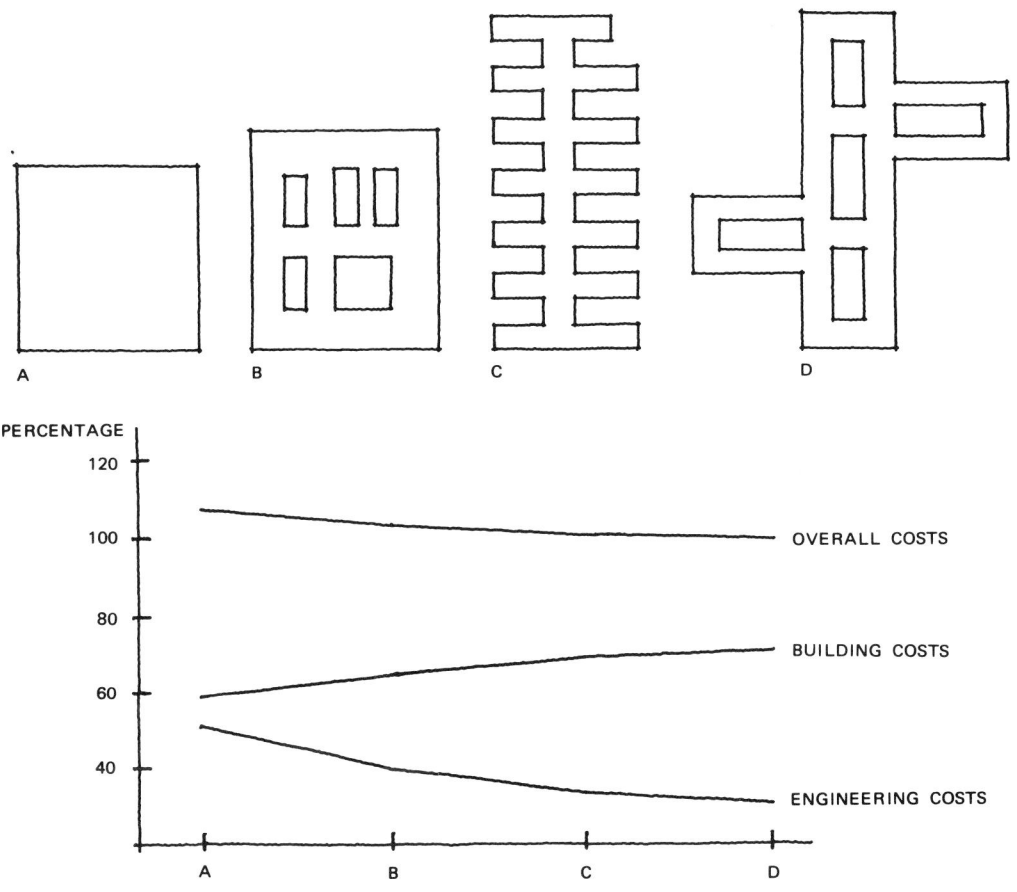

PERCENTAGE

OVERALL COSTS

BUILDING COSTS

ENGINEERING COSTS

Comparative cost of different shaped blocks expressed as an index. When The Department of Health and Social Security in London studied in 1972 the matter, the gross floor area of each study block was 37,161 m^2. Shape D formed the base = index 100.

When air handling systems in high-rise buildings against those in low-rise structures were compared in Canada[18], it was found that an air handling system in a high-rise building is less flexible in coping with change, the horizontal building requires less duct shaft area — 3 per cent versus 8 per cent for the high rise —, that the horizontal building requires less equipment room space — 2.6 per cent versus 9 per cent — and that energy costs be lower in the low-rise building. However, a low rise building requires more ceiling space and their duct work distribution costs and maintenance costs are higher.

18 Peckham Jr Arthur H: Vertical vs. horizontal in hospital design. 1972, Hospital Administration in Canada 14:5:77.

Unlimited adaptability

Believers in inevitability of rapid obsolescence have tried to find solutions which allow alterations easily and immediately without interference to areas adjacent. Their utopian desire to create universal adaptability has led either to unrealisable theories or to hospitals with the wrong kind of adaptability[1].

Some of the monumentally oriented architects believe that the demand for change through addition could be avoided by assuming that remodeling should occur instead. The argument that a hospital chassis — the support structure and the service reticulation — needs to allow infinite flexibility in the planning of rooms and circulation areas seems not to be supported[2].

The needs for functional and/or technical changes in hospitals are not frequent. Some investigations indicate that within 10 years only one to two per cent of the hospital areas — no particular area dominating — require a technical reequipping or shifting of functions[3].

A functional-administrative grouping of localities within a health care facility may remain wholly acceptable up to 20 years. Architects with a shallow knowledge of hospitals and their adaptability requirements believe, that they can create totally adaptable hospitals just by satisfying the few adaptability requirements which are apparent to them.

Most obvious is that in two efforts associated with the creation of adaptable hospital architecture: more or less sophisticated systems of *movable partitions* for room size and function flexibility and *interstitial* engineering floors for exchange and growth of engineering services.

Movable partitions

The movable partitions in hospitals is an outgrowth of the free plans and movable partitions introduced by *Le Corbusier* * in 1914 in his theoretical Dom-Ino System and regarded as an essence of the new architecture[4].

There are movable furniture and wall partitions which are part of a system of modul seamless plastic containers, frames, carts, panels and rails. All space is considered

---

1   Floros Christos: The morphological evolution of the postwar hospital. 1976, World Hospitals 12:177–182.

2   see also Weeks John, Best Gordon, Cheyne James and Leopold Ellen: Distribution of Room Size in Hospitals 1976, Health Services Research 11:227–240.

3   Jaenisch Roland at the 20th International Hospital Congress. Tokyo, May 1977.

*   Le Corbusier (Charles-Edouard Jeanneret) 1887–1965, Swissborn and French, considered as one of the most irrepressibly articulate and yet most engimatic architects in the world.

4   Jencks Charles: Le Corbusier and the Tragic View of Architecture. Harvard University Press. Cambridge, Mass. 1973, p 42.

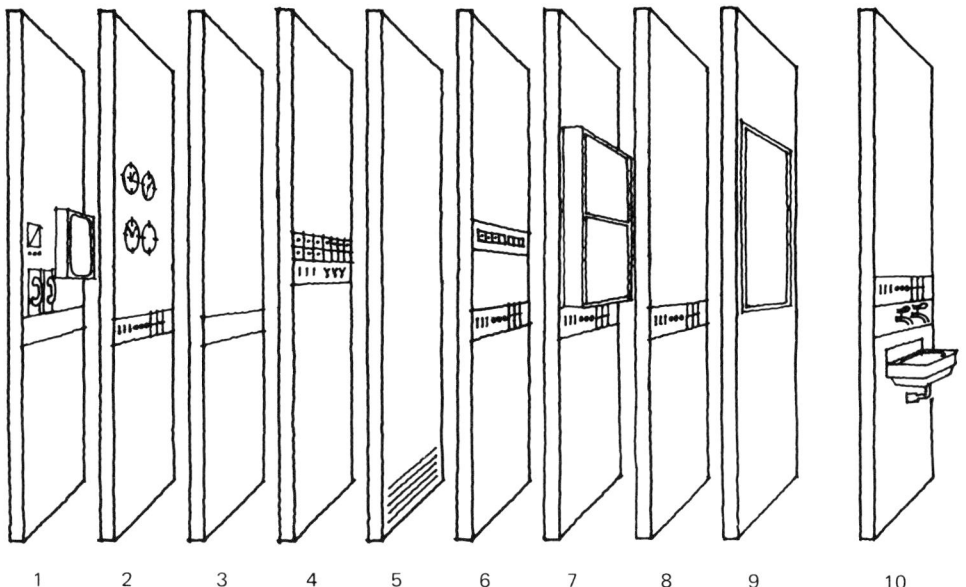

Frederick R Frank and William C Beck (Demountable Metal Partitions as Operating Room Walls: Experimental Study. 1973, The Guthrie Bulletin 43:51-64) have envisioned prefabricated operation room wall panels with standard widths and, three basic heights, but of various functional attainment. All panels could be pre-piped, pre-ducted, or pre-wired to meet the needs of a specified function or group of related functions. Some panels can be developed as wet-panels with an electrical component.

Panel 1 is a communication panel with intercom, audio, telephone, miscellaneous electrical components, panel 2 a time panel with elapsed time, standard time, sweep second and miscellaneous electrical components, panel 3 is a testing panel, panel 4 is for bio-telemetry with jack and electrical outlets, panel 5 is for air supply or air exhaust, panel 6 for medical gases, compressed air, suction, electric service, panel 7 for Xray with viewing boxes, switches, jack and electrical outlets, panel 8 is an electrical panel — 110 V, 208/220/3, panel 9 has an observation window, and panel 10 hot and cold water.

capable of housing any activity until specialized equipment is moved in to create a tailor-made environment.

The use of movable panels and panel-hung work surfaces may enable to dispense with most fixed casework and achieve an anonymity in the various rooms. Rails can be placed at various heights on walls and working surface modules hung from them to set up "action office" stations*.

---

* Action office is a Herman Miller Inc., copyrighted term to describe a system of movable panels and panel-hung work surfaces. Occasionally Co-Struc hanger rails have been integrated with the panels.

Movable walls and partitions by themselves are no guarantee for making variability in functions easy. These and similar provisions for change to the inside of buildings are expensive.

The kinds of change that most often happen are additions and minor modifications in existing area. These occur in a random way that make demountable partitions almost useless and not cost effective[2].

Interstitial spaces

An *interstitial* space is defined as a space above the ceiling and below the floor of two adjacent stories measuring not less than 1.5 m in height and of not less than one-hour fire-resistive noncombustible construction[1]. Its free height varies between 2.2 and 2.8 m.

The interstitial spaces are for the mechanical discipline and can accommodate air handling equipment; transformer rooms; plumbing; fire stand pipe; domestic hot and cold water; acid waste piping; vacuum for cleaning; medical vacuum, high and low pressure compressed air; oxygen, nitrogen, nitrous oxide and natural gas; pneumatic chutes for moving sealed bags of trash and soiled laundry to disposal areas; film and document conveyors, and other distribution systems.

In the US the building standards require in interstitial spaces exhaust ventilation at the rate of not less than two air changes hourly. The fire alarm system, including wiring, has to be insulated against fire.

All kinds of magical results seem to have been expected from that arrangement, which is nothing more than an enlarged structural depth[3].

The thinking behind interstitial floors is obviously akin to the thinking behind music composed according to the probability theory[*]. For the advocates of interstitial floors it is not material whether the space will come to use or not.

The real needs for interstitial accommodations are very limited. The part of a hospital mechanical system which requires maintenance on a continuing basis tends to be the fans, which are most easily dealt with if they are located in an easily access-

2   McLaughlin Herbert and Diaz James: Three hospital projects by Kaplan/McLaughlin. 1978, Architectural Record 163:4:95, 102.

1   Ginsburg David L and Pierson Paul S: Have building codes been worth the cost? 1977, Hospitals 51:3:79–87.

3   Sheoris John V: The Large Scale Planning Module/Unit Theory Design for Hospitals. 1973, World Hospitals 9:1:31–36.

*   Iannis Xenakis (1922–) Greec born Roumanian architect-composer, above all associated with computer music, regards it as immaterial whether a particular note in the partiture is played or not (Sutherland Roger: Xenakis and the Doctrines of Stochastic Music. 1973, London Magazine 13:2:84–95).

ible fan room, which can be located on the roof or on the same floor level as everything else. In terms of other aspects of change, very little happens[3].

If all that interstices can provide, is a bigger *space* there will be some alleviation of mechanical space problems but no improvement in mechanical system performance, building efficiency or flexibility. In fact, unless something vastly better than has been seen to date is produced, it could be easily found a commitment to a completely unworkable structure[4].

Up to 30 m long interstitial trusses to permit widespread columns have been used in connection with interstitial floors. This weaves in some corollary thinking about long-span structures. It is difficult to grasp how the reduction of the number of 40 by 40 cm or 60 by 60 cm columns could increase the flexibility of a 2000 m² squared off mass of space in which no room is larger than 7 by 7 m² and in which no major remodelling is to occur[5].

A theoretically happy result of the interstitial floor thinking is that the exterior visage of these monumental sculptures remains unsullied by ungaining bumps. This can work out also in actual practice, for the interstitial floor is so expensive that additions may not be afforded[6].

One reason for using the interstitial spaces in a hospital is the belief that in the name of the final quality of the hospital, decisions upon hospital functions have to be made as late as possible during the designing and construction stage. However, the postponement of decisions in itself does not mean an automatically improved solution. Indeed, it does not guarantee even a satisfactory solution. For reaching an optimal functional solution not only the size of the available area, but also the shape is decisive. An odd shape of the area may greatly restrict the possibilities to produce an optimal solution.

Also construction components and technical systems, which in this system have been determined independently much earlier enforce the dominance of structure over function. Thus the decision time expected to be gained covers only a limited portion of the medical development process and is in practice mostly of low value.

The true potentials of the interstitial floor system in all hospital areas, have not yet been thoroughly exploited. This concept would be best used when all parts of the facility have equal perennial requirements of considerable changes. The interstitial spaces are initially very expensive and not particularly amenable to growth.

3   McLaughlin Herbert and Diaz James: Three hospital projects by Kaplan/McLaughlin. 1978, Architectural Record 163:4:95, 102.

4   see also Sheoris John V: The Large Scale Planning Module/Unit Theory Design for Hospitals. 1973, World Hospitals 9:1:31–36.

5   McLaughlin Herbert: The Monumental Headache. 1976, Architectural Record 160:1:118.

6   ibid

An American life-cycle cost analysis[7] has shown that in hospitals the interstitial space with long-span construction increases initial construction costs. Their effect on physical and planning on hospital organization adaption remains to be seen.

A solution developed for the unspecified research needs of a collective of eight Nobel prize winners* can hardly be recommended in all hospital areas of all hospitals.

7 Report to the Congress, Study of Health Facilities Construction Costs (B-164031 (3)) by the Comptroller General of United States. November 20 1972. US Government Printing Office 1973. p 60, 85.

* Salk Institute for Biological Studies, La Jolla, California, is strongly connected with the development of the interstitial floor idea. At the start of this institute Dr Jonas Salk stated to Louis Kahn — the Estonia born American architect with profound, uncompromising architectural principles — what he wanted but was not sure what the laboratory should be like.

In the late fifties biological research was new, fast developing, and nobody knew where it would lead and what would be the requirements for the future.

Dr Salk hesitated to give any specific information even about the eight Noble prize scientists who would work in the institute, because he just did not know them so well personally, only their work and achievements (Komendant August E: 18 years with Architect Louis I Kahn. Aloray Publisher. Englewood N J 1975, p 41).

HOSPITAL INFECTION

In the 1850s it was discovered that the way in which a hospital is built affects the health of its patients, even their chances for survival.

In a majority of cases medicine could not cure, and people had begun to suspect that hospitalization in itself might kill those who, if stayed at home under similar care and treatment, would have remained alive. Above all, there was mounting distrust of what was termed vitiated air — air corrupted by many sick housed under one roof[1]. The workings of germs were still not understood.

Since then no single factor has influenced the shaping of the hospital buildings and their departmental lay-outs more than the hygienic aspects, particularly the efforts to eliminate hospital infection.

Infection is defined as a pathologic *i e* harmful process, caused by the growth of pathogenic micro-organisms in living tissues. Infection must not be confused with contamination. Contaminating organisms exist in a commensal state with their host. They live in or on the host without causing infection.

Hospital or nosocomial infection is any hospital aquired infection, which does not exist before entering the hospital and is spread among patients and staff involved with medical care.

It has been maintained that only hospital infections of exogenous origin are nosocomial. Other specialists[2] define as nosocomial infections those which are not apparent on admission but develop afterwards and do not appear to have been incubating at the time of admission, when clinically diagnosed. Nosocomial infection may be considered a multiconditioned phenomenon in ever-changing surroundings[3].

Nosocomial infections can arise from diverse sources. They can be transmitted by diverse routes and generate diverse symptoms. There still are different opinions and the interpretations of some basics vary considerably. Consequently, even the prevention techniques vary.

Cross-infection occurs throughout the hospital and is by no means confined to a single activity, *e g* surgical operation. Nosocomial infection is not a specific disease. The term covers a variety of infections, which are caused by microorganisms, and are grouped into a common category for the purpose of convenience.

---

1 Goldin Grace: Building a hospital of air: the Victorian pavillions of St. Thomas' Hospital, London. 1975, Bulletin of the History of Medicine 49:512–535.

2 Brachman P S cited by Williams R E O and Shooter R A: Infection in Hospitals. Davis, Philadelphia 1963, p 329.

3 see also Michel M F: Nosocomial infections in intensive care patients: the problem and approaches to its solution. 1977, The Netherlands journal of medicine 20:211–219.

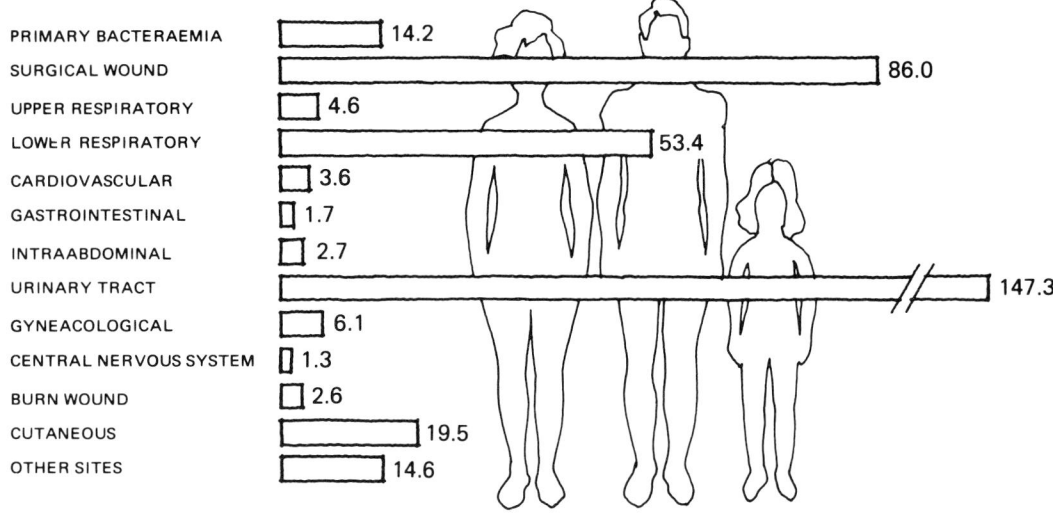

PRIMARY BACTERAEMIA	14.2
SURGICAL WOUND	86.0
UPPER RESPIRATORY	4.6
LOWER RESPIRATORY	53.4
CARDIOVASCULAR	3.6
GASTROINTESTINAL	1.7
INTRAABDOMINAL	2.7
URINARY TRACT	147.3
GYNEACOLOGICAL	6.1
CENTRAL NERVOUS SYSTEM	1.3
BURN WOUND	2.6
CUTANEOUS	19.5
OTHER SITES	14.6

Rates of nosocomial infections, based on each 10,000 discharges from 87 US hospitals according to a United States Public Health Service study (Aspinall Mary Jo: Scoring Against Nosocomial Infections. 1978, American Journal of Nursing 78:1704–1707).

According to an investigation[4] the common sites of hospital-acquired infection are: the urinary tract — 40 per cent, skin and wound — 30 per cent, the respiratory tract — 20 per cent and other sites — 10 per cent. According to another[5] the urinary tract represents 40 to 50 per cent of infections, skin and wound — 16 per cent, the respiratory tract — 12 per cent, and the gastro-intestinal tract — 12 per cent. These figures can be regarded as a kind of general indication, because very wide variations exist[6].

The infectious pool is a complex and distinctive mark of a hospital, as the distribution of bacterial strains varies depending on the time, place, and the operative procedures of the hospital. It varies even from ward to ward within the same hospital[7].

4   Fisher Evelyn J: Surveillance and management of hospital-acquired infections. 1976, Heart and Lung 5:784–787.

5   Stamm Walter E, Martin Stanley M and Bennett John V: Epidemiology of Nosocomial Infections Due to Gram-Negative Bacilli: Aspects Relevant to Development and use of Vaccines. 1977, The Journal of Infectious Diseases 136:S151–S160.

6   also personal communication 1977, Bertil Nyström, Stockholm.

7   see also Gaya Harold: The bacteriology of intensive care. 1974, British Journal of Hospital Medicine 15:853–859.

The usual form of transmission is tactile through *contact*. The hands of the staff can be infected when dressing the wound, giving some treatment, taking the temperature, assisting with bedpan or urine bottle, and when bed making. The microorganisms can then be transmitted to other patients or to door handles, water taps, etc and from there to still other patients.

Contact infection can be prevented by an intangible alerting everyone in the hospital to the problem of infection and by exercising strict aseptic techniques. This means that touching by hand anything that is or may be infected or contaminated must be avoided. A feature of nosocomial infections that contributes to the frustration of the epidemiologists is their sporadic nature.

Hospital infection is dynamic. New problems emerge as some are resolved. New invaders and other disintegrative forces will make their appearance. There will also be changes caused by the constant revision of the concept of pathogenic and non-pathogenic bacteria.

It seems unlikely that the nosocomial infections will ever be completely prevented.

Microorganisms causing hospital infections

The micro-organisms that can give rise to disease are bacteria, viruses, protozoa, Rickettsiae and fungi.

Every micro-organism has its own sources and routes. The relative importance of each route may be different in various surroundings. Every epidemiological situation is unique in space and time. This all makes generalizations undesirable.

Many of the hospital infections are initiated autogenously by self-infection from the micro-organisms in or on the person himself and are called endogenous infections. Other infections are exogenous infections, meaning that micro-organisms from the environment have penetrated into tissues.

Staphylococci — *Staphylococcus pyogenes*, generally called *Staphylococcus aureus* — were for some time the most common cause of localized suppurative infections* and accordingly received most attention. Staphylococci have lost a lot of their one time importance but still represent a common bacterium associated with nosocomial infections in many hospitals.

Gram-negative rods are currently recognized as a major source of nosocomial infections[1]. Data from the Center for Disease Control, Atlanta, Georgia, show that about two-thirds of all nosoco-

---

* According to H W R Siebbeles (Post-operative Wound Infections. in 1971, Archivum Chirurgicum Neerlandicum 23:1:49) 75 per cent of post-operative wound infection were caused by Staphylococcus aureus both in monobacterial and mixed infections.

V I Strutschkow (Kongressbericht: Société Internationale de Chirurgie. 24. Congress. Moscow 21–26.8.1971. in 1972, Zentralblatt für Chirurgie 97:420) stated that out of 2005 infections 79 per cent were caused by Staphylococcus aureus.

1 see also File Jr Thomas M and Vincent Donald J: The Pattern of Gram-Negative-Rod Bacteremia in a Community Hospital. 1977, The Ohio State Medical Journal 73:551–556.

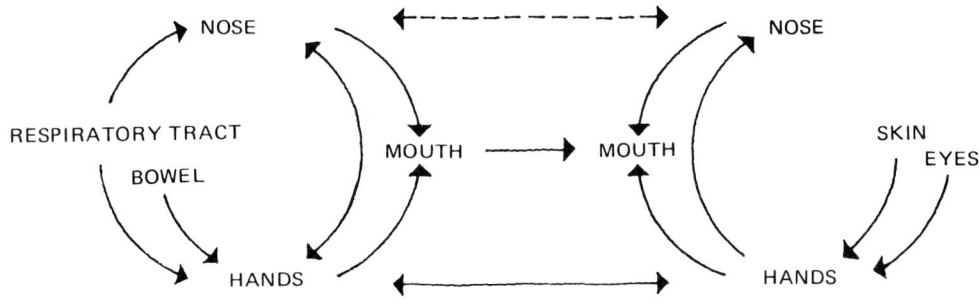

Some possibilities of spreading nosocomial infection.

mial infections are due to Gram-negative bacilli[2]. They have assumed importance also because their infections are severe[3].

Among Gram-negative organisms* *Escherichia coli,* coliform bacteria, Proteus species, Klebsiella species and Pseudomonas species, are a major worry. *P aeruginosa* is unique among pathogens as it infects not only other vertebrates, but also lower animals, terrestial and aquatic, including insects, and even plants. Troublesome infections caused by the *Pseudomonas aeruginosa* (Ps. Pyocyanea) have increased up to more than one third of the current post-operative infection rate. However, there have already been signs that nosocomial infections caused by Pseudomonas and species of Enterobacteriaceae are beginning to decline in frequency and severity[4]. The nonfermentative Gram-negative bacilli, fungi, and viruses seem to be on the way in[5].

As any micro-organism can be a pathogen, infections are being traced to organisms which earlier have been considered benign. For instance, the *Serratia marcescens,* an organism once regarded a harmless saprophyte and used in experiments to track the spread of organisms, has been responsible for an increasing number of serious hospital infections.

Spore-forming bacteria can give rise to tetanus and gas gangrene. *Clostridium welchii, C. oedematiens* and *C. septicum* still remain an uncommon occurence in civilian medical practice[6].

Many hospital infections are caused by mixed organisms including fastidious anaerobes.

---

2   Stamm Walter E, Martin Stanley M and Bennett John V: Epidemiology of Nosocomial Infections Due to Gram-Negative Bacilli: Aspects Relevant to Development and Use of Vaccines. 1977, The Journal of Infectious Diseases 136:S151–S160.

3   see also Hewitt William L and Sanford Jay P: Workshop on Hospital-Associated Infections. 1974, The Journal of Infectious Diseases 130:680–686.

*   The portal of entry for Gram-negative organisms is the urinary tract in 50 to 60 per cent of patients, and the gastrointestinal tract in 25 per cent. The female genital tract is the source in 5 per cent, usually in post-abortal and postpartum women. In 5 per cent the skin and postoperative wounds are responsible. In 10 to 15 per cent the source is unknown (Hassem Ansari: Gram-Negative Bacteremic Shock. 1973, The Medical Clinics of North America 57:1403–1415).

4   see also Teres Daniel: Management of Respiratory Infection in the Intensive Care Unit. Recent advances in respiratory surgical intensive care. ed by T Gordon McNabb and Stephen V Hall. International Anesthesiology Clinics. vol 14 no 1. Spring 1976, p 163–178.

5   ibid

6   see also Shaw James, Vellar Ivo D and Vellar Dominic: Clostridial (gas gangrene) infection in a general hospital. 1973, The Medical Journal of Australia 1:1080–1087.

Oxygen-sensitive anaerobic bacteria comprise the largest group of organisms among the human endogenous microflora. It appears as though these pathogens are to move into a bacteriologic vacuum as willing invaders when antibiotic suppression reduces their natural competitors[7].

Hospital acquired infections due to viruses are recognized, although they — except Hepatitis B, rotavirus and cytomegalivirus[8] — have received little attention, probably because viral isolation and identification are time consuming and expensive, and appropriate laboratory facilities to study and confirm such infections are generally lacking.

Hospital infection rates and the harm done

There is no so-called acceptable general range of level of nosocomial infections as the incidence varies greatly in different specialities. Also the over all incidence of hospital infection varies.

Many hospital-acquired infections are inevitable. According to a study* 65 per cent of bacteremia cases would not most likely have occurred despite rigid adherence to current infection-control practices.

In October 1977 the United States Center for Disease Control reported a lower incidence of 3.6 per cent for general hospitals and 5.1 per cent for surgical services among hospitals**.

Frequencies of 5 per cent[1], 7 per cent[2], 11 per cent[3] and up to 15 per cent[4] of patient population have been reported in complex and industrially developed countries.

University and municipal hospitals generally have reported rates of infection higher than community hospitals of comparable size, and small community hospitals have reported low rates of infection. Lowest nosocomial infection rates have been reported from general military hospitals.

---

7   see also Nobles Jr Eugene R: Bacteriodes Infections. 1973, Annals of Surgery 177:601–606.

8   personal communication: 1977, Bertil Nyström, Stockholm.

*   Mc Gowan Jr J E, Parrott P L, Duty V P: Nosocomial bacteremia: Potential for prevention of procedure-related cases. 1977, JAMA 237:2727–2729.

** cited by Aspinall Mary JO: Scoring Against Nosocomial Infections. 1978, American Journal of Nursing 78:1704–1707.

1   Infection Control in the Hospital. American Hospital Association. Chicago 1974, p 2.
    Fahlberg Willson J: The Administrative Aspects of Infection Control. 1975, Hospital-Hygiene 67:70–73.
    Daschner F: Grundlagen der Krankenhaushygiene und das Hospitalismusproblem. 1977, Intensivmedizin 14:163–168.

2   Wenzel Richard P, Osterman Charles A, Hunting Kathryn J and Gwaltney Jr Jack M: Hospital-acquired infections. 1976, American Journal of Epidemiology 103:251–260.

3   Bernander Sverker, Hambraeus Anna, Myrbäck Karl-Eric, Nyström Bertil and Sundlöf Bo: Prevalence of Hospital-associated Infections in Five Swedish Hospitals in November 1975. 1978, Scandinavian Journal of Infectious Diseases 10:66–70.

4   Grün L at the 8. internationales Krankenhaussymposium. TU Berlin. February 1976.

In nursing home and chronic disease clinic patients, the infection rates rise up to 59 per cent[7].

In intensive care units some reported infection rates have been 4 and 24 per cent[8] and 72 per cent[9]. A nosocomial infection rate of 24 per cent among patients in a newborn intensive care unit has been reported[10].

In spite of the importance which is attached to nosocomial infections, the general and unqualified infection rate of a particular hospital might not be a very meaningful parameter[11].

A total of 1,600,000 nosocomial infections are estimated to occur in patients admitted to acute-care hospitals in the US[12], where the nosocomial infections have emerged on a national scale as a significantly more serious cause of death than automobile accidents[13]. Others have estimated that there are approximately 1,500,000 to 3,000,000 nosocomial infections acquired by the 30,000,000 Americans hospitalized annually[14].

There is an estimate that approximately one of every 5,000 patients entering an American hospital dies of an infection contracted in hospital[15]. Only Gram-negative-rod bacteremia may be the direct cause of 132,000 deaths per year, as current studies indicate[16].

7   Bernander Sverker, Hambraeus Anna, Myrbäck Karl-Eric, Nyström Bertil and Sundlöf Bo: Prevalence of Hospital-associated Infections in Five Swedish Hospitals in November 1975. 1978, Scandinavian Journal of Infectious Diseases 10:66–70.

8   Daschner F: Infektion in der Intensivmedizin. 1976, Intensivmedizin 13, supplement 1, p 79.

9   Bernander Sverker, Hambraeus Anna, Myrbäck Karl-Eric, Nyström Bertil and Sundlöf Bo: Prevalence of Hospital-associated Infections in Five Swedish Hospitals in November 1975. 1978, Scandinavian Journal of Infectious Diseases 10:66–70.

10 Wenzel Richard P, Osterman Charles A and Hunting Kathryn J: Hospital-acquired infections. 1976, American Journal of Epidemiology 104:645–651.

11 see also Greene Velvl and Vesley Donald: Environmental Micro-biology. in Environmental Health and Safety in Health-Care Facilities. ed by Richard G Bond, Georg S Michaelsen and Roger R deRoss. Macmillan Publishing Co Inc. New York and Collier Macmillan Publishers London 1973, p 35.

12 Stamm Walter E, Martin Stanley M and Bennett John V: Epidemiology of Nosocomial Infections Due to Gram-negative Bacilli: Aspects Relevant to Development and Use of Vaccines. 1977, The Journal of Infectious Diseases 136:S151–S160.

13 Haskin Marvin E and McGinley John A: Hospital Ecology and Nosocomial Infections. 1972, The Radiologic Clinics of North America 10:583–588.

14 Wenzel Richard P, Veazey Jr James M, and Townsend Timothy R: Role of the inanimate environment in hospital-acquired infections. in Infection control in health care facilities. ed by Kenneth R Cundy and William Ball. University Park Press. Baltimore, London, Tokyo 1977, p 91.

15 Fekety Jr F Robert: Nosocomial Infections. in Clinical Concepts of Infectious Diseases. ed by Leighton E Cluff and Joseph E Johnson III. The Williams & Wilkins Company. Baltimore 1972, p 72.

16 W R McCabe and M Finland cited by File Jr Thomas M and Vincent Donald J: The Pattern of Gram-Negative-Rod Bacteremia in a Community Hospital. 1977, The Ohio State Medical Journal 73:551–556.

American Center for Disease Control has estimated that patients with hospital-acquired infections spend an average of ten extra days in the hospital per nosocomial infection[16].

A more recent study* indicates that mortality was 14 times greater in patients with nosocomial bacteremia than in matched members of the control group with the same primary diagnoses.

Patients with nosocomial bacteremia had an average hospitalization period that was 14 days longer than the average hospital stay for members of the control group. The authors add that caution must be used when generalizing these findings to other hospital settings.

An itemized cost analysis showed an average excess of approximately US $ 3,600 in direct hospital costs for patients who had nosocomial bacteremias**. At the same time it was estimated that only 24 per cent of the total excess cost to these hospital patients are preventable.

In the USA the annual national cost of hospital infections was estimated in 1974 to be just short of 1,000 million dollars[17]. That cost estimate required an important comment: if patients in tertiary care centres had been included, this amount would have been several times higher.

As the incidence of hospital infections is less in the community hospitals than in the university centre, the US extrapolations based on studies from university centres may be overestimates[18].

This estimate as well as similar estimates have been derived by using the average length of hospitalization of patients with nosocomial infections and subtracting the length of the average stay for all hospital patients. The main problem with these estimates is that the average hospital stay for all patients does not necessarily reflect a group of patients similar to the infected patients in age, sex, use of hospital services, or underlying diseases[19].

In the 55 million population of the Federal Republic of Germany the *per annum* hospital infection cost was estimated 1977 to about 440 million US $. About

16 Wenzel Richard P: Hospital-Acquired Infections: A Medical and Economical Problem. 1978, Virginia Medical 105:429–430.

* Spengler Robert F, Greenough III William B: Hospital Costs and Mortality Attributed to Nosocomial Bacteremias. 1978, JAMA 240:2455–2458.

** ibid

17 Hewitt William L and Sanford Jay P: Workshop on Hospital-Associated Infections. 1974, The Journal of Infectious Diseases 130:680–686.

18 File Jr Thomas M and Vincent Donald J: The Pattern of Gram-Negative-Rod Bacteremia in a Community Hospital. 1977, The Ohio State Medical Journal 73:551–556.

19 Spengler Robert F, Greenough III William B: Hospital Costs and Mortality Attributed to Nosocomial Bacteremias. 1978, JAMA 240:2455–2458.

500,000 FRG patients acquire an infection during their hospital stay, about 25,000 die of infections contracted in the hospitals[19]. According to another source[20] 8 per cent of the patients who die in the hospitals of the FRG, die of hospital-acquired infections.

In Switzerland a single hospital-acquired infection causes an average cost of about 6,500 US $ [21].

Inanimate environment and infection

In the inanimate environment of virtually every area of a hospital potential pathogens are found. Some of them may survive several weeks.

The inanimate hospital environment generally has much less influence than the animate environment — the direct, close, personal, human contact — in transmission of nosocomial disease[1].

The activity of people determines the microbiological condition of an environment and its inanimate surfaces. Humans deposit their own microorganisms, perform manipulations which contaminate, and transfer microorganisms from one location to another.

It is almost impossible to determine retrospectively whether an environmental contamination preceded or followed the patient infections, whether a contaminated hospital environment contaminated the patients or colonized patients contaminated the hospital environment and other patients[2]. Most epidemics within hospitals have occured without an identified source[3].

It would seem that micro-organisms often pass from patient to environment, where they appear to lose at least some of their capacity to infect. They are only rarely transmitted in the opposite direction.

Hospital environment is composed of a large number of materials, furnishings, equipment, and instruments. The microbilogical profile of a hospital reflects the contamination characteristics of each of its environmental components.

19 Daschner G: Grundlagen der Krankenhaushygiene und das Hospitalismusproblem. 1977, Intensivmedizin 14:163–168.

20 Löwe R: Hygiene — auch ein Problem für den Krankenhausplaner. 1977, Der Krankenhausarzt 50:1064–1071.

21 Möller Ove: Das Dilemma der Spitalhygiene. 1975, Hospital-Hygiene 67:359–363.

1 see also Mallison G F: Monitoring of sterility and environmental sampling in programs for control of nosocomial infections. in Infection control in health care facilities. ed by Kenneth R Cundy and William Ball. University Park Press. Baltimore, London, Tokyo 1977, p 26.

2 see also Farmer III John J: Pseudomonas in the Hospital. 1976, Hospital Practice 11:2:63–70.

3 Teres Daniel: Management of Respiratory infection in the Intensive Care Unit. in Recent advances in respiratory surgical intensive care. ed by T Gordon McNabb and Stephen V Hall. International Anesthesiology Clinics. vol 14 no 1. Spring 1976, p 163–178.

Despite numerous investigations into hospital infection, the classification of environmental items into real and imaginary infection hazards is still difficult and often based on guesswork[5].

To enumerate fully the sites in hospitals that have been shown to be capable of supporting the growth of e g the pseudomonas is to review a virtual inventory of essential and accessory hospital apparatus.

Three categories of hazards of infection from inanimate environment have been listed[6].

High risk of infection is connected with operation rooms, ICTUs, premature baby units, transplant and similar units and with equipment in close contact with breaks in skin or mucous membrane or introduced into sterile body area: dialysis equipment, catheters, parenteral and ophthalmic fluids, implants, some endoscopes, e g laproscopes, cystoscopes; surgical gowns and gloves, dressings and swabs.

Intermediate or occasional *risk* of infection consists of close contact with intact skin, mucous membranes of patients, hands and clothing of medical, para-medical and nursing staff involving respiratory and anaesthetic equipment, thermometers, some endoscopes e g bronchoscope, and baby incubators.

In the patient care areas wash bowls, baths, bedpans and urine bottles, nailbrushes and shaving equipment, mouthwash equipment can be mentioned as well as air and bedding (laundry), hand creams, soaps, detergents and antiseptics; food and food preparation surfaces and equipment. Intermediate risks includs also disposal of medico-technical waste, especially syringes and needles.

Low risk of infection — mostly in domestic areas and not in close contact with patient — consists of sinks and drains: mops, buckets, and cleaning equipment: flower vases and aquaria. Low risk includes the disposal of domestic waste.

Infections and floors, walls, ceilings

The risk of infection from floors is generally low[1].

The number of colony forming particles (CFP) on hospital floors shows very wide variations. In operation rooms 1.000 to 3.000 CFPs per m^2 have been found, in regular ward rooms 60.000 to 100.000; in corridors 1.000 to 100.000 and in toilets

5 see also Ayliffe G A J, Babb J R and Collins B J: Environmental hazards — real and imaginary. 1976, Health and Social Service Journal, vol 86, no 4496. Supplement, p 3–4.

6 ibid

1 see also Ayliffe G A J, Babb J R and Collins B J: Environmental hazards — real and imaginary. 1976, Health and Social Service Journal vol 86, no 4496, p 3–4.
   Dietzel W: Angewandte Hygiene zur Infektionsprophylaxe in der Intensivtherapie. 1978, Das Krankenhaus 70:191–194.

80.000 to 300.000. Highest CFP intensity on floor has been found in the showers[2].

There is a positive correlation between the amount of dust on the floor and the number of bacteria that can be found there[3].

The level of microbiological contamination of the floors is a function of the age of the floor, the renovation factor, and the physical conditions of the floor, but it depends also on the density of activities, and housekeeping procedures.

Needle-felt carpet coverings deliver low bacterial flow, terazzo and PVC-coverings the highest[4]. There is no evidence that carpets and other soft-flooring materials are an infection hazard in hospitals[5]. No evidence suggests that carpet harbours pathogenic bacteria and allows them to multiply any more than a sheet vinyl floor covering[6]. Organisms on a carpet will gradually die off if the area is not recontaminated[7]. However, laying of new carpet initially produces a fairly high and fairly constant bacterial count[8].

On the floor or in matwells in the corridor floor at the entrance to surgical department and other comparable areas foam rubber or plastic contamination *control mats* saturated with germicides or shallow *floor baths* with decontaminants have been placed with the intention to eliminate or reduce the bacterial flora on wheels of vehicles carrying patients, various apparatus, and shoe soles. Mats containing pads of cloth-backed adhesive sheets may strip dirt, dust, fluff and grit, even microorganism from shoe soles, bed and equipment wheels.

Tacky mats with replaceable sheets do not remove infection, but transfer tagged bacteria to new contacts. When six different types of the so called contamination control mats in use 1977 at the entrances to UK surgical suites and other clean areas were compared, all mats showed some functional disadvantages[10]. A German study of the S-Entry system indicates that the efficiency of the system is not sufficient[11].

2   Brandberg Åke and Brinkhoff Barbro: Sjukhusstädaren — estet eller bakteriejägare? 1977, Sjukhuset 54:429–434.

3   Bakker P G H and Faoagali J L: The Effect of Carpet on the Number of Microbes in the Hospital Environment. 1977, The New Zealand Medical Journal 85:88–92.

4   Kunze M, Klein H J and Flamm H: Vergleichende Untersuchungen zur Keimabgabe verschiedener Fussbodenbeläge. 1972, Zentralblatt für Bakteriologie, Parasitenkunde, Infektionskrankenheiten und Hygiene 166:437–440.

5   Control of Hospital Infection. ed by E J L Lowbury, G A J Ayliffe, A M Geddes and J D Williams. Chapman and Hall. London 1975, p 109.

6   Bakker P G H and Faoagali J L: The Effect of Carpet on the Number of Microbes in the Hospital Environment. 1977, The New Zealand Medical Journal 85:88–92.

7   ibid

8   Hayman J A: Bacterial flora in carpeted floors. 1972, Hospital and Health Administration 1:12:8–9

9   Laufman Harold: Surgical Hazard Control. 1973, Archives of Surgery 107:552–559.

10 Meddick H M: Bacterial contamination control mats: a comparative study. 1977, The Journal of Hygiene 79:133–140.

11 Vogl J, Wundt W, and Oellers B: Untersuchungen über die Wirksamkeit eines Trockenmattensystems zur Verminderung der Keimzahlen auf Fussböden infektionsgefährdeter Bereiche. 1978, Das Krankenhaus 70:195–197.

Shallow floor baths as decontaminants for wheels and footwear make soon the adjacent floor moist and slippery. Their advantages seem to be illusory and limited to moistening the wheels and to minimal preventing of the dispersal of some dust and bacteria.

Swabs of trolley wheels taken both before and immediately after traversing an antiseptic mat containing 5 per cent phenol have yielded growth of the same organisms: coagulase-negative staphylococci, diphtheroid bacilli and aerobic sporing bacilli[12]. This is not unexpected as antiseptics do not ensure an instantenous kill.

The effect of the mats and floor baths is considered to be mainly psychological[13].

Walls are often clean or with only a poor microbial flora[14]. Organisms from infected patients are seldom found on the walls in their rooms. The levels of contamination are comparable with unwashed walls in conventional patient rooms[15]. Occasionally the walls and doors may be heavily contaminated by the hands of staphylococcal carriers.

Painted walls with smooth surfaces rarely present a contamination problem[16]. However, bacteria can grow on damaged and moist surfaces[17].

Few staphylococci have been cultured from post-operative unit *window sills*[18].

The *ceiling* is a very minor source of hygienic concern.

12 Nuffield House, Musgrave Park Hospital, Belfast. The Case History of a New Hospital Building. London 1962, p 164–165.

13 see also Brandberg Åke and Brinkhoff Barbro: Sjukhusstädaren — estet eller bakteriejägare? 1977, Sjukhuset 54:429–434.

14 see also Froud P J, Alder V G and Gillespie W A: Contaminated areas in operating-theatre. 1966, The Lancet 2:961–963.
   Streptococcal and Staphylococcal Infections. Report of a WHO Expert Committee. World Health Organisation. Technical Report Series No 394. Geneva 1968, p 43.

15 Herzovi F and Barbulescu E: The absence of microbial competition, the main cause of in-hospital infections in children admitted to intensive therapy section. 1973, Romanian Medical Review 17:2:69–74.
   Petersen Norman J, Marshall James H and Collins Diane E: Why Wash Walls in Hospital Isolation Rooms? 1973, Health Laboratory Science 10:23.

16 Infection Control in the Hospital. American Hospital Association. Chicago 1974, p 80.

17 see also Control of Hospital Infection. ed by E J L Lowbury, G A J Ayliffe, A M Geddes and J D Williams. Chapman and Hall. London 1975, p 70.

18 Teres Daniel, Schweers Patricia, Bushnell Leonard S, Hedley-Whyte John and Feingold David S: Sources of Pseudomonas aeruginosa infection in a respiratory surgical intensive-therapy unit. 1973, The Lancet 1:415–417.

Toilets have generally not been shown to constitute a risk to patients. Studies show the potential to be small[1].

However, faecal bacteria occur in large numbers on surfaces which users of washrooms and toilets readily contact: the toilet seat, wash basin overflow, tap handles and the inside handle of the entrance door[2]. Pathogens, if present, can similarly be transmitted. In gynaecological units also gonococci, *Candida albicans* and *Trichomonas vaginalis* can be transmitted via toilet seats[3].

Transmission of disease by possible aerosol formation by *urinals* via the respiratory route cannot be neglected. A possibility of a cross-infection risk from this source has been suggested[4].

Toilet flushing is probably insufficient to produce infection under normal conditions[*].

The provision of a *washbasin* close to the toilet or urinal is essential. Washbasins should be cleaned after use by the user or attendant[5].

Failure to wash hands after visiting the lavatory may spread *E. coli* in the hospital. Bacteria are able to pass through several layers of toilet paper[6], and hands which are not noticeably unclean may be heavily contaminated with bacteria. By transfer on to cistern handles and door handles, bacteria may be carried beyond the lavatory premises.

Although it has been stated that water faucets and drains are not contributing to the transmission of *Pseudomonas aeruginosa*[7], the sinks and washbasins — highly

1   Wenzel Richard P, Veazey Jr James M, and Townsend Timothy R: Role of inanimate environment in hospital-acquired infections. in Infection control in health care facilities. ed by Kenneth R Cundy and William Ball. University Park Press. Baltimore, London, Tokyo 1977, p 77.

2   Merdes M F and Lynch D J: A bacteriological survey of washrooms and toilets. 1976, The Journal of Hygiene 76:183–190.

3   Bergsjø Per: Sykehushygiene og sykehusinfeksjoner ved en obstetrisk/gynekologisk avdelning. 1977, Tidsskrift for Den norske laegeforening 97:705–707.

4   Merdes M F and Lynch D J: A bacteriological survey of washrooms and toilets. 1976, The Journal of Hygiene 76:183–190.

*   Bloomfield Sally F: The Use of Disinfectants in the Home. 1978, The Journal of Applied Bacteriology 45:1–38.

5   see also Control of Hospital Infection. ed by E J L Lowbury, G A J Ayliffe, A M Geddes and J D Williams. Chapman and Hall. London 1975, p 70.

6   Maurer Isobel M: Hospital Hygiene. Edward Arnold. London 1974, p 2.

7   see also Spyros D, Copeland Charles E and Grosiak Barbara: Mode of Transmission of Pseudomonas aeruginosa in a Burns Unit and an Intensive Care Unit in a General Hospital. 1972, Applied Microbiology 23:309–312.
    Zellner P R and Metzger E: Asepsis and Antisepsis bei der Behandlung des Brandtverletzten. 1977, Infection 5:36–44.

contaminated, but mostly with nonpathogenic bacteria — should be regarded as possible, but infrequent reservoirs of Gram-negative bacteria with the hands of personnel as the vehicles of transmission[8]. The shape of sinks should prevent back-splashing.

The floors around ward room washbasins have shown 100,000 to 300,000 CFP, which is considerably more than in other floor areas in the ward room[9].

Floor drainage is considered to be a frequent reservoir of Gram-negative bacteria[10]. The importance of this source may be overestimated[11].

Some hospital areas and items and the infection risk

Operation room environment has since the third quarter of last century been regarded as a most important source of post-operative infection. This belief has to a very great extent influenced the planning and designing of surgical units[*]. A re-evaluation of this historic oversimplification is necessary.

Operations carry their own inherent infection-rate. Exogenous factors are not the most important ones.

A search of literature does not uncover investigations correlating the incidence of postoperative wound infection with directly measured operation room surface contamination[1]. Very little specific information on the environmental contamination in the operation room in general is available.

The level of contamination in regularly desinfected and carefully maintained operation rooms has been found to be low[2].

8   Teres Daniel, Schweers Patricia, Bushnell Leonard S, Hedley-Whyte John and Feingold David S: Sources of Pseudomonas aeruginosa infection in a respiratory/surgical intensive-therapy unit. 1973, The Lancet 1:415–417.

von Graevenitz Alexander: Mögliche Quellen gramnegativer Hospitalinfektionen. 1975, Fortschritte der Medizin 93:385–390.

9   Brandberg Åke and Brinkhoff Barbro: Sjukhusstädaren — estet eller bakteriejägare? 1977, Sjukhuset 54:429–434.

10 see also Kanz E: Transmission von Mikroorganismen im Krankenhaus. 1977, Der Krankenhausarzt 50:334–342.

11 personal communication: 1977, Bertil Nyström, Stockholm.

*
The architecture of the operation room of the surgical department has been developed in many stages. Much thought has been given to the prevention of transmission of infection, although the scientific basis for the proposed architectural solution has seldom been solid.

As the ultimate in ultra-clean environmental control systems surgical isolators and unidirectional flow enclosures have been introduced.

1   see also Weber Donald O, Gooch James J, Wood Walter R, Britt Eugene M and Kraft Richard O: Influence of Operation Room Surface Contamination on Surgical Wounds. 1976, Archieves of Surgery 111:484–487.

2   see also Kanz E: Krankenhaushygiene. 1975, Hospital-Hygiene 67:4–16.

Horizontal surfaces in the operation room are ten times[3] more heavily contaminated than the vertical.

Sedimentation of bacteria seems to be a more important cause of contamination of the operation room floor than the transport of bacteria by shoes and wheels[4].

The redispersal of *Straph. aureus* from the operation room floor dust to air hardly increases the risk for airborne infection of operation wounds[5].

Contact transfer of infection through unintentional touch of the operation room by hand should be regarded as a highly hypothetical possibility.

Pseudomonas aeruginosa has been recovered on the open shelves where supplies are stored[6].

A growth of bacteria has been given by the swabs from the tops of operation lamps[7]. The difference between the contamination on the lamps compared to that on the floors has not been statistically significant[8].

The theoretical frequencies of infection possibly caused by bacteria falling from the operation lamp are unidentified.

In the case of anaerobic infections following clean surgical procedures, the infecting organisms — in most cases *C. perfringens* — may be derived from exogenous sources as a result of some breakdown in the operation room ventilation system. Perhaps more commonly they are of endogenous origins, occuring on the patient's skin as contaminants that are implanted into the underlying tissues during the course of operation[9].

In operation rooms some contamination can be tolerated in air, on surfaces, and on people. The tolerance levels should be the minimum attainable consonant with the technology available at reasonable cost.

3   Hambraeus A, Bengtsson S and Laurell G: Bacterial contamination in a modern operating suite. 1. Effect of a zoning system on contamination of floors and other surfaces. Stencil. Institute of Clinical Bacteriology, University of Uppsala, Sweden 1977, p 12.

4   Hambraeus A, Bengtsson S and Laurell G: Bacterial contamination in a modern operating suite. 3. Importance of floor contamination as a source of airborne bacteria. Stencil. Institute of Clinical Bacteriology, University of Uppsala, Sweden 1977, p 7.

5   ibid

6   Kundsin Ruth B: Microbial monitoring of the hospital environment. in Infection control in health care facilities. ed by Kenneth R Cundy and William Ball. University Park Press. Baltimore, London, Tokyo 1977, p 14.

7   Froud P J, Alder V G and Gillespie W A: Contaminated areas in the operating theatre. 1966, The Lancet 2:961–963.

8   Hambraeus A, Bengtsson S and Laurell G: Bacterial contamination in a modern operating suite. 1. Effect of a zoning system on contamination of floors and other surfaces. Stencil. Institute of Clinical Bacteriology, University of Uppsala, Sweden 1977, p 8.

9   Willis A T: Some infections due to anaerobic sporeforming bacilli. in Anaerobic bacteria: Role in disease. ed by Albert Balows, Raymond M DeHaan, V R Dowell Jr and Lucien B Guze. Charles C Thomas Springfield, Illinois 1974, p 199.

Common sense instead of agitation should prevail when various planning aspects are to be discussed.

Many of the common *childbirth* notions and practices do not seem to be grounded in good scientific principle[10]. For example, the incidence of maternal infection has been found the same in the home and hospital groups. The incidence of neonatal infection has been found slightly higher in the hospital. In the hospital, surgical asepsis was always maintained, whereas in the home, the only sterile items used were gloves worn by the attendant along. The towels or pads beneath the mother were clean.

The hospital's emphasis on asepsis did not seem to change the incidence of infection over the home-group mothers and infants. Given this finding, there seems to be no reason why labour room deliveries in a comfortable double bed, with family and friends present at home, should not be permitted.

The increased risk of infection to patients in the *intensive care and treatment unit* of general hospitals has been emphasized[11]. The ICTU has been called the focal point of hospital hygiene[12].

A high risk has been demonstrated in respiratory intensive care units, nurseries for premature infants, burn units. In each of these facilities a concentration of patients with a major illness, usually complicated by severe depression of the host defense mechanisms, may be found.

Other findings indicate that the intensive care unit might be of less importance than the general wards serving as a reservoir of infecting strains[13]. 59 per cent of staphylococcal infections in patients have been found to be present already at the time of their admission to the unit[14]. Preliminary results from the Danderyd hospital, Sweden, indicate that exogenous infections in general in the ICTU have been rare and that the frequency of endogenous infections is high[15].

10 Mehl Lewis E: Delivery in the home. 1978, Comprehensive Therapy 4:3:18–26.

11 see also Thofern Edmund: Hygieneprobleme im Krankenhaus. 1977, Krankenhaus Umschau 46:690–693.
   Michel M F: Nosocomial infections in intensive care patients: the problem and approaches to its solution. 1977, The Netherlands journal of medicine 20:211–219.

12 Kanz E: Hygienisch-bakteriologische Probleme des Krankenhauses. 1978, Unfallheilkunde 81:43–50.

13 Bröte Lars and Niléhn Birgitta: Wound Infections in General Surgery with Special Reference to the Occurrence of Staphylococcus aureus. in Bröte Lars: Postoperative wound infections in general surgery. Linköping University Medical Dissertations No 33. Linköping 1976, p 9.

14 Harris D M: Staphylococcal infection in an intensive-care unit, and its relation to infection in the reminder of the hospital. 1973, The Journal of Hygiene 71:341–348.

15 Sjukhusinfektioner. Redovisning av enkät vintern 1975/76. Socialstyrelsen. Stencil. Stockholm 1976, p 135.

In a surgical intensive care unit airborne infection is distinctly uncommon[16]. Contamination by contact with hands[17], personnel clothing, and the use of infusion catheters[18] appear to be more influential in the transmission of micro-organisms.

The size of the ward team is related to the rate of infection, a factor to be borne in mind[19].

Physician and nursing personnel handwashing facilities are extremely important, but it has also pointed out, that the hands of the ICTU patients should be regularly disinfected[20].

There is no evidence to suggest that patients returning from the intensive care units to the regular wards transfer infection.

High nosocomial infection rate has been revealed in *neonatal intensive care units*[21], the most important cause of cross-infection — and the most difficult to control — being the NICU staff[22]. Others have concluded that approximately 50 per cent of the affected infants most probably acquired the pathogens during birth. 90 per cent of them must be considered nosocomial infections[23].

Common source epidemics due to contaminated equipment — most notably from isolettes, respirators, umbilical catheters[24] — but also from disinfectants, solutions and medications have occurred[25].

Clean gowns are worn but effective handwashing is probably the most important single measure in preventing the spread of infection in the NICU. Also a report on

16 see also Daschner F: Grundlagen der Krankenhaushygiene und das Hospitalismusproblem. 1977, Intensivmedizin 14:163–168.

   Michel M F: Nosocomial infections in intensive care patients: the problem and approaches to its solution. 1977, The Netherlands journal of medicine 20:211–219.

   Dietzel W: Angewandte Hygiene zur Infektionsprophylaxe in der Intensivtherapie. 1978, Das Krankenhaus 70:191–194.

17 see also Hewitt William L and Sanford Jay P: Workshop on Hospital-Associated Infections. 1974, The Journal of Infectious Diseases 130:680–686.

18 Daschner F: Grundlagen der Krankenhaushygiene und das Hospitalismusproblem. 1977, Intensivmedizin 14:163–168.

19 Cozanitis D A, Mäkelä P and Grant J: Microorganisms in the Hair of Staff and Patients in an Intensive Care Unit. 1977, Der Anaesthesist 26:578–580.

20 Kalmar P, Horatz K, Rodewald G, Schassan HH and Schassek S: Hospitalismus in der chirurgischen Intensivpflege. 1976, Langenbecks Archiv für Chirurgie 342:383–391.

21 see also John Jr Joseph F: Nosocomial Infection Rates at a General Army Hospital. 1977, The American Journal of Surgery 134:381–384.

22 Goldman Donald A: Nosocomial Infection — a hazard of newborn intensive care. 1976, The New England Journal of Medicine 294:1342–1343.

23 Riegel K P: The role of the neonatologist. in Gynecology and Obstetrics. ed by L Castelazo-Ayala and C MacGregor. Excerpta Medica. Amsterdam-Oxford 1977, p 375.

24 Geme Joseph W St: Perinatal and Neonatal Infections. 1975, The Western Journal of Medicine 122:359–365.

25 Goldman Donald A: Nosocomial infection — a hazard of newborn intensive care. 1976, The New England Journal of Medicine 294:1342–1343.

viral infection among neonates indicates that the reason for an outbreak of entero-viral infections was inadequate handwashing by personnel[26].

It is generally believed that airborne bacterial infection occurs rarely in a NICU.

In *burn care units* infections arise from contacts; airborne infection is a minor risk[27] Pseudomonas strains found on furniture and equipment have appeared in the wound area[28]. The milieu has been regarded as the greatest danger for the patient. By exclud-ing common treatment areas, it has been possible to achieve a considerable reduction in the rate of cross-infection among patients[29].

No data are available to demonstrate the effects of architectural design of special care units on nosocomial infections which occur in them[30].

Within the hospital eco-system a hostile microbiological environment confronts patients in the *diagnostic radiology department* and its fomities[31]. There is not one point of patient contact in the system of patient flow from the patient's room via stretcher or wheelchair, to the X ray waiting area, in an X ray room and back again to the patient's room which is free from microbial cross-contamination and infec-tion potential. X ray equipment in itself, unless moisture is present, is very rarely a vector of infection[32]. By Xradiation bacterial and viral mutations can be induced*.

In *physiotherapy units* hydrotherapy equipment, which is not properly cleaned be-tween different patients, may cause trouble for patients with burns[33]. Stainless steel has been found to be an excellent material in hydrotherapy units, when hygienic qualities are concerned[34].

26 Cramblett Henry G, Haynes Ralph E, Azimi Parvin H, Hilty Milo D and Wilder Michael H: Nosocomial in-fection with echovirus type II in handicapped and premature infants. 1973, Pediatrics 51:603–607.

27 see also Ugland O M: Infeksjonsproblemer ved brannskader. 1977, Tidsskrift for Den norske laegeforening 97:704–705.

28 Zellner P R and Metzger E: Asepsis und Antisepsis bei der Behandlung des Brandverletzen. 1977, Infec-tion 5:36–44.

29 ibid

30 see also Laufman Harold: The infection hazard of intensive care. 1974, Surgery, Gynecology & Obstetrics 139:413–414.

31 Haskin Marvin E and McGinley John A: Hospital Ecology and Nosocomial Infections. 1972, The Radiologic Clinics of North America 10:583–588.

LeFrock Jack L, Babu Jegdish P, Klainer Albert S: Nosocomial Infection: Radiology department as source. 1978, New York State Journal of Medicine 78:2039–2043.

32 von Graevenitz Alexander: Environmental surveillance. in Infection control in health care facilities. ed by Kenneth R Cundy and William Ball. University Park Press. Baltimore, London, Tokyo 1977, p 156.

* LeFrock Jack L, Babu Jegdish P, Klainer Albert S: Nosocomial Infection: Radiology department as source. 1978, New York State Journal of Medicine 78:2039–2043.

33 Koepke G H and Christopher R P. Contamination of whirlpool baths during treatment of infected wounds. 1965, Archives of Physical Medicine 46:261–263.

34 Thummernicht W: Der Sanitär-Bereich erfordert mehr Hygiene. 1976, Hospital-Hygiene 68:387–393.

In the *nursing units* the bed of the patient first becomes contaminated and next the curtains, if surrounding the bed[35]. Beds should be washed with detergent or soap and water after discharge of patient[36].

Bedding and blankets reflect the organisms of the people in the environment, but may be less important sources of infection than frequently insisted[37].

Water beds in use in hospitals have been found to be a potential source of *Pseudomonas aeruginosa*[38].

Hospital *furniture* may contain large microbial reservoirs. E g organisms isolated from the wheelchairs and stretchers are the strongest possible reminder that patient's hands spread organisms effectively to such surfaces as wheelchair arm rests, and conversely, patients' hands pick up these organisms[39]. Heavy contamination with haemolytic streptococci and *Staphylococcus aureus* has, as another example, been found also on furniture in a plastic surgery and burn unit[40].

The illuminants are considered to be a very minor source of nosocomial infections*.

The aesthetic and morale-boosting value of *flowers* in hospitals cannot be disputed, but the vases may carry large number of potentially pathogenic bacteria in the water they contain[41]. However, there appears to be no correlation between the types of bacteria isolated from flower water and those responsible for wound infection. For infection control purposes, it would seem reasonable to prohibit flowers from special care units. A burn unit would be an especially inappropriate location[42].

Probably nothing releases more bacteria in various personal activities than the common acts of dressing and undressing. Of all hospital areas studied doctors' *changing*

35 Nothey Dianne, Adess Michael L, Hartsuck James M and Rhoades Everett R: Microbial surveillance in a surgical intensive care unit. 1974, Surgery, Gynecology & Obstetrics 139:321–325.

36 Control of Hospital Infection. ed by E J L Lowbury, G A J Ayliffe, A M Geddes and J D Williams. Chapman and Hall. London 1975, p 72.

37 see also Johnson III Joseph E: Wound Infections. in Clinical Concepts of Infectious Diseases. ed by Leighton E Cluff and Joseph E Johnson III. The Williams and Wilkins Company. Baltimore 1972, p 197.

38 Elhag K M, Baird Rosamund M and Shaw Elizabeth J: Water beds — a potential source of Pseudomonas aeruginosa. 1977, The Journal of Hygiene 79:103–106.

39 Haskin Marvin E and McGinley John A: Hospital Ecology and Nosocomial Infections. 1972, The Radiologic Clinics of North America 10:583–588.

40 Sepsis in a plastic surgery unit. 1976, British Medical Journal 2:1396.

*   Stolzenberg Klaus: Krankenhausbeleuchtung. 1978, Krankenhaus Umschau 47:901–908.

41 see also Taplin David and Mertz Patricia M: Flower vases in hospitals as reservoirs of pathogens. 1973, The Lancet 2:1279–1281.

42 Wenzel Richard P, Veazey Jr James M and Townsend Timothy R: Role of the inanimate environment in hospital-acquired infections. in Infection control in health care facilities. ed by Kenneth R Cundy and William Ball. University Park Press. Baltimore, London, Tokyo 1977, p 72.

rooms were generally the most heavily contaminated[43]. Also according to another study the highest number of bacteria along the staff's route to operation room was found in the so called staff clean dressing area[44].

Likewise changing cubicles in various parts of medical performance area have been identified as rooms with very high degree of aerial contamination[45].

Along the patient route to the operation unit the lowest number of bacteria and *Staph. aureus* has been found in the corridor outside the operation unit holding or waiting area[46]. Otherwise a large amount of bacteria may be found in the corridors.

Few hard facts on bacterial contamination in hospital *lifts* have been collated. Lifts are rarely seen as a potential trouble spot from the view point of bacterial contamination, however, indications are that these problems have remained largely in the stage of potential[47].

Airborne transmission of infection

There is no doubt that bacteria are present in the air of hospitals.

The species involved and magnitude of contamination in each segment of the hospital environment seem to vary according to sampling methods as well as other local variables. These variables include temperature, humidity, air movement, physical structure of the hospital, as well as a seemingly endless list of the clinical features of patients in the area sampled, such as age, underlying illness, and antimicrobial usage.

The ability to document precisely the movement of bacteria from one segment of the environment to another — e g the nares of a carrier of *S. aureus* to the wound of a patient — is fraught with many technical difficulties, and showing that airborne transmission of a specific organism occurs to the exclusion of all other possible

43 Bond R G, Halbert Mary M, Putman Hugh D, Rushmeyer Orlande R and Vesley Donald: Survey of microbial contamination in the surgical suites of 23 hospitals. University Health Service and School of Public Health, University of Minnesota, Minneapolis, Minn. Stencil. March 1964, p 57.

44 Hambraeus A, Bengtsson S and Laurell G: Bacterial contamination in a modern operating suite. 1. Effect of a zoning system on contamination of floors and other surfaces. Stencil. Institute of Clinical Bacteriology, University of Uppsala, Sweden. 1977, p 7.

45 see also Kanz E: Transmission von Mikroorganismen im Krankenhaus. 1977, Der Krankenhausarzt 50:334–342.

46 Hambraeus A, Bengtsson S and Laurell G: Bacterial contamination in a modern operating suite. 1. Effect of a zoning system on contamination of floors and other surfaces. Stencil. Institute of Clinical Bacteriology, University of Uppsala, Sweden 1977, p 8.

47 Schmidt Carlo: Elevators: Benign Neglect? 1974, Hospital Housekeeping 3:18.

modes is extremely difficult. It would also appear from a review of the data that there is no consistently applied method used to study air[1].

The direction of microbial movement from the infected patient to the air or from air to a susceptible patient is unknown. Even if one were to show that the pathogen is more frequently found in the air than on the hands of medical personnel or in the ward environment, it still must be demonstrated further that airborne transmission is the more likely mode. It is conceivable that an organism could be found less frequently on hands, yet be transmitted more efficiently by close contact than by air transmission. Furthermore, the exact airborne infectious dose for colonization/infection is unknown, and the number of organisms transmitted by hand contact may be very large compared to the numbers transmitted by air[2].

Convincing studies on the airborne transmission of infection within hospitals were done during the past ten years. Each study, however, had noticeable shortcomings attesting to the state of the art in the area[3].

If the premise that the airborne route exists is accepted, the magnitude of its role in producing disease must then be determined. Unfortunately, few controlled studies exist that prove the initial premise[4].

Airborne contamination route in hospital infection in general is uncommon[5] and its importance seems to be greatly overestimated, except in the unusual instances of heavy contamination of very infectious organisms or under special circumstances e g during the change of dressings on burned patients[6].

Generally it is agreed that living bacteria, in contrast to spores, are by themselves scarcely present in the air. Only a few pathogens are capable to maintain virulence and viability while suspended in air. Staphylococci and tuberculosis should be mentioned.

1 Wenzel Richard P, Veazey Jr James M, and Townsend Timothy R: Role of the inanimate environment in hospital-acquired infections. in Infection control in health care facilities. ed by Kenneth R Cundy and William Ball. University Park Press. Baltimore, London, Tokyo 1977, p 79.

2 ibid, p 80.

3 ibid

4 ibid

5 see also Winkler K C: General introduction. in Airborne transmission and airborne infection. ed by J F Ph Hers and K C Winkler. Ooesthoek Publishing Company. Utrecht 1973, p 3.
Fisher Evelyn J: Surveillance and management of hospital-acquired infections. 1976, Heart and Lung 5:784–787.
Kanz E: Transmission von Mikroorganismen im Krankenhaus. 1977, Der Krankenhausarzt 50:334–342.
Mallison G F: Monitoring of sterility and environmental sampling in programs for control of nosocomial infections. in Infection control in health care facilities. ed by Kenneth R Cundy and William Ball. University Park Press. Baltimore, London, Tokyo 1977, p 26.

6 Michel M F: Nosocomial infections in intensive care patients: the problem and approaches to its solution. 1977, The Netherlands journal of medicine 20:211–219.

To be transmitted by air, microorganisms must be attached to various particles.

Not every particle carries bacteria. The number of bacteria per bacterial particle has been found to be around 4.6[7].

The chief source also of airborne infection is man.

The most common mechanism for dispersal of microorganisms seems to be the release from the skin, usually with small particles of desquamated epithelium. Some people appear to have a special ability to disseminate their pathogenic flora.

Skin scales play a more important role than the droplet nuclei and the dust particles. The per minute air polluting of particles of 0.3 m μ and larger in size from man, wearing no protective dressing, ranges anywhere from 100,000 to 30,000,000[8].

A person sitting and moving lightly head, hand and forearm emits 500,000 particles per minute. Changing position from sitting to standing gives off 2,500,000 particles per minute.

Males disseminate more organisms into the environment than females. The output of colony forming particles (CFP) from naked males compared to naked females has been found to be considerably greater[9]. Also the pattern of dispersal from the various body sites when undressing is different for females and males[10]. In males the skin count of normal flora on the abdomen and thighs is strongly correlated with dispersal, whereas in females the shin may be more important.

Dispersal from patients in hospital is about half as great during night-time hours as during the day[11].

The sedimentation speed is not constant and depends on the character of ventilation in the room[12]. The medium sedimentation speed for particles of the size 1 to 70 m μ — most of them between 5 and 15 m μ — is 0.3 m/min[13].

---

7   May and Pomeroy cited by Whyte W, Vesley D and Hodgson R: Bacterial dispersion in relation to operating room clothing. 1976, The Journal of Hygiene 76:367–378.

8   Austin Philip R and Timmerman Stewart W: Design and operation of clean rooms. Business New Publishing Company. Detroit 1965, p 77.

9   May K R and Pomeroy N P: Bacterial dispersion from the body surface. in Airborne transmission and airborne infection. ed by J F Ph Hers and K C Winkler. Ooesthoek Publishing Company. Utrecht 1973, p 431. personal communication: 1976, Jan Hoborn, Mölnlycke.

10 see also Noble W C, Habbema J D F, van Furth R, Smith Ingrid and de Raay Carla: Quantitative studies on the dispersal of skin bacteria into the air. 1976, The Journal of Medical Microbiology 9:53–61.

11 Lidwell O M: Clean Air, Less Infection. 1976, Hospital Engineering 30:8:9–17.

12 van der Waaij D, Heidt P J and Wigersma N: Ventilation von Operationsräumen. 1975, medizinische technik 95:47–51.

13 Foord N and Lidwell O M: The control by ventilation of airborne bacterial transfer between hospital patients and its assessment by means of a particle tracer. 1972, The Journal of Hygiene 70:279.

Staphylococcus aureus and other micro-organisms, which have settled on a floor are difficult to redistribute into air[14]. Dust from floors seldom rises above knee-height because of the movement of people in the room. Usually, air velocity in a closed space does not exceed 0.3 m/sec[15]. Dust particles from hard floors are made airborne first when the air velocity is 1.5 m/sec. When carpeting is used, the air velocity has to be as high as 4.5 m/sec.

It is clear that attempts to reduce infection by control of airborne contamination are often unsuccessful. In controlling airborne contamination, directions of air flow are commonly more important than precise volumes[16]. *No advantages will be gained in reducing airborne transfer to less than, say, one tenth of transfer by other means*[17].

Before investing great sums of money on equipment and techniques to reduce or to interrupt the airborne transmission of infectious particles, a cause-and-effect relationship between airborne agents and subsequent illness in well controlled studies must be demonstrated.

14 see also Froud P J, Alder V G and Gillespie W A: Contaminated areas in operating-theatre. 1966, The Lancet 2:961:963.

15 Friedrichs K H, Grün L, Satlow G and Schlipköter H W: Zur Hygiene der Teppischauslegware II. 1970, Gesundheitswesen und Desinfection:7.

16 Lidwell O M: Clean Air, Less Infection. 1976, Hospital Engineering 30:8:9–17.

17 ibid

Post-operative wound infections

The healing of a wound is a complex phenomenon affected by many factors. It occupies a prime position in the priority schedule for body functions.

Nearly half of all post-operative complications seem to be wound complications. Among these, infection, dehiscence, and pathological fibrosis are most common[1]. Of wound complications about 40 per cent have been wound infections[2].

The wound situation is determined in the first place by the surgical techniques. The appreciation of gentleness in handling tissues and the use of careful techniques in sharp surgery are mandatory to minimize infections.

Surgical patients are probably safer with superb surgical techniques and less than perfect antisepsis than they are with less than perfect surgical techniques and superb antisepsis.

The infection rate in clean and clean-contaminated categories has been found[3] almost doubled, when the operation was performed between midnight and 8 a m. This rise was most likely caused by a through weariness lost perfect operation technique.

It has been found noteworthy that the infection rate for emergency operations has always been higher than for elective operations[4].

All wounds are contaminated, but relatively few become infected. Mere presence of bacteria in the wound is less important than the level of bacterial growth. Likewise the mere presence of bacteria in a bone is not enough to cause a disease[5].

Wound healing without infection is less a function of the prevention of the bacterial presence than it is the successful control of the quantitative growth of bacteria below the critical level, which some regard to be 10^5 bacteria per gram of tissue[6].

1   see also de Haan B Bierens, Ellis H and Wilks M: The role of infection on wound healing. 1974, Surgery, Gynecology & Obstetrics 138:693–700.
    Forrester J C: Surgical wound biology. 1976, Journal of the Royal College of Surgeons of Edinburgh 21:239–249.

2   Schilling John A and Heimbach David M: Wound complications. 1977, The American Surgeon 43:682–685.

3   .Cruse Peter J E and Foord Rosemary: A five-year prospective study of 23,649 surgical wounds. 1973, Archives of Surgery 107:206.

4   Wright J E, Hennessy E J and Bissett R L: Wound Infection: Experience with 12,000 sutured surgical wounds in a general hospital over a period of 11 years. 1971, The Australian and New Zealand Journal of Surgery 41:109.

5   Robertson D E: Acute hematogenous osteomyelitis. 1927, Journal of Bone Joint Surgery 9:8.

6   Krizek Thomas J and Robson Martin C: Biology of Surgical Infection. 1975, The Surgical Clinics of North America 55:1261–1267.

Generally, the critical number for bacteria which is needed to produce an infection seems to be one million organisms per one gram of tissues or milligram of biologic fluid[7]. However, not every species of bacteria appears to adhere to the level of greater than 10^6 organisms to produce complications. E g the beta-hemolytic streptococcus has been repeatedly demonstrated to be clinically significant at a much lower level[8].

The balance in contaminated wounds between healing without clinical infection and healing with clinical infection is very narrow and easily tiltable[9].

Moreover, *Irving Enquist* and his colleagues* have found that a certain degree of bacterial contamination appears to stimulate wound repair.

The number of bacteria needed to create a suppurative lesion depends on the physiological state of the tissue in which the bacteria find themselves. A wound with unhealthy, or dead tissue present has very limited resistance to the growth of virulent and non-virulent bacteria.

The presence of a foreign body — e g when a prosthesis is implanted — in the lesion markedly alters local resistance and stimulates infection in wounds which otherwise heal uneventfully. The bacterial transport inside the thread has been found to be of significantly greater importance for the spreading of wound infection than that of the surface of the suture material[10].

Polk Jr[11] has commented the work of *L Marmor* and *D Berkus* on hematogenous infection of total knee implants: beyond any reasonable doubt, these patients all developed infection of their secure, well-incorporated foreign bodies by hematogenous routes from bacterial inflammations, which were not the focus of tissue destructive infection. The patient with an indwelling prosthetic device who subsequently develops an infective process, no matter how mild, is at real risk of hematogenous contamination of his or her prosthesis. The destructive effects of infection in and about virtually any prosthesis leads to loss of function at best and to loss of life at worst. Correlative data suggest that other prostheses are no less risk and, perhaps by virtue of location, e g, intracardiac, are of even greater significance.

7   Robson Martin C, Krizek Thomas J and Heggers John P: Biology of Surgical Infection. Current Problems in Surgery. Year Book Medical Publisher. Chicago 1973, p 17.

8   ibid, p 20.

9   see also Hunt Thomas K: Diagnosis and Treatment of Wound Failure. in Advances in Surgery. Vol 8. ed by R M Zollinger. Year Book Medical Publishers Inc. Chicago 1974, p 287–309.

*   cited by Dunphy J Englebert: Wound Healing. 1978, The Surgical Clinics of North America 58:907–916.

10 Blomstedt Bertil, Österberg Bertil and Bergstrand Anders: Suture material and bacterial transport. 1977, Acta Chirurgica Scandinavica 143:71–73.

11 Polk Jr Hiram C: Late and remote infection — yet another threat to the successful prosthesis. 1978, Surgery 83:491.

As the number of functioning implants increase, almost geometrically, among aging population, the practical significance of the concept posed by Marmor and Berkus will become a part of the practice of medicine.

Experimental and clinical bacteriology has contributed to the advancement of surgical knowledge. However, everyday hospital practice has not been able to keep abreast of all research developments. The number of hospitals which have adequate bacteriological laboratories to give the surgeon* the information which should be available to him is still very limited.

Post-operative infections and the harm done

Although strongly diminished in proportion to their last century occurence, the harm done by post-operative infections is still considerable.

In the beginning of the era of the aseptic surgery, poor risk patients were operated only exceptionally because of the risks involved with anaesthesia and the very limite knowledge of the fluid electrolyte balance, renal and heart function. Currently poor surgical risk patients, whose frequencies of post-operative infections are higher, are included.

Various forces imposed upon microorganisms during the last third of the century have produced reactions in the microbial world, which in their turn have influenced the pattern and nature of post surgical infections. As some infections have been brought under progressive control, other types have taken their place. The overall incidence of infections — as the clinical and laboratory experiences during that period indicate — has not been significantly reduced.

In some areas, e g the post-operative chest infections, despite advances in surgical technique, anaesthetics, and chemotherapy there is some evidence that the incidence of infections has increased[1]. In most cases as the consequence of a post-operative infection, the stay in hospital is prolonged. For some of the involved patients the result of an infection will be so serious that it becomes fatal. Purely in health-service terms, skilled staff is kept occupied with all infected patients and a considerable cost in money is involved.

Substantial variations in the outcome of surgery among hospitals do exist, independent of differences in patient mix[2].

---

* Sir Donald Douglas has stressed that surgeons are not by training and experience competent to express valid opinion upon the bacteriological problems which bear on surgery, though they would give the bacteriologist guidance about clinical matters (Surgical Departments in Hospitals. ed by D M Douglas. Butterworths, London 1972, p 80).

1 see also Presley A P and Alexander-Williams J: Postoperative chest infection. 1974, The British Journal of Surgery 61:448--452.

2 Comparison of hospitals with regard to outcomes of surgery. 1976, Health Services Research 11:112-127.

There is also a security threshold for each surgical department. Beyond a certain number of major or medium operations the mortality and probably the infection rate increases faster than the number of operated patients. In an investigated department this threshold was 22 major or medium operations a week[3].

A large percentage — up to 42 per cent — of wound infections is said to be detected after the patient is discharged[4]. This aspect might gain importance in reappraising wound infection surveillance methodology techniques.

The rates of surgical infections show considerable variations in different countries and areas. They constitute about 25 per cent of all nosocomial infections[5].

In the United States as published in 1974, all surgery considered, the wound infection rate was 3 to 5 per cent[6]. A wound infection was estimated to incur in about 1,000,000 post-operative patients annually. Of these about 100,000 die.

In Canada, an overall infection rate of 5.1 per cent was based on a seven year study of 40,662 operations[7].

In the United Kingdom some 10 per cent of surgical wounds show clinical signs of infection[10]. In the Birmingham region clinical infection has been found in 6.1 per cent of clean undrained operation wounds. Drained wounds had higher sepsis[11].

In Denmark the average general post-operative wound infection rate has been estimated to be 5 to 10 per cent[12], but occasionally, much higher (19.4 per cent[13]) frequencies have been demonstrated.

In Norway 11 per cent of the operated patients have been reported to have contracted post-operative infections, a rate, which in some hospitals is risen to 18 per cent[14].

3   Maillard J N, Flusin J L, Rodary M and Elman Annie: Un nouveau critère de gestion hospitalière. Le seuil de sécurité des malades. 1976, Chirurgie 104:229–234.

4   Weber Donald O, Gooch James J, Wood Walter R, Britt Eugene M and Kraft Richard O: Influence of Operating Room Surface Contamination on Surgical Wounds. 1976, Archives of Surgery 111:484–487.

5   Stamm Walter E, Martin Stanley M and Bennett John V: Epidemiology of Nosocomial Infections Due to Gram-Negative Bacilli: Aspects Relevant to Development and Use of Vaccines. 1977, The Journal of Infectious Diseases 136:S151–S160.

6   Greene Velvl: Sterilization Versus Disinfection. 1974, Hospital Topics 52:5:44–45.

7   Cruse Peter J E: Incidence of Wound Infection on the Surgical Services. 1975, The Surgical Clinics of North America 55:1269–1275.

10 Ventilation in Operation Suites. DHSS London 1972, p 1.

11 Ayliffe G A J, Brightwell K M, Collins B J, Lowbury E J L, Goonatilake P C L and Etheridge R A: Surveys of hospital infection in Birmingham region. 1977, The Journal of Hygiene 79:299–314.

12 Kjølbye Jørgen: Isolationsproblemer for orthopedisk-kirurgiske afdelinger. Amtsrådsforeningen i Danmark. Byggesymposium V. 5–7 december 1972 Helsingør. Stencil. Copenhagen 1973, p 44.

13 see also Jepsen Ole Bent: Contamination of the Wound during Operation and Postoperative Wound Infection. 1973, Annals of Surgery 177:179.

14 Operasjonsavdelinger. Norsk Institutt for Sykehusforskning. Trondheim 1977, p 56.

In Sweden the wound-infection rate in acute disease clinics has been found to be 5.2 per cent[15].

Surgical sepsis has been estimated[16] to increase the period of hospitalization by at least 100 per cent and thus to add considerably to the overall cost of a patient's medical care when an operation is involved.

In a Swedish hospital — the University Hospital, Linköping — the average hospitalization time for patients contracting post-operative wound infections was 9 days longer than for non-infected patients[17]. At Linköping 3.4 per cent of all nursing days were lost owing to excess hospitalization of infected patients. At the University Hospital, Uppsala, the postoperative wound infections increased the stay by 15 to 20 days[18]. At the County Hospital of Falu, Falun, a post-operative wound infection prolonged the hospitalization time by about one week[19].

In a Canadian hospital — the Foothills Hospital, Calgary — hospital wound infections delay the patient's discharge from the hospital by 9.1 days[20]. It is calculated that each infected wound costs $ 1,250 for hospitalization alone. By extrapolation, for the 22.9 million population in Canada the annual cost would be $ 318 million[21].

In the Central Military Hospital in Havanna, Cuba, wound infection delayed the patients' discharge by 9.4 days [22].

Although often quoted in hospital statistics, the overall infection rate is of no value in reflecting a hospital's infection control measures unless the types of operations and the categories of contamination are stated[23]. Neither indicate these values the surgical possibilities of a country.

15 Bernander Sverker, Hambraeus Anna, Myrbäck Karl-Eric, Nyström Bertil and Sundlöf Bo: Prevalence of Hospital-associated Infections in Five Swedish Hospitals in November 1975. 1978, Scandinavian Journal of Infectious Diseases 10:66–70.

16 W E Birkenstock and J W Green and R P Wenzel cited by Joffe Stephen N, Thomson William O, McGavigan James, and Trexler P C: A Closed System Surgical Isolator for Major Elective Abdominal Operations. 1978, World Journal of Surgery 2:123–127.
Wenzel Richard P: Hospital-Acquired Infections: A Medical and Economical Problem. 1978, Virginia Medical 105:429–430.

17 Bröte Lars: Postoperative wound infections in general surgery. Linköping University Medical Dissertations No 33. Linköping 1976, p 17.

18 Bengtsson S, Hambraeus A and Laurell G: Wound infections after surgery in a modern operating suite. 1. Clinical findings. Stencil. Institute of Clinical Bacteriology, University of Uppsala, Sweden 1977, p 8.

19 Leissner K H: Postoperative wound infection in 32.000 clean operations. 1976, Acta Chirurgica Scandinavica 142:433–439.

20 Cruse Peter J E: Incidence of Wound Infection on the Surgical Services. 1975, The Surgical Clinics of North America 55:1269–1275.

21 Cruse Peter: Infection Surveillance: Identifying the Problems and the High-Risk Patient. 1977, Southern Medical Journal 70:suppl 1:4–8.

22 Alacron Dennis Reyes, Cuervo Andres Cazan and Loeches-Fernandez Juan Rodriguez: Infección de la herida guirúrgica según la probabilidad de contaminación: grados y costos. 1976, Revista Cubana de Chirurgia 15:529–537.

23 Cruse Peter: Infection Surveillance: Identifying the Problems and the High-Risk Patient. 1977, Southern Medical Journal 70:suppl 1:4–8.

The information value of the overall wound infection rates as well as the rates for some types of operations is limited as the criteria used to define the wound infection, the time to follow up, the patient's disease, the use of antibiotics, and some other factors vary considerably.

Time and place for initiating post-operative wound infection

It has been frequently claimed that post-operative infections are exclusively initiated in the operation room and that the intraoperative wound contamination is the dominating source of post-operative wound infection.

According to investigations, post-operative infection rarely originates in the operation room and is usually due to a secondary infection of an initially sterile haematoma[1].

The importance of preoperative infection in the genesis of post-operative infection rate has been found 1.1 per cent, with a one-week preoperative stay 2.7 per cent, and with a longer than a fortnight stay 3.4 per cent[2].

Some findings indicate that a longer preoperative stay in hospital does not result in a higher carrier rate[3]. This might be explained by good isolation facilities and ventilation in wards.

A separation of preoperative and postoperative nursing has been recommended.

The risk of acquiring infections during the early post-operative phase through deficiencies in the open intensive care ward, particularly in connection with thoracic surgery[5], has been emphasized. A German investigation[6] indicates that 37 per cent of the post-operative infections involving cardiotomy patients emanated in the intensive care unit.

A wound closed by first intention has no resistance to bacteria swabbed on its surface during the first six hours. After that time it becomes increasingly difficult to infect the wound and at five days it is as resistant as the surrounding skin[7].

Many sources of staphylococcal wound infection have been found in the wards. Much of the staphylococcal infection seem to be attributable to post-operative care.

---

1   see also O'Riordan Colm, Adler Jonathan L, Banks Henry H and Finland Maxwell: Wound Infections on an Orthopaedic Service. 1972, American Journal of Epidemiology 95:448.

Jepsen Ole Bent: Contamination of the Wound during Operation and Postoperative Wound Infection. 1973, Annals of Surgery 177:180.

2   Cruse Peter: Infection Surveillance: Identifying the Problems and the High-Risk Patient. 1977, Southern Medical Journal 70:suppl 1:4–8.

3   Bengtsson S, Hambraeus A and Laurell G: Wound infections after surgery in a modern operating suite. 2. Epidemiological findings. Stencil. Institute of Clinical Bacteriology, University of Uppsala, Sweden 1977, p 8.

5   Lidbom Gunnar: Studies of the Epidemiology of Staphylococcal Infections. 1964, Acta Chirurgica Scandinavica 128:430–433.

Frater R W M and Santos Gil H: Sources of Infection in Open-Heart Surgery. 1974, New York State Journal of Medicine 74:2386–2388.

6   Kalmar P, Horatz K, Rodewald G, Schassan H H and Schassek S: Hospitalismus in der chirurgischen Intensivpflege. 1976, Langenbecks Archiv für Chirurgie 342:383–391.

7   Forrester J C: Surgical wound biology. 1976, Journal of the Royal College of Surgeons of Edinburgh 21:239–249.

Patient and post-operative infection

Since the days of *Pasteur* and *Lister**, it is widely known that the avoidance of infection can be achieved by controlling the environment and a careful handling of tissues. Fewer have stressed the surgical application of the contribution of *Mechnikow*** and others which suggest that also the host resistance is important.

The patient himself contributes significantly to post-operative infection being the principal source for these bacteria. The evidence to document the importance of endogenous sources*** for wound infection is overwhelming.

Mostly normal body defences dispose of pathogenic organisms inoculated during the operation. In newborn, especially in the case of premature birth, the body's defences are not fully developed. The general resistance to infection is lowered in the elderly.

A pilot study has indicated that of the 112 host factors considered there were 11 which showed a trend that suggested that they may be predictive of a serious postoperative infection.

These factors were: malnutrition, the presence of malignant disease, diabetes, or alcoholism, exposure to steroids and/or cytotoxic drugs, hypoalbuminaemia, anaemia, lymphopenia, abnormal immunoglobulins, abnormal results of delayed hypersensitivity skin tests, and the presence of preoperative bacterial contamination. Clearly, some of the factors which were investigated and which did not show such a trend may well prove to be significant in the future and should not be neglected[1].

It could be shown that the greater the number of these risk factors present in any one patient the greater is the risk of a postoperative infection. Thus, if only one risk factor was present the incidence of infection was 17 per cent, but patients with 4 risk factors had an infection incidence of 39 per cent[2].

Large variations in post-operative infections depend on the type of operation — from about 1 per cent in sympathetic and cardiac operations to 50 per cent in operations on the colon and rectum[3].

---

*   Louis Pasteur (1822–1895), French chemist and microbiologist, established the validity of the germ theory of disease.

Lord Joseph Lister (1827–1912), English surgeon, one of the founders of antiseptic surgery.

** Ilja Ilich Mechnikow (1845-1916), Russian-French biologist, established views on the importance of phagocytosis, the dynamic relationship between offending organisms and defence mechanisms in the host.

***Although enormous changes have occured in the etiology of infection within the hospital, there is no conclusive evidence that these changes also occur outside the hospital.

It is not certain whether the problem of the endogenous flora is one that is destined to replace other infectious diseases problems in a more general way, or whether this is a problem largely limited to the susceptible population, which will end up in the hospital for one reason or another (E H Kass in Bacterial Infections. ed by M Finland, W Marget and K Bartmann, Springer-Verlag. Berlin, Heidelberg, New York 1971, p 218).

1   Kune Gabriel A: Life-threatening surgical infection: its development and prediction. 1978, Annals of the Royal College of Surgeons of England 60:92–98.

2   ibid

3   see also Douglas Sir Donald: Wounds and their problems. 1975, Journal of the Royal College of Surgeons of Edinburgh 20:77-95.

Infection in regions near the groin and perineum has always been believed to be frequent. However, the groin incision has not been identified as a significant factor in the development of wound infection[4].

The thigh and especially the leg show significantly less resistance to staphylococcal and streptococcal infection than do the trunk and the arms[5]. The hip region has been found to be a high-risk location, the spine and the knee joint low-risk locations[6].

As *age* increases, wound infections become more frequent. The wound infection rate is highest in the 60 to 74-year old group[7] and lowest in the 20 to 29-year old group. English data suggest a minimum infection rate about the age of 26 years[8]. In the under 10-year old group most infections occur in newborns and in infants younger than 2 years.

It has been found that although the hospital stay increases with age, the additional increase of stay in hospital of infected patients is remarkably constant in all age groups[9].

It is a paradox that youth is an advantage in general surgery but represents a handicap with respect to infectious complications of gynaecological surgery[10].

Sex of the patient has generally not been related to the risk of wound infection. However, in the group of postoperative chest infections, there has been found a statistically significant difference in favour of the female patients — 43 respective 21 per cent[11]. In the infection rates of female and male patients, when only operations common to female and male patients were analysed, infection rates were lower in female patients in all groups except those of 60 to 69 years[12]. Males have been found to be at greater risk of developing a surgical wound infection due to Gram-negative bacilli than the females[13].

Different authors in the field of aetiology of postoperative infection present different conclusions, stress different aspects, and thus support the natural view that several factors may be instrumen-

4   Meech P, Maclean Dorothy M and Stephenson C B S: Postoperative infection in arterial surgery: a review of the incidence and distribution in 386 patients. 1977, The Australian and New Zealand Journal of Surgery 47:745–751.

5   Johnson III Joseph E: Wound infections. in Clinical Concepts of Infectious Diseases. ed by Leighton E Cluff and Joseph E Johnson III. The Williams and Wilkins Company. Baltimore 1975, p 195.

6   Lidgren Lars and Lindberg Lars: Post-operative wound infections in clean orthopaedic surgery. 1974, Acta Orthopaedica Scandinavica 45:161–169.

7   **see also** Davidson A I G, Clark C and Smith G: Post-operative wound infection: A computer analysis. 1971, The British Journal of Surgery 58:333.
    Gierhake F W and Schwick H G: Immunological aspects of post-operative surgical infections. Vingt-quatrième congrès de la Société Internationale de Chirurgie. Brussels, no publishing year, p 72.

8   Ayliffe G A J, Brightwell K M, Collins B J, Lowbury E J L, Goonatilake P C L and Etheridge R A: Surveys of nospital infection in the Birmingham region. 1977, The Journal of Hygiene 79:299--314.

9   Bengtsson S, Hambraeus A and Laurell G: Wound infections after surgery in a modern operating suite. 1. Clinical findings. Stencil. Institute of Clinical Bacteriology, University of Uppsala, Sweden 1977, p 9.

10 Ledger William: Ob/Gyn Infections: Changing Patterns and Management. 1975, Hospital Practice 10:9:115–121.

11 Presley A P and Alexander-Williams J: Postoperative chest infection. 1974, The British Journal of Surgery 61:448–452.

12 Ayliffe G A J, Brightwell K M, Collins B J, Lowbury E J L, Goonatilake P C L and Etheridge R A: Surveys of hospital infection in the Birmingham region. 1977, The Journal of Hygiene 79:299–314.

13 Stamm Walter E, Martin Stanley M and Bennett John V: Epidemiology of Noscocomial Infections Due to Gram-Negative Bacilli: Aspects Relevant to Development and Use of Vaccines. 1977, The Journal of Infectious Diseases 136:S151–S160.

tal. The general and local resistance of the patient, the virulence and size of inoculum of the contaminating organism and a host of other yet poorly understood factors determine whether infection will occur. In addition, these elements vary widely from time to time and from place to place

The measures that can be taken to increase the resistance of the patients are very limited. It is still waited for advances in bacterial vaccines which may radically alter the impact of infections.

Transmission by operating team

People are the primary source of pathogenic bacteria. Most likely, in the operation room the operating team is the greatest single source of airborne bacterial contamination, but the well-draped patient does not appear to be an important source of airborne contamination at the operative site[1]. However, it has been stated that many dispersers shed quite harmless staphylococci[2].

The frequency of carriers of *S. aureus* among one operation unit personnel has been found to be for nurses 21 per cent, for surgeons 33 per cent, for anaesthesiologists 57 per cent and for transient workers handling bedding and refuse as high as 71 per cent[3].

Although the respiratory tract of the operation room staff, particularly the nasopharynges, is frequently given as the main source of pathogenic organisms connected with postoperative wound infections, bacteria emanating from the nasopharynx constitute only a small fraction of the total shed and the hands and noses of the operating team very rarely yield the strain found in the wound[4].

Hair is perhaps a more common site than the nasopharynx[5] for colonization by *Staphylococcus aureus.* However, more microorganisms have been found on the forehead than on the bordering hair[6].

Clean long hair does not appear to be more vulnerable to infection than clean short hair[7], but skin disease masked by unkempt hair is an intolerable bacteriologic hazard[8].

Because of the lack of any quantifiable hazard for the spread of infection from bearded members as contrasted to the unbearded amongst health personnel, perhaps beards which are clean and neatly trimmed could be allowed[9].

---

1   see also Alexakis Peter G, Feldon Paul G, Wellisch Mark, Richter Robert E and Finegold Sydney M: Airborne Bacterial Contamination of Operative Wounds. 1976, The Western Journal of Medicine 124: 361–369.

2   Williams R E O: Airborne staphylococci in the surgical ward. 1967, The Journal of Hygiene 65:207–217.

3   Walter Carl W: Carriers, OR clothing, air changes important in infection control. 1970, Hospital Topics 48:12:65.

4   Johnson III Joseph E: Wound Infections. in Clinical Concepts of Infectious Diseases. ed by Leighton E Cluff and Joseph E Johnson III. The Williams & Wilkins Company, Baltimore 1972, p 197.

5   see also Dineen Peter: Personnel, Discipline, and Infection. 1973, Archives of Surgery 107:603–604.

6   Dathe G: Asepsis und Antisepsis in der Urologie. 1976, Der Krankenhausarzt 49:664–678.

7   Durcel G, Roussianos D and Clerc M-F: Les cheveux dans l'environnement hospitalier. 1971, Hospitalis 41:749–750, 753.

8   Walter Carl W: Cross-Infection and the Anesthesiologist. 1974, Anesthesia and Analgesia 53:631–644.

9   see also York Elihu: Beards and Bacteria. 1972, The Journal of the Maine Medical Association 63:67.

The angle of the jaw, frequently uncovered in the operation room, has been found to be heavily contaminated. The highest counts have been found on the head, neck, axilla, hands, perineum, groin and feet[10]. Of these areas, the head and neck are singled out as a prime source of bacterial contamination[11].

Other investigations had indicated that around 80 per cent of bacterial particles are disseminated from the waist down[12].

Obviously no area of skin can be taken as representative of the whole body surface.

Airborne transmission as a source of post-operative infection

The importance of airborne transmission as a source of post-operative infection is still controversial after having gone through several phases of argument.

In 1890 *Lord Lister* himself wrote in the British Medical Journal[1]: ". . . it seems to follow that the floating particles of the air may be disregarded . . . provided we can . . . avoid the introduction into the wound of septic defilement from other sources". This uncertainty has continued unresolved to the present day[2].

There is little doubt that wounds are contaminated by airborne microorganisms, only the frequency with which it does occur, is not precisely documented. Today's consensus holds that airborne organisms are important in causing wound infection only when an air-handling system is grossly contaminated, when an otherwise effective air-handling system is abused, or during highly specialized procedures in which a large foreign body is implanted[3].

Airborne produced infection must be confined — with a few possible exceptions — to Gram-positive organisms. Staphylococci responsible for post-operative infections are rarely found in the air. Airborne anaerobic bacteria are very rarely found in the operation room[4].

Contamination of the air is not an absolute condition for the occurence of infection*.

---

10 see also Ulrich J A: Surgical team remains prime source of organisms contaminating OR air. 1971, Hospital Topics 49:10:81.

11 Fried Dennis A, Hanback Lawrence D, Hunt Hurshell H and Munster Andrew M: The cotton gown as a barrier against contamination in the operating room. 1977, The American Surgeon 43:52–54.

12 Whyte W, Vesley D and Hodgson R: Bacterial dispersion in relation to operating room clothing. 1976, The Journal of Hygiene 76:367–378.

1 cited by Lidwell O M: Clean Air, Less Infection. 1976, Hospital Engineering 30:8:9–17.

2 see also Lidwell O M: Clean Air, Less Infection. 1976, Hospital Engineering 30:8:9–17.

3 see also Laufman Harold: The control of operating room infection: discipline, defense mechanisms, drugs, design, and devices. 1978, Bulletin of the New York Academy of Medicine 54:472–483.

4 personal communication: 1977, Gunnar Laurell, Uppsala.

* The influence of airborne contamination on post-operative wound infection was studied simultaneously in two hospitals, utilizing the same surgical team and identical pre-operative and operative techniques. A substantial, four to eight times difference in airborne contamination risk at the two institutions was confirmed.

Unexpectedly the infection rates were considerably lower at the institution with higher degree of airborne contamination. This was true of gross and adjusted infection rates in all categories, particularly in clean cases where airborne contamination would be expected to have the most pronounced influence. Factors previously considered to explain institutional variations were uniform in this study. No compensatory factor or reasonable explanation was found to explain the conclusions of this study.

Airborne contamination was clearly not a determining factor in the incidence (Seropian Richard and Reynolds Benedict M: The Importance of Airborne Contamination as a Factor in Postoperative Wound Infection. 1969, Archives of Surgery 98:654–658).

Every member of an operation team may lose up to 20 mg of debris including a number of hairs from the head[5]. The average amount of airborne particles in a conventional operation room[6] can vary from 165 bacteria per m^3 to 665 per m^3.

In the wound area 37 microorganisms per m^3 have been found in comparison with the 197 microorganisms around the assisting nurse and 311 microorganisms around the anaesthesiologist[7]. Increase in bacterial density is linked far more to the activity of the people present than their number[8].

The use of disposable draping is believed to reduce the number of airborne particles — which could carry bacteria — in the operation room and by this way to reduce the incidence of postoperative infections, at least when the patients were operated for the fracture of the neck of the femur[9].

Dispersal of airborne microbial contamination within the operation room is determined primarily by the type of room air distribution system.

About 30 particles might fall during an hour on sterilized instruments, dressings, and other materials, which during the course of the operation are likely to touch the wound. After one hour more than one third of them are contaminated[10].

Because of the thermodynamic phenomena more sedimentation of particles on instruments and other reflecting cooler surfaces can be expected, than in an open wound.

These few bacteria-carrying particles might be of importance e g in a case of burn patient with a great amount of devitalized tissues or in case of transplantation surgery where desensibilized patients are involved. Instead of the number of contaminating micro-organisms rather the concentration of contaminating micro-organisms must be considered.

A self-cleaning effect within operation rooms, if nothing is done to the air at all, has been noted as well as the spontaneous death of bacteria, up to 90 per cent in one hour[11]. The half-value period for airborne microorganisms is 7 minutes, if there is no ventilation system. In operation rooms with 20 air changes per hour, the half-value period is 0.5 minutes[12].

5 Charnley John: Clean air in the operating room. 1973, Cleveland Clinic Quarterly 40:99–114.

6 Whyte W, Shaw B H and Barnes R: A bacteriological evaluation of laminar-flow systems for orthopaedic surgery. 1973, The Journal of Hygiene 71:559–564.

7 Janssen E and Janssen G: Mikroklimatologische Bedingungen im Operationssaal. 1976, Krankenhaus Umschau 45:227–230.

8 see also Shaw Douglas, Doig Caroline M and Douglas Donald: Is airborne infection in operating-theatres an important cause of wound infection in general surgery? 1973, The Lancet 2:18.

9 Bergman Bo R: Resultat av infektionsprofylaktiska åtgärder vid operation av frakturer på övre femurändan. 1978, Läkartidningen 75:787–788.

10 Greene Velvl W: Sterilization Versus Disinfection. 1974, Hospital Topics 52:5:44–45.

11 Petit R, Schvingt E and Grenier J-F: Contamination de plaies opératoires par les germes présents dans l'air des salles d'opération. 1971, Annales de Chirurgie 25:1299.

12 Hambraeus Anna at the ISIMA 78 symposion Planering av operationsavdelningar. Malmö, April 1978.

An authoritative *microbiological standard* on air for use in operation room for general surgery does not yet exist mainly because of the absence of epidemiological data determining the role of air in the transmission of infections.

Therefore it is exceedingly difficult to justify all the exaggerated efforts and large economic investments to eliminate all microorganisms from the operation room air supply and to control completely air movements in units for general surgery. However, before a final statement can be made on the importance of the airborne infection route, further controlled studies on the relationship of air flow rates, filtration, and postoperative wound infections are merited[13].

In some surgical fields where refined clean operations occur[14] *e g* elective craniotomy, orthopaedic and transplantation surgery and where there is a poor blood supply a different view might be adopted, although clean air by itself has been unable to reduce the infection rate below 1.5 per cent[15].

There is no evidence that sterile air has modified the occurence of post-operative wound infection in connection with total arthroplastics of the hip[16]. The need for ultra clean air in operation rooms is deemed to be less urgent than the need to prevent secondary infection after operation[17]. It has also been stated, that if the possibility of haematogenous infection in connection with late infections after total hip replacement is accepted, modifications of the operation environment cannot be expected to reduce the late sepsis rate to nil[18].

13 see also Clark Richard E, Amos William C, Higgins Virginia, Bemberg Kurt F and Weldon Clarence S: Infection control in cardiac surgery. 1976, Surgery 79:1:89–96.

14 see also Polk Jr Hiram C: Diminished surgical infection by systematic antibiotic administration in potentially contaminated operations. 1974, Surgery 75:312–314.

15 see also Charnley John: Clean air in the operating room. 1973, Cleveland Clinic Quarterly 40:99–114.

16 McLauchlan J, Logie J R C, Smylie H G and Smith G: The role of clean air in wound infection acquired during operation. 1976, Surgery, Gynecology & Obstetrics 143:6–8.

17 ibid

18 Late infection after total hip replacement. 1977, British Medical Journal 2:213.

Measures to prevent hospital infection

In the field of applied medical bacteriology progress has not been as spectacular as in the pure medical bacteriology research. The list of sources for bacterial contamination is extensive. Precise and quantitative knowledge of the relative value of each source and each of the pathways is not yet available.

Control of inanimate biocontamination

There are great difficulties of defining the epidemiologic relationship of the environmental biocontamination. The occurence of nosocomial infection in general hospitals has not been related to levels of microbial contamination of air, surfaces, and fomities. Transmission studies appear to have been limited not only because of the complexity of health care delivery but also because it is given 24 hours daily and needs to be observed continuously for extended periods.

Much data, often uninterpretable or irrelevant, about the levels of microbial contamination on floors, walls, and microbes in the air has been acquired. However, until more investigators commit their time and energy to appropriate epidemiological studies of difficult questions, data will continue to be suggestive, possibly erroneous, and definitely inconclusive[1].

Although data about environmental bioloads in itself may be interesting, of practical importance is the understanding of the factors that influence contamination[2]. Ultimately the relevance of the microbes to the health-care institution patients depends on epidemiology rather than on microbiology *per se*[3].

Many hospitals continue to do environmental cultures, and the results are reviewed by the infection control committees. Since no meaningful bacteriological standards have ever been established for the hospital environment, this is an exercise in futility[4].

General routine microbiological sampling of the hospital environment, done with no specific epidemiologic goal in mind, is unnecessary and economically unjustifi-

1 Wenzel Richard P, Veazey Jr James M, and Townsend Timothy R: Role of the inanimate environment in hospital-acquired infections. in Infection control in health care facilities. ed by Kenneth R Cundy and William Ball. University Park Press. Baltimore, London, Tokyo 1977, p 93.

2 see also Greene Velvl and Vesley Donald: Environmental Microbiology. in Environmental Health and Safety in Health-care Facilities. ed by Richard G Bond, Georg S Michaelsen and Roger L DeRoos. Macmillan Publishing Co Inc New York and Collier Macmillan Publishers London 1973, p 33.

3 ibid, p 34

4 T C Eickhoff cited by Laforce F Marc: The Hospital Infection Control Committee: A Personal View. 1977, Hospital Practice 12:3:135–148.

able[5]. More bluntly: routine environmental monitoring of floors and walls is a waste of time[6]. It does not permit one to predict where and when nosocomial infections may be most likely to occur.

The statistical approach to the infection problem is serious: if a precaution could reduce the infection rate from 3 per cent to 2 per cent, more than 3,000 observations would be needed to give the findings statistical significance[7]. Studies with insufficient numbers of observations are not only of little value, they may easily be misleading[8]. When assessing infection rates below 1 per cent, a level is approached where it might be impossible even to mount a properly controlled trial.

The value of infection surveillance rather than environmental monitoring has been stressed[9]. The patient has been rediscovered and regarded as more important than the surroundings[10].

Planning measures through functional planning and construction for the prevention of infection should be based on factual knowledge of all sources and mechanisms of infection.

Every precaution should be directed against a known hazard rather than against a merely theoretical risk[11].

Only evaluated precautions should be recommended. There is also a need to re-test precautions which have been in use for long.

Infections are not controlled by lavish expenditure[12]. They may be controlled only by people using a formula which includes knowledge, skill, care, patience, effort and unrelenting attention to the details of hospital hygiene[13].

5   see also Eickhoff Theodore C: Nosocomial infections. 1975, American Journal of Epidemiology 101:93–97. Daschner F: Grundlagen der Krankenhaushygiene und das Hospitalismusproblem. 1977, Intensivmedizin 14:163–168.

6   Fisher Evelyn J: Surveillance and management of hospital-acquired infections. 1976, Heart and Lung 5:784–787.

7   see also Blowers R: Sources and routes of surgical infection. Vingt-quatrième congrès de la Société Internationale de Chirurgie. Brussels. no publishing year, p 84.

8   Lidwell O M: Clean Air, Less Infection. 1976, Hospital Engineering 30:8:9–17.

9   see also Mallison G F: A hospital program for control of nosocomial infections. 1974, Association Pract. Infection Control. Newsletter 2:1–6.

10 see also Lewis R G and Metcalf E: Settle plate assessment of airborne infections. 1974, Dimensions in health service 51:12:13–17.

11 see also Bagshawe K D, Blowers R, Lidwell O M: Isolating patients in hospital to control infection. Part 1. Sources and routes of infection. 1978, British Medical Journal 2:609–612.

12 Kelsey J C: Personal view. 1973, British Medical Journal 2:104.

13 Maurer Isobel M: Hospital Hygiene. Edward Arnold. London 1974, p 105.

As these measures are part of the working conditions for the staff, they should as little as possible be detrimental to working procedures.

In connection with surgical department planning a general surgeon* has stated: If we allow our highly scientific and highly motivated colleagues in the basic sciences to set arbitrary standards that adversely influence our efficiency, we serve in grave error.

When the precautions which the surgeon and his staff have to observe to prevent infection become so stringent as to restrain the surgical procedures, sepsis risk must be weighed against any possible detriment to the patient.

Hand washing

Hand washing after patient contact remains the single most important method of control of cross infection. Sadly, this procedure often is the most ignored[1]. *Ample* hand washing facilities must be provided.

Hand disinfection should be carried out as soon as there has been contact with anything that is or can be infected. It should be mentioned that colonisation of nurses' hands with *Pseudomonas* may last as long as three days even with hand washing[2].

It has been found a significant increase, averaging 17-fold, in the number of particles carrying viable bacteria released after washing with soap. There increase in bacterial dissemination was suppressed when a surgical scrub was used in place of soap, or when a spirit-based lotion was used without washing. A spirit-based hand lotion might with advantage become a partial substitute for handwashing, in those areas where iatrogenic coagulase-negative staphylococcal infections are more common. Among areas concerned are the intensive therapy units, and the wards where intravenous infusions are commonplace or where patients are nursed after surgery on the urinary tract[3].

Hands should be dried on disposable towels. Towels for common use are important carriers of pathogenic germs and must no longer be available in hospitals.

The nails of hospital staff should be kept short and no nail varnish used. Nail brushes, nail files, and nail scissors, etc, should be used by one person.

Rings and bracelets should not be worn by the hospital staff.

*   Richard O Kraft in 1976, Archives of Surgery 111:488.

1   Fisher Evelyn J: Surveillance and management of hospital-acquired infections. 1976, Heart and Lung 5:784–787.

2   Teres Daniel: Management of Respiratory infection in the Intensive Care Unit. in Recent advances in respiratory surgical intensive care. ed by T Gordon McNabb and Stephen V Hall. International Anesthesiology Clinics. vol 14 no I. Spring 1976, p 163–178.

3   Meers P D and Yeo Gillian A: Shedding of bacteria and skin squamae after handwashing. 1978, The Journal of Hygiene 81:99–105.

Clothes-borne transmission is an important way of spread of infection from patient to patient. It is not interrupted by common hospital cotton gowns[1].

The staff working in the patient areas should wear appropriate hospital clothes, which should be changed as soon as they have become soiled or infected. They should not be worn at meals, during breaks, and when going off duty.

The working clothes should not be kept in the changing room closets together with outdoor clothes.

In places where there is an increased risk of infection, a special protective gown should be worn. However, it has been deduced from studies in an isolation ward for burns, that *S. aureus* is carried via nurses' clothing which is contaminated when dealing with infected patients[2]. Particles are dispersed when the nurse enters another patient room, despite the wearing of protective clothing[3].

Three garment designs, a gown, a loose coverall, and a close coverall, have been compared with each other and with conventional cotton gowns in experimental exercise and nursing procedures. The close coverall was 4 to 7 times better than the loose coverall or gown in preventing the soiling of clothes worn underneath it, but appeared to permit substantially more transfer from garments underneath it to mock patient and to the air than did the looser garments. A cotton gown reduced the soiling of clothes underneath it by more than 10 times and the contamination of a mock patient by more than 30 times as compared with no barrier garment. The close coverall further diminished the contamination of clothes but not the transfer to the patient[4].

Clothes made from materials that in particle transmission tests were 100 times more effective than ordinary cotton were only 5 times better as barrier garments when examined in experimental nursing procedures[5].

Disposable plastic two-piece work suits have been compared with conventional cotton suits, gowns, and plastic aprons by nurses in a burns unit[6]. The plastic suits

1   Hambraeus Anna and Ransjö Ulrika: Attempts to control clothes-borne infection in a burn unit. 1977, The Journal of Hygiene 79:193–202.

2   Hambraeus Anna: Dispersal and transfer of Staphylococcus aureus in an isolation ward for burned patients. 1973, The Journal of Hygiene 71:787–797.

3   Hambraeus Anna: Transfer of Staphylococcus aureus via nurses' uniforms. 1973, The Journal of Hygiene 71:799–814.

4   Hambraeus Anna and Ransjö Ulrika: Attempts to control clothes-borne infection in a burn unit. 1977, The Journal of Hygiene 79:193–202.

5   ibid

6   Clark R P and Mullan B J: Clothing for use in clean-air environments. 1976, The Journal of Hygiene 77:267–269.

allowed fewer micro-organisms to be dispersed into the environment than the other garments but were less comfortable. However, the disadvantages from the aesthetic and comfort standpoint outweighed this and the garments were considered unacceptable for long-period use in a stressful environment.

Disposable gowns as well as disposable sheets and covers are improving in quality and are becoming relatively less expensive. There is, however, no evidence that these items alter the incidence of nosocomial infection[7], although it has been indicated[8] that the using of disposable materials may increase security.

An open-roofed plastic isolator as an alternative to protective garments in isolation rooms is no realistic alternative as it does not appreciably reduce cross-contamination, and gives psychological and practical problems[9].

There is no reason to wear a protective mask regularly in the hospital as the masks contribute little or nothing to the protection of patients in wards against infection[10]. On the contrary, this may lead to a false sense of security with regard to the spread of infection. It is more important to avoid speaking and sneezing.

A mask would, however, seem motivated in some hospital routine work such as examination and care of infants, dressing of burns or extensive open wounds and taking care of isolated patients, who may spread airborne infection.

Although hair may be more contaminated than the hands, the effectiveness of hospital personnel wearing caps while attending patients, even in the intensive care units, is a moot point[11].

Hair covers should be worn only in well-motivated situations. Their use in general wards and intensive care and treatment units seems not to be motivated[12].

7   see also Infection Control in the Hospital. American Hospital Association. Chicago 1974, p 59.

8   see also Operasjonsavdelinger. Norsk Institutt for Sykehusforskning. Trondheim 1977, p 62.

9   Ransjö Ulrika: Isolation Care of Infection-Prone Burn Patients. 1978, Scandinavian Journal of Infectious Diseases, Supplementum 11, p 39.

10 see also Sentralforsyning i Sykehus. Instilling fra en Komité oppnevnt av den Norske Sykehusforening. Drammen 1971, p 57.
    Control of Hospital Infection. ed by E J L Lowbury, G A J Ayliffe, A M Geddes and J D Williams. Chapman and Hall. London 1975, p 101.
    Daschner F: Grundlagen der Krankenhaushygiene und das Hospitalismusproblem. 1977, Intensivmedizin 14:163–168.

11 see also Cozanitis D A, Mäkelä P and Grant J: Microorganisms in the Hair of Staff and Patients in an Intensive Care Unit. 1977, Der Anaesthesist 26:578–580.

12 see also Daschner F: Grundlagen der Krankenhaushygiene und das Hospitalismusproblem. 1977, Intensivmedizin 14:163–168.

A clean hospital has a favourable psychological effect on staff and patients. It is likely to improve the standard of hospital hygiene and asepsis[1]. Hygiene is highly important as an item of health education.

The hospital environment should be particularly easy to clean. The choice of surface materials is as important as the concern about the inevitable obsolescence of finishes.

Good cleaning is a matter of planning, training and organization; cleaning is a form of maintenance, and is the proper responsibility of a trained cleaning manager on the technical staff of the hospital[2].

Housekeeping procedures, such as mopping and dusting, are as important as nursing procedures in many areas, and housekeeping personnel should be educated in the importance of their role in prevention of infection*.

The objective is to remove soil, not to rearrange it. The main purpose of cleaning is to remove physically microorganisms from the various fomities that might transmit them to patients.

Until a scientific standard for all hospital housekeeping is clearly established, cleaning will largely remain on speculation basis. It is exceedingly difficult to relate even the most extensive environmental sanitation to changes in the post-operative infection or other hospital acquired infection rates.

Very few areas need to be kept *aseptically* clean, as distinct from socially clean. The maintenance of even domestic standards demands constant attention, particularly in heavily trafficked areas.

In most hospital areas (in the Federal Republic of Germany) the reduction to about 10 microorganisms per 10 cm^2 floor area is considered fully satisfactory[3]. There are also other recommendations.

Considerable attention has been focused on application of germicides to floors, on room disinfection and on the use of ultraviolet light. All these practices appear to be of little value in the control of infections[4].

---

1 see also Control of Hospital Infection. ed by E J L Lowbury, G A J Ayliffe, A M Geddes and J D Williams. Chapman and Hall. London 1975, p 67.

2 Danielsen Kjell Bård: Hvordan skal renholdet planlegges? 1977, Sykehuset 40:265–269.

* In many hospitals floors are generally washed with a mop dipped in an unnecessarily heavy bucket of filthy water and stored overnight, wet, in a noisome cupboard. Nurses and auxiliaries are taught cleaning methods current 20, 30 or 100 years ago (Danielsen Kjell Bård: Hvordan skal renholdet planlegges? 1977, Sykehuset 40:265–269).

3 S(chäfer) H(ermann): Gebäudereinigung im Krankenhaus. 1977, Krankenhaus Umschau 46:69–71.

4 see also McCabe William R: Gram-Negative Bacteremia. 1973, Disease-a-Month. December, p 36.
   Dietzel W: Angewandte Hygiene zur Infektionsprophylaxe in der Intensivtherapie. 1978, Das Krankenhaus 70:191–194.

The work of cleaning staff — the central cleaning squad — requires careful supervision if they are to be effective and yet unobtrusive.

The primary cleaning activities on daily basis are floor scrubbing, suction cleaning, sanitary fitting cleaning, emptying bins, ash trays. Less frequent procedures are damp mopping, damp dusting, furniture cleaning and shampooing of carpets. Rather infrequent procedures are window cleaning and washing of walls.

Checking the toilets, emptying bins and re-cleaning heavily used areas is needed also during the day.

This applies particularly to toilets in urological, and gynaecological-obstetrical wards[5]

Clinic rooms need checks between sessions.

The time available for cleaning in some hospital areas is both limited and fragmented, because of the long hours it is open to the public and the need for quiet during the clinical sessions. This usually imposes a pattern of work with part-time staff employed, depending on the accessibility of rooms for cleaning.

Wet vacuum pick up has for some time been the method of choice for floor care in hospitals.

Also cleaning floors with a dry, damp or impregnated mop, provided the floor has a homogenous, non-porous surface has been recommended[6]. Mops may be disposable (dry, impregnated or damp) or washable (to be used impregnated or damp). Damp mops must be washed at at least 80°C for at least 10 minutes, spin-dried, and stored under refrigeration. The weekly wet wash is carried out by spreading clean water on the floor with spreader mops and drying it off with clean drying-mops.

A neglected wet mop provides conditions for microbes to multiply. It will distribute many more microbes than it picked up in the first place. Reports of contaminated wet mops in hospitals have been published with monotonous regularity[7].

Some studies indicate that differences between various floor care methods are small, when the air contamination aspect is concerned[8]. A revival of dry vacuum cleaning in many hospital areas has been recommended.

5   Brandberg Åke and Brinkhoff Barbro: Sjukhusstädaren — estet eller bakteriejägare? 1977, Sjukhuset 54:429–434.

6   Danielsen Kjell Bård: Hvordan skal renholdet planlegges? 1977, Sykehuset 40:265–269.

7   see also Maurer Isobel M: Hospital Hygiene. Edward Arnold. London 1974, p 35.

8   Brandberg Åke and Brinkhoff Barbro: Sjukhusstädaren — estet eller bakteriejägare? 1977, Sjukhuset 54:429–434.
    Danielsen Kjell Bård: Hvordan skal renholdet planlegges? 1977, Sykehuset 40:265–269.

In the operation room and similar areas the contact time for antiseptic solution has been five minutes and six to seven minutes the pickup time for the solution[9].

The traditional treatment of operation room floor can be simplified[10]. Treatment between operations should be graded and based on the degree of contamination related to the just finished procedure. A maximal floor treatment should follow septic or contaminated operations. After clean or clean-contaminated cases there is no need of treatment unless gross soilage e g by a bloody sponge has occured. More recent studies indicate that there is no significant difference between the total number of bacteria in the operation room environment after clean and infected operations[11].

The practice of turning hoses on walls in operation rooms may do a lot for staff morale but it does nothing toward combating infection and it is certainly damaging to the building fabric[12]. Cleaning of operation room walls on a rotational basis can not be recommended for daily, weekly, or even monthly routines. If spot disinfection and cleaning is accomplished immediately, there is no justification for regular special cleaning techniques[13].

The walls of isolation rooms need not to be washed routinely between patients, except for grossly soiled areas[14].

Plastered or painted surfaces which are scratched by regular cleaning and scouring may become ingrained with dirt and bacteria, thereby increasing rather than reducing the acceptably low infection hazard*.

Floors in paediatric units must be kept particularly clean, as many of the youngest and young patients may use the floor as a playground[15].

9   see also Kraft Richard O in 1976, Archives of Surgery 111:488.

10 Weber Donald O, Gooch James J, Wood Walter R, Britt Eugene M and Kraft Richard O: Influence of Operating Room Surface Contamination on Surgical Wounds. 1976, Archives of Surgery 111:484–488.

11 Hambraeus A, Bengtsson S and Laurell G: Bacterial contamination in a modern operating suite. 1. Effect of a zoning system on contamination of floors and other surfaces. Stencil. Institute of Clinical Bacteriology, University of Uppsala, Sweden, 1977, p 8.

12 Cowan David: The clean operating enclosure — its effect on the incidence of wound infection and its influence on the design of the operating department of a hospital. Stencil. Pretoria. January 1976, p 70.

13 Peers Jerry G: Cleanup Techniques in the Operating Room. 1973, Archives of Surgery 107:596–599.

14 see also Petersen N J, Marshall J H and Collins D E: Why wash walls in hospital isolation rooms? 1973, Health Laboratory Science 10:1:23–27

*   Bloomfield Sally F: The Use of Disinfectants in the Home. 1978, The Journal of Applied Bacteriology 45:1–38.

15 Brandberg Åke and Brinkhoff Barbro: Sjukhusstädaren — estet eller bakteriejägare? 1977, Sjukhuset 54:429–434.

The cleaners need access at all times of day to a utility room, which has hot and cold water, a 1.2 m worktop with storage underneath, containers for refuse, a drying rack, etc. Space for mechanical cleaning equipment and cleaning utensils is needed. 5.0 m^2 per room should suffice. Large departments will require more than one cleaners' room.

Cleaning equipment including vacuum cleaners and cleaners' carts are stored in decentralized cleaners' rooms. In this area cleaning equipment is decontaminated.

A central changing room with toilets and showers is needed for the cleaners.

When judging the housekeeping department personnel needs in Norway, it has been estimated that in one hour 136 m^2 of ward room or similar floors can be cleaned[16]. This would mean that cleaning 1 m^2 floor area would require 26 seconds.

In Switzerland, the estimated time needed for vacuum-cleaning of 1 m^2 of hospital floor is 12 seconds. To clean a washbasin requires 3 minutes and to clean a lavatory bowl 6 minutes[17].

Disinfection, sterilization

Sterilized respective disinfected objects are used in hospital routine treatments and care.

Disinfection or decontamination is used when sterility is not demanded. Disinfection is the elimination of selected undesirable micro-organisms in order to prevent their transmission. Disinfection is achieved by action of heat or chemical agents on the structure of microorganisms.

When a disinfectant kills the microorganism or permanently disrupts the internal structure and function of microbial cells, a *cidal* process has taken place. The *static* action does not alter the inner structures of the microbial cells permanently and permits the cells to resume growth and reproduction when the disinfectant is neutralized.

The length of time needed to disinfect a surface depends on the type and concentration of the disinfectant, the types of involved microorganisms, and the grade of cleanliness of the object. With massive organic debris present, a disinfection cannot be achieved. A warm surface takes less time to disinfect than a cold one.

Usually hospital linen is disinfected through laundering at 85°C to 90°C. More recent studies indicate that 65°C to 70°C would be sufficient, if there is no risk of hepatitis infection[1].

16 Danielsen Kjell Bård: Renhold i sykehus. 1977, Tidsskrift for Den norske laegeforening 97:725–726.

17 Hofmann D: Die Organisation des Hausdienstes in Kantonsspital Zürich. 1977, Veska-Das Schweizer Spital 41:458–463.

1 Nyström Bertil: Desinfektion, rengöring och sterilisering. 1977, Tidsskrift for Den norske laegeforening 97:695–698.

Before used material and instruments are taken to reprocessing units they should either be disinfected in the unit or ward where used or be wrapped so as to avoid spread of infection.

Sterilization implies complete destruction or removal of all types of micro-organisms from the object. According to the statistical approach[2] an article is regarded as sterile, if the risk of its being unsterile is less than 1:1,000,000.

Objects to be sterilized must be properly cleaned beforehand.

Sterilization can be effected by heat and by means of chemical agents or ionizing radiation. In the case of heat sterilization, steam (autoclave sterilization) or hot air is used.

Brief shocks of 500°C hot air may be used for sterilization of surgical instruments and decontamination of nursing unit utensils.

Sterilization with toxic chemical agents in liquid or gaseous form — ethylene oxide (ETO), formaldehyde, buffered glutar aldehyde — is used for heat-sensitive materials, such as optical instruments.

Gas sterilizers should be installed only in limited access and restrictive areas. No other equipment should be stored in the sterilizer and aerator equipment rooms. ETO sterilizer and aerator rooms should have 6 to 10 air exchanges per hour. Air should be exhausted to the outside[3].

To eliminate human errors the use of a totally automated process has been recommended, when dealing with the ETO sterilization.

Steam and hot air sterilizers should be checked at least weekly, ethylene oxide sterilizers with every load.

Irradiation with either gamma rays or electrons as a method of controlling bacteria has yet to be fully recognized alongside heating and the use of toxic chemicals. Of particular attraction is the irradiation's ability to bring lethal effect even to the apparently inaccessible microorganisms. This property, combined with insignificant temperature rise during treatment, is already exploited in the sterilization of medical devices, pharmaceutical preparates and biological tissues.

Although irradiation is the most recently introduced physical sterilization technique, it enjoys a very advanced and sophisticated scientific background of research[4]. The

2   cited by Nyström Bertil: Desinfektion, rengöring och sterilisering. 1977, Tidsskrift for Den norske laege-forening 97:695–698.

3   Runnells Glenn: Guidelines to assist hospitals in the use of ethylene oxyde. 1978, Hospitals 52:9:119–122.

4   Ley F J: The effect of ionizing radiation on bacteria. in Manual on radiation sterilization of medical and biological materials. Technical Reports Series No 149. International Atomic Energy Agency. Vienna 1973, p 37.

high capital cost of a radiation sterilization unit has militated strongly against the use of the process, even in the largest health care facilities.

Wrapping materials should be impervious to bacteria, but not to steam or ethylene oxide gas, sealable, flexible to permit swift wrapping and unwrapping, to make contamination during unwrapping unlikely, and inexpensive.

A number of fabric and paper wrappers have been used to cover items to maintain sterility after an inhospital sterilization process: 140-thread-count muslin, crepe paper, tightly woven pima cotton cloth, polyethylene bags etc.

A standardization of wrapping procedures and materials is desirable.

Published recommendations contain conflicting information on how long hospital-sterilized goods can be stored and still be sterile.

On open shelves single-wrapped muslin (two layers) sealed in 3-mil polyethylene remains sterile at least nine months and in cabinets single-wrapped two-ways crepe paper (single layer) at least eight weeks[5].

The use of single-wrapped muslin (two layers) packs is not recommended. Closed-cabinet storage is preferable to storage on open shelves.

Soiled utility room

Regardless of whether there are central sterilizing facilities or not, soiled utility rooms are required for taking care of used instruments and bowls, and for the disposal of dressings etc from patient, consulting, and treatment rooms.

Following procedures are carried out in a soiled utility room: soiled *linen* is brought in — trollies may be used — for a temporary storage, but not to be rinsed or washed. Also *bandages and refuse* are temporarily stored in sealed paper or plastic containers to be removed for incineration.

Bedpans and urine bottles — mainly in the ward areas — are emptied, washed and decontaminated in a bedpan washer. If their contents need testing, it will be sent to testing room, kept in specimen cupboard or forwarded to the pathology department.

If no clinical laboratory service and no separate testing room is available, the utility room is the facility for testing and storing of urine samples. About 10 m² is required

After every activity the staff must wash their hands.

Recommended general lighting level is 100 lux, in the testing area 200 lux.

5   Mallison George F and Standard Paul G: Safe storage times for sterile packs. 1974, Hospitals 48:20:77–80.

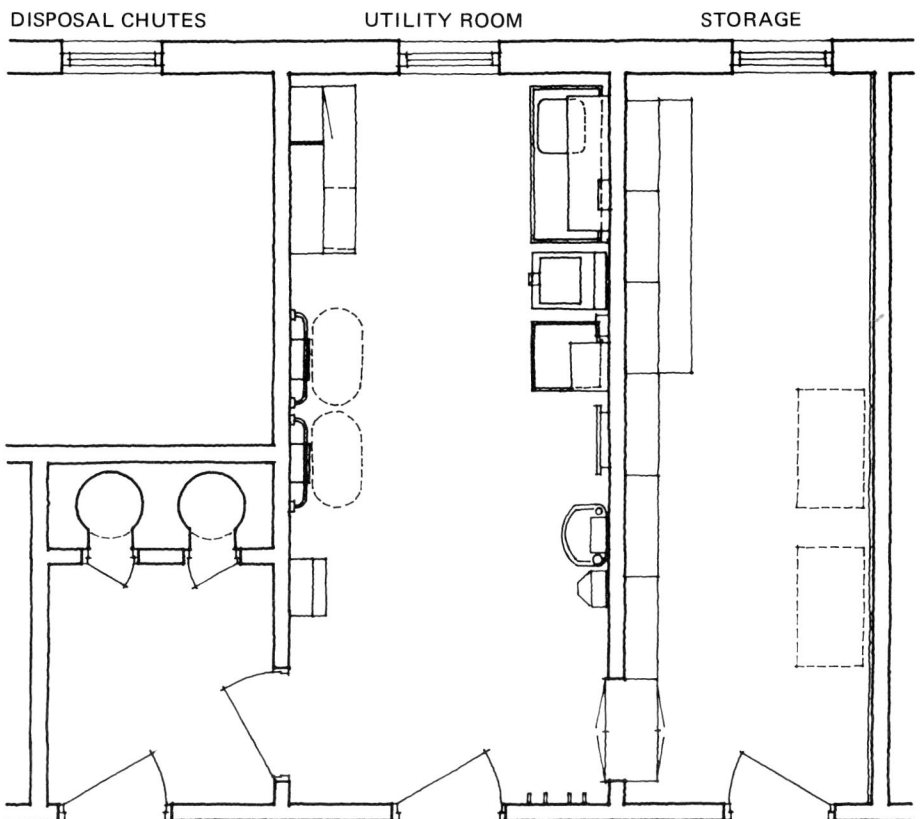

Utility room for ward units combined with a storage and disposal chutes for soiled linen and waste. Soiled utility room equipment may include a worktop 1.2 by 0.6 m, 0.9 m high, an acid resistant top 1.2 by 0.6 m, 0.9 m high, a soap dispenser, a disposable paper towel dispenser, a container for soiled disposable towels, a sink, a urine testing cupboard, shelves for covers, paper bags, a wash basin, a linen disposal trolley 0.85 by 0.45, 0.85 m high, shelves for bed-pans and urine bottles, a bed-pan warming cupboard, a bed-pan washer and decontaminator, and a fume cupboard.

Ventilation should provide suction to outside.

Doors to the utility room should have a 0.6 m high sound absorbing kick-plate and a glass panel at eye level.

In the outpatient area the number of utility rooms required is linked to the number of consulting and treatment rooms. A ratio of 1 soiled utility to 12 examination or treatment rooms could be recommended.

Isolation of patients

Two types of isolation of patients are applied in hospital practice.

The more frequent type — source isolation — is used to prevent spread of infection from a patient to other patients and hospital staff. There are four sub-groups of source isolation: strict isolation; respiratory isolation; wound and skin precautions; enteric precautions[1]. Adhesive colour-coded labels attached to the isolation room would help to inform the staff of the measures to be taken. Blue would be the colour for standard isolation, red for strict isolation[2].

The other type — protective isolation — aims at reducing the infection risk for patients whose resistance to infection is markedly lowered. The amount of protection required varies with the type of patient. Maximum protection includes sterilized food, linen, and other supplies[3].

The methods of protective or reversed isolation in which the patient is protected from contamination with strains of hospital bacteria, seem to be in an experimental stage[4] and have to be improved[5].

It is considered inadviseable to mix accommodation for infected patients — source isolation — with that for susceptible patients — protective isolation. Physically separate units should be provided for these purposes. Separate nursing and ancillary staff are essential[6].

The requirements for isolation accommodation in a hospital are influenced by the patterns of clinical work and type of specialist units. About 2.5 per cent of the beds of a large hospital in a special unit would probably be adequate except during period of unusually high demand[7].

In Norway, a slightly higher percentage — 3 — has been recommended*.

---

1   see also Manual on Control of Infection in Surgical Patients. J B Lippincott Company. Philadelphia-Toronto 1976, p 213.

2   see also Control of hospital infection. ed by E J L Lowbury, G A J Ayliffe, A M Geddes and J D Williams. Chapman and Hall. London 1975, p 122.

3   ibid, p 121.

4   see also Michel M F: Nosocomial infections in intensive care patients: the problem and approaches to its solution. 1977, The Netherlands journal of medicine 20:211–219.

5   Dietrich M, Gaus W, Vossen J, van der Waaij D and Wendt F: Protective Isolation and Antimicrobial Decontamination in Patients with High Susceptibility to Infection. 1977, Infection 5:107–114.

6   Bagshawe K D, Blowers R, Lidwell O M: Isolating patients in hospital to control infection. Part 2. Who should be isolated, and where. 1978, British Medical Journal 2:684–686.

7   ibid

*   Solberg Claus Ola: Isolasjonsavdelinger for pasienter med infeksjonssykdommer. 1978, Tidsskrift for Den norske laegeförening 98:1300–1302.

Facilities for isolation and their use vary from country to country and even from institution to institution: there are separate infectious disease units or clinics for patients requiring isolation, special rooms in various hospital ward areas for isolation procedures, and rooms which are used as the situation requires.

The transfer of infection by the airborne route — e g respiratory infections — can be controlled only by having the patient in a single room. The control of diseases spread by contact depends primarily on barrier nursing, which includes nursing procedures that reduce the risks of transferring infective organisms — by direct contact or by way of fomities — from person to person.

It is strongly felt that also from the aspect of nosocomial infection the placing of all beds in single rooms — at least in the intensive care and treatment units — is for the patient the best solution. All patients must be given rooms, not curtained cubicles[8].

Because isolation may result in a number of additional efforts for physicians, nurses, and patients, sometimes there is reluctance or objection to placing a patient under isolation. E g for the physician extra time may be required, also nursing care may be more time-consuming, for the patient isolation would decrease social contact[9].

The isolation rooms create easily a feeling of false security[10], as the most sophisticated facilities are useless if the staff has not been well trained in the methods of preventing the spreading of infection.

In the process of isolating patients the knowledge of the value of many of the hygienic measures in general use is very incomplete. It is not known for certain how effective are many of the precautions taken to prevent the spread of infection from or to patients[11]. Each of the arbitrarily chosen items of the isolation regimen should be separately assessed[12].

The quantitative contribution of procedures such as washing, changing gloves and gowns, and the air flow in preventing the spread of organisms must be evaluated[13].

---

8   see also Dubay Elaine C and Grubb Reba D: Infection prevention and control. The C V Mosby Company. St. Louis 1973, p 79.

9   Manual on Control of Infection in Surgical Patients. J B Lippincott Company. Philadelphia-Toronto 1976, p 212.

10 see also Brand Lucy: A practical approach to infection surveillance in the intensive care unit. 1976, Heart and Lung 5:788–790.

11 see also Winner H I: Microbiology in patient care. The English Universities Press Limited. London 1973, p 100.

12 see also Tyrrell D A J, Stephany J, Larsson H E and Blowers R: An isolation unit in a district general hospital. 1977, British Medical Journal 2:373–374.

13 ibid

Studies indicate that the protective gowning used by the staff is not sufficient to protect the patients in the isolation rooms of a burn unit. The results were improved when after a visit in a patient room not only the protective gown but also the hospital working clothes were changed [14].

Psychological stress of isolation

Isolation should not resemble solitary confinement. While excessive noise is a frequent cause of complaint in hospital, complete isolation from any audible or visual indications of life outside imposes great psychological stress[15].

Social isolation may affect the patient's welfare. Occasionally elderly patients subjected to prolonged isolation have appeared to suffer from it[16].

Children in isolation wards think that they are being punished, that they have been rejected and are unworthy. They are at risk of withdrawal and regression[17]. Especially for children it is desirable for nurses to spend extra time in the rooms. Mothers may help to look after their babies, if nurses show them the isolation procedures.

Isolation room

An isolation room has to provide uncluttered space around the bed for equipment and the increased number of personnel involved in emergency care. A room area of about 22 m² is adequate within an isolation unit and would greatly reduce the need for an operation room. There should be no unnecessary furniture.

Critically sick patients should have access to oxygen and compressed air. Distribution pipes from the central gas storage should be provided.

The one-patient unit should be self-contained regarding decontamination, toilet, lavatory and sink An isolation room should be provided with a bedpan-flushing equipment in an adjoining room. In the same space equipment for cleaning the isolation room can be stored, used instruments and other equipment decontaminated, and soiled linen kept in containers prior disposal.

Disposable crockery and cutlery items as well as paper or plastic cups are recommended.

The sanitation as well as the heating equipment should be easily cleaned and with few possibilities to collect dust. The backs of radiators should be accessible for cleaning; toilets, bidets etc should be fixed to the wall, leaving the floor free. Floor drains and gullytraps should have an enamel finish on the inside.

Sometimes for visiting relatives and friends speaking panels and glass partitions are provided.

14 Hambraeus Anna: Att förhindra sjukhusinfektioner — vad betyder våra smittskyddande åtgärder? 1978, Läkartidningen 75:2394–2395.

15 see also Lidwell O M: Clean Air, Less Infection. 1976, Hospital Engineering 30:8:9–17.

16 see also Tyrrell D A J, Stephany J, Larsson H E and Blowers R: An isolation unit in a district general hospital. 1977, British Medical Journal 2:373–374.

17 Robertson B A: The Child in Hospital. 1977, South African Medical Journal 51:749–752.

There is almost no information to indicate how large a reduction in airborne exposure should be aimed at in any given circumstance. There is, however, reason to think that reductions of less than a factor of 10 are not valuable*.

For effective isolation a separate ventilation system for each room with controlled air pressures to prevent movement of air into other areas has been recommended.

Each traditional plenum-ventilated isolation room has between the corridor and the room itself a lock-chamber or ante room for donning the protective gown, mask, cap, shoecovers and sometimes goggles. A hand washing facility is included.

Adding an ante room or airlock improves the air isolation, possibly by a factor of ten compared with the simple directional ventilation arrangements. With a ventilated airlock the degree of protection may be about 10,000 times that found in an open situation**.

There should be no cross-circulation or recirculation of air between an isolation unit and other areas of the hospital.

The air distribution should be arranged so that all air escaping through door crevices etc and excess air flows from the corridors, ante rooms and patient rooms to the toilets to be extracted.

The extracted air should be filtered by means of interchangeable filters before discharge into the open air. The provision of temporary microfilters should be possible.

All ventilation ducts should be provided with cleaning shutters to allow for cleaning the inside of the ducts.

Unidirectional airflow in isolation practice

High-efficiency air filters can be used to provide particle- and microbe-free air as a directed nonturbulent flow in the care of highly susceptible patients. Because it is relatively easy to reduce airborne contamination to a level at which contact and autogenous infection become predominant, some of the technical requirements for ventilating patient rooms are less rigorous than for industries. The linear air velocity needed to reduce turbulence sufficiently for unidirectional horizonal flow to be established appears to be no more than 0.1 to 0.25 m/second. Noise control is, however, a major concern.

It is possible to use this form of ventilation to isolate several patients in one room without partitions. Air would enter through the filter bank behind bedheads and

---

* Bagshawe K D, Blowers R, Lidwell O M: Isolating patients in hospital to control infection. Part 3. Design and construction of isolation accommodation. 1978, British Medical Journal 2:744–748.

** ibid

is extracted through slot in roof. Only about 10 per cent of airflow is to pass into downstream end of the room beyond roof slot. Screens or curtains may be positioned between beds.

This arrangement may be advantageous for patients who need much nursing and supervision and for those with claustrophobia in single rooms. Those who come into direct contact with the patients must practise non-contact techniques with regard to clothing, hand preparation, etc. Others who enter the room for activities not needing patient contact need observe only minimal precautions if they remain down stream or to the side of the patients.

With this form of ventilation about 90 per cent of the air can be recirculated with the addition of fresh air to control smells, carbon dioxide, and other gases. Full air-conditioning is required to control heat gain from the fans. The cost is considerable but convenience and comfort are high and the level of isolation that can be attained is limited only by the measures used to reduce contact transfer. The ease of access itself makes considerable demands on aseptic discipline* .

Isolation cart

When a room used for isolation lacks the ante room or lock-chamber, an isolation cart which is not taken inside the isolation room, is used. The isolation cart may be a regular utility table on wheels or a specially designed cart[18].

A pullout front shelf and a stationary side shelf of the cart may be used for a work area, or for placement of diet, medicine, and laboratory trays. A hook on the side of the cart is provided for the physician's or visitor's coat. There is a rack on the side of the cart to hold a box of masks. The cart is stocked with disposable bags, paper or plastic gowns, gloves, contaminated-marked linen, laundry bags, and isolation tape for marking contaminated items[19].

Plastic isolators

When dealing with infections, against which immunization is not at present available to protect hospital staff, it is highly desirable to separate the patient by a physical barrier from the attendants in order to prevent air-borne spread or contamination from blood, secretions and excreta.

* Bagshawe K D, Blowers R, Lidwell O M: Isolating patients in hospital to control infection. Part 3. Design and construction of isolation accommodation. 1978, British Medical Journal 2:744–748.

18 see also Brand Lucy: A practical approach to infection surveillance in the intensive care unit. 1976, Heart and Lung 5:788–790.

19 Dubay Elaine C and Grubb Reba D: Infection prevention and control. The C V Mosby Company. St Louis 1973, p 46.

This can be accomplished e g in the containment type of plastic isolator developed by *P C Trexler*[20]. The isolator consists of a plastic tent with two compartments, one for the patient and one for supplies. When the patient has been placed in the isolator the two separate units are joined together to form an air-tight tent.

Air pressure within the tent is maintained below atmospheric to reduce the risk of leakage in the event of a defect in the fabric. Extracted air is passed through a filter to remove infectious particles. The doctors and nurses wear half-suites welded into the side of the isolator. Storage compartments within the patient's isolator and the supply isolator are stocked before the isolator is brought into use. Subsequent fresh supplies can be introduced through the entry port on the supply isolator.

All contaminated material is removed through the same port into plastic bags which are cut across between two seals and removed for incineration. Terminal disinfection is accomplished by spraying the interior of the tent. Should a dangerous infection be confirmed it would be advisable to dismantle the canopy and destroy it by incineration.

The tent has proved comfortable for patients and acceptable to both nursing and medical staff who have expressed a preference for these isolators for the greater protection they provide[21].

Although it is theoretically possible to nurse infectious patients in these plastic isolators installed in open wards it would be advisable to site them in rooms well separated from other patients in case of failure of isolation techniques or serious tears in the plastic walls of the tent[22].

Some designs incorporate enough space around the bed for the patient to sit, stand, or even walk a few paces. Toilet accommodation can also be provided. Such systems seem to approach the ultimate in isolation, but carry inherent difficulties in management.

20 Emond Ronald T D: Isolation for high-risk patients. 1976, Postgraduate Medical Journal 52:563–566.

21 ibid

22 ibid

Measures to prevent post-operative wound infections

Staff showering

A comparison of the contamination levels in operation rooms and industrial clean rooms where physical activities were comparable, indicates that the industrial clean room was cleaner than the cleanest operation room[1]. This supports the suggestion that the washing procedures by personnel in operation rooms could indirectly be responsible for a good deal of the contamination.

As a means to suppress the number of bacteria to be shed by the staff in the operation room a *shower-bath* before dressing in operation room clothes has been recommended[2] as well as washing the hair[3] by anti-bacterial shampooing.

It has been indicated that shower-bathing and the use of sterilized underwear by operation room staff may reduce dispersing of staphylococci to half in comparison to non-showered staff[5].

Others indicate that showers tend to increase rather than reduce the number of particles dispensed from the skin. Accordingly, staff should not take showers immediately before operations[6].

Although microbial shedding could be reduced greatly by a daily routine of bathing with a germicidal detergent, for the present time there is no certain way of permanently clearing *Staphylococcus aureus* from the bodies of people who carry it.

Concerning the use of germicidals, attention should be paid to what has been said about the use of antibiotics: of critical importance is the relationship of the antibiotics to the organism in its natural habitat — the body surface. In this situation, not only may resistant strains be selected, but also the genes may then be transferred to other strains, and any resistant procency be disseminated to new hosts. The most important aspect to future antibacterial chemotherapy should thus be the limitation of the use of antibiotics, particularly for application to the skin and nose[7].

1   Clark R P and Cox R N: The generation of aerosols from the human body. in Airborne transmission and airborne infection. ed by J F Ph Hers and K C Winkler. Oosthoek Publishing Company. Utrecht 1973, p 414.

2   see also Cleton F J, van der Mark Y S and van Toorn M J: Effects of shower bathing on dispersal of recently acquired transient skin flora. 1968, The Lancet 1:865.

3   Feller Irving, Richards Kathryn E and Pierson Carl L: Prevention of Postoperative Infections. 1972, The Surgi Clinics of North America 52:1361–1366.

5   Gierhake F W: Post-operative Wundheilungsstörungen. Springer-Verlag. Berlin, Heidelberg, New York 1970, p 38.

6   see also Control of Hospital Infection. ed by E J L Lowbury, G A J Ayliffe, A M Geddes and J D Williams. Chapman and Hall. London 1975, p 148.
Operasjonsavdelinger. Norsk Institutt for Sykehusforskning. Trondheim 1977, p 62.

7   Lacey R W: Antibiotic Resistance Plasmids of Staphylococcus aureus and Their Clinical Importance. 1975, Bacteriological Review 39:1–32.

Total elimination of skin bacteria from the hands of the surgeon and the rest of the operating team before performing a surgical procedure and the use of protective gloves are widely believed to be of paramount importance.

The generally used handscrubbing techniques are far from perfect to reduce the bacterial count to zero and to prevent through a residual activity the bacterial growth on the hands for some hours.

The efficacy of the scrubbing method used is dependent to the number of bacteria on the skin before initiating treatment. Individuals respond differently to the same scrubbing methods. Compared to differences between individuals, the differences observed between treatments are of relatively minor significance[8]. Scrubbing for five minutes has been found to be as effective as scrubbing for ten minutes[9].

Some feel that conventional hand scrubbing wastes time, injures skin, and thus promotes colonization by pathogens[10].

To the point of wasting time a comment could be added. Many surgeons have called this time their own, marking the beginning of surgical intervention. In his mind he could — uninterrupted — contemplate and plan the procedure.*

Aerosols emerging at scrubbing can spread to 1.5 from the wash basin[11]. If this means also a spreading of micro-organisms, is not known.

For surgical scrub also the principle of high pressure water jet has been used. Hand and forearm are placed for ninety seconds in a scrub device and subjected to pressure jet lavage which consists of 75 l of warm tap water and 600 ml of a scrub preparation. After lavage, the hand and forearm are rinsed with tap water and dried with a sterilized towel[12].

8   see also McBride M E, Duncan W C and Knox J M: An evaluation of surgical scrub brushes. 1973, Surgery, Gynecology & Obstetrics 137:934–936.

9   Tucci Victor J, Stone Alex M, Thompson Clifford, Isenberg Henry D and Wise Leslie: Studies of the surgical scrub. 1977, Surgery, Gynecology & Obstetrics 145:415–416.

10 Preventing infection at the operation site. 1976, British Medical Journal 2:773–774.

*   see also Morgenstern Leon: Augury and lament for the surgical scrub. 1978, Surgery, Gynecology & Obstetrics 147:758.

11 personal communication. 1976, Jan Hoborn, Mölnlycke, Sweden.

12 see also Cutridge D E, Bhaskar S N, Gross A and Mulcahy D M: A new method of presurgical hand cleansing. 1972, Oral Surgery 33:162.
      Gross Arthur, Selting Wayne J, Cutridge Duane E and Bhaskar Surindar N: Evaluation of Two Antiseptic Agents in Surgical Preparation of Hands by a New Method. 1973, The American Journal of Surgery 126:49–52.

Operation gloves are used by the operation room staff. Although the sizes of the gloves are of importance for the wearers' comfort, no anthropometric studies to define size, have been found[13]. Microorganisms escaping through punctured gloves* have traditionally been included and are still included in the list of agents with high potential for causing post-operative wound infections[14]. However, this question is controversial as other authors indicate that ruptured gloves do not influence the rates of wound infection or the connection is very limited[15].

When super asepsis or ultra asepsis is adapted frequently, double gloving is used. For that purpose a matched pair of gloves, about 1/4 size differential are recommended[16].

Gloves have a role in protecting the surgeon against hepatitis. Average yearly incidences of 5 to 10 per cent among American surgeons have been reported[17].

There is some scientific support to the practice of removing rings before putting on surgical gloves, though this may be unnecessary in subjects who regularly use detergent or antiseptical soap[18].

Operation room clothes

To increase the hygienic standard special clothes are worn in operation units. The procedures in connection with these clothes are time-consuming and expensive.

Surgical costumes should be designed for maximum skin coverage. It is undesirable to leave arms uncovered in the operation room[19], as they have been pointed out as a source of contamination[20].

It has been recommended that operation room clothing including caps and masks should be of nonlinting material, must constitute an effective bacterial barrier,

13 Beck William C: The Surgical Glove. A Continuing Problem. 1977, The Guthrie Bulletin 46:147–151.

* In Sweden up to 50 per cent of the surgeon's gloves have been found to be punctured at the end of the operation. (Hedlund Per: Infektioner på sjukhus. AWE/Gebers. Stockholm 1975, p 113).
In the US evidence has been heard that the incidence of puncture holes developing during operations may reach levels of 50 to 70 per cent (Manual on Control of Infection in Surgical Patients. American College of Surgeons. J B Lippincott Company. Philadelphia-Toronto 1976, p 99).

14 see also Beck William C: The Surgial Glove. A Continuing Problem. 1977, The Guthrie Bulletin 46:147–151.

15 Gad Palle: Glove Damage as a Route of Wound Infection. 1965, Danish Medical Bulletin 12:1–4.

Bröte Lars: Postoperative wound infection in general surgery. Linköping University Medical Dissertations No 33. Linköping 1976, p 19.

Hasselgren P O, Backelin B, Hammersten J and Holm J: Postoperative sårinfektioner. 1976, Svensk kirurgi 33:67–68.

16 Beck William C: The Surgical Glove. A continuing Problem. 1977, The Guthrie Bulletin 46:147–151.

17 see also Jordan Jr George L: Hepatitis — The Surgeon's Disease. 1974, The American Journal of Surgery 127:629–630.

18 Aseptic methods in the operating suite. 1968, The Lancet 1:709.

19 see also Infection Control in the Hospital. American Hospital Association. Chicago 1974, p 127.

20 Kanz E: Transmission von Mikroorganismen in Krankenhaus. 1977, Der Krankenhausarzt 50:334–342.

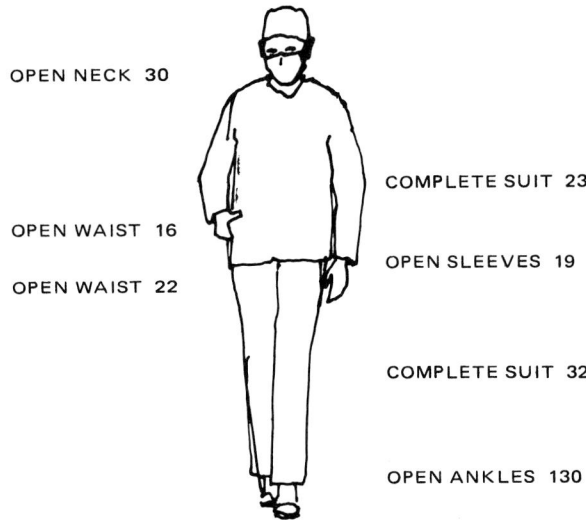

OPEN NECK 30

COMPLETE SUIT 23

OPEN WAIST 16

OPEN SLEEVES 19

OPEN WAIST 22

COMPLETE SUIT 32

OPEN ANKLES 130

Of the escape routes of Staphylococcus aureus from apertures in surgical dress the open ankles are most important. 130 staphylococci per m^2 are dispersed. After R Blowers.

must be comfortable and allow free movement, must transmit heat and water vapour, must not be flammable, and must not have dangerous electrostatic properties[21].

Conventional operation room clothes do not prevent, but may greatly increase dispersal of skin scales which may be contaminated. Male dispersers dressed in ordinary clean operation room clothing disperse as if dressed in ordinary clothes[22].

Bacteria from the surgeon's skin can pass directly to the operative field through the sleeves of conventional surgical gowns[23] and through wet surgical linen[24]. Bacteria penetrate muslin cloth gowns, even in the dry state[25].

When the output of the colony forming particles in relationship to different clothes in operation rooms was studied, the out-put from sterilized regular clothes plus

21 Manual on Control of Infection in Surgical Patients. American College of Surgeons. J B Lippincott Company. Philadelphia-Toronto 1976, p 93.

22 Ayliffe G A J, Babb J R and Collins B J: Dispersal and skin carriage of Staphylococci in healthy male and female subjects and patients with skin disease. in Airborne transmission and airborne infection. ed by J F Ph Hers and K C Winkler. Oosthoek Publishing Company. Utrecht 1973, p 436.

23 Devenish E A and Miles A A: Control of Staphylococcus aureus in Operating Theatre. 1939, The Lancet 1:1088.

24 Propst H D: The effects of bactericidal agents on the sterility of surgical linen. 1953, The American Journal of Surgery 86:301–308.

25 Moylan Joseph A in 1977, Surgery, Gynecology & Obstetrics 145:243.

mask, gloves and caps was less than from regular operation room outfit[26]. This might be explained by the fact that sterilization procedures damage the woven fabric, and makes numerous particles loose which in their turn may carry microorganisms.

It should be mentioned that clothes delivered from the laundry have been shown to be heavily contaminated with microorganisms. Even if the bacteria found on the clothes constitute no great danger for the patient, there is clearly a potential risk if the laundry processing is inefficent[27].

When occluded operation suite trousers are worn, a marked decrease in the amount of bacteria is brought about[28]. Other studies add weight to the suggestion that special attention should be paid to the design and use of impervious trouser suits for both female and male staff[29].

To cover the angle of the jaw in the operation room has been considered to be of great importance[30]. Beards could be regarded as a bigger risk of infection than uncovered hair[31].

Different hooded gowns have come to use. In the Charnley-Howorth enclosure the hoods are fitted to suction outlets to have the expired breath extracted. Per minute about 1.1 m^3 of air evacuated through the suction line[32]. The body exhaust system is said to improve the surgeon's mental concentration, so that the surgeon is in a better position towards the end of an operation session to cope with unexpected surgical complications[33].

26 Wigersma N: Operationskleidung. 1975, medizinische technik 95:51–54.

27 Hambraeus A, Bengtsson S and Laurell G: Bacterial contamination in a modern operating suite. 4. Bacterial contamination of clothes worn in the suite. Stencil. Institute of Clinical Bacteriology, University of Uppsala 1977, p 8.

28 see also Bergman Sven E, Borgström Stig J H and Stenström Sten J: Operating room outfit and the spread of bacteria. 1970, Acta Chirurgica Scandinavica 136:35–38.

Bergman Sven E, Borgström Stig J H and Stenström Sten J: Operating room outfit and the spread of bacteria II. 1972, Acta Chirurgica Scandinavica 138:543–544.

Clark R P and Cox R N: The generation of aerosols from the human body. in Airborne transmission and airborne infection. ed by J E Ph Hers and K C Winkler. Oosthoek Publishing Company. Utrecht 1973, p 425.

29 Noble W C, Habbema J D F, van Furth R, Smith Ingrid and de Raay Carla: Quantitative studies on the dispersal of skin bacteria into the air. 1976, The Journal of Medical Microbiology 9:53–61.

Whyte W, Vesley D and Hodgson R: Bacterial dispersion in relation to operating room clothing. 1976, The Journal of Hygiene 76:367–378.

Dankert J, Zijlstra J B, Lubberding H: A garment for use in the operating theatre: the effect upon bacterial shedding. 1979, The Journal of Hygiene 82:7–14.

30 Böhler J: Ultrareine Operationsräume in der Knochenchirurgie zur Verhütung aerogener Infektionen. 1975, Zentralblatt für Chirurgie 100:28–31.

31 personal communication: 1977, Gunnar Laurell, Uppsala.

32 Charnley John: Sterile Air in Operating Rooms. in British Health Care and Technology. British Operating Theatres. London 1972, p 17.

33 Charnley John: Clean air in the operating room. 1973, Cleveland Clinic Quarterly 40:99–114.

Inside the Pretoria enclosure the staff wear hoods of fibreglass that envelop the head. The hood is integrated with an one-piece gown. The hoods have acryl plastic visors and perforated hollow sections in front of the mouth to extract continuously expired breath. This masking and gowning system can be simplified.

In vertical flow enclosures a plastic helmet with an air slit in the shield is used[34]. An aspiration tube of silicone rubber is fixed around the neck and a sterilized cloth hood is put over the helmet. Bacteriological tests have been performed, comparing the helmet with the mask in the vertical flow enclosures. With both systems, no bacteria could be found in the area of the wound 0.5 m in front of the surgeon. With masks alone, because of the vertical flow of the air, bacteria were to be found on the chest, arms, and hands. With the helmet no bacteria could be found on the suit, over the chest, the arms, or on the gloves.

The hooded gown has received some very high ratings[35].

To check unauthorized visitors a special colour should be reserved for protective clothing to be worn only within the surgical department. This implies that operation room staff must not leave the department dressed in protective clothing.

Different coloured clothing for different categories of the staff in the surgical department simplifies their identification.

All surgical cloths are not necessarily permeable nor are most disposable materials barriers to bacterial penetration. The question of surgical clothing is expected to catch considerable attention and new fabrics anticipated[36].

Surgical masking

A surgical mask may accumulate organisms which may be discharged in bulk on coughing[37] or talking[38]. Anaesthesiologists and circulating nurses talk a great deal

34 Stühmer G, Weber B G, Meierhans R, Janssen R, and Brunner J: Four and a Half Years Experience with a Vertical Flow Sterile Enclosure. 1977, International Orthopaedics 1:95–99.

35 Hambraeus Anna: Att förhindra sjukhusinfektioner — vad betyder våra smittskyddande åtgärder? 1978, Läkartidningen 75:2394–2395.

36 Laurell Gunnar at the ISIMA 78 symposion Planering av operationsavdelningar. Malmö, April 1978.

37 see also Dubac F, Guimont A, Roy L and Ferland JJ: A study of Some Factors Which Contribute to Surgical Wound Contamination. 1973, Clinical Orthopaedics and Related Research 96:176–178.

38 Quesnel Louis B: The efficiency of surgical masks of varying design and composition. 1975, The British Journal of Surgery 62:936–940.

while the scrub nurse remains relatively quiet. The surgeon talks more than his assistant*.

Masks in itself can decrease the amount of air contamination with 90 per cent efficiency[39] but the surgical gauze mask has been shown[40] to be highly inefficient and a possible infection hazard.

The gross efficiency of several types of masks is high, but there is significant difference in efficiency between the best and worst masks[41]. The best masks contain more fabric, are softer and pleated.

The worst are stiffer, smaller and not pleated. Reusable cotton fabric masks are as effective as synthetic fabric masks when made to a good design.

The key characteristic of a surgical mask remains its filtering efficiency. The most efficient filter mask is useless until it's edges are molded to fit the contours of the face, forcing expired air through the filter. A bacteriologically effective mask impedes respiration and may cause fatigue and hypercapnia[42].

In spite of the long time since masking has been regularly used, there is little evidence to suggest inadequate masking of the operation team as a significant factor contributing to the aetiology of post-operative sepsis[43]. It has been stated that the use or non-use of surgical masks makes no difference to the incidence of wound infection[44]. As it is a common reflex action to scratch one's nose in moments of stress, masks are, if nothing more, barriers between noses and fingers[45].

Shoe covers, clogs, stockings

Protective canvas *shoe covers* are condemned[46]. If the soles become even slightly moist, bacteria are dispersed from the undershoes. Also loose fitting surgical boots

* John F Bunker (The Anesthesiologist and the Surgeon. Little, Brown and Company. Boston 1972, p 143) speaks of the surgeon in another role, that of master entertainer, in the operation room. All members of the surgical team indulge in the joking and small talk — which often serves to relieve anxiety — but the surgeon sets the tone. Many surgeons are outrageously funny and enter into this role with enthusiasm.

39 Robson Martin C, Krizek Thomas J and Heggers John P: Biology of Surgical Infection. Current Problems in Surgery. Year Book Medical Publisher. Chicago 1973, p 29.

40 see also Hirschfeld J W and Laube P J: Surgical Masks: an Experimental Study. 1941, Surgery 9:720–730.

41 Quesnel Louis B: The efficiency of surgical masks of varying design and composition. 1975, The British Journal of Surgery 62:936–940.

42 Walter Carl W and Kundsin Ruth B: The Airborne Component of Wound Contamination and Infection. 1973, Archives of Surgery 107:588–595.

43 Davidson A I G, Smith G and Smylie H G: A Bacteriological Study of Immediate Environment of a Surgical Wound. 1971, The British Journal of Surgery 58:331.

44 Wright J E, Hennessy E J and Bisset R L: Wound Infection: Experience with 12,000 Sutured Surgical Wounds in a General Hospital over a period of 11 years. 1971, The Australian and New Zealand Journal of Surgery 41:107–112.

45 see also Walter Carl W: Multiple factors to consider in hospital infection control. 1970, Hospital Topics 48:10:67.

46 Surgical Departments in Hospitals. ed by DM Douglas. Butterworths. London 1972, p 81.

are not recommended as they may cause a pumping action which blows out[47] particles.

Close fitting cotton, paper, and plastic shoe covers are available.

Plastic ones are relevant to cleanliness, but defeat the aims of antistatic precautions. Cotton overshoes are to be preferred[48].

Also fresh, nonwoven, disposable shoe covers are easy to put on, and they are equipped with a conductive strip[49]. Shoe covers are recommended because the usual white shoes with dried secretions on the leather are unsanitary for a number of reasons, including the tendency for flakes to come off with motion and to enter the general ambience. Shoe covers should be worn only under exceptional circumstances. Their value is mainly psychological[50].

Clogs used in the operation rooms and adjoining rooms are heavily contaminated during the day[51].

The wearing of *stockings* by women in the operation rooms increases the disseminations of skin bacteria from the legs[52].

re-operative preparation of the operation site

The bacterial flora of skin is part of the indigenous microflora of the patient. Exchanged with or supplemented by other bacteria during the preoperative hospital stay, the skin could be a source of surgical wound contaminations.

The pre-operative preparation of the operation site with an antiseptic is considered a necessary procedure in reducing a bacterial wound inoculum originated from the skin[53]. Adequate pre-operative skin preparation and local antibiotic irrigation may be most important in preventing clean chest wound infections in patients requiring coronary bypass[54].

---

47 Clark R P and Cox R N: The generation of aerosols from the human body. in Airborne transmission and airborne infection. ed by J F Ph Hers and K C Winkler. Oosthoek Publishing Company. Utrecht 1973, p 425.

48 Vickers M D: Fire and explosion hazards in operating theatres. 1978, British Journal of Anaesthesia 50:659–663.

49 Laufman Harold: The control of operating room infection: discipline, defense mechanisms, drugs, design, and devices. 1978, Bulletin of the New York Academy of Medicine 54:472–483.

50 see also Brandberg Åke and Brinkhoff Barbro: Sjukhusstädaren — estet eller bakteriejägare? 1977, Sjukhuset 54:429–434.

51 Hambraeus A, Bengtsson S and Laurell G: Bacterial contamination in a modern operating suite. Effect of a zoning system on contamination of floors and other surfaces. Stencil. Institute of Clinical Bacteriology, University of Uppsala, Sweden 1977, p 9.

52 Mitchell N J and Gamble D R: Clothing design for operation-room personnel. 1974, The Lancet 2:1133–1136.

53 see also Raahawe Dennis: Antisepsis of the operation site with aqueous cetrimide/chlorhexidine in alcohol. 1974, Acta Chirurgica Scandinavica 140:595–601.

54 Sutherland R D, Martinez H E, Guynes W A and Miller LaWayne: Postoperative chest wound infections in patients requiring coronary bypass. 1977, The Journal of Thoracic and Cardiovascular Surgery 73:944–947.

At the same time it is felt that preparation of the skin tends to become part of an operative ritual that is often more comforting in performance than in fact[55].

To obtain a higher degree of disinfection e g in patients with exceptional susceptibility to infection, the operation site is recommended to be cleansed and disinfected both in the ward on the day before the operation as well as in the surgical unit[56].

Reduction of the bacterial mass of the patient through a *shower* probably reduces the possibility of infection. The patients without shower before operation have had an infection rate of 2.3 per cent[57]. If showered and soap used, the infection rate was 2.1 per cent. If showered using an antiseptic detergent containing hexachlorophene, the infection rate fell to 1.3 per cent.

Preoperative shaving has for some time been a part of the operation routine. Reporting on 23,649 wounds, an infection rate of 2.3 per cent was found[58] in operation sites which had been shaved, 1.7 per cent where the pubic hair had been clipped and 0.9 per cent when no attempt had been made to remove hair. It is felt that these differences are due to by razor caused trauma, which provides a portal of entry to the exogenous organisms. The injured tissues serve as a substrate for bacterial growth.

After eliminating all on-the-ward preparation shaving and so called prepping a decrease in clean operation contamination and wound infection rate has been noted[59].

The *depilatory cream* has proved to be a very efficient alternative to shaving[60] and electric clipping. More than so, it has been concluded, that if hair has to be removed, a depilatory is the agent of choice[61]. In Canada this method has been found to be expensive[62], but in the United Kingdom it has proved to be cheaper than shaving, taking into account the time of staff and the disposable equipment used[63].

55 Hunt Thomas K: Diagnosis and Treatment of Wound Failure. in Advances in Surgery. ed by R M Zollinger. Year Book Medical Publishers Inc. Chicago 1974, p 303.

56 see also Control of Hospital Infection. ed by E J L Lowbury, G A J Ayliffe, A M Geddes and J D Williams. Chapman and Hall. London 1975, p 67.

57 Cruse Peter J E and Foord Rosemary: A five-year prospective study of 23,649 surgical wounds. 1973, Archives of Surgery 107:206.

58 ibid

59 Kraft Richard O in 1976, Archives of Surgery 111:488.

60 see also Seropian R and Reynolds B M: Wound infections after pre-operative depilatory versus razor preparation. 1971, The American Journal of Surgery 121:251–254.

    Powis S J A, Waterworth T A and Arkell D G: Preoperative skin preparation: clinical evaluation of depilatory cream. 1976, British Medical Journal 2:1166–1168.

61 Hamilton H W, Hamilton K R and Lone F J: Preoperative hair removal. 1977, The Canadian Journal of Surgery 20:269–275.

62 ibid

63 Powis S J A, Waterworth T A and Arkell D G: Preoperative skin preparation: clinical evaluation of depilatory cream. 1976, British Medical Journal 2:1166–1168.

Many creams can be readily colonised by pathogenic bacteria and the use of these from multidose containers is potentially hazardous[64].

Draping is a means of demarcating, maintaining, and protecting a limited area which has been prepared for the operation by cleansing and degerming techniques.

Skill, routines, and discipline and post-operative infections

A considerable responsibility for the occurence of post-operative infections is placed upon the operating team. The real hazard to the patient in the operation room seems not to be the personnel *per se,* or the inadequate equipment, but lies in the area of discipline or the lack of it[65].

The aseptic routine consists of reducing and, if possible, eliminating all sources and ways of contaminating the wound.

The innumerable potential interruptions in aseptic routine — even post-operatively — are considered to constitute an important predisposing cause of wound infection.

Shooter has stated that if the surgeon and his team give good observance of aseptic discipline the staphylococcal infection rate for operation room derived infections should not exceed one per cent[66]. *Cruse* has said that the *clean* wound infection rate should be less than 1 per cent. If a rise in the clean rate is found, the operation room, the department, and the surgeon should be quickly notified. Whenever the monthly clean wound infection rate exceeds 2 per cent, a complete review of infection must be instituted. The clean infection rate is the most accurate reflection of surgical technique[67].

It has been suggested that there should be three levels of asepsis: the general operation room asepsis, super asepsis for certain procedures and certain patients when the general precautions may be insufficient, and ultra asepsis for special cases[68].

Ultraasepsis is not necessary by today's criteria for every hospital or possibly even in any hospital[69]. However, the results of its proponents should be observed and their effects assessed.

---

64 Powis S J A, Waterworth T A and Arkell D G: Preoperative skin preparation: clinical evaluation of depilatory cream. 1976, British Medical Journal 2:1166–1168.

65 see also Dineen Peter: Personnel, Discipline, and Infection. 1973, Archives of Surgery 107:603–604.

   Dederich R, Hild A and Wolf L: Zweijährige Erfahrungen mit 2078 orthopädischen Operationen in einem ultrasterilen Operationsraum. 1976, Zeitschrift für Orthopädie und ihre Grenzgebiete 114:113–115.

66 Shooter R A: Infection at the Time of Operation. in British Health Care and Technology. British Operating Theatres. London 1972, p 55.

67 Cruse Peter: Infection Surveillance: Identifying the Problems and the High-Risk Patient. 1977, Southern Medical Journal 70:suppl 1:4–8.

68 Beck William C: Asepsis, super asepsis, and ultra asepsis. 1976, The American Surgeon 42:227–228.

69 ibid

It has been pointed out that super asepsis is possible in any operation room without additional equipment[70]. Every hospital can and should have an established and rehearsed protocol for super asepsis.

Some of the current aseptic rules are based on adequate evidence; some can be recommended provinsionally, but need further evaluation; some are rational and considered to be desirable but cannot be evaluated; and some are traditionally observed practices, which are probably unnecessary* or sometimes potentially harmful[71].

The present routines can also be regarded as a pedagogic instrument which constantly points towards the need of aseptic and technical perfection in performing the operation.

There is no substitute for strict adherence to meticulous aseptic surgical technique. The heady successes of antimicrobial prophylaxis must not overshadow the basic role of surgical asepsis[72].

The number of staff in the operation should be strictly limited to what is needed for the operation in hand. Casual professional visitors should not be admitted.

Physical-chemical treatment of air

Operation room in UV irradiation can reduce the number of pathogenic and apathogenic bacteria in the air considerably. Experimental studies indicate that the number of germs can be reduced to less than 10 per cent of the original amount[74]. UV rays applied over long periods can strongly reduce the number of germs on the surface, even when the rays act only at low intensity and indirectly.

---

70 Beck William C: Asepsis, super asepsis, and ultra asepsis. 1976, The American Surgeon 42:227-228.

* E g when the question whether the scalpel blade used to make the skin incision must be discarded because of the fear of contaminating deeper tissues with skin bacteria was reexamined, the previous work that indicated a low incidence when only one knife blade is used for the incision was confirmed. It was also hoped that these findings will result in abandonment of one superfluous surgical ritual (Coopman Avram M, D'Amico Louis, Sifers Tim and Gavan Thomas L: One scalpel for major surgical procedures. 1975, Cleveland Clinic Quarterly 42:193–196).

71 see also Aseptic methods in the operating suite. 1968, The Lancet 2:831.

72 see also Darrell J H: Antibiotics in Surgery. in Recent Advances in Surgery. Number Eight. ed by Selwyn Taylor. Churchill Livingstone. Edinburgh and London 1973, p 102.

Maki Dennis G: Lister revisited: surgical antisepsis and asepsis. 1976, The New England Journal of Medicine 294:1286–1287.

74 Gundermann Knut-Olaf: Untersuchungen zur Reduzierung des Luftkeimgehaltes in Räumen mit kontinuierlicher Keimfreisetzung. 1974, Zentralblatt für Bakteriologie, Parasitenkunde, Infektionskrankheiten und Hygiene B 159:31–49.

Ultraviolet light cannot clean bacteriologically a deeply contaminated wound[75]. When only ultra-clean cases, such as those in reconstructive surgery, have been considered, the incidence of infection was diminished by the use of UV-rays so that the difference was statistically significant[76].

Many factors influence the incidence of infection to a greater degree than ultraviolet irradiation. Until these other factors are controlled, only very limited benefit if any, could be expected from the use of irradiation in operation rooms. The role of UV in the general operation room may be considerad as terminated[77], although ultra-violet lamps will be used in new operation rooms[78].

There are also serious disadvantages of a practical nature in the use of ultraviolet light[79]. The eyes and skin of the staff and patient must be protected — the ways to protect are both expensive and cumbersome — as ultraviolet photokeratitis is very insidious and incapacitating. The individual does not know when he has been exposed, and symptoms appear first after 4 to 12 hours of latency[80]. if the UV-rays are used, in order to protect the hands, arms and faces of the personnel, there should be no irradiation between the 0.75 m and 2.10 m levels over the floor[81].

Fogging machines have been used for space cleaning but they do nothing for disinfection. Also various *air sprays* and *aerosols* as a backup procedure have been advocated.

When the development of chemical methods in combating airborne infections was critically summed up already in the mid-fifties[82], the suggested methods were found to be incapable of decreasing the incidence of infection to any great degree. Even the cost and inconvenience of the majority of the methods detracted from their practicability. These views have only been deepened.

75 Goldner J Leonard and Allen Jr Ben L: Ultraviolet Light in Orthopedic Operating Rooms at Duke University. 1973, Clinical Orthopaedics and Related Research 96:195–205.

76 Postoperative Wound Infections. Report of an ad hoc Committee of the Committee on Trauma. 1964, Annals of Surgery 160:2. Supplement to 2.

   Goldner J Leonard and Allen Jr Ben L: Ultraviolet Light in Orthopedic Operating Rooms at Duke University. 1973, Clinical Orthopaedis and Related Research 96:195–205.

77 personal communication: 1977, Gunnar Laurell, Uppsala.

78 Kundsin Ruth B: Microbiological monitoring of the hospital environment. in Infection control in health care facilities. ed by Kenneth R Cundy and William Ball. University Park Press. Baltimore, London, Tokyo 1977, p 14.

79 see also Cowan D: The design and development of clean operating enclosures. CSIR Special Report BOU 28, Pretoria 1971, p 2.

80 Pitts Donald G and Tredici Thomas J: The effects of ultraviolet on the eye. 1971, American Industrial Hygiene Journal 32:235–246.

81 Salle A J: Fundamental Principles of Bacteriology. 7th edition. McGraw-Hill Book Company. New York, St Louis etc. 1973, p 666.

82 Körlof Bengt: Infection in Burns. 1956, Acta Chirurgica Scandinavica. Suppl. 209, p 15.

Fogging is considered an unsatisfactory method of decontaminating air and is not to be recommended[83].

The mist which is created has a greater psychological than microbicidal effect. There is also reason to be concerned about potential harm to the respirary tissue from inhaling droplets of phenolic disinfectant solutions and other protoplasmic poisons suspended in the air[84].

83 see also Maurer Isobel M: Hospital Hygiene. Edward Arnold. London 1974, p 45.

Infection Control in the Hospital. American Hospital Association. Chicago 1974, p 63.

84 Spaulding Earle H: Chemical Disinfection and Antisepsis in the Hospital. 1972, The Journal of Hospital Research 9:1:24.

ENVIRONMENT

The spatial features of a hospital have to satisfy both the patients and the staff. Some features are generally valid for everybody. Some create subjective views of various categories of people involved.

The perceiving of built environment is affected chiefly by visual, acoustic, olfactory, and thermal influences. There are no spectators, only participants[1].

A design literally shouts messages of expectations to the occupant[2]. The decoding of the messages given by surroundings is not dependent upon high intelligence. A message requiring a different behaviour pattern from occupants is at once understood, though not always followed.

There is an acceptance limit of information processes of the humans, which is the result of plotting the path of external stimuli via the senses and memory to the reflexe. The total informative capacity is 10^{11} bit/sec* according to *Helmer Frank*[3]. The optical sense conveys 10^7 bit, the acoustical 10^6 bit, the olfactory 20 bit, and the thermal 5×10^3 bit. The brain can absorb not more than 16 bit for 10 seconds, a total of 160 bit. Information elements available above this level will be confused.

Many man-made environments are seldom wholly satisfactory for human beings. Frequently the human body is placed in thermal neutrality and uniform illumination is provided. The widely spread concept of so called optimum conditions for physical environment, meaning that fixed sets of environmental conditions for so-called perfect comfort are implied, is definitely suspect[4].

Already a minor change within the comfort range of temperature, humidity, air movement, illumination and sounds checks the feeling of monotony and thus acts in a beneficial manner.

Fluctuations in thermal conditions increase the effectiveness of the thermoregulatory mechanisms, in particular the vasomotor system, and the sensitivity of the thermoreceptors of the nervous system[5]. Restrictions on temperature swings may be in error. Instead there is a desirability of permitting, or perhaps even artificially creating, temperature swings[6].

---

1   Fitch James Marston: The Aesthetics of Function. 1965, Annals of the New York Academy of Sciences 128:706.

2   Burgun J Armand at the Conference on Health Facility Planning and Design in the Developing Countries. New York. The World Trade Institute. December 1975.

*   bit = binary digit = unit of informative sign

3   cited by Nalbach Gernot: Umweltgestaltung am Beispiel Arbeitsplatz. 1973, Deutsche Bauzeitung 107:1113--1114.

4   see also Rosen A C: Change in perceptual threshold as a protective function of the organism. 1954, Journal of Personality 23:182–194.

    Kendick J D: Human factors affecting design of physical environment in buildings. 1967, The Medical Journal of Australia 2:267–269.

5   Givoni Baruch: Man, Climate and Architecture. Elsevier Publishing Company Limited. Amsterdam, London, New York 1969, p 48.

6   see also Wyon D P: Thermal aspects of the environment in buildings. 1974, Journal of architectural research 3:12–17.

Normal perception, thought, and consciousness of adults, can be maintained only in constantly changing environments. Where there is no change, normal perception fades, the capacity to concentrate deteriorates, and attention lapses.

It is not yet known how far it is possible to compensate a loss of information in one environmental factor by an increased effect of another, and if compensation is applicable to all physical environmental factors. Some reported observations indicate possibilities in this direction: hearing is influenced by the intensity of illumination[7]; visual attention is improved when noise level is reduced[8]; the positive influence of an increased intensity of light by 200 lux on the efficiency of adults is counteracted by simultaneous increasing of the temperature over 25 to 27°C, sounds and textures assume different and even greater significance for the blind[9].

Already *Hippocrates** pointed out: it is not enough for the physicians to do what they do. The patient himself and *his environment* and other external factors must contribute to the cure.

The hospital milieu represents a sensory information complex, which on one side rises confidence and increases optimism, on the other hand is depressive and develops negative emotions[10].

The in-patient therapeutic environment encloses the nursing units, the medical performance rooms in various parts of the hospital and the circulation areas. Traditionally the hospital rooms are believed to be of inferior quality**.

As to-day's patient is more knowledgeable about medicine and more conscious of his surroundings than his counterpart in the past, the quality of hospital architecture, particularly the patient areas, require careful attention.

It is quite natural that in the ward areas out of the three main hospital stay components the psychological milieu and quality of care dominate greatly, when their importance from the patient's point of view was investigated. However, according to various investigations[11] as many as 7 to 19 per cent of patients in somatic wards

---

7   Ruuber Georg: Ilu seaduspärasusest. Valgus. Tallinn 1965, p 9.

8   Hill Henry: In Quest of Quiet. Fred Kenner/publishing projects/. Stackpole Books. Harrisburn, Pa. 1970, p 200.

9   Stephens Suzanne: Hidden barriers. 1978, Progressive Architecture 59:4:94–97.

*   Hippocrates (460–370 B C), Greek physician, founder of the most rational school for medicine that the ancient world had to offer.

10 see also Mälberg Ülle and Siiman Uno: Arsti tegevuse psühholoogilistest aspektidest. 1975, Nõukogude Eesti Tervishoid 18:275–277.

** The following statement is not exceptional: I don't wish to listen to a record which is as thorough and as nude and as devoid of anything as a hospital room (Henryk Szeryng in 1978, Records and Recording 21:7:15).

11 cited by Bjurström Fredrik: Studier i åskådliggörande och värdering av fysisk miljö i sjukhus. in Svenska Sjukhusföreningens Årsbok 1972. Grafisk Reproduktion AB, Stockholm 1973, p 78–92.

considered the hospital physical milieu to be the most important factor. The percentages were still higher — 22 to 28 — in mental care units, but lower — 6 to 13 — in nursing units for chronic patients.

Thus there is a need — sometimes desperate[12] — of people for an environment that responds them in the stressed emotional realm of a hospital. The in-patient areas can have identifiable impact on behaviour of the patient.

To create an atmosphere of warmth, snugness, and dignity for the patients and the staff ought to be the emotional part in health care building design programme. The advocacy for a more humane, dignified, and pleasant environment, particularly in maternity units, seems to be increasing[13].

For many patients sounds, smells, colours, and textures tend to become sharpened and gain special significance. The role which environment plays in influencing the state of mind of a patient facing an operation or another complicated treatment need not to be stressed. It must be admitted that a clear picture has yet to emerge to show how the physical environment affects human beings, particularly the sick.

There is clinical evidence that sensory deprivation may be one element of importance in the etiology of mental disturbance as a complication of various medical and surgical conditions.

Patients placed in isolation* may experience acute sensory deprivation and become psychotic. For this reason, the atmosphere in an isolation room should be as normal as possible[14]. Isolation for prolonged periods of time is better to be avoided[15].

People do not like to be in places where there is no ambiguity and their sensibilities are strongly directed. On the other hand, the tolerance of people for diversity in their built environments is almost limitless.

As an optimum for perception could be regarded changes at random within the range of acceptable environmental conditions.

---

12 Zeidler Eberhard H: McMaster and Beyond. 1975, national hospital and health care 1:7:7.

13 see also Macintyre Sally: The management of childbirth: a review of sociological research issues. 1977, Social science & medicine 11:477–484.

* Hubert Leiderman, Jack H Medelson, Donald Wexler and Philip Salomon (1958, Archives of Internal Medicine 2) have written of hazards of isolation that center around medical care: Volunteers were confined themselves up to 36 hours in a respirator in which they were able to see only a small area of ceiling. Only 5 to 17 could endure the confinement for the full 36 hours. All reported difficulty in concentration, periodic anxiety feelings and a loss of ability to judge time. Eight reported some distortions of reality, ranging from pseudo-somatic delusions to frank visual hallucinations. Four subjects terminated the experiment because of anxiety; two of these in panic tried to release themselves forcibly from the respirator.

14 see also Huffer Virginia: Psychological Disturbances in the Acutely III patient. 1969, Modern Treatment 6:744.

15 see also Roberts Keith D and Edwards Jennifer M: Paediatric Intensive Care. Blackwell Scientific Publications. Oxford and Edinburgh 1971, p 14.

In considering the use of light, colour and pattern, the perceptions of the partially sighted have to be considered.

Design for imperfect vision raises questions about the kind of minimal modern design that minimized distinctions between walls, floors, and furniture and about the tendency toward uniform light levels. Equally questionable in these terms are bold patterns that threaten the visual integrity of major planes or objects in an architectural space[16].

16 Dixon John Morris: Accessible and perceivable. 1978, Progressive Architecture 59:4:6.

Lighting

Not only vision requires light. Light is an environmental factor as much as air, water and temperature. Daylight has perhaps several hundred important effects on human bodily functions. Many of them have a 24-hour rhythm following the daily cycle of light and darkness. Only a few dozens of them are currently known, a few really understood.

The rising cost of energy has stimulated considerable interest in the potentialities of daylight in hospitals.

The need and appreciation of sunshine depends greatly on the activities in the room. A nice view through window is preferred when the choice is between having sunshin into the interiors and an unpleasant view on one side and having a pleasant sunlit view through the window and no sunshine indoors[1].

Sometimes the view is held that sunshine should be excluded from building interior if the solar heat gain requires an excessive increase of the air-conditioning system. This extra cost seems to be a small price for an important psychological benefit.

As a check on the standards of general hospital cleanliness the value of good general lighting cannot be overstressed.

For an in-patient who is away from his familiar environments, the visual comfort in supporting his self-confidence is a factor of paramount importance.

In health care, many critical decisions are based upon the visual appearance of a patient, his tissues, and his tests. The visual impressions may be influenced by the quality of the light. A patient may look healthy under one illuminant and ill under another. The appearance of his tissues may be judged similarly[2].

Studies have been carried out to determine the spectral responses of human complexion, but the tissues — normal and diseased — remain unstudied[3].

---

1 see also Longmore J and Ne'eman: The availability of sunshine and human requirements for sunlight in buildings. 1974, Journal of architectural research 3:2:24–29.

2 see also Schreckendgust Jay, Reynolds Harold, Beck William C, and Geffert John: Light for clinical purposes I. 1978, The Guthrie Bulletin 47:195–203.

3 ibid

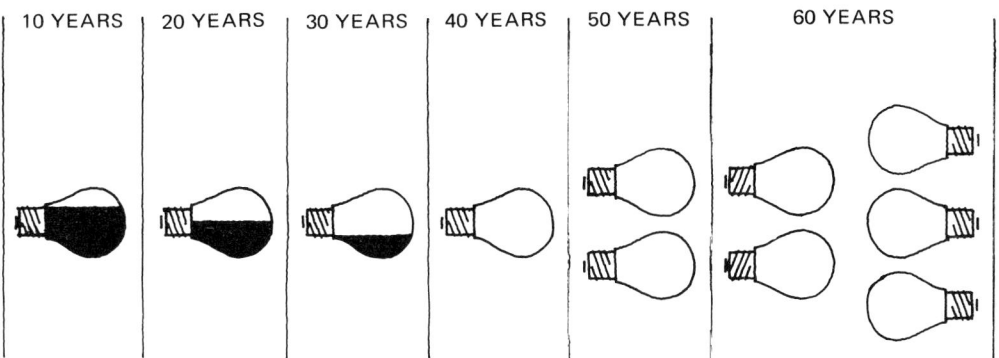

| 10 YEARS | 20 YEARS | 30 YEARS | 40 YEARS | 50 YEARS | 60 YEARS |

Taking the amount needed by a man of 40 as the base, only one-third of the light is necessary for a child of 10, and half for a 20-year-old. A person of 30 needs two-thirds of the amount, and at 50 twice the amount of light. At 60 he needs five times the amount he needed at 40, or about 15 times he needed at 10.

Artificial light sources should not deviate markedly from the lighting environment under which humans evolved in nature. Attempts to change them from the natural sources, either compositionally or drastically by modifying the portion delivered to a living system, can be expected to have some effect[4]. General room lighting, most advantageously, should come from several sources as it is fatiguing to have to work between areas of greatly varying light intensity.

The hospital should strive to minimize or eliminate decorative lighting and to use task lighting whenever possible, because it is more efficient than general illumination[5].

For the majority of ordinary occupations, the desired lighting intensity, based on visual acuity tests, is about one-hundreth of the normal out-of-door midday lighting intensity[6]. 700 lux* of balanced light will be just as good for visual clarity as 1000 lux of cool white light.

The general room lighting level should not exceed 750 lux. A higher level is considered to be a stress factor[7].

---

4   see also Keep P J: Stimulus deprivation in windowless rooms. 1977, Anaesthesia 32:598–602.

5   Frye Jason W: The impact of energy conservation on hospital design. 1978, Hospitals 54:4:105–110.

6   Wurtman Richard J: Biological considerations in lighting environments. 1973, Progressive Architecture 54:9:79–81.

*   10.76 lux = 1 footcandle

7   Hollwich F and Dieckhues B: Kann künstliche Beleuchtung das Tageslicht voll ersetzen? 1978, Krankenhaus Umschau 47:456–461.

General lighting should be free from glare, which seems for a long time to have been the main cause of complaints from patients[8].

The illuminants for direct lighting — if the aesthetically very pleasant indirect lighting is not used — should have the greatest possible reflective area. The contrast between illuminants and the ceiling should be minimal. Particularly during transport to the operation department or other treatment and examination areas, during waiting and procedures in the holding areas the attention of the patient in bed tends to be fixed on the ceiling.

For internal rooms a two level lighting system should be employed: 400 lux during the day and 200 lux during the evening.

Lighting intensities have to be related to the tone of wall and ceiling colours. Light-coloured finishes and interiors will require fewer lights, thereby conserving energy.

Group relamping of fluorescent lighting is said to offer greater efficiency. If group relamping is planned during the design stage, fewer lighting fixtures will be required[9]

A portion of the patients has low vision. Most designers are unaware how the environment appears to them.

Shadows may be hazardous because changes in level or projections cannot be perceived. Surface reflection may cause discomfort and colours are not clearly discernible.

Under uneven light levels the visually impaired person may be more vulnerable to hazardous situations because the eye takes longer to adjust to the sudden changes in illumination[10].

Lighting in anaesthetic room

When complemented with some direct lighting, a total intensity of 400 lux should be achieved in anaesthetic rooms. A variable light source to provide occasionally a higher intensity ought to be installed.

The anaesthesiologist has to rely on his assessment of the patient's colour. Colour temperature is supremely important in enabling the eye to detect the colour shifts in haemoglobin that indicate oxygen lack. Colour temperature at source and on reflection must be towards the red end of the spectrum[11].

8 see also Pütsep Ervin P: Hospital Lighting: Developments in Sweden. 1964, Transactions of Illuminating Engineering Society 29:4:119.

9 Bradley Joseph A: Group Relamping of Fluorescent Lighting for Greater Efficiency/Economy. 1974, Building Operating Management 21:5:24.

10 Jones Michael A and Catlin John H: Design for access. 1978, Progressive Architecture 59:4:65–71.

11 also Foster P A: Planning engineering services from the anaesthetist's point of view. Second Southern African Hospital Symposium. Pretoria. November 1977.

In areas where the anaesthesiologist works some people are awake and vertical, some awake and horizontal. Lying on one's back, half-drugged and unable to avoid bright overhead lights is a form of torture many patients remember after other memories of the intensive care areas have faded[12].

lighting in operation room

Among the hospital's most demanding visual engagements are the surgical procedures performed in the operation room.

Working under a spotlight and additional general lighting the surgeon demands a balance of lighting intensity. The large and unexpected variations in the strength of sunlight in fenestrated operation rooms may make this impossible. Several surgical operations require an entirely darkened operation room. A fenestrated operation room must also be screened against glare and heat radiation[13], occasionally for privacy. The considerable bactericidal properties of daylight and the ease of airing during cleaning might be remembered in that context.

There is little meaning in discussing the psychological aspects of daylight in operation rooms as it is a matter of taste rather than science. There is no scientific evidence on which one could strictly advise. However, the surgical department, as a whole, must possess windows to allow the staff to be conscious of the transitions of the daylight.

Eye fatigue is caused by repeated adaption of the eye to extreme light differences or repeatedly changing distances to the objects. In surgical processes, the surgeon's eye must focus on the patient's tissues, on instruments passed between personnel and on objects across the operation table. Above all the surgeon's eye must adapt to shiny instruments and white sponges on one side and to tissues in the depth of the surgical cavity on the other side.

As a general condition for good working illumination within the special field a disparity not greater than 10:1 should be permitted between the centrum and the periphery of the visual field. When the progressive reduction in intensity from the operation field, through the immediate environment to the rest of the operation room, compounds to the ratios 100 (20):10:1, maximum of visual comfort is achieved[14]. Other experiments indicate that maximum visual comfort arises when brightness of surroundings is only slightly lower than the brightness in the field of a difficult visual task[15].

12 Foster P A: Planning engineering services from the anaesthetist's point of view. Second Southern African Hospital Symposium. Pretoria, November 1977.

13 personal communication: 1977, Ingemar Sjölander, Stockholm.

14 Krochman Jürgen: Tageslicht und künstliches Licht im Krankenhaus. 1973, Deutsche Bauzeitung 107:150.

15 Hopkinson R G and Kay J D: The Lighting of Buildings. Faber and Faber. London 1972, p 212.

Adequate illumination of the operation field is conductive to precision. Rapid adjustments must be reconciled. At the same time the intensity of light in different parts of the operation room has to be comfortable for everybody involved in the operation.

Attention should be given in anaesthetic equipment design to self-illuminating displays against a background of fairly low illumination[16].

To obtain optimal visual conditions in the operation room, the operation lamp, complementary lighting, the colour of scheme of the room, and the textiles must be coordinated.

As extremely high levels of illumination and controlled shadows are required at the area of incision, and glare and heat need to be eliminated, lighting in the operation room presents complex technical problems. It is important that the operation field remains illuminated although the surgeon's head and hands as well as those of his assistance may be directly in the path of a central light beam[17].

A form of operation room lighting comprises movable lamps which either are suspended or on rails above a transparent operation room ceiling.

In the systems developed by *Paul Nelson* resp *Jean Blin* a series of spotlights built into walls and ceiling can be switched on and off either individually or collectively. Their aim was to achieve very great directional flexibility for the light. However, the change of the patient is still required in some situations.

Intensity

Although the general tendency has been towards greater intensities of light, there are differences of opinion concerning the suitable intensity of light in the operation field. Too little light will handicap vision, and too much overtax it.

It would be realistic to require an allround intensity of about 40,000 lux at the plane of incision. The lamp should give an intensity of 8,000 lux at the bottom of an about 13 cm deep and 5 cm wide incision.

The intensity of light from the operation lamp should be variable. The variations in the general lighting in the operation room should be synchronized with the operation lamp.

16 Foster P A: Planning engineering services from the anaesthetist's point of view. at the Second Southern African Hospital Symposium. Pretoria. November 1977.

17 Beck William C: Operating Room Lighting. 1976, The Journal of Hospital Research 2:5-40.

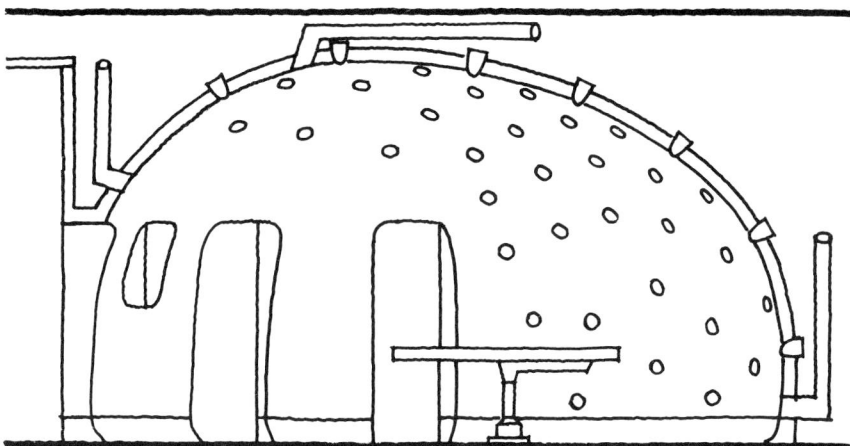

Paul Nelson has suggested about seventy small projectors embedded in the walls and ceiling of an egg-shaped operation room. To alter the position of the illuminated field of the patient's body the operation table must be moved.

Luminance

The normal luminance brightness for the central field during an operation should be 2,000 to 3,000 cd/m^2. Within the central field of the view of the surgeon the relationship between the maximum and minimum brightness – the wound and the surrounding drapes – should be less than 2.5:1, the relation between maximum and minimum luminance should not exceed 1:10 within a base of a 60° cone, which has its point in the eye of the surgeon[18]. Brightness adaption effects the appreciation of colour.

The floor around the surgical table should have a luminance of 200 to 300 cd/m^2, the walls 300 to 500 cd/m^2 and the ceiling lights 1,000 cd/m^2 at most[19].

As surgeons grow older, their resistance to glare decreases[20]. The still acceptable glare index according to the BZ-method[21] is $\leqslant$ 11.

At first visual acuity increases rapidly with increased light intensity, but slows down with subsequent increases until a point is reached where improvement in acuity ceases. From the highest intensities only negative gain of glare can be expected.

In the Federal Republic of Germany an intensity of 100,000 lux is considered desirable. By comparison, the intensity of sunlight on a clear summer day in Europe is more than 100,000 lux, in the shade 10,000 lux, and immediately inside a window on the shade side of a building about 200 lux.

18 personal communication: 1977, Ingemar Sjölander, Stockholm.

19 personal communication: 1972, Ingemar Sjölander, Stockholm.

20 see also Beck William C: Operating room illumination – the state of the art. 1969, Bulletin of the American College of Surgeons 54:5.

21 The IES Code. Recommendations for good interior lighting, The Illuminating Engineering Society 1961.

As a contrast, the Mexican requirement of 10,000 to 15,000 lux could be mentioned[22]. In the United Kingdom the illuminances at the site of operation can be between 10,000 and 50,000 lux[23]. In Sweden 40,000 to 60,000 lux have been required[24].

With age the pupil constricts and the crystalline lens yellows and darkens[25]. For the same visual acuity the elderly members of the operation room staff require more light than their younger colleagues. The latter will, however, not suffer if the level of lighting is designed for the benefit of the former.

Reflectance

Reflectance is the measure of light reflected from the surface of an object and expressed as a percentage of the light striking the surface.

The reflection factors of the operation room surfaces and of especially those of the large instruments play a part. Some examples of reflectance values: surgical wound 9 per cent, surgical drape 30 per cent, light pastel coloured walls 60 per cent, retractors and instruments up to 90 per cent, and white plaster 90 per cent.

Satin finish on all instruments reduces reflectance and disability glare by four-fifth in comparison to instruments with polished chrome[26]. Surgical sponges with pastel shades could reduce glare[27].

A ceiling reflectance of 80 per cent would assist in controlling the luminance contrast ratio between the ceiling and the diffusing enclosures of the general lighting luminaires[28]. The wall reflectances should not be more than 70 per cent.

Directional flexibility

The surgeon operates from a variety of positions. His gaze may rarely be even from below the horizontal. The first assistant views usually from the opposite side of the surgical table at a 45 degree angle from the surgeon.

As important as the intensity control is the directional flexibility of the light. It should be possible to direct operation light to the bottom of a deep incision or cavity. The light must be directed so that the surgical field does not appear flat. It should be possible to appreciate the recesses of the wound in depth. The size of the lit field must be variable.

22 Yañez Enrique: Hospitales de seguridad social. Private publication. Mexico City 1973, p 92.

23 Cockram Alan: The lighting of hospital buildings. 1976, Hospital Engineering 30:18:7–11.

24 Marthin Percy in Ljus, färg & funktion. LTs förlag. Stockholm 1976, p 102.

25 see also Weale R A: The ageing eye. in The Scientific Basis of Medicine. Annual Reviews 1971. University of London. The Athlone Press 1971, p 256.

26 Beck William C: The surgeon's light. 1970, The Guthrie Clinic Bulletin 40:90–95.

27 Beck W C and Goldhamer R D: Discomfort glare and the surgical sponge. A plea for a colored sponge. 1971, The Guthrie Clinic Bulletin 40:157.

28 Cockram Alan: The lighting of hospital buildings. 1976, Hospital Engineering 30:18:7–11.

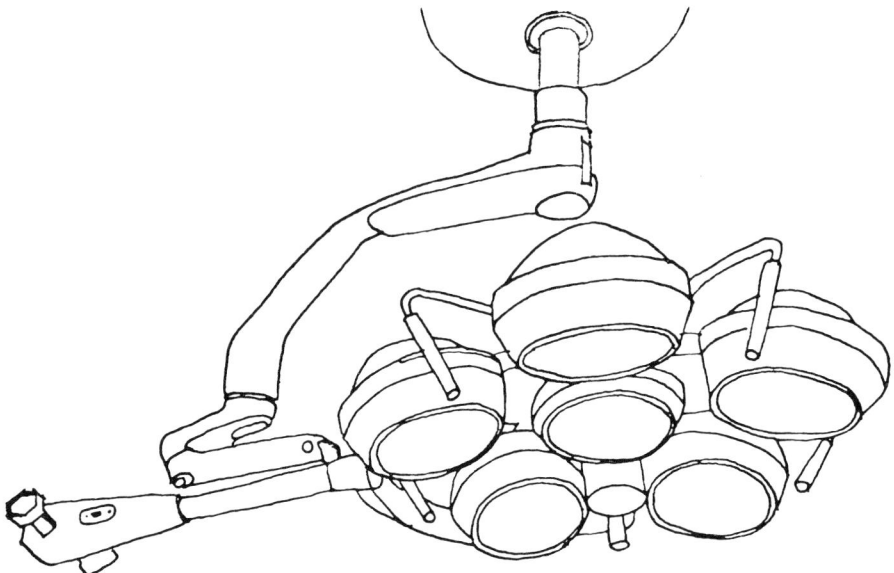

The light of this Castle operation lamp is positioned by a remote control assembly and four satellite control arms.

Colour composition

An operation room lamp should imitate as closely as possible the full radiation in both chromaticity and distribution of the spectral power.

The index of colour reproduction (Ri) can be measured according to the German standards (DIN 6169). Because of the filter-effect of the operation lamp the index value Ri 70 out of the possible 100 should be regarded as optimum[29].

The colour of the light should correspond to about 5000° Kelvin in terms of the correlated colour temperature of the direct light of the sun. Although there is little disciplined research to back up the view, it is felt that 5500°K to 6500°K simulation of daylight with a continuous spectrum would be preferable[30].

The colour characteristics of surgical lighting are not critical for the surgeon, as he can accustom himself to almost any lighting provided that it is sufficiently bright.

The surgeon is concerned with the colour rendering in the cavity, the anaesthesiologist frequently with the skin colour, particularly the face colour of the patient. Although the surgeon and the anaesthesiologist are concerned with different aspects of colour rendering, the spectral composition of the operation room general lighting should be the same as that of the operation lamp.

29 see also Junginger Klaus: Ein Beitrag zum heutigen Stand der Operationsbeleuchtung aus technischer Sicht. 1970, Medizinal Markt/Acta Mediotechnica 18:AM 106.

30 personal communication: 1974, George Weinhold, Fort Washington. Pa.

Changing from one form of light to another interferes with colour appreciation. The interpretation of the colour of blood, lips, fingers and ears may be made exceedingly difficult. The correct spectral composition of light is important for the verification of the patient's skin colour which may warn the anaesthesiologist of poor blood circulation and lack of oxygen.

Tinted light sources may be useful in differentiating tissues by intensifying contrast between them. Warmer lights are better for colour television and for photography.

Heat from illumination

With increased illumination levels the aspect of heat in the surgical field has become a problem. Also the surgeon and his staff feel discomfort.

Generally the heat causes tissues to dry and the loss of body fluids as the patient perspires. If the skin temperature is raised above a critical level of $44°C$, burns occur[31]. When the blood circulation is not normal, the critical level is already at $42°C$[32].

One solution of the heat problem is to surround the operation lamp with a heat-absorbing glass filter that takes heat out of the optical train. Dichromiccoated reflectors reflect selectively only visible light into the surgical field. Up to 80 per cent of the heat generated by the lamp or/and infrared radiations could be dispersed.

Using so called cold light, lighting systems have been developed which claims to have not thermic load for the surgical team and the patient. An illumination adjustable between 30,000 and 135,000 lux without any change of the spectral characteristics in the red is offered.

Operation lamp characteristics

Of a very good operation lamp the following is required:

the fitting be of uncomplicated design and easily accessible for cleaning, maintenance, repair and replacement

a non-splitting glass be used

the intensity of light be variable, but generally at least 40,000 lux[33] at the working plane, and at least 8,000 lux at the bottom of a 13 cm deep and 5 cm wide incision

the fitting be directionally flexible

the area of the lit field be variable

the control be accurate and quick

the colour temperature be at least $5000°K$

the colour reproduction index be Ri 70

31 Fraser Robin: Radiant heat burns and operating theatre lamps: a study of the heat required to cause tissue necrosis. 1967, The Medical Journal of Australia 54:1:1199–1202.

32 Eriksson Ejnar and Holmdahl Martin H-son: Iatrogena värmeskador. 1970, Läkartidningen 67:5085.

33 personal communication: 1977, Ingemar Sjölander, Stockholm.

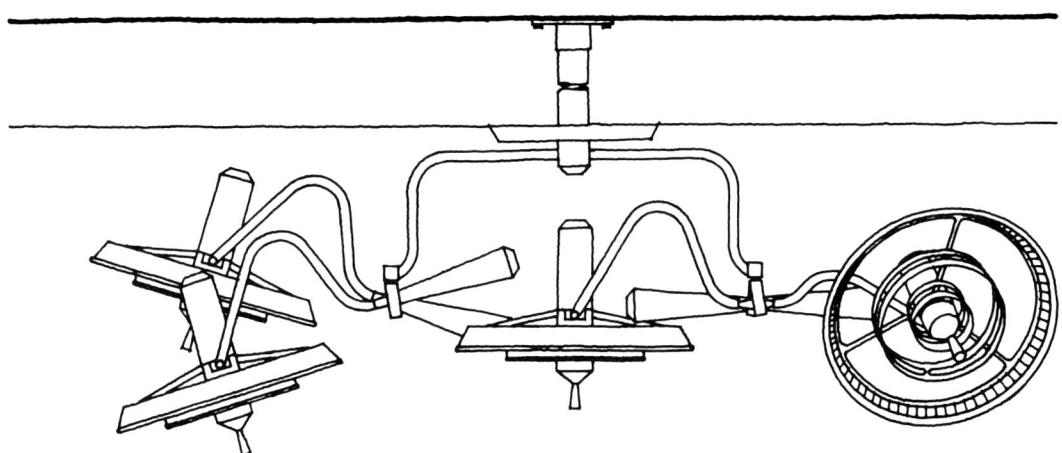

This Pilling operation lamp is designed to give shadow free illumination. It is adapted for the use in unidirectional flow units. There is a nine position intensity control. The light is positioned by using a handle or grasping the reflector ring rim.

a balance be struck between the shadows necessary to the surgeon for the judgement of contour and distance and the disturbing shadows

heat radiation be as small as possible *

the maximum temperature of outer surfaces of luminaires be less than 58°C to avoid injury to the hands of the surgeon or ancillary staff

the national electrical safety regulations be followed

a mirror for the anaesthesiologist to view the progress of the surgical performance be incorporated.

The ability to light secondary fields is an advantage. It would be sufficient to have an operation lamp with secondary light only in a few operation rooms in an operation department.

The operation lamp should with no part hang lower than 2.0 m above the floor.

When evaluating the quality and cost of surgical lights, the life time of the lamp has to be considered. A burn-out during an operation is annoying in a multisource light head and may be critical in a single-source head.

The lamp used in most surgical lights have about two hundred hours of rated life time, which in the case of the quartz-halogen lamps is extended to about two thousand hours.

For use in operation rooms with downward air displacement or vertical unidirectional air flow, less compact lamps have been constructed.

---

* In many cases the radiation from the operation lamp add about 1°C to the surgeon's index temperature.

Fiberoptic operation lamps

In fibreoptic operation lamps light is transmitted through an electrically powered fibreoptic bundle, which is a collection of thousands of coated optical glass fibres. Light enters at one end of each fibre and is transmitted by refraction evenly through its entire length. Infrared radiation is eliminated. Glare, shadowing, and diffusion through air is minimized. The light is uniform and maintains good colour contrast.

Fibreoptic instruments are used for illuminating of deep or small structures within body cavities without obstructing the vision of the surgeon.

The fibre optic light source may be in a self-contained floor-mounted unit or in an attachment to the overhead mounted regular surgical lamp. The floor-mounted fibreoptic lamps should be able to withstand a tilt of 20° and a lateral pressure of 11.3 kg without falling. They should remain where placed so as to be unobstrusive to the vision of the surgeon and his assistants[35].

The optical fibre may be incorporated in the instrument itself to bring the light to the very tip. Fibreoptics furthermore allow the possibility of oblique or retro-illumination even at a great depth in a surgical wound, which is a very valuable asset to microsurgery[36].

The fibre optics in surgery may cause some asepsis problems and the lights can be blanked out by blood splatters.

Fibreoptic luminaires are often called cold lights because the tube itself does not become hot. This is a misnomer for light itself produces heat. A fibreoptic light tip may be cool to the touch, yet a cigarette can be lit from it. Therefore fibreoptics can under some circumstances be dangerous to tissues[37].

General lighting in operation room

General lighting in operation room should attain a minimum of 400 lux[38]. In the US the much higher general illumination capability of 2,000 lux uniformly distributed throughout the room with provision for reducing this level has been recommended[39]

The surgeon alone can judge what are the visually most comfortable conditions for him, and when attention is generally to be concentrated. However, the surgeon should use his power of control regarding the needs of his assistants and the anaesthesiologist*.

34 Operationssalen. Spri project 7064. S7-1974-12-31. Stockholm 1975, p 48.

35 Beck William C and Heimburger Robert F: Illumination Hazard in the Operating Room. 1973, Archives of Surgery 107:560–562.

36 Rich W J: Microsurgery. in Recent advances in surgery. Number nine. ed by Selwyn Taylor. Churchill Livingstone. Edinburgh, London and New York 1977, p 199.

37 Beck William C: Operating Room Lighting. 1976, The Journal of Hospital Research 2:5–40.

38 see also Cockram Alan: The lighting of hospital buildings. 1976, Hospital Engineering 30:18:7–11.

39 see also Beck William C: Operating Room Lighting. 1976, The Journal of Hospital Research 2:5–40.

* E g during laser surgery the operation room lights are often extinguished to aid in determining beam size and location. The patient being operated with lights only on the wound area and the rest of the operation room being in darkness complicates the work of the anaesthesiologist considerably and hazardous situations may arise.

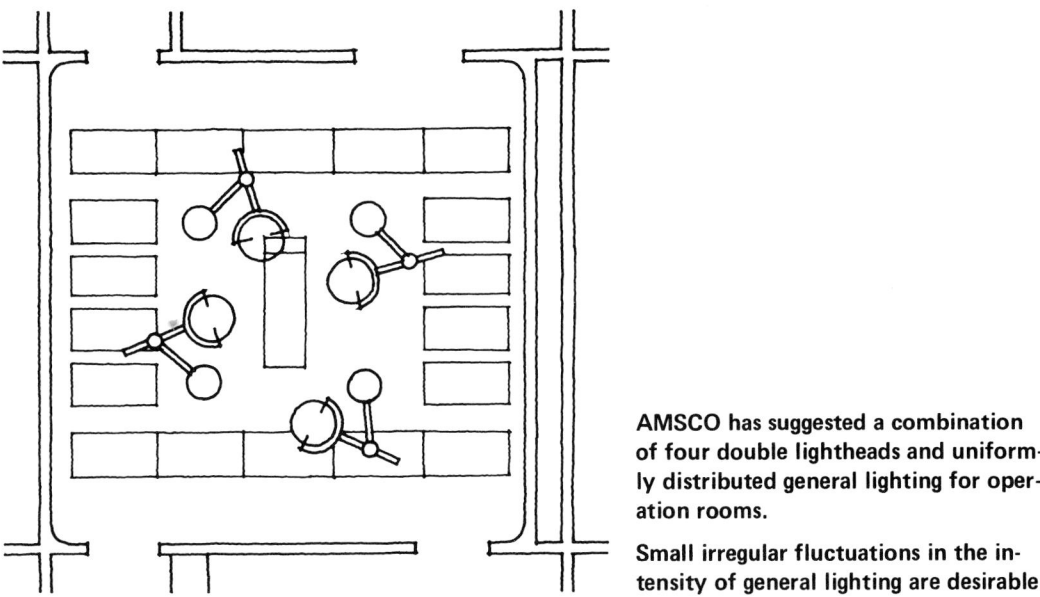

AMSCO has suggested a combination of four double lightheads and uniformly distributed general lighting for operation rooms.

Small irregular fluctuations in the intensity of general lighting are desirable.

lighting in scrub-up room

In order to avoid difficulties in visual adaptation when moving from the scrub-up room to the operation room, the intensity of general lighting in the scrub-up room should be about the same as that in the operation room.

A reasonable level of illumination at washbasins is 300 to 500 lux. In the US for scrub rooms the illumination level of 2,000 lux of the same Kelvin t° as members of the surgical team will encounter in the operation room, has been recommended[40].

lighting in post anaesthetic recovery room

Patients are disorientated and aware of bright lights during the awakening period[41]. Therefore light fittings must be placed where they will not disturb the patient.

40 Beck William C: Operating Room Lighting. 1976, The Journal of Hospital Research 2:5–40.

41 see also Cronin M, Redfern P A and Utting J E: Psychometry and postoperative complaints in surgical patients. 1973, British Journal of Anaesthesia 45:879.

General illumination must be ample, of correct colour and temperature. The anaesthesiologist has to rely on his assessment of the patient's colour even in the post-anaesthetic recovery room. A lighting intensity of about 300 lux is recommendable. Anaesthetic recovery room lighting should be indirect, if provided by tungsten filament lamps.

A mounted wall or ceiling source of higher intensity spot illumination — about 10,000 lux — must be available[42]. However, an operation lamp need not to be provided.

There should be provision for low level illumination for night use.

Lighting in ICTU

The level of illumination in the patient rooms has to be adjusted to the needs of the patients and to those of the staff who will be carrying out their various duties.

The levels must be sufficient for instrument reading, charting, and patient examination. The lighting must be sufficient for head-to-toe inspection. The illumination must not distort colour and complexion. Provision has to be made for varying levels of illumination, especially at the patient's bed. This could be accomplished with general and supplementary sources.

When considering optimal lighting, attention must be given to the reflectance value of walls, ceilings, and floor. The reflectance value is dependent upon their texture and colour. Some recommended reflectance values: ceilings 80 to 95 per cent, upper walls 40 to 60 per cent, lower walls 15 to 20 per cent, floors 15 to 30 per cent, furniture 25 to 40 per cent[43].

General illumination must be of adequate intensity — an intensity of 300 lux has been recommended —, of correct colour and temperature and not disturb the patient. It must not produce electrical noise in monitoring equipment.

The use of fluorescent lights in intensive care and treatment units is considered to be a mistake[44].

For some procedures in the ICTU extra lighting has to be readily available. For each isolation room, and for every two beds in the multibed area, two examination lamps are recommended.

---

42 see also Schowengerdt Carl G: The Recovery Room. in Monitoring in Anesthesia. ed by William H L Dornette. FA Davis Company. Philadelphia 1973, p 365.

43 Hanson John A, Lippert Stanley, Ronco Paul G: Development of Physical and Psychological Measurement Instruments. in Evaluation of Hospital Design. Tufts-New England Medical Center. Boston 1971, p 171

44 von der Mosel H A: Common mistakes in planning intensive care units. 1977, Hospital Engineering 31:5:11, 14–16.

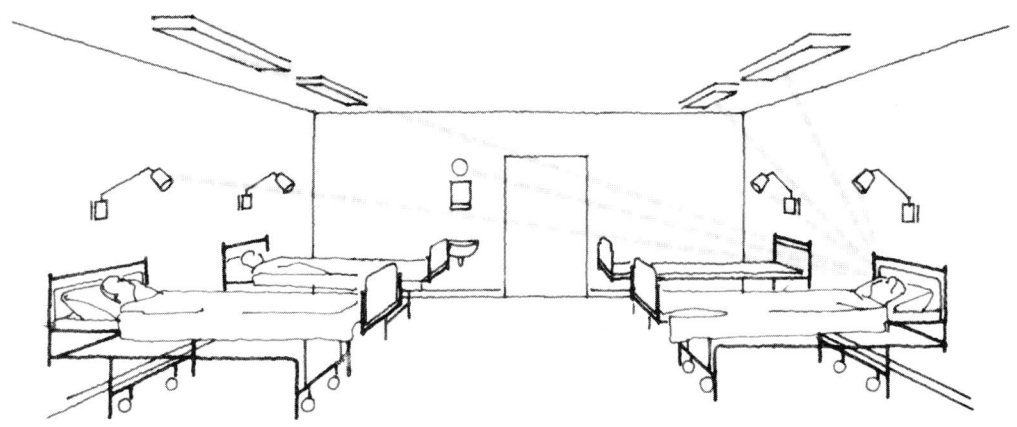

Illumination arrangements in a ward room must not disturb continuously the patient.

While the general room illumination is satisfactory for reading, most individuals when reading prefer that the surface of the article be highly illuminated compared to the remainder of the environment[45].

While an adjustable reading light on a retractable arm would in itself be a good solution, there is a possibility — although remote — for a microelectrocution syndrome. Two separate preaimed incandescent units are considered to be the best solution[46]. For on-off switch there should be a pull-string or pneumatic device.

Night lighting should be variable and to be controlled sectionwise by a dimmer. Nurses need a night light so they can safely enter a room without disturbing the patient with bright lights. The night light should be bright enough to allow the nurse to read a patient's wristband before administring medicine. A night light can also be a reassurance to the patient[47].

On the other hand, hallway lights and those from the other beds in the room can disturb the rest and sleep of the patient.

Lighting in ICTUs, particularly in coronary care units, must not produce electrical noise in monitoring equipment.

45 Goldstein J Richard and Parker Jr William T: The Design of the CCU Patient Room. Stencil. New York. December 1977, p 22.

46 Goldstein J Richard and Parker Jr William T: The Design of the CCU Patient Room. Stencil. New York. December 1977, p 22.

47 see also Dolson Jan, Hesla Loren, Krewson Carol, Parimucha Joe: Around the patient. 1976, Progressive Architecture 57:9:54–57.

In neonatal intensive care units the general lighting intensity of about 100 lux is usually adapted as well as the intensity of 500 lux at the incubators and 1,000 lux for some examinations[48].

Lighting in wards

Generally the elements of ICTU lighting are applicable in patient's rooms in regular wards.

At night the patient only requires a five lux light source, but the nurse will require at least 15 lux when she enters the room from a well-lit corridor.

A special dimmer switch near the door has been recommended for the night light source[49].

Lighting in emergency department

High visual requirements in emergency departments demand in some areas the lighting levels of 600 to 1,000 lux.

Uniform indirect lighting with the level of 400 lux could be recommended as the basic light level, supported by special examination lamps.

Lighting in examination and treatment rooms

The relationship between general examination and treatment room lighting and special area lighting varies according to the type of examination. The ratio between general lighting and special area lighting for examination of body cavities should theoretically be no greater than three to one[50].

General room lighting should come from several sources. Available light quantities should be about 750 lux with dimmer, supplementary luminaires for task lighting 2,000 to 10,000 lux. For orificial purposes the light quantity should be 1,000 lux at the target[51].

---

48 see also Dubois Olivier: Le centre de pathologie néonatale du centre hospitalier d'Arras. 1974, Techniques Hospitalières 30:1:51–60.

49 Pennacchia G: L'illuminazione delle stanze di degenza ospedaliera. 1977, Technica Ospedaliera 7:2:30–39.

50 Beck William C: Lighting considerations for examination rooms. 1971, Hospitals 45:July 1. Reprint.

51 ibid

Red indicating lights should be provided for drug cupboards, to give visual indication when the cupboard is not locked.

Lighting in X-ray room

In X-ray rooms lighting has to be indirect and not ceiling fixed, partly because the lying patient should not have to look up into a light source, partly because the ceiling has to be kept free to hang equipment.

As a general illumination level in a radiodiagnostic room 400 to 500 lux is recommended. In the processing rooms the illumination level ought to be 100 to 200 lux, in reporting rooms and offices 300 to 400 lux, and in record rooms 200 to 300 lux. These values should be applicable at 1 m above floor level.

Lighting in laboratories

When precision instruments are involved or colour have to be judged the illumination level should be about 1,000 lux and when regular instruments 500 to 600 lux. The reasonable level of illumination at work with microscopes is about 3,000 lux.

Lighting in laboratories must not cause reflectance, glare and shadows.

Tungsten lighting has been recommended for radioactive counting rooms[52].

Lighting in mortuaries

In the post-mortem room, lighting should ensure adequate illumination of post-mortem tables and dissecting benches. The lighting has to be satisfactory for colour identification. The lighting fittings should be designed to avoid glare. They should be easy to clean and maintain. Switches in potentially wet areas, as the post-mortem room and body store are, where walls and floors are hosed down, should be of the hose-proof type[53].

Lighting in the viewing room should receive special consideration. A subdued soft light is desirable for viewing, supplemented by separately switched normal lighting.

The reasonable illumination levels are: in the post-mortem room 300 lux, at the post-mortem tables and benches 1,500 to 2,000 lux, in the body store 200 lux.

---

52 see also Everett K and Hughes D: A Guide to Laboratory Design. Butterworths. London & Boston 1975, p 26.

53 Mortuary & post-mortem room. Hospital Building Note 20. Department of Health and Social Security. Welsh office 1970, p 8.

Lighting in offices

At the desk 300 lux is usually adequate for clerical work[54], although illumination levels over 600 lux have been considered[55]. However, the lower the level chosen, the less the heat gain to the room, the need for refrigeration, and the running cost.

Lighting in waiting and holding areas

In waiting and holding areas an illumination level of 150 lux[56] to 300 lux should be available. Indirect lighting ought to be given preference.

Lighting in rooms of social character

Approximately 20 per cent of the light in a room of social character should be in form of a general ambience and come from overhead[57].

To this base specific task lighting is added.

It has been argued for balanced lighting between the natural and the artificial, the direct and indirect. Fluorescent lighting may in many cases be inappropriate for a homelike setting[58].

Light output and dramatic effect may assume as great an importance as surface beauty.

Lighting in corridors

In corridors continuous lighting e g continuously mounted fluorescent tubes — in or on the ceiling adjacent to one of the walls — are used.

The reasonable levels of illumination are about 300 lux at daytime, 200 lux in the evening, and 25 to 40 lux at night.

There should be minimal glare from the fluorescent tubes when viewed by patients on beds or trollies.

The switch positions should be carefully selected.

54 Cockram Alan: The lighting of hospital buildings. 1976, Hospital Engineering 30:18:7–11.

55 see also Fearn R W: Planning for Open Plan. 1974, The Heating & Ventilating Engineer and journal of air conditioning 48:339–347.

56 Cockram Alan: The lighting of hospital buildings. 1976, Hospital Engineering 30:18:7–11.

57 Nuckolls James: Lighting for the future. 1974, Lighting Design and Application 4:11:14–19.

58 Leon Pastalan cited by Stephens Suzanne: Hidden barriers. 1978, Progressive Architecture 59:4:94–97.

Colour

Students of sensation and perception agree that vision predominates among the senses. The human factors literature shows that colour coding reduces search time and facilitates identification better than coding based on brightness, size, or geometrical shape[1].

As *Fernand Léger* has repeated in several of his essays, colour is not a luxury, but a human need like water or fire; it is a raw material indispensable to life[2].

Colour is a sensation, which creates an instant impact.

A human eye does not respond equally to all colours. The response is more to green, yellow, and orange than to red or blue[3]. The individual variations are considerable. One and the same colour evokes innumerable readings[4]. Communication of colour is seriously inhibited by the inability of man to describe in sufficient detail the visual attributes which precisely characterize the object[5].

Colour can delight and soothe, provoke and disturb. A very personal sensitivity to colour is active from the moment of birth.
Likes and dislikes regarding colours are strong.

It has been stated that the positive visual appearance of an environment where much time is spent may reduce absenteeism, rejection rates and increase productivity by 15 per cent[6].
Unpleasant colours can be a psychic burden to those who are particularly sensitive.

There are some popular beliefs concerning the psychological functions of different hues. Thus bright reds, oranges and yellows are believed to be attention-getting; white, light green, light blue would create spaciousness and red-orange, red, orange stimulation and excitement. Distraction prevention is achieved by soft, grayed colours; eye and bodily fatigue reduction by use of colour contrasts. Green, blue, violet are for tranquilization; blues and greens for coolness, and red-orange, red, orange, yellow for warmth[7]. Violet is the colour of highest tension. Many of the

1   T Christ cited by Bornstein Marc H: Chromatic vision in infancy. in Advances in child development and behavior. vol 12. ed by Hayne W Reese and Lewis P Lipsitt. Academic Press. New York, San Francisco, London 1978, p 168.

2   Hyman Timothy: After Léger. 1977, London Magazine 17:6:50–63.

3   Beck William C: Operating room lighting. 1976, The Journal of Hospital Research 46:2:5–40.

4   Albers Josef: Interaction of Color. Yale University Press. New Haven and London 1976, p 1.

5   Schreckendgust Jay, Reynolds Harold, Beck William C, Geffert John: Light for clinical purposes I. 1978, The Guthrie Bulletin 47:195–203.

6   O'Connor James C: Maintenance Painting and Color. 1973, Building Operating Management 20:8:26.

7   see also O'Connor James C: Maintenance Painting and Color. 1973, Building Operating Management 20:8:26.

colour studies have a limited value as the effects of hue have been examined in extremely artificial situations[8] and in many cases relevant experimental data could not be found.

When three experimental rooms which were decorated using either warm (yellow, orange, red), neutral (white), or cool (blue, green) hues were studied[9], it was found that the neutral room was felt like the cool room. Both were different from the warm room in the terms of smooth, like, and light. The neutral room was like the warm room and different from the cool room on the terms adequate, pleasant, and good. Most of the expected effects of room hue were not observed. Failure to find the expected significant differences may have resulted from the confounding of room hue with room design.

The choice of the colour is very strongly influenced by its adaptability both to daylight and artificial light. In order to use colour effectively it is necessary to recognize that colour deceives continually[10].

An interior has to last many years. Therefore the colour scheme should be timeless and unaffected by fashion[11].

Colour and decor in the hospital is a challenge[12].

Quite naturally different groups have arrived at different conclusions on suitable hospital colour schemes and their possible therapeutic effects. Research findings vary: Their significance is arguable. One researcher finds that blue reduces blood pressure; another reports that green, not blue, has that effect[13].

There is evidence that preferred colours may not be therapeutic colours. From same studies, for example, it might be assumed that blue would tranquilize agitated patients and red would stimulate the withdrawn. The reverse, however, has been shown to hold[14].

Reds, dark browns, deep purple and black should be avoided in hospitals altogether[15] The colour red in paint and drapes of a patient's room is said to retard rather than speed up the getting well[16].

8 Pedersen Darhl M, Johnson Michael, and West Jr John H: Effects of room hue on ratings of self, other, and environment. 1978, Perceptual and Motor Skills 46:403–410.

9 ibid

10 Albers Josef: Interaction of Color. Yale University Press. New Haven and London 1976, p 1.

11 see also Bruno Mathsson, 1977, Contract 1:1:3–14.

12 see also Beck William C: Color Problems in Hospitals. 1976, The Guthrie Bulletin 46:1:39–48.

13 Whitehead Clay, Ellison Gail, Kerpen Stephen and Marshall David: The Aging Psychiatric Hospital: An Approach to Humanistic Redesign. 1976, Hospital & Community Psychiatry 27:781–788.

14 ibid

15 see also Janiesch H: Farbe im Krankenhaus. 1973, Der Krankenhausarzt 46:238–240, 242.

16 Kraegel Janet M, Mousseau Virginia Schmidt, Goldsmidt Charles, Arora Rajeev: Patient Care Systems. J B Lippincott Company. Philadelphia, Toronto 1974, p 87.

Orange, yellow, and light green colours attract the attention of people with limited visual abilities. The reds and violets are for them difficult to distinguish[17].

Infants can see, process, remember, and act on chromatic information in their environment. Much of the young infant's behaviour parallels mature behaviour and conforms with expectancies of a trichromatic model of colour vision. The young child is early adapted to process and use the chromatic information in his environment in reasonably sophisticated ways. His first knowledge of the world grows out of the distribution of his visual attention, and the child differentiates and responds to different features in his world according to their colour, organizes his world by colour, just as he may remember different aspects of it on the basis of their colour[*].

Early researchers held the view that no colour preference is discernible before the fourth year of life. Later studies indicate that among the young infants blue and red are most preferred. Also kindergartners have ranked blue and red as more pleasant than yellow and green. 7-, 9-, and 11-year-olds have preferred red to blue to green.

When aged people is involved, two kinds of difficulties may arise. The separation between reds and greens may become visually unstable and the distinction between related colours e g blue and green may be lost[18]. The importance of strong colours in overcoming failing visual perception has to be emphasized despite the objections of the staff[19].

Just as infants appear to follow patterns rather than colour, the design of the wallpaper or curtains appears to be of significance to the aged or senile[20].

The choice of colour should make it easier for the cleaners to discover dirt and substances capable of transmitting infections.

Frequently white is used in a hospital widely as this colour carries the message of cleanliness. However, ophthalmologists have warned about interiors with large areas of bright white, which may cause an effect similar to snow blindness.

In floor colours brown tending towards red and other brown tinges may give a feeling of safety and peacefulness. A dark green tinge may lead to the association of moss or a soft lawn. Light and vague colours should not be used. They may be associated with slipping and falling and produce a feeling of insecurity.

---

17 Braf Per-Gunnar: Miljöplanering och nedsatt syn. 1974, Rapport. Specialnummer p 13.

[*] Bornstein Marc H: Cromatic vision in infancy. in Advances in Child Development and Behaviour. vol 12. ed by Hayne W Reese and Lewis P Lipsitt. Academic Press. New York, San Francisco, London 1978 p 117–170.

18 see also Welter Rudolf: Sinneswahrnehmungen von alten Menschen. 1975, Bauen + Wohnen 29:308–310.

19 see also What are concerned architects doing about the aging's problems? 1977, Architectural Record 161:5:135.

20 Beck William C: Color Problems in Hospitals. 1976, The Guthrie Bulletin 46:39–48.

Colour in surgical department

Very little factual information is available as very little scientific research has been carried out on the use of colour in operation units.

There is a risk of vision disability when looking into a wound which is in strong contrast with the towels and drapes surrounding it. The colour of the drapes should be somewhere between that of the skin and the incision or wound so that the retina need for extra adjustments when the eye moves between the drape and the wound, is reduced. Also the strict application of Schönfelder's law to the problem of choice of the colour of surgical drapes and sponges leads to the choice of colour of raw beefsteak[21].

The medical staff has also to observe the colour of the patient's skin, as any change from the normal could indicate impending surgical shock, respiratory obstruction, or sudden haemorrhage.

The tones of operation room wall and ceiling colours have to be determined in relation to operation room lighting intensities. With high levels of illumination and luminous and warm colours such as yellow, orange, and pink, the body tends to increase its activation in general. With softer surroundings, lower brightness and cooler hues such as grey, blue, green and turquoise there is less distraction, and good inward orientation is furthered[22].

William Beck[23] has suggested that instead of the surgeon's green* on the operation room walls beige, coral, taupe, peach, pearl gray, terra cotta, avocado, aqua, rose, saphire blue, or pale gold would be suitable. In the UK, generally, pale blue, grey and green have been found to be the most suitable[24].

Alan Cockram[25] has recommended to avoid blues and yellows. A light grey colour for the operation room floor has been recommended[26].

The use of patterns on the walls may provide visual respose for the strenuous visual task.

---

21 Beck William C: Color Problems in Hospitals. 1976, The Guthrie Bulletin 46:39–48.

22 see also Birren Faber: Color it color. 1967, Progressive Architecture 48:129–133.

23 Beck William C: Operating Room Lighting. 1976, The Journal of Hospital Research 2:5–40.

* The surgical unit walls have been to a great extent green since 1914 when Harry Sherman in California suggested the true of the spinach leaf as the complementary colour to the red of blood tissues.

24 see also Brigden Raymond J: Operating Theatre Technique. Churchill Livingstone. Edinburgh and London 1974, p 9.

25 Cockram Alan: The lighting of hospital buildings. 1976, Hospital Engineering 30:18:7–11.

26 Ljus, färg & funktion. ed by Perry Marthin. LTs förlag. Stockholm 1976, p 102.

In the colour scheme of the *scrub-up room* there have been some trends towards the use of yellowish or red shades.

The colour of the *anaesthetic rooms* ought to be chosen so that the reflections on the patient's face would not obstruct the anaesthesiologist's judgement of the patient's condition. The colour scheme in the anaesthetic room may be the same as that for the operation room, possibly softer and warmer.

The observation of the patient's colour is frequently of importance also in the *post-anaesthetic recovery unit* and in the *newborn suite.* Patient care areas of these units should have white or slightly off-white walls and ceilings. Use of any other colour will distort true skin tones through reflection of light and possibly will delay early detection of some of the irregularities.

olour in other hospital areas

For *intensive treatment area* cool pure gray, and warm grayed terra-cotta walls have been used[27]. Blues and greens should be avoided in the intensive care rooms[28]. As about 50 per cent of the light reflects from the walls the green and blue colours may make the patients to appear cyanotic.

Blue or blue-green shades should be used in *waiting* and *holding* areas where they are calming.

When choosing the colours in the *laboratories,* there are in principle no restrictions[29].

27 Chaney Patricia S: A behavioral approach to hospital decor can reduce negative responses to hospitalization and thus fasten patients' recoveries. 1973, Hospitals 47:11:61–66.

28 Lawin P and Opderbecke H W: Die Organisation der Intensivmedizin in Praxis der Intensivbehandlung. Georg Thieme Verlag. Stuttgart 1975, p 1–28.

29 see also de bouwkundige opzet van het laboratorium voor klinische chemie. National Ziekenhuisinstituut. Utrecht 1975, p 99.

Signposting, identification signs

Signposting is a systematic arrangement of visual signals to help the individual to reach a particular destination.

The size of the letters, words, and lines has to be chosen for optimal readability. Choice of a type style should take into account legibility and compatibility with the pictographs and the environment.

The signposting contents must be clear and consistent. Consistency means that the text and the pictograph must be identical from the starting point to destination to make it easier for some deaf people who have difficulties talking and being understood.

General signs lettered in blue and underlined with a brown stripe have helped persons with vision problems to read each line[1]. Some investigators recommend that the characters should be white, set against a dark background[2].

One of the most important aspects of good signing is siting. The closer to one's natural line of vision, the better. Exceeding a 10° angle from this line should be avoided[3]

Uniform terminology for signposting ought to be established at least nationwise. Also colours of signs and other markings ought to be determined by national standards associations.

As the ability to remember picture images usually surpasses the ability to retain word messages, pictographs can transcend the language and education barriers. It is important that the picture image always be dark on a light symbol field.

When planning a signposting system, the character of the exterior and interior of the particular health care facility should be considered. To ensure integration of the graphic elements with other architectural features, lighting and colour schemes, the signposting system ought to be developed already at the preliminary design stage.

Although visual acuity diminishes with age, the sight elderly people retain is almost always adequate for the more limited range of activities that characterizes their time of life. However, about 30 per cent of the elderly sustain a gradual loss of central vision while retaining peripheral vision. They will continue to see well enough to move around and to take care of themselves, but their ability to read, to write, to

1   Bright, bold sign program directs people through hospital. 1975, Hospitals 49:3:25.

2   Harkness Sarah P and Groom Jr James N: Building without barriers for the disabled. Whitney Library of Design. New York 1976, p 17.

3   Symbol Signs. National Technical Information Service. Springfield 1974.

  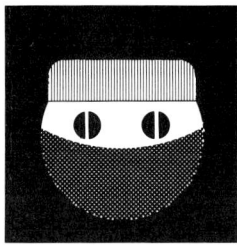 

Pictographs developed by Hänseroth, Federal Republic of Germany.

 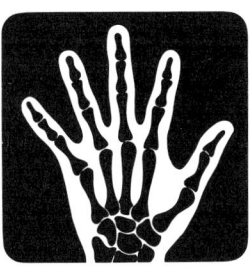  

Pictographs of the Mexican Social Security Organization.

  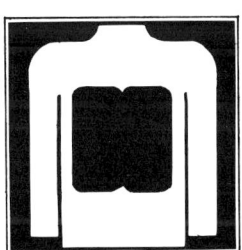 

Pictographs for the health facilities of the City of New York designed by E Christopher Klumb, New York.

enjoy art and to watch television or a movie may be severely impaired[4]. Eye diseases connected with aging will not be entirely resolved in the next 20 to 25 years[5].

Diagrams and maps put up to help people find their way around often fail to help because of too small lettering or surface glare[6].

4   Kornzweig Abraham L: Visual Loss in the Elderly. 1977, Hospital Practice 12:7:51–59.

5   Vodovosov A M: Prognosis for Ophthalmology: Good. 1977, Annals of ophthalmology 9:827–828.

6   Jones Michael A and Catlin John H: Design for access. 1978, Progressive Architecture 59:4:65–71.

When patients with limited or blurred vision are involved, intense colours, which can be perceived easily, should be used to indicate doors to stairways, public facilities, elevators, and emergency exits. The doors should be labelled in large typography for easier identification.

In some US institutions all identification signs have recessed white letters on a black background with Braille beneath. For the 85 per cent of the blind who do not read Braille and for the partially sighted, standards in the US require that identification signs for the general public have letters and numbers of contrasting colours that are raised or recessed. The American Foundation for the Blind recommends that letters and numbers be 15 cm high and 9 cm wide[7].

For identification of hospital rooms, rest rooms, offices, and so on, identification plaques with raised or recessed letters or numerals should be used[8]. They should be mounted about 1.5 m on the handle side of the door opening.

Coloured lines on the floor to direct the people to a hospital destination are not very effective in a crowded corridor.

Signs for accident prevention, safety colour codes

Red danger signs with white and black lettering may be used only where immediate hazard exists. Caution signs are required as warning of potential danger. They are yellow with black letters.

Radiation warning signs are yellow with magenta lettering and standard symbols.

Safety signs must be safe — i e not stick out or cause an obstruction.

Safety colour codes are used for marking caution and physical hazards: *red* identifies fire protection equipment, danger and STOP, *green* safety and first aid equipment, *purple* caution of radiation, *yellow* caution for physical hazards, *orange* dangerous parts of machinery, *blue* caution limited to starting and using equipment, such as lifts under repair.

---

7   Rees Jr Frank W and Burch Emily: Barrier-free design reflects spirit of the law. 1978, Hospitals 52:4:121–125.

8   Rees Jr Frank W and Burch Emily: Barrier-free design reflects spirit of the law. 1978, Hospitals 52:4:121–125.

Architecture is an event itself. It can exist quite independently. It may have no need either of sculpture or of painting.

Art is only one of the numerous parts composing culture as does music, dance, or chess to the true devotee. To understand a work of art fully requires much more ancillary knowledge than to understand a work of literature, music, science, or technology. Psychologists and scientists exploring the phenomena of light and colour have revealed layers of visual complexity, largely unknown to even the cultivated connoisseur[1].

In Anglo-American culture, the visual arts occupy a relatively minor and isolated position[2]. It may be the case even in some other cultures. The societies are for the most part visually illiterate[3]. It has been stressed that the visual memory is very poor in comparison with the auditory memory[4].

The hospital could provide an environment for people to come to some terms with art at a time when many of their connections with the outside world have been severed[5]. This task should, as in museums, not be regarded as a primarily educational function, but as a possibility of providing visual delight. However, the education of the spectator's eye must be taken into consideration. E g the history of abstract art has been punctuated not only by an increasing intellectual acceptance of extreme solutions but also by an increasing optical acceptance[6].

A lot of art in hospital is for seeing while moving.

Visual pollution of any kind must be avoided in hospitals as well as the cosmetic approach*.

Usually the decorated hospital areas have been in and outside of the main entrance, regular nursing units and cultural and worship areas. To these children wards, paediatric out-patient areas, nursing units for infectious diseases and some circulation areas have been added.

---

1   Lee Sherman E: Art museums and education. 1977, Art International 21:1:48–51.

2   ibid

3   ibid

4   Albers Josef: Interaction of Color. Yale University Press. New Haven and London 1976, p 3.

5   see also Senior Peter: The Painter and the Patient. 1976, Health and Social Service Journal 86:1258–1259.

6   Lippard Lucy R: Changing. E P Dutton. New York 1971, p 135.

*   Adam Joseph writes: Many of London's gloomy Victorian hospitals are being revitailised by teams of young artists working through the Job Creation Scheme.
    Healthy splashes of colour, giant murals and big blazing panels are going up on long blank corridors and grey wards and walls. The project is inspired by Shape, the Covent Garden arts organisation which is working with local health authorities to raise the morale of patients waiting for medical attention in drab surroundings (Evening Standard, September 4, 1978).

The hospital areas demanding least attention from the art point of view, are technical areas, industrial areas, administration and out-patient areas[7].

Art in hospitals is part of a non-regular milieu. The conditions for it are not yet firm established. A fact which eases amateurish ideas — they may even be official or sem official — to gain superiority in determining the character of art for hospitals.

An imaginative application of art can contribute greatly to the attractiveness of the hospitals, but it should not turn hospitals to some kind of prestige loaded mini-museums.

To create an artistic hospital milieu does not mean to glue some niceties on the walls towards the end of the construction period, but to have a clear aim for interio quality during the whole planning and construction procedure and to secure the solidarity of all involved towards that aim[8].

In the collaboration of the major arts and architecture, dignity is not an empty claim. If a wall is spoilt, if it is soiled, if the clear, sane language of the architecture is ruined by the introduction of inappropriate painting or sculpture, if the artist is unable to enter into its spirit or goes against its spirits, it is like so many crimes of deceit[9].

The same skill, flair and mental processes that go into making of buildings, also go into making of paintings and sculpture.

In their attempt to be sure that what they are doing is satisfactory, architects make models, perspectives and drawings of parts of the building, interiors and details. In order to gain something from these drawings they must be in a total involvement.

It is unlikely that an outsider will be equally involved. The artists would agree that mostly they would prefer the space to be there, built, before they started work[10].

The artist has to know for whom, what and for which spaces he has to create.

Art placed in the hospital milieu, particularly in its focal points, should have the same qualities as art placed in a civic site. It must be decorative, commanding, easy to take in at a glance, but difficult, stimulating, various enough in receiving light change to provoke continued pleasure, engagement, and surprise.

7 Leucht M, Pahle E, Pietrass M and Zulich Ch: Untersuchungen über Möglichkeiten der Gestaltung von Bauten des Gesundheitswesens. in Das stationäre und ambulante Gesundheitswesen. vol 9. VEB Verlag Volk und Gesundheit. Berlln 1973, p 144–151.

8 see also Rosén Nils Inge: Något om sjukhusmiljö. Svenska Sjukhusföreningens Årsbok 1963. Mejels Bokindustri. Halmstad 1964, p 65.

9 Le Corbusier: The quarrel with realism. in Circle. ed by J L Martin, Ben Nicholson, N Gabo. Faber and Faber Limited. London 1937. Reprint 1971, p 67–74.

10 see also Gardiner Stephen: The Merger. 1967, London Magazine 7:9:84–89.

One of the most profound qualities of sculpture is scale — it can only be perceived intuitively because it is entirely a quality of thought and vision[11].

To become some kind of landmark rather than an indistinguishable element of the hospital collage, a sculpture must retain its autonomy, involve its environment enough to augment but not be absorbed by it[12].

The use of some current distinct art trend should not mark over-clearly the birth-time of a hospital. Neither should the art displayed in various areas of hospitals be purchased only because some artists deserve economic support.

Léger has suggested that for large surfaces, *free colour,* without any figurative reference was the most appropriate language. He seems to have intended a kind of environmental background art[13].

A convincing public art probably demands societal emotions, which also require figures. Something scenic, something showing actions or something suggesting a sense of moving forward with hope is frequently preferred[14].

Margaret Henderson[15] has maintained that so far as known observations went in the UK, sick children rarely, if ever, notice the kind of decor — woodland scenes with animals and traditional characters — which adults image appeals to them. Attempts should also be made to avoid unnecessary strangeness. Reassuring decor more probably is what looks a little like home or school.

Some experiments indicate that infants prefer patterns to colours, and complex patterns like bull's eye and black-and-white checkerboards to simple forms like triangles and squares[16]. Even the youngest infants prefer patterns over colour. An orderly decor with a variety of colours is positively associated with the infant development[17].

Flowers, plants and shrubs provide a pleasant background. Advice about the types of plants and shrubs and their survival in windowless surroundings has been accumulated in the nuclear submarine fleet[18].

11 Hepworth Barbara: Sculpture. in Circle. ed by J L Martin, Ben Nicholson, N Gabo. Faber and Faber Limited. London 1937. Reprint 1971, p 113.

12 Lippard Lucy R: Changing. E P Dutton. New York 1971, p 229.

13 Hyman Timothy: After Léger. 1977, London Magazine 17:6:50-63.

14 see also Paralyzed V A patients create a mural for their dayroom. 1977, Hospitals 51:69-71.

15 personal communication: 1968, Barbara M Duncum, London.

16 Frantz Robert L: The Origin of Form Perception. 1961, Scientific American 204:66-72.

17 see also McVicker Hunt J: Environmental programming to foster competence and prevent mental retardation in infancy. in Environments as therapy for brain dysfunction. ed by Roger N Walsh and William T Greenough. Plenum Press. New York and London 1976, p 232.

18 Innes G S: Design of the therapy department with the future in mind. in The Planning of Radiotherapy Departments. ed by T J Deeley. British Journal of Radiology. Special Report 12. London 1976, p 124.

Sounds

Noise

Hospitals are traditionally supposed to be quiet as libraries. In the last quarter of this century the situation has changed considerably, and hospital noise has become a widely recognized problem.

Much work in a hospital, particularly in a surgical department, depends on the ease of communication. Informative sounds, also from monitoring equipment, alarm signals and the public address system should be clearly audible.

Noise is most disturbing also in two other hospital situations: for the use of audio equipment and for confidential conversation.

Noise is meaningless sound. As the world becomes noisier, it becomes less meaningful[1]. In the form of novel, unexpected and unwanted sounds, noise demands attention, which usually involves the abandonment of a train of thought[2]. Specific noises may evoke fears. However, many reactions are highly individual.

Most likely the hospital staff is in great need of noise control information: much noise arises from lack of consideration of the patient's comfort[3]. Many of the annoying sounds in the patient areas could be eliminated if the employees and visitors would observe the rules of common courtesy: e.e. walking and talking more quietly[4]

Within the hospital, different materials may be used in partition walls to achieve the degree of sound insulation required in any particular department.

Equipment should be of rubber or plastic where ever possible[5].

Sensitivity to noise

The community at large can be broadly divided in two thirds of extreme and one third of average sensitiveness to noise[6]. The sources of external sudden noise and

1   Brett Lionel: Architecture in a Crowded World. Schocken Books. New York 1972, p 115.

2   see also Wyon D P: Noise in Dwellings. 1974, Build International 7:1–15.

3   see also Turner Alvis G, King Charles H and Graddock John G: Measuring and Reducing Noise. 1975, Hospitals 49:15:85.

4   see also Halton Susan and Williams Sylvia: Quiet Zone — The Hospital. 1974, The Guthrie Bulletin 43:114–124.

5   see also Bridges J F: Noise control. 1977, Hospital Development 5:2:29–31.

6   Tarnopolsky A and McLean E K: Noise and Psychosomatic Hazard. in Modern Trends in Psychosomatic Medicine 3. ed by Oscar Hill. Butterworths. London and Boston 1976, p 93.

Just audible	10	rustle of leaves
	15	low voiced conversation
	20	isolation room
	24	empty Royal Festival Hall, London
	25	patient room by night
Very quiet	30	day room in a ward unit
		bed room in apartments
		quiet garden
Generally by the sick accepted noise levels	40	public library
		quiet streets
	45	general areas in a hospital
Quiet	50	warehouses
		restaurants
		typing
		light traffic at 31 m
Generally by the well accepted noise levels	55	business office
	57	bus in city traffic, Tokyo
	60	air-conditioning unit at 6 m
	64	highway-auto traffic at 25 m
	65	normal conversation at 1 m
	70	TV-audio
	75	chamber orchestra
		bus in city traffic, Hongkong
Moderately loud	77	passenger car, 105 km/hr at 8 m
	78	clothes washer
	80	garbage disposal
Very loud	85	crying babies
		symphony orchestra
	88	propeller aircraft flyover at 305 m
Noise level with risk of serious physiologic and physic incidences	90	motorcycles at 8 m
	98	farm tractor
	103	jet flyover at 305 m
	114	rock-n-roll band
	122	youth group disco
Physical pain	130	
	135	jet planes
Noise level with dangerous traumatic incidences	140	test room for jet plane engines
The skin burns	150	
Prolonged exposure would kill	190	
	200	Apollo rocket on take-off

Range of noises in decibels. One decibel is equal to a sound pressure of 0.0002 dyne per cm^2. A dyne is the force which, if exerted for one second, will move a gram one centimeter.

irritation include motor vehicle traffic, particularly motorcycles, lorries, and aircraft, and building construction. The definition external noise embraces also noise sources within the building such as lifts, water and drain pipes, ventilation ducts and fans; pumps, motors and other mechanical installations serving the building.

Complaints can be anticipated when the intruding noise exceeds the usual level by 5 dB. Vigorous reactions may be expected when the usual level is exceeded by 20 dB[7].

When the noise measured in dB is increased from 0 to 20 dB, the true increase of noise is 10 times, to 40 dB 100 times, to 60 dB 1,000 times, to 80 dB 10,000 times and to 100 dB 100,000 times.

Sensitivity to noise increases with age[8]: between 16 and 29 years only 15 per cent of persons are sensitive; in the over 60 years old group this percentage has increased to 34. It would also appear that the patients' illnesses lessen their tolerance of noise[9].

The noise level at which waking from sleep occurs is strongly dependent upon health and age, fatigue and the nature of the noise itself. Even if waking does not occur, noise disturbance can cause a reduction in the depth of sleep and hence a reduction in the rest achieved[10].

Although research trying to define the exact pathological role of noise is still in an early stage, some facts are known. E g it is not possible to get used to disturbing background noises, which always influence the bloodpressure factors.

There are experimental works investigating bodily effects of noise other than deafness in man. Acoustic stimulus has been found to produce alterations of heart rate significantly different from variation under non-stimulus conditions. Properties of this cardio-vascular response are not yet well understood[11].

Noise of 90 dB and over clearly has a variety of adverse effects in addition to the damage it causes in the auditory system[12].

Noise at even relatively low levels causes the tiny peripheral blood vessels in fingers, toes and abdominal organs to constrict and cut down the supply of blood. With less

7   McCord Dickman Donna: Noise and Its Effect on Human. Health and Welfare. 1977, Ear, Nose & Throat Journal 56:36–46.

8   Klosterkötter W and Gono F: Quellen und gesundheitliche Wirkung des Lärms. 1971, Zentralblatt für Bakteriologie, Parasitenkunde, Infektionskrankenheiten und Hygiene 155:303.

9   Halton Susan and Williams Sylvia: Quiet Zone — The Hospital. 1974, The Guthrie Bulletin 43:114–124.

10 see also Wyon D P: Noise in Dwellings. 1974, Build International 7:1–15.

11 Gerber Sanford E, Mulac Anthony and Lamb M Elisa: The Cardiovascular Response to Acoustic Stimuli. 1977, Audiology 16:1–10.

12 Hartly L R: Deafness, Annoyance and Stress. 1976, The New Zealand Medical Journal 83:200–203.

blood in the vessels to pump, the heart reacts involuntarily by reducing its strokes. Experiments carried out at Pavia, Italy[13], show that three seconds after noise of 89 dBs starts, arterioles contract and cut the blood within them by half. When the noise stops, it takes these blood vessels five minutes to recover but they stay constricted as long as the noise continues, whether the subject is awake or sleeping.

The blood vessels on the retina and in the brain show the opposite — they dilate. There is the danger that brain vessels could overdilate and cause headache and migraine. Headache caused by eyestrain through noise can occur.

Noise and infants

It has been required to keep the noise in the delivery room to a minimum while the baby is being born*.

Regardless of any fundamental differences between the effects of noise on children and adults, an important problem could be the sound levels of incubators, intensive care rooms, and oxygen tents.

The infants exposed to high** sound levels of incubators are usually premature, on drugs, and in very poor health. The exposures are continuous and may last several weeks without rest periods. These exposures are well recognized as a potential hazard to the neonate, who may be susceptible to noise-induced physiologic and pathologic alterations[14].

Concern with noise-induced permanent hearing loss in children is not an academic issue[15].

Noise in operation room

In operation rooms where faces are masked any disturbance to conversation may be trying. The deleterious effects of noise may infringe on the verbal exchange of information. Those at a distance from the surgeon may have difficulties in understanding orders. The staff speaks through masks. Voices are muffled and no lip-reading is possible.

The process of anaesthesia may be infringed and psychological disturbances caused.

13 Connell John: The Biological Effects of Noise. 1973, Health and Social Service Journal 83:1249.

* see also Oliver Charlotte M, Oliver George M: Gentle Birth. 1978, JOGN Nursing 7:5:35–40.

** about 60 to 75 dB

14 Shenai Jayant P: Sound levels for neonates in transit. 1977, The Journal of Pediatrics 90:811–812.

15 see also Mills John H: Noise and children: A review of literature. 1975, The Journal of the Acoustical Society of America 58:767–779.

OPERATION ROOM NOISES IN A SCALE DECIBELS[1]

various suction tubes	55
positioning instrument table	60
surgeon's conversation at patient's ear	66–72
walking nurse's orthopaedic heels	68
opening of paper bag	70
crushing of paper garbage	70
suction cleaning of endotracheal tube	73
dropping surgical instruments into bowl	75
crushing of glove package	75
rolling anaesthesiologist's chair	75
adjusting floor platform	75–80
continuos suction bottle	75–80
suction of trachea of patient	78
screwing on aseptic light handle	78
piling surgical instruments	80
sliding bottle on steel shelf	80
taking off surgical gloves	82
placing platform on floor	85
opening package of surgical gloves	86

1   after Shapiro Richard A and Berland Theodore: Noise in the operating room. 1972, The New England Journal of Medicine 287:1236–1238.

Measurements were made with a General Radio 1565–A Sound Level Meter (Serial No. 3109) midway between the surgeon's ear and the patient's ear.

The talk of those in the operation room, including the surgeons, anaesthesiologists, nurses, and assistants, is ever present[16]. Much of their voice communication is, of course, necessary and related directly to the procedures underway. However, it could be readily noted that the conversation frequently slips off the track and involves other subject matter, such as interpersonal relations, current ballgame scores, and even personal aspects of the patient[17].

Much monitoring by the anaesthesiologists is auditory monitoring. In the first place his basic equipment is gas machines, where high-frequency sounds form part of the patient's breathing cycle. Electronic motors use audible signals as well, and it is remarkable how acutely the ear can be attuned to changes in rate, whilst freeing the eyes for other tasks of surveillance. High-frequency noise can also be an important pollutant in the operation room when it interferes with surveillance of equipment[18].

16 Shapiro Richard A and Berland Theodore: Noise in the operating room. 1972, The New England Journal of Medicine 287:1236–1238.

see also Bunker J P: The Anaesthesiologist and the Surgeon. Little, Brown and Company. Boston 1972, p 143.

17 Shapiro Richard A and Berland Theodore: Noise in the operating room. 1972, The New England Journal of Medicine 287:1236–1238.

18 also Foster P A: Planning engineering services from the anaesthetist's point of view. Second Southern African Hospital Symposium. Pretoria. November 1977.

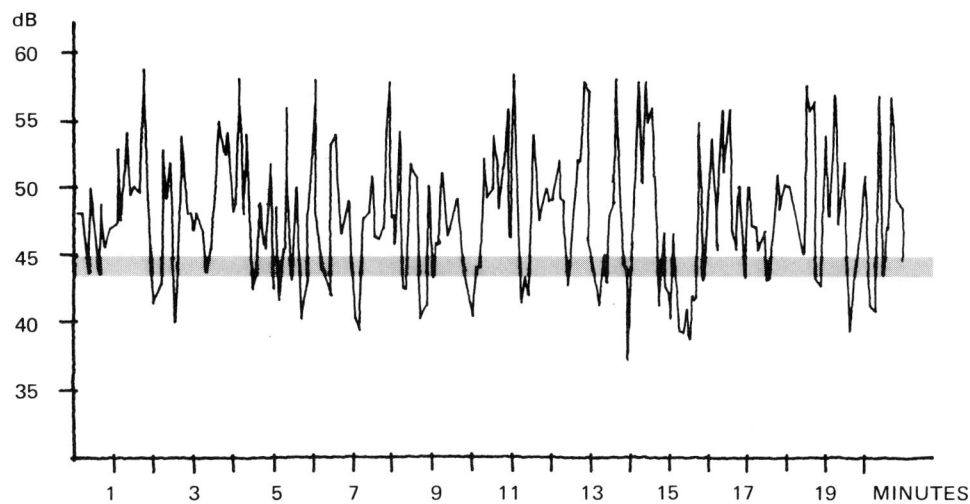

Noise levels throughout an eye operation at a Halle hospital, GDR as found by G Schuschke and L Riedel (Lärmbekämpfung als Krankenhaushygienische Leistungs- und Erziehungsaufgabe. in Das stationäre und ambulante Gesundheitswesen. vol 25. VEB Volk und Gesundheit. Berlin 1976, p 39) and the generally accepted noise level.

Background noise including compressors and suction pumps has a very pronounced effect. Even a background noise level as low as 30 dB A produces a significantly lower speech intelligibility than one of about 20 dB A[19].

Psychological disturbances of sudden noise are even more trying for operation room staff. There are indications, that tasks which require unremitting attention or which place extreme mental demands on the person involved, may be vulnerable to the degrading effects of noise[20]. Working in a quiet environment, the surgeon will suffer less fatigue and can operate with greater accuracy.

Principal internal operation room sources of sudden noise are rubber gloves, paper, objects wheeled across the floor, various hard instruments and implements of metal and glass striking one another, high-pitched compressed-air sounds, sluicing of water and slamming of doors.

The noise in the operation room may exceed that of a high-way. More frequently it approximates that of a ward kitchen, a food blender in operation, a train, or a

19 Kihlman Tor and Nordlund Lars: Taluppfattbarhet i hörsalar. Statens institut för byggnadsforskning. Rapport R 61:1973. Stockholm 1973, p 35.

20 Carpenter A: Effects of Noise on Performance and Productivity. in Control of Noise. Symposium No 12. Her Majesty's Stationary Office. London 1962, p 297–310.

lorry. The noise level in German operation rooms has been found to be about 50 dB A[21], but in the USA operation rooms as high as 90 dB A, which is maximum permissible noise exposure for eight hours according to the United States of America Federal Occupational Safety and Health Act[22]. In Sweden it has been recommended to have a lower noise level than 45 dB A in the operation room[23].

In the anaesthetic rooms as well as in the labour and delivery rooms the noise levels should be below 35 dB A[24].

Noise and newly operated patients

A special sensitivity to noise and need for protection from it is found in newly operated persons whose autonomic nervous system is in disorder[25]. One of the patient's greatest irritations in the recovery area is the laughter and other noises of the staff.

The noise level of 57.2 dB has been recorded as an average in the recovery room[26]. Periods of increased activity, the presence of large numbers of staff, overcrowding of patients, and crying, groaning, and telephone signals produce noise levels of 60 to 70 dB, and occasionally even more than 80 dB[27]. The lowest noise levels recorded were between 40 and 50 dB[28].

The patient's feeling of pain is increased when noise levels are high. Noise is an increased irritant. More pain-killing drugs would be given when noise levels were high than when they were low. Semi-conscious recovery room patients can mis-interpret the quality, character, and meaning of some noises.

In recovery rooms sound absorbent ceiling materials and wall finishes with a reflection factor of about 50 per cent should be used.

21 Sälzer Elmar: Schallschutz im Krankenhaus. 1977, Das Krankenhaus 69 365–370.

22 Shapiro Richard A and Berland Theodore: Noise in the operating room. 1972, The New England Journal of Medicine 287:1236–1238.

23 Akustik i sjukvårdsbyggnader. Spri råd 5.24. Stockholm. 1976, p 44.

24 Akustik i sjukvårdsbyggnader. Spri råd 5.24. Stockholm. 1976, p 44.

25 see also Klosterkötter W and Gono F: Quellen und Gesundheitliche Wirkung des Lärms. 1971, Zentralblatt für Bakteriologie, Parasitenkunde, Infektionskrankheiten und Hygiene 155:312.

26 Falk Stephen A and Woods Nancy F cited in Noise in the quiet zone. 1974, Modern Healthcare 4:4:59–63.

27 Minckley B B: A study of noise and its relationship to patient discomfort in the recovery room. 1968, Nursing Research 17:247–250.

28 ibid

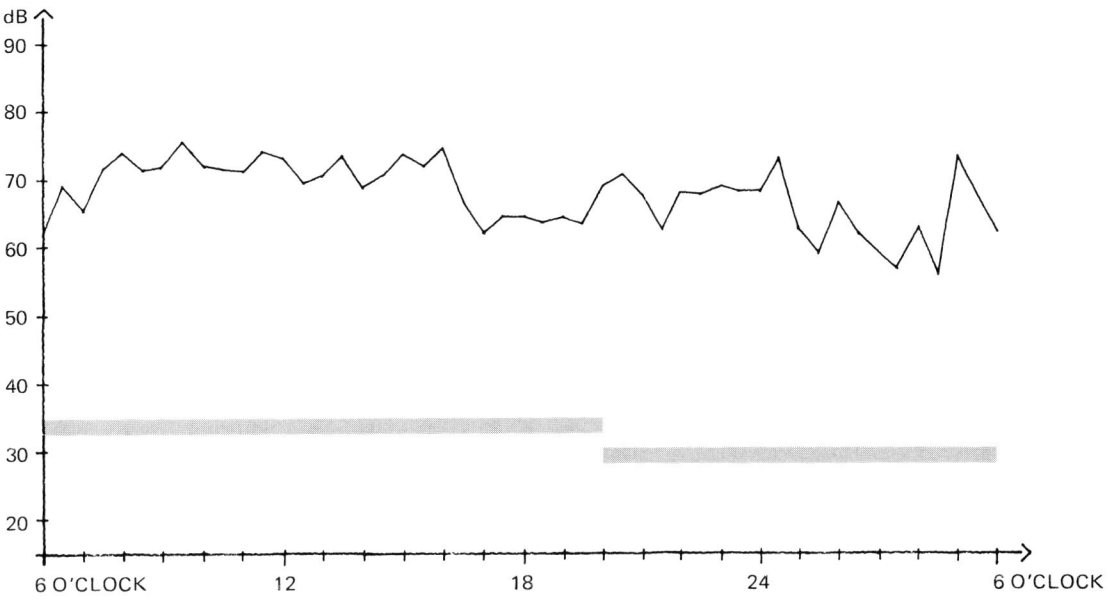

Noise levels throughout 24 hours for a London ICTU as found by S Bentley, F Murphy, H Dudley (Perceived noise in surgical wards and an intensive care area: an objective analysis. 1977, British Medical Journal 2:1503–1506) and the generally accepted noise levels.

Noise and other evidence of activity in adjoining areas should be eliminated[29].

The tom-tom of a multitude of monitors beating out syncopation of cardiac rhytms and rates has been found disturbing in the intensive care unit as well as the noisy mechanical respirators[30] and the noises of fellow patients.

Factors which definitely disturb the patient's sleep are mainly created by staff members, for example talking to each other, and noisy footsteps, but also environmental noises, such as squeaky doors, paper rattling, sudden crashes, oxygen administration equipment and ventilator noises, dragging of chairs, and radio[31].

29 see also Conway Gene F and Haverland Margaret: The Coronary Care Unit. in Monitoring in Anesthesia. ed by William H L Dornette. F A Davis Company. Philadelphia 1973, p 373.

Noury P: L'isolement du malade en unité de soins intensifs cardiaques. 1974, Techniques Hospitalières 30:344:59–66.

30 Badger Theodore L: The Physician — Patient in the Recovery and Intensive Care Units. 1974, Archives of Surgery 109:359–360.

31 Hilton B Ann: Quantity and quality of patient's sleep and sleep-disturbing factors in a respiratory intensive care unit. 1976, Journal of Advanced Nursing 1:453–468.

The movement of routine equipment such as medicine carts and food carts may be disturbing. The squeak of wheels, and bumping against obstructions in confined spaces are cumulatively noticeable[32].

As an average noise level in the ICTU 45 dB[33] has been reported. Average noise levels in the coronary intensive care unit generally just under 60 dB and those in the medical-surgical intensive care unit just above 65 dB have been reported[34]. That means that the noise levels are consistently above speech and sleep interference levels. Noises above 70 dB A have been found to be common in ICTUs[35].

To minimize the adverse effects of noise in intensive care units it is recommended to use individual cubicles[36]. In the ICTU loud conversations tend to develop unchecked and noisy procedures seem to be regarded as a fact of life[37].

Noise exposure has non-auditory effects on man. Noise is more likely to cause a higher rate of errors and accidents than simple reduction of work output. This is most undesirable in intensive care[38].

Noise in ward units

The ability to cope with emotional problems requires quiet in order to collect one's thoughts. *Florence Nightingale** wrote in 1857 in her *Notes on Matters affecting the Health, Efficiency and Hospital Administration of the British Army* that unnecessary noise is the most cruel absence of care that can be inflicted on either sick or well.

An adult patient has expressed his idea of hell as a place where loud noises are moving in from all sides, towards you and on you. To be exposed to noise was like being submerged in water and drowning[39].

32 Clipson Colin W and Wehrer Joseph J: Planning for Cardiac Care. The Health Administration Press. Ann Arbor, Michigan 1973, p 242.

33 Sälzer Elmar: Schallschutz im Krankenhaus. 1977, Das Krankenhaus 69:365–370.

34 Turner Alvis G, King Charles H and Graddock John G: Measuring and reducing noise. 1975, Hospitals 49:15:85–90.

35 Bentley S, Murphy F and Dudley H: Perceived noise in surgical wards and an intensive care area: an objective analysis. 1977, British Medical Journal 2:1503–1506.

36 see also Falk Stephen A and Woods Nancy F: Hospital noise — levels and potential health hazards. 1973, The New England Journal of Medicine 289:774–781.

37 Bentley S, Murphy F and Dudley H: Perceived noise in surgical wards and an intensive care area: an objective analysis. 1977, British Medical Journal 2:1503–1506.

38 Redding Joseph S, Hargest Thomas S and Minsky Stephen H: How noisy is intensive care? 1977, Critical Care Medicine 5:275–276.

* Florence Nightingale (1820–1910), English nurse, one of the founders of modern nursing, whose achievements in public health were almost equally important.

39 cited by Tarnopolsky A and McLean E K: Noise as Psychosomatic Hazard. in Modern Trends in Psychosomatic Medicine 3. ed by Oscar Hill. Butterworths. London and Boston 1976, p 91.

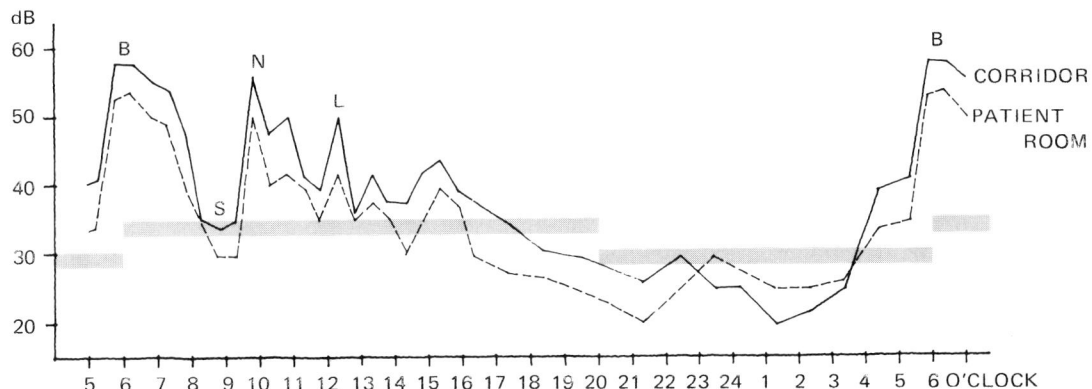

Noise levels throughout 24 hours for a medical ward in a Magdeburg hospital, GDR as indicated by G Schuschke and L Riedel (Lärmbekämpfung als Krankenhaushygienische Leistungs- und Erziehungsaufgabe. in Das stationäre und ambulante Gesundheitswesen. vol 25. VEB Volk und Gesundheit. Berlin 1976, p 40) and the generally accepted noise levels.
B — beds are made, washing bowls, S — staff breakfast time, N — nursing treatments, L — lunches served.

As average noise levels in regular wards the values 30 to 40 dB A have been given[40]. In Sweden as the highest noise level in wards at daytime — 6 to 20 o'clock — 35 dB A is accepted, at night — 20 to 6 o'clock — this level has to be lower by 5 dB A[41].

For patients in the wards or waiting in the medical performance areas staff talk in corridors, particularly noise from nurses and doctors conversing loudly during the night hours, use of clog shoes by staff, noise from the utility rooms, lifts and their doors, other patients in distress, noise from TV sets and radio, coughing, crying and snoring at night, signals from telephones and voice paging, especially the ward kitchen noises[42], trolleys and containers[43], floor polishers[44] and vacuum cleaners[45] have been found disturbing.

40 Sälzer Elmar: Schallschutz im Krankenhaus. 1977, Das Krankenhaus 69:365–370.

41 Akustik i sjukvårdsbyggnader. Spri råd 5.24. Stockholm. 1976, p 44.

42 see also Bächi H: Möglichkeiten der Lärmverhütung und Lärmminderung im technisierten Krankenhaus. in Krankenhausprobleme der Gegenwart. vol 8. ed by E Haefliger and V Elsasser. Verlag Hans Huber. Bern, Stuttgart, Vienna 1974, p 316.

43 Bridges J F: Noise control. 1977, Hospital Development 5:2:29–31.

44 Wilson Lois: Reaction of Patients to Hospital Care. 1977, The New Zealand Medical Journal 86:223–224.

45 Bentley S, Murphy F and Dudley H: Perceived noise in surgical wards and an intensive care area: an objective analysis. 1977, British Medical Journal 2:1503–1506.

Children's wards are not usually allowed to become very noisy places, but they are from time to time the source of the kind of noise which may disturb sick people: for example, a baby may cry insistently.

In maternity units the clattering shoes on hard floors all the time have been found most disturbing[46].

In the USA hospitals voice paging is one of the primary sources of distrubance. It has been found that the average decibel level of these pages is 73. Some pages peake at 83 dB[47]. The unexpected occurence of this noise does not permit one to adapt to it[48].

Use of the public address system should be minimized and the sound level must be lowered after 8 p.m. Also a policy of keeping the patient room doors closed would greatly reduce the disturbance by sounds.

Noise in ambulatory care areas

Confidential matters can even arise unexpectedly during general conversation. There fore internal partitions and doors should be designed to reduce room-to-room transmission of sound to about 40 dB.

Water pipes and cables must be carefully routed to avoid breaching the noise barrier. Sound absorbing finishes and good quality carpets should be used to reduce the impact of intermittent disturbances in waiting areas.

46 Beels Christine: The Childbirth Book. Turnstone Books. London 1978, p 57.

47 Feldman Herman according to Noise in the quiet zone. 1974, Modern Healthcare 4:4:59–63.

48 Halton Susan and Williams Sylvia: Quiet Zone — The Hospital. 1974, The Guthrie Bulletin 43:114–124.

Background noise and music

It has been found that a background noise level of about 40 decibels is desirable if normal incidental people noises are to be satisfactorily masked either by allowing some external or background noise to penetrate or by inducing *muzac* or *white noise*[1].

A favourable effect of soothing music when preparing patients for surgery has been reported.

In the *operation room* the fatigue and boredom arising after long periods of work may cause a slackening of concentration. Conversation may become general. Well chosen light orchestral background music — not in *minor* and in proper *tempi* — might be helpful in mitigating boredom.

The patient in an intensive care and treatment unit frightened by his strange techno-logical environment may benefit from mental diversion. Most ICTU patients like music. Exactly how musical sounds calm, depress or stimulate the nervous system is not known, but it is believed that music can be an aid in patient care. However, some patients, particularly ulcer patients, prefer quiet.

Soothing music decreases minute ventilation, minute oxygen consumption and ba-sal metabolic rate, while exciting music slightly increases these parameters[2]. Exiting music frequently increases the airway resistance and has an unfavourable influence on the respiration[3]. It seems useful to apply soothing music in clinical situations where the reduction of basal metabolic rate and relaxation is required.

Background music in out-patient, and particularly in emergency department wait-ing areas has been recommended[4].

Relayed to waiting areas well chosen background music will make the atmosphere less tense than the use of wall decor. Investigations in Estonia indicate that 5 per cent of culturally interested people preferred art to other sources of emotional enjoyment, but 26 per cent music[5].

1 Green John R B: Health service facility planning and design. Part I. School of Health Administration, University of New South Wales, Kensington, Australia. Stencil. 1974, p 65.

2 Metera Anna and Metera Artur: Influence of Music on the Minute Oxygen Consumption and Basal Meta-bolic Rate. 1975, Anaesthesia, Resuscitation and Intensive Therapy 3:259-264.

3 Metera Anna, Metera Artur and Warwas Ireneusz: Effect of Music on Airway Resistance in Patients. 1975, Anaesthesia, Resuscitation and Intensive Therapy 3:265-269.

4 Evans John and Hawkes Roger: Background music in hospital. 1972, British Hospital Journal & Social Service Review 81:608-609, 611.

5 Laidmäe Virve-Ines: Kunsti nägu ja profiilid. 1975, Looming 1: 126-147.

As already mentioned, background music should be light, orchestral and not continuous. A timing device should be used. For instance, it may be set to play for 20 minutes, to be followed by a 10 minutes interval.

The purveyors of canned music process their tapes to eliminate variations in loudness, which greatly reduces the listner's engagement[6]. In the hospital an improvement of the loudness variations is probably needed. Not all six musical dynamics signs from *pp* to *ff* should be used, but at least two.

Individual speaker volume controls are recommended[7].

The music system has to be separated from the paging and intercom system.

6 see also Pattersson Blake: Musical dynamics. 1974, Scientific American 231:5:78–95.

7 see also Feller Irving and Crane Keith: Planning and Designing a Burn Care Facility. Institute for Burn Medicine. Ann Arbor, Michigan 1975, p 38.

Climate

The development of reliable bio-climatic indices is a basic necessity for effective climate control. Without such indices far more effort/energy and equipment than necessary is put into climate control engineering[1].

Temperature

The body temperature regulating centre is located in the hypothalmus. It receives afferent impulses from sensory receptors in the skin and other areas. The efferent limb is mediated by the sympathetic nervous system. Body temperature adjustments are made either by a fine regulating mechanism such as skin blood flow or by coarse mechanisms such as shivering and sweating.

Temperature and adults

The adult human body homeostatic thermoregulatory mechanism — an exceedingly powerful physiological force — maintains temperatures within the limits of 36.0°C to 37.5°C. Its entire resources may be thrown into an effort to restore the disturbed thermal equilibrium.

Within limits, the healthy human body can adjust its heat production to thermal conditions. Females and males respond differently to dynamic changes in thermal conditions. Males in general tend to feel hotter and react more rapidly[2].

The indoor comfort levels of the humans vary considerably. There has been a trend towards higher temperatures in the industrially developed countries.

A generally preferred indoor temperature for healthy adults seems to be in the region of 21°C to 23°C. When the mean night temperature rises above 24°C, the percentage of those whose sleep is disturbed, increases[3].

The influence of temperature on the viability of microorganisms is small as compared to the effects of relative humidity[4].

1 see also Moorcraft Colin: Solar Energy in Housing. 1973, Architectural Design 43:638.

2 see also Wyon D P, Andersen I and Lundqvist G R: Spontaneous magnitude estimation of thermal discomfort during changes in the ambient temperature. 1972, The Journal of Hygiene 70:203–220.

3 Macpherson R K: Thermal Stress and Thermal Comfort. 1973, Ergonomics 16:611–623.

4 see also Cozanitis D A, Mäkelä P and Grant J: Microorganisms in the Hair of Staff and Patients in an Intensive Care Unit. 1977, Der Anaesthesist 26:578–580.

Temperature and infants

Maintenance of an optimal thermal condition is one of the most important aspects of effective neonatal care[5].

Environmental temperature of 30°C, which might be considered excessively hot to adults, may be too cold for a naked infant. This is due to a small amount of subcutaneous tissue and a large surface in relation to body mass in the newborn infant.

Naked babies in incubator are exposed to serious and unnecessary risks of cooling when the temperature is less than 27°C to 30°C[6]. For older infants temperatures of 26.5°C to 28°C[7] have been required. On the other hand, temperatures hotter than the baby are dangerous[8].

A temperature between 32°C and 34°C has been suggested as a proper range of air temperature for the newborn infant, as then his oxygen consumption is minimal[9].

For preterm infants 35°C to 36°C has been suggested as a range of thermal neutrality in the environmental temperature within which the baby's normal body temperature is kept without extra heat production[10].

Bathing during the first hour after birth appears to decrease body temperature significantly despite previous stabilization of temperature. Delaying the bath would minimize instability of temperature[11].

Temperature in operation room

The character of the thermal environment of the operation room and the anaesthetic room is determined by the need to protect the patient's physical resources — more aberrations of body temperature are seen in the surgical practice than in any other branch of medicine — and to ensure good working conditions for the operating staff

5   see also Kim C B, Ranck Benjamin A, Dean Eileen B and Walker Patricia S: The Temperature in Normal Term Newborns in the First 12 hours. 1977, The Journal of the Indiana State Medical Association 70:863–864.

6   Wilkinson A W: Paediatric intensive care. in Intensive care. ed by W F Walker and D E M Taylor. Churchill Livingstone. Edinburgh, London, New York 1975, p 103.

7   see also Othersen Jr H Bieman and Hargest Thomas S: A New Concept in Temperature Stabilization of Infants in the Operating Room. in Current Topics in Surgical Research. vol. 3. ed by David B Skinner and Paul A Ebert. Academic Press. New York and London 1971, p 77–83.

8   Davies Pamela A, Robinson R J, Scopes J W, Tizard J P M and Wigglesworth J S.: Medical Care of Newborn Babies. Spastics International Medical Publications. William Heinemann Medical Books Ltd. London 1972, p 102–103.

9   see also Silverman William A and Sinclair John C: Temperature Regulation in the Newborn Infant. 1966, The New England Journal of Medicine 274:147.

10 Karlberg P: Management of the preterm infant in the labour ward. in Perinatal Medicine. ed by Z K Štembera, K Poláček and V Šabata. Georg Thieme Publishers, Stuttgart and Aricenum, Prague 1975, p 221.

11 Kim C B, Ranck Benjamin A, Dean Eileen B and Walker Patricia S: The Temperature in Normal Term Newborns in the First 12 Hours. 1977, The Journal of the Indiana State Medical Association 70:863–864.

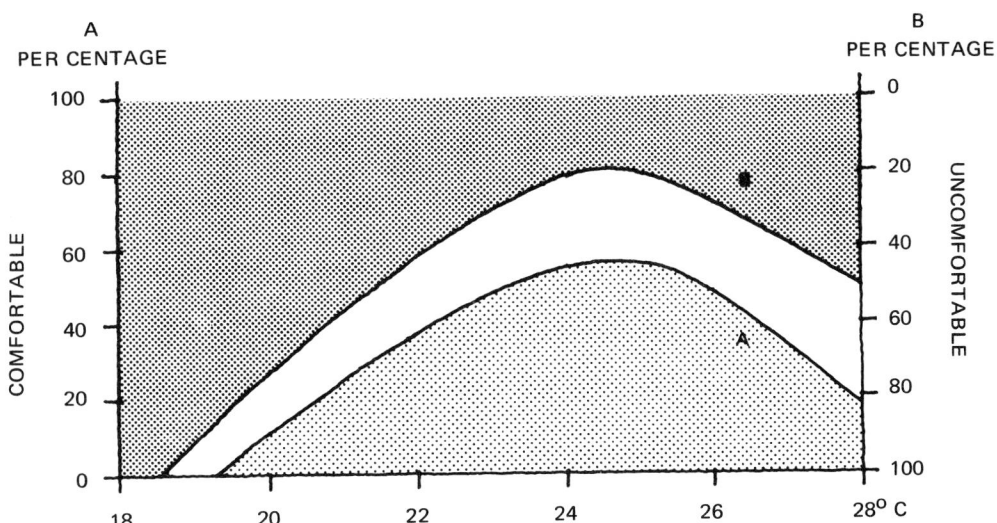

Börje Löfstedt (Luftfuktighetens betydelse minimal för komfortupplevelsen. 1973, Modern Byggteknik Team 3:18) has shown that whatever the temperature in a public local, 20 or 30 per cent of the population is not pleased with it. A indicates those who are satisfied, B — non satisfied. The field between A and B is for the indifferent.

The thermal environment has some effect on the efficiency and accuracy of surgical procedures. However, the extent of this effect is still to be determined.

Whatever the season or the weather, adequate comfort conditions for the surgical team and patient are to be maintained.

The temperature at which unclothed man at rest achieves thermal neutrality with his surroundings is in the British Isles between 24°C and 27°C at the relative humidity of 50 per cent. When conditions change beyond these limits then the body's own temperature control mechanisms are called into play[12].

Heat loss during anaesthesia occurs not only because of low environmental temperatures and humidity but also because of the infusion of cold fluids, ventilation with cold gases, the exposure of body cavities, the absence of muscle movement and subcutaneous vasodilation.

Already a 0.5°C fall in body temperature can result in a doubling of the rate of the patient's energy expenditure. This constitutes an enormous stress on a sick elderly patient undergoing a major operation[13]. From the age of 70 years onward the body's ability to adjust to changes in thermal conditions decreases progressively.

12 Mackenzie A: Hazards in the operating theatre. Environmental control. 1973, Annals of the Royal College of Surgeons of England 52:361–365.

13 Roe C F: Temperature Regulation and Energy Metabolism in Surgical Patients. Progress in Surgery. vol 12. ed by M Allgöwer, S E Bergentz, R Y Calne and U F Gruber. S Karger. Basel, Munich, Paris, London, New York, Sidney 1973, p 97.

There are indications that in operation rooms cooler than 21°C all patients will become hypothermic unless the procedure is very short[14]. In operation rooms with the temperature between 21°C and 24°C about a third of patients will become hypothermic when operations last more than an hour.

In operations lasting a couple of hours, the greatest patient temperature drop usually occurs in the first 30 minutes. This is because of the effect of anesthesia induction, exposure to cold ambient temperature, and preparation of the operative site with cold antiseptic solutions. However, in operations lasting more than three hours there is a further drop in temperature. Patients undergoing intra-abdominal or intrathoracic operations lose more heat than others because of more exposed surface. Irrigation of these surfaces with cold fluids adds to the heat loss[15].

Patients kept at 24°C or warmer will retain their normal body temperature.

There is a large decrease in skin temperature during transfer to the recovery room, despite the beginning of patient activity and maintenance of the environmental temperature.

Hypothermia* has been found in 11 per cent of surgical patients — especially in young children and the aged — admitted to the recovery room[16]. This can only be accounted for by the removal of the drapes from the patient. This decrease is larger than the hourly loss during anaesthesia and, in view of the detrimental effects of hypothermia, should be prevented by suitable covering[17].

In burned patients hypothermia is often initiated by the administration of an anaesthetic and perpetuated by exposed wounds and donor sites. The application of dressings lessens the loss of heat by convection and evaporation. However, hypothermia in itself is not an indication to dress the patient's wounds or donor sites. It is preferred to warm the patient by a source of radiant heat, such as heat lamp[18].

Temperature control in paediatric surgery

Temperature control of the infant is an essential component of paediatric surgery. The responses of infants under general anaesthesia are poikilothermic in character,

14 Morris Roger H: Operating Room Temperature and the Anaesthetized Paralyzed Patient. 1971, Archives of Surgery 102:95.

15 Wanna Hanna T: Temperature Changes During Anesthesia and Surgery. 1978, Journal of the Iowa Medical Society 68:197–200.

* t° below 35.5°C

16 Klingensmith William: Inadvertent hypothermia during surgery. 1971, Texas Medicine 67:5:52–55.

17 Holdcroft A and Hall G M: Heat loss during anaesthesia. 1978, British Journal of Anaesthesia 50:157–163.

18 Boswick Jr John A, Thompson James D and Kershner Cindy J: Critical Care of the Burned Patient. 1977, The Journal of Anesthesiology 47: 164–170.

because shivering is abolished — it appears between the third and sixth month of life — and there is peripheral vasodilation. The effect is greater than in the adult because of the infant's larger body surface in comparison to its total bulk*. Also radiation loss from limbs, head and face is relatively greater.

Low temperatures, particularly for patients less than one year old, as well as high temperature, may be gravely injurious. The hypothermia produced in the air-conditioned operation room in the absence of any heat source has been associated with increased risk of cardiac arrest[19], and morbidity and mortality[20] for the babies.

Low weight new-borns have great tendency to hypothermy although there are wide variations in cold resistance among neonates[21]. The greatest drop in baby temperatures occurs when the baby is removed naked from an incubator, placed on an operation table and left during induction of anaesthesia exposed to a cold environment.

The newborn undergoing operation should be kept warm and the patient placed on some warming device, e g the water blanket, thermostatically controlled to 37°C[22].

Operation room tables with a source of radiant heat are in use to provide a temperature of 37°C to newborns and infants, and to burn patients. This radiant heat and high temperature may be uncomfortable to the surgical team. However, since most heat loss from a child occurs early during anaesthesia induction and preparation for surgery, the room temperature could be lowered and radiant heat turned off later if the child's temperature is stable[23].

If the control mechanisms are not in good order, refrigeration and air-conditioning increase considerably the risk of over-cooling the patient.

When air-conditioning and refrigeration are *not* available, there is a risk of overheating the patient if the weather suddenly turns hot and reasonable precautions are not taken. Excessive external heat tends to produce undesirable vasodilation with a further decrease of the circulating blood volume. As the patient is usually unconscious, this is potentially more hazardous than any situation encountered in hot industries.

* the high surface area — volume is 2.7 times greater in infants than adults (Wanna Hanna T: Temperature Changes During Anesthesia and Surgery. 1978, Journal of the Iowa Medical Society 68:197–200).

19 Henderson W Hardy and Henderson Bruce M: Recent Advances in Pediatric Surgery. 1969, American Journal of Surgery 118:339.

20 Farman J V: Heat losses in infants undergoing surgery in air-conditioned theatres. 1962, British Journal of Anaesthesia 34:543–556.

21 see also Procianoy Guilherme and Procianoy Renato Soibelmann: Termorregulação em recém-nascido. 1972, Jornal de Pediatria 37:344–350.

22 Vivori E and Bush G H: Modern aspects of the management of the newborn undergoing operation. 1977, British Journal of Anaesthesia 49:51–57.

23 Wanna Hanna T: Temperature Changes During Anesthesia and Surgery. 1978, Journal of Iowa Medical Society 68:197–200.

Thermal comfort requirements for surgical teams

During operations, heat is released according to the activity of the human body. The heat gain from senior members of the operating team owing to the nervous energy released is as follows[24]:

surgeon, assistant, operation room sister	640 kJ/h at 21°C
anaesthesiologist	420 kJ/h at 21°C
other team members	320 kJ/h at 21°C

The total heat production per hour caused by the staff, OP-lighting and equipment may be about 2 kW or 1750 kcal/h[25].

Thermal comfort requirements for the surgical team vary in different parts of the world. Requirement changes may be caused also by the seasons.

Views and opinions on what constitutes a comfortable working temperature for the staff in an operation room have changed considerably during the last decades. There has been a reduction of temperature from the general standard of 28°C to 30°C to 19°C to 24°C. However, temperatures of 25°C to 37°C within the operation area are still being measured[26].

Thermal conditions which satisfy the surgeon may lead to the anaesthesiologist complaining of cold. The highest number of so called scrubbed staff have been comfortable at temperatures between 21°C and 23°C, and so called unscrubbed staff between 22°C and 25°C, the average for the former being 22.4°C and for the latter 23.3°C[27].

It is doubtful if it is possible to produce a working environment that is comfortable for all parties involved in an operation without changes in operation room clothing or developing selective air-conditioned zones in the room[28].

Acrylic cements in operation room

The use of acrylic cements is well established in orthopaedic surgery, but few data appear to have been published on the acceleration of the setting-time as a function

24 Kensett R G: Air-conditioning-plant design for operating theatres. 1974, Hospital Engineering 28: Sept:18-2:

25 see also Janssen E and Janssen G: Microklimatologische Bedingungen im Operationssaal. 1976, Krankenhaus Umschau 45:227–230.

26 ibid

27 Lamont S J: Thermal comfort for theatre personnel during surgical operations. 1977, NATnews 14:2:10-12.

28 also Foster P A: Planning engineering services from the anaesthetist's point of view. Second Southern African Hospital Symposium. Pretoria. November 1977.

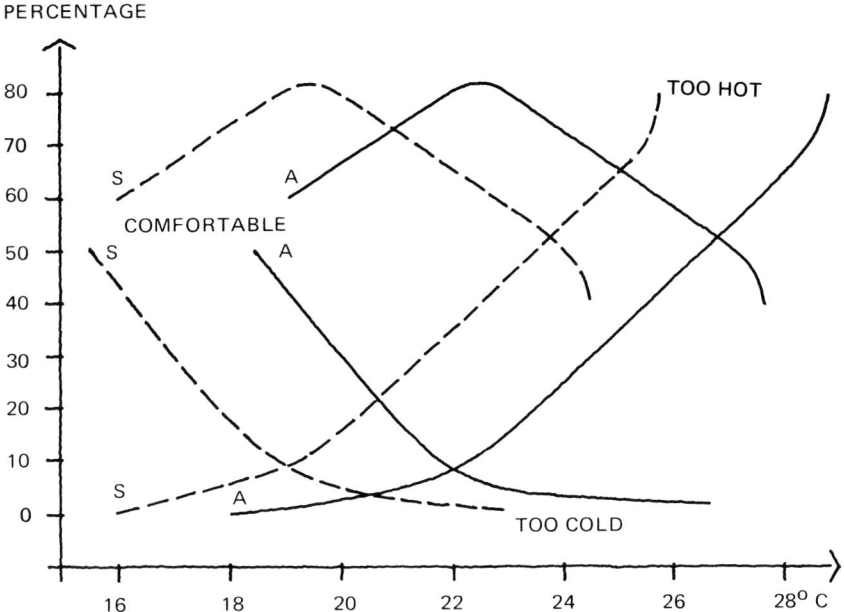

PERCENTAGE

TOO HOT

COMFORTABLE

TOO COLD

Temperatures in operation rooms as preferred or disliked by surgeons and anaesthesiologists. After 1974, Hospital Engineering 28:10:19.

of increasing the operation room ambient temperature. The time to set varies with temperature of polymerisation: $15°C - 21.6$ min, $20°C - 4.9$ min, $30°C - 3.3$ min. Thus between $20°C$ and $25°C$ there is a reduction in setting-time of about 34 per cent. This may be vital during the manipulation and insertion of the cement into the prepared bone cavity. It is recommended that, in order to achieve a desirable extension of setting-time, the unmixed components of the cement should not be stored in the operation room, but be refrigerated to approximately $0°C$ for a period of 10 minutes before mixing[29].

Temperature in delivery room

The most important aspect of newborn care is the maintenance of normal body temperature[30].

---

29 Pearson G P, Jones D F and Wright V: Effect of operating-theatre temperature on the setting-time of acrylic cements for use in orthopaedic surgery. 1975, The Lancet 2:184.

30 see also Dunn P M: "The newborn, Now or Never". 1973, Journal of the Irish Medical Association 66:585–592

The environmental temperature in an air-conditioned delivery room is frequently maintained around 23°C, midway in the thermal comfort zone for lightly-dressed adults, but more than 10°C below the critical environmental temperature for the newborn.

Although fullterm as well as preterm newborn infants have, already at birth, developed mechanisms to maintain normal deep body temperature, in the wet newborn infant exposed at birth to the room temperature the deep body temperature can fall 2° to 3°C unless special precautions are taken[31].

The heat loss that occurs during the first few minutes of life when the infant is exposed to the delivery room environment is significant. Even one minute of delay may cost the infant considerable loss of heat by conduction, convection, radiation, and, most significantly, by evaporation of moisture from its skin[32]. Action taken or not taken during the first five minutes of life can greatly influence the baby's entire future[33].

However, it has been pointed out[34] that a very slight cooling of the infant may be beneficial in the immediate adaption to extra-uterine life by cooling of the skin receptors in initiation of respiration and vasoconstriction by increasing systematic vascular resistance and by reducing right to left shunting of blood through the *ductus arteriosus.* These effects should be restricted to the very immediate period after birth and should be followed by active preventive measures to avoid persistent cooling.

All infants in the delivery room should be provided with a micro-environment which eliminates or reduces body heat loss and minimizes associated metabolic acidosis. Radiant heating devices are sufficient to reduce the baby's body heat loss during the initial examination, cleaning, suction, and performance of other routine procedures.

The facilities for supplying adequate warmth to perinatally asphyxiated and other newborns in need of resuscitation measures are sometimes not satisfactory. Several cases of injuries due to excessive heat have been reported[35].

An extended stay in the delivery room means that for the infant temperature control and monitoring should be provided[36].

31 see also Karlberg P: Management of the preterm infant in the labour ward. in Perinatal Medicine. ed by Z K Štembera, K Poláček and V Šabata. Georg Thieme Publishers, Stuttgart and Aricenum, Prague 1975, p 221.

32 see also Evans James A: Fundamentals of Infant Resuscitation. in Advances in fetal monitoring and obstetric anaesthesia. ed by Barry S Shifrin and Ivor S Smith. Little, Brown and Company. Boston 1973, p 149.

33 see also DeVore Jay S: Resuscitation of the newborn. 1976, Clinical Obstetrics and Gynecology 19:3:607-617.

34 Karlberg P: Management of the preterm infant in the labour ward. in Perinatal Medicine. ed by Z K Štembera, K Poláček and V Šabata. Georg Thieme Publishers, Stuttgart and Aricenum, Prague 1975, p 221.

35 see also Devell Bo and Enockson Erik: Värmetillförsel till nyfödda barn. 1973, Läkartidningen 70:1965-1966.

36 see also Marx F F: Planning and organisation of neonatal intensive care units. in Perinatal Medicine. ed by H Bossart. J M Cruz, A Huber, L S Prod'hom and J Sistek. Hans Huber Publishers. Bern, Stuttgart, Vienna 1973, p 270.

Final value judgements concerning the optimal thermal environment for the new-born infant must await further investigation not only of acute physiologic responses to thermal stimuli but also of their effect on growth and development of the newborn[37].

Temperature in intensive care units

Uncomplicated recovery from anaesthesia and a surgical operation requires control of heat loss. Close control of air temperatures and environmental conditions in general is important in intensive care and resuscitation units.

A temperature of 22°C to 23°C and humidity at 50 to 60 per cent have been found appropriate in the intensive care and treatment units as well as in *isolation rooms.*

Temperature in radiodiagnostic department

Some heating design temperatures for the radiodiagnostic departments[38]:

waiting area	19°C
patients' changing room	22°C
lavage room	21°C
recovery bay	19°C
diagnostic X-ray room	22°C
thermography room	21°C
processing area	19°C
viewing area	19°C
demonstration room	19°C
records	19°C
office	19°C
chemical and film stores	16°C
staff cloak room	17°C
disposal room	17°C

Temperature in laboratories

For laboratories an average temperature of 20°C has been recommended[39].

37 Sinclair John C: The effect of the thermal environment on neonatal mortality and morbidity. in Preventability of perinatal injury. ed by Karlis Adamsons and Howard A Fox. Alan R Liss, inc New York and Elsevier Scientific Publishing Company. Amsterdam-Oxford 1975, p 158.

38 see also Western Regional Hospital Board, Research and Development Unit: Organisation & Design of Radiodiagnostic Departments. Stencil. (Glasgow) January 1973, p 28.

39 see also Taut Anna and Nedeljkov Georgije: Die Gruppenpraxis. Bertelsmann Fachverlag. Dusseldorf 1973, p 167.

The importance of air humidity for a comfortable indoor climate has long been the subject of divergent opinions. In the zone of thermal comfort, the effect of humidity seems to be negligible for grown-ups[1]. The acceptable limits for relative humidity as regards static electricity and comfort are 45 to 60 per cent[2]. For newborn and premature infants a 55 to 65 per cent relative humidity has been considered to be desirable[3].

One of the aspects of humidity is bacteriological. Microorganisms ride on dust particles whose attractibility to one another is favoured by low relative humidity resulting in increased static electricity. Low relative humidity has been reported to be an optimal condition for *Klebsiella pneumoniae* Type A, while *Strasters* and *Winkler* found a threefold decrease in the biological decay of a hospital strain of staphylococcus at 75 per cent relative humidity as compared to 39 per cent relative humidity[4]. High humidity in the hospital enhances the danger of growth of *Ps. aeruginosa*.

Humidity in the *operation* room is believed to contribute to the prevention of dehydration* of exposed tissues.

There have been explosions in the operation rooms. An explosion in the operation room, although statistically extremely infrequent, has nonetheless by its news value for the mass media a psychological impact upon the general public.

At a relative humidity of about 50 per cent a very thin invisible film of moisture forms on operation equipment and other surfaces. This film of moisture conducts static electricity to earth before a sparkproducing potential is built up. Equipment that generate heat in any way, such as lamps and motors, require a higher degree of humidity in the room before this conductive film is formed.

To minimize the explosion risk it has been requested that a standard of relative humidity be fixed for the anaesthetic locations. Recommendations have varied between 40 per cent[5] and 65 per cent[6].

---

1   see also Macpherson R K: Thermal Stress and Thermal Comfort. 1973, Ergonomics 16:616.

2   see also Cozanitis D A, Mäkelä P and Grant J:Microorganisms in the Hair of Staff and Patients in an Intensive Care Unit. 1977, Der Anaesthesist 26:578–580.

3   Hospital care of newborn infants. American Academy of Pediatrics. Evanston, Ill. 1960, p 83.

4   cit. by Cozanitis D A, Mäkelä P and Grant J: Microorganisms in the Hair of Staff and Patients in an Intensive Care Unit. 1977, Der Anaesthesist 26:578–580.

*   during a laparatomy between 500 and 1,000 ml of body fluids are dehydrated (Brümmer P: Die Wertigkeit klinisch-chemischer Laboratorieuntersuchungen für die Chirurgie. 1978, Der Chirurg 49:344–348).

5   see also Ventilation in Operation Suites. DHSS. London 1972, p 6.

6   see also Schmitt Walter: Allgemeine Chirurgie. Johann Ambrosius Barth. Leipzig 1970, p 134.

Broom R A: Operating theatre air conditioning. 1970, Hospital Engineering 24:251.

For the prevention of electrostatic charging the relative humidity should be maintained at 70 per cent[7]. However, when the temperature is allowed to rise above the normal, this degree of humidity is hardly bearable for the patient and the staff.

An authorized standard of relative humidity might give a false sense of security concerning the explosion risks. No device can substitute for the constant alertness of the anaesthesiologist and his awareness of the hazards associated with explosive agents.

When the flammable anaesthetics are not used, it is not necessary to maintain a 50 per cent or greater relative humidity in the whole surgical department. A reduction of humidity in general conditions to more acceptable 40 per cent would be possible. Only when very young children are involved the humidity should be increased.

7   Harder Hans Joachim: Technische Sicherheitsprobleme im Operationstrakt. Springer Verlag. Berlin, Heidelberg, New York 1965, p 66.

The documentation on the temperature-humidity influence on the recovery process is very limited. A study, as an example, indicates that in patients with major fracture the metabolic response to trauma can be abolished by transferring them to an environment of 30°C and 35 per cent humidity[1].

The majority of the investigations in hospitals has tried to find the values, which offer the patients and the staff most comfortable conditions.

In the British Isles the preference in the ward areas is for an air temperature of between 21.5°C and 22°C and a relative humidity of between 30 per cent and 70 per cent, with the air velocity less than 0.1 m/s and the mean radiant temperature close to air temperature[2].

In Western Europe 21°C to 24°C and 50 to 60 per cent relative humidity has been recommended[3].

35 per cent humidity and 22°C in hospitals wards in Sweden are regarded as normal values. Lower humidity values than 35 per cent in wards are not recommended.

In the Baltic area the liked winter room temperature is 18°C to 20°C and in summer 20°C with a relative humidity of 55 per cent.

In the US an individual-room temperature control range of 21°C to 26.5°C and the relative humidity of 30 to 60 per cent has been recommended[4].

In Mexico the favoured temperature range is 22°C to 24°C, and the relative humidity 50 to 60 per cent.

In South Africa a temperature of 18°C to 23°C and a relative humidity of 50 to 60 per cent have been found well tolerable.

There are doubts as to the applicability of the standard thermal comfort assessment techniques to regular ward areas. Even a provision of variable sets of climatic conditions is unlikely to guarantee comfort for everyone. Fortunately, there is a range of air temperatures within which any individual doing light work or similar conditions will be reasonably comfortable. The permissible tolerance in relative humidity is even wider.

1   D P Cuthbertson, C M Smith and W J Tilstone (1968) cited by Curtin Muriel Flavien: Temperature and anaesthesia. 1971, Irish Journal of Medical Science 140:137.

2   Smith R M and Rae A: Thermal comfort of patients in hospital ward areas. 1977, The Journal of Hygiene 78:17-26.

3   Monstadt H: Installation und Wartung lüftungstechnischer Anlagen in Krankenanstalten. 1976, Krankenhaus Umschau 45:434–443.

4   Caplan Knowlton J: Ventilation and Air Conditioning. in Environmental Health and Safety in Health-Care Facilities. ed by Richard G Bond, George S Michaelsen and Roger L DeRoos. Macmillan Publishing Co inc New York and Collier Macmillan Publishers London 1973, p 114.

In the UK *operation rooms* the temperatures 20°C to 22°C and 50 to 60 per cent relative humidity and in other sections of the operation department 18°C to 24°C and 45 to 60 per cent relative humidity have been favoured[5].

In the United States the air temperature of 21°C to 24.5°C with 50 to 60 per cent relative humidity in the operation room has provided a compromise between the supposed requirements of the patient and those of the surgeon.

A following recommendation for operation rooms of highest quality in Scandinavia and areas with similar climate could be made: a full air-conditioning equipment with control mechanisms for variations in temperatures from 19°C to 26°C and in relative humidity between 40 and 55 per cent.

In *laboratories* a fairly stable temperature between 21°C to 22°C and a relative humidity between 40 and 60 per cent should be maintained[6].

5   Kensett R G: Air-conditioning-plant design for operating theatres. 1974, Hospital Engineering 28: July-August:3–12.

6   Rappoport Arthur E, Taylor Wilbur R and Gaulin Richard P: What the modern laboratory must include and where to put it. 1973, Modern Hospital 121:5:55–63.

Ventilation

Operation room ventilation

The operation department and operation room ventilation systems have to be based on rational deduction from scientific investigations and available pieces of clinical evidence. Their cost has to be reasonable.

To maintain oxygenation for ten persons in the operation room, a volume of about 28 m³ of air will be required per hour[1]. This means that less than one tenth of the air volume in a regular operation room — sized 6.2 by 6.2 by 3.2 m — has to be replaced every hour.

To indicate the number of air changes per hour without indicating at the same time the size of the volume of the room considered, is quite meaningless as e g 10 change in a large room have a considerably larger effect than 10 changes in a small room.

A rise of the operation room temperature for the sake of staff comfort can be limited by increased frequency of air exchange using air with proper temperature. This light increase of the air exchange frequencies is usually sufficient also to eliminate from the room radon gas which can have emerged from some building materials.

When subjects smell with a constant concentration of an adorant, the perceived magnitude decays rapidly. Within 2 to 3 minutes it is reduced in dose to an assumptote that equals 30 to 40 per cent of initial magnitude[2]. A high concentration of ozone produces the only notable exception.

How much outside air is required for the dilution of odour will depend on the nature and intensity of odour producing sources. Some experiments indicate that air supplied at 0.24 m³ per minute per person is the critical level for odour suppression It has also been stated that a mechanical ventilation rate of three air changes per hour, with recirculation rates up to 80 per cent provide a level of air quality at which complaints about odour were kept at a low level[4].

1   Edwards Ronald in Operating Theatres and Ancillary Rooms. ed by T Cecil Gray and John Nunn. John Sherrat and Son. Altrincham 1964, p 39.

2   Cain William S: Perception of Odor Intensity and the Time-Course of Olfactory Adaption. 1973, Ashrae Journal 15:12:64.

3   cited by Handler A Benjamin: Systems Approach to Architecture. American Elsevier Publishing Company. Inc. New York 1970, p 140.

4   Rae A and Smith S M: Subjective odour levels in an air-conditioned hospital ward. 1976, Applied Ergonomics 7:27–33.

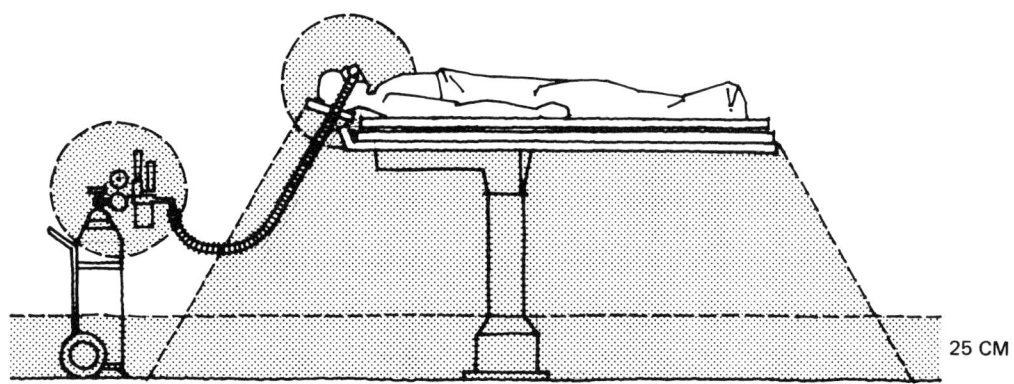

Zones around the operation table, where concentration of anaesthetic gases may occur.

Chemical pollution of operation room air has received increasing attention. Many reports indicate that generally the magnitude of adverse effects of the anaesthetic gases is small[5] and it has been stated that an alarmist view of the healt hazard to anaesthesiologists is not justified by the available evidence[6].

Gas pollution in operation room does not appear to disturb the chromosomal structure in mitosis of cells of females chronically exposed, and it does not seem likely that chromosomes in meiosis would behave differently. Accelerated drug metabolism due to stimulation of microsomal enzymes, shown to occur in anaesthesiologists, may also contribute to the lack of significant effects of the waste gases on the exposed personnel. The increased incidence of reproductive complications in operation room personnel should be attributed to causes other than gas pollution. Physical and emotional stress may disturb the perfusion and oxygen transport to the placenta, and cigarette smoking and occupational infections are other possibilities to be considered[7].

A safe exposure limit or a level above which anaesthetics begin to excert a toxic effect — the toxic limit value — cannot be determined[8].

5   see also Anaesthetics as an occupational hazard. Editorial. 1977, The Medical Journal of Australia 1:427-428.

    Casorbi Helmut F: Is the Operating Room Unhealthy? 1977, JAMA 238:970.

6   see also Fink B R: Professional hazards of anesthesiologists: Introductory remarks — developmental aspects. in Anaesthesiology. Proceedings of the VI World Congress of Anaesthesiology. Mexico City. April 1976. ed by Enrique Hülsz, José Antonio Sanchez-Hernández, Guillermo Vasconcelos and J N Lunn. Excerpta Medica. Amsterdam-Oxford 1977, p 1—5.

    Rosenberg P H and Vänttinen H: Occupational Hazards to Reproduction and Health in Anaesthetists and Pediatricians. 1978, Acta Anaesthesiologica Scandinavica 22:202–207.

7   Rosenberg Per H and Kallio Hanna: Operating-theatre gas pollution and chromosomes. 1977, The Lancet 2:452–453.

8   Milliken Ralph A, Milliken Gerry M and Marshall Betty J: O.R. pollution can have adverse effect on safety. 1976, Hospitals 50:17:97–104.

At present — 1978 — there are no data for establishing permissable levels of anaesthetic gas contamination of areas used by medical and nursing staff. Nonetheless, there are compelling reasons for reducing pollution to the minimum which may be achieved and these are based on common sense rather than any evidence for deleterious effects on psychological performance[9].

It is not possible to prevent completely the pollution of operation room air by anaesthetic gases and vapours. A careless anaesthetic technique on the part of the anaesthesiologist represents the greatest source of pollution in an otherwise adequately equipped operation room[10].

If nonrecirculating air exchange rates in a regular operation room are not greater than 12 times per hour, a waste-gas disposal system, also called scavenging system has to be recommended.

The volume of air flow through an open door or another opening which has to be replaced in the operation room, is related to the area of the doorway or opening and the temperature difference across it, not to the volume of the room. Building Services Research Unit, Glasgow[11], has shown that there is a flow of about 15 m^3 air per minute for each m^2 of doorway, when the temperature difference between the rooms is 1°C.

Despite substantial research efforts, information on the relative contribution of airborne and other routes to the genesis of post-operative surgical wound infection is limited. The available information does not give quantitative estimates on the role of airborne infection in the average operation.

The risk of post-operative infection from airborne micro-organisms, which are introduced into the operation room through ventilation or other air movements, appears to be unimportant. However, the corridors of the surgical department must not connect with the wards and contaminated air must not draw in the operation room from soiled rooms.

A ventilation rate of one change per hour will reduce the level of any contamination present in the air by about 63 per cent, two air changes per hour by about 86 per cent and 10 air changes per hour by about 99 per cent[12]. If airhygienic conditions require ventilation, at least 10 changes per hour are needed to make it meaningful[13].

9   Smith G: Editorial: Pollution and performance. 1978, British Journal of Anaesthesia 50:207–208.

10 Milliken Ralph A, Milliken Gerry M and Marshall Betty J: O.R. pollution can have adverse effect on safety. 1976, Hospitals 50:17:97–104.

11 Ventilation in Operation Suites. Department of Health and Social Security. London 1972, p 3.

12 van Straaten J F: Natural ventilation and lighting of hospitals. Symposium Hospital function and design: a forward look. Pretoria, October 1971.

13 see also Allander Claes and Faxvall Sander: Teoretisk och praktisk undersökning av partikelhalter vid vård-hem med olika typer av ventilation. 1971, VVS 9:61–76.

15 to 20 air changes an hour should be sufficient for comfort, to ensure pressuriza-tion in the operation room, and to maintain considerable control of airborne micro-organisms in an operation room of the size of about 40 m² if an average surgical team is involved.

There are no clear indications what an increasing of 20 air changes to 30 would mean*. Expensive air flow systems add minimal or no benefits[14].

It has been pointed out that increasing the quantity of supply air from 10 to 25 changes per hour in an endwall or sidewall grille installation decreases the concen-tration of microbial contamination in the operation room air, but offers no other special protection to the air above the centre of the operation room from contam-ination arising from any place in the room[15].

Another study shows that bacteriological contamination of the air is markedly re-duced by the use of ultra-clean air, but the wounds themselves are no cleaner than in operation rooms with conventional air conditioning, provided that personnel not in sterilized garments is kept at least 1 m away from the wound area[16].

It is immaterial whether the operation room ventilation system provides fresh air or air that has been made the sanitary equivalent of fresh air.

The particles of outside air are, if air intakes which bring outside air into the hospi-tal are above roof level, of little importance. The only microorganisms of known significance for the outcome of the operation in outdoor air are members of the genus *Clostridium,* which causes tetanus and gasgangrene.

Divergence of opinion on what size of dust particle ** should be excluded from the operation room air supply has been and is considerable. Sizes between 1 to 70 μm have been indicated, although the size of most bacteria-carrying-particles is within 4 to 28 μm range[18]. Obviously it is difficult to motivate the insistence on submicron filtration of air, e g 0.3 μm and 99.97 per cent efficiency with the HEPA filter.

---

*   In the USA 25 air changes are required. Harald M Graning: Minimum Requirements of Construction and Equipment for Hospital and Medical Facilities. US Department of Health, Education and Welfare. Health Resources Administration HRA 74–4000.

14 see also Hunt Thomas K: Diagnosis and Treatment of Wound Failure. In Advances in Surgery. ed by R M Zollinger. Year Book Medical Publishers Inc. Chicago 1974, p 304.

15 Kethley T W and Cown W B: What Is the Quality of the Air in Your Operating Room? 1976, The Guthrie Bulletin 46:1:25:37.

16 Freeman M A R, Challis J H, Zelezonski J and Jarvis I D: Sepsis Rates in Hip Replacement Surgery with Special Reference to the Use of Ultra Clean Air. 1977, Archiv für orthopädische und Unfall-Chirurgie 90:1–14.

** Viruses may be from 0.005 to 0.1 μm, bacteria from 0.4 to 5 μm, and spores from 10 to 30 μm in size.

18 Lidwell O M: Smoke trails and models for exploration of uni-directional flow ventilation systems. I.H.V.E. September 1971.

The use of filters should hinder the outside pathogenic particles over the 1 μm range to enter the operation room. The amount of filtration needed is probably much less than generally assumed, since the infective particles have a size of 10 to 40 μm.

Air distribution systems

Room air distribution systems can be divided into three groups.

First there are turbulent or mixing air distribution patterns which promote uniform mixing of the air throughout the entire room and where dispersion of airborne contamination will be substantially uniform throughout the room, regardless of the location of the source of contamination. The mixing system employs continuous turbulent diluting of clean incoming air with the contaminated operation room air which is exhausted at the same rate.

The designs of the second group diminish transport of contamination arising from peripheral sources and from shedding below the waist to the operation table. The downward displacement piston system takes air in at the top of the operation room. The exhausts are at lower levels. If functional, they offer the greatest promise[19].

A ventilation system that employs partial walls extending 0.76 m from the ceiling, from which the air is allowed to issue freely downwards at an initial velocity of about 0.4 m/sec has been found about 30 times cleaner in terms of airborne bacteria than a well ventilated conventional operation-room. Although the partial-walled system is slightly less efficacious than a full-walled system, the freedom of movement and of communication for the operating team could in some circumstances outweigh this disadvantage[20].

Howorth[21] has reached the conclusion that the ideal air pattern would be to continue to have the very positive pressure and downflow over the operation zone, but then to turn the air outwards so that it moved radially away from the operation zone in an exponential pattern. This exponential air flow pattern is contamination free.

Other advantages of the *exponential* flow according to the inventor are the following: there is clean access to the operation area to a height of over 2.1 m; the effective clean zone extends beyond the perimeter of the 2.8 m diffuser; movement of equipment and personnel within the clean zone is always upstream of the air flow; there can be no entrainment of operation room air.

19 Kethley T W and Cown W B: What Is the Quality of the Air in Your Operating Room? 1976, The Guthrie Bulletin 46:1:25–37.

20 Whyte W, Shaw B H and Freeman M A R: An evaluation of a partial-walled laminar-flow operating room. 1974, The Journal of Hygiene 73:61–74.

21 Howorth F H: The Prevention of Airborne Infection during Surgery. 1976, Hospital Engineering 30:20.19–2

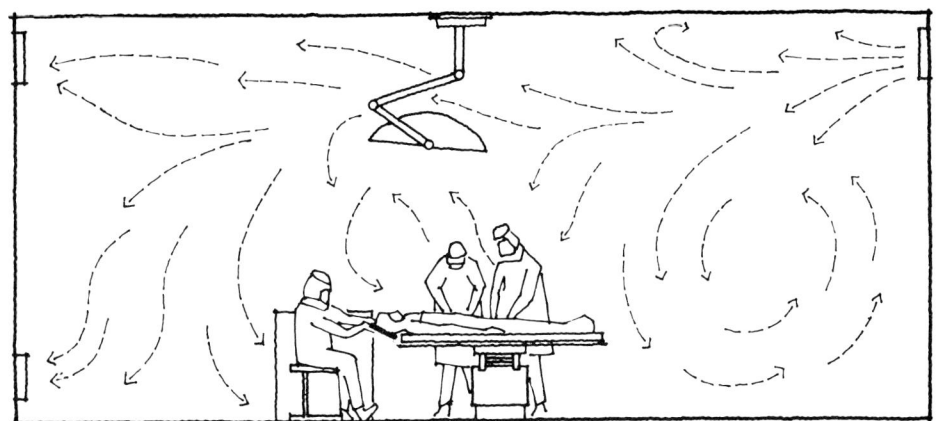

The mixing system employs continuous turbulent diluting of incoming air at the same rate as it is exhausted with the air in the operation room.

The third group of ventilation systems consists of unidirectional, sometimes popularly called laminar* flow and air sealing or curtaining.

Up to 1978 four different unidirectional flow concepts — downflow, the tunnel, the wall-less clean air horizontal or cross flow and the full-wall approach — have been used.

In unidirectional airflow units air (200 to 700 changes per hour) is made to move with a uniform velocity along parallel flow lines with a minimum of eddy currents. Usually 99.97 per cent of 0.3 μm particles are removed from the incoming air by filtering.

The introduction of surgeons, patients, apparatus etc into the airflow system interrupts the air stream and reduces its effectiveness. The same stream of air that will cleanse an area may strip particles from the surgeon and convey them into the wound[22].

There should be no sources of microorganisms upstream above the operation table. Even at a velocity of 0.5 m/sec the source e g the face of the surgeon may not be closer than 0.4 m to the wound to keep the wound area sterile[23].

The efficiency of unidirectional ventilation systems at 0.3 to 0.4 m/sec velocity in operation rooms, where conventional protective operation clothing was worn, has

---

* It has been pointed out (Nelson Carl L and Greenwald Alan Seth: Clean air and total hip arthroplasty. 1972, Cleveland Clinic Quarterly 39:101–107) that the interposition of the surgeon's hands or surgical tools will disturb the air flow pattern over the surgical area creating some air turbulence. The term laminar is therefore inappropriate.

22 Dingwell J S and Proctor E: A Linear Air Flow Chamber for Experimental Surgery. 1975, Journal of Surgical Research 19:121–126.

23 van der Waaij D, Heidt P J and Wigersma N: Ventilation von Operationsräumen. 1975, medizinische technik 95:47–51.

been studied in terms of numbers of airborne bacteria at the wound site. In a horizontal airflow room 11 times less bacteria and in a vertical airflow room 35 to 90 times less bacteria than in a plenum-ventilated operation room were measured[24].

Each type of unidirectional flow operation room has advantages over the other, but at present neither has been shown to be superior*.

In spite of minimal data existing, it has been strongly suggested that there is a substantial tissue dessication directly related to the air flow velocity[25]. It has also been surmised that the high flow of air may contribute to excessive cooling of the patient, but this is yet unconfirmed[26].

In connection with unidirectional flow systems excessive noise interferring with the operating team communication has been reported as well as difficulties with lighting, lack of mobility of the surgeon to change from side to side at the operation table, and increased heat emission from the motors used in the high efficiency particle (HEPA) filters.

It has been indicated[27] that the rate of post-operative infections is lower in connection with procedures done in the unidirectional air-flow operation rooms than after those done in conventional operation rooms. The results of another study[28] have indicated greater knife blade contamination in a conventionally ventilated operation room than in one equipped with unidirectional air-flow. However, the authors concluded that the study did not establish whether or not the environment played a part in post-operative wound infection.

A comparison of wound wash-outs in conventional and unidirectional air flow operation rooms confirms preliminarly that cleaner air does result in less-contaminated wounds[29]. The investigators add a comment: until it is possible to correlate wound contamination with later clinical infection of the same wounds, the importance of the wound wash-out results remains in doubt.

24 Whyte W, Shaw B H and Barnes R: A bacteriological evaluation of laminar-flow systems for orthopaedic surgery. 1973, The Journal of Hygiene 71:559–564.

* Allen Paul, Reynolds D A: Clean air operating environments. 1978, British Journal of Hospital Medicine 20:591–598.

25 Pelosi M: The rationale for low velocity down flow clean rooms. Proceedings of the 8th annual technical meetings. American Association for Contamination Control 1969.

26 Haslam Kenneth R: Laminar Air-flow Air Conditioning in the Operating Room. A Review. 1974, Anesthesia and Analgesia 53:194–199.

27 see also Turner Robert S: Laminar Air Flow. 1974, The Journal of Bone and Joint Surgery 56A:430–435.

28 Ritter M A, French M L V and Eitzen H E: Bacterial contamination of the surgical knife. 1975, Clinical Orthopaedics 108:158–160.

29 Sanderson M C and Bentley George: Assessment of wound contamination during surgery: a preliminary report comparing vertical laminar flow and conventional theatre systems. 1976, The British Journal of Surgery 63:431–432.

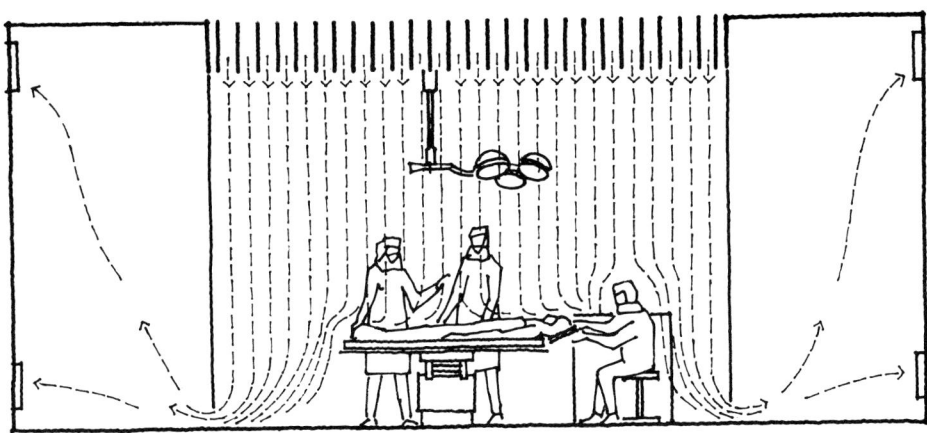

In vertical unidirectional airflow rooms up to 90 times less bacteria than in traditionally ventilated operation rooms have been measured.

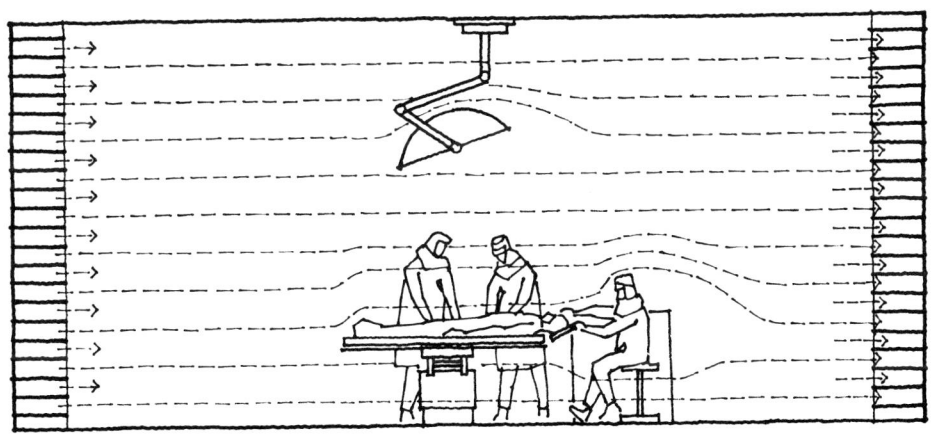

In horizontal unidirectional airflow rooms up to 11 times less bacteria than in traditionally ventilated operation rooms have been measured.

In some operations of long duration with implant of foreign material, as for example in a total prosthetic replacement of the hip, a lower incidence in wound sepsis might be possible[30].

---

30 see also Whyte W, Shaw B H and Barnes R: A bacteriological evaluation of laminar-flow systems for orthopaedic surgery. 1973, The Journal of Hygiene 71:559–564.

Lindberg Lars: "Sterila" operationsrum med laminar air-flow. 1973, Läkartidningen 70:4413–4416.

The evidence that unidirectional clean air flow in itself has a favourable influence on the incidence of post-operative surgical wound infections is not yet conclusive.

There has been the same doubt about the efficiency of the unidirectional air flow as about the operation enclosures with a high rate of air exchange. High rate air exchange systems require to be evaluated in controlled clinical trials before being generally accepted for bacteriological reasons. Certainly, additional data must be obtained.

The essence of the *air curtaining or zonal ventilation system* is the use of thin air-seal streams in a room to limit the area sensitive to particles to an inner zone where a stable rate of air exchanges higher than that in the rest of the room can be maintained by the introduction of air through a perforated ceiling[32].

In operation rooms with zonal ventilation the hourly turnover in the central part is about 80 times. The particle concentration in that part has been found about half that in the periphery. In conventionally ventilated operation rooms the concentration is about the same[33]. Only about one third of particles are transferred from the periphery into the centre, which means that the air current from the ceiling is too slow to create an effective air curtain around the operation table[34].

To choose between different ventilation systems on their special merits is difficult. Before unidirectional units had started to spread, the choice affected only the final 10 per cent of the performance of the operation room air-conditioning system[35] and was thus of relatively little importance.

More recently it has been shown that conventional air-conditioning systems with proper filtering and air flows can provide atmospheres with the same extremely low bacterial contamination as special airhandling devices[36]. In units already running at rates of one per cent or less for wound infections acquired at the time of operation, it is difficult to demonstrate any advantages conferred to different methods of ventilation[37].

32 Allander Claës and Abel Enno: Investigation of a New Ventilating System for Clean Rooms. 1968, Medical Research Engineering 3:28–38.

33 Hambraeus A, Bengtsson S and Laurell G: Bacterial contamination in a modern operating suite. 2. Effect of ventilation on airborne bacteria and transfer of airborne particles. Stencil. Institute of Clinical Bacteriology, University of Uppsala, Sweden 1977, p 1.

34 ibid, p 15.

35 Ma Wm Y I: Air Conditioning Design for Hospital Operating Rooms. 1965, The Hospital Engineer 19:262.

36 see also Haslam Kenneth R: Laminar Air-Flow Conditioning in the Operating Room: A Review. 1974, Anaesthesia and Analgesia 53:194–199.

37 Shooter R A: Infection arising in the operating room. Vingt-quatrième congrès de la Société Internationale de Chirurgie. Moscou 21–28 août 1971. Société Internationale de Chirurgie. Brussels, no publishing year, p 88.

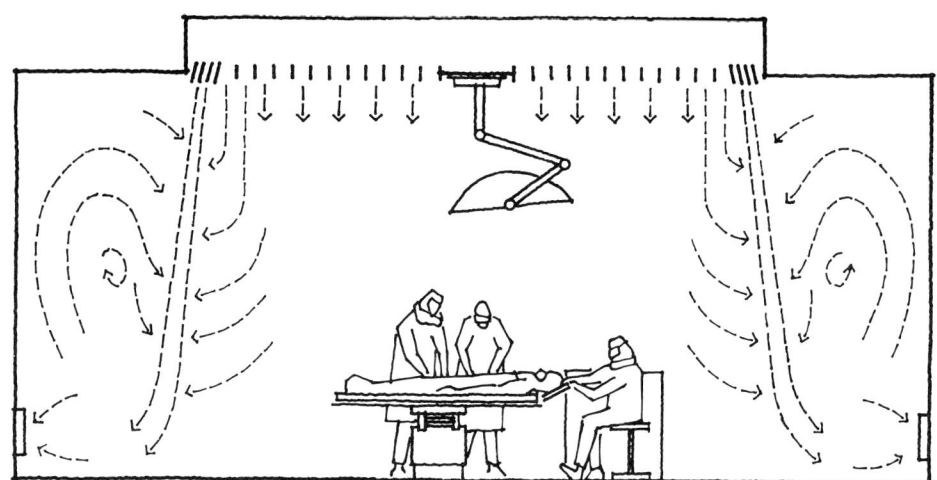

In the air curtaining system by Claës Allander thin air-seal streams are expected to limit the sensitive area to a zone, which is given higher air exchange rates than the room outside the zone.

The method of exhaust is considered to be important. Exhaust ports at 1.0 m above the floor have been found to be more effective in maintaining low airborne microbial population than ports at skirting board level[38].

Each operation room unit with its adjacent services should have its own adjustable air conditioner, easily accessible for maintenance. It should be possible to regulate the amount of clean air entering the operation room and the anaesthetic room, to select any temperature within the range 18°C to 30°C and to vary the relative humidity between 40 and 55 per cent.

The temperature in the operation room is usually registered on a wall thermometer. The wall thermometer does not give an accurate indication of the thermal condition prevailing at the operation table, therefore when making assessments of operation room temperatures, consideration should be taken to radiant heat which is caused by the close grouping of persons and to draughts caused by air circulation.

It is strongly felt that it is impossible to keep pathogenic microbes out of mechanical ventilatory equipment, where humidified air is used.

Detective filter systems and the contaminated water of the humidifying units have proved to be the weakest spots of air conditioning systems in hospitals. The ventila-

38 Ulrich J A, Cribbs W and Michaelsen G S: Recirculation of air in operating rooms. 1976, Medical Instrumentation 10:282–286.

tory equipment has been mentioned as one of the principal vectors of Gram-negative infections[39]. *Pseudomonas aeruginosa* and *Klebsiella/Aerobacter* have been found in humidifiers of the air-conditioning systems[40]. The bacterial concentration in the exhaust ducts may be quite high[41].

For humidifying, if found necessary, deionized or distilled water should be used. Bacterial growth can be prevented in hot-water humidifiers by keeping the temperature at 50°C or above[42].

Attention has been called to the need for rigorous disinfection of them[43]. The entire air transport duct system should be cleaned several times a year[44], and the filters changed according to the maintenance scheme, which has to be provided by the firm, who has delivered the system.

The use of UV irradiators after humidifiers in the air channel system reduces the amount of air-borne germs only slightly[45].

To prevent reverse circulation in the ducts, operation room ventilation should be kept running over-night at reduced volumes.

Before a surgical unit is taken over for use, the ventilation system should be bacteriologically tested. Bacteriological tests should lateron be repeated regularly.

It has been suggested[46], that the entire surgical department, including closets, storage areas and personnel areas, should be ventilated and the air filtered as in the operation room. There is no scientific evidence available to motivate this exquisite standard of ventilation.

The present methods of background heating are by ceiling heating, by underfloor heating, by provision of radiant panels, and by low pressure hot-water radiators.

Heating should be accomplished without appreciable air movement. The heating surfaces should maintain a temperature, which is below the dust carbonization point

39 McCabe William R: Gram-negative Bacteremia. 1973, Disease-a-Month. December, p 36.

40 Grün L and Pitz N: UV-Strahlen in Düsenkammern und Luftkanälen von Klimaanlagen in Krankenhäusern. 1974, Zentralblatt für Bakteriologie, Parasitenkunde, Infektionskrankheiten und Hygiene B 159:50–60.

41 see also Ostertag H: Die hygienishe Überwachung der klimatisierten aseptischen Bereiche im Krankenhaus. 1973, Zentralblatt für Bakteriologie, Parasitenkunde, Infektionskrankenheiten und Hygiene 157:1–22.

42 Lumley Jean: Decontamination of anesthetic equipment and ventilators. 1976, British Journal of Anaesthesia 48:3–8.

43 Peres E J, Criado A, Moreno M and Avello F: Mechanical Ventilators as Vehicles of Infection. 1975, Acta Anaesthesiologica Scandinavica 19:180–186.

44 Feller Irving, Richards Kathryn E and Pierson Carl L: Prevention of Postoperative Infections. 1972, The Surgical Clinics of North America 52:1361–1366.

45 see also Grün L and Pitz N: UV-Strahlen in Düsenkammern und Luftkanälen von Klimaanlagen in Krankenhäusern. 1974, Zentralblatt für Bakteriologie, Parasitenkunde, Infektionskrankheiten und Hygiene. B 159:50–60.

46 Laufman Harold: Surgical Hazard Control. 1973, Archives of Surgery 107:552–559.

A relatively low temperature radiant heating ceiling represents a good solution, although ceiling heating has given rise to some complaints of oppressiveness. Large ceiling surfaces are suitable also for radiant cooling.

Underfloor heating has caused complaints of discomfort, particularly when rubber boots are worn. The problems are considered to arise because of the retention of residual heat within the ceiling or floor. Similar complaints arise from the use of radiant panels.

Conventional radiators very obviously offer dust traps and are a nuisance to clean. Their mere existance gives mostly a feeling that cleanliness has not been bothered about very much.

Ventilation of areas other than operation rooms

The traditional association of smells with dirt and disease makes them in a health care facility particularly undesirable. Some smells arise from volatile fluids used in treatment and may indicate a hazard from inflammable or noxious vapour. They occur intermittently in the course of many clinical sequences and must be dispersed before the next patient enters the room. This implies a speedy air change, meaning the window is effective and the brief entry of external noise irrelevant.

It is important that staff are able to control the natural ventilation easily. In clinical rooms with sealed windows appropriate speedy ventilation may be difficult to achieve, even with mechanical installations.

For the majority of modern buildings the case for air conditioning has rested upon prestige and status. Air conditioning has been regarded as a safeguard against the effects of air and noise pollution, which in itself must, for many reasons, be tackled at the source[49]. Air conditioning application in the general areas in hospitals has to a great extent been based on similar views.

The ventilation installations have seldom met specifications. There has been no action testing, and compromises have been common when the budget must be cut. Some of the most expensive installations have been the worst performers.

Air-conditioning equipment has been poorly maintained because there has been gross ignorance about its function and purpose[50]. In the US about 90 per cent of all air-conditioning problems have been due to poor maintenance or none at all[51].

Air conditioning could be supported in cases where the effective temperature of the built environment inside the hospital exceeds 24 to 24.5°C.

---

49 see also Harper Dennis: Building, Scarce Resources and Limited Energy Supplies. 1974, Advance 15:84–87.

50 Walter Carl W in 1972, Hospital Topics 1:20.

51 van Kirk Jr William K: Preventive Maintenance and Your Air-Conditioning System. 1973, Building Operating Management 20:3:24.

Air conditioning is considered to be a health hazard in its present forms[52]. Rapid cooling and direct draughts must be avoided.

The patient room air conditioning unit should be in a room opposite or adjacent to it; never directly in it[53]. It should not be run throughout the night without precautions taken to avoid draughts and chilling the patient.

The installation of a 2-speed air-conditioning plant is recommended. The lower speed of the plant would maintain a background heating level at 16°C.

Air movements are technically unavoidable where air conditioning is employed. It is advisable for the benefit of comfort to limit the air velocity to 0.15 m/sec.

In *post-operative recovery* areas air treatment is important, because of residual anaesthesia odour and postanaesthesia nausea.

In the *intensive care* and treatment units air inlet is frequently provided by a circular of square diffuser in the ceiling sited over the patient's bed. This siting is objectionable for the patients and nurses. There should be approximately ten to twelve changes of air per hour. The temperature in the individual ICTU rooms should be adjustable.

To prevent a build-up of bacteria released by persons in the open section of the ICTU, and to keep airborne bacteria at low level, it is probably desirable that the section has 15 to 20 air changes per hour[56].

Recirculation of air

In hospitals energy conservation should be applied as far as possible to recover heat and lower investment costs.

At least partial recirculation could be permitted in all areas, including operation departments, post-operative recovery areas, and intensive care units, which have proper filtration. It has been stated[58] that added quantities of cleaned, recirculated air would markedly upgrade the sanitary quality of the air.

The increasing use of non-volatile anaesthetic gases has reduced cold flash and other combustion hazards to a minimum. However, there are no data tolerable concentration of inhalation anaesthetic agents. Until more information is available, some attention should be paid to this circumstance.

52 Benfer Kenneth L: Air Conditioning — Blessing or Curse? 1973, Pennsylvania Medicine 76:4:55–58.

53 ibid

56 Control of Hospital Infection. ed by E J L Lowbury, G A J Ayliffe, A M Geddes and J D Williams. Chapman and Hall. London 1975, p 230.

58 Kethley T W and Cown WB: What Is the Quality of the Air in Your Operating Room? 1976, The Guthrie Bulletin 46:1:25–37.

FLOORS, RAMPS, STEPS, WALLS, SHIELDING, OPENINGS

Floors

Dominating hospital floor coverings are vinyl, resiliant sheet vinyl, asbestos tiles, terazzo, terazzo tile, and carpeting.

American analyses have indicated that considering accumulated costs of 20 years the vinyl asbestos tiles are cheapest[1]. Sheet vinyl was 1.2 times more expensive than vinyl asbestos tiles, terazzo 1.4 times, carpeting 1.45 times and terazzo tiles 1.8 times. Later it has been stated that demanding a quality carpet designed for health care — not to be used in potential high-spillage areas — will result in a higher initial cost than for vinyl, but the long-term maintenance costs are considerable lower[2].

The function of the floor should be the determining factor when choosing floor covering. The blind use sound reflected up from walking surfaces to orient themselves. Carpeting, which absorbs or muffles sound, is not desirable in areas which are used by the blind[3]. However, a live acoustical environment makes hearing more difficult for the partly deaf.

Many of the ambulant disabled prefer a nonskid, carpeted floor as dense, short-pile carpets provide a most desirable walking surface, which provides antislip conditions for normal walking or when crutches are used. Wheeled equipment, and carts will require third-generation nylon of low, thick pile, glued directly to the floor[4].

Considerations, such as acoustical quality *, safety, comfort, and appearance, could make *wall-to-wall carpeting* an appropriate and perferred selection in carefully considered areas, not at least in the patient day-areas and in the administrative section.

When broadloom is impractical because of unequal wear or need to access to the floor beneath carpet tiles, or modular carpet system, could be adapted. The squares, usually 0.45 by 0.45 m, stay put on the floor even under wheeled traffic. Carpet tiles come in various styles and constructions, including velvets, tweeds, and prints.

1   Report to the Congress. Study of Health Facilities Construction Costs by the Comptroller General of United States. Nov. 20, 1972, p 62.

2   Dolson Jan, Hesla Loren, Krewson Carol, Parimucha Joe: Around the patient. 1976, Progressive Architecture 57:9:54–57.

3   see also Harkness Sarah P and Groom Jr James N: Building without Barriers for the Disabled. Whitney Library of Design. New York 1976, p 16.

4   Rees Jr Frank W and Burch Emily: Barrier-free design reflects spirit of the law. 1978, Hospitals 52:4:121-125

*   After carpeting noise levels in patient rooms have been reduced from 49 dB to 41 dB, in corridors from 54 to 48 dB (Michaelsen George S: Noise Production and Control. in Environmental Health and Safety in Health-Care Facilities. ed by Richard G Bond, George S Michaelsen and Roger L DeRoos. Macmillan Publishing Co Inc. New York and Collier Macmillan Publishers London 1973, p 143).

Carpets in hospitals must be of low static resistance to avoid electric sparks. Caution in the use of carpeting and under carpet padding should be exercised both as to fire resistance and potential production of toxic fumes in case of fire[5].

Concerning the microbiological hazards of the carpets, airborne bacteria have been found to be present in similar numbers — in two blind hospital corridors — whether the floors were carpeted or covered with sheet vinyl[6].

Also other studies of soft flooring material, which is waterresistant, has non-absorbent PVC base, is impervious from above and below, has a pile of 2 mm upright fibres, and is cleaned at least once daily with a vacuum cleaner fitted with a filter, suggest that in a clinical area there is no additional microbiological hazard of this type of carpet[7].

However, variations in carpet construction — pile height weight per unit area, weave — have a significant effect on the number of organisms that will be found in that carpet and the atmosphere above it[8]. Busy human motion influences the amount of indoor airborne bacteria to a much higher degree than do most kinds of floor coverings[9]. The interiors of carpets are largely unaffected by treatment. Because of the inaccessibility of the carpet's substance meticulous maintenance is necessary[10].

Smells caused by bacteriological decomposition of spills on carpeted floors are a major drawback to the widespread use of carpets in patient care areas of hospitals. Liquid spills on carpets are difficult to remove completely, because the liquid is absorbed by the fibres and soaks through the backing to the subfloor. The use of non-absorbent pile fibres and an impervious backing can prevent this but necessitate the use of synthetic fibres. It is feasible to produce conventional, woven wool carpets, with a liquid-impervious back, but making wool non-absorbent for water — and oil-based liquids is almost certainly not an economical proposition[11].

At present there is no evidence to indicate that carpeting should be eliminated for hygienic reasons from hospitals, nor is there any evidence on which its unrestricted use can be endorsed unconditionally[12].

---

5   Carroll Walter W: Joint Commission Accreditation Standards for Anesthesia Services and Intensive Care Units. in Public Health Aspects of Critical Care Medicine and Anesthesiology. ed by Peter Safar. F A Davis Company. Philadelphia 1974, p 50-63.

6   Bakker P G H and Faoagali J L: The Effect of Carpet on the Number of Microbes in the Hospital Environment. 1977, The New Zealand Medical Journal 85:88–92.

7   Ayliffe G A J, Babb J R and Collins B J: Carpets in Hospital Wards. Central Sterilising Club. Sixteenth Annual Meeting. Leeds, 1974. A Health and Social Service Journal Supplement. October 1974, p 12-14.

8   see also Bakker P G H and Faoagali J L: The Effect of Carpet on the Number of Microbes in the Hospital Environment. 1977, The New Zealand Medical Journal 85:88–92.

9   Rotter M: Untersuchungen über die Beeinflussung des Luftkeimgehaltes durch Teppichböden. 1974, Sozial- und Präventivmedizin 19:321-328.

10 Bonde G J: Bacterial flora of synthetic carpets in hospitals. 1973, Health Laboratory Science 10:308-318.

11 Bakker P G H and Faoagali J L: Anti-Microbial Treatment for Hospital Carpets. 1977, The New Zealand Medical Journal 85:132-135.

12 see also Shaffer J G: Carpeting in hospitals. 1974, Health Laboratory Science 11:57-60.

It is inadvisable to instal carpets in critical medicine rooms[13] and in spaces where stains from blood, vomit, food, beveridge, and clay can be produced. Moreover, the use of such carpeting is not recommended on floors which are subject to considerable wear, or where carpeting itself is a source of wear, for example, on childrens clothing[14].

Resiliant and acoustical foam backed sheet vinyl would be a good substitute for carpeting[15].

To improve the floor cleanliness standards, colours and patterns that disguise uncleanliness and dirt should be avoided in hospitals.

People with walking difficulties

People who walk with difficulty, with or without a special aid, experience a range of problems. They may have reduced balance, agility, or speed of movement, or combination of these handicaps. Unevenness and raised joints of the walking surface can be hazardous. Very small vertical changes in level are particularly so, as they are not easily seen. Loss of balance, tripping, or falling usually result[16].

When the proportion of blind and partly sighted patients is considerable, changes of materials can be used in floors to indicate the proximity of *entrances, rest-rooms steps* and *stairs,* or potentially hazardous areas[17]. Colour and texture contrasts to the surfaces provide location cues and warnings.

Flooring in operation room and anaesthetic room

For the flooring material in the operation rooms as well as in anaesthetic and equivalent rooms, high demands are made.
The floors should
       be nonslippery, when wet
       withstand intensive application of water and disinfectants
       not absorb physically foreign molecules

13 see also Teppichboden und Gesundheit. 1976, Hospital-Hygiene, Gesundheitswesen und Desinfektion 68:163-164, 185-186.

14 Heltäckande textilmattor i vårdbyggnader. Spri råd 5.20. Stockholm 1974, p 5.

15 personal communication: 1977, K A Klannemark, Ronnebyhamn.

16 Jones Michael A and Catlin John H: Design for access. 1978, Progressive Architecture 59:4:65-71.

17 Harkness Sarah P and Groom Jr James N: Building without Barriers for the Disabled. Whitney Library of Design. New York 1976, p 16.

have a high resistance to breakdown*
be elastic and recover after the removal of heavy objects
be fire resistant
be colourfast
not require treatment with wax or other preservatives.

Coved skirting with a minimum radius of 3 cm and a minimum height of 10 cm should be used for all floors, thereby eliminating junction between skirting and flooring.

It has been required that the floors should be homogenous and not subject to surface cracking. However, no differences in the rates of contamination between sealed and unsealed floors have been found[18].

PVC flooring is the floor finishing probably to satisfy the majority of the requirements of operation room flooring. If a minimum of seams is desirable, PVC should be heat-sealed.

Rubber flooring is satisfactory for comfort, but does — as a rule — not take kindly to heavy loads and will show marks from heavy equipment.

Terazzo is completely satisfactory because of its hardness, noiseness and tendency to craze, and the time taken to repair it. Terazzo can be destroyed by wrong cleaning materials.

Conductivity of flooring

Precaution against explosions** must be maintained in the operation room and where flammable anaesthetics are stored. Also in teaching hospital areas when taught on flammable anaesthetic agents, the flooring should be conductive. The operation rooms should be uniformly protected to avoid restrictions in their use.

---

* When people walk across floors, particles are generated in relation to the inability of the flooring to resist breakdown. 150,000,000 particles, each 1 micron in size, can be generated by wearing away a thickness of 1 micron from a postage stamp sized area (Austin Philip R and Timmerman Stewart W: Design and operation of clean rooms. Business New Publishing Company. Detroit 1965, p 145).

18 Vesley Donald and Michaelsen G S: Application of a Surface sampling Technic to the Evaluation of bacteriological Effectiveness of certain Hospital Housekeeping Procedures. 1964, Health Laboratory Science 1:107.

** Only when a gas which will support combustion, a flammable material, and a source of ignition are assembled simultaneously fires and explosions can occur. Flammable anaesthetic agents are used in many countries only in special circumstances, but it is impossible in the circumstance of anaesthesia to eliminate gases which support combustion, as oxygen-enriched mixtures are almost the rule. (Vickers M D: Hazards in the operating theatre. Fires and explosions. 1973, Annals of the Royal College of Surgeons of England 52:354-357).

Recovery areas are not a practical antistatic problem because of the rapidity with which expired gases become non-flammable after administration ceases[19].

The conductive floor finishes have to conform with the standards and requirements of national agencies.

During the lifetime of an antistatic floor its resistance may change. The resistance of terazzo floors usually increase, whilst that of PVC floors decreases with time. Antistatic rubber has a somewhat limited life and is less convenient in other ways.

When conductive flooring is present in nonflammable anaesthetizing locations, the monthly testing of floors and furniture can be waived provided at least an annual test of the floors is conducted that in no case will show an average resistance of less than 25,000 ohms and no single reading of less than 10,000 ohms. Where the annual check shows an average resistance of less than 25,000 ohms, it has to be reverted to the monthly check of the flooring and furniture in the room[20]. A conductive floor requires systematic maintenance according the manufacturer's maintenance instruction if it is to fulfil its function. Maintenance materials that leave scum or a film on the surface and may counteract its conductivity should definitely not be used.

Flooring in laboratories and radiology units

For *laboratories* special building adaptions, such as deep inserts in the floor, must be taken in planning considerations at an early stage. When heavy equipment might be used, attention has to be paid to floor loading.

All materials to be used for laboratory floors should be tested with strong acids, alkalis, water, solvents, and histological stains. The floors should be of non-slip quality, also when wet, easy to clean, hard wearing, and fire resistant.

Linoleum and tiles are widely used in laboratories. Linoleum floors are slip, when wax-treated. In spite of that they have to be kept well polished in areas where decontamination occurs[21].

Asbestos vinyl tiles are hard wearing and not so slippery when wet. They are, however, attacked by some alkalis and acids. Flexible vinyl is preferred for laboratory floor covering because it is more impervious and therefore a little more resistant to chemical attack[22]. Flexible vinyl is resistant to acids, but not to all solvents[23]. Vinyl sheets should not be laid where it would be subjected to abrasive materials or to heavy point loads[24].

19 Vickers M D: Fire and explosion hazards in operating theatres. 1978, British Journal of Anaesthesia 50:659-663.

20 Portersfield III John D: Building and grounds safety. 1977, Hospitals 51:14:14.

21 Everett K and Hughes D: A Guide to Laboratory Design. Butterworths. London & Boston 1975, p 14.

22 see also Ferguson W R: Practical laboratory planning. Applied Science Publishers Ltd. London 1973, p 33.

23 personal communication: 1977, K A Klannemark, Ronnebyhamn.

24 Everett K and Hughes D: A Guide to Laboratory Design. Butterworths. London & Boston 1975, p 14.

Floor which have to be hosed down should be laid with falls and the channels should discharge into sealed top back inlet gullies outside the building: if open floor channels cannot be avoided, they should have rust-proof, easily cleaned metal grids[25].

To reduce the noise level in the laboratory corridors to a minimum resilient and acoustical vinyl floor covering should come to use. More recently it has been recommended to use in laboratories carpeting in as many areas as possible[26].

In *radiology* units loads of 2,000 kg/m^2 are installed, a fact to be observed when designing the radiodiagnostic department. By using flooring with readily removable tiles the laying or removing of low tension and high tension cables is simplified and an easier changeover of equipment is achieved.

Flooring in rooms with electronic equipment

The use of electrical and electronic equipment in direct contact with the patient, and the introduction of electrodes into body cavities, particularly in the close proximity to or into the heart has increased electrical hazards.

Conductive floors in rooms where electronic equipment is used on patients are needed. No appreciable charge should be allowed build up on the floor, which should have a resistance to limit the current from any defective equipment and simultaneously dissipate the energy through its conductivity.

25 Mortuary & post-mortem room. Hospital Building Note 20. Department of Health and Social Security. Welsh office 1970, p 3.

26 Manual for laboratory planning and design. College of American Pathologists. Skokie III 1977, p 12.

Ramps, steps, stairs

If ramps are to be used by the ambulant disabled as the main means of entry, a minimum gradient of slope is best.

In the US the law requires that pedestrian circulation on the site and in the building be no steeper than a 5 per cent gradation. Any length of circulation steeper than five per cent is considered a pedestrian ramp, the gradation of which may not be greater than 8.3 per cent (1:12). Pedestrian ramps must have handrails. A landing every 6 m is required in Sweden[1], every 9 m in the US[2].

As minimum width of the slanting level 1.6 m could be accepted. All slanting levels should be slip free and fitted with hand rails, one at the height of about 0.9 m and the other at the height of 0.5 m for the ease of visitors in wheel-chairs.

Many of the ambulant disabled find stairs easier to negotiate than ramps, which are necessary for the chairbound[3].

Staircases in health care facilities should have 0.15 m risers and 0.32 m treads.

Handrails should be positioned on both sides of steps and stairs and should extend beyond the first and last steps on at least one side and preferably on both to allow people with long leg braces to pull themselves beyond these points[4].

Steps, stairs, and handrails should not be made of slippery material. Hard, level, non-skid surfaces are essential. The nosings should be nonprotruding so that people with stiff joints, braces, artificial legs or other leg or stability problems will not catch their toes as they climb[5].

1   Svensk Byggnorm 1975. Utgåva 3. Statens planverks författningssamling 1978:1. Stockholm 1978, p 380.

2   Rees Jr Frank and Burch Emily: Barrier-free design reflects spirits of the law. 1978, Hospitals 52:4:121-125.

3   Harkness Sarah P and Groom Jr James N: Building without Barriers for the Disabled. Whitney Library of Design. New York 1976, p 20.

4   Harkness Sarah P and Groom Jr James N: Building without Barriers for the Disabled. Whitney Library of Design. New York 1976, p 21.

5   ibid

Walls, ceilings

Traditionally it has been regarded reasonable to propose that *wall materials* in the high hygienic standard areas like the operation rooms[1] should be hard, robust, impervious, jointless, non-absorbent, easily cleaned and decontaminated. Likewise, it has been recommended that the wall finishes should be unaffected by colour change, staining and mildew[2].

These requirements in perfection are held too high as the hygienic hazards of the walls are extremely small.

Ceramic tile has been criticized because the rough surface of grouting may entrap bacteria. New, smooth grouting materials, suitable for operation room use are available. Other suitable surface materials include laminated polyesters with an epoxy finish and hard vinyl coverings which can be heat-sealed[3].

Good quality coating may be a less costly solution which can be accepted. The glossier the surface, the easier it is to keep clean. High-gloss speciality coating finishes are relatively impervious to stain penetration. Semi-matt wall surfaces reflect less light than high gloss-finishes and are less tiring to the staff.

The corners in the operation room should be rounded and viewing cabinets, switches, plugs, cupboards and door frames in flush with the wall surfaces to make cleaning routines easier.

Factory-made wall units with equipment mounted on them so that they can be maintained from outside the operation room may simplify both maintenance and alteration works. The walls should not cause the build-up of a static electrical charge.

Present trends toward lighter construction affect shielding design. The attenuation by masonry walls often was ignored in the past although equivalent to 1 to 2 mm lead.

Allowance must be made for possible future increases in protection requirements. However, it is expensive and often difficult to add to the shielding after it is installed. Primary protective barriers, rather than secondary, should be provided for all wall and floor areas likely to be exposed to the beam currently or in the future[4].

In laboratories the walls should also have a slow flame-spread characteristic[5].

---

1   see also Manual on Control of Infection in Surgical Patients. American College of Surgeons. J B Lippincott Company. Philadelphia-Toronto 1976, p 203.

2   see also White T: Wall Finishes in Operating Rooms. in British Health Care and Technology. British Operating Theatres. London 1972, p 13.

3   see also Laufman Harold: The control of operating room infection: discipline, defense mechanisms, drugs, design, and devices. 1978, Bulletin of the New York Academy of Medicine 54:472–483.

4   Braestrup Carl B: Radiation protection requirements. Second international symposium on planning of radiological departments. Philadelphia, September 1976.

5   Everett K and Hughes D: A Guide to Laboratory Design. Butterworths. London & Boston 1975, p 10.

In all hospital areas where equipment is moved, protective guards against wall damage should be made of a very heavy material.

The basic colour substances may affect the survival time of bacteria. While the germs on laquer survive for a relatively long time, the germ numbers decrease rapidly on dispersion paint (polyvinylpropionat). The examination of the survival times of bacterial living on coloured surfaces does not reveal any influence of the colour tones on the bacteria[6].

In areas where blind people have to move, sound-reflecting walls are preferred to sound-absorbing walls because the blind use their sense of hearing to guide themselves[7].

Partitions may be used to divide corridors from use areas. From the view-point of fire safety the normal requirement is continuous, slab-to-slab wall with at least one hour resistance[8].

The choice of *ceiling* construction in the medical performance area, particularly in operation rooms and X ray rooms depends on lighting, heating, and ventilating arrangements. Diversified demands for ceiling-mounted equipment require a careful programming.

Basically, the requirements for operation room ceiling surfaces from the view point of cleaning and decontamination are the same as for the walls.

As requirements concerning noise control in operation rooms have increased, the wall surfaces should be relatively non-reflecting. It should be mentioned that domed ceilings in combination with hard surfaces have sometimes created unfavourable acoustic conditions in operation rooms.

6   Gundermann K O and Schmehe G: Untersuchungen zur Überlebensdauer von Bakterien auf Oberflächen und der Möglichkeiten ihrer Beeinflussung. 1970, Archiv für Hygiene und Bakteriologie 154:110–113.

7   see also Harkness Sarah P and Groom Jr James N: Building without Barriers for the Disabled. Whitney Library of Design. New York 1976, p 16.

8   Where there's fire there's smoke. 1976, Progressive Architecture 57:9:58–63.

Electronic measurement of a patient's heart, brain, and other potentials generated by the body involves extremely weak electrical signals. As the recordings on the instruments are obtained by a high degree of amplification of these signals, the physiological recording may be seriously distorted or degraded by interference in the surrounding area.

American studies estimate that ambient electromagnetic noise from radio and TV-transmission, X ray units, even telephone dials, is in and around hospitals about 60 dB. A further estimate is that this noise increases by 3 to 5 dB every year[1].

Electromagnetic interference should be eliminated from rooms in which electro-encephalograph (EEG), electromyograph (EMG), or other equally sensitive equipment, but not electrocardiograph (ECG), is used or where the output of this kind of equipment is fed into a computer for comparison or analysis.

Among such rooms the following can be mentioned
intensive care and monitoring rooms
operation rooms
rooms for catheterization
rooms for angiographic techniques
all rooms for measurements of bioelectric potentials.

The electrical installation on inside or both sides of walls, floor and ceiling of the room should be screened by means of ferrous metal shielding of cables resp metal conduits for cables and wiring. This shielding should be connected only at one point to the protective earth.

Shielding systems vary from copper-clad plywood and modular panels of galvanized steel with a plywood core to transparent vinyl sandwich constructions encasing sheets of bronze screen. The latter permit a visual check for breakages in the metal screen and simplify the location of holes to be cut in the panels to accommodate pipes, ducts, conduits, and equipment.

To ensure radio-frequency interference-proof environment when galvanized steel panels* are used, seams and corners have to be tightly sealed with galvanized steel strips. As duct openings are a potential source of radio-frequency intrusion, supply air must enter the space through baffled wave-guide vents.

Any wire-power, telephone, and intercom penetrating the shield may act as an antenna to conduct radio frequency into the space. Every electrical wire must therefore enter through a radio-frequency electrical filter.

---

1   Aronson Ralph: Shielding spaces against electro-magnetic radiation. 1975, Architectural Record 157:3:160.

*   e g Ray Proof Operation, Keene Corporation, USA.

Because fluorescent lighting introduces its own electro-magnetic contamination into the shielded environment, lighting must be supplied by either incandescent or interference-free cold cathode fluorescent lamps[2].

The shielding of a radiation room shall protect occupationally exposed persons as well as non-radiation workers. It must not be impaired by joints, openings for pipes, ducts, etc. passing through the barriers, or by conduits, service boxes, etc. embedded in the barriers.

Permanent wall radiation screening in X ray department rooms, where the working capacity does not extend 150 kV and radiation is undirected, should comprise of a 2 mm thick sheet of lead or equivalent material. In the X ray department shielded floors will be necessary if there are rooms below the X ray rooms, particularly if tubes pointing downwards are used. When examinations are made with the under-coach tube, ceiling shielding will be necessary for rooms above. Concrete is likely to be the most effective shielding material.

Doors and other means of access to the room and observation windows also require special consideration to ensure adequate protection without sacrificing operational efficiency. The lead lining must also be sandwiched into the doors leading to the room.

For viewing openings between the operator and patient, at least 10 mm thickness shielding glass containing barium or lead should be used.

Similar requirements have been adapted on computer-assisted tomography units[3].

In operation rooms where X ray equipment may have the same capacity as that in the X ray department itself, it is essential to apply the X ray department standards.

The radiation protection relates also to the walls of the rooms in the emergency and in the intensive care unit where X ray equipment is used frequently.

In *nuclear medicine laboratories* safety precautions are much more important in *in vivo* than in *in vitro* studies. Shielding is required not only of the nuclides themselves, but of the surrounding room, so that the floors, walls, and ceilings adequately reduce radiation exposure[4].

2   Aronson Ralph: Shielding spaces against electro-magnetic radiation. 1975, Architectural Record 157:3:160.

3   Gautschi H: Standortbestimmung der computerisierten axialen Tomographie. 1977, Veska — Das Schweizer Spital 41:332–335.

4   Manual for laboratory planning and design. College of American Pathologists. Skokie III 1977, p 40.

Doors must not constrict the space required in different rooms.

Doorways should have 86 cm clear opening width to allow easy passage also for a wheelchair[1]. A level space at least 150 cm wide should extend about 45 cm on either side of the doorway for opening and closing the door by a wheelchair patient.

Door hardware should be designed with single-lever action and should require no more than 4 kg of pressure to open the door[2].

In the operation department, staff dressed in sterilized garments need a minimum door opening width of 90 cm.

A clearance of about 10 cm on either side of the bed including special equipment is required to move it through an opening. A width of 150 cm for (two leaf) door openings can be recommended[3]. If self closing operation room doors are used they should preferably be surface sliding, power operated, and controlled by photoelectric cells.

Any opening device adapted to the surgical department doors must allow them to be opened manually or swung open in case the device fails.

A device that holds the door open must be provided to simplify equipment moving.

Wooden doors to operation rooms are readily marked by knocks from operation tables and other equipment. Doors subject to heavy traffic should be protected at least up to a height of 125 cm with rubber, PVC or stainless steel. The sound insulation properties of the doors should be good. Kick plates should be soundabsorbent.

Operation rooms and anaesthetic rooms should be provided with safety glazed openings with blinds to save unnecessary opening.

Doors to fluoroscopic examination rooms should have no lightleaks into the examination room.

In the postoperative recovery area the doorways should pass beds easily. A door width of about 145 cm is recommended.

1   Harkness Sarah P and Groom Jr James N: Building without Barriers for the Disabled. Whitney Library of Design. New York 1976, p 32.

2   Rees Jr Frank W and Burch Emily: Barrier-free design reflects spirit of the law. 1978, Hospitals 52:4:121-125.

3   see also Karman Jarbas B: Cirurgia. in Planejamento de hospitais. Sao Paulo 1954, p 193.

    Dokumentatie Bouwwezen, Zieken-Huizen. A5. 1.2.1 Rotterdam 1955, p 7.

In the ICTUs handles can be omitted from doors, which can be pushed open[4]. Also here the door width should be about 145 cm. In neonatal intensive care units the door widths of 90 cm have been accepted[5].

X ray doors can generally be shielded by sheet lead, possibly in the form of a wood-lead-wood sandwich. Shielded doors may need an automatic closure to ensure that they are normally shut.

In laboratories 120 cm is considered to be the minimum acceptable door width. For easy exit doors should swing out from the laboratory. Secondary escape exits should be provided. There should be no windows in the doors to exit corridors.

When the number of partly sighted or blind is considerable, doors to dangerous areas should be identified by operating hardware that is knurled or roughened[6].

Generally, there should be no thresholds. Only in noisy workrooms low thresholds of rubber or similar material should be used.

Emergency exits must be clearly labelled. Exit signs may be designed to flash when the emergency alarm is on. However, flashing red lights can cause headaches, nausea and, in extreme cases, epileptic seizures[7].

Farthest point from a room to the nearest exit should be less than 60 m, from a patient-room less than 45 m in the US, in Sweden this distance in the nursing units is reduced to 30 m.

There are fire codes and regulations which require that the doors on patient floors be kept closed or be self-closing to prevent smoke spread. Many patients feel isolated behind closed doors and many nurses feel that they must be able to see their patients from the corridor. As a compromise the doors would be permitted to remain open, if so desired, but there should be provision for automatic or remote release and closing upon detection of smoke[8].

4   see also Burn James M B: Design and staffing of an intensive care unit. 1970, The Lancet 1:1041.

5   Dubois Olivier: Le centre de pathologie néonatale du centre hospitalier d'Arras. 1974, Techniques Hospitalières 30:1:51–60.

6   Harkness Sarah P and Groom Jr James N: Building without Barriers for the Disabled. Whitney Library of Design. New York 1976, p 16.

7   Rees Jr Frank W and Burch Emily: Barrier-free design reflects spirit of the law. 1978, Hospitals 52:4:121–125.

8   Where there's fire there's smoke. 1976, Progressive Architecture 57:9:58–63.

The ability to look out the window is extremely significant to the in-patient[1].

Windowless rooms may cause time disorientation and sensory monotony in patients. Also, staff cut off from visual contact with the outside world, have been reported to lose their orientation of time, the loss being followed by neurosis. However, clear views on the psychological aspects of window-less rooms remain to be formulated.

Attention to the outer world is essential to relieve the sense of enclosure and to provide muscular relief to the eye by allowing it to focus at a distance.

A view may be judged to be 'good' if at least a small portion of each 'layer' — ground, landscape, sky — is visible and it changes as much as possible with each change of the viewing position of the subject[2].

Window size is a compromise between the need to afford a satisfying view and the need to conserve energy and afford privacy. When window size is reduced, the shape and position of windows ought to be adjusted to the view. Near objects seem to require wider windows — 3.1 m — and distant objects narrower — 2.4 m[3]. Satisfaction is generally achieved when the window area occupies 20 to 30 per cent of the window wall[4].

The more constraints are applied, the greater the risk of there being no feasible window solution[5].

Window control devices should be placed within reach of those in wheelchairs.

Windows in the medical performance area must be easily accessible for cleaning. If used for ventilation, they must be equipped with filter screens and locks requiring special keys as precaution against unintentional disturbance to the interior climate.

In cold climate areas windows should be warmed to counteract condensation and downdraughts that discomfort staff and patient, particularly in the operation units.

1   see also Thompson John D and Goldin Grace: The Hospital: a social and architectural history. Yale University Press. New Haven and London 1975, p 271.

2   Thomas A Markus cited by Keep P J: Stimulus deprivation in windowless rooms. 1977, Anaesthesia 32:598–602.

3   E Ne'eman and R G Hopkinson cited by Keep P J: Stimulus deprivation in windowless rooms. 1977, Anaesthesia 32:598–602.

4   E C Keighley cited by Keep P J: Stimulus deprivation in windowless rooms. 1977, Anaesthesia 32:598–602.

5   see also Markus Thomas A: The Real Cost of a Window. in Transactions of the Barlett Society. Vol 8, 1969-70. School of Environmental Studies. University College London 1970, p 33–58.

Although the increased use of the image intensifier in *X ray rooms* has in some cases eliminated the need for complete blackout when carrying out fluoroscopic examinations, there are still times when the need for blackout is required.

Special care is necessary in the placing of windows in the X ray rooms. They may not look out onto areas outside the control of the X ray department or onto public access areas outside the control of the hospital. Windows in the path of direct X ray beam for lateral X ray exposures are hazardous. Window glass is ineffective for X-ray absorption. Even lead glass would be unsatisfactory[6].

Blinds should be provided for shade and privacy in X ray rooms which have windows.

6   see also Terry William and McLaren J W: Planning A Diagnostic Radiology Department. W B Saunders Company Ltd. London, Philadelphia, Toronto 1973, p 195.

Water and steam supplies

Water supply

The general estimate of water supply needs is about 400 to 650 litres per day and bed, a considerable increase from the 300 l in mid-thirties.

Basically, hospitals require a two-temperature range for hot water. Low temperature — about 43.5°C — is required for patient washrooms. For showers 38°C to 40°C is appropriate. Higher temperature systems — between 71°C to 90°C — account for the majority of a hospital's hot water requirements including physiotherapy, kitchen, and cafeteria requirements.

The temperature of hot water supplied to the surgical and similar departments should be regulated between 40°C and 44°C.

Drinking fountains should project out from the wall rather than be fully recessed[1]. It is useful to have both hand- and foot-operated controls.

There should be an arrangement for emergency cold water supply, which, on the failure of normal supply can be turned on.

It is widely held that tap water is free of bacteria whereas it merely has to be free of disease-spreading germs. The contamination of the public water supply with coliform and other bacteria forbids its use for washing and cleaning burns, wounds and internal organs, and makes a specially prepared germ-free water essential.

The supply of *distilled* and/or *sterile water* should be provided in bottles from a central fluids store. There are considerable risks of contamination inherent in a piped supply.

The bottles of water to be used in ultraclean areas should be sterilized in containers, so that they will be sterile on the outside.

Steam supply

Steam should be piped only to departments where nonelectric sterilizers are used.

1 Harkness Sarah P and Groom Jr James N: Building without Barriers for the Disabled. Whitney Library of Design. New York 1976, p 37.

The nature of work in the hospital generally, and in the surgical and similar departments particularly, demands a very high standard of hand cleanliness, and easily accessible washbasins. Of course, the washbasin should not be made a status symbol[1].

Washing should always be done in running water.

Warm water — approximately 32°C to 39°C — is more comfortable than either hot or cold[2]. In public facilities the provision of only fixed-temperature water at approximately 43°C could be considered[3].

For a long time plumbing-systems and fictures were placed in such a manner as to conserve costs instead of stressing the human aspects related to the use of the fixtures themselves[4].

The comfortable working height, when standing, can be set up at about 96 cm, with the water source at about 10 cm higher and the height of the washbasin rim at 91.5 to 96.5 cm[5]. If the washbasin is used by both standing and sitting persons, the basin height has to be lowered to 80 to 85 cm[6]. The minimum dimension of the washbasin from front to back would be 38 cm[7].

Washbasins used by wheelchair patients should preferably be 69 cm deep with a narrow apron to allow knee room underneath[8]. The maximum height for a washbasin for wheelchair patients is 80 cm.

A major problem is the water controls provided. The use of standard lever or wheel controls is unsanitary. It also permits the possibility of the water's not being turned off by the user who is careless or in a hurry. Taps which are fitted with extra-large handles to be operated by elbows or wrists have been introduced in an attempt to prevent recontamination of hands after washing. However, many of these fittings provide an example of expenditure which has achieved little or nothing[9]. Elbow-operated taps not only fail to improve hand hygiene, but may increase hand contamination as the handles offer a greater surface for contamination by dirty hands than the usual hand-operated taps[10].

1   see also Davies Hywel: Modern Medicine. Abelard London 1977, p 19.

2   Kira Alexander: The Bathroom. The Viking Press. New York 1976, p 30.

3   ibid, p 224.

4   ibid, p 8.

5   ibid, p 35.

6   Feurich H: Sanitärausstattung des Krankenhauses. 1975, Krankenhaus Umschau 44:137–144.

7   see also Kira Alexander: The Bathroom. The Viking Press. New York 1976, p 36.

8   Harkness Sarah P and Groom Jr James N: Building without Barriers for the Disabled. Whitney Library of Design. New York 1976, p 46.

9   Maurer Isobel M: Hospital Hygiene. Edward Arnold. London 1974, p 102.

10 ibid

Most of the hospital washbasin water controls should either be self-activating or require minimal contact by the user and should automatically shut off after a predetermined interval of approximately 45 to 60 seconds[11]. This might be accomplished by photoelectric cells, proximity sensors and electronic or pressure-operated timing valves.

To prevent splashing between in the operation department scrub-up washbasins, screens should be provided at each wash place. Scrub-up troughs or sloping screens or wired glass or nonbreakable glass are considered to reduce splashing.

Wall mounted *sinks* with double drainers, will be required also in the operation room disposal room, pantry, sterile service and endoscopy (cystoscopy) rooms.

Floor drains should be provided only in operation rooms, like those for endovasical surgery, where large amounts of water are used.

Water closets, urinals

In the patient areas now there is a general tendency to move in the direction of providing greater privacy for all personal hygiene functions.

Water closets should be wall-mounted and not foot operated. Containers for paper seat protectors as well as soap and paper towel dispensers should be provided. There should be no water closet without a *washbasin*.

Grab-bars next to WC are sometimes needed. 30 to 35 mm diameter will provide most people with a safe grip.

The minimum area for a wheelchair toilet is 2.9 m^2. If the wheelchair patient needs to be helped in the toilet, the toilet area has to be increased to 4.85 m^2. Circulation area outside the wheelchair toilet must be provided.

In wheelchair-toilets grab-bars are a necessity. The space between the wall and the grab-bar is critical. About 3.5 to 4 cm must be adhered to it[12]. If a person with a balance problem or paralysis slips, his or her arm may fall between the hard-rail and the wall. The whole weight of the body would then be taken on the trapped arm and a fracture could result.

All toilets should have aesthetic appeal and quality products to withstand normal hard use. Additional convenience are mirrors, shelves, coat and handbag hooks, and disposal containers. Proper height for toilet mirrors for wheelchair patients is 0.9 m above the floor. Toilet doors should be hung so that they open outwards.

Because of general requirements on cleanliness and of the risk of cross infection there is the need for at least a twice-daily cleaning of patient toilets.

11 Kira Alexander: The Bathroom. The Viking Press. New York 1976, p 225.

12 Jones Michael A and Catlin John H: Design for access. 1978, Progressive Architecture 59:4:65-71.

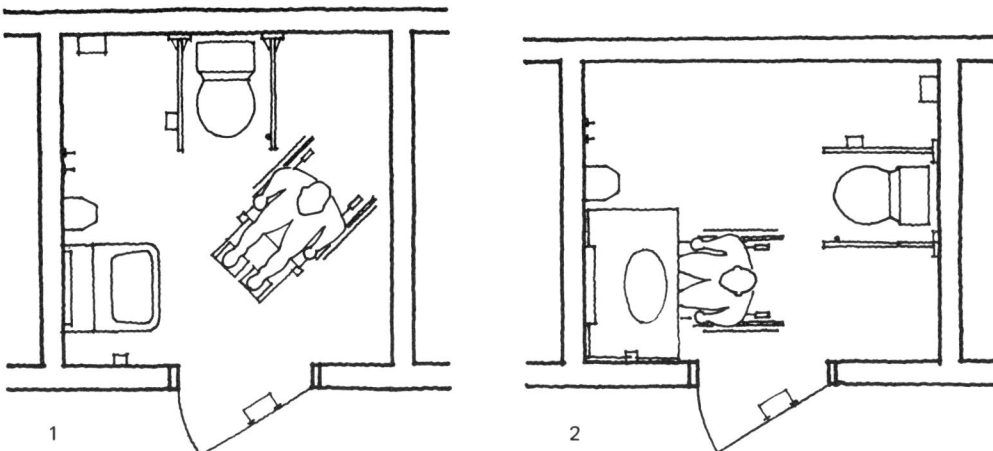

Toilets to be used by unassisted person in wheel chair. Alternative room 1 is sized 2.2 by 2.2 m, alternative room 2 – 2 by 2.4 m.

Urinals in hospital setting are not recommended[13].

Shower, bidet

The basic *shower* container or enclosure should have the dimensions of 106.5 by 91.5 cm[14]. The water source, which should be adjustable both to angle and coarseness of spray, should be set so that at a height of 152.5 to 167.5 cm the centre of the stream would be 30.5 to 38 cm from the wall. The bottom of the shower head itself should be no less than 198 cm from the floor[15].

A 38 cm full bench should be added across the dry end of the enclosure. A positive nonslip surface should be provided. The minimum opening to the shower should be about 61 cm wide, the sill height of not more than 10 cm[16].

Bidet-facilities should be made available in hospitals, not least in maternity units[17].

13 see also Hospital cleaning and patient infections. 1976, Health and Social Service Journal 86:163.

14 Kira Alexander: The Bathroom. Viking Press. New York 1976, p 76.

15 ibid, p 77.

16 ibid

17 Grossman G and Liebetrau B: Hygienische Untersuchungen in geburtshilflichen Abteilungen. 1977, Zentralblatt für Gynäkologie 99:139–146.

Electrical installations

Mains supply

Mains wiring should be arranged so that interference with patient monitoring and data transfer is minimal.

No patient should be permitted to come into direct contact with a potential electrical source. This requires non-electric controls for the nurse call, television, reading light etc. All electrical power should be connected to an isolation transformer[1].

To meet future developments, space should be left in building ducts for additional services.

X ray equipment may require an independent feeder not used for other branch circuits. In radiology departments the position of the switchboards should be chosen to facilitate the access of cables and to shorten the length of cabling to the radiodiagnostic units thus reducing voltage drop.

In several hospital areas a special or general emergency power supply has to be added to the ordinary mains supply.

Electrical outlets, switches

The types of switches, plug outlets, and other appliances using mains current must be approved by the responsible national authority.

Switches, emergency alarms, controls for light, heat, ventilation, and other similar control devices should be placed within reach of those in wheelchairs.

Electrical outlets should not be placed so that power cords between wall-outlets and junction-boxes and apparatus hinder the staff. Power cords must withstand normal cleaning and resist disinfectants.

Power requirements have increased significantly. In operation rooms about 20 outlets are needed for advanced operations. Electrical outlets in the vicinity of the operation table could be combined in a control panel comprising switches, fuses, signal controls, and plug outlets for main voltage and low voltage for electronic appliances. It is preferred to have the control panel hanging from the ceiling.

In the *anaesthetic room* provision should be made for at least six electrical outlets.

1   see also Goldstein J Richard and Parker Jr William T: The Design of the CCU Patient Room. Stencil. New York. December 1977, p 9.

The anaesthetic store light fittings must not produce sparks. The spine of the light fittings, and the transparent part in particular, must be of a material which will not spread flames. The light fittings should be protected from mechanical pressure.

In general *post-anaesthetic units,* up to eight electrical points are necessary for each bed[2]. In post-anaesthetic units for cardio-thoracic and similar surgery the number is up to ten. The outlets must be sparkproof and failsafe. Daily work is facilitated if fuses are placed over each bed.

In *intensive care* and treatment units 10 electrical points per bed are required[3].

In *neonatal intensive care* units 10 to 12 electrical outlets per infant are required[4].

In the *resuscitation room* of the emergency department, there should be for equipment two twin sockets with indicating lights and switches, one general purpose socket outlet, one twin socket outlet for X ray viewing and a provision for fixed electrical apparatus.

In *corridors* electrical outlets with protective ground should be spaced at 10 to 12-meter intervals.

Protective earthing

Any building containing medically used rooms shall have separated neutral and protective earth conductors throughout the building.

The protective earth conductors shall be marked green-yellow. At least inside medically used rooms they shall be insulated.

Illuminated signs

Illuminated engaged signs for operation rooms and anaesthesia rooms are needed in the surgical department corridor, for the X-ray rooms in the radiology department and other similar rooms. These signs should be indicated on an indicator-board within the unit.

There should be a central indicator-board where all electrical apparatus, ventilation pressures etc can be checked.

2   see also Klose R: Intensivtherapiestation   — Planung, Aufbau und Einrichtung. 1975, Medizinische Technik 95:60–64.

3   see also Stoddart J C: Intensive Therapy. Blackwell Scientific Publications. Oxford, London, Edinburgh, Melbourne 1975, p 192.

Clocks

Ordinary electric clocks are needed in waiting areas, nurses' stations, receptions, offices and diagnostic and treatment rooms, but also in special rooms such as post-mortem rooms and body stores.

Operation room, anaesthetic room and radiodiagnostic room clocks should be silent, built-in, prominent with a clearly visible sweeping second hand and connected to the hospital chronometer system.

In the scrub-up area, there should be clocks fitted in a position convenient to surgeons.

TV

TV location is critical. Aesthetics, visibility, and light reflection must all be considered.

In nursing units small TVs mounted on an arm or a larger set on the wall are the two current options[5].

Both alternatives present the same size image to the viewer. Pillow speakers are desirable.

Photoelectrical cell control

Operation room doors and other doors in the surgical unit could be operated by compressed air devices controlled by photoelectric cells.

Ideally, all water controls of washbasins should be automatically controlled either by proximity sensors or photoelectric cells, *or* by electronic or pressure-operated timing valves[6].

Patient calling and paging

The least complicated patient calling system in waiting areas is a simple loudspeaker communicating directly by the doctor and the waiting patient. The direct loudspeaker can be used by all doctors and from all consultation/examination rooms.

4   Tyne Michael D: Concepts for improved nursery design. 1974, Hospitals 48:21:66–68.

5   see also Dolson Jan, Hesla Loren, Krewson Carol, Parimucha Joe: Around the patient. 1976, Progressive Architecture 57:9:54–57.

6   Kira Alexander: The Bathroom. Viking Press. New York 1976, p 225.

All patients can be addressed simultaneously in case of an emergency. This system appears to work well[7].

Other patient calling systems include

> loudspeaker used by the receptionists after a request by the doctor

> loudspeakers with simultaneously illuminated light above the door to consulting suite in question

> nameboard with a light opposite each doctor's name, illuminated and accompanied by a buzz signal when calling the patient, also colour coded to match the colour of the waiting room chairs and consulting room nameboards

> illuminated call board above the door to each consulting suite, and accompanying buzz.

There is an upper limit of six served consulting or treatment units for call systems relying on sound. A larger number of consulting or treatment units sharing a waiting area creates an inevitable disturbance due to the call system, be it buzzer, loud-speaker or personal calling.

Patient-nurse call systems in nursing units seem to give the patient a sense of security[*], which is for them more important than convenience. During the day, the staff initiates more calls than the patients[8].

To meet the patients' needs for security and control, a hard control made up of modules has been recommended[9]. These modules, which include a nurse call, an emergency call, entertainment, window shade and temperature control, could be removed or added to, according to the patients' competencies.

If a coaxial cable system is designed into the building it would significantly decrease wiring costs of the project. Nurse call systems, telephones, TVs will be in the cable. The hospital can implement even more sophisticated systems as they are developed[10].

Acoustic staff paging and calling

In hospitals it is essential to be able to contact key personnel immediately and individually without disturbing others.

---

7   Cammock Ruth M: Health Centre Reception, Waiting and Patient Call. Her Majesty's Stationery Office. London 1973, p 26.

*   A 40 per cent decrease in calls when an entire floor of single-occupancy patients was moved to double-occupancy because of repairs has been observed (One Patient, One Room: Theory and Practice. Editorial. 1975, Modern Healthcare 3:3:65).

8   see also Thompson John D and Goldin Grace: The Hospital: a social and architectural history. Yale University Press. New Haven and London 1975, p 277.

9   Kraegel Janet M, Mousseau Virginia Schmidt, Goldsmith Charles, Arora Rajeev: Patient Care Systems. J B Lippincott Company. Philadelphia, Toronto 1974, p 90.

10 Dolson Jan, Hesla Loren, Krewson Carol, Parimucha Joe: Around the patient. 1976, Progressive Architecture 57:9:54–57.

This can be achieved by installing a radio paging system, which basically consists of a control-encoder, a transmitter with an antenna and a number of pocket receivers with different code numbers. The paged receiver emits an acoustic signal. All the other receivers remain silent because of the selectivity in the system. The system can function also as a group alarm facility, which makes it possible to alert groups of people, *e g* special emergency teams within seconds.

Normally the paging is handled by a central switch-board telephonist. One way or two way speech system provide for the controller the facility to speak directly to the paged individual.

Several clinics and even hospitals in a university teaching facility set-up can be linked together via telephone lines for co-ordinated paging. Systems are available from a few receivers up to more than a thousand. The normal coverage is within a 1.7 km radius from the antenna.

Regular acoustic paging — which must be balanced — is most needed in offices, lounges, changing rooms etc. It should be avoided in operation rooms and anaesthetic rooms.

Communication by *personal microphones* and earphones between the surgeon and the anaesthesiologist in the operation room and the technicians outside, is considered essential in major, *e g* cardiac, surgery.

Each bed in intensive care and therapy unit must be supplied with a call-system which patients or attendants can use to call the staff. A two-way nurse-to-nurse speech facility may sometimes be required.

A loud-speaking intercommunication system has been considered to have advantages in a radiodiagnostic department for location of staff, general enquiries and rapid reporting on results of films[11].

Sometimes visual display of information is given preference over audible systems.

Visual staff paging and calling

The simplest form of visual paging is represented by annunciator lights which indicate that some specific action should be taken. More elaborate visual paging includes a message or instruction on a video display screen, where messages are entered by means of a keyboard. The message remains on the screen until the paged responds or the information remains valid.

Flashing or audible signals attract attention to the screen.

11 see also Western Regional Hospital Board, Research and Development Unit: Organisation & Design of Radiodiagnostic Departments. Stencil. (Glasgow) January 1973, p 32.

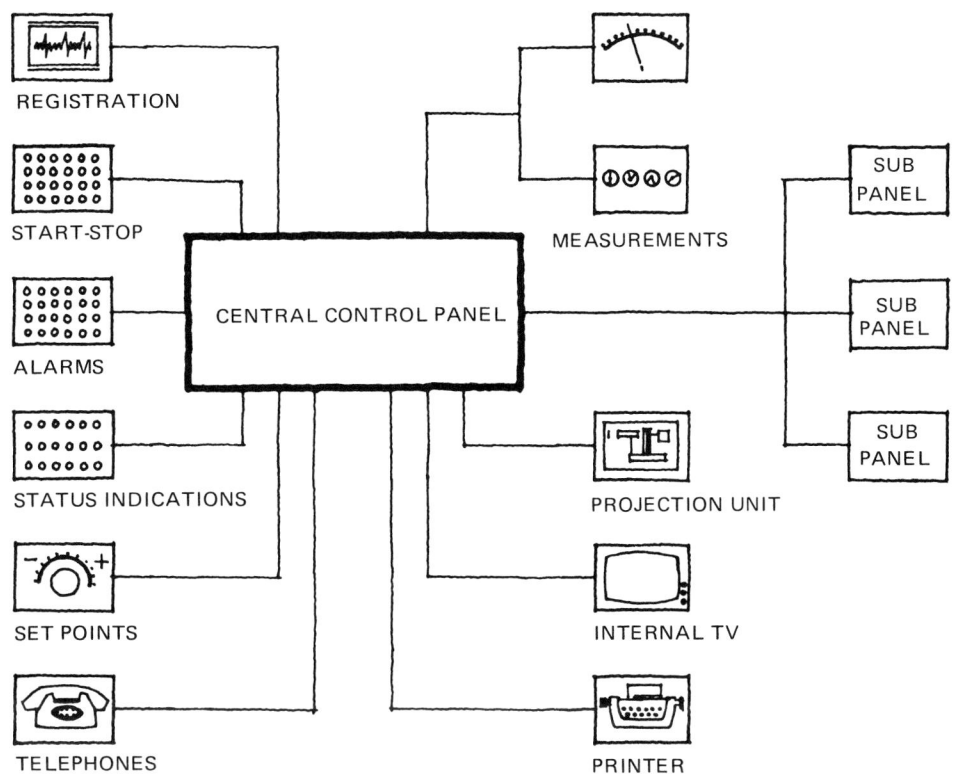

REGISTRATION

START-STOP

ALARMS

STATUS INDICATIONS

SET POINTS

TELEPHONES

CENTRAL CONTROL PANEL

MEASUREMENTS

PROJECTION UNIT

INTERNAL TV

PRINTER

SUB PANEL

SUB PANEL

SUB PANEL

A centralized supervisory system for lighting, heating, ventilation etc as developed by TELE-CONTROL.

Centralized supervisory system

In large hospitals a centralized control and supervisory system of the functioning of technical equipment for lighting, ventilation, heating-cooling etc can reduce the number of maintenance staff.

The various equipment for ventilation, lighting, heating, cooling, etc are first connected to subpanels, which in their turn are connected via coaxial or multiwire cables to a central panel.

13

From the central panel the equipment can be started and stopped automatically or manually. Temperature, pressure, humidity, etc can be checked and set points adjusted.

Main alarm points are monitored. A printer will print out the time of the arriving alarm and the identification number of the locality. The maintenance staff is alerted simultaneously via the paging system and/or acoustic signals.

Centralized supervisory systems are available for from one hundred up to several thousand control points.

Telephones

The number of telephones in a hospital is still increasing.

Telephone facilities for internal and external calls are required in consulting rooms, nurses' room, appointments and reception rooms, and for ambulance drivers. Connections to the hospital telephone exchange are also needed for duty rooms, changing rooms, and staff lounges of the units belonging to the medical performance area.

A telephone connection in the operation room would be for the convenience of the anaesthesiologist.

Telephones should be of desk pattern. For nurses they should be fitted in parallel with an indicating light which is easily visible.

Public call boxes or booths should be sited adjacent to the waiting spaces and in the entrance lobby. The needs of wheel-chaired patients must be observed.

Bed and service lifts

Lifts are needed for moving beds, stretcher beds, and other wheeled carriers. *Bed and service lifts* should have the dimensions 3.3 by 2.7 m, the height of 2.3 m and the capacity of about 1.800 kg. They should be equipped with normal controls and no landing call accumulation devices.

No single lifts should be provided, they should be arranged in groups of two or three

The control system for a group of *staff and visitors' lifts* should be based on normal controls with call-accumulating devices to shorten waiting times. Car-start time should be less than one second.

Lifts must be accessible to handicapped persons on the same level on which they enter the building.

The minimum door opening should be 0.85 m and the minimum inside measurements 1.5 m by 1.0 m. The control panel, including emergency buttons should not be higher than 1.1 m above floor.

Lift doors protected with a rubber safety edge should strike with a minimum impact and should promptly reopen. Doors equipped with a light ray or electronic detector system should reverse before they strike a person or bed in their path. Door reversal should be gentle.

Additional design considerations include automatic or self-leveling lifts to be within 1 cm above or below the adjoining floor.

There is little reason, if any, to supplement lifts with other technical installations to move supply carts and containers.

Goods lifts in which dangerous materials are carried should be provided with an alarm and emergency telephone. The floor of the lift should be able to retain spilled liquid and have reasonable chemical resistance. PVC and rubber are considered adequate for most purposes[12].

12 Everett K and Hughes D: A Guide to Laboratory Design. Butterworths. London & Boston 1975, p 30.

Medical gases, piped air, vacuum

Medical gases

Of medical gases only oxygen (O_2) and nitrous oxide (N_2O) are used in quantities that justify a piped supply economically. It seems unlikely that any other medical gas will be used in equivalent volumes.

Oxygen is the best known of all medical gases, used primarily for inhalation therapy and for anaesthesia. Constant supply and immediate availability throughout the hospital are essential. The non-interruption of oxygen supply is said to be more vital than any other service in the hospital.

Nitrous oxide has been described as the safest anaesthetic known provided it is administered with an adequate supply of oxygen. Together with oxygen it acts as the vehicle for stronger anaesthetic vapours. When inhaled, the gas produces a loss of sensibility to pain, followed by unconsciousness. When discontinued, the gas is rapidly eliminated, with post-operative effects almost unknown.

A Danish study[1] concludes that bacterial infection via contaminated O_2 and N_2O can take place, particularly in connection with unclean ventilatory equipment. The gases were contaminated by low pathogenic micrococci which in patients under anaesthesia must be considered as potentially pathogenic.

To maintain homeostasis the inspired gases should be warm and humidified. There are heated humidifiers which supply gases at 35°C and at 100 per cent relative humidity. The temperature of gases should be monitored to prevent tracheobronchial burn[2].

Piped breathing air may be needed in some hospital areas. The primary use of this air is for inhalation therapy, and in operation rooms and intensive care units for both adults and infants. Air must be both oil free and dry.

Modern ventilators have built-in mixers for oxygen and air whereby the final oxygen concentration can be varied according to the needs of the patient.

Air is also used in laboratories for a variety of purposes. Air is normally supplied from a cylinder manifold or from compressors.

Supply pipes from the gas centre should terminate with self-locking stop valves. Gas outlets points shall be at least 20 cm from electrical components which, correctly used or in case of a fault, could generate sparks.

---

1 Nielsen H, Vasegaard M and Stokke D B: Bacterial contamination of anesthetic gases. 1978, Danish Medical Bulletin 25:93–136.

2 Wanna Hanna T: Temperature Changes During Anesthesia and Surgery. 1978, Journal of the Iowa Medical Society 68:.97–200.

Gas should be released only when an apparatus for its administration is connected to the valve. Plug-in for similar rapid-connection plugs must be used. Gas connections must be non-interchangeable.

Gas pipes must be identified by colours according to national or international standards. Anaesthetic gas termination points should be clearly marked.

Piped oxygen and other gases require the installation of warning lights to indicate when the bank reserve reaches a critical level.

In the preoperative waiting areas only outlets for oxygen are needed.

In all anaesthetic rooms, operation rooms, plaster rooms, and recovery rooms outlets for oxygen, nitrous oxide, and compressed air are needed. In a preferable arrangement of operation room gas outlets, compressed air, and up to four suction pipes are laid in telescopic tubes which extend downward to about 2 m above the floor. The installation should allow variations in the placing of the operation table.

In the post-anaesthetic area two outlets for oxygen, two suction points, and one outlet for compressed air are needed per bed.

In the intensive care and therapy units two outlets for oxygen, one for nitrous oxide, two outlets for compressed air and three suction points per bed are required[3].

X ray screening rooms in the radiology department may require piped oxygen, nitrous oxide, and suction. Alternatively mobile equipment may be provided[4].

Medical vacuum, compressed air

Vacuum is used throughout hospitals in patient treatment areas and in laboratories. In the surgical, recovery and intensive care areas it serves to remove fluids from incisions and body cavities and is used in post-operative drainage. In the laboratory it is used for filtering, cleaning delicate apparatus, and transferring fluids from one container to another.

Vacuum is generally supplied by two or more vacuum pumps operating through a suitable receiver. It is probably a much abused service in the hospital. Frequently it is used for purposes for which it was never intended, such as anti-pollution units on anaesthetic machines. As is rather common to see vacuum being wasted with taps left open although unused, it is generally necessary to over-design on capacities.

At least three vacuum points in an operation room should be provided for surgical equipment, pneumatic motors, suction pumps.

3   see also Strecker Helmut: Zentrale Versorgung mit medizinischen Gasen im Krankenhaus. 1973, Medizinal-Markt/Acta Medico-technica 21:397–401.

4   see also Western Regional Hospital Board, Research and Development Unit: Organisation & Design of Radiodiagnostic Departments. Stencil. (Glasgow). January 1973, p 29.

Surgical suction devices comprise injector pumps, water-jet pumps, and mobile electric suction pumps. Pneumatic injector suction pumps, which have a sealed extractor to isolate contaminated air, are considered most suitable.

The use of hospital piped medical vacuum systems, though feasible, introduces several problems[5]. They should not be used with flammable anaesthetic agents. Anaesthetic agents are soluble in pump oils.

Compressed air tubes or the installation of central compressors is required. Compressed air must be filtered and dry. Condensation moisture must be drawn off from the pipes.

Three outlets for compressed air are needed in the anaesthetic room and in the operation room.

To obtain a reserve of air and a drying effect simultaneously, an air-tank could be used. This reserve may provide a safety margin during power failures.

The compressed air installation must not be placed in a room together with oxygen and nitrous oxide containers.

Piped technical vacuum

Facilities for *floor cleaning* based on wet vacuum pickup procedure include suction points connected with a vacuum plant, which is situated outside the therapeutic and diagnostic facilities.

A central vacuum plant can carry out *refuse removal* in a separate tube system to a separator above an incinerator. Valves and other arrangements shut off refuse chutes from communication with the vacuum system, except when the vacuum is to convey the refuse to the incinerator separator.

Another separate vacuum tube system can be used to convey *soiled linen* to a central soiled linen collection area or to the hospital laundry.

5   Vickers M D: Pollution of the atmosphere of operating theatres. 1975, Anaesthesia 30:697–699.

Life safety, emergency power

Fire alarms

In the US, there is general agreement that smoke kills in hospitals more patients than flames do[1].

A single, all-embracing national code, flexibly and rationally administred, and quickly responsive to new, authentic fire research findings is needed, which is very seldom the case.

A complete life safety system would include[2] a fire-rated construction; an early-warning detection of smoke and fire to block the passage of smoke and confine the fire to its room of origin; an automatic sprinkler protection; a division of each floor into at least two areas or compartments; smoke control facilities; and a trained staff.

The main functions of a detection and alarm system are to alert staff to the malfunction or hazard and to enable staff to move to a place of safety.

All diagnostic and therapeutic units must be connected to the central hospital alarm system.

Advice on the fire-fighting installation proposed should be sought from the local fire authority.

Emergency power

When the hospital is suddenly plunged into darkness at the failure of mains, the major problem is probably the psychological shock.

Few life-support systems are wholly dependent on mains electricity. Cardiac pacemakers are usually battery operated and breathing machines can be manually operated or have their own battery power supplies. All life-supporting facilities shall be provided with a general emergency power supply.

There are areas in which availability of emergency power is essential. The surgical department with its delivery section and the post-anaesthetic recovery area, and the intensive care units, come first. Heart-lung machines, lung ventilators, operation room lighting, pumps, apparatus, and monitoring equipment should be connected to the emergency power supply which, on failure of normal supply, is automatically switched on.

1   Where there's fire there's smoke. 1976, Progressive Architecture 57:9:58–63.

2   John G Degenkolb cited in Where there's fire there's smoke. 1976, Progressive Architecture 57:9:58–63.

Also the laboratory should be connected to the emergency power system: all its loads that are essential for safety, preservation of research data, and for protection of the building and its contents[3].

Lighting in treatment rooms in the radiotherapy units should be provided also by emergency power. The radiocobalt machines must be designed and installed to switch off in such an eventuality[4].

The function of safety lighting in other areas is to enable essential movement of staff and patients and to assist safe, unobstructed means of escape.

Safety lighting is essential in all parts of the hospital.

It is desirable that one lift in each separate section of the hospital should be normally connected to the emergency installation having automatic change-over facilities. These lifts should be suitably indicated by markings at each landing.

Suitable manually operated switching arrangements should be provided for other lifts to enable the stand-by supply to be switched from the emergency lift to each of the other lifts in the group in turn to eliminate the possibility of occupants being trapped.

External emergency lighting will normally be restricted to the emergency entrance areas.

In the operation unit the operation room light should in case of a power supply failure be switched on within half a second, other equipment within about 15 secon The degree and quality of emergency lighting should be approximately equal to that of the normal lighting. In the general lighting a considerable reduction may be accer able.

Ample socket-outlets connected to essential circuits should be available for portable light fittings to be used for tasks outside the critical working area which require a higher standard of lighting, e g in the recovery areas.

The switch-over to emergency power supply should be indicated on a control panel in the duty engineer's office.

A local battery with about one hour capability should be automatically connected to provide uninterrupted supply[5]. Most batteries operate up to three hours. They are easily maintained and for installations up to 20 kW relatively inexpensive. Measures shall be taken that batteries of a special emergency power supply will be recharged from essential circuits.

3   Manual for laboratory planning and design. College of American Pathologists. Skokie, III. 1977, p 9.

4   see also Osborn S B: Radiation Protection in Hospitals — Radiotherapy. 1972, Hospital Building & Engineering 5:3:55–56.

5   see also Emergency lighting — whose standards? 1976, hospital development 4:3:27.

SOPHISTICATED TECHNOLOGY IN HOSPITAL

The biomedical research and development enterprise continually presents health care providers with a wide array of innovations. The medical professional environment encourages the adoption and use of innovations. Possession of modern, sophisticated technology confers prestige on physicians and hospitals, and the public's growing faith in the power of science in general and of curative medicine in particular accelerates the demand for technologically advanced methods of care. In short, technological sophistication is viewed by many — patients, physicians, and administrators — as a surrogate for high-quality care[1].

Electronic equipment for health services can be divided into equipment for general technical purposes: e g ventilation, heating, cooling, communications, laundry, sterilization, and equipment interacting with the patient such as transducers, amplifiers, telemetry devices, large capacity storage systems, high-frequency recorders, high-speed computers, computerized tomographs.

The application of sophisticated electronic equipment to problems of health care has increased very greatly, although approximately 40 per cent of the electronic equipment tested in the US has been found not to meet the specifications of the producer[2]. Technological advances have occured with such a speed that they to some degree appear to be out of control. There is an element of waste perceived to be associated with much existing technology, because the current health care system fosters the production of technology whose social benefits is not worth its social cost. New technology is too widely distributed, and it often diffuses too rapidly and indiscriminately. It is used excessively and in many instances improperly[3].

The public and many professionals view the medical technological revolution as expensive and complex, characterized by resource-intensive capital equipment of unestablished efficacy, which frequently requires hospitalization and serves to inflate the cost of care while delivering little demonstrable health benefit[4].

Increased awareness of the costs of resources devoted to expensive "halfway technology" was poignantly illustrated by C Gaus and B Cooper 1976 at the Conference on Health Care Technology and Quality of Care, Boston, Mass:

In the US 4 billion dollars were spent for new technology (for Medicare patients in 1976) and we do not know if it did any good, much less how much.

If we had continued providing hospital services to the aged, as they were in 1967, then we could have spent that 4 billion dollars last year (to) have brought all aged persons above the poverty line (with at least 3.3 million currently living below it); or

provided the rent to raise 2 million elderly from substandard to standard housing units; or

1 Warner Kenneth E: Effects of Hospital Cost Containment on the Development and Use of Medical Technology. 1978, Milbank Memorial Fund Quarterly/Health and Society 56:187–211.

2 Kane Frank: Programmed maintenance of electronic equipment. 20th International Hospital Congress. Tokyo, May 1977.

3 Warner Kenneth E: Effects of Hospital Cost Containment on the Development and Use of Medical Technology. 1978, Milbank Memorial Fund Quarterly/Health and Society 56:187–211.

4 ibid

brought all the elderly above the lowest accepted food budget and more; or

provided eyeglasses and hearing aids to all who needed them (estimated at 18 million needing or wearing glasses and over 3 million needing hearing aids), and more.

Which would have helped most, (medical) technology or food?

The tendency to overinvest in sophisticated technological services seems to be part of a more general trend to invest too many labour or nonlabour elements in the hospital services and to overuse health care facilities and services. However, the contribution of technology to health care cost rises is not an explicit technology problem. Cost containment has to focus on general reimbursement and regulatory mechanisms, and not to single out the technology aspect.

A basis for developmental considerations in health care equipment is the assessment of the functioning of the product and the end result — the benefit for the patient — when using the product. Considerations on introducing electronic equipment can not be handled differently than considerations on other technologies, such as fluidistics, hydraulics, pneumatics etc[5].

The medical information system must be available at any time, night and day, to authorized users. A clinician becomes an authorized user of a patient's files — full file and/or clinical summary — when the patient seeks his care. A rigid data security system must protect the identified patient files so that only legitimate users can access those records. The ethical guidelines for computer centre handling identified medical records have been compiled. The patient is the "owner" of those parts of the record which are historical and factual data, whereas the physician is the "owner" of those segments of the record which contain his own reasoning and his own diagnostic or therapeutic discussions[6].

The patient's consent as well as the physician's consent must be submitted in order to gain access to protected data. Although no data security design can be absolutely safe, it is feasible to provide a remarkably high level of security for a reasonable cost, amounting to about a ten per cent increase of the data processing cost. This is the price which is to be paid for conserving the confidentiality of the medical data in an electronic data bank.

Different credit card systems have developed the necessary technical measures and experience in this area, the credit card owner controls his own files. A similar data protection system should be used for sensitive medical data. The patient should control his own file[7].

5   Thorp Jan: Economic considerations in adopting electronic equipment. 20th International Hospital Congress. Tokyo, May 1977.

6   Gabrieli E R: Computer support for clinical obstetrics and gynaecology. in Scientific Foundations of Obstetrics and Gynaecology. ed by Elliot E Philipp, Josephine Barnes and Michael Newton. William Heinemann Medical Books Ltd. London 1977, p 840.

7   ibid

Often different opinions are found among experts when asking for advice in evaluating costly equipment. One reason is that they have different sources for their information. Another is that they sometimes are deeply involved in a special system. It should be tried to separate opinions based on objectivity from opinions based on diffuse loyalties and personal obligations.

It is important, that engineers in industry understand the operational problems implicit in the delivery of health care in the hospital. The problems of development within industry must be understood by the health professionals. Mutual cooperation of medicine and technology is the main basis for a sound and purposeful development of new sectors in the health care facilities.

The use of electronic equipment in the hospital environment has to proceed with caution. The motivation must not be the satisfaction of the avid curiosity of research but the advancement of healing, security and wellbeing of the patient. Economical calculations should not lead to loss of medical manpower in order to finance the purchase of computers[8].

One of the reasons why innovation in this field is so fast is that there are hardly any government regulations. In electronics, the free enterprise system still works[9].

There is certainly a wide-open and exiting field in biomedical instrumentation of extremely small components. Their theoretical limits are still very far[10].

Integrated circuits (ICs) are the quantum jump that is about to make a profound technological revolution possible. More than 25,000 applications have been identified. Many of them can be expected to be in connection with health care facilities.

Lately, computers are being developed that can respond to questions phrased in English, or any human tongue, and reply in easily understood terms. The plunging cost of electronic circuits and the discovery of more-efficient ways to store and process information have created computers that can even teach novices — in English — how to operate the computers[11].

Indeed, some computers now know enough English to read newspaper articles, answer questions about complex topics and solve problems written in everyday sentences — even when the human's grammar and spelling are faulty.

8   see also Sulg Ilmar A: Electronics — the key to the enigma of man? in Annals of Estonian Medical Association 1975. ed by Jüri Kaude and Jaan Novek. AB Eesti Post. Malmö 1975, p 69–81.

9   The brainstorm technology. 1977, The Economist, April 16.

10 Morowitz Harold J: On Swallowing the Surgeon. 1978, Hospital Practice 13:4:203, 208.

11 Shaffer Richard A: Computers That Use Plain English Permit Vast New Applications. The Wall Street Journal, March 27 1978.

Within the next several years, experts believe, almost anyone may be able to use his own words to do almost any job on a computer. The Laboratory for Computer Sciences at the Massachusetts Institute of Technology is among those working toward this goal. Its director, *Michael L. Dertouzos,* says, "There are still any number of dangers that could hold us back, but the horizon looks clean and good from here."

All experience has shown that when sophisticated technical devices are introduced in hospitals there is an increase of staff cost. There is further cost for basic technical education, continuous training of and information to the staff regarding the handling and the risks involved in the new methods[12].

Simplifying the use of computers, will lessen dependence on costly and scarce programmers.

An easier and simpler way, however, is not always the best solution from all aspects in the EDP [13]. An easy way and option to programme the computer, e.g. by means of so called basic language, makes even the most advanced computer slower.

In the so called basic terms programmed processing would require 50 to 100 per cent more computer time than the assembly programmed processing. Computer time is mostly more expensive than the costliest programmers.

12 Thorp Jan: Economic considerations in adopting electronic equipment. 20th International Hospital Congress. Tokyo, May 1977.

13 personal communication: 1978, Ilmar Sulg, Stockholm.

Medical monitoring

Monitoring is a continuous or semicontinuous visualization of physiological and physical phenomena by means of analogue or digital display devices.

The data display is presented on a screen or cathode ray oscilliscope. Between data aquisition and data presentation the data are preprocessed, converted, retrieved, processed, and reduced. The information is to draw attention to significant deviations from the accepted or the expected, and to alarm the personnel on duty when some urgent action is necessary.

The monitoring devices include thermal recorders, oxygen analysers, thermistor bridges for multiple site temperatures e g patient's skin, rectum, and oesophagus; cathode ray oscilloscopes for displaying electrocardiograms, electroencephalograms and haemodynamic parameters; blood gas tension recorders; analyzers of drugs and other chemical constituents in blood.

Simultaneous surveillance of several physiological parameters — physiological multiparameter monitoring (PMPM) — rather than their graphic illustration is the main objective of medical monitoring[1]. This surveillance can easily take place without any graphic registration. The value of PMPM lies primarily in the fact that the simultaneous following of the activities of several organs gives more comprehensive information than the data than the separate registration of the same activities. Impaired activity in one organ may lead to a concurrent functional disturbance in other organs[2].

The time intervals between observations vary according to the monitoring situation and the condition of the patient.

The staff of intensive care and treatment unit is under a high level of stress almost continually, and their clinical acumen often is of much more importance than the availability of mechanical equipment in the evaluation of the patient's status. The military experience in which personnel watching data displays such as radar screens have a rapid loss in the ability to recognize significant change after about one hour certainly is applicable in the even more stressful situation of having to interpret several different sources of data as well as the rather nonspecific clinical situation. Specifically, high rates of error in the interpretation of electrocardiograms because of fatigue have been noted[3].

1   see also Sulg Ilmar A: Electronics — the key to the enigma of man? in Annals of Estonian Medical Association 1975. ed by Jüri Kaude and Jaan Novek. AB Eesti Post. Malmö 1975, p 69–81.

2   see also Sulg Ilmar A: Electronics — the key to the enigma of man? in Annals of Estonian Medical Association 1975. ed by Jüri Kaude and Jaan Novek. AB Eesti Post. Malmö 1975, p 69–81.

3   see also Harris III John McA and Cashman William F: Practical Monitoring in the Intensive Care Patient. 1978, The Orthopedic Clinics of North America 9:649–660.

The worst complication of monitoring is misinterpretation of results. Because figures are provided, there is often an unfortunate tendency to attach undue importance to a number, and to disregard or overlook important clinical observations[4].

Extremely sensitive electronic monitors are now commonplace. Many of these amplify signals in the region of 1 mV in low-frequency ranges. They cannot be expected to give accurate results, nor can their alarms be reliable in an electrically 'noisy' environment.

Measurements of physiological variables alone without further processing may not provide the best guide to patient care. The traditional clinical observation is more complex than simple measurements. The ward chart kept by an experienced nurse contains potentially more information than what a monitor writes out about the same variable[5].

As the trend in diagnostic examination is going toward more non-invasive technique the risky invasive diagnostic and monitoring techniques will be reduced. *E g* there are already patient monitoring devices which do not require insertion, injection or punction but utilize a thermistor-transducer which, placed on the skin surface provides accurate reading of the deep body temperature, $p CO_2$, $p O_2$ etc.

MPM by means of telemetry

Telemonitoring has positive psychological effect on the patient by removing the wiring to monitoring instruments.

PMPM telemonitoring can be accomplished by using small portable tape recorders or by radiotelemetry (RTM), a technique still quite new and still with a few problems to be overcome[6].

Mobility after extended period of confinement would help also to improve the effectiveness of diagnostic monitoring, e g by activating cardiac arrhythmias. A cardiac telemonitoring transmitter* — as an example — weighs only about 120 g.

All monitoring units must be interlinked with alarm systems, which operate at predetermined variation extremes of the involved parameters.

4   Allardyce D B: Monitoring of the Critically Ill Surgical Patient. 1978, The Canadian Journal of Surgery 21:75–78.

5   Taylor D E M and Whamod J S: Realiability of Human and Machine Measurements in Patient Monitoring. 1975, European Journal of Intensive Care Medicine 1:53–59.

6   also Sulg Ilmar A: Psychological multiparameter monitoring (PMPM) in differential diagnosis of paroxysmal loss of consciousness. 3rd Nordic meeting on medical and biological engineering. Tampere, January 1975.

*   e g Laser Systems & Electronics, Inc. Tullahoma, Tennessee, USA.

Automatic dataprocessing

Hospitals are so complex and so specialized in their operation that automatic data-processing experience from other fields is often of limited value. The computer by itself is only a piece of machinery, which must be taught everything it does.

Computer research has been characterized by people skilled in one solution (computers) searching for a problem to fit their solution and by the development of relatively inflexible systems that are based on the concept that the existing system must adapt to the programme rather than the other way around[1].

Overenthusiasm, naivety and unmotivated expectations have too often characterized the application of computer technology to health care and hospital management.

Most information systems in hospitals have evolved in a piecemeal fashion rather than through careful planning[2]. The great majority of computer applications to medicine have been excessively modest in scope. Where in other fields the computer has been utilized to perform tasks previously incomprehensive to mankind, in health care delivery we have been — at least in the past — quite satisfied to duplicate the physician. In mathematics, physics, banking, space exploration, etc., the computer routinely is called upon to perform tasks that all mankind working 24 hours a day from creation could not begin to duplicate, but in medicine the measure of success has often been diagnostic accuracy approaching a skilled clinician.

If this timidity were matched in other fields, it is very unlikely anyone could have justified the expense or efforts necessary in these more successful efforts. The disappointing impact of computer technology on medicine may have been caused by the inability to see beyond the single physician and, therefore, the inability to produce tools that do more than emulate the efforts of the individual doctor[3].

To achieve better results, data collectors must gradually progress through phases, starting with a detail and evolving to more details as their perception of information needs changes. This implies that the initial variable definitions should closely correspond to the level of detail currently collected. There must then be rapid modification of the data base as the users change their perception of information needs[4].

The belief that computers can be programmed to perform patient-care functions that human beings are unable to perform is unrealistic[5]. There is also a temptation

1 Friedman Richard Bruce and Gustafson David H: Computers in Clinical Medicine, A Critical Review. 1977, Computers and Biomedical Research 10:199–204.

2 Austin Charles J: Planning and selecting an information system. 1977, Hospitals 51:20:95–96, 98, 100, 202.

3 Friedman Richard Bruce and Gustafson David H: Computers in Clinical Medicine, A Critical Review. 1977, Computers and Biomedical Research 10:199–204.

4 see also Jelovsek Frederick R and Hammond William E: Experience in Computerization of Perinatal Medical Records. 1977, The University of Michigan medical center journal 43:5–8.

5 see also Sheppard Louis C and Kouchoukos Nicholas T: Computers as Monitors. 1976, The Journal of Anesthesiology 45:250–258.

to store and to present ever more data, much of which is irrelevant and trend to obfuscate rather than to elucidate[6]. Computer-data have become an excrescence. They are the very latest kind of pollution[7].

Limited success and numerous failures have been the result of data processing. The majority of projects in the area of Computer Applications to Medicine, once reported, subsequently prove to be impractical, too expensive, or otherwise unacceptable. Unfortunately, there have been very few follow-up articles detailing the causes for these failures[8].

One of the main tasks of automatic dataprocessing is to ensure the rational and maximal use of expensive equipment[9]. Several applications such as historical data acquisition, computer-assisted diagnosis, biosignal analysis, etc., appear intuitively to be of great value in improving patient care.

Although computers appeared on the market more than twenty years ago, the technology became practical for medicine only a few years ago. The cost of vast data banks is becoming reasonable, and the technical know-how is now available for implementing[10].

It seems safe to predict that computer-based medical information systems will enter clinical medicine, and their impact will be substantial. With the support of these information systems, the scientific component of clinical decisions will be greatly enhanced. The clinician will no longer have to recall the hard statistical data of past experience. The information system will provide many answers instantaneously, both on a single patient and on similar cases.

A computer-based reliable information system will become a tool in medicine. The physician will be liberated from some chores of memorizing and recall. However, the computer will not reduce the true human task of the clinician to be firmly in charge of the case, to reassure and show empathy, and to develop rational clinical opinions assisted by the computer-produced statistical evidence. The human's role will not decrease. It will only shift. The technology must remain the servant of the clinician. The ultimate responsibility must be human[11].

No hard evidence has been presented to support the assumption that there is a great value of computers in improving patient care. The inability to demonstrate a definite potential for improving health care prior to the wholesale introduction of a new technology has been a serious problem in all areas of health care delivery.

---

6   see also Casimir H B G: Computers in medicine — why? 1971, Medicamundi 16:174–175.

7   Beer Stafford: Managing modern complexity. 1972, Architectural Design 42:629–632.

8   see also Friedman Richard Bruce and Gustafson David H: Computers in Clinical Medicine: A Critical Review. 1977, Computers and Biomedical Research 10:199–204.

9   see also Automation in Hospitals. Editorial. 1974, The New Zealand Medical Journal 79:1027–1028.

10 Gabrieli E R: Computer support for clinical obstetrics and gynaecology. in Scientific Foundations of Obstetrics and Gynaecology. ed by Elliot E Philipp, Josefine Barnes and Michael Newton. William Heinemann Medical Books Ltd. London 1977, p 840.

11 ibid

The reliability and validity of information collected by computer-based patient interfaces has been demonstrated but not that the providers can make better or less costly decisions because of it.

The cost effectiveness of many computer systems is poorly investigated, much less demonstrated[12]. For computer technology, this inability to demonstrate the potential for significantly improving health care is particularly regrettable, since introduction of computer-based systems requires large investments for equipment and personnel[13].

The computer has, however, improved the hospital recordkeeping, the scheduling of admissions and out-patient sessions. Also storage, retrieval, and analysis of banks of data easily collected and filed has been accomplished.

An electronic picture archive has been proposed which employs optical disk technology to store the bulk of pictorial data contained in X ray pictures[14]. Permanent storage of electronic picture signals is demanded for the rapidly increasing number of computer tomograms. Efficiency of storage would be improved by data compression techniques, which reduce the data volume of X ray pictures without loss of diagnostic image quality. The system may be extended to conventional radiographs if state-of-the-art technology such as laser scanning is applied for conversion into electronic signals and re-conversion into photographic hard copies. X ray TV systems and other electronic imaging systems for infrared, ultrasound, or γ-rays could be directly interfaced.

The visual evaluation process is generally time-consuming and it often makes above-average demands on the individual with respect to concentration and systematic procedure. This is particularly true of light and electron microscope studies and also of the analysis of thermograms. In many problems the observer is obliged by the criteria employed to make subjective decisions which may compromise the reliability and comparability of the results.

Depending on the type and complexity of pattern recognition requirements and evaluation, image analysis with the aid of the computer would afford many advantages. It also appears likely that similar analysis facilities will be available for images which are variable in time. However, the development of the required computer hardware and programmes is a very difficult task[15].

Applications have become known on nuclear medicine, blood cell analysis, and X ray diagnostics.

12 see also Friedman Richard Bruce and Gustafson David H: Computers in Clinical Medicine, A Critical Review. 1977, Computers and Biomedical Research 10:199–204.

13 ibid

14 Meyer-Ebrecht D, Lux P, and Kowalski G: The electronic X-ray archive: an integral approach to filing and remote retrieval of computer-generated radiographs. 1977, Medicamundi 22:3:27–29.

15 Anliker M: Current and Future Aspects of Biomedical Engineering. 1977, Triangle 16:129–140.

In an ECG system, interpretation can be assisted by the computer since the average signal has less artefacts and since the computer can perform physical measurements more rapidly, consistently and accurately than the human eye. It is questionable, however, whether the final interpretation — up to a diagnostic statement — should ever be left to a computer on its own[16].

Computer-assisted axial tomography has resulted in a new field of medical expertise. Parallel to this the computerized methods for ultrasound are rapidly developing.

The main impediments to a successful computer-physician and/or patient-computer communication have been[17]:

> poor engineering of computer terminals, resulting in mechanical breakdowns
>
> placing the computer terminals in out-of-the-way places making them inconvenient to operate
>
> low-speed teletype output (10 characters/sec) or excessive delay between responses (over 3 sec)
>
> long and complicated technical dialogue (sign-on codes)
>
> requirements of knowledge of special passwords, codes, or computer languages.

Computer terminals have been expensive and this has made it difficult to develop accessible, yet cost-effective applications.

To avoid the establishment of a system in which the computer does not function optimally, the application of the following prerequisites has been recommended[18]:

> detailed identification of the clinical needs
>
> precise definition of the problem
>
> establishment of specific objectives
>
> implementation of robust technology
>
> integration of the system into the operation of the unit
>
> follow-through with training, maintenance, evaluation, revision, and updating.

Where a computerized scheme is to be implemented, great care and preparation are required as well as a declared commitment down the head of department and a full discussion with all staff. The installation of a system simply in the hope of general improvement in the service is most unlikely to be successful.

---

16 see also Jansson L, Johansson K, Jonson B, Olsson L G, Werner O and Westling H: Computer assistance in the ECG Laboratory — new look. Introduction. Department of Clinical Physiology, University of Lund, Sweden 1976.

Wolf H K, Gregor R D and Chandler B M: Use of computers in clinical electrocardiography: an evaluation. 1977, Canadian Medical Association Journal 117:877–880.

17 Friedman Richard Bruce and Gustafson David H: Computers in Clinical Medicine, A Critical Review. 1977, Computers and Biomedical Research 10:199–204.

18 see also Sheppard Louis C and Kouchoukos Nicholas T: Computers as Monitors. 1976, The Journal of Anesthesiology 45:250–258.

The computer system demands a rigid medical information input, which has to be imposed on the medical personnel in order to make medical material machine-readable. The present manual systems of medical recording and administration have been built up slowly by small adjustments and gradual agreement of all users over a long period of time. The success or failure of the attempt to computerize the information system is largely determined by the capacity and the willingness of the medical staff to adapt themselves to a demanding new input format system[19].

Automatic dataprocessing enables to store, select and combine large volumes of personal information, which has given rise to dangers of intentional and unintentional invasion of privacy. The risk of uncontrolled distribution and distortion of personal data as well as of the incorrect or illegal use of them has increased.

Protection of privacy must be guaranteed. The introduction of automatic dataprocessing systems with insufficient computer security may have a serious effect on the confidence of the general public in the health service. Those in need of care may be refrained from seeking medical attention or providing the necessary information for adequate treatment[20].

The value of the computer in monitoring has been mainly in the automation of measurement acquisition, display, storage, retrieval, and charting for the medical record[21].

In medicine it is very difficult to give cash termin estimates of the benefits that might be achieved by the use of a computer system.

New uses for the computer in the laboratory are being developed*. They include use of the computer for calculation of hours worked, for workload recording, for individual performance analysis, and for inventory control, all of them administrative tasks whose automation will result in savings. From the patient standpoint, attempts to better assess the effects of drugs on laboratory test results, and either correct the result or alert the attending physician are expected. The computer can be used in microbiology for analysis of organism sensitivity and growth. Storage of coded diagnostic information can lead to better assessment of the meaning of laboratory results.

Although potentially the computer-help can be substantial, the total cost of a computer system remains to be measured with the gains expected to be achieved in term

19 see also Medicine and Computers, Engagement or Marriage? 1973, The Medical Journal of Australia 2:953–954.

20 Sekretess och integritet i samband med ADB inom sjukvården. Spri rapport 10/75. Stockholm 1975, p 6.

21 Sheppard Louis C and Kouchoukos Nicholas T: Computers as Monitors. 1976, The Journal of Anesthesiology 45:250–258.

* see also Groves William E: A Dynamic Computer System for the Clinical Laboratory. 1978, American Journal of Medical Technology 44:575–581.

of genuine saving time for the physicians, in terms of reducing laboratory tests, days of hospitalization and improvement of patient care.

Greater value from instrumental monitoring might lie with systems built around small digital computers. They would provide analysis of biosignals, some diagnoses, information storage, retrieval and display. If designed to require only noninvasive, easily applied transducers supported by reliable peripheral instruments for most cases, these systems would provide a significant improvement of medical care.

Minicomputer devices are already being used for ECG and EEG analysis, for evaluation of cardiac catheterization data, patient monitoring, and pacemaker evaluation reporting. Also here cost effectiveness is clearly a very important issue. The computer system in a catheterization laboratory may constitute 10 to 20 per cent of the cost of a new laboratory[24].

24 see also Alderman Edwin L, Spitz A Lawrence, Sanders William J and Harrison Donald C: Use and Value of the Computer in the Cardiac Catheterization Laboratory. 1977, Chest 71:526–530.

personal communication: 1977, Ilmar Sulg, Oulu, Finland.

Monitoring and dataprocessing in clinical laboratories, X ray departments

Many diagnostic tests, particularly in clinical chemistry have been improved, in spite of the fact that automation of diagnostic tests is only in an early phase[1] of its development.

Though automation, which in itself means improvement of the quality of the test data[2], large numbers of chemical determinations provide a wealth of information. The output also contains a number of previously unavailable determinations. Some controversy persists whether the additional data are needed and are beneficial. The growing number of laboratory reports may obscure the significant values.

In all clinical laboratories irrespective of subdiscipline in the field of computerization the two main tasks are data processing — the clerical work arising from request forms and the generation of reports — and data acquisition — dealing with the output of a laboratory instrument.

The fact that most attention seems to have been given to data acquisition is a hint that data processing is the harder task. This is doubly unfortunate, for processing is in fact more important. The days when specialized hardware — central processor — and complex software — computer programmes — were needed to translate the electric signals from an instrument into an analytical result are gone: most modern instruments are equipped with a standard output that can easily be handled by the computer directly, and this trend will be accelerated by the introduction of microprocessors and cheap memory modules[3].

A busy laboratory might handle 500 or more requests daily, and on each occasion the data base must be checked to find out if the patient is on file, the data verified or a file created, and the investigations and perhaps diagnosis entered. The data base has to contain the set of identifying data for each patient, the requesting source, and files for result of tests on specimens submitted. The results of the tests done have to be merged into the patient files, and the reports generated and then printed. An efficient system should allow these various procedures to occur concurrently, with on-line or off-line acquisition of data from laboratory instruments[4].

The importance of laboratory data processing is now being recognized. Most obvious is the improved quality of service — notably legible reports, a faster turn-round of works, easy inquiry facilities, and fewer errors. The files can be made easily accessible for clinical and epidemiological research.

1 Rexen Arno: Technische Möglichkeiten der Automatisierung im Laboratorium. 1977, Krankenhaus Umschau 46:550–555.

2 see also Trujillo Jose M, Fritsche Herbert A and Wendlandt Gay McC: Laboratory Medicine: Automation and Data Processing. in Cancer Patient Care. ed by R Lee Clark and Clifton D Howe. Year Book Medical Publishers Inc. Chicago 1976, p 745.

3 Hospital laboratory computing. 1978, British Medical Journal 1:387–388.

4 ibid

Such benefits are difficult to measure in financial terms, but some computerized laboratories have reduced staff or avoided the increase of administration costs[5].

There has been a reaction against large multiple analyzers. As response to this criticism small blocks for two to five analytical tests have been introduced as well as instruments with pronounced flexibility which are capable to analyse each sample for one or several tests at the choice of the operator[6].

Many developments could be envisaged. E g in clinical laboratories some challenging problems lie in the smooth sequential formulation and transmission of microbiological test results from the laboratory to clinical records. The manipulation of relevant data by the computer prospectively for the detection and prediction of nosocomial infections or miniepidemics is another[7].

Computer systems have been developed which would help to accurately identify bacteria and thus facilitate proper diagnosis of bacterial infections.

This would be especially useful in identifying organisms seldom encountered. Such organisms may be erroneously identified in routine laboratory practice because the routine test battery is necessarily limited and the laboratory technologist is not always familiar with the characteristic patterns of rare organisms.

A computer system has been introduced for use in epidemiologic studies. Biochemical data on bacteria are stored with information on patient identification and hospital location. Each month the computer puts out information on the distribution of bacteria by patient location. From this and other computer information it would be possible to more rapidly investigate a local outbreak.

The use of computers in diagnostic X ray departments is still controversial. Whilst the use of computerized reporting on its own is possible, real benefit can be expected only where a programme designed for research and departmental management is incorporated. For research purposes the storage of X ray reports will be of doubtful use, but a system to store and retrieve patient data together with a final diagnosis could be of great value.

In some departments a computer can give only marginal improvements, in some total confusion can emerge. The computer system is said to be as efficient as the staff is[8].

---

5   Hospital laboratory computing. 1978, British Medical Journal 1:387–388.

6   see also Holy H W: Trends in the automation of biochemical analyses. 1977, Techniques Hospitalières, nr 380, p 110–113.

7   Kunz Lawrence J: Computerization in microbiology. 1976, Human pathology 7:169–175.

8   James Wilson B: Computers in diagnostic radiology. International symposium on the Planning of Departments of Radiology and Imaging Sciences. Lisbon, May 1978.

A computer system should not require extra work, be simple to operate and give a rapid return-pay off. It also requires a good back up[9].

In the first hand computers in diagnostic radiology can be used for data storage and patient identification[10].

The use of computers in *radiotherapy* permits the accurate computation of detailed dose distributions in the course of planning and executing the usual sequence of investigative and therapeutic procedures[11].

9 James Wilson B: Computers in diagnostic radiology. International symposium on the Planning of Departments of Radiology and imaging Scienes. Lisbon, May 1978.

10 ibid

11 see also Conklin Jeffrey, Munzenrider John, Neurath Peter W and Ross Winifred M: Computer-Aided Medical Decision Making in Radiotherapy. 1977, Radiology 123:441–446.

Monitoring the critically ill

Monitoring the critically ill patients with the aid of the computer has been explored intensively for more than a decade.

There are computerized, integrated systems, modular in nature, available for patient monitoring. Automatic sampling of signals from bedside monitors — ECGs, pressure, respiration, temperature — is possible as well as plotting trends on a scope e g following cardiac output by the dye curve. Monitoring is adaptable for pulse waveform analyse; arrhytmia monitoring in conjunction with a preprocessor; acid-base analyse; logging nurses notes; and generating patient summary reports at the end of each nursing shift.

It seems to be still premature to set instrumentation standards for EEG monitoring of the critically ill[1]. The quantitative methods allowing data reduction offer more comprehensive and reliable results, than the conventional analogue EEG record[2]. Clear distinction should be made between EEG monitoring of the critically ill and the use of the EEG in the establishment of cerebral death.

The electric hazard for patients within the monitoring system, the bulk of which is electronic and dependent on mains power supply must be reduced by providing isolating transformers and by balanced or positively grounded electrical equipment.

Electronic monitoring is only an accessory form of patient surveillance. It can never replace direct visual observation of a patient. *E g*, restlessness in a patient may be a warning sign of cerebral hypoxia even if the cardiac output, electrocardiogram, etc are within normal limits[3].

While automated monitoring equipment might increase the technical effectiveness of the nurses by relieving them of some routine functions, such as charting and checking vital signs, and thus increase the time available to render direct patient care, it cannot substitute human contact and good nursing, especially when dealing with child-patients and patients wakening from anaesthesia who are in particular need of human contact and orientating dialogue.

Only the human mind has the capacity to recognize patterns in illness; there are many developments in the course of critical illness that are infrequent or unpredictable, and no transducer or electronic device has been yet devised that will warn of such events. The colour of the patient's skin, an increase in his respiratory effort, a change in his pain pattern, impairment of cerebration, development of abdominal

1 Handbook of electroencephalography and clinical neurophysiology. vol 3. part B. ed by J D Frost Jr and J S Barlow. Elsevier Scientific Publishing Company. Amsterdam 1976, p 38–61.

2 personal communication: 1977, Ilmar Sulg, Oulu, Finland.

3 see also Roseman David L: Postoperative Monitoring. in intensive Care of the Surgical Patient. ed by Marshall D Golding. Year Book Medical Publishers Inc. Chicago 1972, p 19.

distension, or discharge from a wound can only be observed, and their significance assessed, by an experienced nurse or physician[4].

The computer tends to serve as a partial substitute for nurses performing routine tasks. To capitalize on this substitution the supervisor must make an effort to ensure that the extra available time is channeled into productive activities. However, the actual increases in direct care per patient may not occur if each patient is already receiving an appropriate amount of care for his condition[5].

There seems to be no evidence that the use of computers in ICTU monitoring decreases morbidity, mortality, or cost as there are no adequate studies on cost-effectiveness[6].

When a computerized patient-monitoring system with enormous potentialities in a surgical intensive care unit was evaluated[7], its underutilization surprised the investigating team: of the total computer time available less than 2 per cent was used. When the computer time for automatic data acquisition was included, still only 6 per cent of available time was used. The system's failure to yield objective improvement in patient care was obvious. The output of the system was ignored because the decision maker was unable or unwilling to integrate the more sophisticated data presented by the computer.

The installation of monitoring systems in the *intensive care and treatment units* may not be used as an indication or motivation to reduce the number of nurses. Intensive care patients need continuous bedside attendance. Electronic aids can only lighten the work by immediate and objective recording of physiological data. Unduly elaborate monitoring may actually distract from optimal care[8].

A monitoring period shorter than four hours in intensive care units has been considered to be uneconomical in comparison with manually conducted data registration[9].

4   Allardyce D B: Monitoring of the Critically Ill Surgical Patient. 1978, The Canadian Journal of Surgery 21:75–78.

5   Tolbert Samuel H and Pertuz Alvaro E: Study shows how computerization affects nursing activities in ICU. 1977, Hospitals 51:17:79–82, 84.

6   see also Safar Peter, Benson Don M, Esposito Gerald, Grenvik Åke and Sands Patricia A: Emergency and Critical Care Medicine: Local Implementation of National Recommendations. in Public Health Aspects of Critical Care Medicine and Anesthesiology. F A Davis Company. Philadelphia 1974, p 99.

7   Greenburg A G, McGlure D K, Fink R, Stubbs J A and Peskin G W: Computerization of the surgical intensive care unit: Improvement of patient care via education. 1975, Surgery 77:799–806.

8   Weil Max Harry and Shubin Herbert: Centralized Hospital Care for the Critically Ill. in Public Health Aspects of Critical Care Medicine and Anesthesiology. F A Davis Company. Philadelphia 1974, p 130.

9   Nordström Lars: Elektronisk patientövervakning. Svenska Sjukhusföreningens Årsbok 1969–1970. Västerås 1972, p 128.

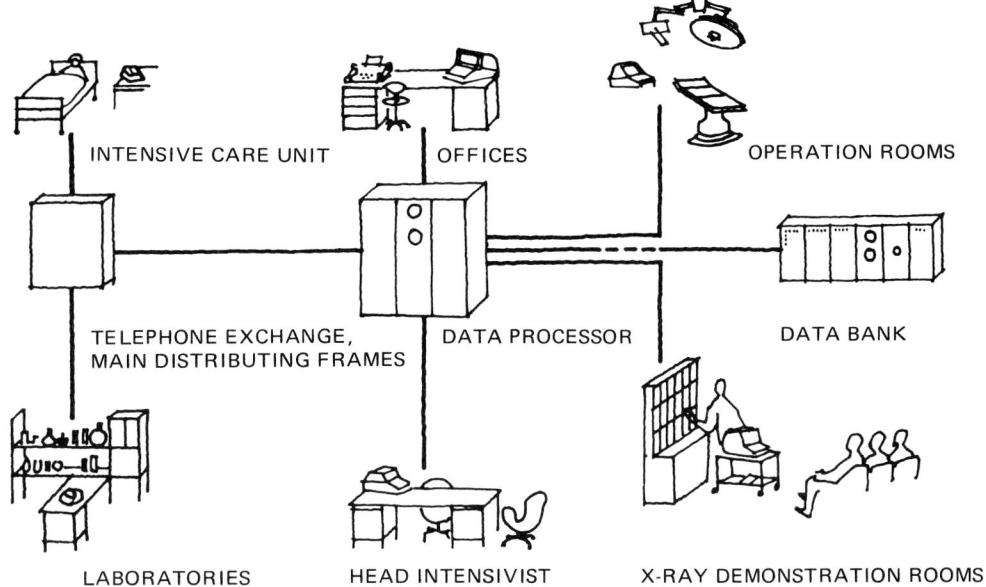

INTENSIVE CARE UNIT   OFFICES   OPERATION ROOMS

TELEPHONE EXCHANGE,
MAIN DISTRIBUTING FRAMES   DATA PROCESSOR   DATA BANK

LABORATORIES   HEAD INTENSIVIST   X-RAY DEMONSTRATION ROOMS

One of the most sophisticated monitoring systems for intensive care was developed by Olaf Norlander at the Karolinska Hospital, Stockholm (Rushmer Robert F: Medical Engineering. Academic Press. New York and London 1972, p 208).

Monitoring devices in *coronary intensive care units* include automatic electrocardiographic writeout on alarms with printout of the patient bed, time, and date of the alarm; ability to recall or freeze the electrocardiographic pattern; nonfade displays; alarms on changes from preset parameters of rate, rhythm, and contour; beat-to-beat rate meters; trend recordings; digital displays; and operational and lead status indicators. In addition, hemodynamic monitoring devices have become part of the CICU.

Unfortunately, continuous monitoring by personnel is difficult to achieve and efforts have been made to develop automatic recording and alarming devices which would eliminate the unreliability of intermittent inspection of the electrocardiogram[10].

A significant reduction in mortality has resulted from improved monitoring facilities[11].

---

10 Uhley Herman N: Present status of monitoring in the coronary care unit. 1978, Heart & Lung 7:67–68.

11 see also Shah Pravin M, Arnold Jeffrey M, Haberern Nancy A, Bliss David T, McClelland Keith M and Bromley Clarke W: Automatic Real Time Arrhythmia in the Intensive Coronary Care Unit. 1977, The American Journal of Cardiology 39:701–708.

The physiological function always monitored in the CICU is the action of the heart by an electrocardiograph (ECG). In modern equipment an ECG recorder is a part of the monitoring machine. Frequently monitored are arterial blood gases and pH and central venous pressure (CVP). Direct arterial blood pressure, and respiration are monitored occasionally. Temperature and EEG are seldom monitored.

Coronary-care systems have been oriented more toward the central monitoring station concept, whereas the majority of cardiothoracic surgical units have required bedside monitoring. In most instances these ideas have been carried over in the subsequent design of newer computer-based systems[12].

There should be a visible alarm at the patient's bedside and a visible as well as auditory alarm at the central monitoring station.

In the ICTUs and CICUs the monitoring equipment should be of a module system with ready interconvertibility to allow modification of the parameters to be measured as requirements are revised.

Multiparameter monitoring and complex investigations may have a legitimate and necessary role in clinical research. There is, however, a risk of complex electronics becoming an end in themselves in intensive treatment units, where they are apt to distract overworked nurses and medical attendants from the direct surveillance of their patients[13].

12 Sheppard Louis C and Kouchoukos Nicholas T: Computers as Monitors. 1976, The Journal of Anesthesiology 45:250–258.

13 see also Morton Anthony: Patient monitoring. 1976, The Australia and New Zealand Journal of Surgery 46:304–309.

Monitoring in operation room

In most major surgical procedures deviations in following physiological phenomena — the oxygen level in the blood; the pH of the blood; the carbon dioxide level in the blood; the pulse rate; the cardiac output and the blood pressure; the blood volyme and the body temperature — may indicate complications.

Especially in pediatric surgery patient monitoring is essential to detect the onset of complications. Monitoring of blood pressure, temperature, and blood loss are advocated. Monitoring of internal temperature is considered particularly adviseable in all infants and young children undergoing major surgery.

There are technical and practical monitoring problems still to be solved. The electronic instruments must transmit the message from the patient without disturbing the operation area and without being electrically interferred by other equipment in the surgical unit.

Miniaturization of circuits has reduced the size and power requirements of instruments, thus enabling the use of several monitors — some of them nonexistent only a few years ago — in the operation room. Telemetric multiparameter monitoring will very probably be the method of choice for surgery in the future[1].

Parallel to visual inspection of the reactivity of the patient, electronic monitoring of brain activity (EEG) can be used. The earliest clinical application of EEG monitoring has been to determine the depth of anaesthesia, an application not more so widely accepted because of the current trend to maintain lighter levels of general anaesthesia, which makes monitoring of other physiological functions such as ECG and $O_2/p\ CO_2$–exchange preferable to the EEG[3]. Nevertheless, EEG monitoring has a definite place in cardiovascular surgery[4], as the possibility of a sudden cardiocirculatory arrest during and after operation is one of the main problems of cardiac surgery[5]. EEG may also be of value for early detection of air embolization in the circulatory system[6].

An ideal system of medical computerization in the operation room would necessitate a screen which gives continuous visual information of events and trends as the operation proceeds. A minute-to-minute alarm system would indicate when a patient is or will be in trouble.

---

1   personal communication: 1977, Ilmar Sulg, Oulu, Finland.

3   see also Matsuo Fumisuke, Butzer John F, Seaba Peter J and Knott John R: Applications of Long-Term EEG Monitoring. 1976, American Journal of EEG Technology 16:59–70.

4   ibid

5   see also Piepenbrock Siegfried and Hempelmann Gunter: Intraoperative and Postoperative Monitoring of Cardiocirculatory Function in Pediatric and Adult Cardiosurgical Patients. in Anesthesia for Open-Heart Surgery. ed by Vieri Wiechmann. Little, Brown and Company. Boston 1976, p 49–61.

6   personal communication: 1977, Ilmar Sulg, Oulu, Finland.

There has to be a facility to deliver black-white paper copies from these display units, so that the essential sequences of the operation could be documented and added to the anaesthesia record[7].

During recent years some cardiosurgical centres have demonstrated that continuous computer-based monitoring of multiple physiological variables in cardiotomy — open heart surgery — patients is both feasible and of practical value[8]. Continuous monitoring may provide the opportunity for prompt and effective reaction to any adverse development in cardiocirculatory function during anaesthesia, operation, and the recovery period, which is especially important in cardiotomy patients[9].

Data suggest that computer-assisted surveillance can play a role in reducing morbidit and possibly mortality in postoperative cardiac surgical patients[10].

7   personal communication: 1977, Ilmar Sulg, Oulu, Finland.

8   Piepenbrock Siegfried and Hempelmann Gunter: Intraoperative and Postoperative Monitoring of Cardiocirculatory Function in Pediatric and Adult Cardiosurgical Patients. in Anesthesia for Open-Heart Surgery. ed by Vieri Wiechmann. Little, Brown and Company 1976, p 49–61.

9   ibid

10 Jurado Roy A, Fitzkee Hillard L, de Asla Richard A, Lukban Salvador B, Litwak Robert S and Osborn John J: Reduction of Unexpected, Life-Threatening Events in Postoperative Cardiac Surgical Patients: The Role of Computerized Surveillance. 1977, Circulation 56:II 44–II 49.

Monitoring in maternity units

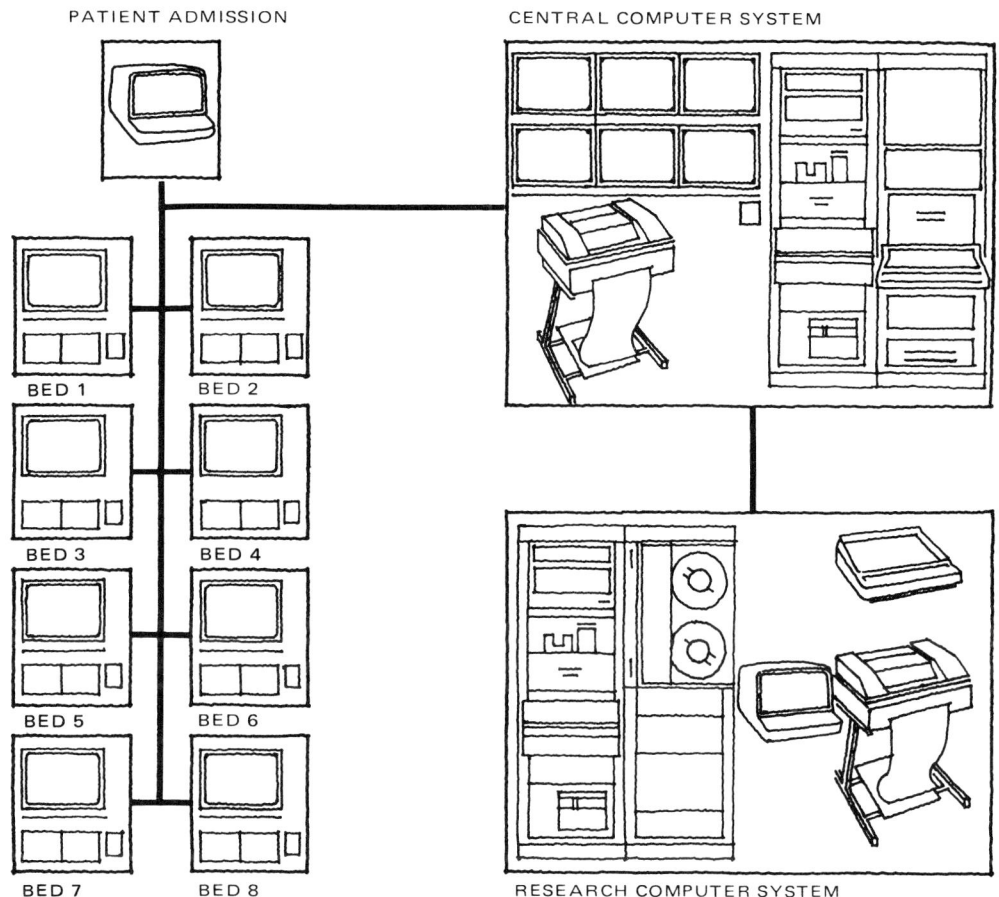

PATIENT ADMISSION

CENTRAL COMPUTER SYSTEM

BED 1 BED 2
BED 3 BED 4
BED 5 BED 6
BED 7 BED 8

RESEARCH COMPUTER SYSTEM

Computer system of a maternity ward as suggested by H Rüttgers, W Grothe, F Kubli (1976). The clinical system is connected to a research oriented computer system.

In maternity units many patients suffer anxiety concerning the welfare of the fetus *in utero* and it seems likely that perinatal monitoring properly explained to the patient, would reduce maternal anxiety concerning the fetus[1] and strengthen the mothers' feeling of safety[2].

1   Renou Peter, Chang Allan, Anderson Ian and Wood Carl: Controlled trial of fetal intensive care. 1976, American Journal of Obstetrics and Gynecology 126:470–476.

2   Övervakning under förlossning. Spri rapport 6/77. Stockholm 1977, p 5.

The benefits of perinatal fetal heart rate monitoring, while at this stage — 1978 — still unproven according to rigid criteria, appear to be a decrease in perinatal still-births, a decrease in neonatal mortality particularly of the low birth weight infant, a decrease in neonatal morbidity as measured by neurologic outcome, and assistance in rational labour management[3].

The established detriments of perinatal monitoring include fetal scalp infection and soft tissue injury, uterine perforation, and increased cost of medical care. The incidence and seriousness of the first two problems do not appear to be large in magnitude, particularly when viewed against the benefits above[4].

The increased monitoring cost would be offset by a decrease in the cost of caring for babies suffering peripartal hypoxic morbidity.

There is also a less optimistic view on that matter[5]. According to that view the monitoring information being assessed is still in a state of flux. Until the electronic data are more clearly understood, clinical computerization will not be justifiable. System available now (1978) are of limited scope, expensive, and of unproved clinical value. Premature attempts at clinical computerization will accomplish little, except to give computers a bad name.

An American study indicates good results in a comparison study of nurse auscultation versus electronic fetal monitoring. Therefore it would seem reasonable to give patients the option of being watched by a person rather than a fetal monitor[6].

A labour cannot be monitored more successfully by a computer than by an experienced clinician[7]. Much of the monitor information given to a capable attentive obstetrician is at best superfluos and at worst may even seem impertinent. However, to the less experienced or the tired clinician much comment could be vital.

Two small surveys of patients' attitudes towards monitoring present no sound information that the monitor *per se* dehumanizes the birth process. Lack of mobility is a serious problem, one, it is hoped, that may be rectified by the development of reasonably priced telemetry kits for fetal heart rate monitoring. Another drawback is the lack of privacy, particularly when the machine is not working properly and various people are called in to rectify mechanical problems[8].

3 Parer J T: Benefits and Detriments of Fetal Heart Rate Monitoring. 1978, Seminars in Perinatology 2:113–118.

4 ibid

5 Rosen Mortimer G, Sokol Robert J, Chik Lawrence: Use of computers in the labour and delivery suite: An overview. 1978, American Journal of Obstetrics and Gynecology 132:589–594.

6 Mehl Lewis E: Delivery in the home. 1978, Comprehensive Therapy 4:3:18–26.

7 Crawford J W: Computer monitoring or fetal heart rate and uterine pressure. 1975, American Journal of Obstetrics and Gynecology 121:342–350.

8 Parer J T: Benefits and Detriments of Fetal Heart Rate Monitoring. 1978, Seminars in Perinatalogy 2:113–118.

losed circuit television patient viewing

Although it has been argued that there is very little useful information derived from a televised view of the patient, as compared to information provided by the physiological monitors, many nurses, particularly in the US, feel more comfortable with closed-circuit television.

The video picture of the patient may be a reminder that the patient is a human being and not just *arterial fibrillation with occasional PVCs*[1].

The provision of TV cameras in the critical medicine areas has been greatly reduced in the recent years[2]. If they are still used, it has to be notified that the bed area is illuminated at all hours of day and night, causing often disturbance or great annoyance to the patients[3]. This disturbance must be avoided, e.g. by using infrared light monitoring cameras.

losed circuit video installations

Videofluoroscopy — TV — screening calls for closed circuit video installations for X ray film demonstration and consultations between operation rooms, out-patient units, and other sections of the hospital on one hand and the radiology department on the other. It can improve collaboration between surgeons and radiologists. A film developed in the radiology department and the commentary by the radiologist can be transmitted to the operation room. In addition a pneumatic tube for sending exposed films from the operation room to the radiology department is needed.

The transmission by TV of a developed X ray picture from the operation room to the radiology department for consultation is not recommended. To secure the best possible diagnosis the original exposure must be examined.

Closed-circuit TV systems can link surgical teams also to other laboratories. TV cameras in the pathology laboratory can be focused over the gross examination area or into a microscope, so that the pathologists will be able to demonstrate the complete specimen or a slide. Prompt delivery of the histological diagnosis, not the televised display of the specimen, is of main importance.

1   Goldstein J Richard and Parker Jr William T: The Design of the CCU Patient Room. Stencil. New York. December 1977, p 30.

2   see also Centralintensiven upprustad. 1978, KS-nytt 17:1-2, 11-13.

3   see also Laufman Harold: The infection hazard of intensive care. 1974, Surgery, Gynecology & Obstetrics 139:413–414.

From an EEG-laboratory with its own computer, which is linked to monitor high risk patients, the quantitative parameters could be transmitted to the operation room and displayed there parallel to other physiological functions[4].

Closed TV systems in operation rooms usually have two circuits for vision and two for sound. One sound and one vision circuit terminate within the lighting complex, servicing the permanent TV camera there. A second pair of circuits terminate in a distribution panel beneath a picture in the operation room and are used in combination with the complementary mobile camera.

Diagnostic and preparatory information as a part of the clinical examination could be obtained by TV, e g televised endoscopy.

As TV control room also the operation room's instrumentation room, if such one is available, could be used.

Recording

For storage of records, also from the X ray department the computer system has high theoretical possibilities. In the UK due to the high expense and large storage capacity it would require only one computer per region for a scheme to be feasible. All departments would be linked to the centre. Information could be transferred at the same time as, say, reporting. The X ray film could be scanned, translated to storage numbers, along with its report and the information stored. The radiologist could then dial for requested past information.

The high initial cost to the region could be helped by the substantial reduction of staff, in every department in the region. No filing staff would be necessary, saving considerable amounts in salaries. Also, if wards and clinics could have a link then clerical staff could be further reduced in line with the decreased number of typed reports to be handled[5].

For recording operations 16 mm film cameras are in many circumstances preferred to closed circuit TV. A mounted camera should be completed by a mobile camera.

It has been emphasized that frequently it takes twice the time to perform the operation with TV-cameras around than without cameras.

For recording microsurgery a combination of TV monitor and videotape recorder have been used. A tiny microphone plugged into the horizontal arm of the micro-

4   personal communication: 1977, Ilmar Sulg, Oulu, Finland.

5   John C: The reported film storage problem solved? 100 mm film miniaturisation using the Oldelft, Delcopex and Odelcard System. 1978, Radiography 44:191–195.

scope provides the sound during videotape recordings[6]. The use of an overhead mirror in spinal, chest and abdominal surgery photography has been recommended[7]. It permits versatility of camera operation, freedom for the operation team, and good orientation for the viewer.

Reflex-cameras with flash attachment are used for medical documentation. Photographic equipment should not cause ignition of flammable gases in operation rooms.

Educational transmitting

When *closed-circuit TV* — educational TV research indicates that there is no clear advantage for colour over black and white[8] — is used in connection with medical education, the system has to be teacher oriented.

Transmitting should be used where TV's distinctive features — image magnification, image multiplication, image transportation, image transformation and image memory — can best be exploited.

TV should not be used when some other method can accomplish the purpose better. It is still salutary to remember that, as was emphasized by Lord *Ritchie-Calder**, with all these new media of communication, first make sure that there is something to communicate.

When also the physiognomy of the patient is involved, monitoring should respect the privacy of the patient**.

Choosing the most appropriate medium is very important for the production of teaching materials. It is quite a simple matter to transfer film to videotape without substantial loss in quality. On the other hand, the transfer of videotape to film is a complicated and expensive process, and there are only a few companies that do this and provide high quality. Therefore, if distribution in either 16 mm or 8 mm is anticipated, it is far wiser to choose film as the original production medium[9].

---

6 see also Machemer Robert and Parel Jean-Marie: An improved microsurgical ceiling-mounted unit and automated television. 1978, American Journal of Opthalmology 85:205–209.

7 Lichtor Joseph: Motion Picture Photography in Surgery Using an Overhead Mirror. 1971, International Surgery 55:42–44.

8 Webster B R and Cox S M: The Value of Colour in Educational Television. 1974, British Journal of Educational Technology 5:1:44–61.

* Lord Ritchie-Calder, born 1906, English author and outstanding scientific, social and political journalist.

**personal communication, 1978, Ilmar Sulg, Stockholm.

9 McPheeters Virginia: Videotape or film? 1978, The Journal of Audiovisual Media in Medicine 1:175-176.

Expensive and complex educational media have produced little positive impact at the continuing educational level. Some very excellent teaching materials have been produced for television — closed circuit, broadcast, and cassette tapes. These have drawn almost unbelievably poor audience responses from physicians. Even more sophisticated teaching exercises have been programmed into the computer-assisted format or as case simulation studies. The fundamental validity of both the materials and the methods are unquestionable. The fact remains that physicians, thus far, have shown little interest. From the cost-benefit standpoint, the loss of funds in these programmes has been horrendous.

The numerous failures in this field have had little publicity. This is unfortunate, because a careful study of the failures may have uncovered some causative reasons[9].

9   Wells Benjamin B: Continuing medical education — pro and con. 1977, Southern Medical Journal 70:645–648.

NURSING UNITS

The main reason for a person entering a hospital environment is that he has a medic problem which causes an inability to meet his vital needs.

The word environment is derived from *environ*, which means *to be* or *extend aroun to encircle, to surround, to envelop.* The hospital environment is to envelop and sur port the patient until he can manage his own self-care again.

The design of a health care environment must be built on the premise of support of the patient's needs as a human being, as well as the provision of his physical deficier cy needs.

A patient needs to have food when he is hungry and can tolerate it, not just three times a day during diet kitchen hours. He has to have privacy of both person and in formation, and the option of sociability when needed. He has the need to be inform as to what is going to take place, so he can best cooperate.

The patient needs also the dignity of being included in the planning of his care. He needs freedom from pain *when* it occurs, and not an hour later. The patient needs immediate decision making by a professional who has both in-depth knowledge of the patient and a scientific knowledge base to put with it. The patient has the need not to be abandoned at time of crisis. The patient needs to have confidence that the people caring for him know his special requirements. And lastly, he needs the frequent reassuring presence of a person who cares about what happens to him and what he is experiencing[1].

A patient's need for air, food, sleep, privacy, identity, must also be included in the environmental considerations, even though these are not directly involved with his deficiency needs. Design must then move out and support required functions and procedures in ever widening rings of environmental design — each decision based on the patient's needs[2].

A territorial instinct is part of people's innate behaviour. Therefore an attempt to define the patient's own areas — the room, bed, chair, closet — should be made.

Yet into this territory will come a parade of health professionals, who seem to exhibit more of a right to be there than he does. The patient, in a strict sense, becomes the trespasser on the territory of health professionals[*].

Members of the medical staff enter often without knocking, carry out activities often without introduction or explanation, and depart, seldom leaving the patient's territory as it was before they arrived.

1 Kraegel Janet M, Mousseau Virginia Schmidt, Goldsmith Charles, Arora Rajeev: Patient Care Systems. J B Lippincott Company, Philadelphia, Toronto 1974, p 94.

2 ibid, p 88

* Stillman Margot J: Territoriality and Personal Space. 1978, American Journal of Nursing 78:1670–1672.

When activities involving the patient's personal space are necessary, the manner in which they are carried out is important. This includes recognizing the patient as an individual, providing explanations where indicated, not leaving his body exposed, working quickly to minimize bodily contact, and recognizing the physical and psychological discomfort that may arise from an invasion of privacy*.

Patients in rooms with several inhabitants are subjected not only to territorial encroachment by staff, but by neighbours.

The efficient and economic running of hospital in-patient services is probably one of the most difficult problems of all continuously operating services.

Over the years a considerable amount of research has been done to devise ways of assessing workload with a view to calculating the number and mix of nurses required for a definite load[3].

The literature shows conceptual confusion surrounding attempts to develop criteria of quality of care.

Nursing care can be divided into three areas: the technical-professional, the educational and the trusting relationship areas. The technical-professional area seems to be the most important to both the nurses and patients.

Basically the question of quality of care is a question of supervision and of good management of the available resources.

The organization of nursing care constitutes a subsystem that very directly aims at achieving the hospital's overall objectives.

A Belgian study[4] bases integrated nursing on three clear and intervowen objectives: The nursing organization has to be patient oriented, it has to assign nurses a broad responsibility. By way of an organizational framework the professionalization of nursing practioners is to be encouraged.

Individual nurses would be assigned full responsibility for the total nursing care of a number of patients during their shift. This responsibility involves not only providing nursing care, but also plannnig and evaluating that care. The individual nurse

*   Stillman Margot J: Territoriality and Personal Space. 1978, American Journal of Nursing 78:1670-1672.

3   Watt Elizabeth: Lengthy look at way forward for nursing. 1978, Health and Social Service Journal 88:160–162.

4   Grypdonck M, Rodenbach M Th and Windey T: Het model integrerende Verpleegkunde: voorstel tot her-orientëring. 1977, Acta Hospitalia 17:124–145.

would, when necessary, rely on the active support group, colleagues who are able to give advice and to participate in decision making. Such a group of nurses would be coordinated by a group leader, who does not hold a position above the group members but has a temporary, purely functional authority to coordinate the work and to ensure its smooth running.

The transferring of some of the head nurse's executive tasks to other nurses in this way frees the head nurse for genuine leadership functions, both group and task oriented, and for defining the policies of the unit.

The head nurse leads the training of new personnel and the improvement of nursing care. Administrative tasks which have little or no nursing content are to be performed by a ward secretary under the head nurse's direction. The coordinator is a staff member with the responsibility to see that new ideas and developments in nursing are brought into practice. When nurses take upon themselves more responsibility for total care, their instructions must be carefully specified. The nursing plan must give a clear overview of all that must be done for the patient including the observations which must be done, tests, medications and other nursing care that can be carried out by the nurse on her own initiative. At the same time information has to be collected to clarify future tasks, e g diagnosis.

Group discussions are primarily patient-related, but they also absorb tensions and stress, promote group cohesion and reduce uncertainty in individual nurses' functions.

When staffing patterns are not flexible, the patient profile offers the opportunity to establish priorities between what can and can not be accomplished with a greater degree of precision.

The nursing unit remains one of the most important elements in a hospital. Yet little has been done to re-evaluate its needs and functions[5]. Most effort has been devoted to better organization and administration. Development has been geared toward better material handling and better nursing organization, towards designing spaces which will save personnel steps, a measure believed by some health care consultants to have great importance for gaining efficiency in operation.

The basic reason for the hospital's existence — the patient and his human needs — seems to have been neglected, or at least subordinated, as a design consideration[6].

Hospitals which have been designed primarily to meet health professionals' needs and so called efficiency in operation, usually fail to develop an environment which appropriately meets the patient needs[7].

5   see also Zeidler Eberhard H: Healing the Hospital. The Zeidler Partnership. Toronto 1974, p 64.

6   ibid

7   Kraegel Janet M, Mousseau Virginia Schmidt, Goldsmith Charles, Arora Rajeev: Patient Care Systems. J B Lippincott Company. Philadelphia, Toronto 1974, p 88.

The personnel environmental needs must be balanced with those of the patient.

It is now recognized that it is dangerous, inefficient, and expensive to base the design and staffing of an inpatient unit on the average needs of patients during their hospital stay[8].

Supervision is deliberately optimized in critical care units when the patient is very ill and privacy reduced. When the patient is getting better, observability can be reduced and privacy has to be increased in more general nursing units.

Gradually the recovering patient is transferred to medically less sophisticated areas or units.

Different kinds of units, that offer varying degrees of patient adjusted care have to replace standard nursing units.

The primary needs of the patient as well as the basic nursing care methods alter very slowly, although clear definitions concerning the needs of and the patient himself are still lacking.

Lasting requirements for the nursing unit design could be established by basing them on to-days intellectually and economically above average standing patient, who while hospitalized, should not be expected — when leaving the intensive care area — to alter his routines and his normal standard of living considerably.

8   also Robert J O'Connor et al, M A Rockwell cited by Thompson John D and Goldin Grace: The hospital: a social and architectural history. Yale University Press. New Haven and London 1975, p 313.

Critical care units
Definition and scope

There is no general agreement at this time (1978) concerning the definition and scope of critical medicine[1], the parent of intensive care and therapy units — ICTUs.

With intensive therapy it is usually meant the treatment of patients during a period of their critical illness. It requires extraordinary care, qualified staff, strict supervision, and very often mechanical aids to support vital functions. The patient may require artificial ventilation, treatment for shock, cardiac monitoring, pacemaking, peritoneal or haemodialysis, biochemical correction of severe metabolic disorders and special protection against infection[2].

Intensive observation is adapted until complications requiring ventilatory or circulatory resuscitation no longer are a threat[3].

Intensive or critical care is a method of organizing medicine and nursing so that expertise and sophisticated equipment are concentrated where they are most needed and efficiently utilized. Intensive care is considered to be a very constructive therapeutic method. On the other hand, it has been felt that the development of ICTUs has suffered from overemphasis on gadgets and spatial designs and underemphasis or personnel[4].

ICTU patients require careful study and accumulation of experience. The days are over, when it was thought that they were merely more severely ill examples of other patients[5].

Any patient without terminal illness deserves initial admission to an intensive care unit. In each medical speciality and subspeciality there are patients eligible for intensive treatment. Advanced age *per se* is no reason for rejecting a patient from an ICTU. The recovering patient should have an active life of some sort to look forward to.

---

1   see also Safar Peter and Grenvik Åke: Organization and Physician Education in Critical Care Medicine. 1977, The Journal of Anesthesiology 47:82–95.

2   Wiklund Per Erik, Fjeldborg Nils, Suutarinen Toivo, Gjengstö Haavard, Feychting Hans and Norlander Olof at the Tenth Congress of the Scandinavian Society of Anaesthesiologists. Lund, June 1971.

3   ibid

4   see also Safar Peter: Health Care Delivery Problems and Goals: A Personal Philosophic Appraisal. in Public Health Aspects of Critical Care Medicine and Anesthesiology. ed by Peter Safar. F A Davis Company. Philadelphia 1974, p 2–32.

5   see also Freeman R: Infection and Intensive Care. in Selected Topics in Clinical Bacteriology. ed by John de Louvois. Baillière Tindall. London 1976, p 19.

A strong case can be made for intensive care units if their individual guidelines are set within a general ethical framework that takes account of human rights, and that such guidelines give careful consideration to the salvageability of patients and the condition of salvageability. It is difficult to justify the admission and retention in intensive care units of patients whose needs and rights are not served by this care.

The intensivist has an obligation to ensure that there is no case in which the only so called right that remains to an intensive care patient is the right to utilize medical technology[6].

In return for whatever benefits it bestows, intensive care exposes the seriously ill to an especially high level of risk from the procedures intended to help them[7]. There is also the danger of overenergetic treatment i e so called overtreatment of minor cases and unnecessary treatment of hopeless cases[8]. The fact that it is possible to maintain and prolong life, does not inevitably and in all cases mean that to do so is justifiable or even desirable[9]. Reverence for life must be tempered by restraint and an equal respect for the dignity of death[10].

6   Cohen Cynthia B: Ethical Problems of Intensive Care. 1977, The Journal of Anesthesiology 47:217–227.

7   Russel Louise B: The diffusion of new hospital technologies in the United States. 1976, International Journal of Health Services.6:557:580.

8   see also Pessi Teuvo T: Experiences gained in intensive care of surgical patients. 1973, Annales Chirurgiae et Gynecologiae Fenniae 62:suppl. 185, p 10.

    Binkert E: Zur lebensrettenden Funktion einer Intensivstation. in Krankenhausprobleme der Gegenwart. vol 7. ed by E Haefliger and V Elsasser. Verlag Hans Huber. Bern, Stuttgart, Vienna 1974, p 188–193.

9   see also Spencer G T: Special care units. in A practice of anaesthesia. ed by W D Wylie and H C Churchill-Davidson. Lloyd-Luke. London 1972, p 530.

10 Peaston M J T: The Intensive Care Unit. in Recent Advances in Surgery. Number Eight. ed by Selwyn Taylor. Churchill Livingstone. Edinburgh and London 1973, p 319.

Need for intensive care and treatment beds

There is a very important statement: If intensive care is defined as observation and treatment of patients with imminent or manifest failure of vital functions, the need for intensive care beds is much lower than if it is defined as heavy nursing care[1].

On an average, most large hospitals will need only about 2 per cent of the number of beds in the clinics which make use of the critical care* or intensive care and treatment unit[2]. This percentage may rise to 3 per cent[3].

The need for surgical intensive care may increase from 4.1 per cent to 5 to 6 per cent of surgical bed capacity, the reason being the increasing share of outpatient surgery[4]. In the Federal Republic of Germany the amount of ICTU beds in a hospital has been maximized to 5 per cent to the total number of beds[5].

In the US about 5 per cent of total medical-surgical beds are represented by intensive and coronary care units[6], although it has been recommended[7] that 10 per cent of the total number of beds in a hospital should be allocated for use in the intensive care unit.

Wiklund[8] recommends for intensive observation 1.5 to 2 beds per operation room or 5 to 7 per cent of surgical beds or 5 per cent of acute beds; and for intensive therapy 2.5 to 3 per cent of beds in clinics in need of intensive therapy.

In thoracic surgery and neurosurgery the needs are far bigger. If these units are segregated, the ICTU bed need is about 15 per cent of the clinic beds.

Whether a hospital should have an ICTU for a single speciality or for a group of them, or a multispeciality ICTU, depends on the type of hospital and on the regional health care organization.

1 Dannert Friedrich, Hedstrand Ulf and Holmdahl Martin H:son: Patient Material in Multidisciplinary Intensive Care Units. 1975, Acta Anaesthesiologica Scandinavica. Supplementum 57, p 64–70.

* Sometimes three step-down sections in a unit for critical care are distinguished — critical care, intensive care and concentrated care.

2 see also Juraszyński Janusz, Nitsch Andrzej, Porebowicz Stefan and Radwański Zygmunt: Projektowanie obiektóv sluzby zdrowia. Arkady. Warsaw 1973, p 149.

3 Poulsen H: Probleme der Organisation und Leitung von Intensivtherapie-Abteilungen. 1973, Zentralblatt für Chirurgie 98:1073–1082.

4 Pessi Teuvo T: Experience gained in intensive care of surgical patients. 1973, Annales Chirurgiae et Gynecologiae Fenniae 62:supplement 185, p 48.

5 see also Mindestvoraussetzung für die Anerkennung von Intensivstationen. 1973, Krankenhaus Umschau 42:568.

6 Safar Peter, Benson Don M, Esposito Gerald, Grenvik Åke and Sands Patricia A: Emergency and Critical Care Medicine: Local Implementation of National Recommendations. in Public Health Aspects of Critical Care Medicine and Anesthesiology. ed by Peter Safar. F A Davis Company. Philadelphia 1974, p 99.

7 Bregande B J: Design of intensive care units. 1973, Hospital Topics 51:10:41–42.

8 personal communication: 1977, Per Erik Wiklund, Danderyd, Sweden.

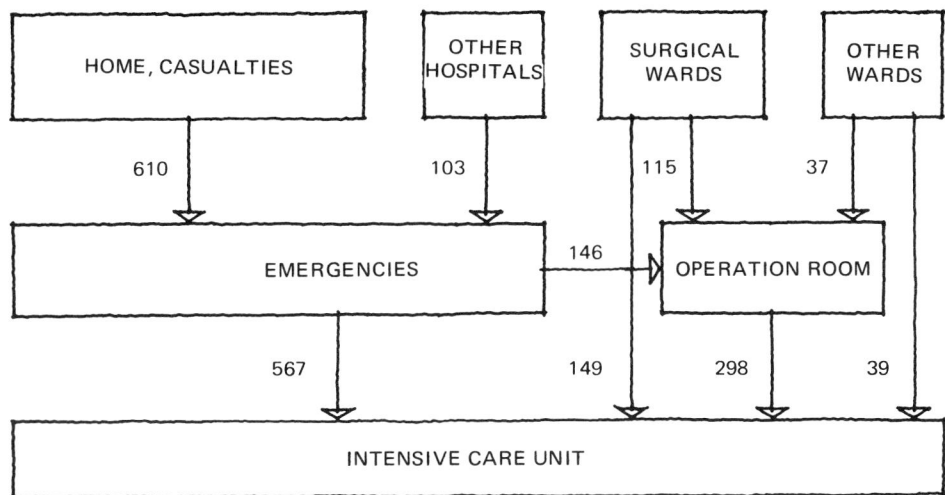

Route of admission of 1053 surgical patients to intensive care unit as found by Teuvo Pessi in Finland 1973.

Organ systems, clinical syndromes, and patient population may be the basis for grouping the patients, as illustrated by cardiac care units, burn units, and paedriatric units.

A general intensive care unit, a coronary care unit — as far as possible, heart patients should not be nursed with non-coronary patients — a burn unit, and a neonatal and premature unit have represented the physical subdivisions of critical care areas commensurate with efficient staffing, best patient care, and maximum economy[9].

In hospitals which have about 1,000 or more beds other types of ICTUs could be added, primarily for patients who have been subjected to cardiac surgery, neurosurgery, or thoracic surgery[10]. Although the concept of a stroke intensive care unit or neurovascular care unit — NCU — has been in existence for ten years, there still is conflict of opinion regarding its advantages[11].

9   see also Boutros Azmy R: Anesthesiology and Intensive Care. 1974, The Journal of Anesthesiology 41:319: 320.

    Feller Irving and Crane Keith: Planning and Designing A Burn Care Facility. Institute for Burn Medicine. Ann Arbor, Michigan 1975, p 26.

10 see also Battersby E F: Anaesthesia and intensive care. in Recent advances in paediatric surgery. Number 3. ed by Andrew W Wilkinson. Churchill Livingstone. Edinburgh, London and New York 1975, p 31–41.

    Dannert Friedrich, Hedstrand Ulf and Holmdahl Martin H:son: Patient Material in Multidisciplinary Intensive Care Units. 1975, Acta Anaesthesiologica Scandinavica. Supplementum 57, p 64–70.

11 see also Norris J W and Hachinski V C: Intensive Care Management of Stroke Patients. 1976, Stroke 7:573–577.

The importance of gastrointestinal intensive care units is underscored by an examination of the rapidly emerging clinical, educational and research needs in gastrointestinal disease[12]. However, the idea to take surgical gastroenterology away from general surgery is opposed in some quarters[13].

Some experts favour only interdisciplinary ICTUs.

Intensive care and therapy wards are for a group of patients an extension of the immediate post operative care[14].

The ICTU ought to be linked with the post-anaesthetic recovery area, the emergency area and the delivery section.

Paediatric beds

The intensive therapy units have been designed predominantly for adults. Two-thirds of the nurses on adult ICTUs have considered the environment of the adult intensive therapy unit unsuitable for children[15].

The optimum care of the child is accomplished in an area specifically designed as paediatric, and by personnel trained in the care of children.

The paediatric skills are the main considerations for the critically ill child. It is decidedly easier to give children's nurses training in intensive care — a six-months course — than ICTU nurses training in paediatric care — a course of 13 months[16].

One ICTU-bed for twenty paediatric beds, including sub-specialities, has been recommended[17]. It has also been assumed that the beds in paediatric intensive care units should constitute 6 per cent of all beds in the paediatric clinic[18], or 8 per cent of the average hospital paediatric census[19].

12 Den Besten L: The Gastrointestinal Intensive Care Unit. 1976, Surgery, Gynecology & Obstetrics 142:404–405.

13 see also Allgöwer Martin: General surgery and trauma. 1975, Annals of the Royal College of Surgeons of England 57:133–138.

14 see also Pütsep Ervin and Linneroth Anna: Die Planung von Intensivpflegestationen. in Modernes Krankenhaus 2. Verlag für Gesamtmedizin. Berlin 1960, p 85–104.

15 Harper J R and Verakis G: Children in adult intensive therapy units. 1970, British Medical Journal 1:810.

16 Appleyard James and Joseph Michael: Intensive care within a children's ward. 1971, Guy's Hospital Report 120:337–345.

17 Appleyard James and Joseph Michael: Intensive care within a children's ward. 1971, Guy's Hospital Report 120:337–345.

18 see also Poppelbaum H Ferdinand: Children's Intensive Care Unit in the Municipal Clinical Hospital Berlin-Buch. 1974, Anaesthesia, Resuscitation and Intensive Therapy 2:65–70.

19 Benzing III George: Pediatric Multipurpose Intensive Care Unit. 1974, American Journal of Diseases of Children 127:795–796.

Intensive care in hospitals uses up a large sector of personnel.

It is difficult to evaluate and compare costwise the results of intensive care[1]. The questions on the ICTU financial and personnel costs, as well as those on the circumstances of their usefulness and selection of treatments have — until now — been rarely asked and even less frequently answered[2].

In the USA an intensive care patient is given 16.76 nursing man-hours per day[3], which is 2.85 times more than in medical and surgical units.

Although in the intensive care units efficient use of staff is made, the cost of maintaining it is from 2.5 to up to 20 times higher per bed than in regular bed care. In the US between $ 24,000 to 232,523 has been spent to allow one patient to survive by adapting intensive care[4].

It has been estimated that the laboratory procedures may account for about 30 per cent of the ICTU cost[5].

Benefit from intensive care is currently impossible to access because patient populations differ, treatment protocols vary widely, and persistence in life support may reflect the ethical climate of the unit[6].

One sad comment could be cited: intensive care medicine is extraordinarily expensive, yet results in only a small number of patients surviving to a useful and productive life. Far more likely is death or survival with poor functional recovery[7].

It has been assumed that the introduction of an intensive care unit would significantly affect the work pattern in acute wards and move the peaks and troughs of productivity. Experience has proved this to be untrue[8].

1   see also Pessi Teuvo T: Experiences gained in intensive care of surgical patients. 1973, Annales Chirurgiae et Gynecologiae Fenniae 62:suppl. 185, p 10.

2   Vayda Eugene: When Is Surgery Indicated? 1977, The Milbank Memorial Fund Quarterly/Health and society 55:495–504.

3   Data now available on specialized nursing units. 1977, Hospitals 51:11:33.

4   Cullen David J: Results and Costs of Intensive Care. 1977, The Journal of Anesthesiology 47:203–216.

5   see also Russell Louise B: The diffusion of new hospital technologies in the United States. 1976, International Journal of Health Services 6:557–580.

6   Cullen David J: Results and Costs of Intensive Care. 1977, The Journal of Anesthesiology 47:203–216.

7   ibid

8   Watt Elizabeth: Lengthy look at way forward for nursing. 1978, Health and Social Service Journal 88:160–162.

Some staff aspects

The intensivist

A specialist in critical medicine, also called the intensivist, must be expert in many areas in such a manner as to transcend the traditional divisions inherent in today's practice of medicine. The collective expertise of the anaesthesiologist, the pulmonary medicine specialist, the cardiologist, the nephrologist, and the clinical pharmacologist must be combined. Understanding of fluid and electrolyte balance, of the effects of severe trauma and major operative procedures on the functions of various organs, and of the proper use of parenteral feedings and antibiotics must be possessed. The intensivist must be expert in applied physiology, especially as it pertains to the cardiovascular, pulmonary, and renal systems. He must have superior knowledge of mechanical ventilators and electronic devices. This extensive expertise is available to only a few physicians[1]. The fact, that there was 1977 no comprehensive work published in English on the whole field of critical care medicine[2], is very significative.

The intensivist must also care. He must learn to discover the individual who lies obscured beneath a maze of tubes and numbers and find the thinking, feeling human being hidden behind the anxieties of those entrusted with the lives of patients. He must understand the bond that unites him and his patient in the common human enterprise. For when a patient is lost among a welter of technology, when no longer his face can be recognized, his pain felt and his silent anguish heard, the medical profession is diminished also[3].

Increasing emphasis is being placed on the role of the psychiatrist in the intensive care unit[4]. A quietly deluded or silently hallucinating patient is often unnoticed by the medical or surgical staff. Psychiatrists can help greatly in the detection and management of such patients as well as in aiding in the adjustment of all patients to the unusual environment of the intensive care unit. Likewise the psychiatrist can help to resolve interpersonal conflicts among the staff that are peculiar to the intensive care unit.

1 Boutros Azmy: Anaesthesiology and Intensive Care. 1974; The Journal of Anaesthesiology 41:319–320.

2 Safar Peter and Grenvik Åke: Organization and Physician Education in Critical Care Medicine. 1977, The Journal of Anesthesiology 47:82–95.

3 see also Caroline Nancy L: Quo vadis intensive care: more intensive or more care? 1977, Critical Care Medicine 5:256.

4 Theodore Nadelson cited by Harris III John McA and Cashman William F: Practical Monitoring of the Intensive Care Patient. 1978, The Orthopedic Clinics of North America 9:649–660.

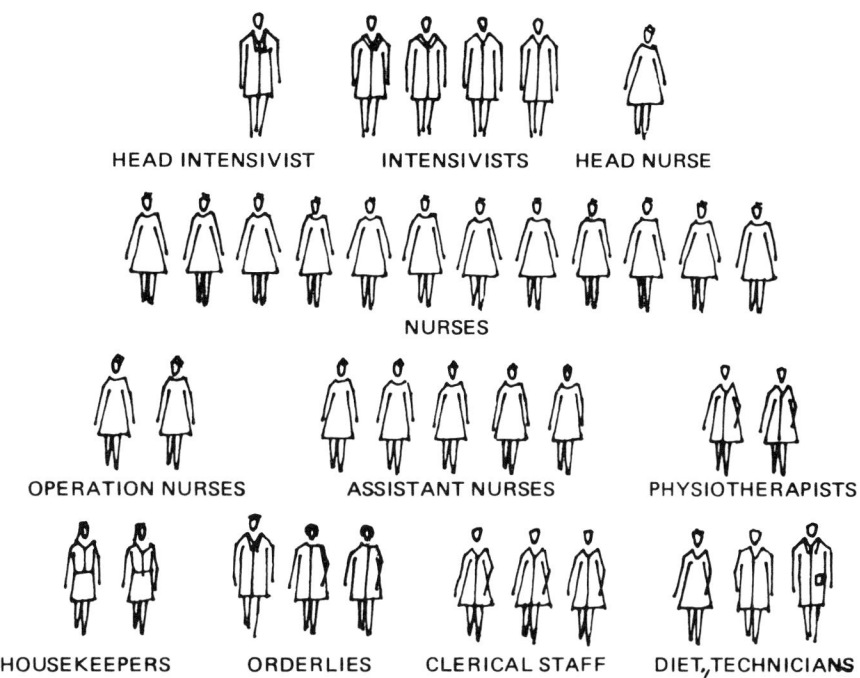

Staff requirements of a Hungarian 12 bed ICTU (Varga Peter, 1977).

...ursing care

ICTU work is much more demanding than most forms of the hospital work. It is a great challenge and it requires of nurses the highest qualities of competence and character[5].

The range of nursing in an intensive care unit is of great extent including the observation of the patient, the basic care of the patient, the observation of apparatus, the interpretation of recordings, and the emotional support of the patient and his relatives.

The lack of communication with patients hinders basic nursing care and detracts from job satisfaction[6]. The strains on staff are considerable e g dealing with the

---

5 see also Harris E A, Neutze J M, Richard Margaret P, Seelye Eve R and Simpson Marie M: Intensive Care of the Heart and Lungs. Blackwell Scientific Publications. Oxford, London, Edinburgh, Melbourne 1975, p XV.

6 Shircore Richard: Stress and intensive care staff. 1976, Health and Social Service Journal 86:1476–1477.

apparently hopeless cases of irreversible brain damage following incomplete respons to resuscitation[7].

The repetitive exposure to death and dying is a major problem as well as the work overload, lack of gratification from patients, and feeling of personal failure. Stress enters the situation when the nursing staff are trying to cope with a role beyond their capabilities or where there is no co-operation and support from the medical staff[8].

Paramedical staff

The sophistication of intensive care has created various categories of paramedical personnel. These include respiratory therapists and technicians, physical therapists, radiology technologists, laboratory technicians, biomedical equipment technicians, bacteriology technicians, physiologists, computer technicians, programmers, electrical safety officers, and social workers. With development of therapeutic methods, including on-line computerized monitoring, use of artificial organs, and extra-corporeal circulation. The number of paramedical specialists in ICTUs must be expected to continue to increase[9].

Many of these positions illustrate the point that, while sophisticated equipment may provide speed and convenience, it does not reduce the need of staff.

Staff-patient ratio

The recommended nurse-patient ratio* has been estimated between 1 to 1 and 1 to 2 during the day and evening shifts and between 1 to 2 and 1 to 3 on the night shift[10]. A Swiss estimate requires the relationship of 2 to 2.5 staff to 1 patient in 6 to 8 bed ICTUs and 1 to 1.5 staff to 1 patient in 12 bed ICTUs[11].

7   see also Bourke A M, Bresnihan P C, Clarke D M, Leahy E, Lucey C, Taaffe J, Lehane S and Solan J:
    An Intensive Care Unit in a County Hospital. 1973, Irish Medical Journal 66:205–207.

    Tomlin P J: Psychological problems in intensive care. 1977, British Medical Journal 2:441–443.

8   see also Melia Kath M: The Intensive Care Unit — a stress situation? 1977, Nursing Times 73:5:17–20.

9   see also Safar Peter, Benson Don M, Esposito Gerald, Grenvik Åke and Sands Patricia A: Emergency and
    Critical Care Medicine: Local Implementation of National Recommendations. in Public Health Aspects of
    Critical Care Medicine and Anesthesiology. ed by Peter Safar. F A Davis Company. Philadelphia 1974,
    p 102.

*   When a working week of 36 hours, the day pass not exceeding six and the night pass of eight hours is
    adapted, a staff increase may be expected.

10 see also Teres Daniel: Management of Respiratory Infection in the Intensive Care Unit. in Recent advances
    in respiratory surgical intensive care. ed by T Gordon McNabb and Stephen V Hall. International Anesthe-
    siology Clinics. vol 14 no 1. Spring 1976, p 163–178.

11 Die Planung einer Intensivpflegeabteilung und deren Ausstattung mit Überwachungsgeräten. 1976, Veska
    40:348–350.

A British observer has noted that when standard working hours and absenteeism are taken into account, the relationship works out to 4.3 nurses per bed[12]. Another UK writer has 4.25 nurses per bed including the allowances for holidays and occasional absences[13].

In Hungary 8 to 16 beds require a staff of 30 to 55, the average being 3.5 to 3.75 per bed[14].

A paediatric intensive care unit — PICU — should be staffed by a minimum of one nurse for every two patients and, in the case of the very ill child who requires constant attention, one nurse per patient. At all times there should be at least one nurse in the unit who has had additional training in the critical care and resuscitative skills[15].

12 cited by Russell Louise B: The diffusion of new hospital technologies in the United States. 1976, International Journal of Health Services 6:557–580.

13 Tinker Jack: The staffing and management of intensive therapy units. 1976, British Journal of Hospital Medicine 16:399–406.

14 Varga Peter: Az intenziv betegellátás elvi-szervezési kérdései. in Az intenzív betegellátás elmélete és gyakorlata. Medicina Könyvkiadó. Budapest 1977, p 35.

15 Stewart David R and Malley Betsy: Tenets of Treatment: Critical Care of the Pediatric Patient. 1978, The Journal of the Kansas Medical Society 79:121–122.

Patient in the intensive care and treatment unit

The critically ill patient in an intensive care unit may be scarcely visible, let alone identifiable as human, among all the paraphernalia of life support. Monitors and ventilatory equipment surround him like sentinels. Charts and flow sheets hang at the end of the bed, chronicling the vicissitudes of a dozen parameters. The distractions may be limitless. But there are also tears, pain, sadness, lonelineness, uncertainty, fear, helplessness, despair. These are not on the flow sheet. These cannot be read off a monitor or determined by cannulation of a vessel. These cannot be measured or computed[1].

Obviously the busy intensive care environment is frequently the opposite of peace and quiet required for the recovery from serious illness.

Background sound levels measured in four US ICT units were found to be comparable to those in the hospital cafeteria at noon, and only somewhat lower than in the boiler room[2].

The noise of the unit creates adverse physiological effects and an emotional strain on the patient, disturbing his rest by day and sleep at night. E g after heart surgery sleep may become fragmented and amount only to a total of 1 to 4 hours for 2 to 3 days.

It has been pointed out that incidence or severity of simple reactive apathetic depression, which is extremely common in patients whose stay in the intensive care unit is prolonged, is unchanged when ambient lighting or noise is reduced[3].

Sleep may be disturbed in any patient admitted to an intensive care unit. Patients with severely disturbed sleep patterns tend to have significant residual disability compared to those with a similar clinical state but normal sleep records[4].

Frequent unnecessary awakenings are due to a general lack of awareness by the intensive care unit staff of noise levels, lighting conditions and other factors that would be conductive to sleep[5].

Medical thinking has not yet grasped that tissue healing may be accelerated by sleep. There persists an assumption that degradation and synthesis in tissues not

1   Cardine Nancy L: Quo vadis intensive care: more intensive or more care? 1977, Critical Care Medicine 5:256.

2   Redding Joseph S, Hargest Thomas S and Minsky Stephen H: How noisy is intensive care? 1977, Critical Care Medicine 5:275–276.

3   Tomlin P J: Psychological problems in intensive care. 1977, British Medical Journal 2:441–443.

4   Norris J W and Hachinski V C: Intensive Care Management of Stroke Patients. 1976, Stroke 7:573–577.

5   see also Orr William C and Stahl Monte L: Sleep Disturbances After Open Heart Surgery. 1977, The American Journal of Cardiology 39:196–201.

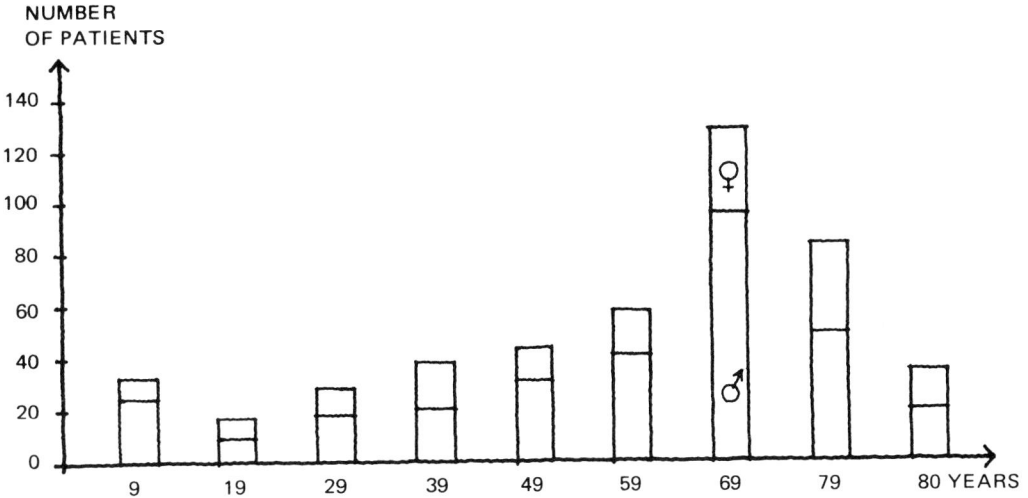

A one-year study by I Gustavsson and E Johansson (1976) shows that in surgical intensive care two thirds of the patients are men. 50 per cent of the patients belong to the age group of 40 to 70 years.

only continue all the time — as they do — but they are continually equal — which they are not[6].

The phenomena which can occur for the ICTU patients in various degrees include confusion, disturbed memory, disorientation in place, time and sometimes in person, and delusions and hallucinations in which the design, colours, sounds and equipment of the ICTU may be involved. The sound of the air-conditioning unit, for example, can become a voice, and a stain on the ceiling a face[7].

Visual obstruction between the patients is desirable. On the other hand, an exterior view is essential. Daylight* and clocks — perhaps with digital readings — and calendars with large type and pull-off pages contribute towards the well-being of the patient. In the US tackboards suitable for mounting get-well cards have been recommended[8]. A surface for flowers and plants, should as far as possible be coordinated with the window location and natural light.

6   Adam Kirstine and Oswald Ian: Sleep is for Tissue Restoration. 1977, Journal of the Royal College of Physicians of London. 11:376–388.

7   Bazelmans J: Intensive care: virtue or vice? 1977, The Netherlands journal of medicine 20:220–226.

*   Two to three times greater delirium frequencies have been reported from windowless units than from those with windows. (see also Keep P J: Stimulus deprivation in windowless rooms. 1977, Anaesthesia 32:598–600).

8   Goldstein J Richard and Parker Jr William T: The design of the CCU Patient Room. Stencil. New York. December 1977, p 28.

Appearance of familiar objects give considerable assistance in overcoming disorientation and visiting by loved ones becomes very important. Petty restrictions placed upon visiting are unjustified and appear only to be for nursing convenience[9].

Providing a television set and letting the patient choose his favourite programme appears to give a prolonged boost to the patient's morale[10].

The management of the psychological components is of paramount importance for patients in an ICTU[11].

Length of patient stay

The patient's stay in the ICTU — the variations in the average length are considerable — should be kept as short as possible.

The average length of stay in an ICTU unit in Sweden has been 3.5 days[12], but some patients may remain in the unit for a month or more.

The average length of stay in the United Kingdom, quoted in a British Medical Association's working party report, was five days with a range of two to twelve days[13]. Later, an average stay of two to three days has been reported from a university hospital[14].

In the Federal Republic of Germany the length of stay has been calculated at four days for observation and seven days for therapy[15]. From one teaching hospital an average length of stay of 5.1 days has been reported[16].

In the German Democratic Republic the average length of stay in the ICTU is four to five days[17], in Hungary seven to twelve days[18]. According to a Finnish study[19]

9   Robinson J: A Patient in the Intensive Care Unit. Abstracts of the Spring Meeting of the Intensive Care Society. 1978, Intensive Care Medicine 4:169–170.

10   Tomlin P J: Psychological problems in intensive care. 1977, British Medical Journal 2:441–443.

11   Robinson J: A Patient in the Intensive Care Unit. Abstracts of the Spring Meeting of the Intensive Care Society. 1978, Intensive Care Medicine 4:169–170.

12   Intensivvård — verksamhet och resurskrav. Spri rapport 18/73, p 10.

13   Bain W H and Mackey W A: Intensive Therapy and Care in Surgical Departments in Hospitals. ed by D M Douglas. Butterworths. London 1972, p 92.

14   Tomlin P J: Psychological problems in intensive care. 1977, British Medical Journal 2:441–443.

15   Deutsche Krankenhausgesellschaft. Richtlinien für die Organisation der Intensivmedizin in den Krankenhäusern: Empfehlung vom 9. September 1974. 1974, Das Krankenhaus 66:457–460.

16   Schuster H P, Baum P, Schönborn H and Schölmerich P: Intensiv-medizin in Bereich der Inneren Medizin. 1977, Der Krankenhausarzt 50:18–31.

17   Bauers H G at the V UIA International Public Health Seminar. Nairobi. November 1974.

18   Varga Peter: Az intenzív betegellátás elvi-szervezési kérdései. in Az intenzív betegellátás elmélete és gyarkorlata. Medicina Könyvkiadó. Budapest 1977, p 31.

19   Pessi Teuvo T: Experiences gained in intensive care of surgical patients. 1973, Annales Chirurgiae et Gynecologiae Fenniae 62:suppl. 185, p 48.

the average duration of treatment of surgical ICTU patients is 6.2 days. Another Finnish study[20] indicates that the average duration of intensive care for thoraco-surgical patients is 4.1 days.

In the United States the average length of stay has been about four days. A study from western Pennsylvania indicates that the average ICTU stay is five days[21].

In New Zealand less than three days average duration of stay has been reported[22]. In Australia the mean duration of stay for medical patients has been three days, and for surgical patients six days[23].

In neurosurgical ICTUs the average stay is nine days.

As there is a tendency that the stay in the ICTU is being prolonged, as the average length of stay five to six days could be suggested for planning purposes.

In the paediatric cases, most patients stay for a short time only[24].

20 Merikallio E M, Vilkko P G and Tala P: Thoracic surgical patients in the intensive care unit. 1974, Annales Chirurgiae et Gynecologiae Fenniae 63:265–270.

21 Safar Peter, Benson Don M, Esposito Gerald, Grenvik Åke and Sands Patricia A: Emergency and Critical Care Medicine: Local Implementation of National Recommendations. in Public Health Aspects of Critical Medicine and Anesthesiology. ed by Peter Safar. F A Davis Company. Philadelphia 1974, p 66–135.

22 Shaw H A: The Place of a General Intensive Care Unit in a Metropolitan Hospital. 1975, The New Zealand Medical Journal 81:337.

23 Gilligan John E, McCleave David J, Worthley Lindsay and Price Lynne: The role of intensive care units. 1976, The Australian and New Zealand Journal of Surgery 46:301–304.

24 see also Poppelbaum H Ferdinand: Children's Intensive Care Unit in the Municipal Clinical Hospital Berlin-Buch. 1974, Anaesthesia, Resuscitation and Intensive Therapy 2:65–70.

ICTU size

The views on the optimal number of beds in an intensive-care-treatment unit have varied. An intensive care unit of less than 6 beds is clearly uneconomical[1]. However, to reduce the risk of nosocomial infection for most highly susceptible patients the sizing of the ICTU to four to six patients has been discussed in the US[2].

In the Federal Republic of Germany[3] the optimal number of beds per unit is put at 12 with a minimum of 6 and a maximum of 16. The choice of 6 to 16 beds has been recommended also in Denmark[4]. In the United Kingdom the optimal size of an ICTU is considered to be between 8 and 10 beds[5]. In Hungary, the size 8 to 16 beds is considered as recommendable[6]. In Switzerland 12 beds have been felt to be the maximum in an intensive care unit[7].

Too big ICTUs become ineffective[8].

The need for more beds than in one ICTU should be met not by fragmentation and multiplication of ICTUs, but by grouping several units into a critical care medicine centre, which enhances the utilization of beds.

As optimal ICTU occupancy rates 65 to 70 per cent[9], and 80 per cent[10] have been suggested.

1   see also Tinker Jack: The staffing and management of intensive therapy units. 1976, British Journal of Hospital Medicine 16:399–406.

2   Hewitt William L and Sanford Jay P: Workshop on Hospital-Associated Infections. 1974, The Journal of Infectious Diseases 130:680–686.

3   Deutsche Krankenhausgesellschaft. Richtlinien für die Organisation der Intensivmedizin in den Krankenhäusern: Empfehlung vom 9. September 1974. 1974, Das Krankenhaus 66:457–460.

4   Poulsen H: Probleme der Organisation und Leitung von Intensivtherapie-Abteilungen. 1973, Zentralblatt für Chirurgie 98: 1073–1082.

5   Tinker Jack: The staffing and management of intensive therapy units. 1976, British Journal of Hospital Medicine 16:399–406.

6   Varga Péter: Az intenzív betegellátás elvi-szervezési kérdései. in Az intenzív betegellátás elmélete és gyakorlata. Medicina Könyvkiadó. Budapest 1977, p 31.

7   Die Planung einer Intensivpflegeabteilung und deren Ausstattung mit Überwachungsgeräten. 1976, Veska 40:348–350.

8   also personal communication 1976, Jon Gjessing, Sundsvall.

9   Varga Péter: Az intenzív betegellátás elvi-szervezési kérdései. in Az intenzív betegellátás elmélete és gyakorlata. Medicina Könyvkiadó. Budapest 1977, p 32.

10 Tinker Jack: The staffing and management of intensive therapy units. 1976, British Journal of Hospital Medicine 16:399–406.

patial requirements

The spatial needs of the ICTU have been almost always underestimated.

The current average overall spatial need in the ICTU is about 50 m^2 per bed[1], although lower figures, such as 20 to 30 m^2, have been published[2].

ntrances

If the ICTU is not planned with single occupancy rooms exclusively, the entrance to the ICTU should be planned as an anteroom, where staff, visitors or personnel from other sections of the hospital must, before entering the patient area, be submitted to the gowning routines adapted in the ICTU.

There should be an *emergency entrance* for patients.

The corridor should be at least 2.5 m wide.

atient rooms

The goal should be a patient area, in which the requirements of psychologically pleasant environment and some elements of a scientific laboratory are balanced.

Of the two basic design possibilities — the open ward and the single-bed accommodation — the single-bed accommodation has gained preference[3]. The provision of privacy without isolation, in which communication is essential, has been recommended[4] — not least for the purpose of noise reduction — for all intensive care patients[5].

1   see also Stoddart J C: Intensive Therapy. Blackwell Scientific Publications. Oxford, London, Edinburgh, Melbourne 1975, p 192.

2   Schneider M, Schattenberg W, and Opitz B: Hygienische Probleme der Intensivtherapie. 1976, Das stationäre und ambulante Gesundheitswesen 25:26–29.

    Atkinson R S and Rushman G B: A synopsis of anaesthesia. Eighth edition. John Wright & Sons Ltd. Bristol 1977, p 875.

3   see also Gaya H: Infection control in intensive care. 1976, British Journal of Anaesthesia 48:9–12.

    Burrell Jr Zeb L and Burrell Lenette Owens: Critical Care. The C V Mosby Company. St Louis 1977, p 379.

4   Hay D and Oken D: Psychological stresses in intensive care unit nursing. 1972, Psychosomatic Medicine 34:109.

5   see also Falk S A and Woods N F: Hospital noise-levels and potential health hazards. 1973, The New England Journal of Medicine 289:774–781.

Nurses may have a different view on this issue. Open-plan intensive therapy areas where the nurses could have social contacts with other nurses have been recommended[6].

The spatial need for an ICTU bed in a single-bed room is 17 to 21 m^2.

The bed is an environmental influence which the acutely ill patient cannot escape.

The patient's bed should provide conditions for his effective existence and his progr toward an improved state of health. A knowledge of the detrimental effects of bed-rest must be a part of bed designers' armamentaria. Such pathologies as bedsores, muscle atrophy, thrombophlebitis, constipation, syncope, atelectasis, and osteoporosis could be alleviated with proper bed mattress and bedding design[7].

The bed should be capable of providing a comfortable working height for the female and male staff. The comfortable height would be 97.5 cm for women and 107.5 cm for men. The optimum zone for manual and visual tasks *i e* adjusting a drip and reading dials will be 127.5 to 150 cm[8]. For the patient to get safely in and out of the bed the compressed mattress height would need to be as low as 32.5 cm.

The bed should be readily adjustable to various therapeutic positions, easily moved for transport, should have a locking mechanism for a secure stationary position, anc where feasible, a removeable headboard.

Since the advent of the high/low electric bed with its thick, plasticized mattress, mi mal attention has been given to the basic design of this essential part of the patient' environment[9]. Fancy, lighted side consoles have been added. The side rails may disappear out of sight when not in use. The bed may go into eight or more esoteric positions — but it continues to be a hazard to the very life and limb of the patient. Th is not a bed on the market which will drop to the height of 32.5 cm — the height re quired to allow the weakened patient to place both feet firmly on the floor in order to most effectively and safely rise to a standing position.

Electric stretcher-beds in iniself have possessed shock risks and have been latently hazardous. They have not operated as rapidly as manually-controlled beds, and have cost far more to purchase and maintain. They have been more complex and less safe than conventional equipment.

---

6   Kilgour D Y: Nursing in intensive therapy units — personnel problems. in Intensive Care. ed by W F Walker and D E M Taylor. Churchill Livingstone. Edinburgh, London, New York 1975, p 229.

7   J Carpendale and L Finkelstein cited by Kraegel Janet M, Mousseau Virginia Schmidt, Goldsmith Charles, Arora Rajeev: Patient Care Systems. J B Lippincott Company. Philadelphia, Toronto 1974, p 87.

8   Bretten Pauline: The ergonomics of the hospital bed. 1973, Hospital Health Services Purchasing, no vol: 154–156.

9   see also Kraegel Janet M, Mousseau Virginia Schmidt, Goldsmith Charles, Arora Rajeev: Patient Care Systems. J B Lippincott Company. Philadelphia, Toronto 1974, p 87.

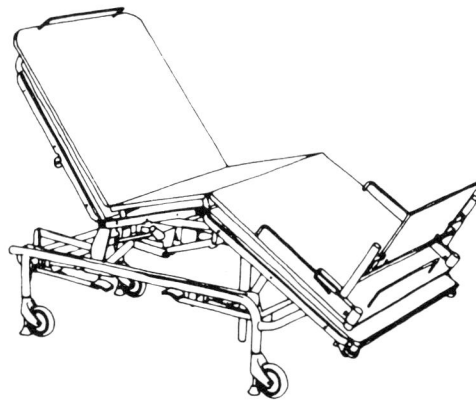

A typical manually controlled intensive care bed: length 208 cm, width 95 cm, height of bedstead bottom 50-85 cm. It has a frame of chrome-plated steel tubing and steel profile sections, and an Xray transparent bedstead bottom.

An overbed table for holding food trays and for grooming should contain a compartment for personal items.

For multiple organ support ample space should be provided around the bed. Bulky equipment may be accommodated.

The space around the bed in a single-bed accommodation can be used most efficiently when the shape of the floor is close to a square[10]. The length of the room may be the critical dimension.

In the ICTU clinical policy decisions on individual patients tend mostly to run from hour to hour rather than from moment to moment[11].

Close and often invasive monitoring is adapted to allow for early recognition of problems leading to appropriate treatment before a very critical situation occurs. Such trends are often best seen if the data not only are instantly available but are stored so that they can be recalled as new data are recorded. The simplest method of data storage is the clinical chart kept at the bedside, which represents a discontinuous series of observations. Electrocardiographic material and similar electronic data can be stored either on paper or in a computer system with recall[12].

The amount and sophistication of that equipment varies greatly. There should be shelves upon which equipment and instruments can be mounted and a place for patient charts.

---

10 Peaston M J T: The Intensive Care Unit. in Recent Advances in Surgery. Number Eight. ed by Selwyn Taylor. Churchill Livingstone. Edinburgh and London 1973, p 301.

11 see also Himsworth R L: Acute medical care in hospitals in the 1980s. 1976, British Journal of Hospital Medicine 16:605–611.

12 Harris III John McA and Cashman William F: Practical Monitoring of the Intensive Care Patient. 1978, The Orthopedic Clinics of North America 9:649–660.

A dual-channel, nonfading oscilloscope and a computer terminal can be mounted on the wall behind the head of the bed.

Locating the beds permanently away from the wall of the room gives the staff a 360° access to the patient, except for ECG leads — if not telemonitored — nasogastric suction, and respiratory connections. All tubes and wires could be run through a junction box under the bed.

All tubes, pipes, and wiring for the patient could also be organized and contained in a panel or column at the head of the patient's bed. The utility unit may contain an intercommunication system between the patient and the nurses' station and a telephone for the patient's personal use.

One of the panel's important features is that almost everything required for life support can be done for the patient or to the patient from either side of the bed. Under usual conditions, no wires or tubing pass over the patient or over his bed. The equipment cannot be seen by the patient, therefore, he is almost unaware of the instruments and machines that are needed to support his life. If and when a patient gets to an ambulatory stage while he is still receiving critical care, a screen can be used to temporarily cover the panel, so that the area does not look so much like a critical care room[13].

It has been recommended that monitoring equipment should be maintained outside the patient's room. Bedside monitors could be turned on only when needed. This will reduce the monotony of any constant rhytmic signal and diminish anxiety in those patients who are aware of the significance of these devices[14].

Individual patient wardrobe units are not required to be located in the patient's room. They could be placed near the nurses' station or in some other area of the ICTU[15].

In some ICTUs viewing windows have been provided in the partitions between rooms to permit a nurse caring for one patient to observe simultaneously another. Some nurses believe this is desirable, provided the windows are placed to prevent patients from seeing one another. It has been reported that in the interest of privacy draperies are practically always drawn across such windows[16].

13 O'Brien John F: Hospital-designed support system offers top efficiency, accessibility. 1978, Hospitals 52:3:85–88.

14 Kornfeld Donald S: Psychiatric aspects of patient care in the operating suite and special areas. in Modern Perspectives in the Psychiatric Aspects of Surgery. ed by John G Howells. Brunner/Mazel, Publishers. New York 1976, p 611.

15 see also Goldstein J Richard and Parker Jr William T: The Design of the CCU Patient Room. Stencil. New York. December 1977, p 28.

16 see also Bobrow Michael L and Craft Nina B: ICU and CCU facilities. 1971, Hospitals 45:10:47–51.

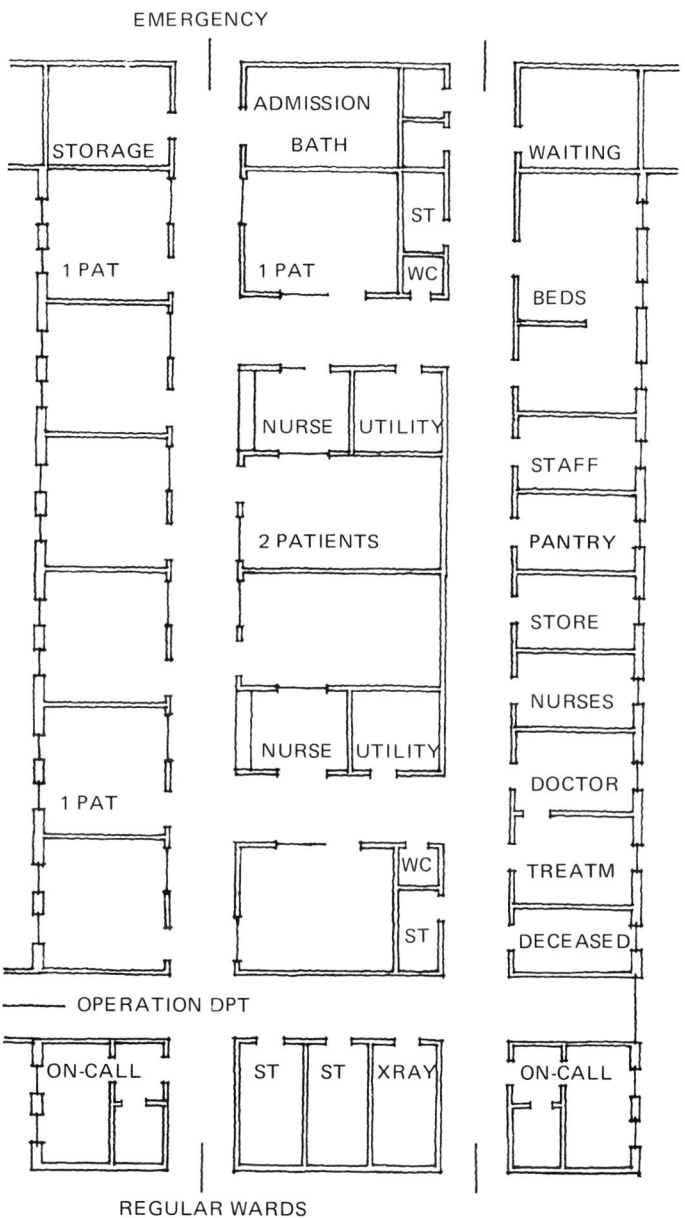

EMERGENCY

STORAGE

1 PAT

1 PAT

ADMISSION

BATH

1 PAT

ST

WC

WAITING

BEDS

NURSE UTILITY

2 PATIENTS

NURSE UTILITY

STAFF

PANTRY

STORE

NURSES

DOCTOR

WC

ST

TREATM

DECEASED

OPERATION DPT

ON-CALL

ST ST XRAY

ON-CALL

REGULAR WARDS

373

A 12 bed intensive care and treatment unit with two nurses' stations. Pütsep International 1976. Coronary care and burn care patients are not treated in this unit.

A room adapted for *maximum care* may be needed as well as a room for *hyperbaric oxygen* and a room for *induced hypothermia,* where the ambient room temperature has to be decreased to 10°C[17].

In cooled rooms desired environmental conditions may be achieved by ceiling cooling systems.

For each bed in the *open* ICTU — which as already indicated should be avoided — an average area of about 20 m² should be allowed, with about 3.5 m between bed centres. 15 m² for one bed is a minimum[18].

The paediatric intensive care unit — PICU — should be designed to have at least 12 m² allotted for each bed space. This allows room for extensive monitoring equipment, portable X ray machines, and working space for special diagnostic or resuscitative procedures. There must be at least six electrical outlets per bed space. Ceiling or wall suction as well as oxygen lines must be provided. The two parameters most commonly recorded are the ECG and the arterial blood pressure[19].

Patient toilets

It has been maintained that the intensive treatment patient is too ill to use the toilet and therefore it is unnecessary to provide one in the ICTU. However, the toilets are badly needed for the recovering patients, who should not be deprived of the accustomed privacy.

The number of patient toilets depends wholly on the ICTU admission policy. All the toilets must include a washbasin.

Bathroom

A bathroom for shower baths and where the patient could be washed is a considerable advantage. An area of about 12 m² is needed.

For *reheating* patients with significant hypothermia the use of a warm water bath at 40°C for young age group of acute poisoning, if hypothermia is reasonably recent, has been indicated. For the older age-group an alternative procedure is to immerse

17 Barker J: Postoperative care of the neurosurgical patient. 1976, British Journal of Anaesthesia 48:797–804.

18 Nunn J F: Design of the Intensive Therapy Unit at Northwick Park. Abstracts of the Spring Meeting of the Intensive Care Society. 1978, Intensive Care Medicine 4:169–170.

19 Stewart David R and Malley Betsy: Tenets of Treatment: Critical Care of the Pediatric Patient. 1978, The Journal of the Kansas Medical Society 79:121–122.

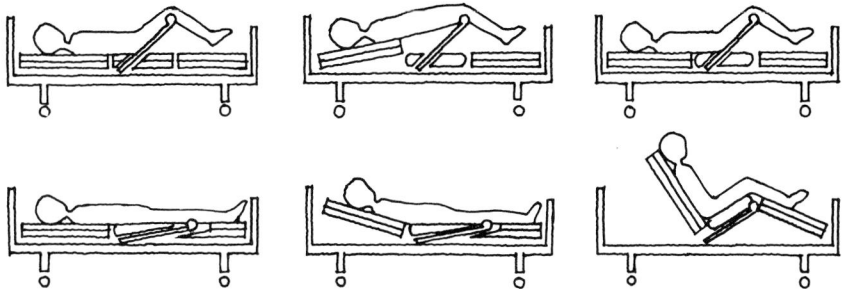

Arrangement to ease the use of bedpan.

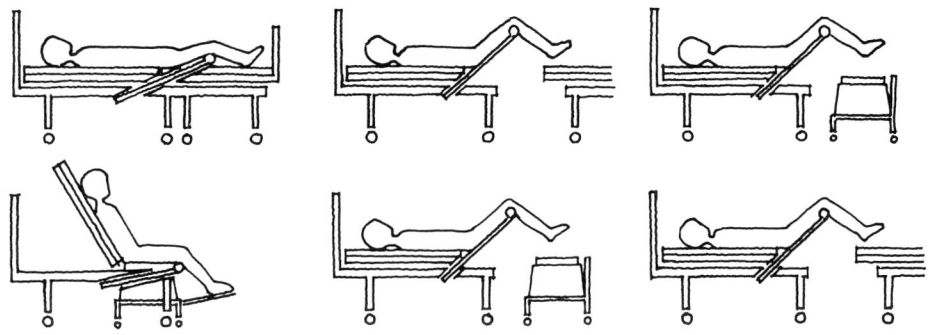

A for the patient more comfortable substitute for the bedpan.

Elimination arrangements for non-ambulant patients.

one forearm in water at 43°C with the patient otherwise wrapped in blankets and kept in a warm environment[20].

Nurses' station

The nurses' station, to be located centrally within the ICTU, may to some extent also serve as a physician's office. The desk should accommodate charts and provide working space for several people. There should be an acoustically shielded telephone and the central monitoring recorder.

Units that have a central command area where all data are read out and all records kept are very satisfactory from the point of view of administration but can lead to

20 Lawson A A H: Intensive therapy of acute poisoning. 1976, British Journal of Hospital Medicine 16:333–348.

isolation of the patient from data critical to his care at exactly those times when maximal bedside information and minimal bedside confusion are important[21].

In units with a large number of isolation rooms two nurses' stations may be needed.

Preparation area

Linked to the nurses' station there should be a preparation area with a supply of drugs and sera, parenteral solutions, blood, sterile sets, emergency equipment, etc.

A refrigerator for drug storage is needed.

Unit office

The nurse requires a separate accomodation, of about 15 m^2, where she or the physician can talk with relatives and members of the staff in privacy.

Utility room

Utility rooms of about 8 m^2 size, both clean and soiled, are needed. There should be a refrigerator for pathological specimens *e g* for twenty-four-hour urine.

Treatment room

Frequently there is a treatment room of about 30 m^2 size within the ICTU.

Laboratory services

There may be up to about 20 laboratory determinations routinely done at the outset and repeated at 2 to 24-hour intervals.

The intensive care unit should have access to clinical laboratory services on a 24 hour basis, particularly for arterial blood gas and arterial pH analysis. Laboratory apparatus includes equipment for electrolyte and osmotality determinations, gas-liquid chromatography, flame spectrophotometry, and autoanalysis equipment for assays of serum or plasma components as blood glucose, urea, bilirubin and enzymes as SGOT, LDH, CPK etc within a matter of minutes.

An area of about 18 m^2 has been required.

21 Harris III John McA and Cashman William F: Practical Monitoring in the Intensive Care Patient. 1978, The Orthopedic Clinics of North America 9:649–660.

ray service

The ICTU is dependent on a round-the-clock service from the diagnostic radiology department.

As radiological consultation and reporting is best carried out within the ICTU, high-powered mobile equipment capable of taking films should be available.

An X ray technologist would cover the intensive care unit portable X ray work. The films should be reviewed by the ICTU physician and radiologist at the same time.

ourishment area

The ICTU has to rely on the general food distribution system of the hospital. Naso-gastric diets for intubated patients and other special diets may need to be prepared on the spot.

A refrigerator for food and beverages is needed.

An area of about 10 m² is needed for patient catering.

ork room for technicians

There is a need for a room of about 18 m² with working space for technicians responsible for the maintenance of the increasingly elaborate technical equipment.

ed cleaning room

A facility for cleaning and decontaminating ICTU beds within the unit or adjacent to it should be available. The recommended area is about 12 m².

Whereas the bed cleaning and decontaminating room improves the work in the nursing units, the total centralization of bed cleaning is a very exotic method that invariably creates less productivity at higher costs[22].

tore rooms

Materials needed in immediate patient care should be available close to where used.

A clean supply store should be in the core of the ICTU.

A commodious storeroom is required for bulky equipment, such as respirators, defibrillators, oscilloscopes, dialysis machinery, special beds, oxygen tents, bed scales, and patient's lifts.

22 see also Bromberg-Richter Hildegard: Planning and building health care facilities in view of operational techniques — the supply system. 1975, World Hospitals 11:124–128.

Free and easy passage to the equipment is essential when a defibrillator or a respiratory machine is urgently needed as no time may be wasted.

It has been estimated that there should be about 9 to 10 m² storage space per ICTU bed[23]. In Hungary, at least two storages 18 m² each, are required in an ICTU[24].

Staff changing room

Changing rooms both for male and female staff should be adjacent to the ICTU entrance.

Staff toilets and showers should be provided.

Offices, conference room, room with teaching aids, library

Offices for physicians and secretaries, and a conference room should be available.

The systematic teaching of qualified nurses and junior doctors, which is an essential part of intensive care, requires in the unit a room with standard teaching aids, blackboard, slide-tape machine and mannequins for teaching resuscitation[25].

For discussions and lecturing the unit's library could be used. In small units, the staff lounge can serve this purpose.

Staff lounge

A well-ventilated room of about 12 m², clearly separated from the ward area, is needed for coffee or tea breaks.

In enclosed ill-ventilated spaces, smokers may expose other people to harmful concentration of tobacco smoke. Apart from discomfort, such exposure may lead to impaired psychomotor performance, cause distress to asthmatics and other susceptible, often allergic, subjects, and prejudice the cardiac function of people with coronary heart trouble. Measurable levels of nicotine have been found in the blood and urine of non-smokers exposed to tobacco smoke[26].

Pantry or vending machine should be provided. Comfortable noninstitutional furnishing is important.

23 Safar Peter, Benson Don M, Esposito Gerald, Grenvik Åke and Sands Patricia A: Emergency and Critical Care Medicine: Local Implementation of National Recommendations. in Public Health Aspects of Critical Care Medicine and Anesthesiology. ed by Peter Safar. F A Davis Company. Philadelphia 1974, p 99.

24 Sandor Janos: Intenziv betegellátó osztályok épitészeti kialakitósa. in Az intenziv betegellátós elmélete és gyakorlata. Medicina Könyvkiadó. Budapest 1977, p 48.

25 see also Sherwood Jones E: Teaching and educational value of intensive care. in Intensive Care. ed by W F Walker and D E M Taylor. Churchill Livingstone. Edinburgh, London, New York 1975, p 115.

26 Smoking and disease: the evidence reviewed. 1975, WHO Chronicle 29:402–408

On-call rooms

There is a need for a sleeping room with a toilet and a shower for the physician on-call.

Rooms for visitors

Humanitarian reasons may make a visit by relatives or persons in primary relationships highly desirable.

A visitors' waiting room is needed as the patient's condition often precludes visiting from more than a few minutes at a time. There should be a generous allocation of space, comfortable furnishing — tables may not be needed[27] — pleasant decor, and, if possible, a window to look out.

Partially secluded sections are desirable for particularly worried or emotionally distressed relatives to obtain some anonymity or to confer in privacy with a physician, if no unit office is available.

There should be at least one public telephone. Access to a pantry or vending machine is an advantage.

Relatives and friends who wish to stay for longer periods close to a seriously ill patient need adjacent the ICTU *over-night-rooms* of about 10 m² area with telephone, toilet, and shower.

Room for deceased

Although it has been stated that a nurse enters the profession to care for live patients and a deceased patient enters the domain of other professionals, and therefore should be immediately removed to the hospital mortuary[28], a room of about 8 m² is frequently provided for the deceased prior to removal of the body to the mortuary.

In some Swedish hospitals this room, with proper lighting, decor and flowers, is used to give the relatives and friends a peaceful and dignified chance for taking the last farewell from the deceased[29].

27 Cooper Cheryl: The Waiting Room. 1976, American Journal of Nursing 76:273.

28 Melia Kath M: The Intensive Care Unit — a stress situation? 1977, Nursing Times 73:5:17–20.

29 personal communication: 1977, Per Erik Wiklund, Danderyd.

Coronary intensive care unit

This term as well as the term *cardiac* or *coronary care unit* is used to identify the units restricted to patients who have or are thought to suffer from acute myocardial infarction, arrhythmias or some other cardiac emergency conditions.

A CICU should not be part of a general purpose intensive therapy unit or of a general medical ward[1]. It has to contain an intensive care section (IC) and an intermediat care section (IMC) as significant patient risk continues beyond 12 days of hospital admission.

There is, as yet, no satisfactory study documenting the need for intermediate coronary care units, but much presumptive evidence is available to indicate that this is so[2].

In the United Kingdom the usual length of stay in the CICU for the patients is 2 to 5 days[3]. In Sweden the length of stay usually is 1 to 3 days in the intensive care section and 8 to 30 days in the intermediate care section[4].

The CICUs are widely spread. E g in the United States in 1974 CICUs were found in 80 per cent of all voluntary hospitals with 300 or more beds[5].

One of the reasons for spreading the CICUs is that in case of cardiac emergencies* long transportations must be avoided[6].

In Sweden it has been suggested that between 6 and 8 CICU beds should be available for every 200,000 of the population served[7]. In the United Kingdom between 6 and 8 CICU beds are required for every 250,000 to 300,000 of the population[8].

---

1   see also The Care of the Patient with Coronary Heart Disease. 1975, Journal of the Royal College of Physicians of London 10:1:28.

    Pentecost B L: A critical appraisal of the success of coronary care units in the United Kingdom. in Progress in Cardiology. ed by Paul N Yu and John F Goodwin. Lea & Febiger. Philadelphia 1976, p 352.

2   Resnekov Leon: The intermediate coronary care unit. 1977, British Heart Journal 39:357–362.

3   ibid

4   personal communication: 1977, Torbjörn Lundman, Stockholm.

5   Russell Louise B: The Diffusion of new hospital technologies in the United States. 1976, International Journal of Health Services 6:557–580.

*   It has been shown that when the period of anoxia — the time from cardiac arrest to initiation of effective resuscitation — was less than 1 minute 61 per cent of patients survived, when it was 1 to 5 minutes 17 per cent survived, when it was 5 to 10 minutes 9 per cent survived, and when it was more than 10 minutes fewer than 1 per cent survived (Lund and Skulberg cited by Webster A C: Evolution of emergency cardiac care in Canada. 1977, Canadian Medical Association Journal 117:1383–1386).

6   see also Östberg Henrik, Ulfberg Jan, Carling Lasse, Lööf Lars and Wennerholm Mats: Hjärtinfarktvård vid ett normallasarett. 1977, Opuscula medica 22:160–161.

7   Vården av patienter med akut hjärtinfarkt. En rapport om hjärtinfarktavdelningar baserad på 1969 års hjärtinfarktstudie i regi av Svenska Cardiologföreningen. Stockholm 1971, p 10.

8   The Care of the Patient with Coronary Heart Disease. 1975, Journal of the Royal College of Physicians of London. 10:1:27.

In the US the optimal number of CICU beds per million population (in the state of Massachusetts) would be 60, assuming that no patient should have a travel time of more than 30 minutes and that he would have a 95 per cent chance to find an available bed in the nearest CICU[9].

It is believed that the level of a CICU performance drops when less than 60 acute myocardial infarctions are admitted yearly[10].

Advances in coronary care have led to a substantial reduction in hospital mortality and to an increase of life expectancy[11], but they also entail in survivors an increase in the number of myocardial infarction hospitalizations for subsequent attacks[12].

There have been positive achievements, but many of the therapeutic procedures which are used routinely in the CICUs have never been validated scientifically[13].

Treatments currently available have progressed little beyond that of nine or ten years ago, although there is no doubt that the understanding of natural history and disturbed physiology of myocardial infarction has advanced considerably[14].

Some reports indicate that coronary care units appear to have disappointingly little effect on the mortality of patients with heart attacks and they do not support the view that some sort of specialized accommodation for the care of patients after cardiac infarction is essential*.

Although proof of effectiveness of CICUs is lacking, their continued use is assured[15]. They do not have to be an unnecessary burden for the health care system[16].

The future advances in coronary care hold the prospect of reducing mortality and late disability.

9 Baumann Peter C: Prehospital and Hospital Coronary Care. 1978, Intensive Care Medicine 4:5–11.

10 The Care of the Patient with Coronary Heart Disease. 1975, Journal of the Royal College of Physicians of London 10:1:27.

11 see also Cretin Shan: Cost/Benefit Analysis of Treatment and Prevention of Myocardial Infarction. 1977, Health Services Research 12:174–189.

12 ibid

13 Pentecost B L: A critical appraisal of the success of coronary care units in the United Kingdom. in Progress in Cardiology. ed by Paul N Yu and John F Goodwin. Lea & Febiger. Philadelphia 1976, p 351.

14 Pentecost B L: A critical appraisal of the success of coronary care units in the United Kingdom. in Progress in Cardiology. ed by Paul N Yu and John F Goodwin. Lea & Febiger. Philadelphia 1976, p 351.

* Hampton J R: Are coronary care units and coronary ambulances effective? in Advanced Medicine 14. ed by D J Weatherall. Pitman Medical. Tunbridge, Wells. 1978, p 156.

15 Bloom Bernhard S, Jonsson Egon and Dolk Marie-Louise: Utilization of Coronary Care Units in Sweden. 1977, Scandinavian Journal of Social Medicine 5:141–144.

16 Hugenholtz P G, Laird-Meeter K, Balakumaran K, Ritsema van Eck H J, and Hagemeijer F: Reflections on Current Coronary Care. 1978, Intensive Care Medicine 4:1–3.

Size

For coronary intensive care units the sizes of 6 to 10 beds have been most frequent. In some countries there seems to be a tendency towards smaller coronary intensive units. *E g* in the Netherlands a frequent CICU size has been 3 to 5 beds[17].

A separate nursing station is considered feasible when the CICU contains 4 to 8 beds[18]. For the economies of scale the units of at least with 8 beds have been suggested[19].

Units of less than 4 or more than 10 beds create difficult staffing problems[20]. More than 10 beds in a unit increase the problems in patient supervising[21].

Location

The CICU should be adjacent to a general emergency admission unit or be situated near a medical ward in which progressive care of the patient with acute myocardial infarction can be undertaken.

Many clinicians seem to prefer that the CICU be close to the general medical wards, for it is to these areas that the survivors will be transferred[22]. Some experience from Norway indicates that the unit adjacent to the admitting area is probably preferable[23].

CICU nurses

The nurses' task in the CICU is very demanding. Even if the patient is spared knowledge of all possible complications of a myocardial infarction, the staff of the coronary care unit are not. Their reactions to the development of a potentially fatal complication such as cardiogenic shock are an important feature of experience in the coronary care unit[24].

17 Dekker E: Hartbewakningseenheid. 1974, Acta Hospitalia 14:12–37.

18 Clipson Colin W and Wehrer Joseph J: Planning for Cardiac Care. The Health Administration Press. Ann Arbor, Michigan 1973, p 362.

19 Bloom Bernard S and Peterson Osler L: Patient needs and medical-care planning. 1974, The New England Journal of Medicine 290:1171–1177.

20 Oliver Michael F, Julian Desmond G and Brown Myra G: Intensive coronary care. World Health Organization. Geneva 1974, p 29.

21 personal communication: 1977, Torbjörn Lundman, Stockholm.

22 see also Pentecost B L: A critical appraisal of the success of coronary care units in the United Kingdom. in Progress in Cardiology. ed by Paul N Yu and John F Goodwin. Lea & Febiger. Philadelphia 1976, p 352.

23 Skjaggestad Ø, Lippestad C and Sivertssen E: Medical intensive care units in Oslo; a comparison between the ur.its. 1977, Journal of the Oslo City Hospitals 27:121–127.

24 Cassem Ned H and Hackett Thomas P: Psychological Aspects of Myocardial Infarction. 1977, The Medical Clinics of North America 61:711–721.

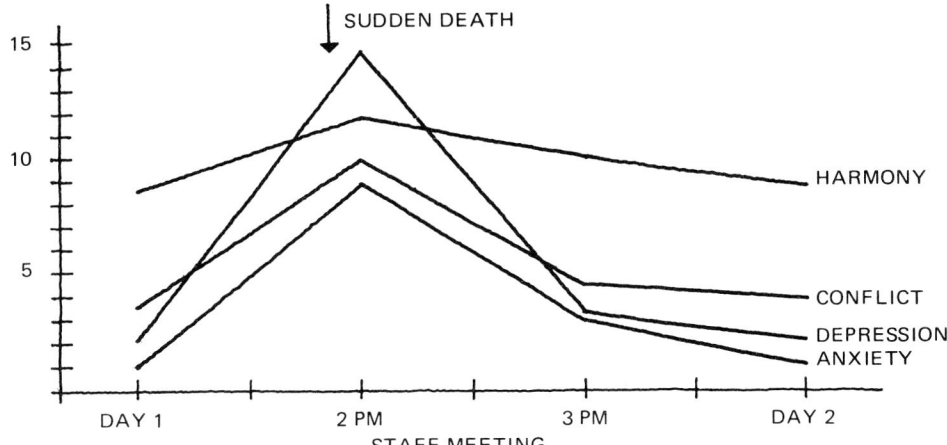

Morale scores of CICU nursing staff according to Atmosphere Assessment Scale after a sudden death on morning rounds, with assessments before and after a staff meeting, after Croog, Shapiro, Levine 1971.

Another problem for the CICU nurse is boredom by the repetitive nature of her duties and the narrow clinical field of her activities[25].

These factors may contribute towards tension among staff. General areas of conflict have been identified[26] as nursing administration — conflicts and disagreements about the size of the unit and proper furniture —, scheduling and staffing, and the patients' families. The patient appeared on the conflict list as number six. The first item on frequency and even severity score was heavy lifting, as the coronary artery disease tends to spare the thin.

atient in CICU

Patients with acute myocardial infarction are anxious to a greater or lesser extent. *Blacher* has underlined the universality of fears about the heart[27]. Earlier it has been found that 80 per cent of patients exhibit some form of anxiety[28]. Another author

25 Pentecost B L: A critical appraisal of the success of coronary care units in the United Kingdom. in Progress in Cardiology. ed by Paul N Yu and John F Goodwin. Lea & Febiger. Philadelphia 1976, p 353.

26 Cassem Ned H and Hackett Thomas P: Sources of Tension for the CCU Nurse. 1972, American Journal of Nursing 72:1426–1430.

27 cited by Cassem Ned H and Hackett Thomas P: Psychological Aspects of Myocardial Infarction. 1977, The Medical Clinics of North America 61:711–721.

28 Hackett T P, Cassem N H and Wishnie H: Detection and treatment of anxiety in the coronary care unit. 1969, American Heart Journal 78:727.

has stated that only about 30 per cent of coronary care patients are either anxious, depressed or show minor behavioural problems[29].

The physiological and haemodynamical condition of the cardiac patient is in some way correlated with the patient's style of coping with stress, and his history of previous life stress situations[30].

If it cannot be avoided that the patients notice and are disturbed by an alarm reality to another patient, everything should be done to increase their feeling towards security and to relieve their anxiety.

It seems to appear that not only is it humane to minimize the distress caused to patients when they are being cared for in a coronary care unit but their treatment will be more effective if they can be tranquil[31].

Preferably the patients of the intensive care area of the CICU should be for the most part out of sight of each other but within view of the nursing staff[32] and seem to be best accommodated in individual rooms separated by walls or opaque and sound-proof partitions[33].

The advantage of single-roomed CICU is felt to be that patients cannot compare their progress with that of any other patient and they do not witness the resuscitation procedures or the death of a neighbouring patient[34]. According to another study, the closed ward, as compared to the open ward, has not resulted in reduced anxiety levels, but rather in somewhat higher levels[35].

To maintain the patient's sense of time and place, windows with a view to outside, clocks and calendars are important. A specific location for a limited display of the personalizing items should be provided[36]. This personal space must not infringe on space required in normal and emergency procedures.

29 Dudley H A F: Affective disturbances in patients in intensive care. in Intensive Care. ed by W F Walker and D E M Taylor. Churchill Livingstone. Edinburgh, London, New York 1975, p 223.

30 Pancheri Paolo, Bellaterra Marilia, Matteoli Sergio, Cristofari Massimo, Polizzi Carlo, and Puletti Mario: Infarct as a Stress Agent: Life History and Personality Characteristics in Improved versus Not-Improved Patients after Severe Heart Attack. 1978, Journal of Human Stress 4:1:16–22, 41.

31 Hill Oscar: The coronary care unit. 1977, The Chest, Heart and Stroke Journal 2:34–36.

32 see also Lundman Torbjörn, Mogensen Lars and Orinius Erik: Akutvård vid hjärtinfarkt. Private publication. Stockholm 1973, p 50.

The Care of the Patient with Coronary Heart Disease. 1975, Journal of the Royal College of Physicians of London 10:1:28.

33 Oliver Michael F, Julian Desmond G and Brown Myra G: Intensive coronary care. World Health Organization Geneva 1974, p 29.

34 see also Cay E L, Vetter N, Philip A E and Dugard P: Psychological reactions to a Coronary Care Unit. 1972, Journal of Psychosomatic Research 16:437–447.

35 Leight Hoyle, Hofer Myron A, Cooper Jerome and Reiser Morton F: A psychological comparison of patients in "open" and "closed" coronary care units. 1972, Journal of Psychosomatic Research 16:449–457.

36 Clipson Colin W and Wehrer Joseph J: Planning for Cardiac Care. The Health Administration Press. Ann Arbor, Michigan 1973, p 138.

In the coronary intensive care unit the patient is also exposed to physical discomfort in the form of thoracic electrodes for ECG — telemetry can greatly reduce this —, IV drip, oxygen catheter in the nose, or face mask. There are generally visual or acoustic alarm devices.

Provided the monitoring apparatus is silent, unobtrusive, and out of the immediate view of the patient, the monitoring is usually tolerated well by patients if they have been informed that it saves work for nurses and doctors[37].

There are psychological implications caused by the obstrusion of machines into the intensive care environment. Some patients have paid, in psychological terms, a price for it[38]. However, there is little indication that CICU equipment, activities, or procedures bring about longlasting psychological disturbances in modal CICU patients in British, Scottish and American hospitals[39].

More strain may come from medical visits. Patients can become very tense, expecting oracular pronouncements, and are often mystified and misled by ill-comprehended discussions at the bedside[40].

oronary intensive care area

Some American studies[41] indicate that about 13 m² is a workable and perhaps desirable size for a patient room. According to some Swedish experience more space is needed and the size of 18 to 22 m² is recommended. One of the IC rooms should be even bigger — about 30 m².

In the case of cardiac arrest the attending physician or nurse must have access to the patient's head. It must be possible to insert a board behind the patient's back without difficulty. Therefore the bed must be away from the wall.

As there are therapeutic advances in having the patient to spend some time seated rather than lying by the third day, a comfortable bedside armchair has to be provided. It has to be located so, that a nurse can easily assist the patient to chair. The chair ought to be in position for comfortable supervision.

At the head of each bed there should be notice boards to display vital data. Another feature which should be attached to the headwall is an equipment organiser. It could take some of the equipment, which traditionally is placed on a cart.

37 Oliver Michael F, Julian Desmond G and Brown Myra G: Intensive coronary care. World Health Organization. Geneva 1974, p 33.

38 see also Bowden Paul: The Psychiatric Aspects of Cardiac Intensive Therapy: A Review. 1975, European Journal of Intensive Care Medicine 1:85—91.

39 Doerman Steven R: Psycho-social aspects of recovery from coronary heart disease: a review. 1977, Social science & medicine 11:199—210.

40 see also Hill Oscar: The coronary care unit. 1977, The Chest, Heart and Stroke Journal 2:34—36.

41 Clipson Colin W and Wehrer Joseph J: Planning for Cardiac Care. The Health Administration Press. Ann Arbor, Michigan 1973, p 381.

There must be a resuscitation panel — both oxygen and suction are essential — and a panic button to alert the staff when cardiac arrest occurs. Sometimes medically pure compressed air is provided to power some types of breathing apparatus. No service should have less than two outlets. Each service connection should be located as close to the point of use as possible. It is believed[42] that there are functional advantages when oxygen, vacuum, compressed air and the electrical outlets are provided on both sides of the patient's bed.

With the current popularity of prefabricated modular headwall systems in several countries, notably in the US, and the willingness of several manufacturers to customize the headwall to the specific requirements of the staff, the architect often believes that all the functional requirements necessary for patient care — electricity, oxygen, compressed air, vacuum, nurse call, reading light and physiological monitoring — have been solved with the selection of a headwall unit. If the headwall is not properly designed and installed to integrate with the other elements in the room — IV track, examination lights, bed, work space — serious operational problems will occur[43].

Bedside equipment includes oscilloscopes, which need to be simple, large faced, and provide a stable electrocardiogram[44].

Telemetric equipment reducing CICU stresses is gaining greatly in importance.

When computerized monitoring is used in the CICU, the following parameters are monitored: ECG, arterial blood pressure, left atrial pressure, right atrial pressure, pulmonary artery pressure, temperature, chest drainage, urine, cardiac output, respiratory cycle, pulse, tidal volume, peak oral pressure, blood in/out, and fluid in/out.

Sequential films of uniform high quality are most valuable in monitoring the progress of patients with acute heart failure[45].

A minimum of 8 adequately earthed electrical outlets per room are needed.

In case of power failure emergency electrical supplies must be available.

There should be washbasins to all patient rooms.

An enclosed toilet in connection with the patient room in the intensive care area is not needed[46], as long as the majority of CICU patients are wired to the monitors.

42 see also Goldstein J Richard and Parker Jr William T: The Design of the CCU Patient Room. Stencil. New York. December 1977, p 8.

43 ibid, p 5.

44 see also Pentecost B L: A critical appraisal of the success of coronary care units in the United Kingdom. in Progress in Cardiology. ed by Paul N Yu and John F Goodwin. Lea & Febiger. Philadelphia 1976, p 353.

45 Murray J P: The chest in critical care. 1978, Radiography 44: 173-178.

46 also personal communication: 1977, Torbjörn Lundman, Stockholm.

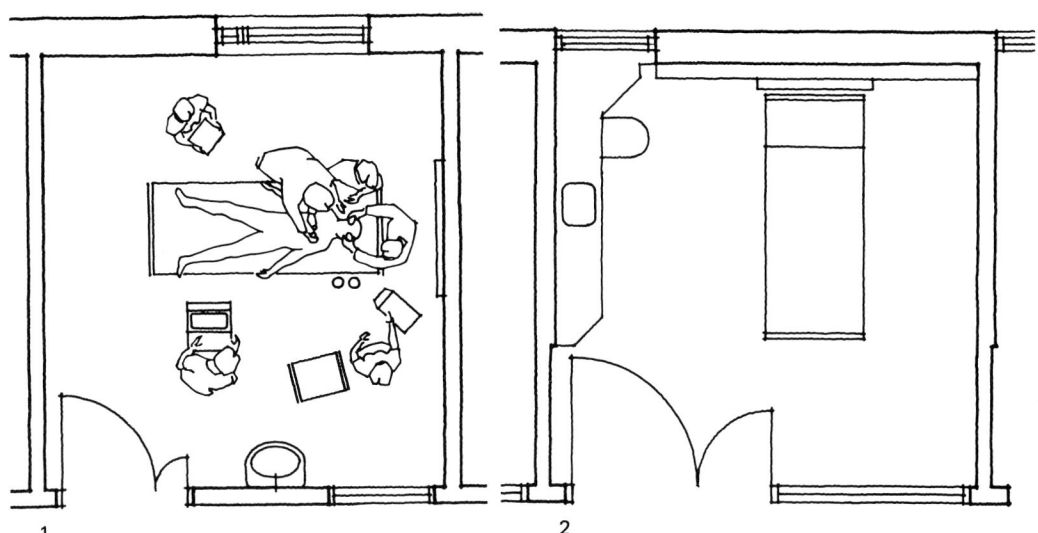

1   2

J Richard Goldstein and William T Parker Jr have indicated that the goal should be to develop a patient room which balances the requirements of the scientific laboratory and those of a psychologically comfortable environment.
A workable patient room (1), sized 3.8 by 4.1 m. Pütsep International. Goldstein-Parker Jr suggest a room (2) including a Pullman toilet and toilet privacy curtain.

It is not necessary to provide a shower in this area.

A central nurses' station should be provided.

Laboratory data, medication, nurses' notes, and vital signs are entered manually via the terminal keyboard. Also, most of the automatically monitored parameters can be manually charted[47].

The need for central multichannel monitors at the nurses' station largely depends on the design and the number of staff[48]. However, no amount of sophisticated monitoring is a substitute for the trained nurse's direct observation of the patient.

Utility rooms and storages are needed.

47 Tolbert Samuel H and Pertuz Alvaro E: Study shows how computerization affects nursing activities in ICU. 1977, Hospitals 51:17:79–82, 84.

48 see also Pentecost B L: A critical appraisal of the success of coronary care units in the United Kingdom. in Progress in Cardiology. ed by Paul N Yu and John F Goodwin. Lea & Febiger. Philadelphia 1976, p 353.

Intermediate care area

In the intermediate care section, which ought to have twice the number of intensive area beds, multibed rooms — with 4 to 6 beds — are recommended[49].

The multibed rooms seem to be the provision of more social contact, with associated freedom of expression of hostile feelings, while lack of privacy leads to higher levels of shame and anxiety[50]. In a multibed-patient room the reciprocal assistance among patients can be considerable as viewing each other is easy.

The closed rooms provide privacy at the expense of human inter-actions resulting in increased loneliness and displacements of hostile feelings.

Considering both the high physiological and psychological stresses in toiletting, particularly in the act of elimination, it only could be concluded that much more design attention should be paid to reducing the anxiety and the resulting stress attending this inevitable function. The bedpan is probably used more frequently than is generally believed to be justifiable[51].

An enclosed toilet room but the door without locks, should be provided close to each patient room. Access to showers is needed.

Radio for the intermediate care patients is generally favoured. The question of providing TV is still controversial. On the issue of its potential for involving the cardiac patient in stressful viewing there is little doubt that TV can be stressful. Allowing limited TV viewing may reduce anxiety for some patients, especially if TV viewing is an important aspect of their lifestyle. The use of video tapes and closed circuit TV for the purpose of rehabilitation and health education might be generally considered to be a constructive and safe use of the media with significant benefits for the recuperating patient[52].

Equipment

The CICU requires ECG apparatus, defibrillators — machines which deliver electrical impulses to the heart —, respirators, ventilators, intravenous infusion units and monitoring systems.

Having within the CICU laboratory equipment that determine e g the acid base levels depends greatly upon the availability of centralized pathological services[53].

49 personal communication: 1977, Torbjörn Lundman, Stockholm.

50 Leight Hoyle, Hofer Myron A, Cooper Jerome and Reiser Morton F: A psychological comparison of patients in 'open' and 'closed' coronary care units. 1972, Journal of Psychosomatic Research 16:449-457.

51 Clipson Colin W and Wehrer Joseph J: Planning for Cardiac Care. The Health Administration Press. Ann Arbor, Michigan 1973, p 139.

52 ibid, p 140.

53 see also The Care of the Patient with Coronary Heart Disease. 1975, Journal of the Royal College of Physicians of London 10:1:32.

Outlets for mobile X ray apparatus — a separate 220 volt power source — should be located as far as practicable from the patient beds[54].

If a portable image intensifier is to be used, the part of the bed that supports the patient's chest must be radiotranslucent, which is not always the case.

To avoid the transport of seriously ill patients elsewhere for introduction or placing catheters, ready access to fluoroscopy apparatus is important in coronary care units. A cardiac fluoroscopy room should be adjacent to the CICU. Alternatively portable fluoroscopic image intensifiers are used.

For *pacing* within the CICU a specific area should be set aside. Appropriate radiation protection should be established.

ommon areas

An *admission room* where early diagnosis is made, is necessary.

A *physicians'* room, a *nurses'* room, a *medicine preparation* room, a *secretary'*s room, a room for *interviewing relatives,* a *visitors'* room with a toilet, and a physicians' *overnight* facility are needed.

There should be a ward *kitchen, storages* for equipment, linen and trolleys, a room for *record-keeping,* staff *changing* facilities and toilets, *janitor's closets* and an *equipment maintenance* room.

The CICU staff should have access to a *conference room* equipped with a conference table, chairs, a chalkboard, an X ray viewing screen and a provision for audio-visual display and to a comfortable, geographically separate *lounge* for tea or coffee breaks.

54 see also Conway Gene F and Haverland Margaret: The Coronary Care Unit. in Monitoring in Anesthesia. ed by William H L Dornette. F A Davis Company. Philadelphia 1973, p 373.

Pulmonary intensive care unit

Chronic obstructive lung disease has been increasing at a faster rate than many other major health problems. Acute respiratory failure is a frequent occurrence in a comprehensive pulmonary care programme. A pulmonary intensive care unit — PICU — is the major key in such a programme[1].

In order to provide a good environment sufficient room must be provided to accommoderate ventilators, resuscitation equipment, fluoroscopy units and rehabilitive eff. A minimum space is about 1.8 m each side of the bed centre.

Each bed must be equipped with oxygen, suction, compressed air and space for intravascular pressure and electrocardiographic monitoring.

Every effort should be made to provide a bright, cheery environment. Sound absorbing materials such as curtains, acoustical ceilings and carpeting should be used[2].

The length of stay in a PICU is about seven to ten days[3].

The patients are more prone to ICU psychosis secondary to continuous bombardment by high noise levels from ventilators, oxygen equipment, frequent stimulation from suctioning with postural drainage, and by central nervous system stimulation from bronchodilator medications possibly superimposed on hypoxic confusion.

Patient rooms should have a window with a view.

The nursing station must be equipped with remote monitoring having a simultaneous display of each patient's cardiopulmonary data. The monitors should include crisis monitors with a memory loop or delay capacity so that crisis precipitating events can be recorded.

Utility and supply rooms are needed.

A laboratory for around-the-clock determination of arterial blood gases immediately adjacent to the PICU is required, since these patients are very unstable. A logistic delay due to laboratory remoteness or unavailable technical assistence is not acceptable[4].

This laboratory can also function as an additional facility for supporting specialized ventilatory studies and sputum examinations.

1   Lampton Lawrence M and Brashear Richard E: The Pulmonary Intensive Care Unit. 1977, The Journal of the Indiana State Medical Association 70:644–646.

2   ibid

3   see also Grass Jüri, Vaiguste Aime and Gross Ruth: Ägeda kopsupõletiku intensiivravi kogemusi. 1977, Nõukogude Eesti Tervishoid 20:492–495.

4   Lampton Lawrence M and Brashear Richard E: The Pulmonary Intensive Care Unit. 1977, The Journal of the Indiana State Medical Association 70:644–646.

A closeby intermediate care unit would allow the patients to be continuously observed and monitored by telemetry for arrhythmias. This arrangement facilitates increased rehabilitative efforts while the patient convalesces toward self care.

From the PICU the recovering patient is taken to a nearby conventional nursing unit specializing in completing the comprehensive pulmonary care programme.

Neurovascular care unit

Neurovascular or stroke cases are admitted predominantly from the emergency department, not later than 48 hours after the event has occured. The great majority is admitted within 10 hours of their stroke. Usually there are no age limits.

The patients are preferably discharged from the unit to a neurology ward when their general and neurological conditions have become stable, and continuous vital sign monitoring no longer is necessary. Continuous observation of vital sign thus is routine. ECG and, in some cases, EEG are routines. As soon as possible after admission, all patients should have a skull X ray, sometimes echoencephalogram, EEG, brain scan, serial ECG, cardiac enzymes over three consecutive days and a lumbar puncture[1].

The use of computerized axial tomography — CT — has considerably enhanced the diagnostic acuracy in stroke patients[2].

Many patients need a cardiological opinion shortly after admission[3].

1   see also Norris J W and Hachinski V C: Intensive Care Management of Stroke Patients. 1976, Stroke 7:573–577.

2   Feindel W: Head and body scanning by computer tomography. 1976, Canadian Medical Association Journal 113:273–274.

3   Norris J W and Hachinski V C: Intensive Care Management of Stroke Patients. 1976, Stroke 7:573–577.

Burn care unit

An indigenous nursing service in the burn care unit cannot be overemphasized, since its members not only provide the intensive care for survival but assist in the identification of clinical problems deserving of study and resolution[1].

Two phases of the burns illness — the shock period and the healing period — have to be accommodated. Experts have clearly advocated special burn care units. However, there are studies which do not identify any advantages to treating burn patients in special facilities[2]. The investigators admit that instantly accepting the study results would certainly be unwise, but point out that, if these results are really true, it means that at the present time costly intensification of burn care does not improve outcomes because of the limits in ability to treat burn patients.

Special equipment to meet the peculiar needs of burned patients, such as Circ-O-Lectric beds, ropes, weights, and pulleys for positioning and applying traction to extremities, should be available[3].

Many patients in burn care units have emotional problems. For a child no trauma, injury or illness is as severe or complex as a major thermal injury[4].

The burned patients are susceptible to many complications. Infection is responsible for nearly 30 per cent of burned patient complications[5] and for 35 per cent[6] to nearly 50 per cent[7] of the deaths.

Airborne transfer of bacteria is of little importance as a cause of cross-contamination between plenum ventilated isolation rooms. In such rooms, transfer of bacteria is mainly via clothes contaminated by contact. Patients with small burns can be important sources of contact contamination although they disperse little bacteria to the air[8].

1 Pruitt Jr Basil A: Multidisciplinary care and research for burn injury. 1977, The Journal of Trauma 17:263–269.

2 Linn Bernard S, Stephenson Jr Sam E, Bergstresser Paul R and Smith Jane: Are Burn Units the Best Places to Treat Burn Patients? 1977, Journal of Surgical Research 23:1–5.

3 Boswick Jr John A, Thompson James D and Kershner Cindy J: Critical Care of the Burned Patient. 1977, The Journal of Anesthesiology 47:164–170.

4 Seligman Roslyn: Emotional response to burns in children. in Modern Perspectives in the Psychiatric Aspects of Surgery. ed by John G Howells. Brunner/Mazel, Publishers. New York 1976, p 468.

5 Feller Irving and Crane Keith: Planning and Designing a Burn Care Facility. Institute for Burn Medicine. Ann Arbor, Michigan 1975, p 21.

6 Müller F E: Probleme der Intensivtherapie Schwerverbrannter. 1976, Langenbecks Archiv für Chirurgie 342:369–381.

7 Feller Irving and Crane Keith: Planning and Designing a Burn Care Facility. Institute for Burn Medicine. Ann Arbor, Michigan 1975, p 21.

8 Ransjö Ulrika: Isolation Care of Infection-Prone Burn Patients. 1978, Scandinavian Journal of Infectious Diseases. Suppl. 11, p 38.

The quickest and easiest source for germs in a burn wound is from elsewhere in or on the same patient. Cross-infection from other patients is uncommon[9]. Others state that exogenous spread of resistant hospital organisms is often the source[10].

Burn patients have malfunctioning polymorphonuclear leukocytes (PMN), particularly during the first and second week after injury, which coincides with the maximum growth of bacteria in the burn wound. The monitoring of PMN functions can give guidance as to when the patients need protective isolation[11].

Complete reverse isolation can be a significant factor in the prevention of bacterial contamination of individuals incurring major burn injuries.

The recommended number of beds in a burns ward has been between 6 and 15 beds. The total spatial requirements of about 50 m^2 per bed in the smallest unit are reduced to about 30 m^2 per bed when the size of the unit increases to 15 beds[12].

An adequate staffing for 10 beds at an average occupancy of 100 per cent is in the US[13] as following:

physicians	general surgeon (director), surgical resident, intern
nurses	head nurse, 13 registred nurses, 8 licensed practical nurses, 4 burn care technicians, 4 nurse aides
other paramedicals	laboratory technicians, social worker
service personnel	1.4 janitors, 1.4 maids, 2.8 secretary-clerks.

Part time assignments include an anaesthesiologist, a dietitian, an inhalation therapist, a microbiologist, an occupational therapist, and a physical therapist.

On-call staff includes a pediatrician, a psychiatrist, and an education teacher.

atient rooms

Plenty of space is essential for the treatment of acutely ill patients, who usually will remain in the shock room for two or three days. The shock room should be of about 26 m^2 in size.

9   Vilain Raymond C: Is the burn center a septic ghetto? 1977, Plastic and Reconstructive Surgery 59:733–734.

10 Demling Robert H, Moylan Joseph A, Ellerbe Snellyn and Jarrett Fredric: Experience with laminar airflow in the management of major burns. 1977, Wisconsin Medical Journal 76:S149–S150.

11 Ransjö Ulrika: Isolation Care of Infection-Prone Burn Patients. 1978, Scandinavian Journal of Infectious Diseases. Suppl. 11, p 38.

12 Feller Irving and Crane Keith: Planning and Designing A Burn Care Facility. Institute for Burn Medicine. Ann Arbor, Michigan 1975, p 26.

13 ibid, p 19.

The ordinary patient room should be about 20 m² in size. Special beds or cranes and other apparatus for handling heavy patients may require additional space as well as such procedures as application of grafts.

A few double rooms in the burns unit have been accepted.

Supply of oxygen, a suction apparatus and hand washing facilities are needed.

Floor drains are an advantage in bed rooms[14].

Each room should have separate lavatory premises. Access to utility rooms must be easy.

Each patient must have individual supplies for his exclusive use. Decontamination of equipment before use by another patient is always necessary.

Burned patients require chest and other X ray films because of possible inhalation of gases, complications, trauma, or prolonged immobility. The burns unit demands on X ray department are average[15].

In all patient rooms outlets for portable X ray apparatus are needed.

In the management of the burned patient, to decrease evaporative cooling and fluid loss, the room temperature should be regulated to 29°C and humidity to about 30 per cent[16]. Many burned patients require an air temperature of 30°C at relative humidities of 50 to 60 per cent[17]. When the patient has to lie naked in the shock room a temperature of 32°C is required[18]. Infrared light has been used to maintain the patient's body temperature.

Air condition with a high number of changes per hour is desirable[19].

Various types of unidirectional flow units and axenic chambers are among the techniques for regulating the air conditions. Unidirectional flow in treating the 40 to 65 per cent burn victims has been suggested[20].

14 see also Feller Irving and Crane Keith: Planning and Designing A Burn Care Facility. Institute for Burn Medicine. Ann Arbor, Michigan 1975, p 35.

15 see also Feller Irving and Crane Keith: Planning and Designing A Burn Care Facility. Institute for Burn Medicine. Ann Arbor, Michigan 1975, p 100.

16 Headley Barbara J, Robson Martin C and Krizek Thomas J: Methods of Reducing Environmental Stress for the Acute Burn Patient. 1975, Physical therapy 55:5–8.

17 Clark R P and Mullan BJ: Clothing for use in clean-air environments. 1976, The Journal of Hygiene 77:267–269.

18 Ugland O M and Drabløs P A: Brannskader. 1976, Tidsskrift for Den norske laegeforening 96:864–867.

19 see also Müller F E: Probleme der Intensivtherapie Schwerverbrannter. 1976, Langenbecks Archiv für Chirurgie 342:369–381.

20 Demling Robert H, Moylan Joseph A, Ellerbe Snellyn, and Jarrett Fredric: Experience with laminar airflow in the management of major burns. 1977, Wisconsin Medical Journal 76:S149–S150.

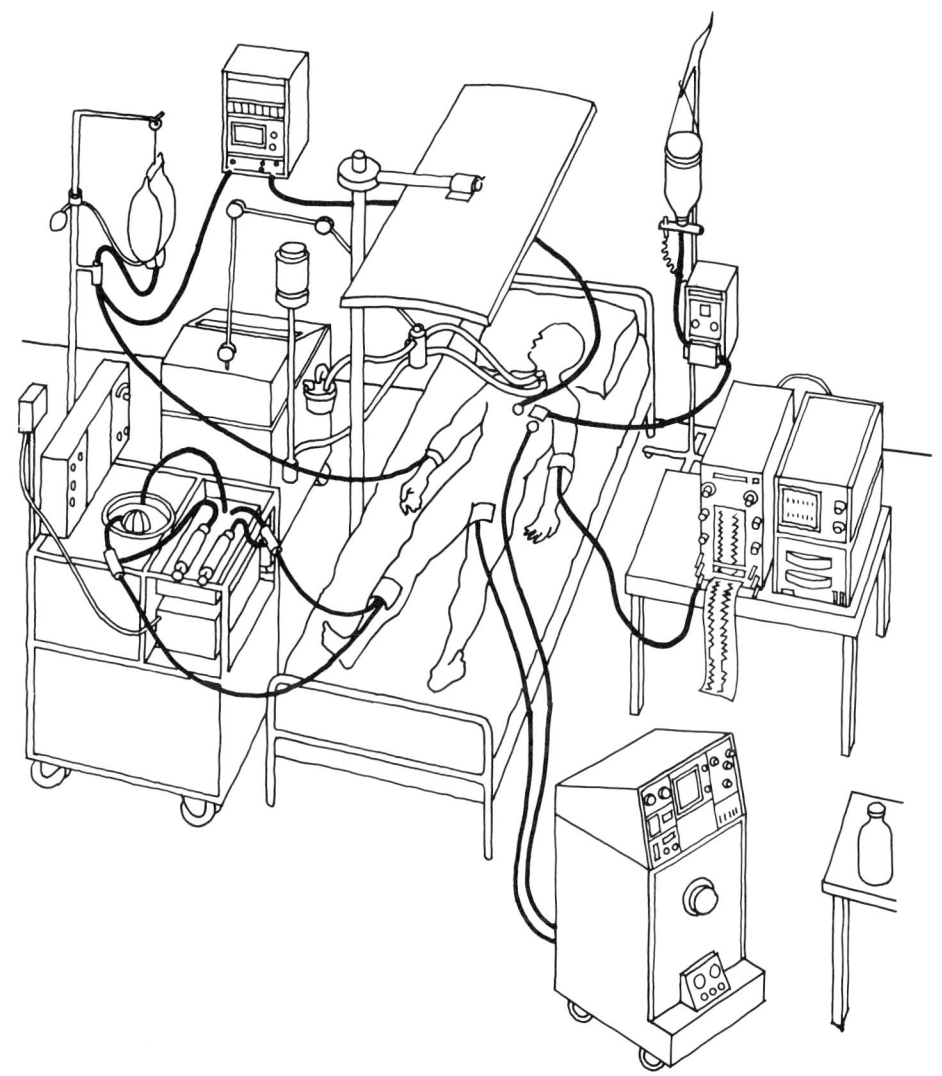

In a burn room a multiple organ support system may require a haemodialysis unit, a respirator, an arterial blood pressure catheter and transducer unit, a monitor for ECG and blood pressure, a heater, an IV drip regulator, a pulmonary artery and wedge pressure monitor, and an intra-aortic balloon pump (Waisbren, Burton A Simultaneous Multiple Organ Support. 1976, Hospital Practice 11:5: 102-112).

Another study of an unidirectional flow burn unit indicates that at an ambient temperature of 25°C and relative humidity of 44 per cent patients are able to maintain their water balance *ad libitum* without difficulty or the need for supplemental routes of water administration. Additional benefits of the unidirectional flow unit were that nutrition was easily maintained and weight loss was minimal. Also, septic complications were reduced in this series[21].

A patient who has experienced a major burn has a high degree of anxiety. In addition to the actual pain and discomfort caused by the injury, the memory of the accident itself is likely to be painful. The extent of the injury and disfigurement is uncertain at first, and this causes worry. There are many other anxiety-provoking aspects of the experience, such as concern about the possible work loss, and the effect of the injury on the patient's family[22].

All medical procedures, including their purpose and what will be expected of them should be explained to the patient. Physiologic stress, as well as psychologic stress, should be prevented if possible. Energy expenditure on the part of the patient should be kept to a minimum. He should be moved slowly and gently only when it is essential for his care or comfort. Quick postural changes or rough handling can cause hypotension or cardiac arrest. The environment should be kept warm to minimize heat loss, but not so warm as to cause perspiration[23].

The burned patient is surrounded by strange equipment and noises. The surroundings are foreign, the staff frequently masked. He may lie on his abdomen or back for lengthy periods. Because of the severe physical and chemical stresses placed on his central nervous system he may lose track of time and place.

The facility must provide an atmosphere of reality and comfort. Windows should be low enough to look out. There should be clocks and calendars. TV has been found to be excellent for preventing boredom and maintaining morale[24].

Lighting should be reduced at night.

A day room is required for burned patients who are ambulant and are considered suitable for mixing with others at a similar stage of their illness. An occupational therapy room is an asset.

---

21 Larkin James M and Moylan Joseph A: Evaporative Water Losses in Patients Treated in a Laminar Flow Burn Unit. 1978, Journal of Surgical Research 24:65–69.

22 Hayter Jean: Emergency Nursing Care of the Burned Patient. 1978, The Nursing Clinics of North America 13:223–234.

23 ibid

24 Muir I F K and Barclay T L: Burns and Their Treatment. Lloyd-Luke (Medical Books) Ltd. London 1974, p 168.

As the patient runs a greater risk of being contaminated when he is outside of the unit, it would be best to provide all of the direct care services required by the burn patient within the unit itself[25].

At least one air conditioned dressing-room with a stainless bath and mechanical hoist should be provided. A disposable sterile polythene liner-sheet is recommended to be used for each bath.

To save the backs of the staff, apparatus have been designed to carry the patient on the stretcher between bed and bath[26].

Plenum-ventilation of dressing-room with an exhaust ventilated air lock has been shown to reduce infection in a burns unit[27].

Recently it has been pointed out that it is possible to achieve a considerable reduction in the rate of cross-infection among burn care unit patients by excluding common treatment areas[28].

An operation room within the burn unit is frequently favoured. A patient with a burn up to 20 per cent total body surface will require an average of one to two debriment and/or grafting procedures during his initial hospitalization. Patients with a burn of 20 to 40 per cent will require an average of four procedures. A burn of over 40 per cent requires four to five procedures[29].

A small laboratory is recommended within the unit to perform the large number of white blood counts and haematocrits required by burned patients[30].

ledication room, nourishment area, storages

The medication refrigerator would suffice also for storing the daily needs of homograft and heterograft skin. A specially controlled blood or plasma refrigerator within the burns unit may be necessary.

---

25 see also Feller Irving and Crane Keith: Planning and Designing A Burn Care Facility. Institute for Burn Medicine. Ann Arbor, Michigan 1975, p 22.

26 see also Walden J R and Bell R C: A bath unit transporter system designed to save nurses' backs. 1976, British Journal of Plastic Surgery 29:317–321.

27 Control of Hospital Infection. ed by E J L Lowbury, G A J Ayliffe, A M Geddes and J D Williams. Chapman and Hall. London 1975, p 102.

28 Zellner P R and Metzger E: Asepsis and Antisepsis bei der Behandlung des Brandverletzten. 1977, Infection 5:36–44.

29 Feller Irving and Crane Keith: Planning and Designing A Burn Care Facility. Institute for Burn Medicine. Ann Arbor, Michigan 1975, p 94.

30 ibid

Many burned patients require high oral fluid and high caloric intake. Unless a complete kitchen is planned, the nourishment area can be combined with e g the medication room[31].

Storage spaces should be ample, as many items of bulky equipment in occasional use in burn wards should be readily available. Storages for linen — burned patients require two or three times as much linen as the average patient — and supplies are needed.

Housekeeping storages are required.

Staff area

Male and female changing rooms with lavatories and showers are needed.

The clothing requirements for the medical and nursing staff in burn units are fairly rigorous[32]. The garments have to be light in weight, they must allow the wearer to remain cool at fairly high work rates, and they must absorb sweat. They should also be aesthetically pleasing, fashionable and be quickly and easily changed. They have to prevent the transmission of microorganisms.

There should be a *visitor's gowning* room.

The burns team has to be provided with comfortable rooms for breaks, reports, conferences, and classes as it is important that the team members can get away from the many stresses for short periods of time[33].

For many of the staff the stresses are very great. It has become clear[34] that the strong aversion to the burn unit and its patients is directly related to the intense stresses engendered by working with maimed and disfigured persons, who frequently remain maimed and disfigured after multiple surgical procedures and months of hospital care.

Additional facilities

Adjacent the burns unit there should be a *visitors' waiting room* with a lavatory, a *skin bank, office* for the burn care facility director and possibly a *social worker's office.*

31 Feller Irving and Crane Keith: Planning and Designing A Burn Care Facility. Institute for Burn Medicine. Ann Arbor, Michigan 1975, p 60.

32 Clark R P and Mullan B J: Clothing for use in clean-air environments. 1976, The Journal of Hygiene 77:267–269.

33 see also Müller F E: Probleme der Intensivtherapie Schwerverbrannter. 1976, Langenbecks Archiv für Chirurgie 342:369–381.

34 Morris James, McFadd Adrienne: The Mental Health Team on a Burn Unit: A Multidisciplinary Approach. 1978, The Journal of Trauma 18:658–663.

Obstetric intensive care unit, fetal intensive care

For patients with diabetes, Rh-incompability, hypertension, cardiac complications, renal disorders, with a history of reproductive difficulty, for high-risk eclampsia patients, and particularly for those in premature labour under 33 to 34 weeks gestation a special ante and intra partum unit also referred to as an obstetric or labour or maternal intensive care unit should be provided[1].

The ante partum unit could also be regarded as a fetal intensive care unit (FICU) for all high-risk pregnancies. The fetal intensive care could be associated with improved neurologic and biochemical status of the neonate[2].

When the high-risk patient has reached her term or it appears that labour may have to be induced or operative interference considered, she is transferred to the intrapartum unit.

Some 5 per cent of maternity patients have been considered to need intensive care[3].

Paediatric coverage and obstetric anaesthesia should be constantly available. The minimum nurse requirement is one to two patients. Monitoring of physiologic parameters in both the mother and the fetus requires an additional number of staff. For wholly satisfactory care the nurse-to-patient ratio should be at least 1 to 1.

To motivate an obstetric intensive care unit of about 10 beds — 8 antepartum and 2 intrapartum — the annual delivery rate of the hospital should be about 3,000.

---

1   see also Quilligan Edward J: The Obstetric Intensive Care Unit. 1972, Hospital Practice 7:6:61–69.

    Thompson T and Reynolds J: The results of intensive care therapy for neonates. 1977, Journal of Perinatal Medicine 5:59–71.

2   Renou Peter, Chang Allan, Anderson Ian and Wood Carl: Controlled trial of fetal intensive care. 1976, American Journal of Obstetrics and Gynecology 126:470–476.

3   van Gelderen C J: Maternal Intensive Care. 1978, South African Medical Journal 53:838–841.

Neonatal intensive care unit

An intensive care nursery is to provide the best chances of saving life and of improving physical and developmental status for survivors of serious perinatal illness[1].

Ideally, reduction of neonatal death should be accompanied by reduction in the persistence of permanent handicaps. Yet, some infants are saved from early death only for an existence which few persons would consider worth living[2]. *D B Allbrook* has stated that 30 per cent of very low birth weight infants are grossly abnormal and need permanent institutional care[3].

Like any specialized care, the cost of neonatal intensive care is high: in Canada between $ 200 and $ 500 per patient per day[4].

In the US a study[5] indicates that the average cost of insuring that a premature infant will leave the hospital healthy and what is considered normal is $ 115,356. The average daily cost for infants who died in the NICU within 1 to 165 days were $ 825 per infant. Total charges ranged from $ 72 to $ 124,624. The average total cost per nonsurvivor was $ 14,236. Due to less time spent in the NICU, the average daily cost for surviving infants was less than for nonsurvivors. The approximate cost was $ 450 per day, for an average stay of 89 days. Total charges per survivor ranged from $ 10,744 to $ 106,050, with the average total equalling $ 61,641.

A breakdown of the total charges indicates that room charges were as high as 43 per cent, ventilator and oxygen support 19 per cent, blood gases 11 per cent, pharmacy 9 per cent, laboratory 8 per cent, central supply 5 per cent, radiology 4 per cent, miscellaneous 1 per cent. Physicians' fee represented less than 5 per cent of the total bill and were not included[6].

The equipment cost for each baby[7] may be greater than $ 10,000.

The costs as a part of cost of a single life saved from handicap should be weighed against $ 140,000 which is the average cost per severely handicapped child according to French experience[8]. In Ca-

1   see also Davies Pamela A, Robinson R J, Scopes J W, Tizard J P M and Wigglesworth J S: Medical Care of Newborn Babies. Spastics International Medical Publications. London: William Heinemann Medical Books Ltd 1972, p 11.

2   Jonsen A R, Phibbs R H, Tooley W H and Garland M J: Critical issues in Newborn Intensive Care: A Conference Report and Policy Proposal. 1975, Pediatrics 55:756–768.

3   cited in Technology and health care. 1976, The Medical Journal of Australia 1:376–378.

4   Segal Sydney: Perinatal intensive care: pediatric aspects. in Perinatal medicine. ed by James W Goodwin, John O Godden and Graham W Chance. The Williams & Wilkins Co. Baltimore 1976, p 606.

5   Jeffrey J Pomerance, Christina T Ukrainski, Tara Ukra, Diane H Henderson, Andrea H Nash, Janet L Meredith cited in Newborn intensive care an expensive proposition: study, 1978, New York State Journal of Medicine 78:2038.

6   ibid.

7   Merenstein Gerald B: Outcome of Neonatal Intensive Care. 1975, Military Medicine 140:190–191.

8   cited by Matthews Thomas G: Perinatal Medicine — Can We Afford It? 1977, Irish Medical Journal 70:249–250.

nada the financial cost of inadequate or delayed life support during the lifetime of two to four such children has been estimated at about $ 1,000,000, which the community will spend on health, custodial and special educational services. This figure does not include loss of the individual's productivity or the emotional and psychologic cost to his family[9].

Infants admitted to the NICU include pre and postsurgical patients, mostly up to one month of life, outborn neonates transferred from hospitals not provided with special skills, and neonate trauma and burn victims. The maximal admission age of one month is an arbitrary determination. All infants of a size the incubators or bassinets can accommodate could be included.

Many of the low birth weight neonates will spend only a few hours in this area for immediate postnatal observation. However, very low weight infants — about 750 g — may remain in the NICU for a month of longer.

Full time availability of physicians, the services of a neonatalogist, paediatric surgeon, radiologist and inhalation therapist are required[10].

The staff needs are one per two patients to one per one patient[11]. In some cases two nurses per patient and one physician per two neonates has been required[12].

At the birth of a premature infant or an infant with serious medical problems, the parents often experience intensive anxiety, and simultaneously grieve the loss of their desired normal infant. Their ability to begin to deal with these psychologic problems is further hampered when circumstances dictate separation of the parents from their infants, such as a needed transfer to a neonatal intensive care unit[13].

There are questions that remain to be answered[14]. Should there be more human contact and stimulation of tiny babies during their prolonged hospital stays? With the concern that bonding not be restricted to mothers and fathers, should *families,* in some way, be allowed to participate in the intensive care nursery?

Recent advances indicate that parents should be encouraged to visit as often as possible, to touch and handle their babies from the earliest stages, and to feed them

9   Segal Sydney: Perinatal intensive care: pediatric aspects. in Perinatal medicine. ed by James W Goodwin, John O Godden and Graham W Chance. The Williams & Wilkins Co. Baltimore 1976, p 606.

10 Merenstein Gerald B: Outcome of Neonatal Intensive Care. 1975, Military Medicine 140:190–191.

11 see also Serrage John C: The Neonatal Intensive Care Center. 1976, The Journal of the Maine Medical Association 67:291–293.

12 Vivell O and Bäppler E: Intensivmedizin in der Neugeborenen-periode. 1977, Der Krankenhausarzt 50:87–91.

13 see also Kopelman Arthur E, Simeonsson Rune J, Smaldone Arlene and Gilbert Linda: Does a Photograph of a Newborn about to be Transferred to an Intensive Care Center Promote Mother-Infant Bonding? 1978, Clinical Pediatrics 17:15–16.

14 see also Dweck Harry S: The Tiny Baby: Past, Present, and Future. 1977, Clinics in Perinatology 4:2:425–429.

in convalescence. Though no figures exist to prove the point, there can be little doubt that these measures lead to a more confident and healthy parent-infant relationship by the time of discharge from hospital, and are a step in the direction of diminishing the problems in management which have always been a troublesome feature of the later development of preterm babies[15].

Current knowledge concerning the transmission of pathogens has left all the routines which have been adapted for hygienic reasons, only meticulous hand washing is in use. Measures like isolating cubicles and special gowning are now recognized as impediments to effective observation and necessary care[16].

The importance of enforcing strict visiting regulations and to keep all personnel with any infectious illness away from the NICU, especially during a community epidemic has been emphasized[17].

The best estimates currently available suggest that at least 60 of every 1,000 infants will need some form of neonatal intensive care, if death and disability are to be minimized[18].

Neonatal care has to be regionalized. To justify administratively a neonatal intensive care unit the basis of about 4,000 deliveries a year is needed.

The number of NICU beds in a hospital can be estimated on basis of the number of high risk neonates in the catchment area of the hospital, the occupancy rate and the length of patient stay.

$$\text{The number of NICU beds} = \frac{L \times (IB + OB)}{OR}$$

L is the average length of patient stay, IB the number of inborn babies requiring intensive care, OB the number of outborn babies requiring intensive care and OR the average occupancy rate.

A neonatal intensive care facility must have a close working relationship with the obstetrical service. It could be part of it. There should be an intensive care area and an intermediate care area.

15 Burnard E D: New approaches in neonatal intensive care. 1977, The Medical Journal of Australia 2:835–837.

16 Segal Sydney: Perinatal intensive care: pediatric aspects. in Perinatal medicine. ed by James W Goodwin, John O Godden and Graham W Chance. The Williams & Wilkins Co. Baltimore 1976, p 593.

17 Meibalane R, Sedmak Gerald V and Sasidharan P: Outbreak of influenza in a neonatal intensive care unit. 1977, The Journal of Pediatrics 91:974–976.

18 Jonsen Albert R and Lister George: Newborn Intensive Care: The Ethical Problems. 1978, The Hastings Center Report 8:1:15–18.

It is estimated that 2 per cent of live births need intensive care and 3 per cent intermediate care[19].

Three level NICUs have been required. A 28-bassinet unit might have three intensive care spaces, 20 intermediate care areas and 5 transitional care places for short-term observation[20].

Intensive care is provided for the care and observation of all premature and low birth weight infants, infants of high risk mothers, infants with low Apgars, suffering neonatal asphyxia, birth defects, traumatic births, postsurgical patients, trauma, and burn victims.

The intermediate care area provides care for the essentially well infant who still requires some specialized care, though graduated from the intensive care area.

A British expert group has recommended that a unit for intensive care of the newborn should contain at least 24 cots[21]. A smaller NICU containing less than 10 to 12 bassinets is not adviseable[22].

A neonatal intensive care unit would include ward rooms of about 14 to 15 m^2 with three incubators in each. Wards with six cots or incubators have been accepted[23]. Each incubator needs a regular intensive care bed outfit including individual 100 per cent oxygen, 50 per cent oxygen, vacuum leads, and electrical outlets.

There should be shelf space available for placing respirators, resuscitators, infusion and feeding pumps, monitors for respiration or apneic episodes, for heart rate and blood pressure.

A washbasin for each three to four bassinets is needed. Value of washing hands must be stressed rigidly.

The requirement for visibility between the wards in neonatal nurseries limits the choice of materials available. Glass is generally an easy surface to keep clean. Problems may arise where it is supported at its edges. Smooth surfaces with rounded corners and lack of dust traps are important.

19 Serrage John C: The Neonatal Intensive Care Center. 1976, The Journal of the Maine Medical Association 67:291–293.

20 Segal Sydney: Perinatal intensive care: pediatric aspects. in Perinatal medicine. ed by James W Goodwin, John O Godden and Graham W Chance. The Williams & Wilkins Co. Baltimore 1976, p 604.

21 Alberman Eva, Cotlingwood Julia, Pharsah P O D, Vaizey Jane and Oppé T E: Arrangements for special and intensive care of the newborn. 1977, British Medical Journal 2:1045–1047.

22 Waner R R, Wolf S and Granel E L: Personelle Besetzung einer neonatologischen Intensivtherapiestation. Teil I: Mittleres Medizinisches Personal. 1976, Kinderärztliche Praxis 44:49–55.

23 see also Keay A J and Simpson R McD: Prevention of infection in nurseries for the newborn. 1977, Postgraduate Medical Journal 53:583–587.

To have an *admission* room for infants admitted from other hospitals is an advantage

A facility to carry out microchemistry, haematology, blood gas analysis, and bacteriology is needed as well as access to ECG, EEG, and blood bank services[24]. Biochemical determinations must be based on micromethods to limit blood loss.

Radiography by usually a mobile X ray unit is one of the most important diagnostic tools in the initial and follow-up evaluation of high-risk neonates. Virtually, none of the causes of respiratory distress in the new born can be diagnosed without good quality chest radiography[25].

A *procedure room* may be incorporated into the NICU, but preferably it is sectioned off to reduce traffic and to allow better control of techniques such as exchange transfusion, umbilical vessel catherization, and human puncture[26].

If neonates are to be operated in the NICU, a *minor operation room* is needed. It should include a special operation table, instrument and anaesthetic trolleys, rails for infusion bottles, and a viewing box for X ray radiographs. Neonates as well as very small children do not need an anaesthetic room. There ought to be a sluice room with an incinerator for soiled nappies, dressings etc[27].

In larger NICUs clean and soiled *utility rooms* are needed.

A chart *storage* at the working area in the wards and an instrument room for storage and maintenance of respiratory and electronic equipment is needed.

The NICU should include a *nurses' station* with patient data storage for clerical work

The importance of a *staff lounge* for moral purposes has too often been underestimated. It could be used as a study facility.

A *parents' room* to allow feeding, bathing, and in select instances breast feeding, is an essential facility. Another facility should be provided for interviewing the parents

The corridors should be at least about 1.8 m wide.

24 Segal Sydney: Perinatal intensive care: pediatric aspects. in Perinatal medicine. ed by James W Goodwin, John O Godden and Graham W Chance. The Williams & Wilkins Co. Baltimore 1976, p 604.

25 Murray J P: The chest in critical care. 1978, Radiography 44:173–178.

26 Segal Sydney: Perinatal intensive care: pediatric aspects. in Perinatal medicine. ed by James W Goodwin, John O Godden and Graham W Chance. The Williams & Wilkins Co. Baltimore 1976, p 604.

27 Rickham P P: Neonatal surgical unit: layout and equipment. in Neonatal Surgery. ed by P P Rickham, James Lister, Irene M Irving. Butterworths. London 1978, p 19–26.

Acute nursing care units

The optimistical assumption that the introduction of an intensive care unit elsewhere in the hospital would significantly affect the work pattern in acute wards and move the peaks and troughs of productivity has proved through experience to be untrue.

Findings have differed between medical and surgical specialities: surgical patients change dependency, but a sizeable majority of medical patients seem to remain in the same dependency category throughout their stay[1].

Also staying in a regular acute ward unit disrupts an individual's normal mode of operation. He is inable to carry on his regular activities in work, recreation, religion. The loss of contact with family, friends, and co-workers may be felt as much as the physical confinement.

The ward unit activities — wide variations exist — are illustrated by the pattern of an in-patient day[2]:

6.30— 7.00	cups of tea or coffee for patients who are awake
	special early breakfast
	special 6- or 8-hourly medicines given
	fluids charted
	sanitary round for patients not allowed up to visit WC
	output charted
	urine specimens collected and tested
	patients prepared for operations
	temperatures taken in special cases only
7.00— 8.00	test meals commenced
	preparation for X ray
	special treatments performed
	IV infusions maintained
	dressings
	beds made or tidied
	seriously-ill patients bathed, attention to care of mouth
	washing bowls given to those patients not allowed up to wash, and cleared
	attention to pressure areas
	mouth-washes given and cleared
	patients prepared for operation room list
	fresh water jugs and glasses given out
	medicines and drugs given, also pre-dedication
	newspapers distributed

1   Watt Elizabeth: Lengthy look at way forward for nursing. 1978, Health and Social Service Journal 88:160–162.

2   see also The Pattern of the In-Patient's Day. Ministry of Health. Central Health Services Council. Her Majesty's Stationery Office. London 1961, p 23.

8.00— 9.00	patients accompanied to operation department service of breakfast and special diets seriously-ill patients feeded fluids charted patients' mail distributed
9.00— 9.30	sanitary round for patients not allowed up washing bowls given and cleared medicine round laboratory technician collects specimens
9.30—12.00	nursing treatments preparation for X ray bathing of patients in bathroom collecting and testing urine specimens medicines and injections given prior to lunch radiography with mobile X ray beds of discharged patients stripped and clean beds made up
12.00—13.00	lunches served seriously-ill patients fed fluids charted sanitary round for patients not allowed up output charted hand washing bowls given and cleared medicine round
13.00—14.30	patients' rest period
14.30—15.15	nursing treatments
15.15—16.00	teas or coffees served seriously-ill patients fed fluids charted
16.00—16.15	sanitary round and hand washing bowls for patients not allowed up output charted
16.15—17.15	patients assisted in getting up
17.15—18.00	urine specimens taken, collected, tested sanitary round and hand washing bowls
18.00—18.15	medicines given temperatures taken in special cases
18.15—19.00	suppers served seriously-ill patients fed fluids charted sanitary round and hand washing bowls
19.00—20.00	mouth-washes, dressings sanitary round and hand washing bowls
20.00—21.30	milk drinks given beds made for seriously-ill patients pressure areas dressings sanitary round and hand washing bowls

406

21.30 on– wards	night nurse on duty
	drugs given
	lights lowered

The objectives of the hospital system and particularly of the nursing units frequently dictate that the patient be treated as a *sick person,* not as a *person, who is sick*[3]. The patient is expected to adjust and adapt. To an ill individual the stress of hospital life may seem unending. Unfortunately, the criterion for patient well-being is rather nebulous.

The nursing unit design can contribute towards the patient's coping with the psychological effects of the hospital routines. However, the facility is only one component of a system[4].

There are ward units also in most unusual shapes and design. In many cases the main aim has been to reduce the walking distances, as in many circles the only argument for nursing economy has been mileage*.

In the US the nursing unit designs include square units, round units, rectangular units, pinwheels and cloverleaves; single-loaded corridors with patient rooms on only one side and double-loaded corridors with patient rooms on both sides, schemes for simple circulation and schemes for redundant circulation. Dozens of styles could be shown[5]. Wide variations exist also in other countries.

Nursing units in the US have also shown the greatest number of changes of any hospital department studied[6].

This all indicates very clearly that there is no solid basis for nursing unit design yet, the large amount of philosophies, practices and policies involved being unbalanced, their relationships being unsettled. And still, in broad lines the nursing unit development in various countries has followed the same pattern.

---

3 Hanson John A, Lippert Stanley, Ronco Paul G: Development of Physical and Psychological Measurement Instruments. in Evaluation of Hospital Design. Tufts—New England Medical Center. Boston 1971, p 147–208.

4 Hanson John A, Lippert Stanley, Ronco Paul G: Development of Physical and Psychological Measurement Instruments. in Evaluation of Hospital Design. Tufts—New England Medical Center. Boston 1971, p 147–208.

* The walking activity of the nurses and aides in the nursing units is approximately 2.5 km per day shift, on the average (see also Hanson John A, Lippert Stanley, Ronco Paul G: Development of Physical and Psychological Measurement Instruments. in Evaluation of Hospital Design. Tufts—New England Medical Center. Boston 1971, p 147–208).

5 Thompson John D and Goldin Grace: The hospital: a social and architectural history. Yale University Press. New Haven and London 1975, p 282.

6 McLaughlin Herbert, Kibre John and Raphael Mort: Remodeling and Expansion: Study Tells Which Areas Change most often and Why. 1973, Modern Hospital 120:3:97–98.

The lowest level nursing unit consists of an open ward, where all the beds are facing the centre of the room. The nurses station consists of a desk, some storage space, and water supply facilities. At the far end of the ward there is a serving kitchen, a soiled utility room, toilets and a bath room and a storage.

On the next higher level, the nursing unit is divided into units with four or more beds in each and a line of service rooms is added. The added service area contains the nurses unit with a treatment room, a clean utility room, a nurses' station, a sluice, a soiled linen room, and also administration space, a household unit with kitchen, and wardrobes for the patients. Additional sanitary facilities are arranged.

The next step is the adding of a few isolation rooms for critical cases or for contagious diseases.

In the last phase day spaces are provided, some storages added, and sanitary facilities differentiated.

Single occupancy room

In well-run hospitals single occupancy rooms have been regarded axiomatic for both medical and social reasons, this meaning mainly privacy in relationship to a sick roommate and to his visitors.

In 1925, it was suggested in the US, that 14.4 per cent of hospital patients should be placed in separation rooms[7]. This figure was quoted as gospel for decades and turns up even currently in American hospital literature, although the background to the figure has completely changed.

In 1952, 73.7 to 84.4 per cent of the patients in the US would have preferred a private room. They rated the value of private toilet highest *, companionship lowest. The third-most-important item in that patient survey was privacy, which meant even more to patients over fifty years[8]. According to a 1957 study only 20 per cent of the American patients of *lower* income groups would have chosen a private room[9].

At the same time, in the UK, the need of provision for privacy was estimated to about 25 per cent.

A study in Northrhine — Westphalia, Germany, in 1974, indicates that only 6.6 per cent of the patients favoured single occupancy rooms and 45.7 two-bed rooms. 39.6 per cent favoured three-bed rooms and 8.1 per cent rooms with four or more beds[10].

7   S S Goldwater and E M Bluestone cited by Thompson John D and Goldin Grace: The hospital: a social and architectural history. Yale University Press. New Haven and London 1975, p 214.

*   The use of toilets was greatly increased by early ambulation.

8   Charles Lotreck cited by Thompson John D and Goldin Grace: The hospital: a social and architectural history. Yale University Press. New Haven and London 1975, p 220.

9   Thompson John D and Goldin Grace: The hospital: a social and architectural history. Yale University Press. New Haven and London 1975, p 224.

10 Wünsche und Wirklichkeit in Krankenhäusern. 1974, Krankenhaus Umschau 43:590.

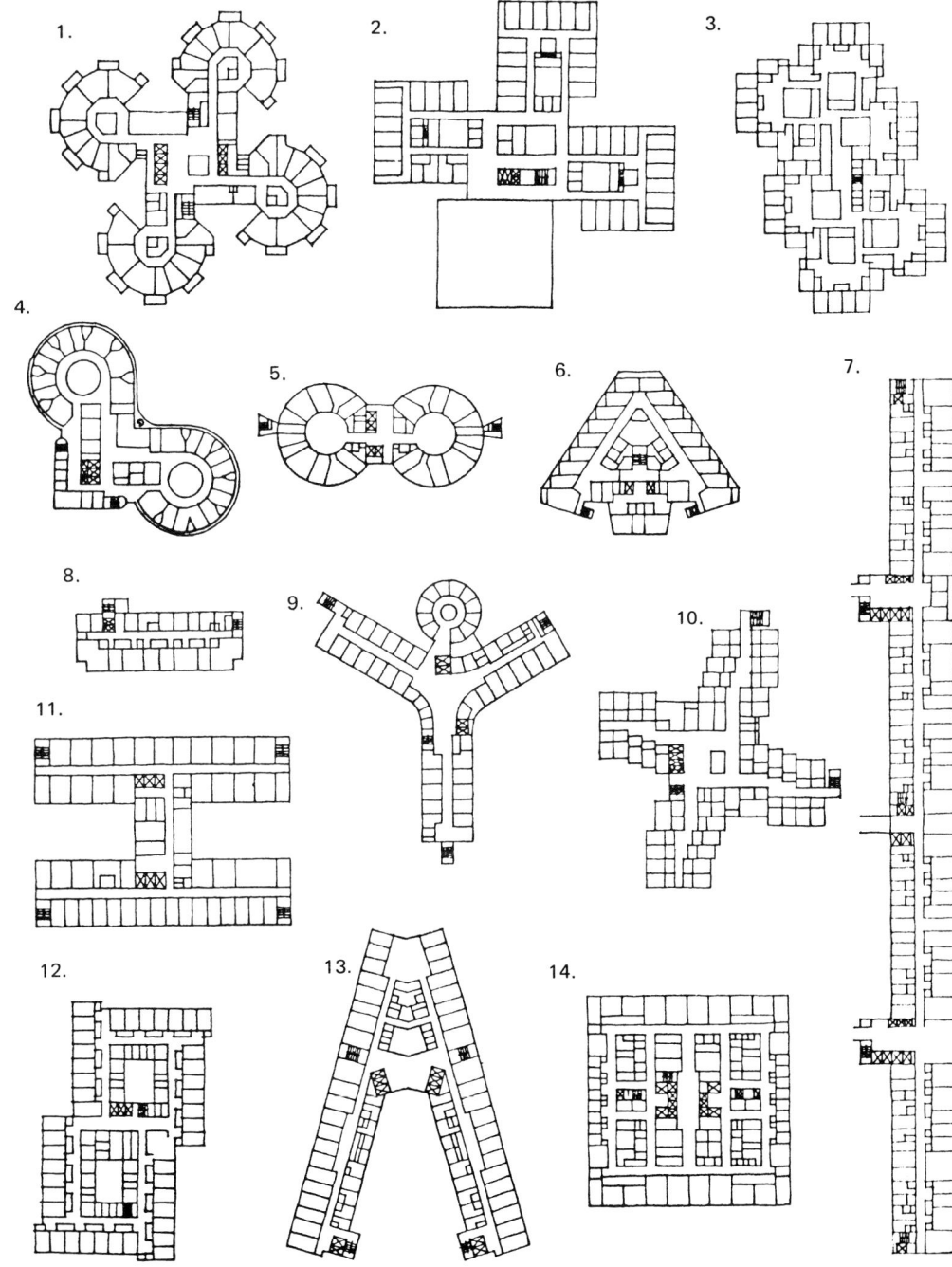

1. 80 bed unit-Göppingen, German Federal Republic (F Novotny, A Mähner),
2. 116 bed unit-Nuremberg, G F R (Walter Mayer),
3. 100 bed unit-Ravensburg, G F R (Hans Riempp),

4. 60 bed unit-Münster, G F R (Schachner, Weber, Brand),
5. 46 bed unit-Panorama City, Calif. (C W Mayhew, L H Thiederman, S R Garfield),
6. 48 bed unit-Sulz am Neckar, G F R (Franz Brümmendorf),
7. 136 bed unit-Hannover, G F R (Gutschow, Nissen),

8. 30 bed unit-Wolhusen (Brechbühl, Itten),
9. 44 bed unit-Louisiana US (Perry Segura),
10. 80 bed unit-Freudenstadt, G F R (Hans Egon Hahn, Werner K Hahn),
11. 72 bed unit-Carmichael, Calif. (Rex Whitaker Allen),

12. 105 bed unit-Nagold, G F R (Hans Egon Hahn),
13. 100 bed unit-Berlin-Kreuzberg, G F R (Peter Poelzig),
14. 112 bed unit-London (Yorke, Rosenberg, Mardall).

The number of variations in ward unit design is almost limitless.

An increasing trend toward more privacy in every aspect of life accounts in part for an emphasis on the single occupancy room in hospitals.

It has been found that patients prefer what they are familiar with and tend to preserve the *status quo*.

However, no strong preference for or against privacy should be stated as an axiom. People, who were alone in their lives, resent being left alone in a hospital.

The additional cost for the single occupancy has become a very small part of the very large total cost per day[11].

Nurses like the privacy of the patient, which would give them a closer rapport with the patient, who would be less embarrassed to ask for advice or help.

In single occupancy fewer medication errors occur, and there is a superiority in emergency situations[12].

A hospital patient room is a sick bay, but also an individual territory. It is a hotel room, an emergency unit, a family reunion centre. Fulfilling these demands requires more than one specialist.

The inadequacies of space in patient rooms have been criticized very frequently.

Space restrictions can lead to limited freedom of movement, absence of privacy, and lack of personal facilities. All these conditions can have serious psychological, physiological and social consequences. It has been suggested that the recovering patients should be given at least the possibility to control the microclimate: light quality, room temperature, air movements, odours, humidity.

The patient rooms rarely are designed to take into account the psychological influences of proportion and size. Also the windows, open doors and screens affect the patient to perceive the conditions of his socio-physical environment.

The configuration of the patient room has to be functionally appropriate.

In order to arrive at a suitability, the activities of both patients and staff which are carried out in the room as well as the space requirements of furnishings relevant for the medical treatment and for the convenience of the patient have to be analyzed carefully.

E g there is a definite advantage in storing each patient's clothing in a wardrobe cupboard within his bed area. It improves security, and can even improve bed turnover by removing delays due to patients' clothing not being immediately available.

11 Templer John, Wilson Richard, Taylor Joe: The architecture of health facilities. Current trends in North America. 1976, architecture in greece 10:129–138.

12 One Patient, One Room: Theory and Practice. Editorial. 1975, Modern Healthcare 3:3:65.

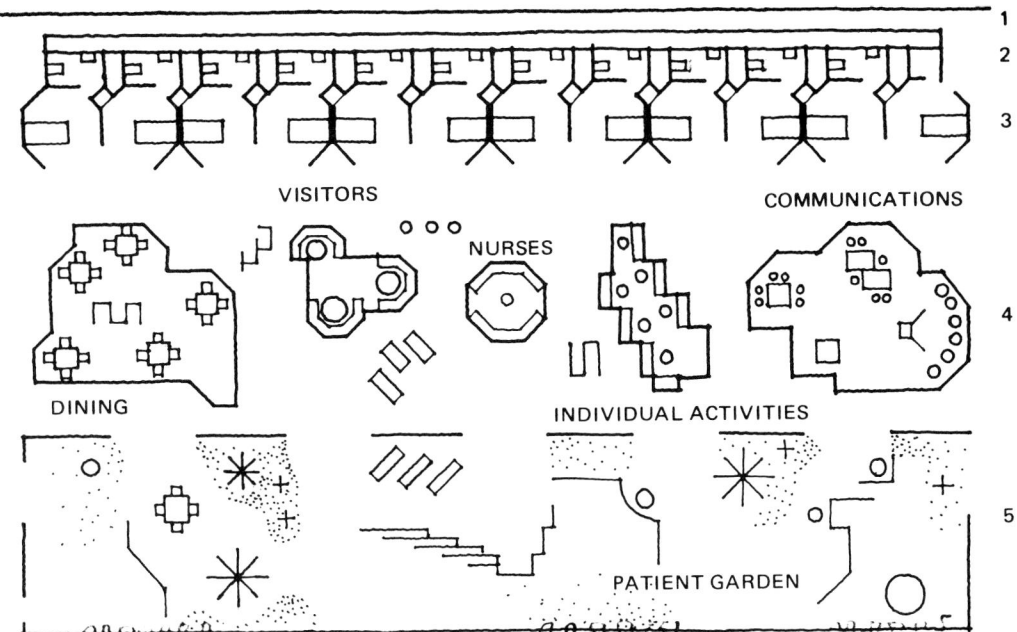

A diagrammatic so called cellular system for standard care based on single occupancy rooms as suggested by Walter Mayer (Prognosen der Zukunft. 1971. Bauen + Wohnen 25:219–222). 1 — technical installations, 2 — sanitary zone, 3 — bed area, 4 — therapy, rehabilitation, communication, movements, occupation, 5 — external, open air zone.

The corner bed constitutes nursing problems, a fact recognized already in the 1920s. Only the free-standing bed is admissible in hospital practice, when the acutely ill patients are involved. For patients not acutely ill, there is an average of only 2.4 movements of the bed in 24 hours[13].

The ideal room size for treating different conditions must be known, but also the limits below and above which room size should not go. Figures reflecting dynamic anthropometry and function and the perceptual responses of people should enter the calculations[14].

When designing the patient's room, many strive to make them as much like home as possible. Not recognizing the wide diversity of environments from which patients

---

13 John F O'Connor cited by Thompson John D and Goldin Grace: The hospital: a social and architectural history. Yale University Press. New Haven and London 1975, p 220.

14 Hanson John A, Lippert Stanley, Ronco Paul G: Development of Physical and Psychological Measurement Instruments. in Evaluation of Hospital Design. Tufts—New England Medical Center. Boston 1971, p 147-208.

come, planners project their own ideas of home onto this patient space. What is the scientific foundation of the belief that the homelike atmosphere will meet the patient's needs when he has an illness, it has been asked[15].

All patient rooms must be as self-contained as possible and, in particular, should be directly linked to WC and washing facilities. Washing compartments should be separate from WC compartments, self-contained, and doors should be provided. Some of the WC and washing compartments should allow easy access for wheelchairs.

Apparently in the field of providing showers or bathtubs in patient bathrooms research has never been done[16]. Because it is so difficult to find out what are the cultural habits of the clientele to be served, it would be well worth the expense of having bath-tub-shower combinations for all rooms. This meets the individual needs for every patient.

In Finland in 1969 97 per cent of the female patients and 72 per cent of the male desired to use a bathing facility daily. 78 per cent of females and 65 per cent of males had the shower as the most popular bathing alternative[17].

Multipatient rooms

For reasons of the ease of observability — privacy's very opposite — the single room have been opposed, maybe most in the UK because of the from *Florence Nightingale* derived military emphasis on supervision.

It could be hardly assumed that a patient feels better cared for, if he sees the nurse in the room more often, attending to someone else.

At a conference at the Hospital Centre in London a member remarked that he had never understood why it was so important that a patient should be seen to fall out of bed. A principal matron observed that a nurse could stand at the bottom of a patient's bed and not realize he was dead[18].

Sharing a room in a general hospital is a source of some positive and some negative experiences. It is good to have a roommate to talk to and very important that room mates try to help each other, but it is undesirable to have a very ill roommate and

15 Kraegel Janet M, Mousseau Virginia Schmidt, Goldsmith Charles, Arora Rajeev: Patient Care Systems. J B Lippincott Company. Philadelphia, Toronto 1974, p 89.

16 Kraegel Janet M, Mousseau Virginia Schmidt, Goldsmith Charles, Arora Rajeev: Patient Care Systems. J B Lippincott Company. Philadelphia, Toronto 1974, p 90.

17 Kokko Kauko: The general hospital ward. University of Oulu. Oulu 1971, p 77.

18 cited by Thompson John D and Goldin Grace: The hospital: a social and architectural history. Yale University Press. New Haven and London 1975, p 215.

a great difference between the ages of the roommates, it has been said[19]. The room-mates who have too many visitors are quite annoying to other patients. There is no privacy no matter how much it is wanted. Smoking does not cause many problems; neither do odours, but noise is an annoying factor.

Roommates who would not snore, smell, smoke cigars, who would like the same TV programmes and have attractive, quiet visitors, are preferred.

In the 1960s Americans came to feel that a two-bed compromise between the private room and the four-bed* ward was too much of a compromise because it simultaneously attempted to satisfy administrative need for flexibility, the patient's need or desire for privacy, the physician's preference for privacy, the nurse's need to save steps by working in a shorter corridor, and the necessity to keep costs down. One room could not do all that. The two-bed room really satisfied nobody[20].

Although some medical professionals agree in principle with a four-bed maximum requirement, many believe that a larger room configuration has additional therapeutic value in patient care[21].

Experience from Oslo, Norway, indicates that about 30 per cent of the female patients could be treated in large multiple occupancy units[22]. A 20 bed room has been suggested.

However, savings in personnel have not been indicated and the bed-landscape reduces the possibilities of good patient-staff contact[23]. Also most of the sheer physical surroundings of large wards are inimical to good communication, because they make private, intimate conversations between doctor and patient very difficult to achieve, and quite impossible if the patient is hard of hearing[24].

Large multi-bed rooms in acute wards for adults represent a significant loss of amenity and of flexibility in the allocation of beds.

Their only means to provide some privacy for highly sensitive physical examinations are privacy curtains. They should be provided in any situation in which the patient could be unwittingly exposed.

---

19 Reid Elizabeth Anne and Feeley Ellen M: Roommates: To Have and Have Not. 1973, American Journal of Nursing 73:1:104–107.

* In 1978 a regulation limiting the number of patients per hospital room to four was being considered.

20 Thompson John D and Goldin Grace: The hospital: a social and architectural history. Yale University Press. New Haven and London 1975, p 217.

21 Sprague Joseph G: Codes, regulations and compliance: a never-ending dilemma. 1978, Hospitals 52:4:90–92.

22 Lotsberg Jostein, Wiik-Larsen Else, Enger Erik, Ranvig Eivind: Sengelandskap. 1978, Tidsskrift for Den norske Laegeforening 98:74–78.

23 ibid

24 Reynolds Maureen: No news is bad news: patients' views about communication in hospital. 1978, British Medical Journal 1:1673–1676.

Single and multibed accommodation mix, ward unit size

Needs which have emerged through development of sub-specialities and changes in the pattern of morbidity, can be effectively met by the provision of single rooms and four-bed rooms in the wards.

The optimal mix of single and multibed accommodations in a ward cannot easily be expressed as a single universal percentage, as it depends on a combination of medical, social, and economical factors. The proportion of each type of bed arrangements will vary with the quality level of the clinic, its therapeutic philosophy, and the social characteristics of its patients. However, it could be generally stated that at least 40 per cent of the ward unit beds should be provided in single bed rooms.

In the size of acute wards there have been wide variations in basic units — 12 to 30 beds — as well as in the ward unit combinations — 60 to 120 beds. A ward of 24 beds has received broad support, as well as the combinations 2 x 24 and 4 x 24 beds. Larger ward unit combinations, which make the practicing of progressive patient care easier, are being encouraged[25].

Day room

Within each multi-bed room a small sitting area should be provided to meet some of the requirements of early ambulation. A central dayroom or rooms of a domestic character should also be provided for the convenience of the ambulant patients, who could converse with others, have a different window view, change of activity, books to read, and cards to play. A change in environment would help stimulate a patient's senses and makes him more ready for sleep and rest at night. It would help him move out of the invalid role into progression towards a more normal living pattern[26].

The dayroom should not be used as a smoking room.

Most dayrooms and lounges are designed for sitting. Why not have hobby corners, game activity centres, and the like, it has been asked[27]. Why not a music centre with records and tapes and earphones where patients could listen to their favourite music?

For active pursuits of leisure activities, appropriate settings and equipment has to be provided. While some provision could be made within the patient rooms for activi-

25 see also Watt Elizabeth: Lengthy look at way forward for nursing. 1978, Health and Social Service Journal 88:160–162.

26 Kraegel Janet M, Mousseau Virginia Schmidt, Goldsmith Charles, Arora Rajeev: Patient Care Systems. J B Lippincott Company. Philadelphia, Toronto 1974, p 93.

27 Hanson John A, Lippert Stanley, Ronco Paul G: Development of Physical and Psychological Measurement Instruments. in Evaluation of Hospital Design. Tufts—New England Medical Center. Boston 1971, p 147–208.

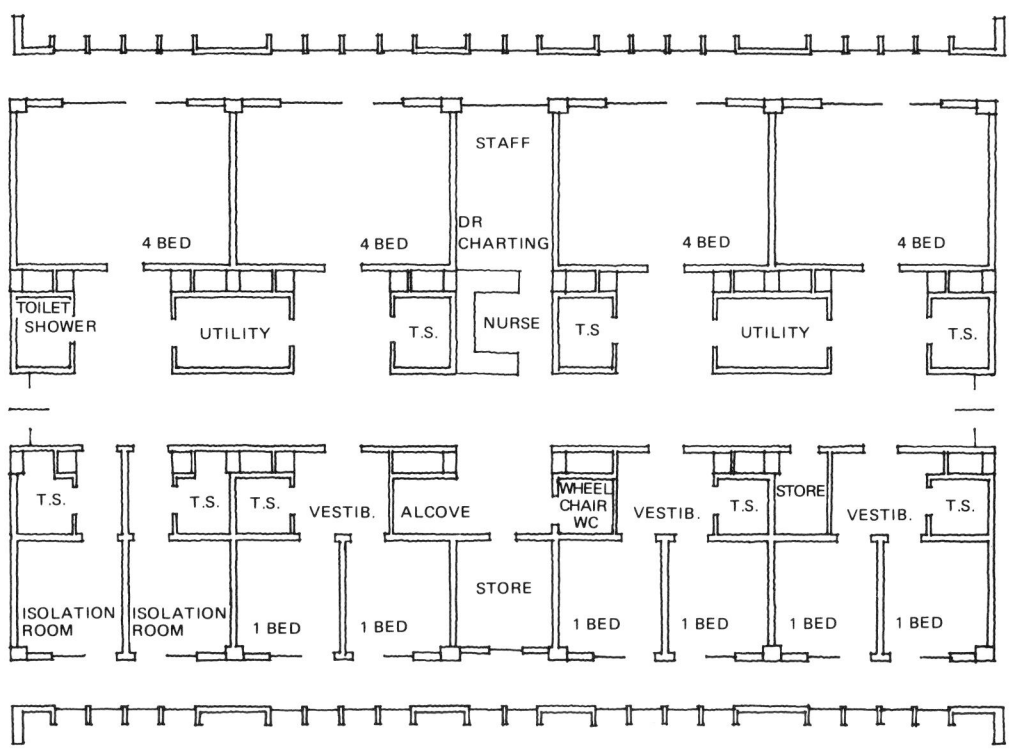

A basic 24-bed ward unit with inner and peripheral corridors. Pütsep International.

ties such as craft-work, it is perhaps more feasible and desirable to locate such activities outside the patient room in special units.

Decentralized day spaces seem to be better for debilitated patients and may more effectively contribute to early activation.

A separate patients' dining room is intended for ambulant and wheelchair patients to encourage an early return to normal life. Although this arrangement is mostly met with approval, sometimes a less generous solution, where the day room's function is widened by the dining function, is advocated[28].

The kind and size of the ward kitchen or pantry depends on the catering policies of the hospital. Whatever the catering policy practised, meals have to be served hot, patients' expectations and dietary demands considered, transportation distances kept reasonable and perfect cleanliness maintained.

28 see also Kokko Kauko: The general hospital ward. Acta Universitatis Ouluensis. Series C. Technica No 1. Architectura No 1. University of Oulu. Oulu 1971, p 93.

Rooms for nursing procedures

Analysis of nursing procedures in acute wards shows that all procedures conform to a broad pattern made up of giving and receiving oral or written instructions; preparation or assembly of items for nursing procedures; carrying out the procedure in the bed areas, treatment room or bathroom; recording results of the procedure, and cleaning or disposal of used items.

These activities require an instructions and recording area, and a preparation area.

The instructions and recording area consists of the nurses' station, sister's station and the doctor's office. The nurses' station should be acoustically closed as it is a source of noise.

All clean and sterilized items for nursing and medical procedures should be selected and assembled in one preparation room. Space must be provided for trolley setting.

A disposal room is required for the temporary storage of used items awaiting reprocessing and disposal or destruction. Some items are reprocessed in this room and returned to the preparation room, e g treatment trolleys.

In the US, *Gordon Friesen* and others have rejected the central nursing station in favour of decentralized nurse servers at each patient room.

The combination of inner and peripheral ward corridors is considered to improve the nursing conditions. The inner corridor is mainly the work area for hospital personnel and to a limited extent used by the patients. The peripheral corridor serves th visitors, but is used to some extent also by the patients. When only one circulation space — the inner corridor — is provided, attention should be paid to the corridor width. 2.4 m, which has almost become an international standard, is obviously insufficient and the width of 2.8 m would better meet the operational needs[29].

Storages

Linen store for bed linen, patients' pyjamas and other clothing and various items used by the staff, but not for storage of mattresses, blankets, pillows and dust generating supplies, should be provided. It should be realized that the supply space is only one part of a complex distribution system which extends to the receiving docks of the hospital. If a cart or twin-cart system is to be operated, there are considerable consequences on the ward spacing.

An equipment store has to be provided for spare parts for beds, plints, crutches, examination lights, wheelchairs, etc.

29 see also Kokko Kauko: The general hospital ward. Acta Universitatis Ouluensis. Series C. Technica No 1. Architectura No 1. University of Oulu. Oulu 1971, p 113.

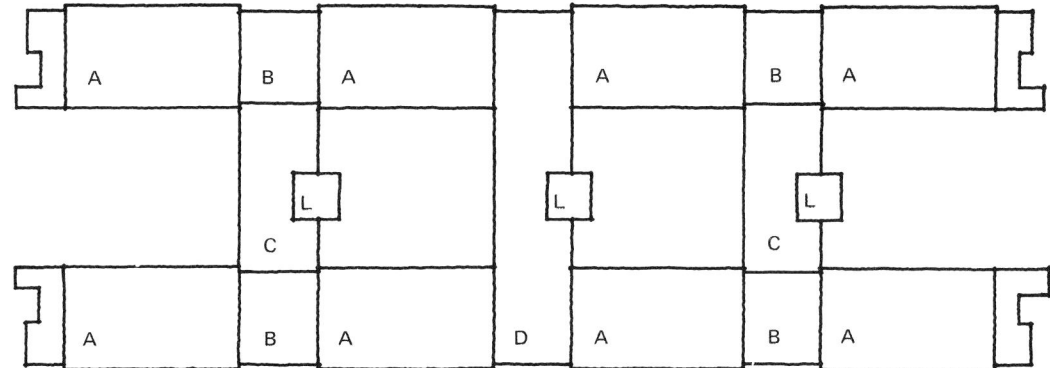

A 192-bed combination of basic 24-bed ward units. Pütsep International.
Area A: basic 24-bed ward unit; area B: examination and treatment room, doctors' and nurses' offices, pantry, bathroom, storage, janitor's, closet; area C: patients dining and day areas, ward kitchen, bed cleaning and store, store for used items; area D: staff cloakrooms, offices and instruction rooms, storages; area L: lifts.

Additional facilities

Offices, staff refreshment break room, interview rooms, laboratory, female and male staff cloaks, domestic service room and some stores are examples of rooms required at ward level but not related to any particular group. They may serve more than one nursing charge.

A room for visitors' waiting and relatives' overnight stay is considered relatively useful. A centralized overnight accommodation would meet most requirements[30].

Wherever possible, centralized services should be provided with the consequent removal of many avoidable activities at ward level. The range of central services provided will affect the location and size of some of the working areas. The main central services which nowadays are provided are sterile and other supplies, catering and housekeeping.

Communications and management systems are important elements of the supply and distribution system.

30 Kokko Kauko: The general hospital ward. Acta Universitatis Ouluensis. Series C. Technica No 1. Architectura No 1. University of Oulu. Oulu 1971, p 94.

A clear statement of an institution's goals, establishing its objectives and categories of inpatients for whom care is to be provided, is needed to determine the character of its ward units.

CLINICAL LABORATORY SERVICES

The primary function of clinical laboratories, also called the pathology department, is to provide accurate and timely information for the diagnosis, monitoring and treatment of the patient, i e for the medical evaluation and decision-making. Qualitative and quantitative scientific tests and measurements of body fluids, tissues and products are carried out.

Clinical chemistry is concerned with the analysis of the biochemical composition of body fluids and composition and functions of tissues, *clinical microbiology* with microorganisms and viruses found in the body and in the environment, and with immunologic phenomena, *clinical physiology* and neurophysiology with the functions of various organs and systems, and *clinical pathology* and cytology with the macroscopic and microscopic structural changes in tissues and cells. Larger hospitals may have a separate unit for *blood transfusion* service.

The increase in the type and volume of tests performed in the hospital laboratories over the past decades has been extraordinary. E g in the late fifties the repertoire of the average laboratory for clinical chemistry and haematology was of the order of 60 methods. Today, 1978, well over 350 chemical tests on blood, faeces, saliva, sweat and biopsy specimens covering enzymes and other specific proteins, hormones, intermediary metabolites and drugs are available to the physician[1]. In the US there has been an annual increase of about 6 per cent in the number of procedures[2]. Probably this will continue at a similar rate. The development of new analytical methods is reflected in an augmented workload in the laboratories. The yearly increase has been reported as 10 to 15 per cent in Sweden[3] and 20 per cent in the United Kingdom[4]. In the US more than 5,000 million laboratory tests were performed in 1975, and this number may reach 10,000 million by 1984[5].

Much of this is due to better diagnostic distinction and other benefits to the patient by the new tests. However, a sensible part may originate in the use of multiple screening tests or biochemical profiles which implies ordering at the samt time a large number of analyses as an endeavour to hasten the diagnostic considerations by detection of clinically more or less unsuspected deviations from the normal pattern.

To test the validity of this, a study[6] was performed in which a group of patients was subjected to a primary screening test battery and compared to a group in which the doctors were free to select the timing and nature of tests done on their patients. The

1 personal communication: 1978, Bo Norberg, Stockholm.

2 Gitelman H J: Future shock from the laboratory. 1975, Annals of Clinical and Laboratory Science 5:319–323.

3 de Verdier Carl-Henrik, Hjelm Magnus, Sandblad Bengt, Wadman Bengt, Wengle Bo and Östling Göran: Klinisk kemi — effektivitet och kostnader. 1976, Nordisk Medicin 91:321–326.

4 Stevens John F: Current trends in automation: a review. 1973, Medical Laboratory Technology 30:139.

5 Trujillo Jose M, Fritsche Herbert A and Wendlandt Gay McC: Laboratory Medicine: Automation and Data Processing. in Cancer Patient Care. ed by R Lee Clark and Clifton D Howe. Year Book Medical Publishers Inc. Chicago 1976, p 745.

6 Durbridge T C, Edwards F, Edwards R G and Atkinson M: Evaluation of benefits of screening tests done immediately on admission to hospital. 1976, Clinical Chemistry 22:968–971.

authors conclude: The screening procedure added to the cost of hospitalization without associated evidence of benefit to the patient.

Inappropriate or excessive use of procedures and technologies that are not expensive on a pre-use basis is also a significant factor in cost inflation. For example, the proliferation of laboratory tests has added greatly to the charges for care without producing an obvious commensurate gain in health outcomes. *Scitovsky* and *McCall* found that from 1951 to 1971, the average number of laboratory tests for a set of common diagnoses grew from two to six times, while prognoses remained essentially unchanged. The causes of such a profusion of technology adoption and use are numerous and complex[7].

The situation in laboratory approaches is by no means stabilized yet. E g blood and urine contains enormous amounts of chemical and physiological information, which must be discovered, identified and decoded. The data must be correlated and synthesized to describe the integrated organism of man during his varying reactions in health and disease. This task is only in the design stage[8].

The laboratory technology will permit further increase in the number of methods and in the number of tests for a given patient. But it is not in the interest of the patient and the doctor that a lot of factual, though irrelevant information is delivered. It is important and rational to select carefully in relation to the clinical problem the analyses to be performed on the individual patient, in addition to a moderate general screening programme. The clinician and still more the practising physician may need and get assistance in this respect from physicians trained in laboratory services and responsible for the laboratory reports, as is the case in the Scandinavian countries[9].

The second generation of multichannel analytical machines are designed for individualizing the analytical programme. As already indicated, there is no evidence that larger and larger amounts of random data will improve physicians performance or lead to better medical care. The use of problem-oriented laboratory requisitions would develop a more logical approach to the use of laboratory information[10].

When planning a laboratory, the aim is to create an efficient and economical facility for the laboratory services needed by the medical institution. The design has to follow a simple and logical pattern. It should be easily comprehensible. It should be adaptable for changes.

7   Warner Kenneth E: Acquisition and Use of New Medical Knowledge. 1978, The Journal of Anesthesiology 48:396–398.

8   Williams George Z: Advancing Technology of Clinical Laboratory Practice. 1973, MCV/Q 9:293–297.

9   personal communication: 1978, Bo Norberg, Stockholm.

10 Conn R B: Clinical laboratories. Profit center, production industry of patient-care resource? 1978, The New England Journal of Medicine 298:422–427.

For a general hospital the clinical laboratory must be prepared to perform certain services at any time, day or night.

At start the composition of the laboratory services and the medical policies have to be determined and the administrative patterns indicated. With the aid of production statistics and estimates the volume of analytical work is calculated, the number of staff members indicated, and the space requirements assessed. The scope of the interdepartmental relations has to be determined.

When choosing the location for laboratory, less importance should be attached to the proximity of out-patient departments and nursing wards than to the considerations which are concerned with the efficient functioning of the laboratory itself[11], which includes the expansion possibilities of the main service lines. The laboratories should be located in areas where there is no excessive vibration or excessive fluctuation of electrical power[12]. Offensive noise and obnoxious odours should not be transmitted into adjoining areas.

The location on the ground floor is the most adviseable. There must be at least two distinct escape routes from the principal work areas. For the receipt of bulk deliveries of chemicals and large items of equipment the doors, corridors and lifts should be given proper dimensions.

The laboratory should be isolated from the other sections of the hospital with protective barriers against spread of fire.

Laboratory elements

There should be a direct connection between the laboratory entrance and the reception area. Also the consulting and examination rooms should be close to the entrance.

The reception area is for patients and hospital staff members who come to the laboratory. It also includes space for receiving requisitions and specimens as well as for sample collection.

The patient waiting room should be provided with comfortable furnishings. It should be well-ventilated and arranged with appropriate consideration of infection risks through contamination of the air[13].

---

11 see also det bouwkundige opzet van het laboratorium voor klinische chemie. Nationaal Ziekenhuis-instituut. Utrecht 1975, p 94.

12 see also Musser A Wendell: The planning, operation and function of a clinical laboratory in a teaching hospital. 1975, CRC Critical Reviews in Clinical Laboratory Sciences 6:47–66.

13 Nikodemusz I: Bakteriologische Untersuchung der Luft im Polikliniklaboratorium. 1976, Hospital-Hygiene 68:385–387.

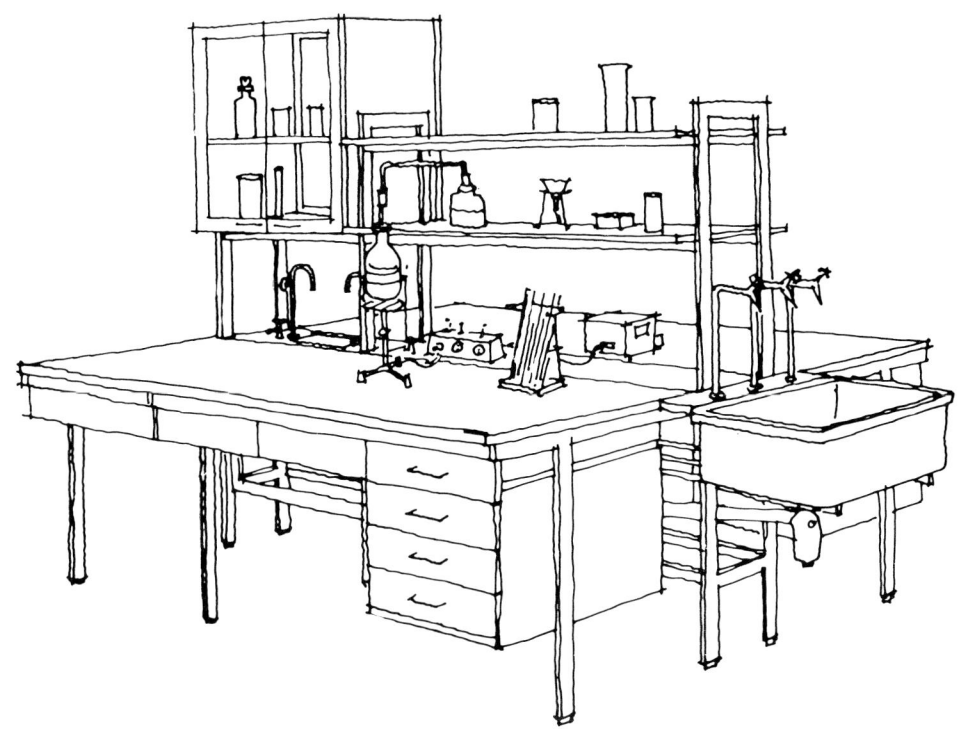

A free standing laboratory bench as developed by Tranås Rostfria.

In the phlebotomy or venepuncture rooms blood specimens are drawn from ambulant patients either sitting or lying on a coach. Racks for hanging coats are needed. An area of about 6.5 m² is sufficient.

An adjacent toilet for collection of specimens of urine, stool, seminal fluid should be provided with a pass-through hatch directly into the technical area. The lavatory space is about 3.0 m². Doors should allow the passage of wheelchairs. Recommended general lighting level is 100 lux, in the testing area 200 lux.

In larger hospitals special rooms for collecting, checking, sorting, temporary storing, and sometimes testing of blood and urine specimens from out-patients can be provided within the out-patient consultation area, to reduce the amount of circulation in the hospital. These rooms should have intercom contact with the laboratory.

Instrumentation is one of the main factors in clinical laboratory planning. The development of automated or mechanized methods do not necessarily save the overall space as has been expected. Older methods may still be retained for the handling of single or small number of tests.

To obtain a good degree of multifunctional use, laboratories should be modular. Frequently as the first module unit choice is 3.0 m considered, as the second 3.6 m. Each laboratory should be two modules in depth. Rooms deeper than 7.2 m pose problems of lighting and ventilation. In the United Kingdom it has been assumed that the most suitable arrangement could be achieved by using parallel benches running the length of a 6.1 by 3.3 m module[14].

A laboratory which has equipment and working space on one side of the room only, requires a width of 2.3 m.

Each pathology assistant needs about 16 m length of laboratory benches. The total functional area per one assistant is about 25 m². This corresponds to 35 m² when all traffic and technical areas are included.

As an acceptable laboratory room height 2.4 m has been accepted[15], but it ought to be about 2.8 m.

For psychological reasons it has been considered desirable to provide for some fields of work separate rooms or by partitions separated[16] areas in the laboratory.

In the recent years an open laboratory planning has frequently been given preference because it has been believed that this system would improve the use of available space. Walls are eliminated and the spatial division is achieved with cupboards and screens. The disadvantages of the open laboratories are lack of psychological security[17] and noise interference.

In the open plan surface absorptivity must be maximized to reach acceptable anechoic properties of the room[18]. Installing carpeting in as many laboratory areas as possible has been recommended[19].

All laboratory furniture should be modular, readily interchangeable and standardized

For the laboratory tables there seems to be a ratio of 1.0 m table length to 2.4 m² net laboratory floor area[20]. Tables should permit to place refrigerators and cabinets on wheels under them. Under-table space is also for drawers. Preference is given to short tables, which can be assembled to fit specific work situations[21].

14 Pathology Department. Hospital Building Note 15. Department of Health and Social Security. Welsh Office. Revised 1973, p 11.

15 Svensk Byggnorm 1975, Utgåva 3. Statens planverks författningssamling 1978:1. Stockholm 1978, p 460.

16 see also de bouwkundige opzet van het laboratorium voor klinische chemie. Nationaal Ziekenhuisinstituut. Utrecht 1975, p 94.

17 see also Purvis M J: Laboratory Planning. Balliere Tindall. London 1973, p 3.

18 Pirn Rein: Acoustical misconceptions in open planning. 1972, Progressive Architecture 53:8:74–75.

19 Manual for laboratory planning and design. College of American Pathologists. Skokie III 1977, p 12.

20 de bouwkundige opzet van het laboratorium voor klinische chemie. Nationaal Ziekenhuisinstituut. Utrecht 1975, p 96.

21 see also de bouwkundige opzet van het laboratorium voor klinische chemie. Nationaal Ziekenhuisinstituut. Utrecht 1975, p 100.

The mechanized equipment can be housed on adjustable shelves or tables rather than on conventional tables[22].

Under-window tables not requiring pipes or drainage are used mainly for writing.

The Swedish recommended height for the laboratory table when the work is performed standing is 0.9 m and when sitting 0.7 m[23]. In the US a uniform table height of 0.9 has been recommended[24].

The depth of wall tables should not exceed 0.85 m and of the island tables 1.7 m[25].

The height of conveniently reached over-table cupboards is up to 1.5 m.

In most chemical and biochemical laboratories the table surfaces should be resistant to water, alkalis, acids, solvents and heat. Cracks and joints should be avoided. It is an advantage if the bench-top can be formed into a shallow tray, about 0.5 cm deep, to contain spillages and also be provided with an integral or carefully attached upstand where it backs on to a wall[26].

In histopathology laboratories the working surfaces should be heat and stain resistant. In microbiological laboratories the surfaces should be easily cleaned and in some sections resist UV-waves.

For wooden tables teak is excellent. Also wooden table tops finished with a synthetic material — melamine — are found to satisfy requirements well[27].

Laminated plastic tops are excellent for most bacteriology and biology laboratories. Plastics are restricted to temperatures below 155°C, in some cases as low as 40°C, and some burn readily[28].

Stainless steel is very good in radioisotope laboratories and also for work with virus and mercury[29]. When heat-resistance is required mainly tiles and ceramic material are used. Impregnated natural stone tops are excellent for heavy chemical use, but when the coating wears off, they may absorb liquids[30]. Glass tops are very good, but have vulnerable edges and low resistance to impact. Glass also limits on-the-job modifications.

22 Pathology Department. Hospital Building Note 15. Department of Health and Social Security. Welsh Office . Revised 1973, p 16.

23 see also Laboratorieanvisningar. Utfärdade av Kungl. Arbetarskyddsstyrelsen i juni 1971, Stockholm 1971, p 47.

24 Rappoport Arthur E, Taylor Wilbur R and Gaulin Richard P: What the modern laboratory must include and where to put it. 1973, Modern Hospital 121:5:55–63.

25 see also Purvis M J: Laboratory Planning. Bailliere Tindall. London 1973, p 36.

26 Everett K and Hughes D: A Guide to Laboratory Design. Butterworths. London & Boston 1975, p 20.

27 de bouwkundige opzet van het laboratorium voor klinische chemie. Nationaal Ziekenhuisinstituut. Utrecht 1975, p 100.

28 Everett K and Hughes D: A Guide to Laboratory Design. Butterworths London & Boston 1975, p 16.

29 Manual for laboratory planning and design. College of American Pathologists. Skokie III. 1977, p 12.

30 ibid, p 13.

Laboratory tables should not be bolted down or supported on base cabinets which should have an independent structure.

At a laboratory table following services may be required:

> piped distribution: cold water*, hot water, distilled water, deionized water, steam, compressed air, vacuum, town's gas, oxygen
>
> electrical services: power supplies, telephones, chronometers
>
> collection services
>
> environmental services: lighting, ventilation control, heating and/or cooling control, black-out facilities, fire detection
>
> fume cupboard**

Ready access to the services behind them for inspection, maintenance and subsequent modifications, as well as for normal cleaning, should be provided.

The fume-cupboards should be glazed in toughened glass or in other appropriate safety material. In a fume-cupboard there should be no provision of shelves for the storage of hazardous chemicals. The fume-cupboards should be kept as far as possible from the entrance and the emergency exit, so that in case of an accident the line of retreat is away from the hazard area[31].

Selected stainless steel is an attractive material to use in integral *sink* and *drainer* units, but it is susceptible to attack by some chemicals, in particular by hydrochloric acid. Alternative materials are earthenware and polypropylene[32]. The sinks must be designed and installed so that they do not harbour contamination.

Washbasins should be well distributed.

Emergency drenching showers should be provided at strategic positions to be used in the event of acid spillage and clothing fires. The floor under the showers should be drained into gullies.

The laboratory mechanical distribution and collection systems should be devised both in principle and in routing so that access for local isolation for maintenance or updating does not disrupt services in other areas.

The number of socket outlets — some of them for vacuum cleaners — should be sufficient to make radical changes in work procedures possible. The outlets should not be too near water supplies. Some equipment require special voltages separate

---

* Cold water requires frequently pressure control, filtering and softening.

**Turbulence should be avoided around the fume cupboard's front opening, at the front stiles, and at the bench top level where a counter flow occurs. Fume cupboards are only as efficient as the extraction system to which they are attached. Sockets are needed for the mantles and hotplates to heat chemicals.

31 Everett K and Hughes D: A Guide to Laboratory Design. Butterworths. London & Boston 1975, p 66.

32 Everett K and Hughes D: A Guide to Laboratory Design, Butterworths. London & Boston 1975, p 23.

circuits, or three-phase supplies. High-speed centrifuges should have separate circuits and high power fuses. There should be a cut-out switch away from the machines in case of an emergency.

Some laboratory areas should incorporate drainage and shielding for radiation laboratories, reinforced floors for heavy equipment and vibration-free laboratories.

Generally, drainage pipes of acid-resistant QVF glass are considered ideal in laboratories. Being transparant they make the locating of a blockage in the pipe easy. Vulcathene pipes and joints of PVC and black polythene are vulnerable to solvents[33]. Acid waste disposal devices as well as mercury traps should be installed according to the local building code requirements.

Clinical laboratories require comfortable general ecological conditions, and some special conditions of hygiene, temperature, light and darkness.

Most people would prefer to work in a laboratory which has windows. Daylight, preferably north light, can be of advantage for examining plates in the clinical microbiology department[34]. However, the windows are not always absolutely necessary. In a few cases e g in the electron microscope rooms they are a disadvantage.

Large glass areas and infill panels of low thermal mass ensure high solar heat gain, and can result in conditions which require artificial cooling. Overheating of air can become a problem for gas cylinders and some solvents.

Much is to be gained by the avoidance of glazing exposed to the sun, or by limiting the extent of the glass and ensuring its effective external shading. Internal shading, whilst effective in shielding the occupant from the direct rays of the sun, has only a limited effect in reducing heat gain into the laboratory[35].

In the US it is being postulated that with proper ventilation, lighting, surface finishes, and colour selection, the proper balance for a desirable laboratory working environment can be achieved without windows[36].

The assets in windowless laboratories are increased wall space and complete shielding from the sun and thus a possibly more accurate temperature control.

For heating the convector system seems to be very satisfactory. Radiators are not easy to clean and occasionally occupy valuable space.

Heat emitting equipment such as Bunsen burners, ovens, refrigerators and the like, which, together with the natural heat emission of the personnel, can amount to a

33 Purvis M J: Laboratory Planning. Bailliere Tindall. London 1973, p 20.

34 Pathology Department. Hospital Building Note 15. Department of Health and Social Security. Welsh Office. Revised 1973, p 16.

35 Doe L N: The Servicing of Laboratories. in Symposium on hospital engineering services-present and future. Institution of Heating and Ventilating Engineers. London 1965, p 107–114.

36 Manual for laboratory planning and design. College of American Pathologists. Skokie III. 1977, p 11.

considerable temperature rise in the laboratory. This circumstance has to be taken into consideration during the planning stage.

The need for laboratory ventilation is extensively dependent on the type of work undertaken, the nature and location of the laboratory itself and the country in which it is situated.

Cooling plant should be included in the ventilation system when without excessive number of air changes the internal temperature could be expected to rise more than 3°C above outside temperature in the United Kingdom and in countries which have a climate similar to the United Kingdom's. The temperature difference between entering air and room air should not be more than about 6°C[37].

Primary supply air filters of the dry type, capable of removing at least 90 per cent of all particles down to 5 micron size have been recommended[38].

It has been stated[39] that the risk of accident is greater in a fume cupboard than elsewhere in the laboratory. The fume cupboards can create problems of laboratory ventilation and could even control the required rate of ventilation of the laboratory. Substantially varying air flow or pressure is, in many circumstances, unacceptable.

In fume cupboards for general use there should be a minimum average face air velocity of about 22 m per minute[40]. A system whereby the fume cupboard extract system operates continuously should be adapted. The exhaust fan from all laboratory hoods in which infectious or radioactive materials are processed should be equipped with filters which have a 99 per cent efficiency[41].

Fire extinguishers must be placed so that they can be easily seen and used in case of emergency.

Recording

Many laboratory results are recorded on recorder charts. The pattern of handling and storing records is changing with the introduction of automatic data processing systems.

Automated laboratory reporting systems* transmitting 85 per cent of chemistry and haematology test results to hospital wards are available. Chemistry findings

---

37 Pathology Department. Hospital Building Note 15. Department of Health and Social Security. Welsh Office. Revised 1973, p 33.

38 ibid, p 34.

39 Ferguson W R: Practical laboratory planning, Applied Science Publishers Ltd. London 1973, p 15.

40 Manual for laboratory planning and design. College of American Pathologists. Skokie, III 1977, p 8.

41 ibid

* e g Veteran Administration, Boston Hospital, USA.

from automated instruments go directly to the laboratory computer while haematology and manual chemistry results are introduced into the computer through cathode-ray tubes. Whenever new tests are conducted for a patient, the computer prints out a summary of all laboratory findings to date.

Other systems use reporting by means of transferable labels[42].

torages

Storage space is needed for specimens of blood, urine and tissues; biochemicals requiring temperatures below ambient; chemicals, flammable solvents, alcohol, drugs, poison, radioisotopes; gas cylinders; liquid gases; glassware and glass tubing; plastic items; instruments, electronic and electrical spares; and stationery. Mobile racks and static racking can be used.

It has been recommended to provide adjacent to the laboratory an outdoor flammable goods store, where the major proportion of gases and of highly flammable liquids should be stored[43].

Cold rooms

The chemical pathology, haematology and microbiology departments need cold rooms for storing specimens and media.

Usually two compartments are required to be kept at 4°C and –20°C respectively and to be entered via an air lock.

The 4°C compartment should accommodate a working area for some tissue preparations, cold pactionations etc.

Cold rooms need electricity supplies for compressors which can be water or air cooled. All light switches and sockets must be of the safety type. Light fittings must be covered. For rooms where the temperature falls below –10°C, an alarm system is necessary.

A centrally located control panel should be installed to show the temperature in all cold storages. The panel has to be viewed around the clock.
Local flashing lights have to be provided to indicate when the cold room door is open.

---

42 personal communication: 1978, Bo Norberg, Stockholm.

43 Pathology Department. Hospital Building Note 15. Department of Health and Social Security. Welsh Office. Revised 1973, p 18.

Hot rooms

Hot rooms are primarily needed in the microbiology department for incubating cultures at the temperature of 37°C.

A hot room should be provided with a work table. Local flashing light have to be provided to indicate when the hot room door is open.

Wash-up and handling of glassware

Cleaning and sterilization of glassware can be arranged either in dispersed or centralized units.

In many hospitals a central wash-up facility serving all laboratory departments would provide the most economic service from both capital and revenue aspects[44]. The central wash-up and sterilization units should be located near the microbiology department, which is their major user, in order to minimize staff movements and reduce the possible dangers arising from transport of discarded microbiological cultures for terminal handling[45].

A pressure sterilizer, a hot air oven, a water still, and a pipette washer are located within the glass-washing and sterilization area. Where glassware is washed, catchpots should be fitted under sink units to avoid the pipes being blocked by pieces of broken glass, small tubes and stoppers.

For disintegrating blood clots, which may clog waste lines a waste grinder should be installed under a specific sink[46].

Preparation facilities

Special rooms are needed for assembly of glassware, making media plates — as far as industrially produced media are not used — and dispensing and bulk solutions.

The use of commercially prepared plates is strongly increasing. Most laboratories undertake only a portion of their media preparation depending on cost, quality and fluctuations in demand rate.

The pouring of plates for bacteriological tests should be done on a level table in draught-free conditions. The media pouring room requires balanced mechanical ventilation, with an extract fan providing an even, draught-free and dust-free flow of air

44 Pathology Department. Hospital Building Note 15. Department of Health and Social Security. Welsh Office. Revised 1973, p 18.

45 ibid.

46 Rappoport Arthur E, Taylor Wilbur R and Gaulin Richard P: What the modern laboratory must include and where to put it. 1973, Modern Hospital 121:5:55–63.

over the poured plates while they gel. The rate of flow of the supply air should slightly exceed the capacity of the extract fan[47].

The media preparation room should be close to the central wash-up and sterilizing room in order to share the sterilizing equipment[48].

Cleaners' rooms

In cleaners' rooms cleaning equipment including vacuum cleaners is stored. One room would cover the housekeeping needs for approximately 400 m² to 1,000 m² of floor space, depending on the operative policy and departmental layout.

Hot and cold water and a drainer are needed.

Handling of wastes

Laboratory wastes can be hazardous. Some of the test products from experimental programmes can be extremely dangerous if released without destruction.

All organic laboratory wastes should be incinerated. Space is required in various departments for holding bagged items prior to taking them to the disposal unit.

Chemical waste disposal is usually controlled by codes, although most of these controls seem to be based on hazards to plumbing rather than to people.

Broken glass including hypodermic syringes and needles, should be kept separate from all so called soft waste. Special containers and collection and disposal bins must be provided[49].

Arrangements should be made for the temporary storage of waste, if disposal cannot be carried out within the laboratory facilities.

Switchgear rooms

Clinical laboratory services are heavy users of electricity. For ease of maintenance one walk-in switchgear room for each 1,000 m² has been recommended[50].

---

47 Pathology Department. Hospital Building Note 15. Department of Health and Social Security. Welsh Office. Revised 1973, p 38.

48 ibid, p 17.

49 see also Everett K and Hughes D: A Guide to Laboratory Design. Butterworths. London & Boston 1975, p 118.

50 Pathology Department. Hospital Building Note 15. Department of Health and Social Security. Welsh Office. Revised 1973, p 19.

Emergency power

Emergency power sources[51] should cover the following personnel safety needs: all exit lights, lighting of all corridors, stairwells, switchboards, motor control centres, emergency generators and controls, fume cupboards for hazardous chemical, biological and radiological materials, forced ventilation, where required to sustain life.

Other areas that require emergency power are: areas and rooms for bed patients, blood bank refrigerators, warm rooms and incubators as well as cold rooms and refrigerators containing biological research materials, critical research apparatus, and animal rooms to maintain a minimum ventilation.

Administrative and staff area

The administrative and staff area of the laboratory includes offices for pathologists, technicians, and secretaries and conference rooms.

The best location for laboratory offices is controversial, the alternatives being offices within the laboratory and offices adjoining the laboratory.

A *conference room* for meetings, teaching, demonstrations etc should be planned when its average use will be at least three hours a day. It should have electrical outlets for audio-visual and dimming capabilities, chalkboard and tackboard, book shelves and possibly a rear screen projection. A small storage as well as a kitchenette and a toilet facility would be an asset.

If this room is used for demonstration purposes, a small preparation-work room should be provided. In larger laboratories it may be necessary to provide a small ante-room where the lecturer can prepare for his presentation[52].

Minor *library* facilities are an asset.

Staff *changing facilities* with lockers and toilets, and a staff *lounge* is needed. The lounge should have a tackboard on which employee notices, bulletins, inservice teaching programmes etc can be displayed. A separate lounge for smokers is desirable.

A *retirement room* per every ten woman employees for rest and emergencies is needed[53].

There may be a need for *on-call rooms*.

51 Manual for laboratory planning and design. College of American Pathologists. Skokie, Ill 1977, p 9.

52 ibid, p 11.

53 ibid, p 185.

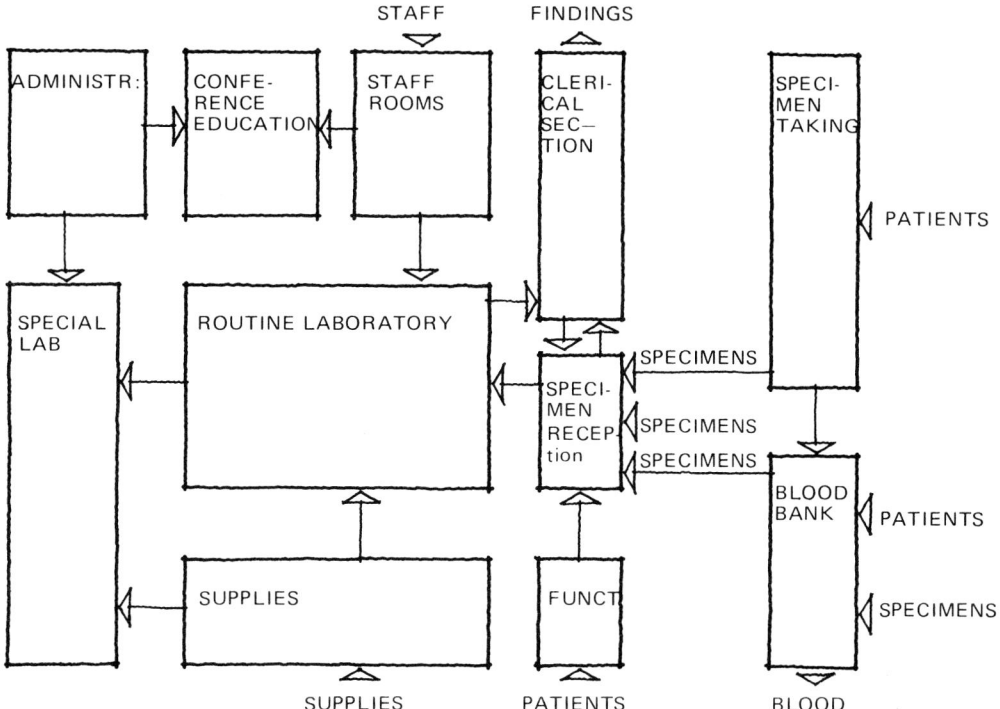

Main functions and primary connections in a clinical chemistry laboratory for 1,200-bed hospitals. All areas proportional. After SPRI.

aboratory for clinical chemistry

In a laboratory for clinical chemistry or chemical pathology department specimens of blood, urine, other body fluids and faeces are examined qualitatively and quantitatively to investigate disease processes.

After receipt of the material — mostly in the mornings — administrative recording and preparation takes place. Urine and faeces specimens are measured, blood centrifuged to separate serum and plasma. The prepared specimens must be identifiable all times.

The aim of the *qualitative* analytic work is to determine the presence or absence of a certain substance in mainly urine and faeces. For these analyses generally only simple instrumentation is required.

33

The major part of analytical work is *quantitative* — the assessment of the level of or or more substances in the specimens, mainly serum or plasma. The number of substances of which the level must be assessed is on the increase.

The result may be indicated directly through the measurement or calculated on the basis of the measurement. A wide range of apparatus from simple mechanical disper ing apparatus to computerized analytical machines is available.

A considerable development of mechanized analyzers has taken place. More than 80 per cent of routine biochemistry could be undertaken on mechanized equipment[54].

Two approaches have been distinct: the continuous flow analysis and the discrete analysis.

In a *continuous flow system* chemical reactions take place in continuously flow air segmented streams, which are pumped through a series of changeable modules. Each modul carries out a different analytic function: sampling the specimen, adding reagents, purification by dialysis, heating, incubation, detection, and recording results. The sample and reagents are mixed in coils under controlled conditions which allow the chemical reaction and subsequent colour development to occur. The colour intensity of the stream is measured in a colorimeter.

Alternative methods of detection include spectrophotometers, flame photometers, fluorimeters, and atomic absorption spectrophotometers.

It is quite likely that development in ion electrodes, radio-immunoassy, gas-liquid-chromotography, mass spectrometry and nuclear magnetic resonance will continue and make available equipment to analyze the concentration of the constituents bot in the plasma and the cells themselves[55].

Analyses can currently be performed at 120 to 160 samples per hour. This sample rate probably will be increased to at least 200 per hour.

In a *discrete analysis system* individual samples are processed in separate tubes. The interaction between successive samples is reduced, which makes it possible to process them at the higher rate about 300 samples per hour.

A request for *emergency analysis* may interfere with the organization of quantitativ analytical work[56]. To avoid this there should be a laboratory consisting of a few tables and spaces kept free of series of specimens which are analyzed with mechanical analyzers.

---

54 see also Pathology Department. Hospital Building Note 15. Department of Health and Social Security. Welsh Office. Revised 1973, p 7.

55 see also Stevens John F: Current trends in automation: a review. 1973, Medical Technology 30:144.

56 see also det bouwkundige opzet van het laboratorium voor klinische chemie. Nationaal Ziekenhuisinstituut. Utrecht 1975, p 93.

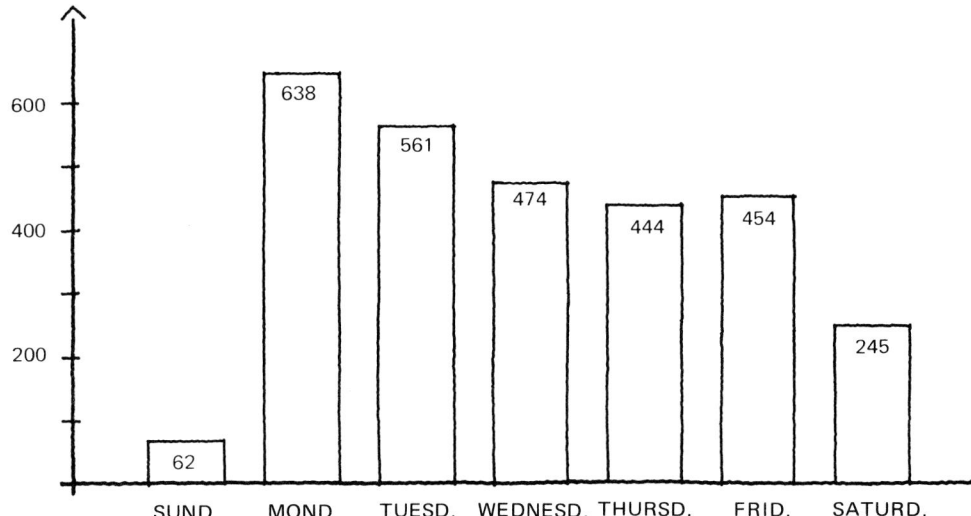

NUMBER OF CASES PER DIEM

The daily work load in clinical chemical laboratories shows considerable variations. A study by G Kaminsky and G Wobbe (1977).

Following rooms can be envisaged in the clinical chemistry laboratory:[57]

Reception area:
> reception office,
> waiting room for ambulant patients,
> cubicles and toilets for specimens, recovery room
> receiving room with fume hoods for urine and faeces samples
> receiving room for blood samples and preparation of plasma/serum with centrifuges which may be housed into separate compartments or cabinets to reduce the noise.

Analytical area:
> emergency laboratory, preferably near the reception area, may contain an automatic multi-channel analyzer, a blood gas analyzer and an analyzer for haematological parameters, haematology and coagulation laboratory

> general clinical chemistry laboratories or sections for flame- and atomic absorption photometry, preferably at outer wall and with fume extracts,
> gas-chromatography with fume cupboards,
> liquid chromatography with fume cupboard

57 personal communication: 1978, Bo Norberg, Stockholm.

protein laboratory (electrophoresis),
lipid laboratory,
enzyme laboratory,
micro-analysis room,
spectrophotometry room,
urine and faeces laboratory with fume cupboard,
isotope laboratory (radioimmunological analyses),
laboratories for chief clinical chemist and biochemist.

Administrative and special area:
office for medical laboratory director and secretary,
office for chief clinical chemist,
office for biochemist,
office for head-analyst,
office for computer operator,
computer room,
laboratory for preparative work including reagents,
balance room,
cold storage room,
storages,
repair workshop,
disposal of refuse,
cleaners' room,
utility room,
staff area.

Laboratory layout must include at least two distinct escape routes from the principal work areas. If one route is obstructed by smoke, an alternative route has to be available[*].

[*] the maximum size of a compartment is specified by local fire regulations.

	WORK TABLE		GERM-FREE INPLANTATION CABINET
	MICROSCOPE TABLE		INCUBATOR
	STAINING TABLE		HOT AIR STERILIZER
	TITRATION TABLE		VERTICAL STERILIZER
	BALANCE TABLE		GLASS WASHING MACHINE
	FUME CUPBOARD		REFRIGERATOR
	LABORATORY TABLE		BLOOD BANK
	AUTOMATIC ANALYZER		WATER STILL
	COMPUTER		CENTRIFUGE
	PRINTER		SHAKING MACHINE

Some symbols of medical chemistry and haematology laboratory equipment designed by Netherlands Hospital Planning Consultants.

Laboratory for haematology, blood bank

Independent haematology laboratories are mostly affiliated to teaching hospitals or other larger scale hospitals. In most hospitals the haematology service is supplied by the laboratory for clinical chemistry.

The investigations of the laboratory for haematology comprise haemoglobin estimation and blood morphology, blood-gas equilibria, haemophilia and other coagulation measurements, morphology and possibly histochemistry of bone marrow, and for blood transfusion service the blood-group serology[58].

137

58 personal communication: 1978, Bo Norberg, Stockholm.

Considerable amount of the work is done while seated. Extensive use is made of microscopes. Mechanical analytical apparatus and auxiliary apparatus is increasingly coming into use[59].

A haematology laboratory needs the following rooms:

> room for haematologist
> routine laboratory for haematologist
> laboratory for morphology
> laboratory for coagulation and electrophoresis
> centrifuge room
> balance room
> cleaners' room
> storages
> staff area
> disposal of refuse

In many cases the laboratory for haematology not only keeps blood in reserve but also controls the bloodtransfusion service *in toto*. In some cases blood transfusion service is considered to be the principal function of the laboratory[60].

The requirements on the *blood banks* are influenced by the level of blood donating and the size of the hospital. The highest level hospitals require annually about 6 l blood per bed, large general hospitals about 5 l per bed and the smaller hospitals about 4 l per bed[61]. The possible influence of intraoperative autotransfusions has not been taken into account.

In a Swedish university hospital** the blood bank delivered in 1976 31 per cent of its volume to thoracic surgery, 14 per cent to the internal medical clinic, 9 per cent to radiotherapy, 7 per cent to general surgery, 6 per cent to orthopaedic surgery, 6 per cent to the paediatric clinic, 5 per cent to neurosurgery, 3 per cent to intensive care, 3 per cent to obstetrics-gynaecology and 2 per cent to the emergency department.

For a blood bank a blood typing room, a blood donating room, a recovery room, a plasma extraction room, a sterilization room and storages are needed as well as a comfortable reception room with waiting room and easily accessible lavatories. Comfortable chairs, table lamps and magazine racks should be provided in the waiting area.

If there is no interview room, the desk for receptionists should be placed so, that the donor can answer questions for the record in relative privacy. Maintenance of donor records requires the use of office space, files and secretarial help.

59 see also det bouwkundige opzet van het laboratorium voor klinische chemie. Nationaal Ziekenhuisinstituut. Utrecht 1975, p 93.

60 see also Heistø Helge: Laboratorium for immunhematologi og medisinsk immunologi — funksjoner. 1976, Sykehuset 39:203–215.

* In Europe they are lowest in Norway — 31 donations per 1000 inhabitants — and highest in Switzerland — 82 donations (Heistø Helge: Laboratorium for immunhematologi og medisinsk immunologi–funksjoner. 1976 1976, Sykehuset 39:203–215).

61 Heistø Helge: Laboratorium for immunhematologi og medisinsk immunologi-funksjoner. 1976, Sykehuset 39:203–215.

** Karolinska Hospital, Stockholm.

There should be an examination room for donors. For privacy the blood donating area should be divided into cubicles of about 10 to 12 m² size. Spotlights for focusing on the work area may be useful. A blood donating procedure takes about 90 minutes.

The processing, typing, and cross matching of blood should be performed in the blood bank area. About 20 m² are required. In order to minimize any risk of error which may have fatal consequences the environment must be undisturbed[62]. Telephones should be muted in this area.

For preparation of blood components about 15 m² are needed. Work with blood plasma need access to a refrigerated room and a freeze room and an ultra clean room, which has high quality air filters.

A centrifuge room requires about 15 m².

After processing the blood is kept in refrigerators or cold storage rooms. The temperature should be kept at 4°C as constantly as possible. Under no circumstances the blood temperature may fall under 0°C or rise above 10°C.

Three refrigerators may be needed: one for the blood bank proper, one for compatibility-tested blood, and one for the night bank. At daytime access to them should be controlled. At night the access should be easy for the departments involved.

Also an administrative room, a doctor's room, stores, also for disposable material and cleaners' rooms are needed.

Preparing for blood transfusion includes the following functions: preparation, cross matching, routine serology and BT development.

Tissue bank

The function of a tissue bank is collection, determination of the basic chemical and biological pattern of the tissue, and storage of tissues and their distribution.

One section of the bank deals with the taking of tissues, the second with their classification and the third with preservation.

62 Pathology Department. Hospital Building Note 15. Department of Health and Social Security. Welsh Office. Revised 1973, p 7.

Medical microbiology laboratory

The bulk of the medical or clinical microbiology work load requires inspection of cultures and the use of microscope for examination of slide preparations.

In general bacteriology culture media are inoculated with specimens and then incubated in incubators or hot air rooms, usually over night. TB cultures have to be incubated for at least six weeks preferably eight weeks[63]. The specimen may be examined under a microscope with or without staining. New instruments such as automatic colony counting equipment and bacterial detection devices using radio-isotopes are beginning to make an entry into microbiology.

A microbiology laboratory may include the following:

general microbiology laboratory
special bacteriology room
virology laboratory
immunology laboratory
media preparation and plate pouring room, autoclaves
incubator room
cold room
serology room
TB bacteriology test room
chief technician's room
consultant's office
consultant's laboratory
dishwashing room
sterilization room
room for destruction of infected material
storages
apparatus room
cleaners' room
staff area.

As the medical microbiology section is the mainstay of hospital infection control, an office and a *laboratory for the hospital hygiene officer* should be included.

Conditions in the laboratory section pose an infection hazard to the personnel and a contamination hazard to the specimens. When discussing the use of safety equipment in microbiological laboratories, the fume cupboard is often identified as the most important item, which, of course, cannot substitute for good laboratory trainin

63 see also Pathology Department. Hospital Building Note 15. Department of Health and Social Security. Welsh Office. Revised 1973, p 17.

When the use of open bench, an exhaust-ventilated fume cupboard and a unidirectional flow cabinet for the microbiological examination of blood were compared, the highest contamination rates were found in the unidirectional flow cabinet, the lowest on the open bench. As the safety factors involved in working next to a Bunsen flame make the working on an open bench unacceptable, the use of exhaust-ventilated safety hood was recommended[64].

Usually two laboratory bench heights are used: for sitting personnel 0.75 m and for standing 0.9 m[65].

Sit-down areas for microscopy work should be ample enough to provide space also for lamps, slides, racks, other accessories and writing materials. Pull-out drawers or overhead shelves are needed for storages. Gas and electric outlets, vacuum supply and a staining sink equipped with a nozzle for washing slides are necessary. The benches should be open underneath for leg room. The microscopy work area should not be compromised for a considerable amount of technician time is spent here[66].

The fluorescent microscopy area must be enclosed and completely free of light. If all the preparations for fluorescent microscopy are performed in this area, there should also be stand-up benches, a sink, storage, refrigeration and incubation facilities. Gas and electric outlets are necessary[67].

UV-light has been recommended to be used during night over TB laboratory benches[68].

Fume cupboards are used also in the TB test room, where the bacteriology tests are carried out on sputa, urine and pus and the infectious material from the specimens may be dissipated into the atmosphere[69].

A complete *virology department* probably is practical only if it provides about 1,000 bed coverage[70].

The area to be used must be completely enclosed and traffic-free, and protect workers from infection and culture specimens from contamination.

64 Spencer R C and Savage M A: Laboratory contamination of blood cultures. 1975, Journal of Clinical Pathology 28:980–982.

65 see also Jensen Aase Marum: Laboratorium for medisinsk mikrobiologi-mikrobionomens syn. 1976, Sykehuset 39:264–267.

66 Manual of laboratory planning and design. College of American Pathologists. Skokie III 1977, p 36.

67 ibid

68 see also Jensen Aase Marum: Laboratorium for medisinsk mikrobiologi – mikrobionomens syn. 1976, Sykehuset 39:264–267.

Manual of laboratory planning and design. College of American Pathologists. Skokie III 1977, p 35.

69 see also Pathology Department. Hospital Building Note 15. Department of Health and Social Security. Welsh Office. Revised 1973, p 7.

70 Manual of laboratory planning and design. College of American Pathologists. Skokie III 1977, p 52.

The area should be well ventilated and air-conditioned. A negative pressure would not let the infectious particles to escape into the surrounding environment.

Fume cupboards must be provided. Ultraviolet light sources must be available[71].

Microscopy techniques use light microscopy, fluorescent microscopy, and electronic microscopy.

Laboratory counter heights should accommodate microscopy work as well as stand-up work.

The smallest immunology section, which is concerned with the diagnosis of disease by the detection of antigens of pathogenic organisms, particularly micro-organisms, requires a basic module: about 3.6 m of bench space, a centrifuge, a refrigerator, a 1.2 m table and a 2.4 m desk[72].

In this area precipitation, complement fixation, and agglutination is carried out. In addition following activities may be included: fluorescence microscopy, radioisotope work, immunodiffusion and immunoelectrophoresis, which spacewise require another module.

No recirculation of the laboratory air is allowed. The exhaust air from laboratories should be filtered. There should be negative pressure in the exhaust duct, which should be fabricated from noncorrosive materials[73]. In order to maintain air pressure differentials, all doors should have automatic closing devices. Doors in potentially contaminated areas should be provided with glass viewing-panels and plastic diaphragms to improve visual and oral communication while limiting traffic into the rooms[74].

Washbasins should be easily accessible.

Drinking water for personnel should be available from a foot-operated fountain, preferably outside of any potentially contaminated work area. Water for the drinking fountain should be supplied from a single line with no other connections and the line should be connected to the water supply before the back flow preventor[75].

It is felt[76] that in microbiology laboratories handling more than 100,000 requests a year, in spite of the comparative expense of computing time, some form of computerized reporting is desirable if not essential.

---

71 Manual of laboratory planning and design. College of American Pathologists. Skokie, Ill 1977, p 52.

72 ibid, p 44.

73 Rappoport Arthur E, Taylor Wilbur R and Gaulin Richard P: What the modern laboratory must include and where to put it. 1973, Modern Hospital 121:5:55–63.

74 Sansone Eric B and Slein Milton W: Application of the microbiological safety experience to work with chemical carcinogens. 1976, American Industrial Hygiene Association Journal 37:711–720.

75 ibid

76 Andrews H J and Vickers M: An assessment of one year of computer-assisted microbiology reporting at Charing Cross Hospital. 1974, Journal of Clinical Pathology 27:185–191.

Regardless of the microbiology section's size, it should be enclosed and completely isolated, so that it is not entered by the non-laboratory personnel.

All contaminated items must be disposed of in a manner that precludes dissemination of microorganisms. Contaminated tubes should be autoclaved. Petri dishes and other disposable contaminated materials should be disposed in bags in garbage cans.
The bags should be incinerated. The disposal area, about 7 m² in size, should be outside the work flow of the laboratory.

Engineering support zones should be located outside of the potentially contaminated laboratory areas together with clean offices, conference rooms, etc., with shower and changing rooms placed in transition zones between the laboratories and clean areas. Access of maintenance personnel to ducts and utility lines that supply the laboratories should be via pipe chases in the walls adjacent to relatively protected corridors and via the attic or basement to minimize possible exposure of personnel and equipment to aerosols. All points at which utility lines traverse laboratory walls, ceilings and floors should be carefully sealed to prevent the transport of aerosols from one laboratory to another or to clean areas[77].

77 see also Sansone Eric B and Slein Milton W: Application of the microbiological safety experience to work with chemical carcinogenes. 1976, American Industrial Hygiene Association Journal 37:711–720.

Clinical physiology laboratory

In most cases the patients to be examined in the clinical physiology laboratory are ambulant. Separate waiting areas for in- and out-patients are preferred.

Undressing cubicles and resting rooms are needed.

Multifunctional examination rooms are to be recommended.

Most frequently are examined cardiovascular functions, pulmonary functions, blood circulation, gastroenterological functions, neurophysiological functions, auditive functions, phoniatric functions, and vestibular functions.

Cardiological examinations

Electrocardiography (ECG) constitutes the major part of investigations of cardiovascular functions. The electrocardiogram is a record of the electrical phenomena associated with muscular activity of the heart, plotting voltage variations against time.

The electrocardiographic unit requires rooms with a space for a bed or stretcher to perform the ECG recording on a patient, recumbent or seated in a chair. Often cardiograms are repeated immediately after exercise either over a two-step staircase device, or on an ergometric bicycle. Simultaneously with the ECG could also the gas exchange studies be performed.

The ECG room should be soundproof. A shower after an exercise cardiogram is an asset.

Telephone outlets must be in the office or desk area to convey ECG data from the laboratory to a physician's office for interpretation and reporting. Space must be set aside in the office for processing electrocardiographic strips, for copying and for entering results in the patient's record[78].

The *cardiac catheterization room* containing radiographic equipment must be shielded, eg with lead. The diagnostic radiographic unit includes a fluoroscope and an image intensifier, capable of bi-plane cine recording or a videotape permitting live transmission to monitors elsewhere. There should be a separate room for pressure tracings with catheters in place and monitoring equipment.

Areas should be provided for the X ray equipment, preparation of catheters; immediate gas analysis[79], and scrubbing and gowning of personnel.

78 Manual for laboratory planning and design. College of American Pathologists. Skokie III 1977, p 30.

79 Harrell George T: Planning Medical Center Facilities. The Pennsylvania State University Press. University Park and London 1974, p 113.

Physiological data obtained by a noninvasive technique might open an entirely new field in the cardiovascular physiology[80].

linical neurophysiology, pulmonary function laboratory, gastroenterology

Recording of bioelectrical activity from the brain (EEG — electroencephalography), nerves (ENG — electroneurography) and muscles (EMG — electromyography) requires very high amplification. The examination procedure is therefore sensitive for electrical interference from the environment. No other instruments, including electric typewriters, clocks or any other devices that cause line voltage fluctuations[81] should be connected to EEG lines.

Neurophysiology has required rooms with shielding built into the walls, ceiling, floor and doors. Recent recording devices are generally less sensitive concerning external interference[82]. The Faraday cage is no longer the prerequisite for sufficient neurophysiological recordings. Grounded shielding of all wires and cables from mains is, however, necessary.

Electroencephalograms are taken frequently over long periods of time, as in studies of sleep patterns, and the records are very large.

The EEG room has to be in a quiet area. There should be no noises so that the patient may be at complete rest and even sleep. The surroundings should be pleasant and conductive to rest and relaxation.

The introduction of computerized tomography has demonstrated no change in the frequency of EEG testing[83].

A separate shielded and grounded room should be provided for recording electric muscular activities.

About 12 to 15 m² is needed for the technician to process EEG strips to be prepared for charting. There should be extensive file cabinets.

The pulmonary function laboratory uses bulky breathing equipment and a treadmill.

80 see also Irisawa Hiroshi and Hirakawa Senri: Evaluation of Cardiac Functions Through Non-Invasive Technique. 1977, Japanese Circulation Journal 41:476.

81 Manual for laboratory planning and design. College of American Pathologists. Skokie III 1977, p 31.

82 personal communication: 1977, Ilmar Sulg, Oulu, Finland.

83 Knaus William A, Schroeder Steven A and Davis David O: Impact of New Technology: The CT Scanner. 1977, Medical Care 15:533–542.

In the gastroenterological laboratory specimens are collected by means of esophago-scopes, gastroscopes, rectoscopes etc. Fluoroscoping should be available. A toilet must be provided.

Retention of the original graphic recording for archival purposes is the most convenient method of storing as long as there is no problem of space.

Continuous-flow and single sheet microfilming provides a convenient method to store compactly laboratory documentation, which can be viewed on a microfilm reader[84]. By means of continuous electrostatic copying or by other printing methods a complete reproduction of the originals can be obtained from the microfilm.

84 see also Handbook of electroencephalography and clinical neurophysiology. vol 3. part B. ed by I D Frost Jr and J S Barlow. Elsevier Scientific Publishing Company. Amsterdam 1976, p 3 B:13.

Clinical histopathology department

The study object for histopathology or morbid anatomy is the diseased human body. Histopathology is the study of the micro-structure of diseased tissues.

A bench with adjacent sink and slop-hopper is required for *dissection of specimens.* Space is needed for (automatic) *processing of specimens,* block making, moduling, trimming and note taking.

There may be up to four cutting positions with microtomes, waterbaths and hotplates and areas for routine and special stains.

Urgent specimens from the operation department may be frozen and sections cut, if this service is not available within the operation department. Two cryostats of freezing microtomes are needed.

Stores for formalin specimens and for morbid anatomy slides and paraffin blocks are needed.

For gross specimens space should be provided to permit storage for two weeks[85]. Some laboratories store specimens for a longer period.

Clinical pathology department must have excellent ventilation.

An office for the chief technician is an advantage.

The pathologist's office should provide seating space for four other people. There should be room for files, dictation equipment, a microscope, and bookshelves. Autopsy files should be kept permanently, autopsy materials for at least ten years: the more recent ones in the laboratory area, after a year in a remote area[86].

In the *cytology* sub-department following units may be found: routine methods laboratory, special methods laboratory, technician's office, technician's laboratory, punction rooms, examination rooms, waiting room, patient lavatories, and telephones.

One person can stain and mount about 150 smears in an eight-hour day, a cytology technician can screen approximately 60 smears[87].

General purpose rooms and administration include administration rooms, clerical staff rooms, cloak rooms, reception-registration, filing*, medical library, general

---

85 Manual for laboratory planning and design. College of American Pathologists. Skokie III 1977, p 34.

86 ibid, p 49.

87 ibid, p 30.

* cytology files and slide files should be retained for 20 years.

stores, store for chemicals, store for glassware, staff changing rooms, showers, staff lavatories, staff lounge and cleaners' room.

Transmission electron microscopy

Transmission electron microscopy is considered to be a necessary complementary method to diagnostic pathology. It is to study the ultrastructure of various cells in a tissue from which conclusions regarding disease process may be deduced.

Not every hospital may have request for ultrastructure studies regularly. Due to many limitations and current fragmented knowledge on ultrastructural pathology positive answers cannot always be expected. There will be occasions in which TEM studies will give limited answers only, or no answers at all[88].

In the TEM unit several rooms should be set aside for tissue preparation and film processing.

Fume cupboards, refrigerators and electric ovens are needed.

An electron microscope does not tolerate building vibrations. It requires air conditioning.

A library of histology and ultrastructure of the cell is most useful.

88 see also Hoffmann E O: Diagnostic Electron Microscopy: Uses and Limitations. 1978, The Journal of the Louisiana State Medical Society 130:119–121.

RADIOLOGY SERVICES

In the medical diagnostic system, the radiologist supported by technicians, physicians and file clerks, responds to the inflow of patients and patient information, which includes radiographs. His activities include selection* and maintenance of equipment, control of radiation hazards, and administration of radiology services.

Nearly 90 per cent of all patients are believed to require sooner or later the services of radiology[1].

Two basic types of diagnostic imaging — transmission type and emission type — are available.

X ray and ultrasound units fall under the category of transmission imaging because their images are created by X rays or sound waves transmitted** from the machine into the body.

Emission imaging involves giving a patient a dose of radioisotopes and recording the distribution of radiation of gamma rays emitted from the radioactive material in the patient's body by gamma or scintillation cameras.

Radiology services consist of units for general diagnostic-skeletal, digestive, chest, and urinary systems; angiography; mammography; thermography; sonography; nuclear medicine; computed tomography; and radiation therapy.

A review of these services will remind primary care physicians and the public of the astronomic growth and diversification of the available services[2].

In its first 75 years diagnostic radiology — roentgen, nucleonics — progressed to the third largest clinical speciality in teaching hospitals in terms of the number of physicians employed[3]. The total number of X ray apparatus in the hospitals all over the world[4] was in 1976 about 160,000.

However, reliable estimates suggest that about 30 per cent of all diagnostic X ray units are out of order in many countries at any given moment. Government-operated

---

* In 1973, the British National Health Service spent approximately 17.1 million dollars on the purchase of diagnostic X ray equipment. This figure had increased by some 20 per cent per year for the past few years.

The choice of apparatus had often been arbitrary, since little objective information had been available upon which a rational choice could have been made (Assessment of diagnostic X ray equipment. 1974, The British Journal of Radiology 47:205).

There should be advice available for acquisition of apparatus for new departments and replacement of existing units to eliminate unnecessary expenditures that may be redundant within the foreseeable future.

1 also Terry William G: The architect, the doctor and the hospital. A paper prepared for the International Symposium on The Planning of Departments of Radiology and Imaging Sciences. Lisbon, May 1978.

** Examples of X ray transmission are common chest X rays — general radiography — and an upper or lower gastrointestinal tract test — fluoroscopy.

2 see also Osmond Jr John D, King Richard L, De Marco Victor J, Klein Howard J, Farmer James P, Storaasli John P and Sykora Glenn F: Radiology and the Primary Care Physician. 1977, The Ohio State Medical Journal 73:389–395.

3 Maurer H J and Soila P: Future of diagnostic radiology. 1975, Annals of Clinical Research 7:295–300.

4 Junod A: Le Scanner. 1976, Veska 40:326–327.

maintenance and repair services are, very often, insufficient to cope with the problem. This, compounded with the maldistribution of personnel and facilities, accounts for the fact that two-thirds of the world population do not have access even to the most elementary radiodiagnostic services[5].

In the western world about 500 examinations *per annum* are made per 1,000 inhabitants. The examination frequencies vary widely both nationwise* and hospitalwise.

A 5 to 15 per cent *per annum* increase in the work load of X ray departments in western countries was observed for some time. Although it has been expected that the volume of X ray work is to increase by 10 per cent *per annum*, the expansion of the number of conventional radiological examinations has not grown. It is very unlikely to grow at the rates earlier predicted[6].

There is obviously no international standard growth rate as the growth resp decrease rates of radiological examinations in some European countries indicate[7]:

Denmark	1970–76	6 — 8 per cent
Finland	1972–75	1 per cent
France	1965–75	10 per cent
Germany	1975–76	decreasing
Italy	1970–76	8.5 per cent
Netherlands	1972–75	4 — 6 per cent
Spain	1970–76	13 per cent
Switzerland	1970–75	0 per cent
United Kingdom	1970–76	3 per cent

In the US during the last five years the classical X ray examinations have been reduced by 20 per cent[8].

Ultrasound has taken over from conventional radiology in quite a few instances. Isotopes and thermography have become adjuncts to conventional radiological examinations. Computer-assisted tomography — CT —, synonyms computed transverse axial scanning — CAT —, automatic computerized transverse axial scanner — ACTA — and EMI scanning, and xero-radiography have replaced some methods of the X ray examination.

---

5   Kaprio L A: Medical technology: blessing or problem? 1977, Acta Hospitalia 17:301–311.

*   In 1976 the examination workload per 1,000 population was in Finland 1,200, Canada 890, US 700, Scandinavia 640 to 700, Netherlands 525, UK 500. In many countries the workload varies between 2 and 400.

6   also Kormano M and Tähti E: Follow-up of ISPRAD I: The past four years in retrospect. Second international symposium on the planning of radiology departments. Philadelphia, September 1976.

7   C B A J Puijlaert cited by Martins da Silva: Modifications and growth rate of the radiology department of the Hospital de d'Estefania. A paper prepared for International Symposium on the Planning of Departments of Radiology and Imaging Sciences. Lisbon, May 1978.

8   Olivia Luigi: Basic functional concepts in planning of image forming systems departments. International Symposium on the Planning of Departments of Radiology and Imaging Sciences. Lisbon, May 1978.

Also the cost of equipment e g in US diagnosis facilities — about 40 to 50 per cent of the world market — indicates that conventional X rays are on the decrease[9]:

	1972	1973	1974	1975	1976
Conventional X ray	86%	86%	80%	69%	57%
C T scanners	—	—	2%	12%	23%
Sonography, nuclear medicine, thermography	14%	14%	18%	19%	20%

The development of computer-assisted tomography has been seen as the most significant advancement in the X ray field since the discovery of the X ray. With astonishing clarity details of morphology previously seen only at necropsy or in anatomy atlases are revealed[10]. Although conventional medical roentgenography is valuable in evaluating tissues with large differential densities, it cannot clearly distinguish most soft-tissue structures, and displays overlapping, superimposed shadows of the area under investigation[11].

In conventional X ray, the transmitted X ray is recorded on sheet film; in computer assisted tomography scanners, the transmission is picked up by a detector and the information is reconstructed by the computer on a video screen. A hand-copy reproduction can be made with Polaroid or sheet film.

Because of the non-invasive natur of the CT scan, outpatients as well as very ill patients are being studied by CT with increasing frequency.

All CT scanners are axial. Longitudinal CT scanners may not be needed, because once the computer receives the data for a section of the body, it can reconstruct longitudinal-slice images for that part of the body.

A scanner requires 4 to 20 seconds for each head scan.

To date already four so–called generations of CT scanners have been introduced*. It will most likely be possible to reduce scanning times to less than 1 second

9   Combee B: Beheersing van de medische technologie. Visie vanuit de industrie. 1977, Acta Hospitalia 17:343–356.

10 Ter-Pogossian Michel M: The Challenge of Computed Tomography. 1976, American Journal of Roentgenology 127:1–2.

11 Ledley Robert S: Introduction to computerized tomography. 1976, Computers in Biology and Medicine 6:239–246.

*   In 1976 about 20 firms had manufactured 19 CT models, additional 6 prototypes were being developed. The total number of CTs and similar equipment in the hospitals of the world was less than 600.

    In the spring of 1977, there were 587 computer-assisted tomography (CT) scanners operating in the United States only. Almost certainly the one thousandth CT in the US commenced operation some time during the first half of 1978.

    According to Spri (Spri informerar 4/78) in March 1978 there were 4.4 CTs in use per one million inhabitants in the US, 2.6 in Japan, 1.6 in Sweden, 1.5 in Norway and the FRG, 0.9 in the UK, 0.6 in Denmark, 0.2 in Finland and France.

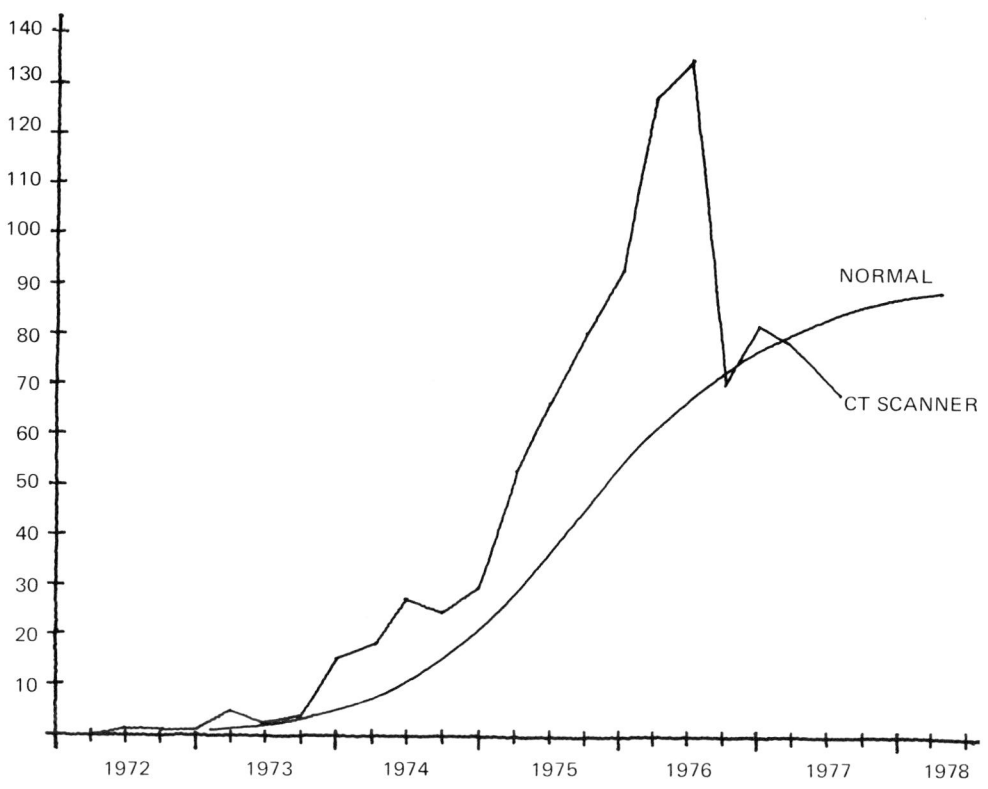

CT scanner spreading — quarterly order units — in the US has been markedly different from the curve of normal expectations for new medical technology. A study by J Lloyd Johnson Associates (1977).

— scanning times of 10 to 100 milliseconds have been mentioned — by using a rotating X ray source and a circular or arcuate arrangement of 300 to 600 stationary or co-rotating detectors. This would largely eliminate the movement artifacts caused in chest and abdominal tomograms by respiration and peristalsis. The limitations to whole-body tomography in the trunk region would be greatly reduced[13].

Computer assisted tomography may be expected to make rapid strides when it becomes possible to demonstrate anatomical structures in three dimensions and measure them; when truly quantitative data on material densities and chemical compositions can be produced; or when the resolving power in time is sufficiently increased for

13 see also Computer Tomography. Editorial. 1976, The New Zealand Medical Journal 84:487–488.

Anliker M: Current and Future Aspects of Biomedical Engineering. 1977, Triangle 16:129–140.

Computer-Tomographie: lieb und teuer. Neue Zürcher Zeitung, May 23, 1978.

the dynamics of the heart and the circulatory system to come within the scope of investigation[14].

CT can reduce total medical care costs by decreasing the number of examinations needed, expediting diagnosis on an outpatient basis, and reducing the need for exploratory surgery.

In spite of this optimism, it has been said that although each year will no doubt bring us closer to machines with fewer artifacts, less patient motion, lower cost, more flexible display, more rapid reconstruction, and lower patient dose, certain laws of physics will always apply. The ideal machine will never be achieved[15].

The current potential and practical applications of CT technique have been summarized[16] as follows.

Computer assisted tomography of the body has specific and expanding applications. It does not replace other diagnostic imaging methods but narrows and complements their applications. Although radionuclide scanning is proving more valuable in screening for the spread of malignant disease and in studying physiologic processes, CT appears to be proving itself as the method of choice for depicting anatomic detail and tumour localization. The chief uses of ultrasound, with its unique ability to image in the longitudinal plane, are for evaluation of pregnant patients; for study of cardiac disease; and, together with CT, for differentiation of solid and cystic masses and for needle biopsies. Angiography is still necessary for detailed study of blood vessels and lymphatics.

Computer-assisted axial tomography has revolutionized diagnostic neuroradiology, but for many abdominal conditions ultrasound scans are as accurate and substantially more cost-effective than CAT body scans[17].

Computer assisted tomography of the chest and abdomen has become available also to the paediatric medical community.

The only preparation used in children before undergoing a CT is the familiarization with the examination room and equipment. The machinery has to be broadly explained to the child in an attempt to allay as much anxiety as possible. Prescan sedation has been necessary with the younger children, but general anaesthesia has not been required[18].

---

14 Anliker M: Current and Future Aspects of Biomedical Engineering. 1977, Triangle 16:129–140.

15 Crowe John K: Scanning and Planning. 1977, Mayo Clinic Proceedings 52:399–400.

16 Carter Barbara L and Ignatow Stanley B: Computed body tomography — how useful is it? 1978, Postgraduate Medicine 63:5:66–80.

17 Baker Christopher and Way Lawrence W: Clinical Utility of CAT Body Scans. 1978, The American Journal of Surgery 136:37–43.

18 Vinocur Charles D, Dinn W Martin and Dudgeon David L: Computed Tomographic Scanning in Children. 1977, Journal of Pediatric Surgery 12:847–855.

The complexity of paediatric diseases and the character of infant care will necessitate a hospital CT practice both for paediatric inpatients and outpatients rather than an isolated CT diagnostic unit. It is likely that for a paediatric hospital or division with over 100 beds, a total-body CT system can be utilized full time[19].

The acceptance of CT by the radiologic community has been immediate, unreserved, and overwhelming, even without well documented proof of its clinical usefulness[20] and radiation risks.

The patient's exposure to radiation was initially estimated to be less than with a conventional series of X rays. In 1977, it was known that multiple head scans with the use of contrast agents may give as much as 10 R to the patient and it was believed[21] that the whole body scanner may give a much larger dose than this, which in itself is an enormous dose.

Two serious problems have arisen since the advent of CT scanning. First is the enormous cost of these machines, and second the cost and effectiveness of service and maintenance contracts[22].

The devices now under development are technologically impressive.

They provide information about the living body — in health and in disease — that doctors could never get otherwise, even with C T scanners.

The technique is called emission tomography, to distinguish it from transmission tomography, which uses X rays.

Also under development are machines that produce images not of the shapes of organs but of the spatial distribution of a given metabolic process or chemical reaction.

For example, where a conventional X ray film or C T scan might show only the contours of a normal brain, one of the new devices could produce a picture showing that the brain was failing to carry out a necessary metabolic process. The image would appear as a cross section with gray tones varying according to the rate of the metabolic process under study.

Although many doctors see great potential in positron emission tomography, one barrier to its spread is the cost of a cyclotron — just over $ 1 million. A machine to detect and construct the image can cost an additional $ 800,000.

19 American Academy of Pediatrics. Committee on Radiology: Computerized Tomography: A Perspective in the Pediatric Patient. 1977, Pediatrics 59:305–308.

20 Ter-Pogossian Michel M: The Challenge of Computed Tomography. 1976, American Journal of Roentgenology 127:1–2.

21 Wright J T: Computerized tomography: the greatest discovery since Röntgen rays? 1977, The Medical Journal of Australia 1:425–426.

22 Pevsner Paul H: Computed tomograph: the problem of service and maintenance. 1977, Southern Medical Journal 70:1029–1030.

And given today's increasing skepticism over whether extremely expensive medical technology is worthwhile, many authorities on health care are coming to believe that just because something is technologically possible does not mean that it is necessarily in the patient's interest*.

In *xeroradiography* the roentgen film is replaced by a plate of aluminium covered with a layer of amorphous selenium which is electrostatically charged. When roentgen photon are absorbed within the layer, a local reduction of the charge takes place in the exposed area. The image relief within the radiation is transformed into a charge relief visualized by electrostatically charged, coloured plastic particles and specially prepared paper.

Xerograms are characterized by a remarkable contrast, especially of soft tissues. Its best known application is in the diagnosis of breast tumours, but it is used also in direct assess of profilo-plasty in maxillo-facial surgery and to gain radioanatomical data of the nose prior to rhinoplasty[23].

The building and equipping of a radiological department is probably the most costly of all hospital departments[24]. In 1975 the diagnostic radiology departments represented more than 5 per cent of all US hospital expenses[25]. Of all medical equipment cost in a hospital, the share of radiology may be as much as 40 to 50 per cent[26].

In teaching hospitals diagnostic radiology may consume some 10 per cent of the yearly hospital budget[27].

Of the total running cost for the radiology department the share of the staff is about 60 per cent and of the technical equipment about 40 per cent. Other cost factors are negligible[28].

It has been stated that for an improved radiology service emphasis should be directed towards the design of the management system and scheduling techniques, and not the

* Rensberger Boyce: Nuclear Medicine in U.S. Devices Allow View of Body Functions. International Herald Tribune. November 16, 1978.

23 see also Le Pasteur J, Sarazin J and Tristant H: La Xérographie. 1976, Annales de Chirurgie Plastique 21:169–174.

24 see also Gajjat R D: Physical planning. in The Planning of Radiotherapy Departments. ed by T J Deeley. British Journal of Radiology. Special Report 12. London 1976, p 13.

25 Radiology expenses. 1976, Hospitals 50:11:41.

26 Olsson Olle: Position of diagnostic radiology in a Hospital. International Symposium on the Planning of Departments of Radiology and Imaging Sciences. Lisbon, May 1978.

27 Soila P and Maurer H J: Future of diagnostic radiology. XIII Congreso Internacional de Radiologia. Madrid, Octubre 1973, Excerpta Medica. Amsterdam, Princeton, London, Geneva, Tokyo 1973, p 22.

28 Oberhofer Franziska: Analyse der Leistungs- und Kostenstrukturen von Röntgenabteilungen in Akut-Krankenhäusern. 1973, Das Krankenhaus 65:2:57–67.

staff and/or facilities[29]. In this statement the role of functional and anticipatory planning of this most costly service rendering unit has been grossly underestimated.

For securing a safe planning ground, realistic frequencies of examinations in a planned hospital have to be established. It is necessary to know the amount and the types of examinations to be adapted, the length of time of these examinations and the hours during which the diagnostic facilities can be made available.

The strong limitations which traditional working hours have impressed on radiology departments have been criticized. In Finland the concept of 1 1/2 shifts a day or 2 shifts a day has been found to be very acceptable. This concept contains a great cost benefit as the construction and equipment expenses are reduced. A department may be designed to operate to the capacity of an eight-hour shift. Some of the future work expansion can be met by extended hour coverage.

Depending on the character of the examinations, the X ray room capacities vary between 5,000 to 20,000 examinations *per annum.*

In Sweden an examination room has been used averagely 1,300 hours a year[30]. This would mean 5,200 to 13,000 annual examinations per room.

In Scotland[31], for planning purposes, the number of annual examinations per room is 7,500.

In the Netherlands, the usual estimate has been 5,000 to 6,000 examinations per room and year. The average is expected to go down to 5,000[32].

If the proportion of neuro-radiological and vascular examinations is large, the normal output of the examination rooms is reduced to between one third and a half.

In the US the proportion of out- and in-patients in many general hospitals has been two to one[33]. In Sweden, the proportion is roughly the same: 70 per cent of the investigations are made on ambulatory patients, 30 per cent on hospitalized patients. 14 per cent of all investigations are emergencies[34]. In Brazil, 79 per cent of investigations are made on out-patients, 21 per cent on in-patients[35].

---

29 Lev B et al: Patient flow analysis and the delivery of radiology service. 1976, Socio-Economic Planning Sciences 10:159–166.

30 Röntgendiagnostikavdelningar — lokalprogram, planutformning m m. Spri råd 5.6. Stockholm 1972, p 15.

31 Western Regional Hospital Board, Research and Development Unit: Organisation & Design of Radiodiagnostic Departments. Stencil. (Glasgow), January 1973, p 6.

32 Puijlaert C B A J: Factors determining planning of X ray departments. International Symposium on the Planning of Departments of Radiology and Imaging Sciences. Lisbon, May 1978.

33 see also Lindheim Roslyn: Uncoupling the Radiology System. Hospital Research and Educational Trust. Chicago 1971, p 72.

34 Olsson Olle: Position of diagnostic radiology in a hospital. International Symposium on the Planning of Departments of Radiology and Imaging Sciences. Lisbon, May 1978.

35 de Magalhaes Alvaro and Kisil Marcos: Planning in Macro-Radiology Departments. International Symposium on the Planning of Departments of Radiology and Imaging Sciences. Lisbon, May 1978.

The knowledge of the total number of examinations to be carried out does not automatically include information on space and procedure time requirements and a thoughtless reliance on the basic figure may result in grave planning and designing errors.

Some average values[36], which in itself may represent considerable variations, would illuminate the point. Thoracical examinations represent about 26 per cent of the total work load of an X ray department, whilst accounting for about 9.5 per cent of the examination time; skeletal 38 resp 26.5 per cent; kidney, gall bladder 6 resp 15 per cent; angiography 3 resp 12.5 per cent; GIs 14 resp 18.5 per cent; tomography 3 resp 4 per cent, neuroradiology 7 resp 7.5 per cent.

In Sweden, a simplified formula has been used for calculation of the number of personnel needed for the different tasks[37]: the basic unit, a work team consisting of five people — one radiologist, one radiographer, one nurse's aid, one film technician and one secretary — has a capacity of 5,000 to 7,500 patient examinations per year. This corresponds with 100 to 150 examinations per week in a 40 hour week or 20 to 30 work-days of 8 hours.

When estimating the capacities, the duration of all the main components: diagnosis, examination, and discussion have to be considered very carefully.

At a teaching hospital the workload should not exceed 5,000 examinations/year/radiologist. At general hospitals the number is usually 8,000 to 12,000, but may be as high as 18,000*.

In Scotland 2.5 radiographers are needed per one X ray room, as well as 0.3 to 0.5 technicians[38]. One nurse is needed per 6 rooms and supporting nurse staff per 7 to 10 rooms. The clerical-secretarial needs are not defined.

There may be changes for this capacity calculation as 10 to 12 hours usage time for the equipment has rightfully been required.

The staffing aspects may become influenced by some studies which indicate that a considerable amount of the staff time is unproductive: 15.5 per cent of the radiologist's time, 29.1 per cent of the radiographer's time, 31.7 per cent of the nurse's time and 25.9 per cent of the secretary's time[39].

---

36 personal communication: 1978, Lothar Ackermann, Lisbon.

37 Holm T: A simplified model for dimensioning of personnel at roentgendiagnostic departments. International symposium on the planning of radiological departments. Otaniemi, Finland, August 1972.

* There are wide variations in the averages of various countries. According to C B A J Puijlaert (Expansion of radiodiagnosis and diminishing workloads. International Symposium on the Planning of Departments of Radiology and Imaging Sciences. Lisbon, May 1978) the average is 7,000 in Italy, 6,000–8,000 in Sweden, 8,000 in the US, 15,000 in the UK, and 18,000 in Spain.

38 McCreadie D W A and Montgomery R: Staffing of radiodiagnostic departments. International symposium on the planning of radiological departments. Otaniemi, Finland. August 1972.

39 Wobbe G and Kaminsky G: Datenerfassung in der Röntgenabteilung eines Krankenhauses mit Hilfe von messenden Zeitstudien und Multimomentaufnahmen. 1978, Krankenhaus Umschau 47:443–446.

There is no reliable criterion for determining the appropriate number of CT scanners.

It has been predicted that by the end of 1980 general hospitals with 500 or more beds would have at least one scanner in operation, many would have two or more[40]. By 1985, EMI believes, about 6,000 computer-assisted scanners would be needed worldwide[41].

It has also been estimated that a hospital with more than 300 beds would require a CT. A hospital with 8 to 10 X ray rooms would need one CT, with 12 rooms — two, with 14 to 20 rooms — three, and with 24 to 36 rooms — four[42].

A CAT room should take 2,500 brain scans or 1,500 whole body scans a year[43].

A 12 to 14 hours a day running time has been recommended, requiring a staff of 4.5 persons[44].

Data to enable a profound discussion of the CT's cost effectiveness are not yet available, although there are some indications that the length of stay of the patients to be diagnosed in the hospital is shortened.

Reports have been centered on the accuracy of diagnosis and on the non-invasive nature of the CT examination. Little has been done to measure the resulting change in the health of those who receive CT scanning. There have been some indications that the improvement in health of those served might be negligible, which could occur when the ability to diagnose some diseases outstrips the ability to treat them. The changes in morbidity and mortality rates for those receiving CT examinations as compared to other diagnostic tests have to be quantified[45].

For estimating the spatial needs of an X ray diagnostic department, studies indicate that if the X ray room's share in auxiliary rooms is included, the total area per X ray room amounts towards 200 m^2 in the surface[46].

40 Phillips Donald F and Lillé Kenneth: Putting the leash on 'CAT'. 1976, Hospitals 50:13:45–49.

41 The Times, May 17, 1977.

42 Oliva Luigi: Basic functional concepts in planning of image forming systems departments. International symposium on the Planning of Departments of Radiology and Imaging Sciences. Lisbon, May 1978.

43 Computer-Tomographie: lieb und teuer. Neue Zürcher Zeitung, May 23, 1978.

44 Gautschi H: Standortbestimmung der computerisierten axialen Tomografie. 1977, Veska — Das Schweizer Spital 41:332–335.

45 Swartz Robert and DesHarnals Susan: Computed Tomography: The Cost — Benefit Dilemma. 1977, Radiology 125:251–253.

46 see also Puijlaert C B A J: Planning and calculation of surface of X ray department based on workload to be expected. Second international symposium on the planning of radiological departments. Philadelphia. September 1976.

Cobben J J: Facts and figures in radiodiagnosis. International Symposium on the Planning of Departments of Radiology and Imaging Sciences. Lisbon. May 1978.

Diagnostic departments and subdepartments

The diagnostic X ray department planning is primarily based on balanced patient and professional staff circulation. The efficiency of the personnel engaged to expedite the examinations and treatments should be maximal, their fatigue minimal. Concurrently attention should be paid to the convenience, privacy, and comfort of the patient. The secondary planning concerns the X ray film flow.

As the demands made on Xray departments change over a period of time, the character and the work load of individual departments should be assessed and analysed at intervals.

A diagnostic X ray department usually consists of following subdepartments: inpatient, outpatient, emergency, and special procedures departments as well as a section for diagnostics in the operation unit.

The description and operational problems of one widely scattered department are said to be a tale of woe[47]. According to some estimates decentralization is said to give 25 per cent loss in efficiency[48]. However, the pattern of conducting of *all* X ray examinations in one centralized department — although generally advocated — is by no means self-evident, at last in larger hospitals.

The different needs of inpatients and outpatients in terms of attention, facilities, and furniture and equipment indicate that a large hospital organization should be improved by dividing the radiology diagnostic department facilities. The inpatient facilities should be located close to bed areas, and the outpatient X ray facilities close to the outpatient departments.

Paediatric Xray has some special characteristics[49]. There is no collaboration by infants and younger children, which increases the number of staff members, particularly radiographers. The extremely unquiet patients have a greater transparency, which requires sophisticated devices to fix the patients and high powered apparatus with short exposure times. Paediatric patients must be accompanied and need continuous attention as well as spacy and special waiting areas.

A diagnostic unit consisting of about 10 examination rooms is easily supervised. From the functional-architectural viewpoint good solutions can be offered. Also a large hospital's immense circulation problems can through X ray differentiation be simplified.

---

47 MacEwan Douglas W: Editorial. 1977, The Journal of The Canadian Association of Radiologists 28:94.

48 Puijlaert C B A J: Factors determining planning of Xray departments. International Symposium on the Planning of Departments of Radiology and Imaging Sciences. Lisbon, May 1978.

49 also Knap Klaus: Planning of paediatric Xray departments. International Symposium on the Planning of Departments of Radiology and Imaging Sciences. Lisbon. May 1978.

In large hospitals, separate Xray facilities can be envisaged for emergency and admittance, intensive care department, out-patients, paediatrics, prematures, otolaryngology, urology, neurology, orthopaedics, general medical-surgical areas, gynaecology, neuro- and cardio-surgery, and epidemical diseases or a combination of some of the mentioned specialities.

Following programme-orientated medical groupings, each of them containing a diagnostic radiology unit, have already been established[50]:

> *musculosceletal:* orthopaedics, rheumatology, physical medicine and rehabilitation
>
> *cardiopulmonary:* cardiac and thoracic surgery, laryngology and bronchoesophagology, cardiology, pulmonary diseases
>
> *gastrointestinal:* gastroenterology, urology

The groupings without an own radiology unit and which have to rely on above mentioned groupings when radiology is concerned are:

> *community medicine:* emergency and accident services, screening clinics and
>
> *human growth and development:* paediatrics, obstetrics, gynaecology.

Decentralization may shorten waiting periods; simplify scheduling; speed up diagnosis; reduce the amount of hospital infections; diminish the need for use of portable Xray units and achieve a more intimate closeness between the clinicians and the radiologists. However, a deal of the interaction between members of the radiology departments is lost, and some duplication of Xray rooms for radiologists and technicians is required.

---

50 Lapayowker Mark S, Kundel Harold L and Shea Francis J: Planning of vertically orientated radiology department in a program-floor hospital. International symposium on the planning of radiological departments. Otaniemi, Finland, August 1972.

Centralized Xray diagnostic department

Patient area

Waiting

According to Swedish experience 3 per cent of the patients are taken directly to Xray rooms. 17 per cent are bed or stretcher cases. 80 per cent are ambulant or use wheel-chairs or are minors who are carried by their parents[1]. It has been estimated that 5 to 10 per cent of the department's patients will be children[2].

Through proper scheduling systems excessive waiting periods can be avoided. Not more than two patients per room should be scheduled at a time. It has to be stressed that not all scheduled cases show up. E g in Spain this percentage is about 6[3].

It is essential that the reception office is easily reached by all categories of waiting patients or those who accompany them to simplify the registration and production of previous records and films, if they exist.

Small interview rooms are of great value to distressed and embarrassed patients and should be a part of the reception area complex.

From the main reception area the patients are directed to the sub-waiting areas close to the X ray room where the examinations are to take place. Thoughtless stacking of patients at the entrance to the diagnostic room produces or increases patient stress.

A nurses' station controlling the entrance to the waiting areas is needed. In-patients often wear dressing gowns and may even be taken to the X ray department bed-ridden with drip and drainage bottles connected to them.

Waiting areas for in-patients and out-patients should be segregated. In some countries the segregation of male and female waiting areas is required.

The provision of minor waiting rooms is beneficial to patients who are embarrassed or distressed.

A particular waiting area for children and accompanying mothers and nurses should be provided. The sight of an obviously ill person might be frightening to a child. As much emotional refinement as possible should be provided for.

The patient waiting areas have to be planned with utmost care.

---

1   Tengrud Harry at the International symposium on the planning of radiological departments. Otaniemi, Finland, August 1972.

2   see also Truman Graham: Children as patients. 1977, Radiography 43:259.

3   Pedrosa Cesar: Some computers' applications in scheduling. International symposium on the Planning of Departments of Radiology and Imaging Sciences. Lisbon, May 1978.

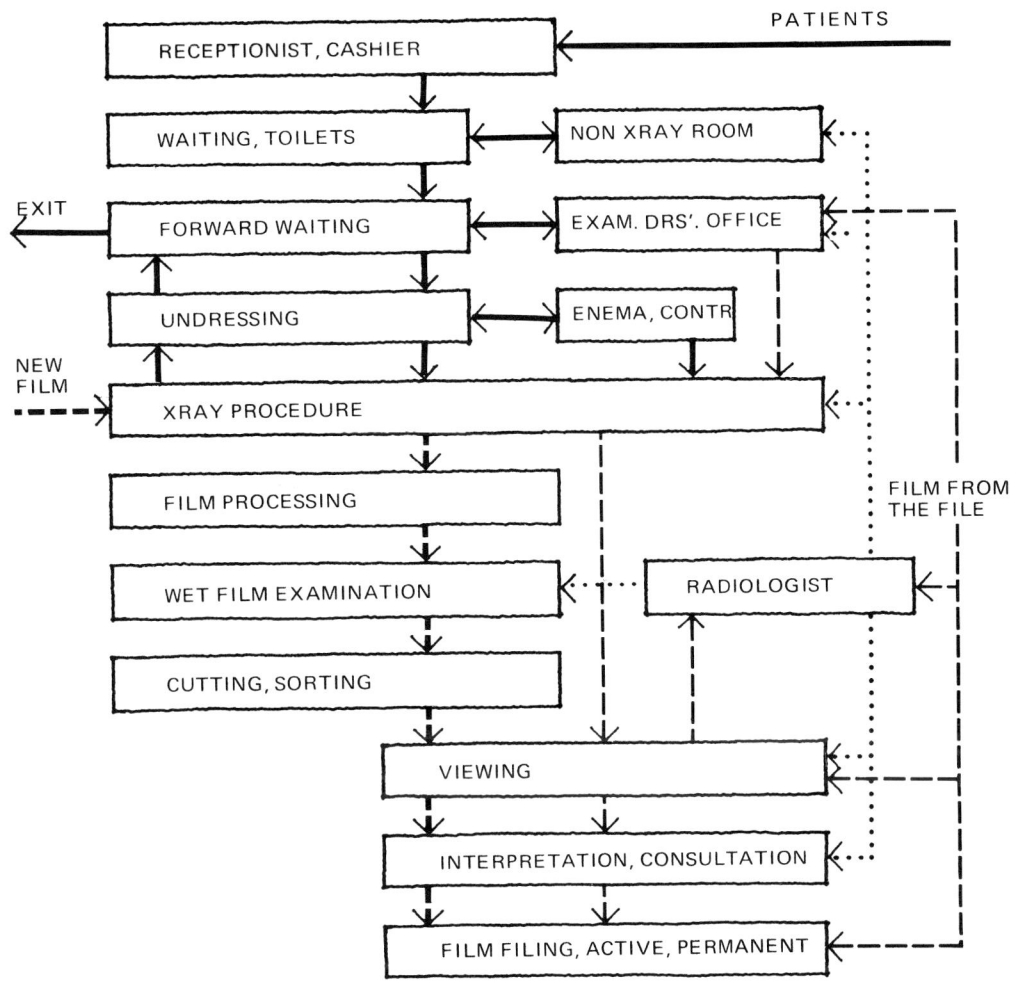

Patient, radiologist and film flow in radiodiagnostic departments.

A floor area of about 1.3 m² should be allowed for each waiting patient. If relatives or friends are allowed to accompany the patient in the waiting areas, additional space is needed.

Parking areas for beds and trolleys should be provided. The corridors must be 2.8 m wide for bed traffic.

As the number of elderly patients is increasing, low and soft easy chairs should be avoided. As once down an older person almost impossibly gets up unaided.

The use of loudspeakers to request the patients to go to the examination rooms or to give them other information, has not proved successful.

463

It has been pointed out that particularly in the times of epidemic respiratory infections nasopharyngeal contamination may endanger the people in the waiting room[4]. A higher rate of ventilation than usually is recommendable.

There should always be a separate entrance for accident and emergency cases. These patients should have their own waiting area and should not mix with other patients. A special enclosed area for the injured or seriously ill who require special attention is needed.

Lavatories

Lavatories should be easily accessible to waiting patients. Some should be larger so that an attendant could assist. Handgrips on the wall for the patient are recommended. Some wheel-chair lavatories of about 4 m² size should be provided. Doors to lavatory compartments should open outwards.

All lavatories must have a washbasin.

Changing cubicles

The patients who are to be X rayed require either complete undressing, or stripping to the waist*, or removing from head and neck items which are radiopaque.

Each X ray room requires 2 to 4 well lit and ventilated comfortable cubicles of about 1.3 m² size. Some of the cubicles should be at least of about double size and be designated for wheelchair patients, children and aged and their attendants.

There should be an arrangement to lock up personal possessions in the cubicles.

Changing cubicles can be designed either as the pass-through type or as opening off a sub-waiting area.

The pass-through type of cubicles gives the patient privacy and is mostly considered to be more practical[5]. The pass-through cubicle door leading into the radiodiagnostic room requires to be lead lined.

4   see also Nikodemusz I: Bakteriologische Untersuchung der Luft in Polikliniklaboratorium. 1976, Hospital-Hygiene 68:385–387.

*   For routine chest X rays the practice of not undressing patients could be adapted. Re-X raying because of clothing shadows is seldom required (see also McEwin Roderrick: A study of Radiology Departments. 1971, Australasian Radiology 15:1:71).

5   see also Koivisto E and Vuorinen P: Some Experiences of the Roentgen Diagnostic Departments at the New University Hospital in Oulu. in Planning of Radiological Departments. ed by Martti Kormano and Friedrich Ernst Stieve. Georg Thieme Publishers. Stuttgart 1974, p 244.

The changing cubicles of the non-pass-through type are associated with sub-waiting areas, which should be given non-institutional character. The cubicles should be easy to identify for the patient when returning. Each patient using the non-pass-through type cubicles should be given a clean (disposable) gown.

The custom of using the changing cubicles as a second stage waiting room is unfortunate. Generally patients dislike longer waiting in the confined space of a cubicle.

The rapid turn-over rooms need more changing cubicles than the time consuming types of investigation. However, lavatories, washing rooms and utility rooms are generally not needed in the rapid turn-over X ray room area.

Patient recovery area

There should be one individual *resting cubicle,* about 2.5 m² in size, with a couche per each radiodiagnostic room. The cubicles should be provided with curtains.

Contrast media preparation room

In the vicinity of the undressing cubicles and X ray rooms there should be a room where contrast media, frequently barium powder, is mixed for investigations.

Lavage room, bidet facility

The lavage or enema room of about 8 m² size should be associated with both the X ray screening, particularly fluoroscopy rooms and the recovery area. It should be provided with a sink and a lavatory cubicle opening off the lavage room.

A *bidet facility* for personal cleaning after enema is sometimes recommended.

Xray screening rooms and suites, auxilliary rooms

Tailored rooms in the radiology department have been suggested[6], although basically the design for a diagnostic X ray room should be multifunctional.

The degree of room standardization is increasing. In Sweden[7] the standard screening room floor areas of 25, 30 or 40 m^2 have been recommended. The Scottish Home and Health Department[8] has for examinations only one size — 37 m^2, the long axis of the room being not less than 6.7 m. Lately, a standard size of 40 m^2 has been recommended[9].

The depth of the screening room should not be less than 5.8 m.

In the room a working height of about 3.3 m could be recommended*.

When only ambulant patients are involved e g in departments for out-patients, the diagnostic room area can be reduced[10].

In all X ray rooms a stainless steel unit with a sink and a washbasin is needed because of the microbial cross-contamination and infection potential.

In an X ray room in which remote control is to be used, it is essential to have a lead-glass window to protect the radiologist who is in line with the X ray table in floor level so that the operator can see and communicate with the patient. The lower edge of the protective screen should be about 1.15 m from use in the erect position. The television monitor should be placed so that it can be easily seen through the lead-glass window. Simultaneously the patient should be kept in view. The control panel should be close to the X ray table so that the patient showing any signs of distress could be quickly reached.

Door openings should be at least 1.3 m wide.

Doors between X ray room and staff corridor are frequently erroneously left open during X ray examinations giving rise to an increased radiation level in the staff corridor. In Denmark[11] the idea of introduction of mazes between staff corridor

---

6 see also Cadmus Robert R: Radiology Suites. in Functional Planning of General Hospitals. ed by Alden B Mills. McGrax-Hill Book Company. New York, Toronto, Sydney, London 1969, p 224.

7 Röntgendiagnosavdelningar — lokalprogram m m. Spri råd 5.6. Stockholm 1972, p 29.

8 McCreadie D W A and Montgomery R: Design and organization of radiodiagnostic departments. International symposium on the planning of radiological departments. Otaniemi, Finland. August 1972.

9 Cobben J J: Facts and figures in radiodiagnosis. International Symposium on the Planning of Departments of Radiology and Imaging Sciences. Lisbon, May 1978.

* Western Regional Hospital Board, Research and Development Unit accepts as a minimum clear ceiling height in radiodiagnostic rooms 3.1 m (Organization & Design of Radiodiagnostic Departments. Stencil. (Glasgow) January 1973, p 23).

10 see also Taut Anna and Nedeljkov Georgije: Die Gruppenpraxis. Bertelsmann Fachverlag. Dusseldorf 1973, p 109–111.

11 Hjardemaal Ole: Mazes between staff corridor and X ray room from a radiation protection point of view. Second international symposium on the planning of radiological departments. Philadelphia. September 1976.

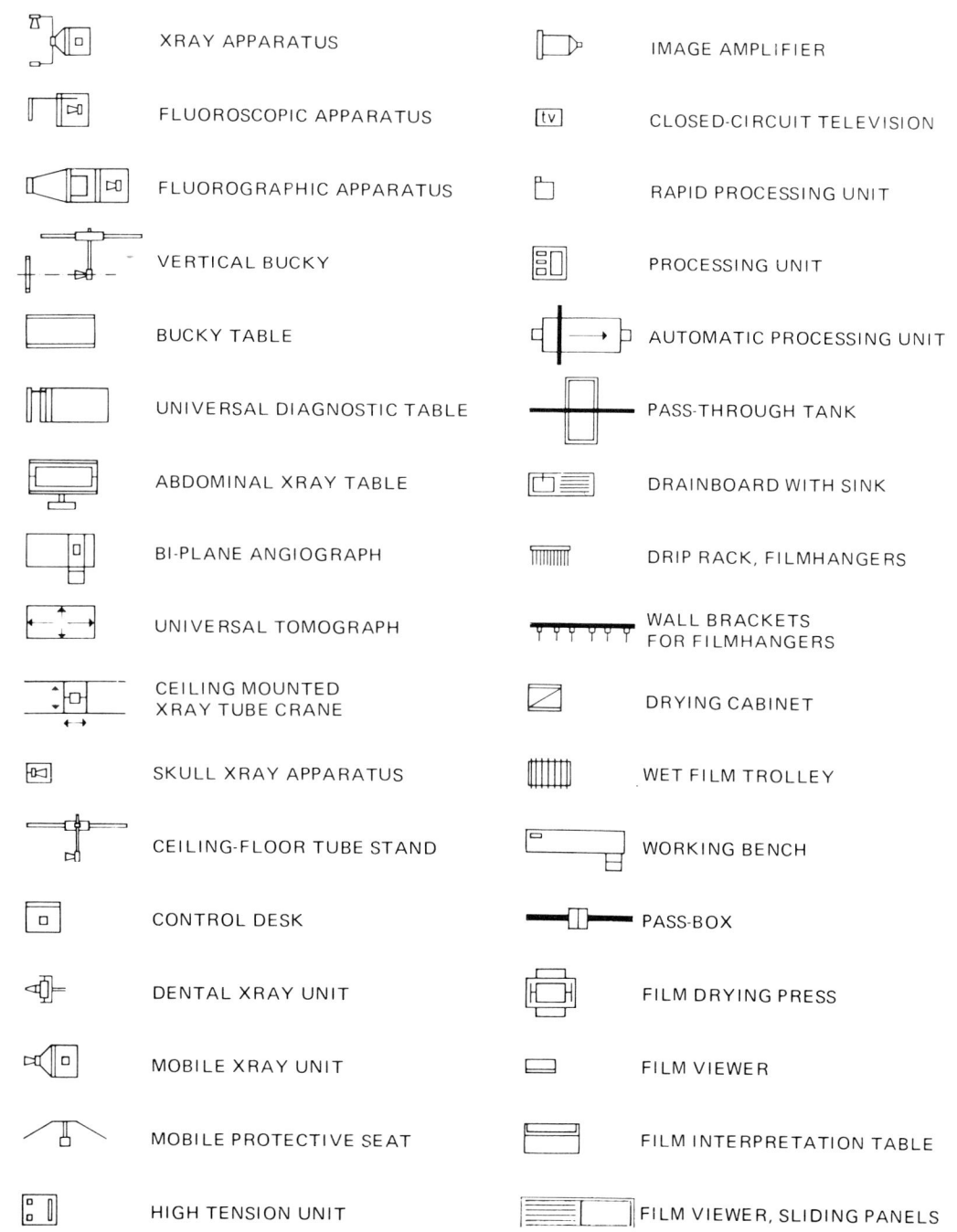

XRAY APPARATUS		IMAGE AMPLIFIER	
FLUOROSCOPIC APPARATUS		CLOSED-CIRCUIT TELEVISION	
FLUOROGRAPHIC APPARATUS		RAPID PROCESSING UNIT	
VERTICAL BUCKY		PROCESSING UNIT	
BUCKY TABLE		AUTOMATIC PROCESSING UNIT	
UNIVERSAL DIAGNOSTIC TABLE		PASS-THROUGH TANK	
ABDOMINAL XRAY TABLE		DRAINBOARD WITH SINK	
BI-PLANE ANGIOGRAPH		DRIP RACK, FILMHANGERS	
UNIVERSAL TOMOGRAPH		WALL BRACKETS FOR FILMHANGERS	
CEILING MOUNTED XRAY TUBE CRANE		DRYING CABINET	
SKULL XRAY APPARATUS		WET FILM TROLLEY	
CEILING-FLOOR TUBE STAND		WORKING BENCH	
CONTROL DESK		PASS-BOX	
DENTAL XRAY UNIT		FILM DRYING PRESS	
MOBILE XRAY UNIT		FILM VIEWER	
MOBILE PROTECTIVE SEAT		FILM INTERPRETATION TABLE	
HIGH TENSION UNIT		FILM VIEWER, SLIDING PANELS	

467

Symbols of Xray diagnostic and darkroom equipment designed by Netherlands Hospital Planning Consultants.

and X ray room has been supported. Mazes have advantages as well as disadvantages for staff and patients. They consume more space than doors.

Radiodiagnostic rooms should have natural lighting and ventilation whenever possible.

All artificial lighting in the screening room should be wall mounted. The ceiling has to be free from air ducts, pipes, etc and should be weight bearing in all directions for the installation of ceiling mounted equipment.

To help the rheumatoid and arthritic patients in getting on to the X ray table a ramp with a rubber matting walking surface has been recommended[12]. The ramp is 1.70 m long and 0.50 m wide, has an initial step of 3.5 cm and rises to 27.5 cm from the floor. The patients walk up the ramp using the X ray table edge as a hand support on their best side, until reaching a convenient height.

As ergometric studies have been used only on a very limited scale in developing regular diagnostic tables, some developments and changes could be expected for them.

An examination room suite for general examinations including chest, abdomen, skull, extremities, spine and IVP; a suite for special procedures including cardio-vascular, neurological and urological procedures, and suites for tomography, for routine fluoroscopy and for rapid chest examinations could be envisaged.

The number and function of X ray rooms allocated for special procedure suites depends on the character of the particular hospital.

A very good size for a radiodiagnostic unit is about 8 to 10 X ray rooms. It should not include more than 12 X ray rooms.

In a small radiology department the principle of multiplicity of functions in a diagnostic room may be followed. In larger hospitals the increased volume tends to justify single-purpose accommodations.

A typical range of major radiodiagnostic equipment which should be provided for a six roomed radiodiagnostic department has been described, the object having been to endeavour to double cover each function[13].

Room	Function	Equipment
1	General	tomographic table, dental unit, chest stand
2	General	Bucky table, universal Bucky stand, chest stand

---

12 Ramp for Disabled X ray Patients. 1970, British Hospital Journal and Social Service Review 80:1684.

13 Western Regional Hospital Board, Research and Development Unit: Organisation & Design of Radiodiagnostic Departments. Stencil. (Glasgow) January 1973, p 9.

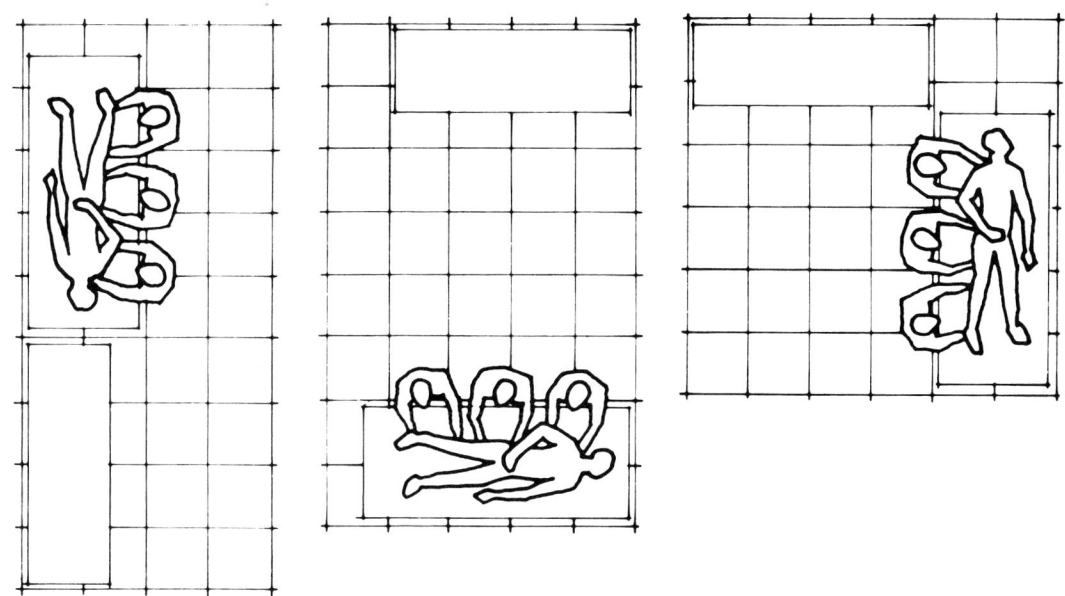

Spaces needed to lift a patient from a trolley to an operation table or Xray table.
Planning grid 0.5 by 0.5 m.

3	Fluoroscopy	tilting table, image intensifier and closed circuit television, over couch tube for use with film changer
4	Fluoroscopy	tilting table, image intensifier and closed circuit television, over couch tube and chest stand
5	I.V.P.	two Bucky tables, tomographic attachment, vertical Bucky stand
6	Accident	Bucky table, Bucky stand with trolley and skull unit.

Two rooms have been provided for fluoroscopy procedures, chests, vertical Bucky work and tomography. In the event of an apparatus failure, the work would be transferred to an adjoining room, which contains the same type of equipment and has the same functional relationship with the ancillary service.

All rooms will have a control, tube, tube stand or support and cabling. A generator may serve two rooms.

Th Holm[14] has based his five room department on Swedish examination distributio

1	General radiography (47 per cent)	Bucky table, ceiling mounted tube, skull unit, vertical Bucky
2	Chest examinations (31 per cent)	specialized chest unit or vertical Bucky
3	Radiography with fluoroscopy (13 per cent)	tilting fluoroscope with image intensifier and Bucky, ceiling mounted X ray tube
4	Urography and tomography and spine examinations (6 per cent)	Bucky table, ceiling mounted tube, pendulous tube stand, tomograph
5	Angiography and other special procedures (2 to 4 per cent)	Bucky table, film changers, image intensifier etc.

The distribution of examinations varies in various countries. In the Netherlands, as an example, chest examinations take only 23 per cent, but radiography with fluoro scopy is increased to 18 per cent[15].

When only out-patients are involved, following units may be the answer to the X ra facility problems*:

1	General radiography 1	tilting table, image intensifier, 100 mm spot film camera, ceiling stand, wall Bucky stan
2	Urography	Bucky table with tomoequipment, ceiling stand
3	Skeleton	cranio-skeleton stand, cranio-skeleton tabl Bucky table, ceiling stand
4	Tomography	tomograph
5	General radiography 2	distance controlled tilting table, image intensifier, 100 mm camera
6	Special examinations	angio-table, image intensifier

Several film sizes are used, one of the most frequent being 240 by 300 mm.

As a full-size radiograph can be achieved on 100 mm film, with the same radiation dose, there seems to be no reason why 100 mm film should not be introduced as a standard film[16]. This would have advantages as follows: no cassettes and intensifying screens; patient details on every film; costs reduced; storage problems simplifie

14 Holm T: Basic Equipment for General Roentgendiagnostic Departments. in Planning of Radiological Departments. ed by Martti Kormano and Friedrich Ernst Stieve. Georg Thieme Publishers. Stuttgart 1974, p 245–251.

15 Cobben J J: Facts and figures in radiodiagnosis. International Symposium on the Planning of Radiology and Imaging Sciences. Lisbon, May 1978.

* as recommended by a major producer of equipment.

16 White John: Miniaturisation of X ray films. 1978, Radiography 44:185–190.

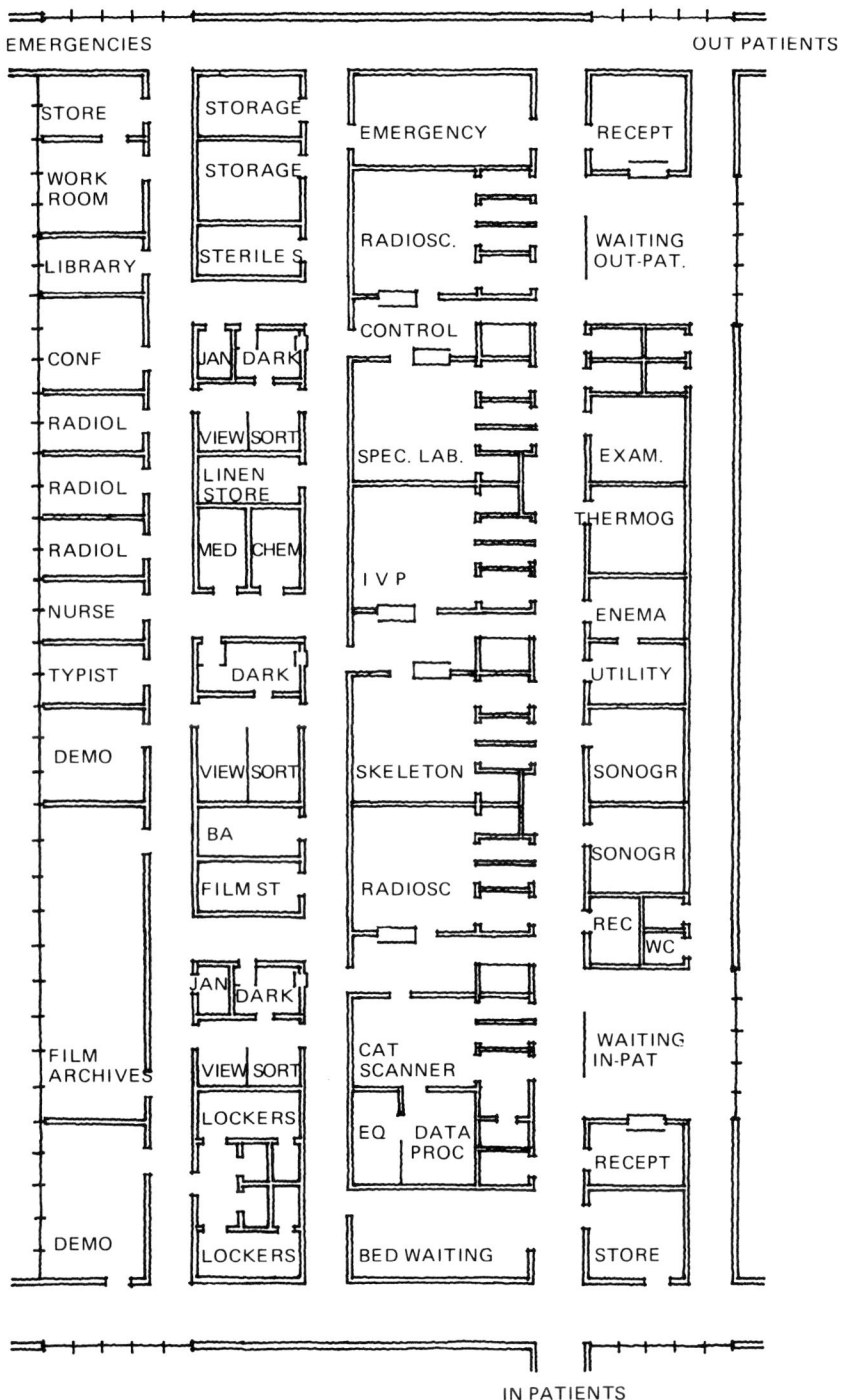

EMERGENCIES

OUT PATIENTS

STORE

WORK ROOM

LIBRARY

CONF

RADIOL

RADIOL

RADIOL

NURSE

TYPIST

DEMO

FILM ARCHIVES

DEMO

STORAGE

STORAGE

STERILE S

JAN DARK

VIEW SORT

LINEN STORE

MED CHEM

DARK

VIEW SORT

BA

FILM ST

JAN DARK

VIEW SORT

LOCKERS

LOCKERS

EMERGENCY

RADIOSC.

CONTROL

SPEC. LAB.

I V P

SKELETON

RADIOSC

CAT SCANNER

EQ   DATA PROC

BED WAITING

RECEPT

WAITING OUT-PAT.

EXAM.

THERMOG

ENEMA

UTILITY

SONOGR

SONOGR

REC
WC

WAITING IN-PAT

RECEPT

STORE

IN PATIENTS

71

A linear radiodiagnostic department for a 600-bed hospital. Pütsep International.

A further important factor would be the reduction of dosage to the public[17].

A new 14″ image intensifier[18] is expected to have a great influence on the working procedures in X ray diagnostic departments[19]. The 14″ image intensifier is the nucleus of a new X ray system. It will make full size imaging on X ray film superfluous for the major part of all routine examinations. This would also mean an easier film handling and filing. It would be a solution of the problem of automatic film supply of various sizes in universal X ray systems[20]. Some of the practical problems for the design of a large-format image intensifier are the result of the limited space available on existing X ray diagnostic equipment[21].

A linear arrangement of X ray rooms with separate patient corridors and work corridors could be recommended. The single corridor plan in which staff and patients mix is not effective for patient comfort, pleasing work conditions and high volume productivity.

In the recent years there has been a tendency — not always gladly accepted by the staff — to replace the individual control rooms of 4 to 10 m² in size by a common control corridor with a width of about 2.3 m, where separation of the control desk is maintained to avoid interference.

The linear system is usually combined with multiple dark rooms.

In larger departments the rooms could be folded round. E g the first and last four Xray rooms of a twelve room complex can be moved through ninety degrees so that the three darkrooms will all look into a common viewing and quality control area[22]. This cluster is still a two corridor system, the patients moving externally and the staff internally.

In larger departments such clusters can cover specific functions, so that according to the nature of the work being carried out, appropriate ancillary rooms and activities can be associated with them. There may be clusters of general rooms, fluoroscopy rooms, genito-urinary rooms, special procedure rooms, and so on.

17 John C: The reported film storage problem solved? 100 mm film miniaturisation using the Oldelft, Delcopex and Odelcard System. 1978, Radiography 44:191–195.

18 Kühl W and Schrijvers J E: A new 14 in. X ray image intensifier tube. 1977, Medicamundi 22:3:9–10.

19 personal communication: 1978, J M J van der Sommen, Eindhoven.

20 personal communication: 1978, J M J van der Sommen, Eindhoven.

21 Kühl W and Schrijvers J E: A new 14 in. X ray image intensifier tube. 1977, Medicamundi 22:3:9–10.

22 Terry William G: Pre-planning considerations. A paper prepared for the International Symposium on the Planning of Departments of Radiology and Imaging Sciences. Lisbon, May 1978.

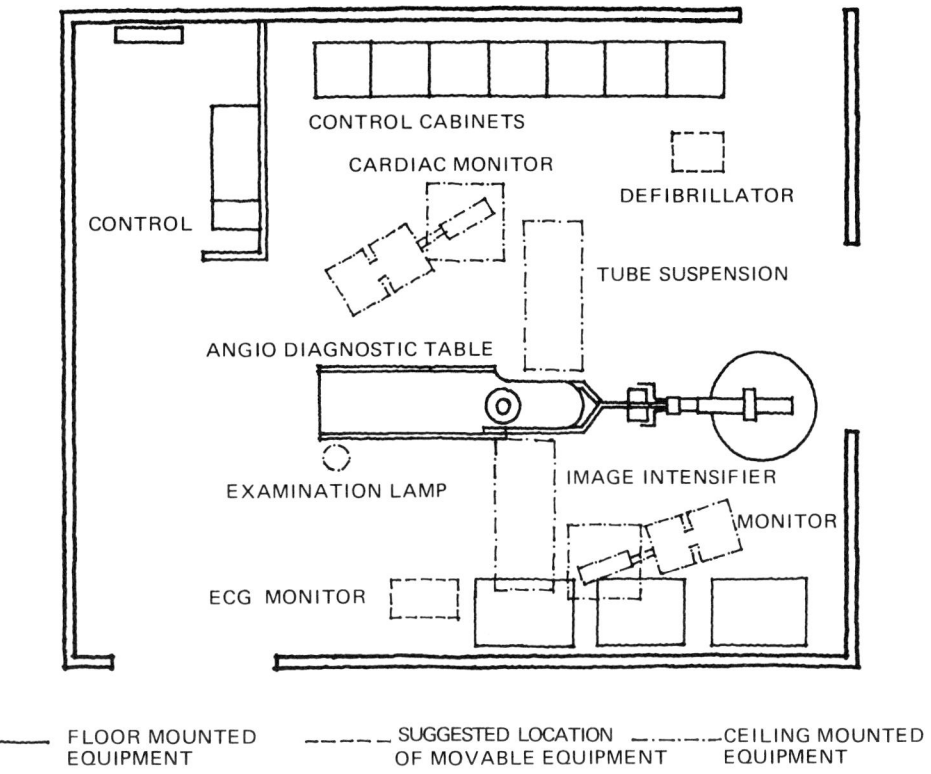

CONTROL CABINETS

CARDIAC MONITOR

DEFIBRILLATOR

CONTROL

TUBE SUSPENSION

ANGIO DIAGNOSTIC TABLE

EXAMINATION LAMP

IMAGE INTENSIFIER

MONITOR

ECG MONITOR

——— FLOOR MOUNTED EQUIPMENT ————— SUGGESTED LOCATION OF MOVABLE EQUIPMENT —·—·—·—CEILING MOUNTED EQUIPMENT

Xray equipment for investigation and diagnosis of cardio-vascular disease as installed in the Northern General Hospital, Sheffield 1977.

giographic procedure suite

In major hospitals, particularly in teaching hospitals, an angiographic procedure facility is needed. It may consist of following procedure units: a room for angiocardiography, a room for neuroangiography, a room for abdominal and peripheral angiography, a room for pneumoencephalography and gas myelography, a room for pacemaker implants, and support facilities. There should be provisions for use of radioisotopes for angiography[23].

23 see also Paulin S: Design of a modern angiographic procedure suite. Radiologic, architectural and administrative considerations. XIII Congreso Internacional de Radiologia. Madrid, Octubre 1973, Excerpta Medica. Amsterdam, Princeton, London, Geneva, Tokyo 1973, p 466.

For cardiac catheterization* because of the size of the medical team involved and the ancillary equipment used, a total floor area of 55 to 60 m² is suggested. A preparation room may be required.

The core of the system is the examination table. The X ray tube may be mounted over or underneath the table. Further components in the system are: image intensifier for catheterizations, and equipment for stop-motion 70 mm fluorography and cine-films; film changers for morphological studies; TV chains for display of fluoroscopic images and visual control in cinefluorography; high pressure injectors for undiluted contrast flow, and electronic equipments for monitoring, displaying and recording the physiological data.

Adult cardiac-catheterization laboratories should perform about 300 studies *per annum*[24] to be justified.

Processing areas

Good-quality X ray film processing reduces the necessity to repeat X ray exposures.

The processing devices have until very recently been concentrated to dark rooms, which in a sense have been the central point of the department.

Xray film processing systems in which the film is not touched by hand after removal from the cassette until leaving the automatic processing unit have been preferred.

The classical *darkroom* contains processor-loading chutes, a dry bench, a washbasin, film hoppers and pass-through hatches. When two processors are installed side by side, partitioning must be provided to allow the processors to be withdrawn without interference.

Cine-film processing should be possible. No viewing boxes are needed.

The size of the darkroom depends on the number of staff working in it. For the first person about 8 m² is required, for each additional person about 2 m².

Darkroom entrance by a single door is considered to be insufficient.

Citrus fruit colour and pastel shades are suitable for the walls and ceiling of the darkroom. Dark colours, above all black, should be avoided.

Ten changes of air per hour are recommended.

---

* The radio-nuclide gamma camera provides the kind of information that in many cases can make cardiac catheterization unnecessary. The gamma camera method is a relatively small fraction of cost of cardiac catheterization.

24 see also Mc Gregor Maurice, Pelletier Gerald: Planning of specialized health facilities. 1978, The New England Journal of Medicine 299:179–181.

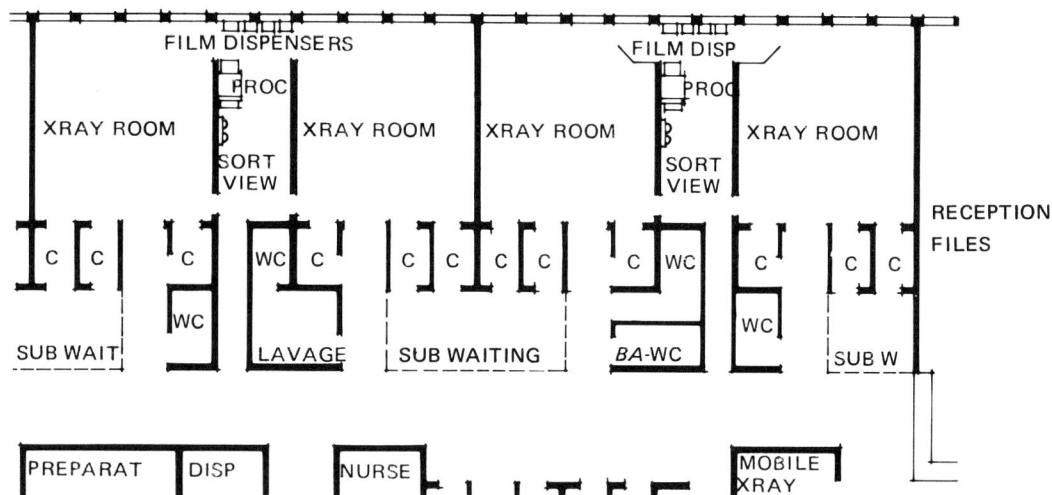

A section of a Scottish six room radiodiagnostic department based on the Du Pont daylight system. After Mc Creadie and Montgomery.

Since automatic processors have largely taken over from manual systems, there have been changes in the darkroom planning development. The cost reduction has made it possible to have several automatic processing units within one X ray department instead of a large, centralized darkroom, Decentralized units simplify the technical planning of larger radiology departments, and their working procedures.

The advantages of having a processing, viewing and sorting area for each pair of radiodiagnostic rooms are: fewer cassettes required and the use of conveyors avoided, the quality control of films by the radiographer facilitated, the physician's work accelerated and made easier, the assistant's work facilitated, and the patient's waiting time shortened.

The further development of automatic film processors directly connected to the diagnostic apparatus can be expected.

Daylight Xray film processing

Medical Xray films can be cassette-loaded, exposed, unloaded and processed entirely in daylight. About 90 per cent of all Xray examinations could be performed without access to a darkroom[25].

25 Ackermann Lothar: How elimination of the darkroom can influence the planning of diagnostic X ray departments. International symposium on the Planning of Departments of Radiology and Imaging Sciences. Lisbon, May 1978.

One of the systems* involves automatic daylight film dispensers for five film sizes, taking up to 100 sheets of X ray film for exposure. There are automatic daylight cassettes for exposing the film in the normal X ray exposure equipment. An automatic cassette unloader, that receives the cassettes, unloads and deposits the exposed film in a removable storage bin of the daylight transport feeder. The transport feeder accumulates 50 sheets of X ray film for daylight transfer to the processor. A daylight combination adapter unloads in daylight the X ray films from single cassettes or from the transport feeder into the processor.

Another system** provides loaders for six sizes of film which can be mounted as required in the racks of the loader, which is 1.52 m high, 0.66 m long and 0.70 m in width.

The automatic cassette unloader can be fitted on to processors with a horizontal feed table. This operation can be carried out in daylight conditions.

There should be an X ray processor for every two to three rooms. There seem to be advantages of these systems over traditional work procedures, provided that the X ray film is of excellent quality. The radiography staff can work in fenestrated rooms as the automatic system needs no darkroom. All equipment, including the processor, can be set up in the diagnostic room. The automatic system reduces the physical work load of carrying the cassettes by the radiographer. It has been calculated that during the course of one month a radiographer usually carries cassettes in the weight of a London double decker bus[26].

'Daylight' processing system may increase the work load of each radiographer on day shift by about 30 minutes, but reduce the work load of the dark room technicians by about 2.5 hours per shift and reduce the work load of radiographers at night by about 45 minutes. Only limited darkroom facilities are required. Technicians are not required for routine film processing[27].

Many speakers at the Second International Symposium on Planning of Radiology Departments at Philadelphia, September 1976, pointed out the benefits of daylight loading systems or cassette-less radiology in chest, skeletal and 70 or 105 mm gastrointestinal fluorography. A recent US department was designed for 18 rooms on the basis of conventional wisdom; using the new methods it can do all its work with 10 rooms; 8 rooms are surplus. The impact and efficiency of the new methods were not fully appreciated until about a year ago[28].

---

*   Du Pont Daylight System

** Gevamatic L by Agfa-Gevaert.

26 Mountford Grahame: Shedding the weight of a London double decker bus in one month. 1977, Health and Social Service Journal 77:678–679.

27 X-ray department: daylight processing of X ray films. Abstracts of Efficiency Studies in the National Health Service No 177. Her Majesty's Stationery Office. London 1977.

28 MacEwan Douglas W: Editorial. 1977, The Journal of The Canadian Association of Radiologists 28:94.

Viewing and interpreting

At the first stage films are viewed from the radiographic point of view: to have further radiography or to terminate the examination.

More than 60 per cent of all exposed films can be interpreted and reported upon immediately by the radiologists.

To view is best to be alone. When viewing in a larger viewing room, a neutralizing background noise is essential. Fatigue of viewing is the most important cause for errors. Not more than 50 to 60 cases should be reported upon a day by a radiologist. A larger workload means that deleterious effects on quality increase clearly[29].

An efficient method for viewing radiographs for both radiologists and typists should permit concentrated film reporting sessions. The magazine mode, which employs multipanel viewers with preloaded panels has been shown preference for.

An early reporting is to be favoured. TV-communication with other departments, particularly with operation rooms, is needed.

A comprehensive, automatic, diagnostic radiographic reporting system can replace conventional dictation and transcription[30]. Radiologists using this system report diagnostic interpretations directly by probing terms on a visual display terminal linked to a computer. The information appears instantly on a cathode ray tube for confirmation, followed by printout, report dispersal, and storage. The system can be run from a large time-sharing computer or dedicated minicomputer. Costs are regarded to be comparable to stenography[31].

A disadvantage of the system is that the radiologist must look away from films while probing the terminal. Also the number of radiologists reporting simultaneously is limited by the number of terminals.

Computer down-time has averaged to about 2 hours a week. Terminal breakdowns can be frustrating interruptions for the radiologist[32].

Another radiodiagnostic data-handling system — Roentgen-Tele-Data — with telephones connected to the hospital exchange has been described[33]. Time, data, and location of examination are automatically recorded. The system can deliver spoken instructions from the computer and warns if data are not valid. Diagnoses, their degree of verification, and cases of special interest are added at display terminals. Costs are believed to represent 1 per cent of the department's expenditures. Future plans include a booking system, rapid access, and on-line connection to the main data system.

29 see also Soila A Pekka: For what are we planning in diagnostic radiology? Second international symposium on the planning of radiological departments. Philadelphia. September 1976.

30 Wheeler Paul S, Simborg Donald W and Gittin Joseph N: The Johns Hopkins Radiology Reporting System. 1976, Radiology 119:315–319.

31 ibid

32 ibid

33 Madsen Bent and Nehl Jørgen: Roentgen-Tele-Data: A Radiodiagnostic Recording System. 1977, Radiology 123:627–630.

The final stage in the development of Roentgen-Tele-Data will be on-line connection to our hospital's larger system for the automatic processing of information. Thus, the radiologists will have rapid access to further clinical information, and a short free text, representing the result of radiographic examinations, will be included in the information registered for each patient.

Computer-assisted tomography – CT – unit

The CT room has to accommodate the CT scanner, an anaesthesia machine as also an anaesthesiologist is involved, a ventilator, routine monitoring equipment, and a patient bed. Toilet facilities for the patient adjacent to the scan room should be provided.

The CT scan rooms tend to be cold, with the temperature under 21°C, and control of patient temperature may become difficult[34]. The neonate or infant is especially prone to develop hypothermia, and facilities to add or conserve heat, especially during anaesthesia, should be established[35].

The induction facilities – to eliminate delays in the CT schedules – should be in an adjoining room with storage space for anaesthestic equipment and defibrillator. When not employed for anaesthetic purposes, the induction room would be available as a holding room for patient preparation.

Piped anaesthetic gases and vacuum with connectors for anaesthesia machines should be provided in both CT and induction rooms. To accommodate ventilators an appropriate electrical power source and oxygen connection are required.

Provisions have to be made for waiting with toilet facilities and dressing rooms.

For postanaesthetic observation there should be a nearby recovery unit.

The computers, generally situated adjacent to the scan room, are so temperature critical that frequently the room must be air conditioned. A temperature of about 21°C is required.

The difficulty of working in a limited space in an environment not conductive to intensive-care support of potentially high-risk patients – head injuries etc – is often not appreciated. A complete CT unit would require an area of 100 to 120 m².

34 see also Altman William S: CT scanning and patient inconvenience. 1977, The New England Journal of Medicine 297:226–227.

35 Aidinis Sydney J, Zimmerman Robert A, Shapiro Harvey M, Bilanuick Larissa T and Broennte A Michael: Anesthesia for Brain Computer Tomography. 1976, The Journal of Anesthesiology 44:420–425.

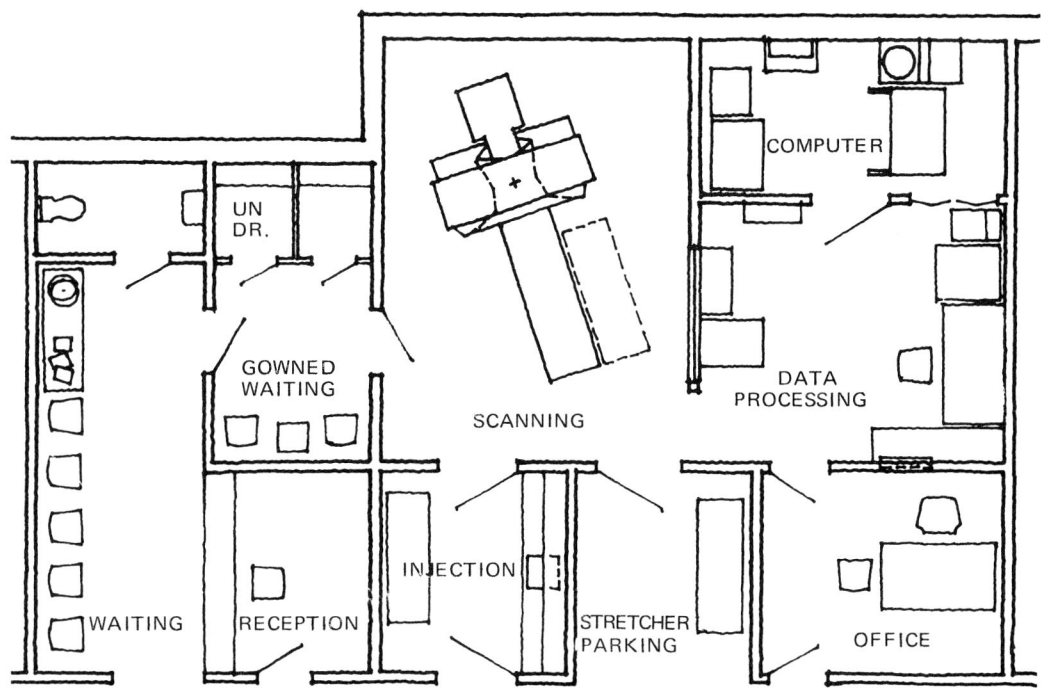

A computer assisted tomography suite, inspired by architectural planning of General Electric. Required ceiling height 2.8 m.

Xray diagnostic consultative session room

For X ray film diagnostic and consultative sessions, where doctors from all involved clinics participate at pre-arranged fixed times, large and small film demonstration rooms are needed.

30 to 35 seats require 35 m² of space, 20 to 25 seats 25 m², 14 to 18 seats 20 m² and 8 to 10 seats 15 m².

In the large room about 400 films are to be demonstrated per session on examining screens.

X ray diagnostic screens have a very low brightness. As the radiologists differ in their sensitivity to glare, control of the screen brightness is desirable. The details should be revealed without creating glare discomfort. The rooms should be illuminated during the sessions to the very low level of 1 lux.

Typing pool

The typists in the immediate interpreting area usually perform only a fraction of the secretarial and typing tasks of the radiological department. Most of the work is done in the typing pool of the department, which has to be planned after office planning principles.

A considerable saving of typing time can be achieved by increased precision in dictated reports. It has been found to be usual that up to two thirds of the X ray report wordings are insignificant and unnecessary[36].

X ray file room

The active film files with a capacity of about 2 years must be immediately available at the reception office of the department. The need of previous films in daily routine roentgenological work is limited, because the value of the filed film decreases very quickly[37].

The long term filing usually covers a period of 10 to 12 years.

Old films must be found without delay. The length of the filing period, the type of filing and the principles on which old films are discarded are important for the functioning of the film files. No system seems to be undoubtedly the best. The advantages must always be weighed against disadvantages[38].

In a department with an output of 100 examinations per day, anything between 100 and 180 changes have to be made in the files[39].

Roughly 1,000 examinations per meter of frontage and five shelves on top of each other would be equal to a capacity of 3,000 to 3,500 examinations per m² of floor space. For 20,000 yearly examinations during a 20 years period 250 m² is needed, corresponding to 900 shelf meters[40]. Insufficient space allocation for filing has been one of the frequent errors in radiologic diagnostic facility planning.

To make the handling of film files easier, when traditional film sizes are used, only 80 per cent of the shelves should be used and there should be not more than four

36 Thornbury J R: The Radiologist as a Reporting Computer. 17th Annual Meeting of the Association of University Radiologists. San Francisco, May 1969.

37 Brolin Inger: Problem vid arkivering av röntgenfilm. 1973, Läkartidningen 70:383–389.

38 ibid

39 Puijlaert C B A J: The expansion of radiodiagnostics. 1969, Medicamundi 14:147.

40 see also Puijlaert C B A J: Planning and calculation of surface of X ray department, based on workload to be expected. International symposium on the planning of radiological departments. Otaniemi, Finland, August 1972.

shelves on top of each other. Six shelves should be used in non-active film files. The depth of the shelves should be about 0.45 m and the height about 0.45 m. The distance between two shelves should not be less than 0.8 m and the total lenght of a shelf should not exceed 7 m, when open circulation is possible. If a dead-end system is applied, the length of a shelf should not exceed 5 m.

Mobile filing racks, which run on rails and can be either hand or motor driven, increase the storage capacity by between 90 and 150 per cent. They are not favoured when several people work in the filing room.

Record miniaturisation is aimed at increased efficiency and less cost in storage system.

The 100 mm copies are small enough to offer a high ratio of space-saving per number of films[41]. They are a convenient handling size. The size makes them large enough to be read with a naked eye against an ordinary light source. Simple enlargers can be obtained for viewing, but many medical staff find a simple magnifying glass satisfactory.

This size allows sufficient fine details to be retained in the copy. Areas of specific interest can be individually copied and enlarged on the 100 mm up to a size ratio of almost 1:1.

The 100 mm film is also a convenient size to fit in patient's notes. A copy would be made for this purpose so that earlier radiographs and a copy of the report are always available in the notes. This would offer one of the greatest savings in departmental clerical time.

Filing and retrieval of films is currently almost entirely performed manually by clerical staff. Automated electronically controlled systems have been developed. Computerization is changing the filing and information distribution systems.

X ray images might be stored also as video tape or video disc recordings. Objections to this system, in addition to cost, are the risks of loss or degradation of images through technical electronic difficulties[42]. Some see the way to be with 35 mm film plus computerization for medical records[43].

There is some doubt about the value of microfilming in general. It is not recommended in very active files where current information is added.

The future must bring developments in the field of X ray record storage, it has been stated[44]. Maybe it will see the complete abolition of the departmental film file. Indeed what real need is there for it now? If it is acceptable that a miniaturised copy, accompanied by a radiological report, is all that is necessary then would not storage in the patient's notes be sufficient? The common argument against this is that the films will be easily lost. But this should not happen to any section of the patient's notes at all. Keeping one copy only would place the onus of responsibility fairly on the medical staff.

---

41 John C: The reported film storage problem solved? 100 mm film miniaturisation using the Oldelft, Delcopex and Odelcard System. 1978, Radiography 44:191–195.

42 see also Fisher Harry W: Communication in Diagnostic Radiology. 1972, Australasian Radiology 16:1:12–22.

43 see also White John: Miniaturisation of X ray films. 1978, Radiography 44:185–190.

44 John C: The reported film storage problem solved? 100 mm film miniaturisation using the Oldelft, Delcopex and Odelcard System. 1978, Radiography 44:191–195.

Consultation rooms

It is advisable to separate the consultation rooms from the radiodiagnostic area. Eac consultation room requires an area of about 10 m². Washbasin is needed in all consu tation rooms.

Library

A departmental library of about 10 m² is an asset.

Store rooms

There should be a clean supply store and a store for contrast media, medicaments and drugs.

Materials and equipment stored in the clean supply room comprise procedure packs sterilized syringes and needles, comercially processed sterile disposable items, bandages, linen, etc.

In the store for contrast media, medicaments and drugs, also sterilized topical fluids external lotions and disinfectants are kept.

The minimum size for a store is about 2.5 m².

Unexposed Xray film store

The from radiation well protected film store should cover the department's needs* of about five weeks.

Building materials for facilities where unprocessed photographic materials would be stored must be chosen with the greatest care. If the fog level is to be kept low, the film shielding has to be about 100 times higher than for staff shielding[45].

In all countries there should be a list of available low radiation building materials, gravel and like, which can be recommended for X ray departments. Materials that have a gamma activity around 10 $\gamma\mu$ C/g are fully accepted. An upper limit is set at 15 $\gamma\mu$ C/g. Cosmic radiation usually plays a smaller part than radiation from building materials.

---

* 10,000 yearly examinations correspond to a length of 2.75 m shelving for a month's X ray film needs.

45 Lundh A: Storing conditions for X ray films. International symposium on the planning of radiological departments. Otaniemi, Finland. August 1972.

Open film packages require a humidity of 40 to 60 per cent.

The storage temperature should not exceed about 20°C. Cooling is needed only in tropical countries.

Good ventilation is essential to keep the radon gas level low.

hanging rooms for staff, retirement room

Changing rooms should have toilets and showers.

A retirement room for rest and emergencies for every ten female employees should be provided.

ffices and conference room

Offices for radiologists, supporting medical and clerical staff, and a conference room are needed.

For lectures and discussions the unit's *library* could be used.

taff lounge

The staff refreshment room-lounge has to be comfortable and fenestrated.

A pantry or vending machines for tea and other refreshing drinks should be available.

As long as smoking is tolerated in hospitals, the lounge must be extremely well-ventilated.

echnological section

In large hospitals workshop, offices and laboratories for radiophysicists, X ray engineers, as well as film and TV engineers should be available.

This section — not necessarily within the diagnostic department area — includes also the video centre, a technical development shop and staff training facilities.

Cleaners' rooms

One cleaners' room per about 400 to 600 m² floor space is needed. There should be a drainer and access to cold and hot water. An area of about 5 m² would be sufficient for the purpose.

The formula of one hour per 10 m² of floor area per week could be used when calculating the number of cleaning staff required[46].

Disposal room

An area of about 12 m² is required for the collection and temporary storage of items such as used syringes and needles, soiled linen, awaiting return for re-processing; materials for destruction by the hospital's incinerator; and materials *e g* glass, that cannot be destroyed by incineration.

The disposal room should be provided with a sink, a disposal unit and storage for urinals, bedpans, disposal bins, soiled laundry bags, shelves, and a washbasin.

46 Western Regional Hospital Board, Research and Development Unit: Organisation & Design of Radiodiagnostic Departments. Stencil. (Glasgow), January 1973, p 20.

Sonography, a diagnostic ultrasound technique consists mostly in waves of frequency between 2.25 and 10 MHz and not audible for human ear. The ultrasound facility should provide scheduled services and be available for emergency cases[1].

Diagnostic sonar methods can be used to demonstrate* soft-tissue structures and to study physiological movements, using exposure conditions which seem to be harmless[3].

Sonography provides answers to some clinical questions without discomfort, or great expense that otherwise demand hazardous, invasive, and costly investigation.

In the field of cardiology and obstetrics, it is indispensable as a source of diagnostic information not duplicated by other techniques. The use in obstetrics, excepting pelvimetry, of any other form of radiant energy is generally considered substandard practice[4].

Ultrasonic diagnosis is useful in distinguishing between cystic and solid tumours in the abdomen, thyroid and breast[5]. Being harmless, it must remain the first choice imaging technique in many cases of abdominal disease, to include liver, pancreas and other organs[6]. Ultrasonic echography in nephrology has proved itself to be both benign and effective[7]. Sonography is used in ophthalmology, cardiology, paediatrics, surgery, neurology, neurosurgery, urology, in diagnosing soft tissue tumours, and in radiotherapy planning.

---

1   System design of a clinical facility for diagnostic ultrasound. 1978, Hospitals 52:11:99–110.

*   The received echoes can principally be displayed in four forms:
    in the A mode the coordinate along the trace of the oscilloscope represents time, the amplitude of the echo is displayed as a deflection of this coordinate;
    in the B mode the coordinate along the trace of the oscilloscope represents time, the amplitude of the echo is represented as brightness or intensity of the appropriate portion of the trace;
    in the AB mode the coordinate along the trace of the oscilloscope represents time while the amplitude of the echo is displayed both as a deflection of this coordinate and brightness of the trace;
    in the M mode the trace is moved to display the pattern of movement of echoes but the transducer is kept stationary.

3   Wells P N T: Ultrasonics in Medicine and Biology. 1977, Physics in Medicine & Biology 22:629–669.

4   see also Cimmino Christian V and King Donald L: The General Radiologist and Ultrasound. 1976, American Journal of Roentgenology 127:867.

5   see also Goudie E G; Myers J B and Morley J E: Ultrasonic Diagnosis in General Surgery. 1974, South African Medical Journal 48:203–205.

6   see also Meire H B: Ultrasound — current status and prospects. 1977, The British Journal of Radiology 50:379–380.

7   see also Kellerman Edwin, Goldberg Barry B and Pollack Howard M: Ultrasonic Echography in Renal Disease. 1976, Hospital Practice 11:6:109–115.

Ultrasonic equipment is expensive. New machinery appears all too frequently. In spite of the many available advantages and its great potential, proper caution must prevail until the limitations of diagnostic ultrasound are completely defined[8].

In the US it has been estimated that the caseload of a comprehensive ultrasound service will undergo a rapid growth phase up to about one examination per year for every 50 people in the population served[9].

It is estimated that about 50 per cent of sonography investigations are gynaecological-obstetrical. 38 per cent of investigations are made in the fields of internal medicine, surgery and urology, 12 per cent in angiological, cardiological, neurological and ophthalmological fields[10].

Technology is rapidly extending the field of ultrasound, and there are no grounds for complacency. Apparatus is likely to grow more refined, become more penetrating, and yield an ever-increasing flow of information. If there is a threshold past which damage occurs, it may one day be exceeded, although it was not known 1977 what that damage might be or what form it would take[11]. No adverse effects have yet been shown using the power levels and frequencies commonly employed in medical ultrasonic diagnosis[12].

It has been feared that the advent of computer assisted body tomography will pale ultrasound into obscurity. This seems unlikely to happen for many different reasons[13]. Probably sonography will assume greater importance with regard to the prevention of birth damage and strokes and also in the identification of anatomical and functional changes in the body in general. However, these new diagnostic possibilities will be realized only if there is substantial improvement in the quality of ultrasonic tomograms, if ultrasonic angiograms can be produced successfully, and if prices are reduced sufficiently for the necessary equipment to be afforded by wider practices[14].

Computer storage and analysis, and holography belong to the future arsenal of ultrasonics.

---

8   see also Heins Jr Henry C and McCarter Linda M: Diagnostic ultrasound in obstetrics and gynecology. 1978, Comprehensive Therapy 4:3:38–44.

9   System design of a clinical facility for diagnostic ultrasound. 1978, Hospitals 52:11:99–110.

10 Oliva Luigi: Basic functional concepts in planning of image forming systems departments. International Symposium on the Planning of Departments of Radiology and Imaging Sciences. Lisbon, May 1978.

11 Donald Ian: Further developments in diagnostic sonar in obstetrics and gynecology. Obstetrics and gynecology annual. vol 6. Appleton-Century-Crofts. New York 1977, p 61.

12 Robinson H P: The current status of sonar in obstetrics and gynecology. in Recent advances in obstetrics and gynecology. number 12. ed by John Stallworthy and Gordon Bourne. Churchill Livingstone. Edinburgh, London, New York 1977, p 244.

13 Meire H B: Ultrasonic — current status and prospects. 1977, The British Journal of Radiology 50:379–380.

14 Anliker M: Current and Future Aspects of Biomedical Engineering. 1977, Triangle 16:129–140.

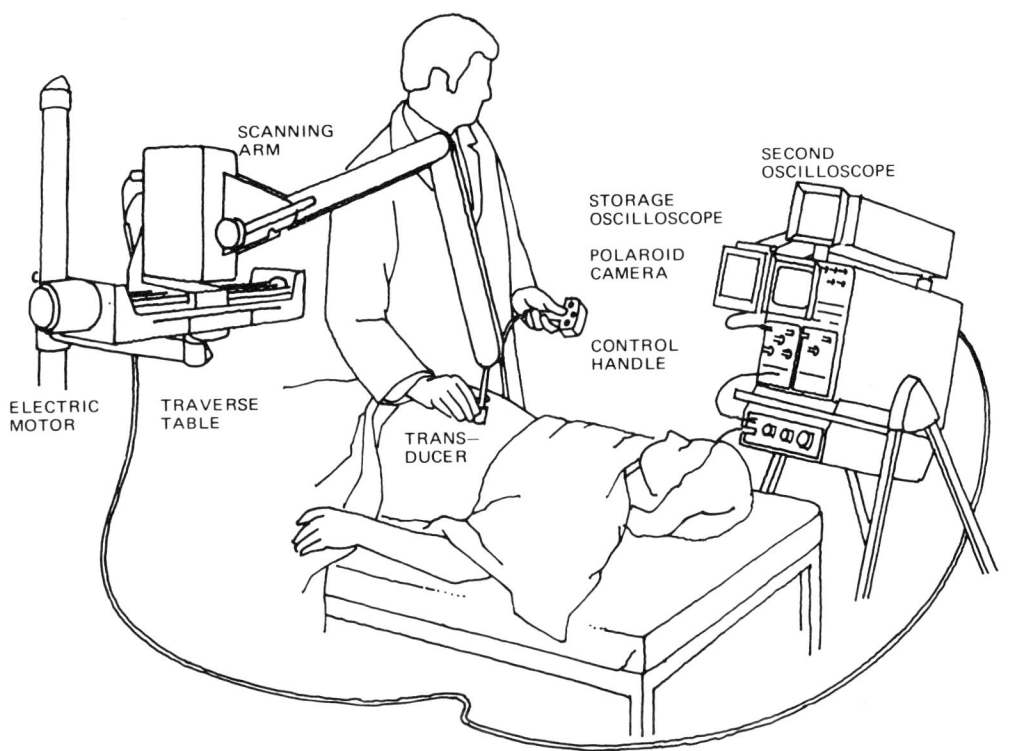

Sonography in obstetrics. After Bruce D Doust (1973).

The centralized diagnostic sonography unit should be located close to or established as a section within the diagnostic radiology department. In cases in which a speciality group controls the diagnostic sonography unit and only those speciality procedures are done, the obvious location is within the speciality area.

The scanning time e g for obstetrics is about 30 min, for lymph node assessment up to 60 minutes. Until an average time per patient has been established, 45 minutes can be used as a basis for scheduling appointments[15].

The maximum contact-B scanner work load that one sonographer (technologist) using one machine can accommodate is estimated to be between 10 and 18 cases per day[16].

15 System design of a clinical facility for diagnostic ultrasound. 1978, Hospitals 52:11:99–110.
16 ibid

A (part-time)physician and two sonography technicians are always needed. The work load necessary for a physician in charge to maintain proficiency is estimated to be at least 4 cases a day[17].

Space requirement for a sonography room is about 25 m². Hot and cold water should be available as well as suction and oxygen supply. Space for staff, for storage of material and for patient reception, waiting and toilets which admit also a wheelchair is needed.

Waiting room should have separate areas for inpatients and outpatients as well as for two stretcher patients.

Two changing cubicles of about 2 m² size should be available for each ultrasound room. They should be equipped with hooks, mirrors and means of locking up the patients' valuables.

A 10 to 12 m² physician's office is required. It should include viewboxes for imaging interpretation and for correlating ultrasonic images with Xray or other studies. Secretarial space is needed.

Records should be filed outside the examination room. 1 to 1.5 m² of space is required for one year's storage[18].

Echocardiography

Pulsed ultrasonic Doppler technique afford opportunities for making transcutaneous measurements on the cardiovascular system and to provide information which other approaches can not make available.

Echocardiography has steadily gained in precision and is achieving broader application in cardiac diagnosis, even on infants and young children. It is non-invasive and causes no discomfort and needs little co-operation from the patient, but it requires a high level of skill. The procedure itself took in 1976 approximately 15 minutes, and the success rate in expert hands was 80 to 90 per cent[19].

The maximum echocardiographic work load that one sonographer using one machine can accommodate is estimated to be between 4 and 6 cases per day. The work load possible from one machine may double or triple when multiple sonographers are used[20].

Assessment of cardiac performance with the use of ultrasound is in its infancy. Continued investigations regarding cardiac function should improve the credibility, re-

17 System design of a clinical facility for diagnostic ultrasound. 1978, Hospitals 52:11:99–110.

18 ibid

19 Cahill Noel S: Echocardiography: A Review. 1976, Irish Medical Journal 69:213–218.

20 System design of a clinical facility for diagnostic ultrasound. 1978, Hospitals 52:11:99–110.

liability, and validity of the technique[21]. A major limitation is its image quality: the picture is by no means as clear as an angiocardiogram taken by X rays; fine detail is notably absent[22].

In spite of these limitations echocardiography is regarded indispensable to management of cardiac diseases. In hospitals with a cardiologist but without facilities for cardiac surgery it has special value as a screening method for patients who are being considered for further examination in a specialist unit or for operative treatment. Echocardiography may speed diagnosis, reduce unnecessary referrals to other hospitals, reduce time spent in hospital, and limit the more hazardous, uncomfortable, and expensive invasive diagnostic procedure.

When less than five echocardiographic studies are performed a week, technical and interpretive capabilities of the operator tend to deteriorate[23].

Echocardiography can be combined with non-cardiac diagnostic ultrasound examinations in a multi-purpose diagnostic ultrasound facility located either in a radiology department or in a sonography department. With increasing clinical applications, the economic necessity for combining echocardiography with other diagnostic ultrasound examinations is decreasing[24].

The echocardiography equipment is portable and easily used at bedside. For some cardiac diseases this diagnostic method has a specific diagnostic value and can be easily performed without any risk in the critically ill patient in the ICTU[25].

The space required for echocardiography is about 20 m^2. The door width should be 1.3 m.

Use of an adjustable bed instead of an examining table enhances patient comfort and makes changes in position easier. There should be commonly grounded electrical outlets, a dimmer switch to adjust room light, and a washbasin.

There are no radiation protection requirements[26].

If high risk cardiac patients are examined in the echocardiography unit, support facilities for cardiopulmonary resuscitation should be immediately available.

About 15 m^2 will be needed for administrative functions, case reviews, and reporting. An additional 15 m^2 is needed for waiting, toilets and storage.

21 Meyor Richard A: Echocardiography – Application in Assessing Cardiac Performance in Clinical Care. 1978, The Journal of Anesthesiology 49:71–77.

22 Partridge John: Echocardiography. 1978, The Chest, Heart and Stroke Journal 3:13–17.

23 Report of Inter-Society Commission for Heart Diseases Resources. Gramiak Raymond, Fortuin Nicholas J, King Donald L and Popp Richard L. Fligenbaum Harvey. 1975, Circulation 51:A1–A7.

24 ibid

25 Hanrath P, Sonntag F and Bleifeld W: Wertigkeit der Echokardiographie in der Intensivmedizin. 1978, Intensivmedizin 15:150–155.

26 Report of Inter-Society Commission for Heart Diseases Resources, Gramiak Raymond, Fortuin Nicholas J, King Donald L and Popp Richard L. Fligenbaum Harvey. 1975, Circulation 51:A1–A7.

Thermography is an infrared scanning system for measuring changes in distribution of surface temperature and presentation of the temperature distribution and develop ment.

Colour thermography is performed by the use of colour filters in front of the camera which select different isotherm levels. In superimposition photography the various isotherms are displayed according to the various colours of the filters.

Warm areas may represent inflammatory or cancerous processes. Cool areas may signify inadequate blood supply. From this the pato-physiological state of the body can be determined and applied to diagnose various diseases.

Although of established value in industrial and military usage, the potential of thermography as a clinical diagnostic technique has yet to be fully recognized. First used clinically in the diagnosis of breast disease, medical thermography has many other applications[27].

Thermography is used for diagnosis and therapy appraisal as a complement to conventional methods in connection with peripheral vascular disorders, plastic surgery, burns and tissue viability, some inflammatory conditions, bone metastases, some cranial diseases, in connection with intensive care and the monitoring of drug therapy in rheumatology.

Nearly the whole thermal spectrum emitted by the human body[28] is covered. It is now possible to obtain a continuous pattern of the surface temperature resolution, which may be as high as 0.03 to $0.1°C$[29].

Although the thermography equipment is simple and quiet in operation, further research in the engineering section is required, including the problems of scanning surface for body curvature; colour display; image processing of thermograms; analysis of the thermogram by computer; miniaturization of apparatus, and reducing the cost of apparatus[30].

The temperature information from the infrared camera, which is normally displayed as a picture or an oscilloscope screen, is particularly suitable for computerization[31].

27 Carter Linda M: The clinical role of thermography. 1978, Journal of Medical Engineering & Technology 2:125–128.

28 Aarts N J M: Thermography in retrospect and prospect. XIII Congreso Internacional de Radiologia. Madrid, Octubre 1973. Excerpta Medica. Amsterdam, Princeton, London, Geneva, Tokyo 1973, p 129.

29 Atsumi K: The past studies and developments on bio-medical thermography in Japan. 1977, Acta Thermographica 2:67–82.

30 ibid

31 see also Feasey C M, Evans A L and James W B: Thermography in breast carcinoma: results of a blind reading trial. 1975, The British Journal of Radiology 48:791–795.

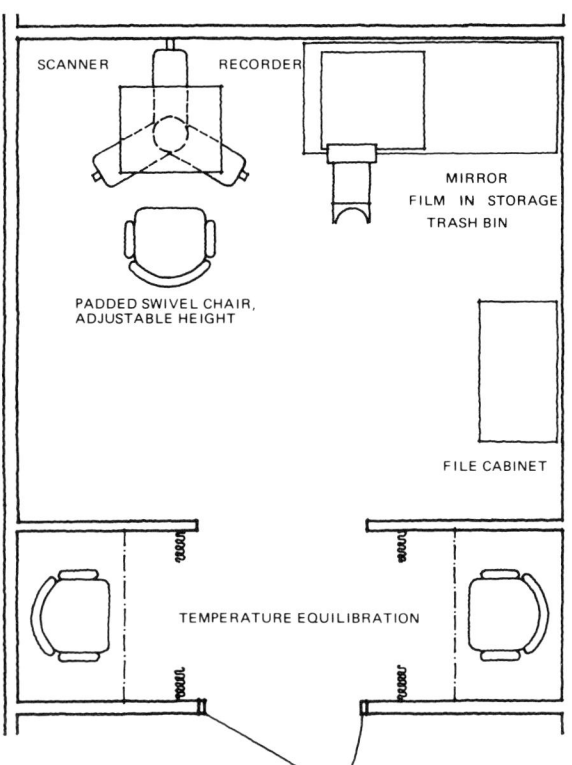

SCANNER   RECORDER

MIRROR
FILM IN STORAGE
TRASH BIN

PADDED SWIVEL CHAIR,
ADJUSTABLE HEIGHT

FILE CABINET

TEMPERATURE EQUILIBRATION

A thermography room needs cubicles for temperature equilibration.

Thermograms could be assessed using a computer without loss of accuracy and without the necessity to use expensive personnel for examination and interpretation.

A complete independent medical thermography unit[32] should include one room each for thermography, sonography and radiology, with separate waiting rooms and changing cubicles, a reception room, two examination rooms with washbasins and all the regular storages, staff and additional facilities. Thermography rooms require a size of about 18 m² and a height of 2.5 m. The room should not be smaller than 3.5 by 3.5 m[33].

The thermal environment must be controlled with great accuracy. There should be no heat sources or draughts. No sunlight should enter the room and it is best if not even daylight comes in[34]. Light should be provided by fluorescent tubes.

There should be no glass or polished metal surface near the subject. The walls of the room should not have glossy paint.

32 Largillière Serge: La Thermographie Médicale. 1975, Techniques Hospitalières 31:11:54–64.

33 Chudáček Zdeněk: Medical Thermography. Acta Universitatis Carolinae Medica. Monographia LXXVI. Prague 1977, p 21.

34 ibid

The thermography room should be maintained at a temperature of 21 ± 1°C[35] and at a humidity of 50 per cent. According to other specialists the temperature should be maintained between 19 and 21°C[36] or 18 and 20°C[37].

The patient should be exposed without clothes to this environment for 5 to 10 minutes in order to remove all thermal artifacts on the skin surface. A woman who calls for examination of her breast should not wear a brasier on that day.

The waiting room and the changing cubicles adjacent the examination room should have the climatic conditions of the examination room proper. The waiting and ante-rooms should be equipped to allow the subject to acclimatize in the position he is going to be examined, e g prior to examination of the breast the axilla should be exposed for 15 to 20 min. Since elderly women have difficulties in holding their arms above the head, the waiting room should have bars or other means to hold on to.

35 Gautherie M and Gros Ch M: Contribution of infrared thermography to early diagnosis, pre-therapeutic prognosis and post-irradiation follow-up of breast carcinomas. 1976, Medicamundi 21:135–149.

36 Chudáček Zdeněk: Medical Thermography. Acta Universitatis Carolinae Medica. Monographia LXXVI. Prague 1977, p 21.

37 Carter Linda M: The clinical role of thermography. 1978, Journal of Medical Engineering & Technology 2:125–129.

Chudáček Zdeněk: Medical Thermography. Acta Universitatis Carolinae Medica. Monographia LXXVI. Prague 1977, p 22.

uclear medicine services

Nuclear medicine is the speciality in which radioactive tracers (radionuclides) are applied to medical situations. In a broader sense, the nuclear medicine specialist should be part of the diagnostic imaging team[1]. As such, he would fit his expertness into a broader concept of diagnostic imaging, which includes ultrasound, computed tomography, and radiography. The result could be a more efficient and effektive use of powerful diagnostic techniques in medicine.

Nuclear medicine includes all aspects of radionuclide use in medicine[*], including radioimmunoassay methods (purely in vitro); wet studies such as absorption tests, excretion tests and haematology tests (partially in vivo and partially in vitro); imaging studies (in vivo); and therapeutic applications (thyroid and blood diseases). However, it is not unusual to find a division of effort wherein the in vitro studies being performed in the clinical laboratory of the pathology department, the imaging studies being done in the radiology department, and aspects of thyroidology and haematology, including therapeutic applications, being managed by the internal medicine department[2].

In the radioisotope unit of the nuclear medical services short-lived isotopes are used diagnostically as tracers to locate lesions and tumours. The more long-lived isotopes are used therapeutically.

Through scanning the distribution of radioactive material in the human body is mapped. If a particular organ accumulates radioactive material selectively, an image may be produced which shows the position, size, and shape of the organ. The degree of radioactive material concentration may supply information about its function and lesions.

The trend of new instrumentation and the efforts of radiopharmacists indicate that nuclear medicine is returning to an analysis of body functions and metabolism[3].

The safety and relative simplicity of the nuclear examination methods suggest a considerably increased application on different organ systems than heretofore.

Moving detector instruments — rectilinear scanners or scintillation cameras — and stationary detector instruments, the so-called gamma cameras are used. Emission CT scanners do the same thing as gamma cameras. The difference is that emission CTs can provide either cross-section slices or slices the entire lenght of the body, whereas gamma cameras do not. The image of the emissions is reconstructed by a computer on a video screen; data can be stored in the computer for later analysis or manipulation.

---

1   Johnston Gerald S: Nuclear Medicine. 1978, Military Medicine 143:527–531.

*   There are two major facets: in vivo studies require injection of a radionuclide into a patient; in vitro tests require no injection.

2   Johnston Gerald S: Nuclear Medicine. 1978, Military Medicine 143:527–531.

3   Budinger Thomas F: Instrumentation Trends in Nuclear Medicine. 1977, Seminars in Nuclear Medicine 7:285–297.

Emission CT scanners come in two types. The low-energy type, also known as single-photon, uses commonly available radioisotopes that are routinely used by nuclear medicine departments. These low-energy radioisotopes can be active in the body for up to an hour, in some cases, and can be stored.

High-energy emission CT scanners, also known as positron ECTs, positron cameras or annihilation coincidence detection devices, use high-energy radioisotopes that have a short half-life and cannot be stored. Most often used isotopes are the radioactive forms of carbon, oxygen and nitrogen. These must be manufactured in a readily-accessible cyclotron, one that is usually no further away from the treatment area than in the adjacent building.

Although positron emission CT scanners have been around longer than single-photon units, there are very few installations due to the necessity for a nearby cyclotron. The cost of acquiring both devices, if not nearby cyclotron is available, is prohibitive for most facilities — close to $ 1 million. For this reason positron cameras are, for the most part, limited to research facilities[4].

Radioactive wastes are clearly defined. Methods of their management are established. No reason for variance exists. Adequate installations must be provided to deal safely with radioactive wastes in liquid or solid form, whether from the laboratory or excreted by patients, and for the storage of unsealed sources in accordance with safety requirements. A storage tank for radioactive waste is an advantage when isotopes with short half-life are used.

The patients who have died briefly after an injection of a significant dose of radioactive isotopes require the morgue to be equipped with a radiation protected refrigerated chamber[5].

Experience suggests that, in general, special precautions are not necessary for post mortem examinations or embalming of corpses containing less than 5 mCi of colloidal ^{90}Y or ^{198}Au, 10 mCi of ^{32}P or 15 mCi of ^{131}I. Embalming of corpses containing greater activities should not normally be carried out*.

Little information is available regarding the extent of radionuclide usage within hospitals[6].

It is estimated that in many countries about 1 per cent of the population is annually exposed to nuclear medical examinations[7]. About 50 to 60 per cent of the nuclear

4   New devices extend nuclear imaging. 1977, Modern Healthcare 7:8:41–42.

5   Alexander N N and Sukovatykh L S: The equipment of modern radiological departments in oncological institutions. Abstract. International symposium on the planning of radiological departments. Otaniemi, Finland. August 1972.

*   The Handling, Storage, Use and Disposal of Unsealed Radionuclides in Hospitals and Medical Research Establishments. Pergamon Press. Oxford, New York, Frankfurt 1977, p 20.

6   Henry David A, Gray Jane M B, Guthbert Georgina, Greig William and Lawson David H: Frequency and Pattern of Radionuclide Administration to Medical Patients in a General Hospital. 1977, European Journal of Nuclear Medicine 2:133–135.

7   Rootwelt Kjell: Laboratorium for nucleaermedisinfunksjoner. 1976, Sykehuset 39:198–202.

medical services are conducted on the out-patient basis, at least in Sweden and in the Federal Republic of Germany[8].

In the US teaching hospitals about 30 per cent of the patients are diagnosed using radionuclides[9].

Nuclear medicine is a field in which technological advances are rapid and the demand for procedures is expanding, making planning difficult.

In Sweden, it has been estimated that a population of 200,000 would require annually 4,000 scintigraphies, 2,000 other examinations and 10,000 *in vitro* analyses[10].

At least 5,000 examinations are said to be needed yearly in the Federal Republic of Germany to make a nuclear medical unit economically rational[11].

Internationally the nuclear medical services have not a uniform organizational position. There are complete, independent units, but also units, where some of the activities are spread to X ray diagnostic units, to radiotherapy, clinical chemistry, clinical physiology and medical physics. It has been stressed that there is an ever growing association between nuclear medicine and diagnostic radiology[12]. E g when isotopic techniques are compared with the standard chest radiograph, it is evident that the two are complementary. Their combination provides a powerful tool[13].

The office or control centre, located at the point of patient arrival, would be the hub of the department.

The size of a procedure room or laboratory should be about 27 m² and of a scanning room about 15 m².

In the procedure room there is a patient examination table, work counters, a disposal sink, a scintillation well counter, wall cabinets, a ventilated cabinet, a desk, a refrigerator, and a washbasin.

Electronic devices for locating the site of the tumour within the body is placed in the procedure room. Instead of a separate procedure room for each major instrument, larger rooms or bays in which two or more instruments can be operated simultaneously can be used.

---

8   Rootwelt Kjell: Laboratorium for nucleaermedisinfunksjoner.1976, Sykehuset 39:198–202.

9   ibid

10   Nosslin B, Rinquist I and Vikterlöf K J: Isotopverksamhetens omfattning och ställning inom servicesektorn i den framtida sjukvården. Promemoria juni 1974 på uppdrag av Socialstyrelsen, Stockholm.

11   zum Winkel K: Organisation moderner nuclear-medizinischer institute. 1972, Der Radiologe 12:1:10.

12   Terry William G: Pre-planning considerations. A paper prepared for the International Symposium on the Planning of Departments of Radiology and Imaging Sciences. Lisbon, May 1978.

13   see also Fazio F, Lavender J P, Steiner R E: Radioisotopes, chest radiology and lung physiology. 1978, Journal Belge de Radiologie 61:219–228.

As patients are fully clothed during nuclear medicine procedures, there is no need for privacy in conventional sense. On the contrary, the area's open atmosphere seems to help patients to feel less fearful during the diagnostic process, and the surrounding activity helps to provide them with some interest. However, use of these open spaces does require that the staff members have considerable insight into patient anxiety[14].

The large scan area approach seems to provide staff efficiency improvement, good visual contact among staff members, easier modification to accommodate new techniques and equipment[15]. A folding, sound-absorbing wall is recommended to be used to close one bay of the procedure area when a seriously ill or particularly noisy patient is treated[16].

For radionuclide-therapy a limited number of radiation protected single patient rooms is needed.

The well protected *radiopharmaceutical preparation room* or hot laboratory is to provide radioactive compounds to the patient scan areas. In this room these materials are stored and dispensed. A shower for use in case of radiation contamination should be located near the radiopharmaceutical preparation room.

No office should be located near a source of high radiation, such as the hot lab. The high radiation levels in the hot lab may interfere with procedures in adjoining rooms so the hot lab should be isolated, adjoining an area such as the storage area.

In the handling and storage area the departmental layout has to be compact. Sophisticated remote handling equipment is used to reduce personal exposure. Lead is used in shielded areas. The weight of shielding may cause construction problems.

Liquid radioisotopes may present problems relating to vaporization, contamination, ingestion, and waste disposal. The shielding arrangements, however, are considerably simpler in comparison with solid source shielding.

The room temperature in the storage area should ensure that stored liquids do not freeze. As stores may be visited infrequently, attention shall be paid to fire risks. Advice should be sought from fire authorities, also concerning an automatic fire detection and warning system.

Outside each store there must be a clear warning sign, including the standard radiation symbol and the name of the person responsible for the store.

Rooms are needed for film viewing areas, files, patient waiting, and staff lounges and lockers.

---

14 Simple, efficient departmental design suits functions, growth of nuclear medicine. 1977, Hospitals 51:10:30–32.

15 ibid

16 ibid

In all rooms where radioactive nuclides are stored, dispensed, or manipulated chemically, exposed   surfaces require appropriate treatment to prevent contamination. Adequate shielding and security of such rooms must be ensured. These rooms should be separated from rooms where highly sensitive counting of low activities takes place.

Safety precautions are much more important in *in vivo* studies than in *in vitro* studies.

Laboratories and clinical rooms where large amounts of nuclides or highly radioactive patients are handled should be as far as possible from counting rooms where low activities are being measured. In multistorey buildings this may be a three dimensional problem and permissible floor loadings for heavy equipment and shielding have to be considered.

All surfaces in the procedure rooms should be for ease of decontamination and cleaning of nonporous, continuous and smooth material.

Plastic laminate covered benches are excellent, although joints and sinks present problems. Stainless steel benches easily incorporate formed sinks, but can be corroded by chemicals.

Taps of the sinks for washing up contaminated glassware and other articles should be operatable without using the hands. The drain should be connected directly to a main sewer. The taps should be accessible for periodic monitoring*.

Floors can be covered with sealed PVC except where hot objects or some organic chemicals may fall on them. Then linoleum may be preferable if cut so that joints do not occur where spills are most likely.

A floor drain is sometimes justified[17]. The drains could be of any material except poly-ethylen which tends to absorb radioiodine.

Hand washing facilities should be provided and sited conveniently by each working area.

Washing facilities ought to be elbow or foot operated.

Where large quantities of radionuclides are handled, a shower should be available for use in an emergency.

About 10 changes of air per hour should be provided.

---

*   The Handling, Storage, Use and Disposal of Unsealed Radionuclides in Hospitals and Medical Research Establishments. Pergamon Press. Oxford, New York, Frankfurt 1977, p 12.

17 see also Osborn S B: Radiation Protection in Hospital — Radioisotopes. 1972, Hospital Building and Engineering 5:5:50–53.

Ventilation should be designed so that air from rooms where radionuclides are used and which could under accident conditions be contaminated will not be recirculated or taken into inactive areas. In a suite of rooms used for work at different levels of activity, ventilation should ensure that the air flow is from low to high activity areas*.

In adverse climatic conditions it is important that the entire department be air-conditioned to guarantee good working conditions for the staff and to protect the measuring equipment[18].

The crystals in the gamma camera heads can tolerate temperature variations only from $10°C$ to $40°C$, but cannot adjust to rapid fluctuations. The camera also requires a non-condensing relative humidity between 35 and 60 per cent[19].

The primary purpose of *electrical design* in a nuclear medicine suite is to provide an uninterrupted and constantly even source of power. Noise on the electrical lines, pure circuit noise on the electrical input panels, sudden voltage surges that occur as other large equipment is turned on or off, and similar problems necessitate the use of isolation transformers to filter the electrical flow[20].

At the present time a complete radioisotope service is possible only in hospitals of the highest standard.

A complete nuclear medical service[21] would include the following sections and rooms:

> *diagnostics:*
> radiopharmaceutical preparation — hot laboratory, application room; area for diagnoses including two gamma–cameras; room for radiochromatography etc; data room; two examination rooms; dark room; physical laboratory; electronic shop; radiation-protected store for isotopes; laboratory; waiting room for non–ambulant patients; waiting room for ambulant patients; two patient lavatories; room for physicist and chemist; two bio-chemical laboratories; sample preparation; room for liquid-scintillation-counter; room for autoradiography; film viewing room; film filing room**; staff changing rooms; staff lounge and radioactive waste room.

---

* The Handling Storage, Use and Disposal of Unsealed Radionuclides in Hospitals and Medical Research Establishments. Pergamon Press. Oxford, New York, Frankfurt 1977, p 12.

18 see also Nuclear Medicine. World Health Organization Technical Report Series No 591. World Health Organization. Geneva 1976, p 22.

19 Simple, efficient departmental design suits functions, growth of nuclear medicine. 1977, Hospitals 51:10:30–32.

20 ibid

21 see also zum Winkel K: Organisation moderner nuclear-medizinischer Institute. 1972, Der Radiologe 12:1:12.

** about 400 scans can be filed on one linear m of space.

counting:
counting room; room for electronics; two dressing cubicles; patient lavatory; patient shower and staff room.

therapy:
two operation rooms; preparation room; room for dosiometric planning and radiation-protected isotope store.

nuclear medical ward:
twelve single rooms with shower and lavatory; two four patient rooms with shower and lavatory; day room; nurse's station; doctor's room; pantry; utility room; two changing rooms for staff and staff lounge.

experimental animal unit:
two animal rooms; preparation room; operation room; staff room and feed supply room.

central administration
Major nuclear medicine equipment in an university medical centre covering about 5,000 nuclear medicine procedures *per annum*[22] may include two scintillation cameras, one thyroid uptake system, two gamma-cameras, one multi-channel analyzer and scaler, one liquid scintillation counter, one dose calibrator, one automatic well scintillation counter, one stationary *in vivo* multiprobe counting system, and equipment for radio-pharmaceutical preparation.

22 see also Harris N Jeanne and Bennet Leslie R: Planning a nuclear medicine service. 1973, Hospitals 47:20:84–94.

Radiotherapy units

Radiation therapy is a speciality in the field of oncology.

For many of the most common cancers — cancers of the lung, breast, bladder, and ovaries, for example — surgery is the treatment of choice and data suggest, for the major cancers, that radiation's total contribution is measured in terms of relatively small increments to the survival rates achieved by surgery[1]. However, a large portion of the benefits of any radiation — mainly palliative — must be measured in terms of relief from the symptoms of an incurable cancer, rather than by the relatively simple yardstick of survival times[2]. Chemotherapy, which is exceptionally demanding in medical time both in the clinic and the laboratory, is given as an adjunct to radiotherapy or as a continuing treatment[3].

The majority of the radiotherapy patients can be treated on out-patient basis, and also in limited radiotherapy facilities.

Radiation therapy can be divided into following categories[4]:

Brachytherapy — ionizing radiation using radium or the equivalent, or radioactive cobalt, cesium, or iridium. These isotopes are used in the form of needles for implantation of tumours, or in applicators to be placed against the tumour or inserted into a cavity containing a tumour.

Superficial therapy — ionizing radiation with energies from 8 to 140 kilovolts. Relatively soft X rays are used for noninfiltrating cancers, such as skin cancers.

Orthovoltage therapy — ionizing radiation with energies from 150 to 400 kilovolts. This equipment has been replaced largely by megavoltage units. It is used in the treatment of infiltrating surface malignancies and often as a supplement to megavoltage therapy such as interoral and intervaginal treatment.

Megavoltage therapy — ionizing radiation of greater than one million volts. This includes cobalt 60 and a variety of accelerators using high-energy X rays. The term cobalt therapy enjoys the reputation as being synonymous with all megavoltage therapy. This, of course, is not true. In addition to cobalt, most of the radiation therapy centres have more sophisticated accelerators which deliver radiation at 4 to 12 million volts. A few of the large centres have accelerators and betatrons which produce X rays at 25- to 35-million-volt.

In the linacs of linear accelerators, electrons are accelerated in a linear tube by high frequency power generators. Electrons are emitted from a gun, travel down the tube gaining energy all the way to hit a target and produce X rays at the end of the tube or to be let out. The main ad-

1   see also Russell Louise B: The diffusion of new hospital technologies in the United States. 1976, International Journal of Health Services 6:557–580.

2   ibid

3   Bratherton D G: Considerations in the planning of new radiotherapy departments. in The Planning of Radiotherapy Departments. ed by T J Deeley. British Journal of Radiology. Special Report 12. London 1976, p 44

4   see also Osmond Jr John D, King Richard L, De Marco Victor J, Klein Howard J, Farmer James P, Storaasli John P and Sykora Glenn F: Radiology and the Primary Care Physician. 1977, The Ohio State Medical Journal 73:389–395.

vantages over the cheaper cobalt machines are the higher quantum energy of the radiation, better depth dose curves and better collimation and the much higher radiation intensities of the X-rays[5]. The maintenance of a linac is more complicated and costly than that of a cobalt unit[6].

In the betatron, electrons are accelerated by induction and guided by magnetic fields. The betatron is basically a very simple and reliable, though expensive machine for producing very high energy electrons. Unlike radiation from other common sources, the dose it delivers drops off very sharply after a certain depth and, in general, a lower amount passes through the patient on the side away from the point at which the radiation enters. These advantages are countered to some extent by the fact that an electron beam is not particularly well focused and radiation is scattered to tissues around the cancer.

A betatron and a linac are complementary and can serve most needs. It has been stated that the ideal combination is a matched pair of supervoltage machines either cobalt or preferably linear accelerators[7].

Where both machines are readily available, a clinical preference for linac treatment leads to a higher linac/cobalt ratio. This element seems usually to outweigh the factors which might otherwise tend to increase the observed cobalt unit caseload. Among them the slightly longer down time required for maintenance and repair of accelerators. Where choice exists, cobalt is used for a higher population of the simpler palliative treatments requiring fewer, less accurately defined fields than the conditions treated by linear accelerator[8].

Evaluating and comparing the patient benefits of the different types of radiotherapy is a complex matter. Whatever the medical benefits of the radiation, they must also be weighed against its side-effects, which range from the almost immediate skin reactions and radiation sickness to possible longer-term complications involving the heart, the lungs, and deep tissue reactions.

On account of the high-dose-rates, the irradiation times have become so short that the setting-up times for the full utilization of these expensive units have become extremely significant.

Radiation therapy, for optimal use of professional staff and equipment, and economy consistent with high quality care would still be best performed in a limited number of medical centres.

According to the UK estimates, a population of one million requires in a radiotherapy department, two cobalt machines or one cobalt machine and one linear accelerator or betatron machine. In addition there is a need for a superficial X ray

5   Wideröe R: Recent trends in cancer radiation therapy. Symposium on the value and application of high-energy accelerators in medicine. Johannesburg. March 1972.

6   see also Russell Louise B: The diffusion of new hospital technologies in the United States. 1976, International Journal of Health Services 6:557–580.

7   Bratherton D G: Considerations in the planning of new radiotherapy departments. in The Planning of Radiotherapy Departments. ed by T J Deeley. British Journal of Radiology. Special Report 12. London 1976, p 47.

8   Raison J C A: Policy, scale and location of radiotherapy departments. in The Planning of Radiotherapy Departments. ed by T J Deeley. British Journal of Radiology. Special Report 12. London 1976, p 40.

machine and a deep X ray machine — 200 or 250 KV — for palliative therapy or for use when one of the supervoltage machines is not working[9].

To establish a radiotherapy unit in the Federal Republic of Germany 7,000 to 10,238 medical treatments and/or examinations per annum are requested[13]. In the German Democratic Republic this figure is 12,000[14].

A regular 700-bed hospital in the Federal Republic of Germany, as an example, requires in addition 12 to 24 beds when radiation therapy is introduced in the hospital, a 1,000-bed hospital 40 to 60 beds and a hospital of the highest medico-technical standard about 50 to 80 beds[15]. In these ward units special precautions against radiation have to be taken.

The assumption as a broad guide for planning has been that a cobalt machine can treat 300 to 400 patients annually, and the linear accelerator 600 to 800. *Raison*[11] has found some lack of reciprocity in these figures and suggests on the basis of 400 cobalt-patients per annum 560 linear accelerator patients and on the basis of 800 patients taken on an accelerator 500 patients for a cobalt machine.

According to *Snelling* a cobalt unit can treat thirty to forty patients in a day of seven hours with two radiographers to each machine and a linear accelerator treats sixty to seventy patients in the same time. Because of the very short treatment times the number of radiographers has to be doubled[12].

All machines should be replaced in 12 to 15 years[10].

9 Snelling Margareth: Basic principles in the planning of radiotherapeutic and oncological departments. International Symposium on the Planning of Departments of Radiology and Imaging Sciences. Lisbon, May 1978.

10 ibid

11 Raison J C A: Policy, scale and location of radiotherapy department in The Planning of Radiotherapy Departments. ed by T J Deeley. British Journal of Radiology. Special Report 12. London 1976, p 40.

12 Snelling Margareth: Basic principles in the planning of radiotherapeutic and oncological departments. International Symposium on the Planning of Departments of Radiology and Imaging Sciences. Lisbon, May 1978.

13 Kaufmann Horst: Die Leistungsbewertung in der Strahlentherapie. 1976, Röntgenpraxis 29:197–202.

14 ibid

15 see also Scherer E: Strahlentherapie-Institute und —Kliniken. 1972, Der Radiologe 12:1:6.

Elements of radiotherapy unit

The *clinical examination section* of a radiotherapeutic clinic includes a reception area including a registration room, examination and consultation rooms, rooms for medical staff and social workers, waiting areas including bed or trolley bays, storages, toilets and telephones.

The consultation rooms should be separated from the treatment area. The ratio of examination and treatment rooms has to be high as many patients are old and slow to undress. The inevitable number of follow up examinations often produce large clinics. Insufficient rooms may result in insufficient use of medical staff[16]. A darkened cubicle or room should be provided for examining otolaryngological patients.

An acceptable clinic room design from the functional point of view does not necessarily become acceptable when a mirror image of this is produced[17].

The *treatment section* comprises the treatment planning room for time-consuming dosimetric planning which requires access to a computer assisted scanner, simulator, mould room, medical staff — medical officers, physicists and technicians — and secretarial and record facilities, rooms for the unit stands, spaces for machinery including the power supply components and the control room. The planning procedure may require the taking of check X rays and the use of simulator.

This simulator is an essential piece of equipment and mandatory for all megavoltage units[18]. The accommodation will comprise the main simulator room and control area, an Xray processing room, and a clinical room for the preparation of the patient for minor surgical procedures[19].

A computer assisted tomography coupled with computerized treatment planning and dosimetry offers a great potential for improving radiation therapy through accurate localization of tumour and critical normal structures within the host and by utilizing the tissue density and X ray attenuation coefficients to increase the accuracy of dose computations. Such a system will utilize measurements from the

16 Bratherton D G: Considerations in the planning of new radiotherapy departments. in The Planning of Radiotherapy Departments. ed by T J Deeley. British Journal of Radiology. Special Report 12. London 1976, p 46.

17 see also White W F: Late modifications preparation for commissioning: prevention is better than cure. in The Planning of Radiotherapy Departments. ed by T J Deeley. British Journal of Radiology. Special Report 12. London 1976, p 189.

18 see also Doppelfeld E and Frik W: Erfahrungen beim Einsatz eines Therapiesimulators zur Bestrahlungsplanung. 1976, Strahlungstherapie 152:504–508.

19 see also Crooks S H: Supporting services: their need and size. in The Planning of Radiotherapy Departments. ed by T J Deeley. British Journal of Radiology. Special Report 12. London 1976, p 102.

actual patient for corrections necessary for dose perturbations resulting from tissue heterogeneity[20]. A special CT scanning unit is needed in larger radiotherapy units.

A treatment room needs about 45 m^2 — 56 m^2 has been preferred[21] — for its irradiation area including the 1.75 m wide maze, about 15 m^2 for the stand, and 35 m^2 for the machine room.

Various methods are used for providing access to the treatment or radiation room. The most convenient is achieved by means of a door leading directly into the room. In the case of megavoltage installations, however, such a door requires heavy shielding, even when located in a wall exposed only to leakage and scattered radiation. It may be very heavy and require an expensive motor drive as well as means for emergency manual operation. A maze arrangement is generally the most economical, as shielding of the door can be greatly reduced, usually to less than 6 mm of lead if it is exposed to multiple scattered radiation only. The required lead equivalence of the door will depend upon radiation energy, maze design, weekly workload and beam orientations. The principal objections to the use of a maze are increased space requirements and sometimes less convenient access to the treatment room, particularly for stretcher patients[22].

Direct window viewing is used in most superficial and orthovoltage installations. For megavoltage installations the cost of the high-density glass and its lead frame may be significant. Indirect viewing by means of mirrors is more economical but may be less satisfactory.

Closed circuit TV provides considerable flexibility, as both camera and display can be located for maximum convenience. Therapy equipment control panels and TV displays for several facilities may be placed in close proximity to each other; several cameras may be used to view the patient from different angles; a pan-tilt mechanism for the camera may be operated from the control panel to view any portion of the treatment room; and additional displays may be located elsewhere. Disadvantages of such a system include the need for auxiliary viewing in case of TV equipment failure, and the cost of maintenance[23].

In therapy installations means of oral communication between the patient and control room shall be provided.

The people outside the treatment room must be protected from accidental radiation. The walls of the treatment room likely to be hit by the direct radiation must be made of baryt concrete, the other walls may consist of normal concrete.

20 Stewart J Robert, Hicks John A, Boone Max L M, and Simpson Larry Dean: Computed tomography in radiation therapy. 1978, International Journal of Radiation Oncology Biology Physics 4:313–324.

21 Innes G S: Design of the therapy department with the future in mind. in The Planning of Radiotherapy Departments. ed by T J Deeley. British Journal of Radiology. Special Report 12. London 1976, p 121.

22 Buitendag J J: User evaluation of engineering services and equipment in radiation protection. Second Southern African Hospital Symposium. Pretoria. November 1977.

23 ibid

In treatment rooms, there is a hazard due to high concentrations of ozone and the oxide of nitrogen[24]. An air flow across the room to reduce rapidly the gas concentrations and about 12 air changes per hour should be provided.

The *machine control room* or station needs not border on the treatment room. It should allow adequate space for the radiographer team and some students, altogether approximately six people.

The radiotherapy *mould room* suite is a key supporting facility. Its activities are diversified over a range of technical skills[25]. The prime function of this suite is to produce skills and applicators for tumour sites. Here patient impressions are taken, appliances constructed, plaster of Paris technique applied as well as cold setting resin formulations, epoxy/polyester techniques etc practised.

The main work laboratory should have benching, cupboards, and drawers. Work cubicles should be provided for construction and fitting procedures to afford privacy to patients.

The plaster room of about 11 m^2 size should have tiled surfaces and floor drainage.

A vacuum forming and injection moulding bay is required as well as a store for materials. As the mould room uses inflammable materials, good ventilation is essential.

To reduce the hazard of transporting radioactive sources, the insertion of radioactive materials is undertaken in the operation room. A single-operation-room *operation unit* is needed. Extra space must be allowed for radiation protection equipment.

The place of *chemotherapy* in radiotherapy-oncology department is increasing steadily — palliative at first but sometimes curative when combined with other disciplines[26].

As many patients may attend for multi-agent injections, there must be adequate waiting space, rooms for injection therapy and a recovery unit containing at least three couches for out–patients awaiting transport after treatment, and toilets.

The *radioisotope laboratory* has for its solid sources a general service area where applicators and accessories are stored together with shielded containers and appliances for transporting radioactive materials. Records of radioactive material in stock and in transient use must be kept.

24 Innes G S: Design of the therapy department with the future in mind. in The Planning of Radiotherapy Departments. ed by T J Deeley. British Journal of Radiology. Special Report 12. London 1976, p 122.

25 see also Crooks S H: Supporting services: their need and size. in The Planning of Radiotherapy Departments. ed by T J Deeley. British Journal of Radiology. Special Report 12. London 1976, p 103.

26 Snelling Margareth: Basic principles in the planning of radiotherapeutic and oncological departments. International Symposium on the Planning of Departments of Radiology and Imaging Sciences. Lisbon, May 1978.

A *radiopharmaceutical* room is needed to produce under aseptic conditions substances which are injected intravenously into the patient.

Rooms for general *in vivo* and *in vitro* counting are needed, where gamma cameras and rectilinear scanners are used. Additional rooms will be required for imaging equipment[27].

A sub-waiting area will enable to separate patients who have received radioisotopes from other waiting patients.

Offices for registration, consulting rooms, and rooms for secretarial staff and data recording equipment are needed as well as a Xeroxing bay. Any large radiotherapy unit has to allow a *seminar room* for daily meetings to review case reports, notes and films and to keep the staff generally informed.

A staff *library* with a section for medical slides is needed as well as offices for *photography,* and *documentation* and *statistics,* as well as accommodation for research.

Provision for ample *storage* space is essential. Equipment not in regular use should not be left around in treatment rooms as it can be unsightly in departments and worrying for ill patients[28].

There should be mechanical engineering and electronic *workshop* facilities.

Hospitals where radiotherapeutical experimental studies are conducted, require *animal quarters.*

Whereever possible, rooms should have outside windows.

Radioactive waste

Radioactive waste from telecurie and brachycurie treatment is in the kilocurie or 100 millicurie range with a half life of about five years. These preparations, as well as cobalt 60, are regarded as no longer useable after a few years. These wastes are not bulky but are highly active and need to be fully screened at all stages.

Waste from nuclear medicine and other applications are bulky but with a half life of less than 14 days can be treated as inactive waste after 24 half life periods. Iodine 125, with a half life of 60 days, needs special storage. When providing facilities for storing of these wastes, the national regulations have to be observed.

27 Crooks S H: Supporting services: their need and size. in The Planning of Radiotherapy Departments. ed by T J Deeley. British Journal of Radiology. Special Report 12. London 1976, p 104.

28 Deeley T J: Considerations in the expansion of existing radiotherapy departments. in The Planning of Radiotherapy Departments. ed by T J Deeley. British Journal of Radiology. Special Report 12. London 1976, p 53.

OPERATION DEPARTMENT

Surgery is the branch of medical science which relates to body injuries, deformities and morbid conditions requiring remedy by drugs and by surgical intervention. Surgery may alleviate pain, restore or maintain the normal function of the body and eliminate a threat to life.

The emphasis on treatment should not be allowed to create a false image that the operation procedure is the essence of the discipline, which compasses preoperative care, intraoperative judgement and management, and postoperative care.

For thousands of years surgery practices were simple mechanical endeavours. The results depended on the plastic skills of the operator and the then unknown ability of the body to heal. A more profound understanding of normal body functions was gained only in the past half-century.

Before the nineteenth century surgery was almost restricted to five procedures whic incredibly to the contemporary reader, could be performed on the unanaesthetized patient: amputation, lithotomy, trephining of the skull, incision of abscess, and operation of cataract.

Although the introduction of anaesthetics had greatly extended the scope of surgery as far as to the last quarter of the nineteenth century the results of the common ope ations were alarming[1]. The average level of competence in the medical profession remained depressingly low until the beginning of the twentieth century.

Up to the second quarter of our century clinical surgery was not a science. It was a profession, or perhaps a kind of art, the quality of performance depending on the ability, skill and training of the surgeon. His activities and interests were almost entirely limited to the performance of the operation itself[2].

Surgical advances have been largely dependent on basic scientific research, experimental surgery and parasurgical innovation. Most of them have taken place in terms of pre-operative and post-operative care. Particularly, chemistry, biophysics, instrumentation and synthetic prosthetics have contributed towards the recent development in surgery.

The great amount of hardware and electronics which have been introduced in the operation room have sometimes given rise to the erroneous belief that increased technology substitutes for good procedures.

The significance of classifying operations in major and minor operations has been seriously questioned. Statistics based on this classification will not produce meaningful data[3]. Surgical operations may instead be broadly classified as emergency and elective operations.

1 McKeown Thomas: Medicine in modern society. Georg Allen & Unvin Ltd London 1965, p 26.

2 Nielubowicz J: The impact of basic science on clinical surgery. 1977, European Surgical Research 9:suppl 1·5–9.

3 see also Bowden Lois A: Statistical information in surgery. 1974, Hospitals 48:13:14.

An *emergency* operation must be carried out as soon as practicable after the diagnosis has been made and the patient prepared in a proper way. Exogenous emergencies include patients who are admitted as urgent cases. In the case of endogenous emergencies, e g wound dehiscence or post-operative intestinal obstruction, the decision to operation is made by the surgeon in charge of the patient.

Elective operations, which are the majority, are carried out some time after the diagnosis has been made and when they suit best for the patient or the hospital.

Because of dissimilarities in professional policies indications for operation are not the same in all countries. *Brian Abel-Smith*[4] has asked: Why is twice the amount of surgery done in the United States than in the United Kingdom? Why are there as many appendicectomies done in the Federal Republic of Germany as in the United States, although the latter has three times the population?

The number of operations in an area seems to depend directly on the number of general surgeons in that area[5]. Some in the US feel that the demand for surgical services is to increase when the public becomes more informed of the benefits of surgical services[6]. Other investigators indicate that higher-education groups tend to have fewer operations[7].

In Sweden, there have been changes in the frequencies of some operations during the last decade:

appendectomies	–
ventricular operations	–
operations of varices	–
operations of colon-rectum	+
operations of gall bladder	–
arterial surgery	+
ablatio mammae	+

In gynaecology no major changes in the operation frequencies have been observed, but in obstetrics the frequencies have been doubled.

A reduction in the volume of general surgery is expected as well as an increase in orthopaedics. The total volume of operations is not believed to increase[8].

---

4   Abel-Smith B: Value for money. in Health care planning. ed by J CJ Burkens, C L C van Nieuwenhuizen and A H Wiebenga. Excerpta Medica. Amsterdam-Oxford 1976, p 37–44.

5   Bunker J P: Surgical Manpower: A Comparison of Operations in the United States and in England and Wales. 1970, The New England Journal of Medicine 282:135.

6   see also Bunker John P and Brown Jr Byron Wm: The physician-patient as an informed consumer of surgical services. 1974, The New England Journal of Medicine 290:1051.

7   see also Bombardier Claire, Fuchs Victor R, Lillard Lee A and Warner Kenneth E: Socioeconomic factors affecting the utilization of surgical operations. 1977, The New England Journal of Medicine 297:699–705.

8   Zederfeldt Bengt: Förväntade förändringar inom operationsverksamheten. Symposon Planering av operationsavdelningar. ISIMA 78. Malmö, April 1978.

It is also believed, that although extirpative surgery will remain important, clinical surgery will move in the direction of supplementing bodily functions by adding rather than removing something. Many mechanical artificial organs are meeting with increasing sucess[10].

All operative methods are not perfect. There are alternative methods of doing almost every operation. Many of the so-called surgical rules are the result of cumulative experience based on a long series of surgical situations.

In the history of surgery many operations regarded one time as classic have been replaced by other methods. There is always a possibility of further development, even if for some men of science it would appear that surgery is now heading for an era of conservatism[11].

Currently there are at least fifteen surgical specialities or subspecialities. Each speciality has its own triumphs and shortcomings.

Surgical specialists include *tissue* specialists e g the neurosurgeon and the vascular surgeon; *organ* specialists e g the ophthalmologist, the cardiac surgeon, the otologist; *system* specialists e g the urologist, the gynaecologist, (perhaps) the thoracic surgeon; and *disease* specialists, who operate upon whatever part of the body becomes involved as in the case of rheumatoid arthritis[12].

Surgery can also be classified on a regional basis into that of the brain, head and neck, back, heart, respiratory system, abdomen, lower extremity, upper extremity, and genitourinary system, both female and male[13].

Paediatric surgery is primarily the surgery of congenital malformations in widest sense[14]. It has to be carried out by surgeons in close co-operation with paediatricians. The aim of paediatric surgery is not, as has been sometimes mistakenly assumed, to operate on all children with surgical conditions. A well trained general surgeon should certainly be able to operate on the common, simple surgical conditions in infancy and childhood.

It is strongly felt that paediatric surgeons still belong to the large, university connected hospital centres[15].

10 Corry Robert J: Glimpses Into the Future — Surgery. 1977, The Journal of the Iowa Medical Society 67:125

11 see also Nanson Eric M: Recent advances in general surgery. 1977, The Australian and New Zealand Journal of Surgery 47:438–441.

12 see also Boyes Joseph H: The regional surgeon — a new kind of specialist. 1975, Plastic and Reconstructive Surgery 56:199–201.

13 Boyes Joseph H: The regional surgeon — a new kind of specialist. 1975, Plastic and Reconstructive Surgery 56:199–201.

14 Rickham P P: European paediatric surgery, triumph, and problems. 1975, Acta Chirurgica Belgica 74:353–357.

15 see also Rickham P P: European paediatric surgery, triumph, and problems. 1975, Acta Chirurgica Belgica 74:353–357.

Small size is not always a barrier to surgical procedures. Brilliantly illuminated magnification enables the surgeon to enter another dimension with vastly improved visual acuity.

In every surgical discipline the need for the use of magnification, should be recognized. In general surgery, for instance, there are many areas of dissection where the use of magnification x2 or x4 would be a greater advantage.

The relative crudity of routine surgical procedures, even when performed carefully by experienced hands, contrasts largely with the same surgeon's suddenly selfimposed precision when operating with magnification and *microsurgical techniques*. The field of vision is governed by the magnification employed. At x6 magnification the diametre of the field is 30 mm, at x40 magnification 5 mm. The field of vision which the surgeon covers is greatly increased by mobile microscopes.

Microsurgery may be defined as surgery performed under magnification: the purist restricts it to surgery using the operation microscope, while the generalist includes loupes and other ocular aids.

Microsurgery has proved its usefulness in otorhinolaryngology, ophthalmology, neurosurgery, particularly peripheral nerve surgery, vascular, plastic and hand surgery.

Most advances in surgery have been due to a greater emphasis upon precise repair of the defect. Microsurgery further advances this precision to almost the cellular level of repair. The results, as seen in microneural repair, have been a far greater percentage of successful operations for the patients[16].

Despite the longer operating time entailed, shorter hospitalization renders microsurgery more economic than conventional methods. Yet with experience, operating times are gradually being reduced[17].

Microsurgery, embodying a technique that is by far the most advanced operative skill yet known, is expected to play an increasing role in almost every field of surgery where fine structure are involved[18].

An observation that has called for reflection[19] is that in the past the surgeons were limited not by unsteadiness of the hand, but by the acuity of the human eye. Now that they have excellent magnification and instrumentation they are limited only by the human mind.

---

16 Graham John Kirkland: Microsurgery. 1977, The Journal of the Louisiana State Medical Society 129:239.

17 O'Brien Bernard McC: Microsurgery: a rapidly expanding field. 1977, The Australian and New Zealand Journal of Surgery 47:263–264.

18 see also Rich W J: Microsurgery. in Recent advances in surgery. Number nine. ed by Selwyn Taylor. Churchill Livingstone. Edinburgh, London and New York 1977, p 207.

19 Kleinert Harold W, Roberts III Thomas L: Microsurgery: its development, current status and future potential. 1978, Southern Medical Journal 71:753–755.

Cryosurgery is based on the use of liquid nitrogen at a very low temperature. Nitrogen is brought through a hollow probe into contact with diseased tissue, which after being briefly exposed to freezing dies and sloughs away. The local pain is absent.

The value of cryosurgery is becoming increasingly apparent. Its procedures are being standardized[20]. Thermography has improved the cryosurgery technique[21].

It is likely that the future use of cryosurgery will include an increased number of sites within the body and the treatment of a wider range of diseases[22].

The *biomedical laser* — light amplification by stimulated emission of radiation — is one of the ways to make the conventional scalpel obsolete. The absence of physical contact between the CO_2-laser beam and the tissues and the cutting without mechanical pressure makes the operation relatively nontraumatic. The risk of infection is reduced because of the sterility of the tool and because microorganisms are killed by heating.

The medical laser has proven operationally feasible in some areas. However, neither as a general surgical instrument nor as a source of significant nonocular trauma does the laser yet seem worthy of consideration by the general surgical clinician.

The *anaesthesiologist* shares, as a rule, the responsibility for the patient's general condition during the operation with the surgeon, so that the surgeon can devote more of his attention to the technical problems of the moment and less to the acute physiological changes.

The anaestesiologist is not only a partner to the surgeon but also to the obstetrician, the paediatrician, the internist, the cardiologist and the psychiatrist. Anaesthesiology has developed far beyond the confines of the operation room and the recovery room.

Anaesthesia is the administration of a drug or gas which produces unconsciousness and usually excellent relaxation. Complete muscle relaxation is important to the success of many procedures. Unless the patient's condition or circumstances contraindicate, general anaesthesia is selected.

The practice of anaesthesiology consists of reversibly altering a patient's neurophysiologic status to conditions suitable for an operative procedure, yet restoring as soon as possible his normal status. Obviously, significant and remarkable strides have been made during the past decade to introduce more effective anaesthetics and develop simpler and safer methods to effectively control pain during surgery. However, in 1977, not all in anaesthesiology was wine and roses[23].

20 see also Lloyd Williams K and Holden H B: Cryosurgery in general and ENT surgery. 1975, British Journal of Hospital Medicine 14:14–25.

21 see also Bradley P F: Thermography as an aid to cryosurgery. 1977, Acta Thermographica 2:83–90.

22 see also Fraser James: Cryosurgery. 1975, Progress in Surgery 14:136–159.

23 Corssen Guenter: Anaesthesia. 1977, the alabama journal of medical sciences 14:385–386.

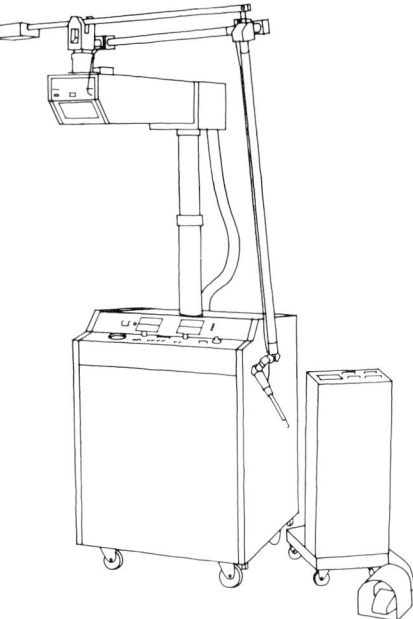

A surgical laser system, which requires about 0.8 by 1 m of floor space. The height is about 2.2 m. The five sections of the system are the focusing head, the manipulator arm, the laser, the control console, and external water and dry nitrogen.

Some of the anaesthetic techniques are likely to change as search for nonpharma-cologic methods continues.

Paediatric anaesthesia is difficult to define. Most paediatric anaesthesiologists in Britain would agree that paediatric anaesthesia applies to children up to about 3. Under this age the differences between the child and the adult — and, indeed, the differences between the young child and the older child — are considerable.

Surgical staff

About one hundred members of the hospital staff — medical specialists, nurses and skilled technicians — may be involved in preparation for and performance of a major operation and in the postoperative care of a patient.

The surgical services* involve a major cost. In North America the operation room service represents about 6 per cent of the total hospital budget. 60 per cent of that money is spent on the services of personnel, about 35 per cent on supplies. An analysis from the United Kingdom[1] indicates that the basic cost — salaries and maintenance — is about 51 per cent of the total cost; materials used require 33 per cent of the cost; the anaesthetic room 12 per cent, and autoclaving 4 per cent.

The cost of the use of operation rooms is escalating.

The immediate success of an operation depends on the judgement and skill of the surgeon. Operation tools and operation room equipment cannot substitute for the surgeon's skill, but they as well as good facility planning, can contribute to it.

As the number of prolonged and complicated operations is on the increase, and generally more mechanical and electronic equipment is required, the operation room environment gains value.

For the patient's welfare, a good interpersonal relationship within the surgical department and particularly in the operation room is extremely important. All frustrations of the team, which may lead to errors of judgement and performance should be eliminated.

Films and television have pictured the operation room as an area of permanent drama. This image is destroyed after a few day's study. However, there is a pace and tension due to the worry about the patient or operation itself which not all persons can adjust to.

The physical work performed by the surgeon during operation often reaches a level which requires very good physical fitness. Working in operation rooms causes significantly increased non-adrenaline excretion in the urine and pronounced variations in the systemic blood pressure of the operation room personnel[2].

---

* An operation room or surgical theatre is the space where surgical operations are carried out.

An operation suite consists of an operation room, anaesthetic room, disposal room, scrub-up and gowning room and sterile storage-preparation room.

A surgical or operation department comprises one or more operation suites together with change and rest rooms, reception, holding and recovery areas, various common-use rooms and circulation space.

1 Miller A: The cost of an operating session. 1974, NAT News 11:4:14.

2 Kratholm Svend: Pollution and stress-reactions in operating rooms. in Anesthesiology. Proceedings of the VI World Congress of Anaesthesiology. Mexico City, April 1976. ed by Enrique Hülsz, José Antonio Sánchez-Hernández, Guilermo Vasconcelos and J N Lunn. Excerpta Medica. Amsterdam-Oxford 1977, p 13-14.

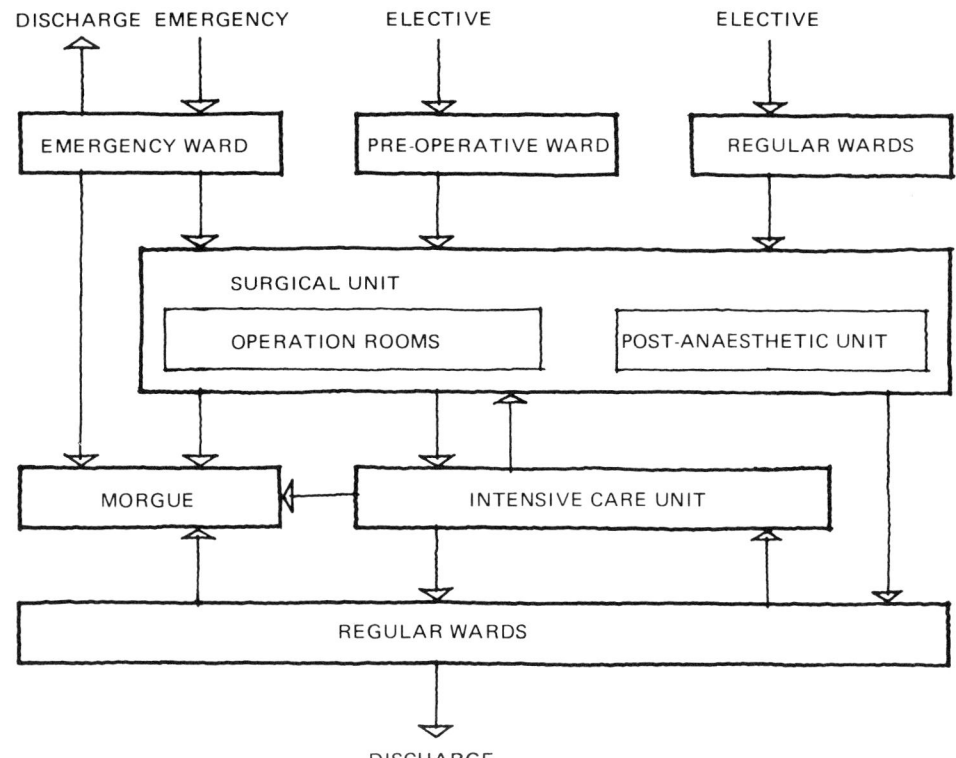

Patient movements in the course of surgical operations.

There is an increase in the surgeon's body temperature and a decrease of body weight after all operations[3]. As a one per cent decrease of body weight due to loss of water might cause a ten per cent decrease of work capacity[4], during prolonged operations the lost body water should be replaced.

In long lasting operations a decrease of grip force has been noted[5].

The provision of perfect environmental conditions cannot be overemphasized, and still, most frequently the surgical centre milieu has been dreary and discontented[6].

3   Lereim Paul and Rö Johannes: Physical work performed by surgeons during orthopaedic operations. 1975, Acta Orthopaedica Scandinavica 46:31-37.

4   Staff P: Vaeskemangel som begrensende faktor vid langvarig muskelarbeid. 1971, Sanitetsnytt 17:38-50.

5   Lereim Paul and Rö Johannes: Physical work performed by surgeons during orthopaedic operations. 1975, Acta Orthopaedica Scandinavica 46:31-37.

6   Sahl R J: Planung von Operationsanlagen. 1974, Das öffentliche Gesundheitswesen 36:14-22.

Patient and the approaching operation

Established techniques of anaesthesia provide mostly a safe and rather comfortable journey through the operative period for the vast majority of patients, and yet they still think of surgery as a harrowing experience[1]. According to some studies about 75 per cent[2] experience moderate fear and anxiety[3] about the approaching operation and not at least about anaesthesia, a few are terrified[4].

This fear has several causes: the amount of pain which can be expected is often unknown and may be imagined as worse than in reality, the risk is often exaggerated and patients may not have had a chance to voice their fears, many patients think they have cancer when they have not[5]. Some patients, before the operation, are often so apprehensive that they have a retrograde amnesia and do not remember important discussions with their surgeons. Indeed, after the operation, some even do not remember coming to the hospital[6].

The incidence of complaints of anxiety is about equal for both sexes, but females — who account for more surgery than men* — are more likely to assess their anxiety as being in the highest grade[7].

Fears increase with increasing age[8], but there is less fear expressed at both ends of the age scale of the grown-ups.

The patient's psychological readiness for operation and the expectation of success is often as significant to the outcome as is his general physical readiness.

Usually the physiology and psychology of people with acute surgical problems form a true psychophysiologic reaction[9]. Negative emotions during the pre-operative

---

1   see also Birkinshaw K: Pre-operative approach to patients. 1978, Anaesthesia 33:483–487.

2   see also Cronin M, Redfern P A and Utting J E: Psychometry and post-operative complaints in surgical patients. 1973, British Journal of Anaesthesia 45:879–885.

3   see also Stahl William M: Supportive Care of the Surgical Patient. Grune & Stratton. New York and London 1972, p 245.

4   see also Ellis Harold and Wastell Christopher: General Surgery for Nurses. Blackwell Scientific Publications. Oxford, London, Edinburgh, Melbourne 1976, p 20.

5   Birkinshaw K: Pre-operative approach to patients. 1978, Anaesthesia 33:483–487.

6   Beck William C: Color Problems in Hospitals. 1976, The Guthrie Bulletin 46:1:39–48.

*   Canadian and United States sources report surgical procedure rates for women 1.5 times the comparable rates for men.

7   Cronin M, Redfern P A and Utting J E: Psychometry and post-operative complaints in surgical patients. 1973, British Journal of Anaesthesia 45:879–885.

8   Ramsay M A E: A survey of pre-operative fear. 1972, Anaesthesia 27:396–402.

9   see also Huffer Virginia: Psychological Disturbances in the Acutely III Patient. 1969, Modern Treatment 6:732–745.

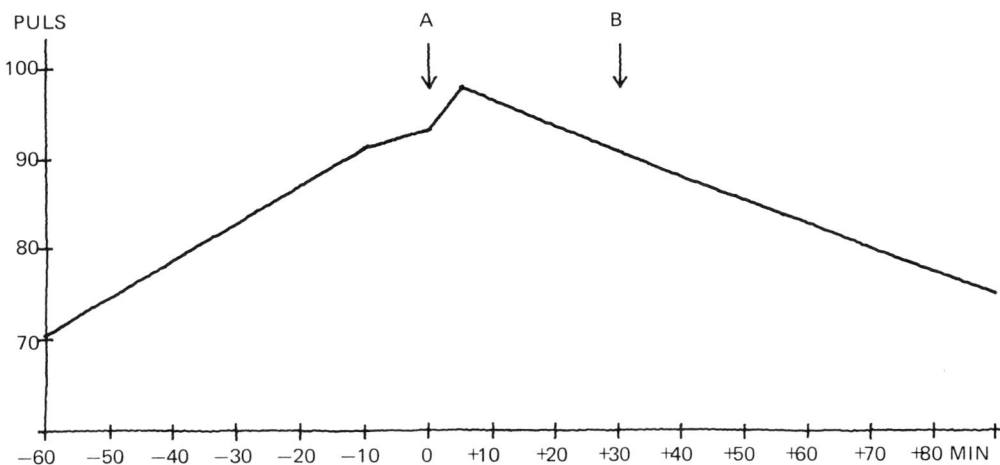

PULS

Fear and anxiety about the approaching operation can be measured. The study of P Kielholz (Psychische Krankheit und Stress. 1977, Schweizer Archiv für Neurologie, Neurochirurgie und Psychiatrie 121:12-19) shows the stadia of patient alarm. A — local anaesthesia commences, B — operation commences.

period may cause pathological changes in the function of several organs[10]. Malignant anxiety may even lead to death[11]. The fear of dying and cardiac arrest show significant relationship[12]. Arrhythmias may be noted unexpectedly in the surgical patient before operation[13].

The intensity of suffering varies with the mood and emotional state of the individual.

The aspect of losing one's personal identity is disturbing:

> . . . stretched on the table,
> You are a piece of furniture in a repair shop
> For those who surround you, the masked actors;
> All there is of you is your body
> And the 'you' is withdrawn[14].

10 see also Flink Robert: Psychische Probleme in der Chirurgie. in Krankenhausprobleme der Gegenwart. Band 4. ed by E Haefliger and V Elsasser. Verlag Hans Huber. Bern, Stuttgart, Vienna 1970, p 60.

11 Bücherl E S: Schlusswort. in Der Postoperative Verlauf. ed by Emil Sebastian Bücherl. Georg Thieme Verlag. Stuttgart 1969, p 137.

12 Peterson Clare Gray: Perspectives in surgery. Lea & Febiger. Philadelphia 1972, p 27.

13 Mulder Donald G and Kattus Albert A: Electrocardiography for the Surgeon. in Advances in Surgery. volume 10. ed by William P Longmire Jr. Year Book Medical Publishers. Chicago 1976, p 7.

14 Eliot T S: The Cocktail Party. Faber and Faber Ltd. London 1958, p 26.

The immediate hours and minutes before an operation may be the time of extreme apprehension for the patient. The dreadful loneliness of the pre-operative surgical patient after the relatives or friends have left has to be experienced to be understood. *Harold Rodgers,* himself a surgeon, has described these feelings in the poem *No one called me by name*[15]:

> Long strange processions of ceilings are gone
> I roled recumbent in ritual white
> Rolled on a trolley raised up in a lift
> Purification with changing of sheets
> Lying alone under a dish of light.
> I hear no voice now I have heard before
> Behind that bright light, beyond that din
> Is that loud voice said: "I must go in
> Just to look — on the list — for tomorrow".
> And now on the list, here I lonely lie
> Alone, and no one calls me by name.
> What will it be like this chemical sleep?
> How will it subdue my wondering brain?
> In this the waited moment come to pass?
> Awesome translation to Eternity.
> If only darling you here to see
> And softly say a silent prayer with me
> But I am alone and struggling to pray
> And so to pray as not to be alone.

What to doctors and nurses may appear a straightforward or trivial operation is neither of these things to the patient. Also for the planners it is very easy to overlook this uniqueness in the experience of patients.

The patient with aesthetic sensibilities will be distressed by unpleasant sights, sounds and odours, and is intolerant of disarray.

The patient should not see preparations being made for his operation, nor should he be subjected to inconsequential chatter, joking, loud laughter, and instrument clatter.

15 1973, Proceedings of the Royal Society of Medicine 66:324.

In a well planned and run hospital bed occupancy would be high, waiting lists short and operation sessions fully used.

It has been found ironic that a hospital with too few operation rooms tends to be more efficient than the one with too many[1]. This statement has been backed up by other observations. However, a hospital that has no shortage of operation rooms, staff, and equipment would not find itself in a state of recurrent crises in which minor difficulties are spread by a chain-reaction and become matters of wide-spread concern[2].

Frequently, the number of operation rooms in a general hospital or surgical department has been determined by some general estimates or it has been related to the number of hospital beds, particularly surgical beds.

In Mexico one operation room has been recommended for every 50 general beds[3], in the United Kingdom for 30 to 40 surgical beds[4], and in Norway for 25 surgical beds[5].

The proper number of operation rooms has also been indicated to be 5 per cent of the total number of surgical beds[6].

To determine the operation frequency including emergencies in larger hospitals — a thumb rule, 0.1 operations per bed and day, has been used[7].

It has been assumed that approximately one hour's operation time is required per surgical bed per week. A proper monthly work load for an operation room has been considered to be about 65 operations.

The number of operation rooms* in a hospital could be more exactly determined[8] when it is related to the number of surgical and equivalent beds**, the percentage

1   Hyde Jacobs Jr Robert: Prototype designs reflect innovations in O R Planning. 1969, Hospitals 43:12:124.

2   see also Luck G M, Luckman J, Smith B W and Stringer J: Patients, Hospitals, and Operational Research. Tavistock Publications. London 1971, p 2.

3   Yánez Enrique: Hospitales de seguridad social. Private Publication. Mexico City 1973, p 7.

4   Control of Hospital Infection. ed by E J L Lowbury, G A J Ayliffe, A M Geddes and J D Williams. Chapman and Hall. London 1975, p 144.

5   Operationsavdelinger. Norsk Institutt for Sykehusforskning. Trondheim 1977, p 12.

6   Laufman Harold: Surgical Hazard Control. 1973, Archives of Surgery 107:552–559.

7   see also Lindahl Jonny et al: Produktionsplanering vid regionsjukhuset i Örebro. Spri Projekt nr 7012. Bilaga C:1, p 3.

*   the provision of endoscopy, cystoscopy and plaster rooms and operation rooms in surgical day-care sections would be additional

8   see also Cowan David: A method for estimating the number of operating theatres required in a general hospital. Council for Scientific and Industrial Research. Report No 201, Pretoria 1963, p 6.

** separate facilities for treatment of burns should be provided.

rate of bed occupancy, the average length of stay for patients in surgical and equivalent clinics, the length of the daily operation session, and to the length of the hygienic interval*.

The number of operation rooms required is $\frac{T}{C}$, T being the total number of operations to be performed in the hospital and C the estimated capacity of one operation room.

The total number of operations — T — is determined by using the following formula

$$T = \frac{B \times 365 \times P}{L \times 100}$$

B is the number of beds in the surgical block, P — the percentage of bed occupancy and L — the average length of the patient stay in the hospitals, in days.

By using the average percentage of the three busiest months both for bed occupancy and length of stay, rather than the medium annual values, the influences of seasonal variations** are eliminated.

When the factors that cause the current unpredictability of the duration of surgical convalescence are identified, the length of hospital stay may be shortened.

To estimate the operation room capacity — C —, the following formula could be used:

$$C = \frac{D \times H}{A}$$

D is the number of working days a year, H — the average number of daily working hours, and A — the average operation length in hours.

A five-day-working-week corresponds to at the most 1,500 annual regular operation hours per operation room.

In Sweden, 64 per cent of all operations are started between 8 and 12 o'clock Monday through Friday, 24 per cent between 12 and 16 o'clock Monday through Friday[9].

---

* the time needed for operation room cleaning and resting.

** Seasonal variations vary in different countries. E g in the Scandinavian countries demand for surgery is lowest during the summer months.

In the US people prefer to be operated on during their summer vacation. During the winter colds cause many cancellations and postponements of operations.

9 Bo Arnesjö at the symposon Planering av operationsavdelningar. ISIMA 78. Malmö, April 1978.

In the UK operation room utilization above 95 per cent is generally considered high, and below 80 per cent low[10]. The UK values are generalizations. They may be suitable for some, but not for all specialities. It may be reasonable to expect 85 per cent operation room utilization in ENT, for example, but unreasonable in thoracic surgery where operations tend to be long and it may only be possible to schedule one case for most sessions[11].

Frequently the utilization of surgical department facilities and personnel is limited to less than 60 per cent of a light working day. A study undertaken by the American Society of Anaesthesiologists[12] showed that the mean operation room utilization of all hospitals sampled was only 45 per cent. In the Netherlands, in a medium-sized hospital, the operation room utilization rate was as low as between 30 and 40 per cent[13].

In Sweden, the average utilization of operation rooms has been even lower — 12 hours per room/week — 30 per cent — in largest hospitals and 7.9 hours — 20 per cent — in small hospitals[14].

Up to 35 per cent of operation time has been kept available for emergencies etc[15], although usually the emergency operations represent only about 15 per cent of the work load, also in terms of time.

In some quarters the present amount of utilization of the operation rooms is considered to be a disgrace to the profession of medicine as well as to hospital administration[16].

A fairly full use of the operation room for at least 8 hours a day should be the target. If a seven-day-week would be adopted in the surgical department, an increase of operation capacity by 40 per cent could be expected. Alternatively the number of operation rooms could be reduced by about one third.

Recorded average times in minutes per operation show considerable variations, having varied between 35 and 65 minutes.

10 see also Weir Michael: Making the most of beds and theatres to shorten the waiting. 1977, Health and Social Service Journal 87:564–565.

11 ibid

12 cited by Finarelli Jr Hugo James: An algorithm for scheduling the hospital admission of elective surgical patients. University of Pennsylvania. Stencil. Ann Arbor 1971, p 2.

13 Ir W Wijnja, cited by Cremers A G P: Verwerking en toepassing van patiëntgerichte medische en medisch-organisatorische informatie in het ziekenhuis. 1976, Acta Hospitalia 16:192–222.

14 Inge Dahl cited by Bo Arnesjö at the symposion Planering av operationsavdelningar. ISIMA 78. Malmö April 1978.

15 Elzinga E and Tuinman H: Statistiek operatiekamers als planingsinstrument. 1976, Ziekenhuis 6:442–446.

16 see also Letourneau Charles U: The Anesthesiologist in the Hospital. 1973, International Anesthesiology Clinics 11:4:55–63.

As an example of variations of operation lengths in various specialities some figures from Chur, Switzerland, could be given: general surgery 78.4 minutes, orthopaedics 23.8 min*, urology 32.2 min, neurosurgery 206 min, gynaecology 50.7 min, otorhin laryngology 44.5 min and ophthalmology 20.5 min[17].

Within a particular group of operations the variations are wide. E g in the group of abdominoperineal resections for rectal carcinoma the operation times range from 55 minutes to 445 minutes, with an average time of 205 minutes[18].

The list of operations for each session should not be so long that the time for careful cleaning and preparation between each operation is insufficient[19]. There is a possibility of hygienic failures when the work-load is increased[20].

The time used to clean and service an operation room for the next case varies. In the US the cleaning times have ranged from about 5 minutes in the small operation room to about 7 minutes in the large rooms for an experienced servicing team[21]. In the everyday Swedish practice, the average interval is about 17 minutes, varying between 10 to 20 minutes[22].

About 12 minutes would be needed for setting up operation rooms for normal and 20 minutes for complicated procedures.

As concluded from the available evidence, 75 to 80 minutes, including the hygienic interval between operations, could be regarded as the average length of time of oper ation for the purpose of calculating the total number of in-patient operation rooms in a hospital.

The formula $\frac{T}{C}$ is not enough to calculate the number of operation rooms. Conside ation must also be given to the capacity of other functions in the medical performan area.

* The average length of orthopaedic operations in 1976 at the Karolinska Hospital, Stockholm, was 89 minutes.

17 Raeber U, Rückert C and Rohner H: Ziel- und Gesamtplanung im Krankenhauswesen. 1976, Veska 40:630–635.

18 Voitk Andrus J and Mazzara Salvatore: Abdominoperineal Resection for Carcinoma in the Community Hospital. 1974, Annals of Surgery 176:843.

19 see also Blowers Robert: General Aspects of Infection Control in the Operating Room and Intensive Care Unit. in Infections and Sterilization Problems. ed by Robert Bryan Roberts. International Anaesthesiology Clinics. Summer 1972, vol 10:2:28.

20 Bröte Lars: Postoperative wound infections in general surgery. Linköping University Medical Dissertations No 33. Linköping 1976, p 19.

21 see also Aquaviva Gretchen and Loring June: Team cleaning does better O R job. 1969, Modern Hospital 112:1:124.

22 see also Vogt V and Lieb W: Planung von chirurgischen und poliklinischen Abteilungen. 1976, Zentralblatt für Chirurgie 101:204–214.

The practice of medicine deals with persons in their constant inter-relationship, each affecting the others. Re-evaluation and re-definition of the activities in surgical department as well as introduction of new devices, and changes in administrative and personnel policies may influence the utilization of the operation rooms and the organization of the surgical department.

The smallest operation department, which guarantees a good standard must have three operation rooms, including one room for endoscopy. About 20 operations could be performed daily[1].

The views on the size of a very well administrated operation room units vary. In the Federal Republic of Germany[2] 6 to 8 operation rooms are considered to make a good solution, in some circles in Sweden[3] this number is higher — 8 to 10 operation rooms, in some others[4] lower — 5 to 6 rooms. In Norway[5] a surgical department should not contain more than 12 operation rooms.

When a hospital requires over ten operation rooms, two or more separated surgery departments may be preferred. Certainly, by avoiding huge operation departments a considerable amount of planning difficulties and of later administrative complications are eliminated.

Before the surgical department is planned in detail, its location in the hospital set-up has to be determined using the intensities of communication with other hospital departments.

Important are the links with the intensive care and treatment units, with the emergency unit, X ray department and with pathology.

Obviously for all these services a case for horizontal propinquity is built up.

To achieve most freedom in planning and designing the surgical department, it should be given its own wing, a part of the podium of the hospital building. Also later expansions or alterations can be undertaken with the least possible disturbance to the department, its services and the remainder of the hospital, when the independent low building approach is adapted.

---

1   Vogt V and Lieb W: Planungen von chirurgischen und poliklinischen Abteilungen. 1976, Zentralblatt für Chirurgie 101:214.

2   Gundermann K O: Anforderungen an die funktionell-bauliche Gestaltung von Krankenanstalten unter besonderer Berücksichtigung lüftungstechnischer Anlagen. 1977, Gesundheits-Ingenieur 98:123–127.

3   Vogt Victor: Operationsavdelningar förr och nu. Symposion Planering av operationsavdelningar. ISIMA 78, Malmö, April 1978.

4   Tillander Hans: Hygieniska aspekter, konsekvenser för operationsavdelningens utformning — infektionsprofylaktiska synpunkter. Symposion Planering av operationsavdelningar. ISIMA 78, Malmö, April 1978.

5   Operasjonsavdelinger. Norsk Institutt for Sykehusforskning. Trondheim 1977, p 13.

Surgical department build-up

Procedures

The *basic procedures* which encircle the act of surgery are, as a rule, the following:

    reception and identification of patient
    pre-operative supervision of patient
    depilation of patient
    transfer of patient to operation table
    administration of anaesthesia
    intubation
    positioning
    preparation of the operative area and surrounding skin
    draping of patient
    the act of surgery — OPERATION — which may involve blood transfusion, parenteral
     fluid administration and X-ray examination.
    wound sewn up and dressed
    drapes removed and bagged
    extubation
    transfer of patient from operation table to trolley or bed and to the post-anaesthetic
     recovery area
    post-operative supervision of patient

The *supporting procedures* are

    staff changing to operation room garments and shoes
    putting on cap
    masking
    aseptic washing of hands
    gowning
    putting on gloves
    putting on apron
    laying out, checking and re-checking the number of instruments and dressings to be
     used during the operation

The *administrative procedures* include

    preparation of operation lists, duty schedules and rota
    requisition of patient
    notification to wards of time for patient transport to and from the surgical department
    distribution of messages
    staff paging
    requisition of records, equipment and material
    contacts with other departments, laboratories, workshops and suppliers

The *clerical procedures* include

> preparation of operation records
> preparation of operation room records
> filing
> statistical interpretation of operation room records

The *housekeeping procedures* include

> collection of used instruments
> collection of used materials, and soiled surgical instruments, dressings and underlays
> cleaning of operation rooms and other areas in the surgical department
> disposal or incineration of refuse

Storekeeping and repairs conclude the list of surgical unit functions.

A study indicates that the effective working time for staff in operation garments is only 30 per cent of the total working hours, and for assisting staff even less — 24 per cent. Each surgeon-minute requires 14 supporting minutes[1].

When the activities of the surgical department nursing were analyzed, little proved to be simple repetitive tasks[2]. The largest single function, still not amounting for more than 10 per cent of the analyzed time, was the handling of instruments, sutures and sponges during operation.

1 Hallén Olle, Holmquist Jörgen and Jeppson Pål-Henry: Kan operationer mätas? 1973, Läkartidningen 70:4038–4040.

2 Blumberg Mark S: Hospital Automation: The Needs and Prospects. 1961, Hospitals 35:15:39.

Circulation and zoning

One of the aims of designing the surgical department is to use architectural means for influencing the conduct and circulation of the patient and the surgical department staff according to the principles which are supported by the current science.

As the patient proceeds through the whole course of the operation, requirements on the environmental character and cleanliness vary.

The case is the same concerning the members of the surgical staff.

A surgical department could be divided into zones*, where the quality of environment is to conform with the cleanliness policy adapted by the individual hospital.

Five surgical department cleanliness zones (4, 3, 2, 1, 0) — some of the lower zones not always clearly marked — have been used. They could be distinguished from each other by using a colour scheme, which may also conduct the behaviour of the staff.

In the *general zone* — zone 4 — the requirements on the cleanliness correspond to usual hospital cleanliness standard.

This zone accommodates waiting rooms for relatives, cloakrooms for street clothes, reception offices, catastrophe and triage areas, plaster rooms, offices, record rooms, rooms for preparation, pathological laboratories, stores for non-sterile materials, changing rooms, doctors' offices, rooms for maintenance of anaestetic apparatus, repair shops, photographic laboratories, developing rooms, cleaners' rooms, porters' rooms, apparatus stores, rest rooms, staff lounge-refreshment rooms, pantries, disposal rooms, soiled linen rooms, incineration rooms, and toilets.

Clean zone 3 provides for the surgical department reception ward, anaesthetic rooms delivery rooms, endoscopy rooms, stores for blood, medicine, parenteral solutions, etc., stores for tubed medical gases, the sterile service area, the general post-anaesthetic area, Xray apparatus stores, and clean bed stores.

Super clean zone 2 accommodates scrub-up and gowning areas, operation rooms, operation room stores, sterile linen stores, and thoracic post-anaesthetic rooms.

Ultra clean zone 1 is determined by a circle with a 1 m diameter from the wound.

Aseptic zone 0 is limited to the area of incision.

---

* The idea of zoning the bloc operatoire was initiated in France in a vogue of bacteriological fetishism in the 1930's when it was assumed that air has a paramount importance in the aetiology of post-operative infections.

The first project which showed a careful preoccupation with zoning within the surgical department was by Paul Nelson in 1932.

The main traffic routes for *patients* can be identified as follows: from the regular ward or emergency unit or intensive care and therapy unit (via the holding area) to the anaesthetic room and to the operation room. After operation the patient is taken via the anaesthetic room to the postanaesthetic recovery area and then to a regular ward or an intensive care and therapy unit.

The *surgical staff* route is from the entrances via changing areas and scrubbing and gowning areas to the operation room. After finished operation they may proceed to rest rooms and/or changing area and then to the exit.

The *anaesthetic staff* moves from the entrance to the changing area, to the gowning area, to the anaesthetic room, and to the operation room. After operation they go back to the anaesthetic room and may visit the post-anaesthetic recovery area. Alternatively they proceed to the rest rooms and/or changing area and to the exit.

For *other members of the staff* the route is from the entrance via changing area to the respective working areas and rest rooms and later via changing areas to the exit.

The circulation patterns of the staff have to be uncomplicated and direct. A separation of staff circulation from the patient circulation is impossible.

Clean equipment and supplies are routed from the entrance over the supplies area to the point of use, the *sterile equipment and supplies* from the instrument centre via the operation room storage to the point of use, and the *used and soiled equipment and supplies* from the point of use to the disposal area or to the laundry or to the destruction unit or to the sterile service unit.

Some of the routes are represented by corridors, some may be goods serving channels.

Departmental planning approaches

Departmental space planning should ensure the avoidance of unnecessary movement and obstruction. It must provide for easy, simultaneous circulation of various categories of staff and supplies.

The most prominent errors in the surgical department designs are poor space planning and creating of underdimensioned areas.

Surgical department corridors should be not less than 2.85 m, preferably 3.2 m wide.

There are several departmental planning approaches. The one-time dominating one-corridor system has been replaced by the so called central-island, by segregated corridor and by double corridor systems, the last one being probably the most practicable.

The *central-island* system — not so long time popular in America — is based on a spatial core, where sterile supplies are handled and sometimes the scrub-up facilities located. The core is surrounded by operation rooms. The peripheral route of this system is used for patients both before and after operation as well as for disposal of used materials.

Tests of the environment in the core have found it to be the dirtiest in the surgical suite[3]. In practice, personnel working in the clean core move about in short sleeves with masks down. Skin squames, lint, and dust constantly are shed and circulated. People who work in this area constantly leave and reenter it. These observations bring to the conclusion: this unavoidable activity and other abuses which contaminate the environment make one question the validity of the entire architectural concept[4].

The system with *segregated corridors* in surgical departments has provided corridors classified as clean for circulation of patients and staff and corridors classified as regular for transport of materials. Separated corridors have been provided for postoperative patients and used instruments. The latter element seems to be ludicruos. Considering the patients, it is impossible to distinguish between the relative cleanliness of a patient before his gallstones are removed and thereafter.

In the *double corridor* system the operation rooms and the supporting ancillary rooms are positioned between a corridor classified as regular and another classified as clean. In this arrangement the patient and the anaesthesiologist have access via the regular corridor route into the operation room. The patient's exit route via the

---

3 Laufman Harold: The control of operating room infection: discipline, defense mechanisms, drugs, design, and devices. 1978, Bulletin of the New York Academy of Medicine 54:472–483.

4 Laufman Harold: The control of operating room infection: discipline, defense mechanisms, drugs, design, and devices. 1978, Bulletin of the New York Academy of Medicine 54:472–483.

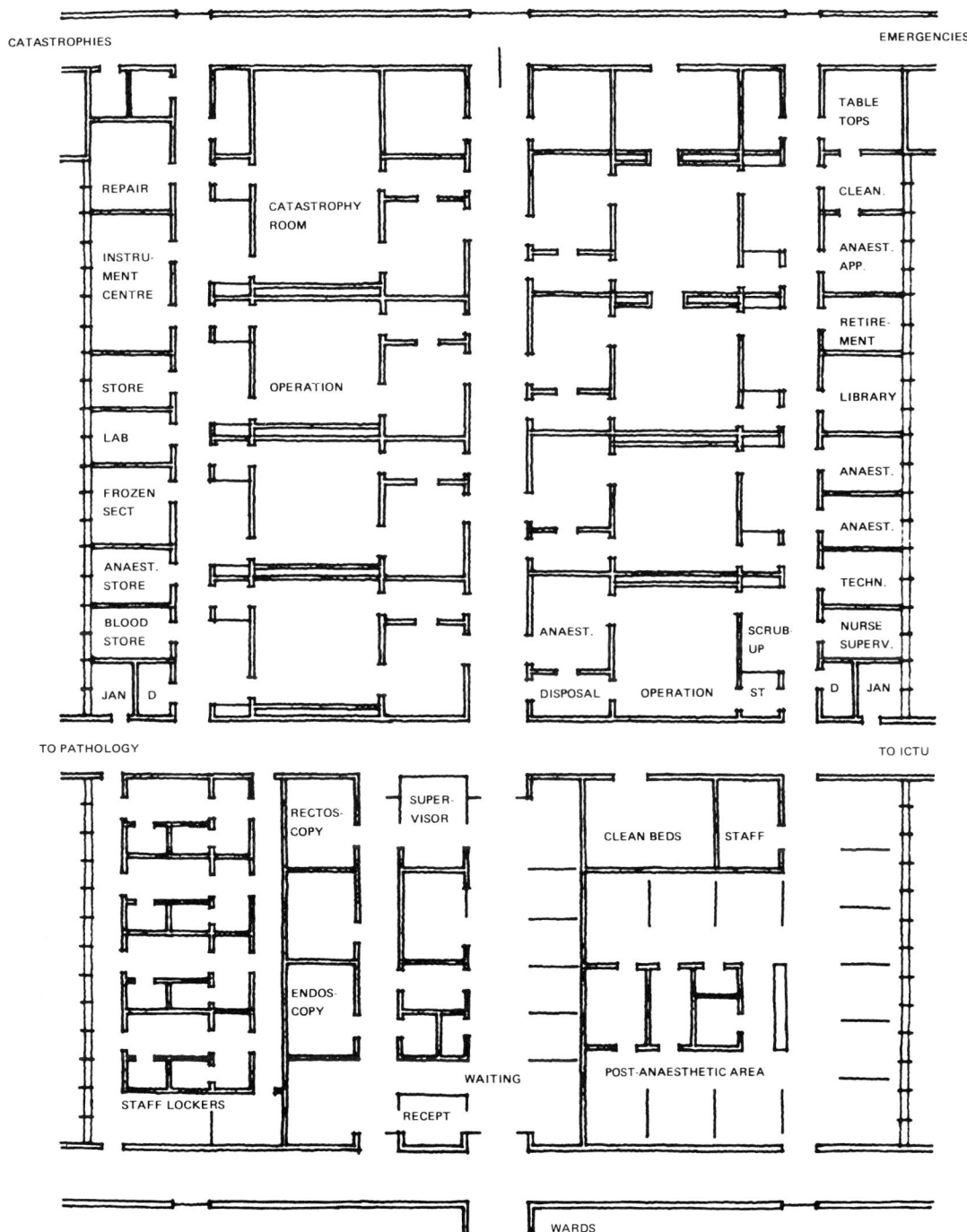

CATASTROPHIES

EMERGENCIES

REPAIR

INSTRU-
MENT
CENTRE

CATASTROPHY
ROOM

TABLE
TOPS

CLEAN.

ANAEST.
APP.

STORE

LAB

FROZEN
SECT

OPERATION

RETIRE-
MENT

LIBRARY

ANAEST.

ANAEST.
STORE

ANAEST.

BLOOD
STORE

TECHN.

JAN   D

ANAEST.

DISPOSAL

SCRUB-
UP

OPERATION   ST

NURSE
SUPERV.

D   JAN

TO PATHOLOGY

TO ICTU

RECTOS-
COPY

ENDOS-
COPY

STAFF LOCKERS

SUPER-
VISOR

WAITING

RECEPT

CLEAN BEDS   STAFF

POST-ANAESTHETIC AREA

WARDS

529

Surgical department with 9 operation rooms, a section for endoscopies and a post-operative area for 12 patients. Pütsep International.

same corridor is shared with the disposal route. The surgical team enters and leaves via the clean corridor. The clean corridor is used also for the delivery of sterile and clean supplies.

The principle for having ultraclean enclosures for surgical procedures in a rather regular micro-biological hospital surrounding has been followed by a natural suggestion to have several enclosures in one large operation room, in a kind of *operation landscape,* to achieve savings in the anaesthetic service and in the use of monitoring equipment.

At the Eugéne Marais Private Hospital in Pretoria a five-enclosure department serves the needs of general surgery, orthopaedic surgery, and neurosurgery. An approximate area saving of 30 per cent over conventional departments has been achieved[5].

In general, the surgeons have found in this multi-enclosure system advantages over the traditional surgical suites. However, the size of the individual enclosure and the quality of used operation lights has been criticized.

The anaesthesiologists have been less definite in their judgement. An anaesthetic ante-room has been considered to be desirable as well as wide passages between enclosures to make the circulation of patients and equipment easier.

The nursing staff has been positive feeling that their work load is reduced. The multi-enclosure unit is felt to be sociable.

The operation room matrons have found the department easier to supervise than conventional operation departments they have had to control in the past[6].

Some interesting changes in the surgical department planning concepts, when this basic idea is adapted, can be expected. The enclosures may simplify the planning of operation departments and enable to achieve low post-operative infection rates within the simplified architectural lay-out.

Appraisal of architectural circulation control

Opinions regarding the character of the movement patterns have always diverged. The appraisal of the role of zoning in space planning, and the architectural circulation control is complicated and impracticable.

The influence of such designing principles on the frequencies of the post-operative wound infection — although zoning contributes to a lower degree of bacterial contamination of surfaces in the operation room[7] — might be only marginal. More likely they just cannot be evaluated.

---

5   personal communication 1974: David Cowan, Pretoria.

6   Cowan David: The clean operating enclosure — its effect on the incidence of wound infection and its influence on the design of the operating department of a hospital. Stencil. Pretoria. January 1976, p 50.

7   Hambraeus A, Bengtsson S and Laurell G: Bacterial contamination in a modern operating suite. 1. Effect of a zoning system on contamination of floors and other surfaces. Stencil. Institute of Clinical Bacteriology, University of Uppsala, Sweden 1977, p 13.

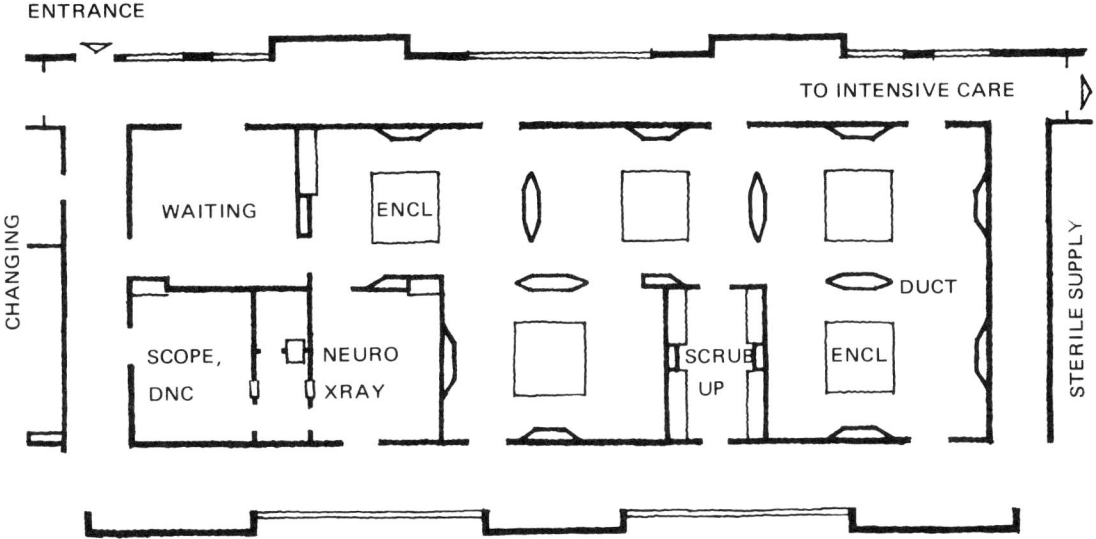

ENTRANCE

TO INTENSIVE CARE

CHANGING

STERILE SUPPLY

WAITING

ENCL

DUCT

SCOPE, DNC

NEURO XRAY

SCRUB UP

ENCL

Five enclosure operation department of the Eugene Marais Hospital, Pretoria. Hurwitz, Murray & Pokroy.

It has been stated that it is obvious that a zoning system and a positive pressure ventilation do not in themselves diminish the postoperative infection rates[8].

The margin of permissible errors and deviations in operation department design seems to be great as equally good operations may be performed in many different types of departments[9].

A surgical department design which satisfies everybody involved in detail can not emerge.

Whatever structural and technical precautions are taken, it is the attitude of the staff to the hospital hygiene generally and asepsis particularly, which determines the results of the aspired aseptic techniques within the surgical departments. No technical precautions can succeed, unless the staff understands their purpose and applies them thoroughly.

8   Bengtsson S, Hambraeus A and Laurell G: Wound infections after surgery in a modern operating suite. 1. Clinical findings. Stencil. Institute of Clinical Bacteriology, University of Uppsala, Sweden 1977, p 9.

9   see also Manual on Control of Infection in Surgical Patients. American College of Surgeons. J B Lippincott Company. Philadelphia — Toronto 1976, p 201.

Spatial elements

Staff area

Entrances

Operation room staff and service personnel should enter the surgical department at one point.

It is essential to prevent the supplies entrance being used by the staff as a back door.

Cloak rooms

For the staff, visitors and students there should be cloakrooms for street clothes near the entrance to the surgical department. Cloakroom equipment includes fixed hangers, hat and shoe racks, lockers, and a mirror.

An adequate number of *toilets* — to be used before entering the changing rooms — should be provided.

In the cloakroom and in the corridor after leaving the changing rooms provision should be made for the general bulletin and notice boards and for the operation department scheduling boards which have a grid system indicating 15-minutes period

The operation-schedule should include

the surname and other names, age, sex, and room and ward number of the patient
the nature, site and side of operation
the names of the surgeon and his assistants
the names of the anaesthesiologist and his assistant
the nursing team number
the names of the scrub and circulating nurses
the number of the operation room
the time for the patient to leave the ward
the time of anticipated commencement of the operation
the anticipated time of completion of the operation
clean-up time
X-ray notification
additional notices

Chalk and grease pencil boards should not be used.

To suit the needs of different groups of the staff, the changing rooms — preferably of passage type — ought to be divided into eight to twelve person units equipped with showers and washbasins.

In the changing area, operation room clothes, including stockings, and caps, which may be stored in protective containers, are donned. Gowning of those, who take direct part in the operation, should take place after scrub up.

On completing the operation and before returning to the changing room the staff, students and the visitors have to put in the operation room their used protective operation room clothes in hampers, which are then kept in the disposal room of the operation room.

The used items are to be removed from the surgical department after the operation session. Alternatively vacuum driven disposal chutes can be used.

Staff showers are needed for comfort reasons to be used after the finished operation session. The shower cubicles should be spacious enough for people to undress and dry themselves within the compartment.

Adjacent to the changing rooms on the operation room corridor entrance side there should be lavatories provided with wall hung (foot-manoeuvred) toilets and washbasins.

Changing rooms should be provided with telephones and intercom.

ounge-refreshment room

The comfortably furnished operation staff lounge should be designed to hold not more than half of the regular staff plus some visitors. One larger lounge is preferred to several smaller lounges[1].

A pantry with a refrigerator should be available.

As long as smoking is tolerated in hospitals, the lounge must be particularly well ventilated *.

---

1 Timmermans C J: Die Operationsabteilung und ihre Bewohner. 1975, medizinische technik 95:55–59.

* The main known acute effect of exposure to environmental tobacco smoke on no-smokers is an acute irritation of the eyes and the respiratory passage. The effects may occur at very low concentrations among atopic persons or persons who otherwise have a reactive respiratory tract (Environmental Tobacco Smoke Effects on the Non-Smoker. ed by R Rylander. Munksgaard. Copenhagen 1974, p 89).

Offices

Surgeons need individual *cubicles* within the operation unit — one per three to four operation rooms — for dictation, writing and typing, communicating with the relatives of the patient by telephone, and also for some discussions and study.

The area of a cubicle ought to be about 4 m². The cubicles need not be concentrated in one place within the surgical department.

The surgical department *(nurse-) supervisor** should have an office with an area of about 12 m². The office furniture includes a desk, a table, a bulletin board, book shelves, a telephone, and a filing cabinet. It is essential that the supervisor is provided outside the surgical department with another facility, where she can interview staff and talk with visitors in private.

Depending on the size of the operation department there may be one or more *assistant OR supervisors.* Below supervisory level the next position is called *head nurse* or *nurse specialist* or *clinical nurse.* There may be one or several head nurses. Offices for these categories are needed.

For the *clinical teacher* or *operation room in-service instructor* for student nurses the facilities of the operation room and of a formal seminar room are needed. An office of about 20 m² with a bulletin board and blackboard should be provided alternatively. This room could be used also for the closed circuit TV-viewing.

Offices for *clerks* typing medical records — if there is no central typing pool — should be adjacent to the surgical department and furnished with desks, book shelves, chairs, filing cabinets, telephones, and intercom. The space required is about 12 m² per room.

For computerized operation records different routines and spatial requirements are adapted.

Large surgical departments have an office of about 12 m² for the *photographer.*

Retirement rooms

A retirement room of about 7 m² size and provided with a washbasin should be planned for every ten female employees for rest and emergencies.

On-call rooms

For surgeons, anaesthesiologists, and nurses sleeping accommodations in single-occupancy rooms have to be provided outside the operation department.

All on-call rooms should have their own lavatories. Access to showers is highly recommendable.

* even the titles OR executive, director of OR nursing and assistant director of nursing — OR are used.

Patient area

Holding area

The patient may gain his initial and sometimes lasting impression of his surgical experience from the manner in which he is received into the preoperative holding area and treated there. However, this subject is difficult to investigate scientifically[1].

On the arrival, the patient's identity must be checked at the entrance. The identification of the patient prior operation must follow a written instruction as several factors have increased the risk of making errors. The nurses have less opportunity to develop personal relationships with the patients and as the average age of patients undergoing surgery has increased, some patients cannot always be relied on to identify themselves[2]. A bracelet which cannot be removed by the patient and is worn during the whole hospital stay is used in many hospitals.

The patient's medical records including the X ray pictures should always accompany him into the operation room so that the surgeon and anaesthesiologist can obtain immediately the information they may need.

While staying in the holding area the patients must remain under supervision. Their pulse, respiratory rate, and blood pressure may be measured. Some of the pre-operative medications are administrated in the holding area. Catheters may be inserted.

The patient is also depilated or shaved*. While it is true that skin with hair can be prepared, the presence of hair can interfere with skin closure and dressings.

In some hospitals lipstick and nailvarnish is moved generally from female patients. This practice being bitterly resented by the ladies serves no useful purpose[3], unless the hand is to be operated[4].

Respect for the dignity of the patient must be maintained.

Views are held that the surgical preparation in the holding area can be performed more efficiently than in the regular ward[5].

1   Cronin M, Redfern P A and Utting J E: Psychometry and post-operative complaints in surgical patients. 1973, British Journal of Anaesthesia 45:879–885.

2   see also McEwin Roderick and Dearlove T P: Identification of Patients for Surgery. 1971, Hospital and Health Care 1:10:3—5.

*   Frequently patients for elective surgery are shaved the evening before operation. This should be avoided.

3   Stephens K F: 'Patientese': Some Thoughts on Pre-operative and Post-operative Patient Psychology. 1971, Proceedings of the Royal Society of Medicine 64:883–885.

4   personal communication 1977, Herbert Sunzel, Varberg, Sweden.

5   see also Brown Eli M, Bonk Sandra M and Wilkins Elvira: Centralizing presurgical preparation. 1972, Hospitals 46:17:116–124.

The spatial needs are one to two[6] bed cubicles of 7 m² size per operation room. For patients with respiratory tract infection, who may heavily contaminate the environment, a separate holding room should be provided.

Washbasins are needed. Good illumination is essential.

The *reception room* in the holding area should be equipped with a writing desk, telephone, and intercom. The recommended floor area is about 8 to 10 m².

There should be a *disposal room,* sizing 7 to 9 m².

Special *waiting rooms* for children and accompanying mothers should be provided.

Children need recognizable individuals. They should be accompanied to the anaesthetic room, if parents not available, by a nurse or attendant with whom they are familiar. A paediatric nurse should play with, talk to or comfort a particular child during the immediate pre-operative period. The nurse should remain in the anaesthetic room until the child is asleep. Instead of a uniform, that makes for the child all nurses look alike, private clothes have sometimes been recommended.

No instruments or apparatus need to be visible.

Taped music helps to divert and tranquillize many children.

The children's waiting area must be closed to all traffic, and extraneous conversation should not be allowed.

Immediate pre-operative ward

It has been recommended that early in the operation day, patients undergoing elective surgery would be taken for premedication to an immediate pre-operative ward, which is part of the operation suite. The ward would be run by an anaesthesiologist and by nursing staff who can allay to some extent the fears and anxieties of the patient.

The patients in a pre-operative ward or area, if the surgical department is provided with one, should be harboured in separate, elaborately equipped cubicles.

Transfer areas, patient bed in the surgical department

To keep the patient bed, which can be tipped and has removable ends[7], outside the anaesthetic room during the operation — there is in itself no particular reason to do so — special transfer areas or rooms of at least 16 m² of size, adjacent the holding area have been suggested for transferring the patient from his bed to the operation table or operation table top or from a ward trolley to an operation room trolley.

6   Operasjonsavdelinger. Norsk Institutt for Sykehusforskning. Trondheim 1977, p 78.

7   Farman John V: The work of the recovery room. 1978, British Journal of Hospital Medicine 19:606–616.

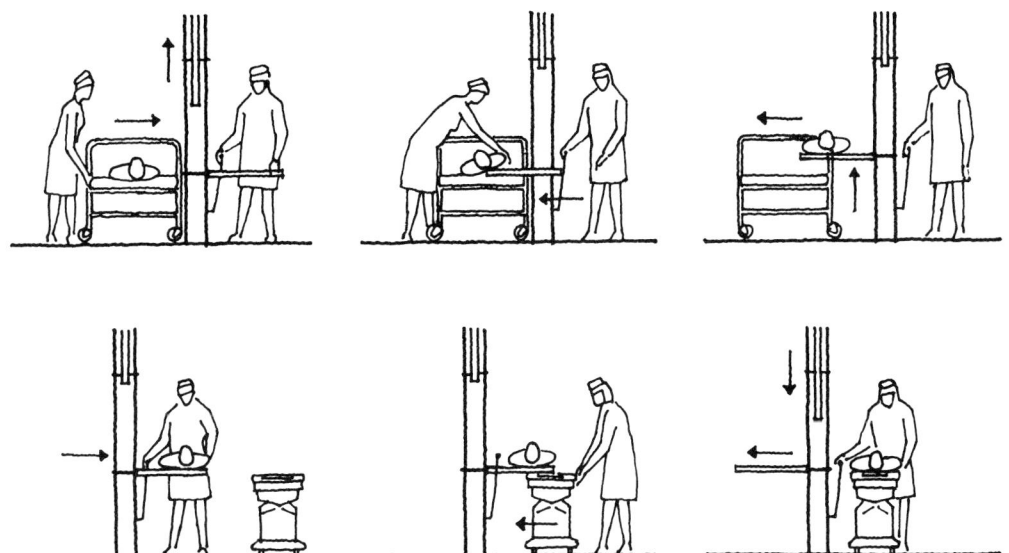

A hatchway in the surgical department might contribute towards a stricter hygienic discipline. However, the time needed to carry out the procedure may be considerable.

A considerable total transfer area is needed in a major surgical department, as each transfer may take 6 to 10 minutes[8].

A technical refinement of the transfer room idea is the patient transfer *hatchway* between the holding area and the operation room suite area. It may consist of a prefabricated wall element of stainless steel incorporating a motor driven elevating column which receives the operation table top, and operates automatically a sash of safety glass. The ascent mechanism is controlled on the operation room side.

There is no evidence to demonstrate the value of transfer practice in reducing the risk of infection[9]. Operation rooms without transfer areas do not have more contamination of their floors than do operation rooms in suites provided with such areas[10].

8   Nedeljkov G: Beziehungen der chirurgischen Fachabteilungen und ihrer diagnostischen Sondereinrichtungen zum OP-Bereich im neu-zeitlichen Krankenhaus. Veska. Aarau 1968, p 27.

9   see also Williams R E O, Blowers R, Garrod L P and Shooter R A: Hospital Infection. Lloyd-Luke (Medical Books) Ltd, London. 1966, p 225.

    Operasjonsavdelinger. Norsk Institutt for Sykehusforskning. Trondheim 1977, p 16.

    Laufman Harold: The control of operating room infection: discipline, defense mechanisms, drugs, design, and devices. 1978, Bulletin of the New York Academy of Medicine 54:472–483.

10 see also Lowbury E J L: Zeroing in on infection. 1972, Hospitals 46:1:80.

    Laufman Harold: Surgical Hazard Control. 1973, Archives of Surgery 107:552–559.

As a result of another study it has been indicated that concerning the total number of bacteria and *Staph. aureus* there is no difference between the waiting room and the soiled and clean side of the transfer area[11].

The use of ward beds within the surgical unit has not been attended with a higher rate of infection than the transfer to a stretcher bed used within the surgical department[12]. The procedure of transferring the patient to a clean trolley and the availability of a trolley transfer area in the operation suite can be omitted[13]. This view is applicable also on the use of hatchways as — although strongly recommended[14] — there is no documented proof yet that they have reduced the post-operative wound infection rate.

From the economical point of view the use of ward beds is to be preferred[15]. To transfer a patient in a ward bed from the ward to the surgical department obviates the problem of lifting the patient in the ward as well as later from his bed to the operation table.

11 Hambraeus A, Bengtsson S and Laurell G: Bacterial contamination in a modern operating suite. 1. Effect of a zoning system on contamination of floors and other surfaces. Stencil. Institute of Clinical Bacteriology, University of Uppsala, Sweden. 1977, p 7.

12 see also Berry Edna Cornelia and Kohn Louise: Introduction to Operating Room Technique. Fourth Edition. A Blakinston Publication. McGraw-Hill Book Company. New York 1972, p 9.

13 see also Control of Hospital Infection. ed by E J L Lowbury, G A J Ayliffe, A M Geddes and J D Williams. Chapman and Hall. London 1975, p 151.

14 Ostertag H: Die hygienische Überwachung der klimatisierten aseptischen Bereiche im Krankenhaus. 1973, Zentralblatt für Bakteriologie, Parasitenkunde, Infektionskrankenheiten und Hygiene 157:1–22.

15 Operationsverksamhet — funktionsbeskrivning och krav. Spri rapport 18/71. Stockholm 1971, p 14.

Procedure area

Anaesthetic room

In an anaesthetic room, also called preparation or induction room*, the patient is transferred to the operation table or to the operation table top. He is depilated with a depilatory cream — if this procedure has not already been carried out in the holding area — given a cap, prepared, and his anaesthesia commenced. Also intubation and induction of sterile parenteral solutions etc may be carried out in this room.

Patients who are not too heavily sedated may move to operation table by their own effort. If the patient is too drowsy to move unassisted, he must be lifted by personnel. To lift correctly up to four persons are needed.

The employment of various fixed or mobile lifting devices, though slow in operation, may be of value where male assisting staff is not available. It could be advantageous to the patients as well.

Provision should be made for the easy movement of both patient bed or other transport vehicle and operation table or top into the anaesthetic room where they will be placed either side by side or with the head ends together under 90° angle for the transfer of patient.

To wheel the anaesthetized patient and anaesthetic equipment from the anaesthetic room to the operation room requires approximately half a minute. This interference in started anaesthesia is considered theoretically dangerous by some anaesthesiologists. In spite of that, the practice of anaesthetizing the patient outside the operation room is not opposed. On the contrary, there are strong psychological reasons not to commence anaesthesia and pre-operative procedures in the operation room, even if the patient is premedicated.

In many cases anaesthesia is terminated in the operation room[1], but it seems to be preferable that it is terminated in the anaesthetic room.

The post-operative patient is in the anaesthetic room transferred from the operation table or from the operation table top to the patient bed or an operation department transport vehicle, which brought the patient to the anaesthetic room and remained there during the operation.

---

* Jean Walter introduced on grounds of air hygiene a double unit — a preparation room and an anaesthetic room. The anaesthetic room was placed as a buffert between the operation room and the preparation room (Walter Jean: Renaissance de l'Architecture Medicale. Imprimerie E Desfasses. Paris 1945).

1 Operasjonsavdelinger. Norsk Institutt for Sykehusforskning. Trondheim 1977, p 46.

In the unconscious patient almost any region of the body is postoperatively susceptible to damage by pressure, stretching, or other adverse forces[2]. Care should be taken in proper positioning the patient and during transport from the anaesthetic room to the post-anaesthetic recovery areas.

In the anaesthetic room space is required also for a writing desk, medicine cabinets with glazed doors, storage racks for screens which separate the patient's head from the surgical field, for operation table fittings, diathermy plates, a work bench, an anaesthetic table and apparatus, two transfusion stands, and one or two washbasins. There have to be oxygen and nitrous oxide outlets and a suction device.

The anaesthetic table requires a space of 0.6 by 0.4 m. When activities around the table during the preparation stage are considered, an area of 0.5 by 1.4 m is needed[3]. When circulation needs are added, the total spatial need for the anaesthetic table is 1.1 by 2.6 m.

For anaesthetic apparatus and activities around it an area of 0.5 by 1.5 is needed, which is increased to 1.1 by 1.5 when circulation needs are considered[4].

The dimensions 5 by 4 m can be recommended for an anaesthetic room as they cover the needs of the majority of the anaesthesiologists, although a room with an area of 17 m² has been accepted[5].

For complicated thoracic and neurosurgical procedures an increase in the anaesthetic room area to 25 m² would be required.

To achieve *hypothermia** additional space and arrangements are needed.

Hypothermia is practiced in open heart surgery and neurosurgery. By whole-body cooling the activities and requirements of the tissues are greatly decreased and a circulatory arrest will cause damage to tissues and organs after a much longer time than under normal conditions. The patient is transferred to the operation table, when patient's temperature has been reduced.

Still larger anaesthetic rooms are needed for teaching and demonstration purposes.

---

2   see also Berkebile Paul E: Postoperative care. in Anesthesia and Ophthalmology. ed by R Brian Smith. 1973, International Ophthalmology Clinics 13:209.

3   Operationssalen. Spri projekt 7064. S7. 1974-12-31. Stockholm 1975, p 15.

4   ibid, p 17.

5   Operasjonsavdelinger. Norsk Institutt for Sykehusforskning. Trondheim 1977, p 42.

*   The term hypothermia is used as a rule to indicate a condition in which the body temperature has been reduced by physical means at least 2°C below the normal physiological range. The degrees of hypothermia are subdivided into mild — 37° to 28°C, moderate — 28° to 20°C and deep hypothermia — 20° to 0°C.

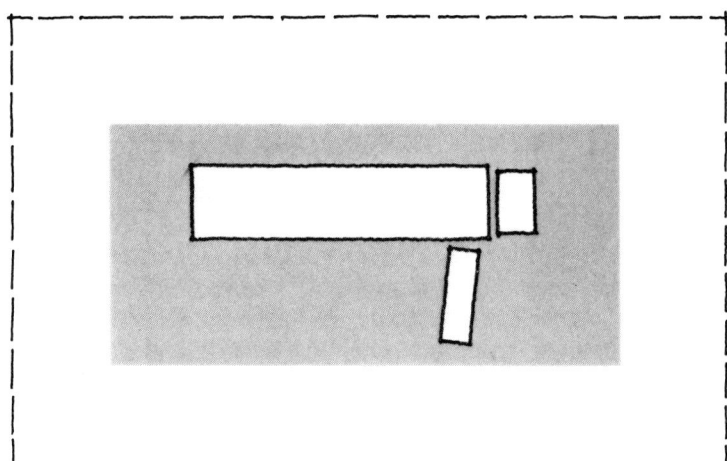

A minimum of 1.5 by 3.1 m of floor space is needed to carry out procedures on patients on the table. The surrounding circulation area ought to be not less than 2.7 by 4.3 m.

All stimuli unpleasant to the patient should be eliminated. The anaesthetic room should be both visually and acoustically well screened from the surgical department so that the patient is not in any way disturbed.

Particularly at the beginning of anaesthesia noises are greatly exaggerated for the patient. Even low voices and minor sounds appear loud. A sudden loud noise in the early stages of anaesthesia can provoke life threatening cardiac arrhythmias[6].

Conversation around the patient should always be discreet, both in topic and sound level. Earplugs for patients are of value, especially when the operation demands very light anaesthesia, or high oxygen percentage, e g in connection with Caesarean sections and poor risk cases.

The need for silence during the induction of anaesthesia can be emphasized by warning signals in the operation department corridors.

During induction of anaesthesia the chest and usually also the abdomen are exposed. The preparation of the skin with volatile antiseptics substantially increases the rate of heat loss. A temperature of not less than 23°C should be maintained.

It should be remembered that frequently the sedation of the patient brings periphery vasodilatation and some heat loss, another reason to have a warm anaesthetic room.

6   Martin John T: Modern Architecture Design in the Operating Room. 1974, Hospital Topics 52:5:41–42.

There is no absolute request for windows in anaesthetic rooms. Large areas of a sing colour outside a window might be reflected by the ceiling and interfere with colour values in the room. Furthermore, variations in daylight from hour to hour may inter fere with the anaesthesiologist's judgement of the colour of the patient. The glare from windows may tire the eyes of the anaesthesiologist. For the sake of consistenc of quality and intensity, artificial light has been considered more satisfactory.

Egress room

Instead of using the anaesthetic room for terminating anaesthesia and for extubatior the provision of an egress room with an area of 10 to 20 m^2 has been suggested[7].

The egress rooms may increase the capacity of surgical departments by about 5 per cent, causing at the same time an increase in operation costs by 5 per cent[8].

The egress room might be justified in operation-room-set-ups with very rapid turn-overs to shorten waiting for the operating staff[9].

A 1977 tour of European hospitals revealed that the extubation room almost never is used for the purpose intended[10].

Scrubbing and gowning area

The scrub-up room should be close to the operation room.

All those taking a direct part in the operation have to disinfect their hands and arms, which thereafter sometimes are immediately powdered or oiled. Automatic dispensers for sterilized nailbrushes are used. Sterilized towels are needed for dry-ing hands.

Two or three members of the operation team will sit and scrub simultaneously.

Although it is sometimes recommended that donning of sterilized operation outfit be carried out in the operation room[11], sterile gowns, caps, masks and gloves could be donned also in the scrub-up room.

7   see also Wåhlin Åke: Effektivare operationsrum med särskilt avvecklingsrum. 1970, Moderna Sjukhus 5:11:36.

    Gundermann K O: Anforderungen an die funktionell-bauliche Gestaltung von Krankenanstalten unter besonderer Berücksichtigung lüftungstechnischer Anlagen. 1977, Gesundheits-Ingenieur 98:123–127.

    Operasjonsavdelinger. Norsk Institutt for Sykehusforskning. Trondheim 1977, p 46.

8   Melander Klas et al: Operationsverksamhet — Kapacitet, ekonomi. Spri rapport 3/7. Stockholm 1970, p 22.

9   personal communication: 1977, Peter Heimann, Bergen.

10 Laufman Harold: The control of operating room infection: discipline, defense mechanisms, drugs, design, and devices. 1978, Bulletin of the New York Academy of Medicine 54:472–483.

11 Heimann Peter: Operasjonsavdelinger. 1977, Tidsskrift for Den norske laegeforening 97:726–729.

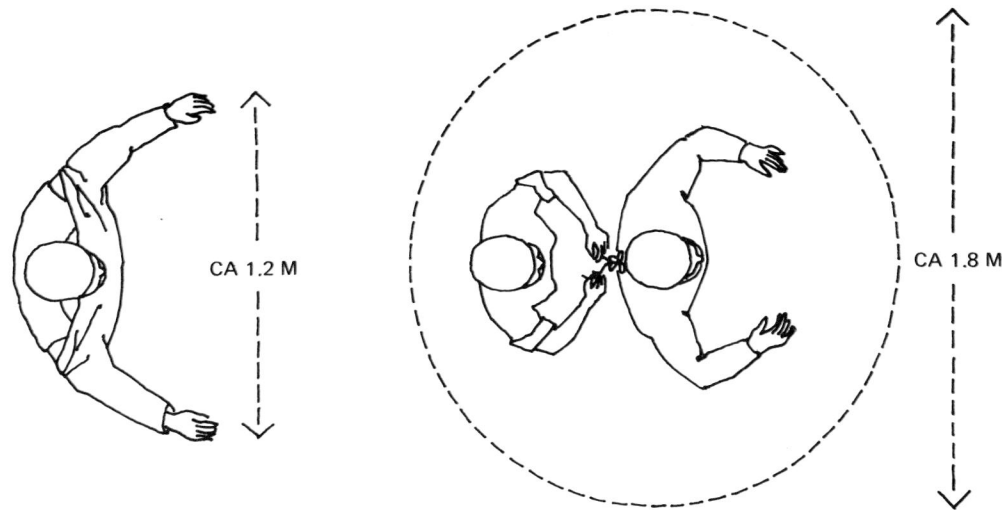

CA 1.2 M

CA 1.8 M

Donning of a sterilized operation outfit requires about 3 m^2 unobstructed space.

If it is likely that the gown may become wet with blood or other fluids, the surgeon should wear a sterilized plastic apron or an impermeable gown. In donning most operation gowns currently used the assistance of a second person is needed.

An area of about 3.0 m^2 is required for donning a gown. A scrub-up and gowning area to serve one operation room equipped with three scrub-up places requires about 11 m^2. Under some circumstances one scrub-up and gowning area may be shared by two operation rooms[12].

The scrub-up room should be designed so that scrubbing and gowning may proceed simultaneously without detriment to either activity.

Space has to be reserved for a (trolley) storage, for sterilized gowns, caps, masks, gloves and aprons.

12 see also Operasjonsavdelinger. Norsk Institutt for Sykehusforskning. Trondheim 1977, p 84.

The operation room or surgical theatre should provide good comfort for both the surgical team and the patient. The operation room should not provide for activities that can be performed outside it.

A division of operation rooms into septic and aseptic groups does not appear to be necessary[13] or even possible[14], although it is adapted[15], advocated[16] and even required[17]. That a wound is obviously contaminated, in no way excuses its treatment with anything other than the strict aseptic technique and the attention that would be given to a clean surgical wound[18].

Aseptic operations carried out in operation rooms belonging to the septic group do not seem to be followed by a higher infection rate than normally[19]. During operation on a septic patient, or indeed, after the patient had been in the operation room, no significant bacterial colony count has been found in the operation room atmos-

13 see also Laufman Harold: Surgical Hazard Control. 1973, Archives of Surgery 107:552–559.

Binner Werner-Helmut: Vorstellungen über den zeitgemässen HNO-Operationsraum aus der Sicht des Operateurs. 1974, Krankenhaus Umschau 43:1036–1039.

Operasjonsavdelinger. Norsk Institutt for Sykehusforskning. Trondheim 1977, p 75.

Tillander Hans: Hygieniska aspekter, konsekvenser för operationsavdelningens utformning — infektionsprofylaktiska synpunkter. Symposion: Planering av operationsavdelningar. ISIMA 78. Malmö, April 1978.

14 also Vogt Victor: Operationsavdelningar förr och nu. Symposion: Planering av operationsavdelningar. ISIMA 78, Malmö, April 1978.

15 Bengtsson Stellan, Hambraeus Anna, Laurell Gunnar: Postoperativa sårinfektioner på en ny centraloperationsavdelning. 1978, Läkartidningen 75:2690–2696.

In Canada one special operation room for contaminated cases was found in 30 per cent of larger hospitals and in 20 per cent of small hospitals (O.R. Report. 1973, Hospital Administration in Canada 15:7:25).

16 see also Kanz E: Praktische Hygienemassnahmen auf der septischen Station. 1975, Hospital-Hygiene 67:149–153.

Anforderungen an eine zeitgemässe Operationsabteilung. 1977, Veska — Das Schweizer Spital 41:31–34.

Gundermann K O: Anforderungen an die funktionell-bauliche Gestaltung von Krankenanstalten unter besonderer Berücksichtigung lüftungstechnischer Anlagen. 1977, Gesundheits–Ingenieur 98:123–127.

17 see also Teodorescu Aurelia, Mihailescu Mihai, Machedon Emilian and Popescu Viorel: Constructii spitalicesta. Editura technica. Bucarest 1971, p 107.

Evrard J: Etat actuel de la prévention de l'infection en chirurgie orthopédique. 1977, Acta Orthopaedica Belgica 42:517–535.

18 see also Caswell H Taylor, Schreck Kenneth M, Learner Norman et al: A three year study of staphylococcal disease with observations on control. 1960, Surgery, Gynecology & Obstetrics 110:530.

Dathe O: Asepsis und Antisepsis in der Urologie. 1976, Der Krankenhausarzt 49:664–678.

19 see also Gillquist Jan: Sårinfektioner på en gammal och en ny operationsavdelning. 1967, Läkartidningen 64:1220.

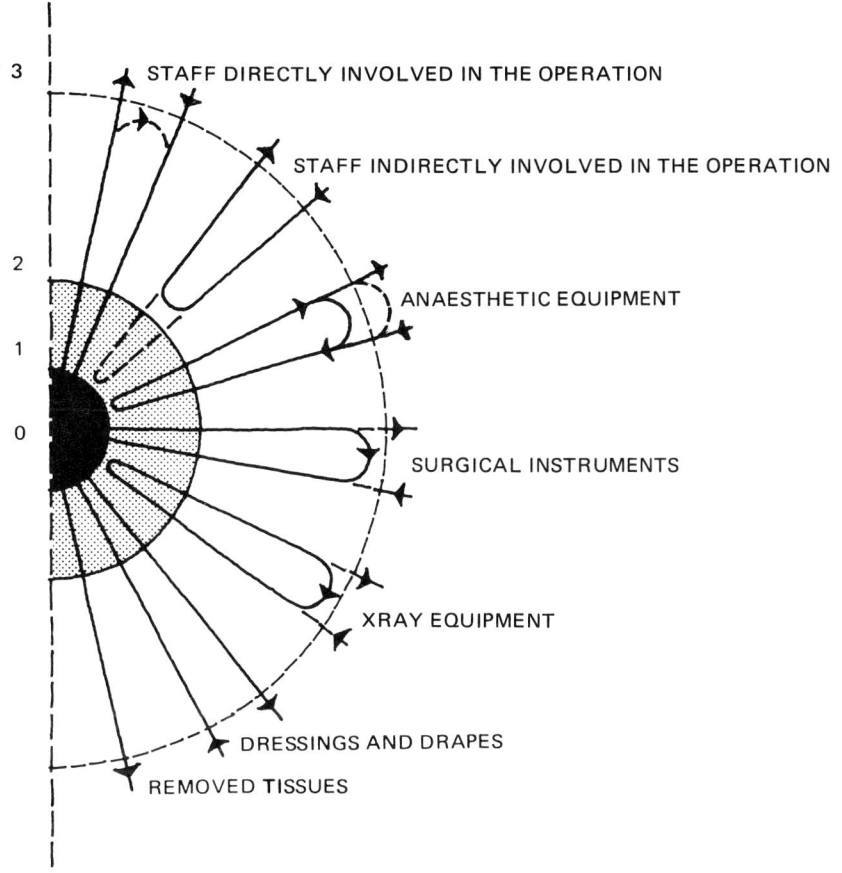

STAFF DIRECTLY INVOLVED IN THE OPERATION

STAFF INDIRECTLY INVOLVED IN THE OPERATION

ANAESTHETIC EQUIPMENT

SURGICAL INSTRUMENTS

XRAY EQUIPMENT

DRESSINGS AND DRAPES

REMOVED TISSUES

Circulation in the cleanliness zones of an operation room: 0 — aseptic zone, 1 — ultra clean zone, 2 — super clean zone, 3 — clean zone.

phere[20]. There is no significant difference between the total number of bacteria after operations on clean and infected cases[21].

There seems to be no need for more extensive cleaning procedures with the use of disinfectants after so called dirty operations as compared with so called clean operations[22].

20 Wiley A M and Bernett Michael: Clean Surgeons and Clean Air. 1973, Clinical Orthopaedics and Related Research 96:168–175.

21 Hambraeus A, Bengtsson S and Laurell G: Bacterial Contamination in a modern operating suite. 1. Effect of a zoning system on contamination of floors and other surfaces. Institute of Clinical Bacteriology. University of Uppsala, Sweden 1977, p 8.

22 ibid, p 13.

The concept of quarantine of operations rooms following the so called dirty cases and the doing of contaminated procedures at the end of the day's schedule could be dispelled[23]. However, for care of instruments and equipment, and for cleaning rooms between cases proper techniques must be conscientiously adapted.

With all main operation rooms regarded as equal, preparing of operation schedules is made easier.

In transplantation surgery the recipient and donor should be in two adjacent operation rooms. A *double* operation room suite is needed.

Operative team

The actual team for routine general surgery procedures varies usually between four and seven persons*. Cardiovascular surgery may require an overall staff of about twenty or more.

The operative team may consist of a surgeon, an anaesthesiologist, an assistant who helps with ligatures, retractors etc, a scrub nurse who passes instruments to the surgeon, a circulating nurse, who makes general preparations for the operation and sees that all instruments the surgeon may come to need are available, and an anaesthesiologist nurse. There may be up to four assistants. The operative team is assisted by radiographers, technicians and porters as well as a sterilizing staff and a disposal staff. If intra-operative autotransfusion is part of the surgical procedure one operator has to give undivided attention to the autotransfusion equipment[24].

The surgeon's position at the operation table is determined by the character of the operation and the physical qualities of the surgeon. The anaesthesiologist's position demands ample space and should be nearest to the anaesthetic room.

Operation table and other equipment

The main item of the operation room furniture is the operation table. One table per operation room is required. The number of reserve tables, if mobile tables are used, depends on the frequency of operations.

Mostly the operation tables are constructed for the surgeon operating standing. It has been pointed out[25] that to operate sitting means increased precision. This, however, requires modifications in the traditional operation table construction.

Another disadvantage that is found in many table constructions is the faulty assumption that the back of the patient is flat[26].

---

23 see also Peers Jerry G: Cleanup Techniques in the Operating Room. 1973, Archives of Surgery 107:596–599.

*   an average Swedish surgical team has 4.3 members (Hälso- och sjukvård inför 80-talet. Socialstyrelsen. Stockholm 1973, p 167).

24 Raines Jeff, Buth Jacob, Brewster David C and Darling R Clement: Intraoperative autotransfusion: equipment, protocols, and guidelines. 1976, The Journal of Trauma 16:616–621.

25 Mandal A C and Gundersen Gunnar: Hospitalsergonomi. 1977, Tidsskrift for Danske Sygehus 53:74–90.

26 ibid

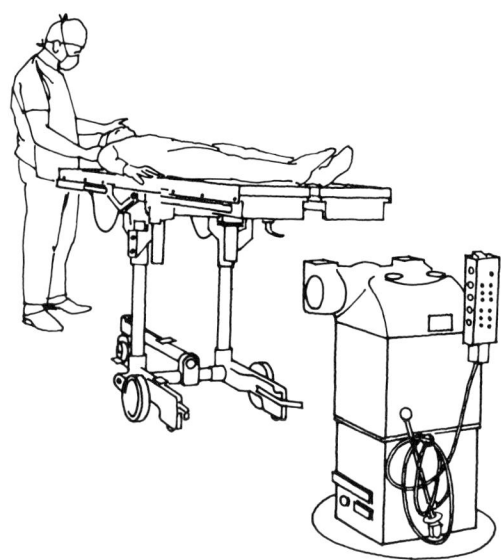

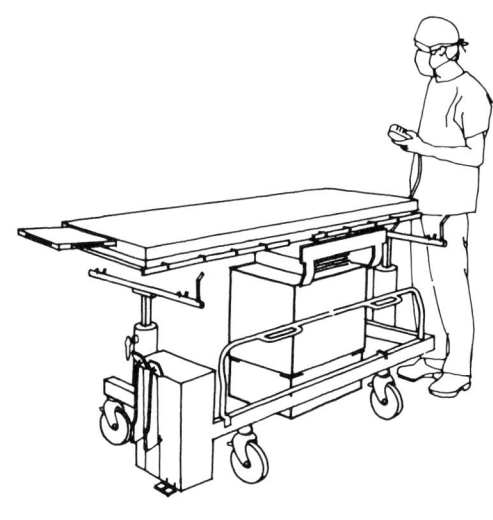

The MAQUET operation table system is based on a fixed column, which gives the operating team as well as the Xray apparatus and image intensifier free access under the table tops. The variety of table tops meets the requirements of surgical specialities.

The KIFA H table-system includes a trolley, several types of transportable table tops, and a permanently mounted base. The patient can be transported from bed or ambulance to operation room and post-anaesthetic units without changing position. The table top can be clamped firmly on the base in desired position.

There are operation table tops that can be detached from their permanently fixed pedestals. When released from the pedestal the table top fits on to a wheeled trolley for transfer of the patient between the anaesthetic room and the operation room and *vice versa*. The patient is anaesthetized on the trolley in the anaesthetic room and transferred to the operation table in the operation room.

The pedestal accommodates gas and electricity supplies and other services and hydraulic power to manoeuver the table top.

All operation tables should allow a convenient insertion of X ray cassetts.

Reservations have been expressed concerning the fixed operation table[27]. A mobile table leaves the floor space free and might make easier to accommodate changes in practice.

When a mobile table is used, the patient is anaesthetized on it in the anaesthetic room and then wheeled into the operation room. Services are from wall, ceiling or pendant fittings. The pendant fitting should hang not lower than 1.90 m over the floor[28].

A common problem with heavy mobile operation tables is their damaging effect on floor surfaces.

27 Green John, Moss Raymond and Jackson Colin: Hospital Research and Brief Problems. King Edward's Hospital Fund for London. London 1971, p 121.

28 see also Operasjonsavdelinger. Norsk Institutt for Sykehusforskning. Trondheim 1977, p 41.

For microsurgery *microscopes* with remote controls for functional alterations are used. These alterations include coarse and fine focusing, zooming from low to high power slowly or rapidly while remaining in focus, moving in anterior-posterior and X–Y directions and even axially. The surgeon is allowed the free use of both hands while either the feet or face control the microscope. Stereoscopic colour video-microscope has come into use.

The body size of the microscope has been reduced and ceiling and wall mounts reduce operation room clutter about the table.

Furniture and equipment should whereever possible be wall hung. A wall desk 0.45 m by 0.6 has been found useful for writing up notes, swab registers, etc[29].

Mobile equipment used in the operation room may include anaesthetic apparatus and anaesthetic tables, X ray equipment, diathermy equipment, electrical suction apparatus, acoustic pulse monitors, respirators, and devices for physiological and isotope investigations.

All surfaces, wheels etc of equipment should be easily accessible for cleaning and decontamination.

No piece of equipment which stands on the floor should have a height exceeding 1.8 m.

Operation room size

The size of the operation room depends on the number of staff involved and the amount of furniture, fittings, and mobile equipment.

The continuous development taxes the conformations of the space in which they are performed. There is a kind of accordeon effect. To accommodate the new instrumentation, the space must be enlarged. Then, through miniaturization, the new devices shrink. For the second simultaneous procedures the space must expand again, and again after perfecting the method some spatial requirements may be rendered unnecessary[30].

Mostly only about one third of the operation room space is planned for surgical intervention. The remainder is to house support systems.

For the surgical moment exclusively, the area can be reduced to less than 2.13 by 2.13 m as indicated by the Charnley enclosure, which will be described later.

Activities around the operation table require 3.05 by 1.45 m[31]. The circulation needs increase the required area to 4.25 by 2.65 m.

On the anaesthesiologist's side a minimum distance of 1.8 m between the patient's head on the operation table and the operation room wall is requested.

29 see also Brigden Raymond J: Operating Theatre Technique. Churchill Livingstone. Edinburgh and London 1974, p 27.

30 see also Frank Fredrick R and Beck William C: Demontable Metal Partitions as Operating Room Walls: Experimental Study. 1973, The Guthrie Bulletin 43:51–64.

31 Operationssalen. Spri Projekt 7064. S7. 1974-12-31. Stockholm 1975, p 19.

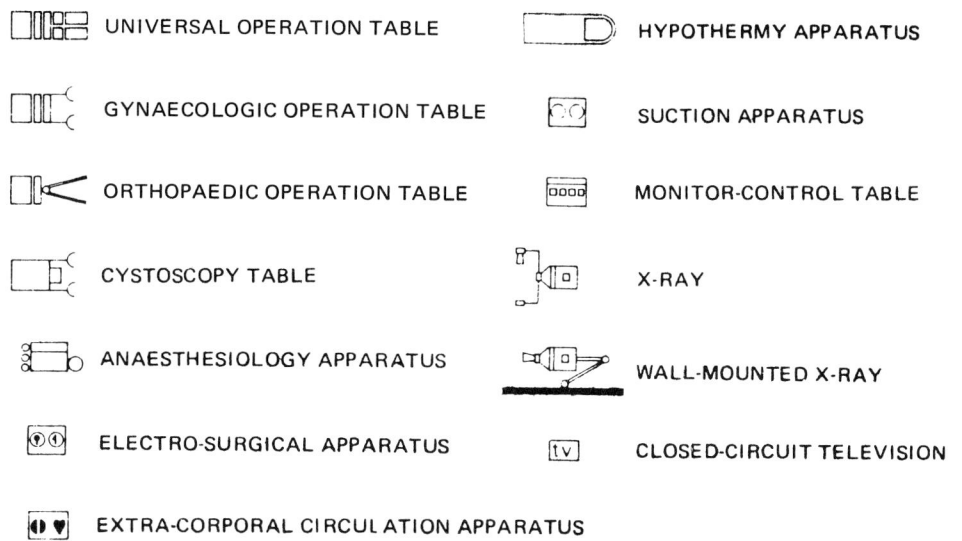

UNIVERSAL OPERATION TABLE		HYPOTHERMY APPARATUS
GYNAECOLOGIC OPERATION TABLE		SUCTION APPARATUS
ORTHOPAEDIC OPERATION TABLE		MONITOR-CONTROL TABLE
CYSTOSCOPY TABLE		X-RAY
ANAESTHESIOLOGY APPARATUS		WALL-MOUNTED X-RAY
ELECTRO-SURGICAL APPARATUS		CLOSED-CIRCUIT TELEVISION
EXTRA-CORPORAL CIRCULATION APPARATUS		

Operation room equipment symbols designed by the Netherlands Hospital Planning Consultants.

The *minimum area* of a contemporary operation room for general surgery, where standard aseptic techniques can be easily applied is 29.4 m² (5.25 by 5.6 m).

A suitable size for an operation room for most forms of surgery has been for some time in the region of 40 to 42 m². The measurements 6.5 by 6.55 m have been recommended[32].

Operation rooms for neurosurgery, thoracic surgery, eye surgery, orthopaedics, and ear, nose and throat surgery are now so specialized in their equipment that a considerable variation in the operation room lay-outs is justified.

As an outcome of a London study[33], which indicates that low sepsis rates could be obtained in conventional operation room environments, when the staff in not sterilized garments is not allowed to approach within 1 meter of the wound area, whatever ventilation employed, there is a recommendation that the practice of painting (green) lines on the operation floor to restrict the movement of operation room personnel should be made standard practice.

32 Operationssalen. Spri Projekt 7064. S7. 1974–12-31. Stockholm 1975, p 45.

33 Freeman M A R, Challis J H, Zelezonski J and Jarvis I D: Sepsis Rates in Hip Replacement Surgery with Special Reference to the Use of Ultra Clean Air. 1977, Archiv für orthopädische und Unfall-Chirurgie 90:1–14.

Operation room shape

It has been suggested that shapes other than the rectangular would contribute to an improvement in operation room standard. Circular, oval, dodecagonal as well as various asymmetrical plans and ceiling forms have been introduced and tried. It remains highly doubtful whether these shapes with their higher building costs have any advantage over the usual rectangular operation room. A rectangular oblong operation room with rounded internal corners to ease the cleaning procedures meets most of the surgeons' needs.

Consistency of construction should extend to an identical shape and the very same placing of doors and equipment as well as of the outlets for electricity, medical gases, compressed air in all operation rooms of a department.

Mirrored operation rooms as found in twin operation room suites should definitely be discouraged, as only one of them is functionally correct.

The free ceiling, with or without a suspended ceiling, should preferably be 3.5 m high and not less than 3.1 m to maintain a good volumetric proportion to the people and equipment, although in many cases the ceiling height has been as low as 2.5 m.

Maximum height for the operation room is about 3.65 m when the ceiling light is considered.

Auditory effects

It is a basic requirement that reverberation times have to be minimized in all areas of the hospital, except in large lecture rooms where too short a reverberation time would be detrimental to speech comprehension.

Little attention has been given to the design of the operation room itself and of its furnishing and instruments in terms of auditory effects. Hard reflective walls and ceilings contribute to long reverberation time of the noise, both original and reverberant. The situation is worsened in orthopaedic operation rooms in which motorize instruments are used.

The reverberation time in operation rooms should be reduced to below one second.

Measured sound from ventilation systems should not exceed 35 dB in anaesthetic rooms and 40 dB in operation rooms.

Wall, ceiling, and floor materials that without lowering housekeeping requirements decrease reverberation time should be used in operation rooms. Silent running apparatus, stretcher wheels, operation tables etc should be chosen. All sanitary installations, including sinks, should be constructed and mounted so as to minimize noise.

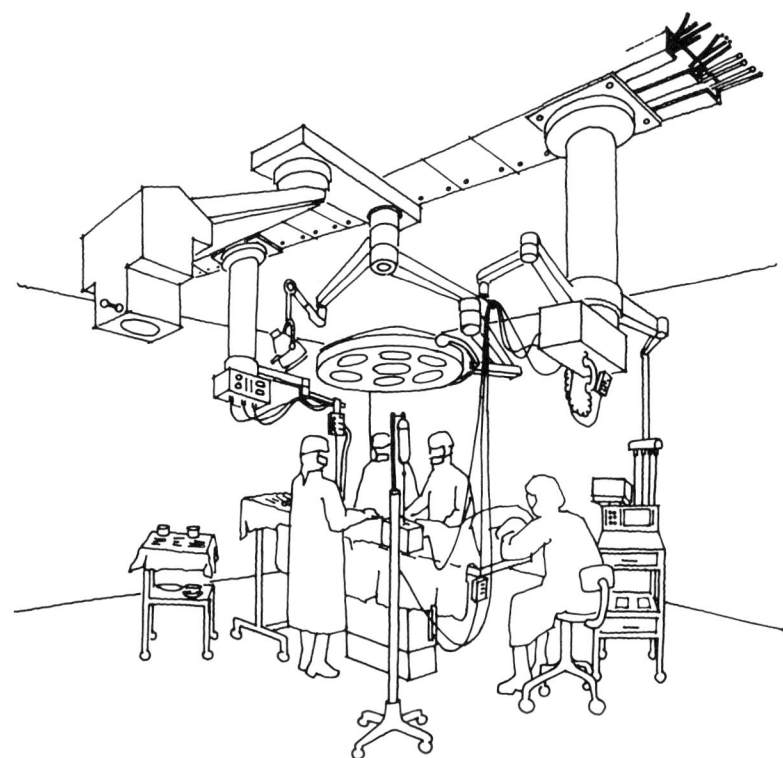

In operation rooms outlets for oxygen, nitrous oxide, and compressed air as well as suction pipes are frequently laid in telescopic tubes, which must not extend downwards lower than 2 m above the floor.

Many noisy instruments could be replaced by quieter heat-resistant plastic instruments. By adapting noise control methods on surgical technology a less nerve-irritating operation room could be achieved.

Operation viewing

Closed circuit TV has reduced, but not eliminated, the need for observation domes.

Viewing rooms have a value in paramedical training curricula and for giving insight into the management of operation and anaesthetic rooms and the encircling events which occur before, during, and immediately after operation.

For monitoring and communication viewing rooms can be electronically connected with the operation room.

Traumatological and orthopaedic operation room

Traumatological therapeutical interventions are mostly surgical acts to reduce bone fractures by closed fracture treatment or by an operation and to treat injuries to soft tissues, internal organs, blood vessels, brain.

For operation of injuries to cavity organs an operation table complemented with an extension table and extension devices is needed. For treating bone fractures hooks, fastened in the operation room ceiling or in the wall, are used.

In case of multiple trauma, multiple fractures of a limb, simultaneous fractures of several limbs, or a combination of limb fractures with injuries to the skull, spine, thorax, abdomen, the four extremities as well as the body should be brought into posture which is desirable for the simultaneous treatment of the injuries or for treating the various injuries one after the other.

For carrying out the adjustment of the body needed both for closed treatment of fractures and for their semioperative or operative treatment, special traumatological operation tables are available.

To make radiographic examinations possible, some elements of the table have to be of a substance permeable to X rays, and there should be an arrangement to extend the limbs for reducing bone fractures in such a manner that the operation table does not interfere.

A traumatological operation room requires a size of about 42 to 50 m^2.

Plaster room

Whenever possible, plastering, and especially the removal of plaster with attendant dust, should be performed in a special plaster room and not in the room, where operated.

The plaster room, connected to an operation room, should have an area of about 40 m^2. Usually, also an anaesthetic room is required.

The equipment in the plaster room includes an orthopaedic table, a suspension frame, slop sinks with plaster traps, and access to X ray apparatus.

To maintain proper air cleanliness, 20 air changes per hour have been recommended.

The splint and plaster store should be located between the orthopaedic operation room and the plaster room.

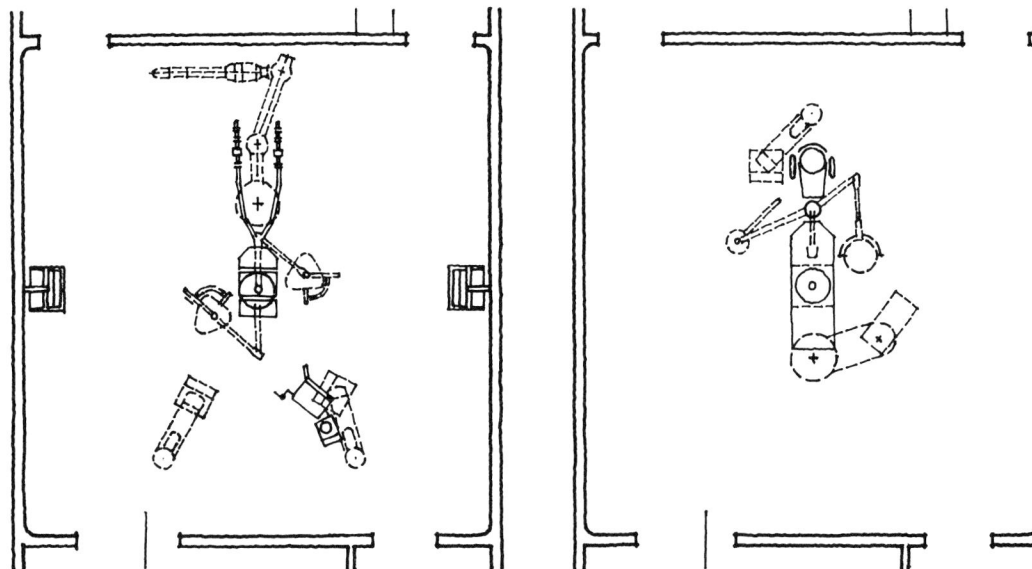

Equipment in orthopaedic operation room should include according to Maquet an operation table column with an extension table top, an anaesthetic monitoring box, gas box, anaesthetic apparatus, a surgery box on swivel stand, Xray image intensifier-TV unit on overhead support, a TV-monitor on console. Operation lamp is Hanaulux-London.

Equipment in eye operation room should include an operation table column with a table for microsurgery, a ceiling-mounted unit with anaesthetic apparatus, a surgery-box on universal swivel stand, an operator's stool, a ceiling-mounted microscope. Lighting equipment is Hanaulux-Hamburg.

In ophthalmic surgery, two contradictory trends have been forecast[34]. One emphasizes on doing the least, using minimal surgical intervention in order to attain the final goal, the other is toward massive resection of the eye.

An operation room for minor eye surgery should have a size of about 30 m², for major eye surgery about 40 m².

The eye operation room includes a from the ceiling suspended equipment column, a pedestal attached to the floor, control consoles connected with both the columns and the pedestal, and equipment cabinets.

The main equipment column, which can be raised or lowered, would provide support for the surgical instrument tray with canopy, a high-intensity twin light, the surgical microscope suction pump for phacoerysis, cautery, diathermy unit, microphone and, coaxially mounted television

34 see also Vodovosov A M: Prognosis for Ophthalmology: Good. 1977, Annals of Ophthalmology 9:827–828.

cameras. In some cases cryosurgical units and wet-field bipolar coagulators have been added[35]. To reduce potential vibration the horizontal arms that carry the operation microscope should be sturdy, have as few joints as possible, and be as short as possible.

The surgeon's chair is an integral part of the system in which foot controls are used if surgery is performed under high magnification.
Flexible foot controls extending from the pedestal or the chair allow an easy up-and-down adjustment of the microscope, focusing, variation of the microscope zoom magnification, activation of cautery, diathermy, and vacuum.

As mostly only single man microscopes are made, the assistant has to wear loupes.

It is essential for the surgeon to be comfortably seated around the patient's head. As all movement is with surgeon's fingers, the forearms should be immobilized by resting the wrists. This is often hard to achieve with the present design of operation tables and operation room stools*.

The best way to avoid traumatizing microinstruments** at operation is to have them presented in their rack on a separate Mayo stand, which is plentifully draped to give it some padding. The instruments should remain in their rack except when they are in use[36].

For operations of retinal detachment suspended tables have been designed.

Ophthalmological surgery is often time-consuming and the room may be in darkness for several hours. Switches for light and for the electric motion of curtains or blinds, in case the operation room has windows, should be at the equipment column.

More than half of all eye procedures are done with local anaesthesia[37], and the surgeon cannot work without the patient's cooperation. Therefore the atmosphere in the eye operation room must enhance the patient's confidence.

Because sounds are exaggerated, the room must be quiet. The staff must talk in normal tones. Whispering aggravates the patient's apprehension.

35 Machemer Robert and Parel Jean-Marie: An improved microsurgical ceiling-mounted unit and automated television. 1978, American Journal of Ophthalmology 85:205–209.

*Treplin M C W, Arnott Eric J: Seeing eye to eye. 1978, Nursing Mirror 147:18:30–33.

** A deformation of less than 0.1 mm will put a good pair of microforceps or scissors out of alignment so badly that they cease to function. This amount of trauma is produced very readily, for example by dropping a pair of jeweler's forceps onto a hard surface from a height of 12 mm.

36 Acland Robert D: Instrumentation for Microsurgery. 1977, The Orthopedic Clinics of North America 8:281–291.

37 personal communication: 1977, Peep Algvere, Stockholm.

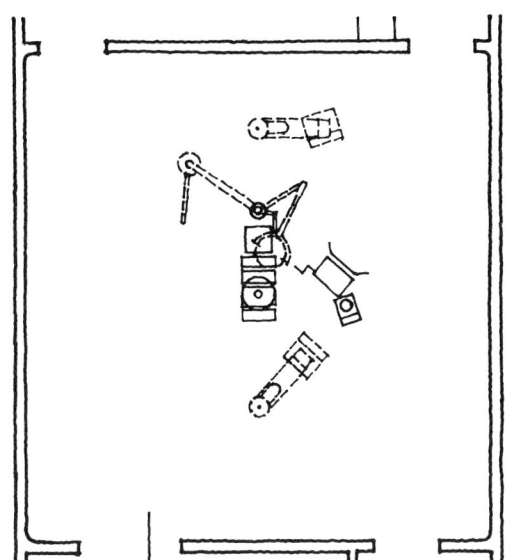

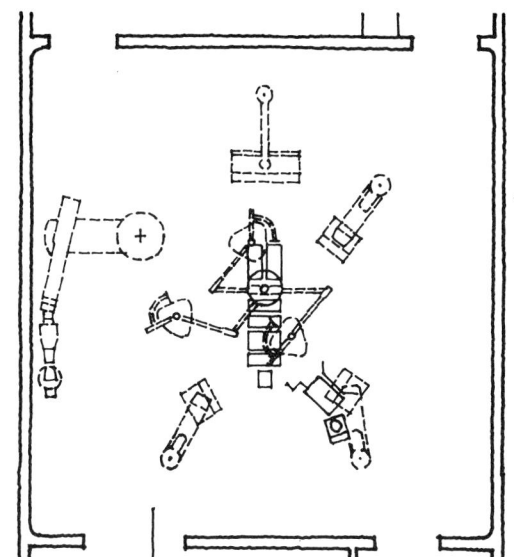

Equipment in an ENT operation room should include according to Maquet a table column and a top with ENT accessories, an anaesthetic box on swivel stand with monitoring system and gas box, an anaesthetic apparatus, a surgery box on swivel stand. Lighting is Hanaulux-Duo Hamburg special.

Equipment in a cardiac-thoracic operation room should include a table column and a universal table top, an anaesthetic box on swivel stand with monitoring system and gas box, an anaesthetic apparatus, a surgery box on swivel stand, an Xray image intensifier TV-unit on overhead support, a monitor for physiological variables, a cardiotherapy box on swevel. Lighting is Hanaulux-London with satellite London.

ENT operation room

In the ENT operation room the surgeon sits at the head and the anaesthesiologist at the side of the preferably special ENT operation table. The column of the operation table must be near the foot end to allow space for the surgeon's feet and foot switches. It must be possible to transport the patient head first on to the operation table. The table top must tilt with either the head end or foot end down.

Suspended from the ceiling a fitment should enable the microscope, and the satellite with all instruments and connections to move freely on independent arms.

No part of suspended equipment may be hang lower than 1.8 m above the floor.

A special operation lamp with the intensity of 80,000 lux has been recommended for the otolaryngologic purposes[38].

---

38 Binner Werner-Helmut: Vorstellungen über den zeltgemässen HNO-Operationsraum aus der Sicht des Operateurs. 1974, Krankenhaus Umschau 43:1036—1039.

Cardiovascular operation room

The complexity of cardiovascular surgery, a large staff and special equipment involved require an area of 56 m² (7.2 by 7.8 m) and a third major light in addition to the usual dual overhead system.

To justify the installation of a cardiovascular operation room, at least four major cardiac operations have to be performed a week.

In units carrying out open-heart surgery, there seems to be no reason to encourage a turnover much over 200 operations per year[39].

Microvascular operation room

Major surgical departments should possess for small vessel surgery a microvascular set-up and an operation room of about 30 m².

In microvascular work visual aids should be simple to handle without contamination of the operation field. Portable stereoscopic operation microscopes which are clamped to the side of operation table are used. Usually the magnification is x6 and x40.

Fiberoptic lighting systems avoid heat discomfort to the surgeon and heat damage to the tissues in the operation field.

For much microvascular work ophthalmic instruments are used.

Stereotaxis room

Stereotaxis* in-man is based on the X ray visualization of the target or suitable reference structures. Neurological technique, specially pneumoencephalography and angiography, are suited for this purpose. Open stereotaxic operations use radiofrequency heat lesions and closed intra-cranial radiosurgery high energy gamma rays through the intact skull.

The radiosurgical equipment for *closed operations* is the Gamma Unit. The beam sources in the Gamma Unit are 179 in number and consist of radioactive cobalt (Co^{60}).

39 McGregor Maurice, Pelletier Gerald: Planning of specialized health facilities. 1978, The New England Journal of Medicine 299:179–181.
* see also Leksell Lars: Stereotaxis and Radiosurgery. Charles C Thomas Publisher. Springfield 1971.

During the period of irradiation the patient is observed in a mirror and movements of the head and stresses on the axis are continuously recorded.

When the procedure is performed with the patient awake, a two-way radio or intercom facilitates communication between the patient and the operator.

Of all irradiation units only the Leksell system requires no shielding of the operation rooms*.

The stereotaxis room should have a temperature of 18°C. The humidity percentage should be about 50.

Spatial needs for a stereotaxis room only are about 30 m².

During an operation the neurosurgeon may be confronted with a wide variety of responses to stimulation, which must be optimally interpreted in order to determine the lesion site with the greatest possible accuracy. An intraactive online computer system has been developed[40] to process data collected during stereotaxic neurosurgical procedures, in order to facilitate more accurate localization of subcortical target sites.

Endoscopy rooms

Endoscopic examination is the examination of organs through natural or artificial ortifices. Endoscopic methods comprise e g bronchoscopic, laryngoscopic, cystoscopic, gastroscopic and similar methods. The importance of co-operation with anaesthesiologists is expanding.

The co-operation with radiological department is essential as well as in some cases, such as gastroenterologic endoscopy, with the department of clinical physiology[41].

The demand for endoscopic services is likely to increase considerably. Continuous progress in the miniaturization of electronics and the accompanying development in the construction of TV cameras is opening up possibilities in endoscopic investigational and therapeutic techniques. These techniques would lead to further reductions in the frequency and severity of some traumatic procedures. An extension of out-patient treatment could be expected. However, the realization of new endoscopic methods implies also efforts in the field of micro techniques, especially with regard to apparatus for manipulating tissues during surgical procedures[42].

*Personal communication: 1978, Tiit Rähn, Stockholm.

40 Hawrylyshyn P, Rowe I H, Tasker R R and Organ L W: A computer system for stereotaxic neurosurgery. 1976, Computers in Biology and Medicine 6:87–97.

41 Reutsch I, Müller P and Gärtner U: Planung, Einrichtung und instrumentelle Ausstattung der gastroenterologischen Endoskopieabteilungen im städtischen Krankenhaus Bremen. 1976, Das Krankenhaus 68:381–383.

42 Anliker M: Current and Future Aspects of Biomedical Engineering. 1977, Triangle 16:129–140.

The number of endoscopy rooms in a larger hospital is frequently estimated to half of the hospital's operation room number.

Endoscopy requires operation room-like facilities, even stereomicroscopy is practiced, with minor operation room lamps. The room needs sometimes to be darkened

In larger endoscopy units special rooms for septic endoscopy have been provided[43].

All groups of endoscopy are functionally well served in a room with an area of 28 to 32 m². The harmonious integrations have placed an endoscopy room beside an X ray room. About half of the endoscopy is performed with radiological assistance. Extreme approaches of placing all endoscopy in radiology department or all endoscopy in other sites of the hospital have not been as fruitful[44].

Staff scrub-up has been traditionally performed within the endoscopy rooms. Nowadays a separate scrub is frequently preferred.

Undressing cubicles, resuscitation facilities, X ray facilities, an anaesthetic room, a recovery room, and a waiting room with a toilet are needed as well as a room for administrative purposes.

A disposal room should be directly accessible from each endoscopy room.

Provision for gas-sterilization is needed as a portion of instruments is sterilized on the premises.

Pressurized operation rooms

The main indications for clinical treatment in a hyperbaric chamber where surgery is dependent upon oxygenation or pressure have been found in cardiac surgery[45]. *Boerema's* original purpose in establishing a hyperbaric chamber in Amsterdam with the intention to increase the time for elective cardiac arrest turned out to be a disappointment because the gained extra time was insignificant, even when hyperbaric oxygen therapy was combined with hypothermia[46].

Only very few of the clinical applications suggested for hyperbaric oxygen therapy have withstood critical appraisal. In spite of this it is still used in situations where the evidence for its value is unproven[47].

43 see also Ruhr-Universität Bochum. Programm Praktische Medizin. Institut für Krankenhausbau. Technische Universität Berlin. Berlin 1976, p 269.

44 MacEwan Douglas W: Editorial. 1977, The Journal of the Canadian Association of Radiologists 28:94.

45 Meijne N G: Hyperbaric oxygen, increased pressure and the activities in this field in Boerema's department in the period 1956—1972. 1973, Archivum Chirurgicum Neerlandicum 25:195–213.

46 Walder D N: Surgery and the hyperbaric environment. in Recent Advances in Surgery. Number 9. ed by Selwyn Taylor. Churchill Livingstone. Edinburgh, London and New York 1977, p 220.

47 ibid

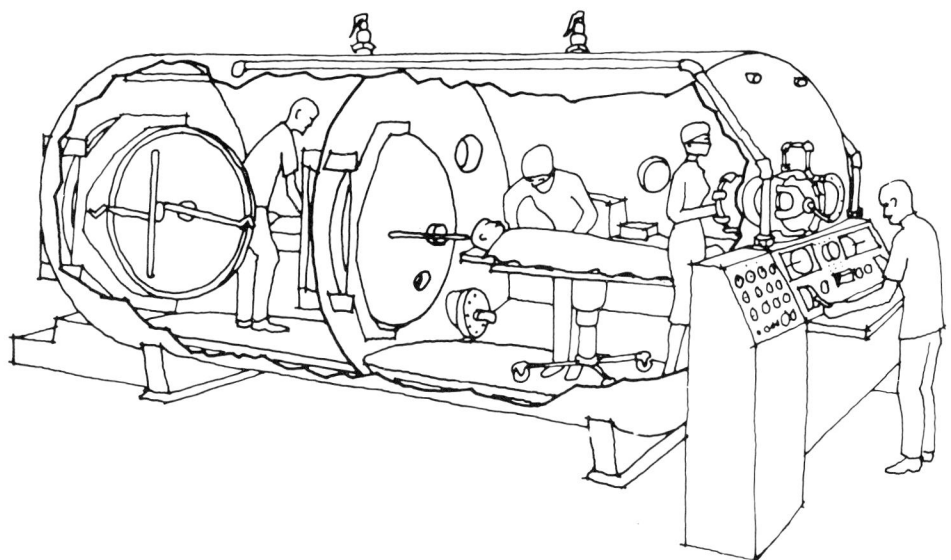

Hyperbaric chambers were introduced with the intention to increase the length of time for elective cardiac arrest.

A double-locked hyperbaric chamber is mostly 5 to 15 m in overall length and 3.5 to 5 m in diameter.

The chamber is housed in a unit which has a compressor with a working pressure of about three atmospheres absolute, a low pressure compressor which keeps the circulation throughout the chamber constant, and banks for air and oxygen supply.

The chamber proper has an air conditioner, based on filtered recirculation; a control for automatic pressure regulators, and a humidity and temperature control. The air temperatures between 15 and 25°C, and the humidity of 55 to 60 per cent have been adapted[48].

The hyperbaric chamber is equipped with an operation table; a medical lock for passing instruments in and out of the chamber without decompression; cold and hot water; bloodgas analysis equipment for pressures and cardiac output; a conduit panel to transmit signals from sensors within the chamber to recorders outside the chamber; and fire extinguishers.

TV monitors as well as laminated glass portholes allow observation and control of conditions inside the clinical hyperbaric chamber.

48 see also Bureau Jacques: L'oxygénation hyperbare et sa technique. 1973, Techniques Hospitalières 29:12:67–70.

In a clinical hyperbaric unit the colour of the chamber walls and the character of lighting have to alleviate any feeling of claustrophobia.

In hyperbaric operation chambers the noise of the compressor, blowers and air conditioner is often trying. For continuous operation, a noise level below 45 decibels should be maintained. Well chosen piped-in music helps mask the noise to some extent.

Hyperbaric chambers are hazardous environments with regard to fire and explosion risks. Precautions to be taken in their construction are similar to those taken in connection with any high pressure oxygen unit. They include explosion-proof construction of all electrical installations, uninterrupted wiring for lights, placement of all circuit breakers and electric motors outside the chamber, earthing of conductive floor, and controls on air inlet and outlet lines.

Clean air isolators and enclosures

For strong reducing or eliminating airborne microorganisms during surgical operations isolators of impermeable materials and clean rooms are available.

A slightly turbulent enclosure without equipment for ultra-filtration has been suggested[49], as to filtrate air to less than 2 μm is not considered necessary. For the surgical team a body exhaust system and impermeable all-investing gowns and hoods are foreseen.

Evidence appears to be incompatiable with the view that airborne infection plays an important role in general surgery and that the use of isolated cubicles with a high air exchange would be helpful[50].

The proof for or against the clean air enclosures suffers from the statistical defects and the incompleteness of the investigation process. Infection rates depend very much on the clinical material[51].

For the present the decision whether or not to embark upon the considerable expense of installing clean-room facilities in new or existing operation units cannot be made solely on the scientific data available*.

Many users of clean enclosures or isolators remark about the increased emphasis on the discipline of technique which these enclosures seem to impose. The surgeons seem to be less disturbed within an enclosure and can increase concentration on the act of surgery. On the other hand, a significant conclusion drawn from long experience in providing clean air enclosures[52] is that the side walls and hanging panels may impose irksome restrictions on procedures, and on the movement of personnel and equipment.

Isolators

The basic unit which is being used in Glasgow[53] consists of a gamma-irradiated, disposable plastic film envelope which is 240 cm in length and 90 cm in diameter. A surgical drape forms a panel in

49 Eftekhar N S: The Surgeon and Clean Air in the Operating Room. 1973, Clinical Orthopaedics and Related Research. Number 96, p 188–194.

50 Douglas Sir Donald: Wounds and their problems. 1975, Journal of the Royal College of Surgeons of Edinburgh 20:77–95.

51 Stühmer G, Weber B G, Meierhans R, Janssen R, and Brunner J: Four and a Half Years Experience with a Vertical Flow Sterile Enclosure. 1977, International Orthopaedics 1:95–99.

* Allen Paul, Reynolds D A: Clean air operating environments. 1978, British Journal of Hospital Medicine 20:591–598.

52 Howorth F H: The Prevention of Airborne Infection during Surgery. 1976, Hospital Engineering 30:20:19–20.

53 Joffe Stephen N, Thomson William O, Mc Gavigan James and Trexler P C: A Closed System Surgical Isolator for Major Elective Abdominal Operations. 1978, World Journal of Surgery 2:123–127.

the floor, and clear plastic forms the roof. No structural alterations are required of the operation room.

The time required to prepare the surgical isolator for use is approximately 10 minutes. This is carried out during the induction of anaesthesia.

The anaesthetized patient is prepared and placed on the operation table in the usual way. A conventional skin preparation is carried out.

The skin is dried, the surgical isolator inflated, and the skin of the operation site sprayed with a sterile aerosol adhesive. The surgical drape on the floor of the isolator is uncovered and stuck to the operation site.

The envelope is inflated with sterile filtered air, which escapes through a flutter valve in the roof of the isolator to maintain a continuous circulation of air.

The members of the surgical team operate on the patient outside the surgical isolator through a series of sterile surgical sleeves and gloves. The sleeves along each side of the isolator end blindly at the cuff. Gloves of the appropriate size for each surgeon are passed into the isolator and fitted to the sleeves. Metal rings, 10 cm in diameter, are slipped into the cuffs of the gloves which are then placed against the blind end of the invaginated sleeves. The sleeve is invaginated carrying the glove and ring with it. The two are held together and sealed by elastic band applied from the outside. When the surgeon is ready to begin the operation, the end of the sleeve, which forms the diaphragm across the cuff of the glove, is torn away and the surgeon puts his hands into the gloves. If a glove is punctured during operation, a second glove could be simply placed over the first, which is removed by cutting it off.

A special table for instruments is placed at the foot of the operation table on which the supply end of the isolator is mounted, and beneath this table are housed the pump and filter. The air is filtered by using an ultra-high efficiency type filter, 30 by 30 by 15 cm. The air in the isolator is changed about 60 times per hour. Drying of the wound is not a problem.

By opening or closing the exit valve, the amount of distension of the plastic envelope could be controlled.

The air filter would be sterilized twice a year.

Air sampling at the exit valve of the surgical isolator reveals that the air which has circulated through the isolator is sterile.

At the supply end of the isolator is an air-supported entry port for the introduction of sterile instruments and supplies. The flutter valve and air-supported entry port are opened and the nurse receives the instruments and other supplies. The outer wraps of the sterile instrument packs are removed by an assistant in the stream of air issuing from the entry port, and the packs are taken by the operation room nurse into the isolator.

Electrical leads for diathermy and suction hoses are introduced as sterile supplies. The end of the leader hose is then pushed into one of the small cones fitted to the surgical isolator, the tip of the cone is cut, and the leader hose fed through. The hose is taped to the cone and, since air flows outwards, sterility is maintained.

Swabs and packs could either be removed through the entry port or placed into the swab sump. These could be removed at any time during the operation for counting and weighing without danger of contaminating the isolator.

The surgical isolator is easy to dispose of by incineration.

Some limitations may be imposed. The surgeon cannot change his position around the table without changing gloves. For anastomosis of small vessels it may be necessary to insert a rigid support

EXIT VALVE

AIR SUPPORTED
ENTRY PORT

FILTER BLOWER

ACCESS SLEEVES

Diagram of a closed system plastic isolator (Stephen N Joffe, Willam O Thomson, James McGavigan, P C Trexler: A Closed System Surgical Isolator for Major Elective Abdominal Operations. 1978, World Journal of Surgery 2:123–130).

ring in the wall to provide a flat field of view. Occasionally light is reflected from the surface of the plastic. This requires a slight shift of either the plastic or the light source. Spurts of blood must be wiped off.

Surgical isolators are considered to be ideal for use when operations have to be performed in makeshift or unhygienic surroundings[54]. Their future value may be in high-risk groups of patients[55]. Others believe that they will prove to be of benefit to much larger groups of patients[56].

Extensive clinical trials will be required to evaluate the effectiveness of the isolators in hospitals as a means of reducing post operative infection.

Charnley enclosure

The Charnley enclosure, more precisely called the Charnley-Howorth Sterile Operation Unit, which was developed at the Wrightington Hospital, in Lancashire, England, is an armour plate glass box with an area of 2.1 by 2.1 m[57]. The armour plate glass sides of the enclosure are relatively inflexible[58]. The bottom edges of the enclosure rest on metal feet.

54 Preventing infection at the operation site. 1976, British Medical Journal 2:773–774.

55 Joffe Stephen N, Thomson William O, McGavigan James, and Trexler P C: A Closed System Surgical Isolator for Major Elective Abdominal Operations. 1978, World Journal of Surgery 2:123–127.

56 Levenson Stanley N: Invited Commentary. 1978, World Journal of Surgery 2:127–130.

57 Charnley John: A Clean-air operating enclosure. 1964, The British Journal of Surgery 51:202–205.

58 Cowan D: The design and development of clean operating enclosures. CSIR Special Report BOU 28. Pretoria 1971, p 7.

The present system* has a floor area of approximately 2.4 by 2.4 m, which allows room for the surgeon, two assistants, and a scrub nurse.

The air is supplied in the enclosure through three filter bags in the ceiling opening and escapes to the surrounding room either through a space which is left above floor level or through the 3 mm vertical gap which is between the edges of the glass plates forming the enclosure. Up to 400 air changes per hour are provided.

Within the enclosure special gowns and hoods are worn. The body-exhaust system makes refrigeration of the surgical enclosure unnecessary[59]. The surgeon is spared fatigue and his sweating is reduced[60].

The patient's body exhaust is to prevent self infection which might be caused by body vapour emissions.

The provision of monitoring systems for early warning of clean air installation failure and methods of quickly and cheaply changing the filtration elements has been emphasized[61].

When the enclosure had been used for about five years, *John Charnley* stated: I certainly have to agree that sterile air is not the sole answer to the problem of postoperative wound infection, though I believe it has played a very important part in reducing our infection rate from the 3 to 5 per cent level to its present 1 per cent[62].

When summarizing his ten year experience with the enclosure he repeated, that air cleanliness in the operation room is important, but not the only factor[63]. He concluded that the dosage of organisms to produce infection must be less than previously imagined and maintained that air cleanliness cannot reduce wound infection below a level of 1 per cent**.

* Allen Paul, Reynolds D A: Clean air operating environments. 1978, British Journal of Hospital Medicine 20:591–598.

59 Charnley John: Operating-theatre ventilation. 1970, The Lancet 1:1054.

60 Charnley John: Experiences with germ-free environments in surgery in relation to design. in Aerobiology. ed by I H Silver. Academic Press. London, New York 1970, p 191.

61 Charnley John: Sterile Air in Operating Rooms. in British Health Care and Technology. British Operating Theatres. London 1972, p 17.

62 Charnley John: Experiences with germ-free environments in surgery in relation to design. in Aerobiology. ed by I H Silver. Academic Press. London, New York 1970, p 195.

63 Charnley John: Postoperative infection after total hip replacement with special reference to air contamination in the operating room. 1972, Clinical Orthopaedy 87:167.

** Harold Laufman has surveyed five orthopaedic surgeons in the US who performed 3,622 hip replacements in operation rooms not equipped with laminar flow systems. The infection rate was 0.45 per cent in patients followed 9 to 42 months (1973, Modern Hospitals 120:4:92).

Robert H Fitzgerald Jr, Declan R Nolan, Duane M Ilstrup, Robert E van Scoy, John A Washington II and Mark B Coventry have reported (Deep Wound Sepsis following Total Hip Arthroplasty. 1977, The Journal of Bone and Joint Surgery 59 A:847–855) an 0.8 per cent incidence of deep sepsis in hips operated with 28 to 32 room-air exchanges per hour.

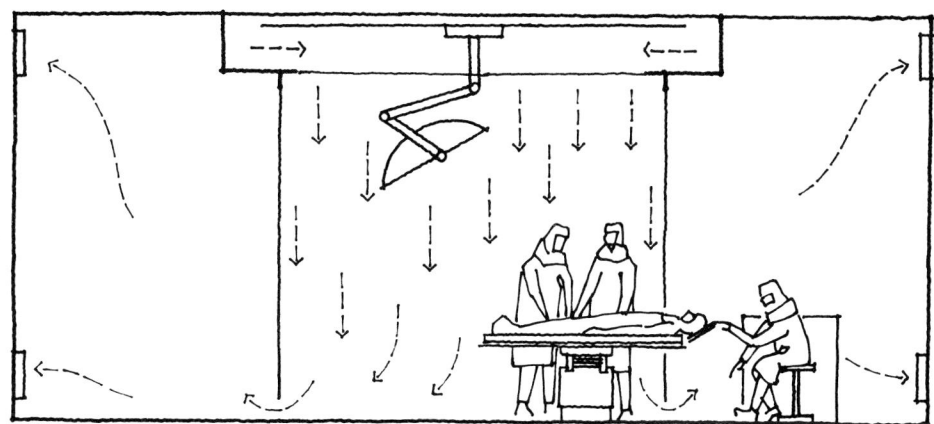

When the Charnley enclosure is used only the operating team — up to four persons — is in the enclosure. The patient is positioned within the enclosure, but the anaesthesiologist, anaesthetic equipment, drips and monitoring equipment remain outside the enclosure.

An American study group concluded of their material that in Charnley enclosures early acute post-operative infections can be prevented; but it is highly unlikely that these environments have any effect on late deep wound infections[64].

The study did not answer the question: Is the environment of the Charnley enclosure the primary reason for the low infection rate or is it the discipline required by the environment?

Later it has been stated that perhaps the greatest contribution of the Charnley school has been its insistence on meticulous asepsis at the time of operation[65].

Unidirectional air flow systems of the type pioneered by Charnley afford less absolute protection than surgical isolators[66]. As Charnley enclosure was designed for arthroplasty in hip operations, it has limited application, although the idea has been elaborated for an ophthalmologic service in France[67].

64 Brady Louis P, Enneking William F and Franco Jorge A: The Effect of Operating-Room Environment on the Infection Rate after Charnley Low-Friction Total Hip Replacement. 1975, The Journal of Bone and Joint Surgery 57-A: 80–83.

65 Moore B: Antibiotics in cement. 1977, The Journal of Bone and Joint Surgery 59-B: 139–142.

66 Preventing infection at the operation site. 1976, British Medical Journal 2:773–774.

67 Hervonet F: Un bloc operatoire sterile. 1977, Annales d'Oculistique 210:549–551.

An industrial clean enclosure incorporating the down flow unidirectional air principle was modified and adapted for various types of surgery in Pretoria[69].

The recommended size of this enclosure is 3.0 by 3.0 m, the clear height 2.44 m. A system of electrically operated vertical sliding PVC sides is used. The use of transparent PVC sides excludes the use of flammable anaesthetics. The instruments are passed during the operation to the enclosure through a permanent aperture measuring 0.61 by 0.45 m in the curtain at the patient's foot end. Any one of the other three curtains can be lifted during the operation to a height of about 1.4 m to allow large equipment to be passed through without affecting the airflow pattern and the pressurization.

After changing to basic operation outfit in the staff changing room, the team puts on the suction apparatus and the mask and proceeds to scrub up. Thereafter they enter the enclosure and help each other to gown up.

Inside the enclosure the staff wear moulded fibreglass headpieces that completely envelop the head and are integrated with a special one-piece gown.

The anaesthetized patient is positioned within the enclosure, but anaesthetic equipment, drips and monitoring equipment remain outside the enclosure. The anaesthesiologist has easy access to the patient's head and arm and can control the movements of the operation table. A loosely fit cloth closure around patient an operation table allows at the anaesthesiologist's end of the enclosure to project the patient's head outside the enclosure while operation on the torso and limbs is carried out. To provide the anaesthesiologist with a view of the operation clear PVC is fitted to the cloth closure.

The packs with sterilized items are opened within the enclosure after all sides are closed. When additional instruments are delivered, the circulating nurse retains the protective wrapping of the set and the nurse in the enclosure receives through the already described opening the required instruments sterile.

After the completed operation the curtains are opened and the patient taken to the plaster room or to the post-anaesthetic area. The removed head dresses and gowns of the staff are taken to the disposal room.

General illumination — 4630 lux — at the table level is provided by twelve fluorescent lamps. Four additional satellite lamps have proved to be adequate for most surgical procedures. For operating in body cavities a fibre optic light is added.

---

69 Cowan D: The design and development of clean operating enclosures. CSIR Special Report BOU 28. Pretoria 1971.

Beck William C: South Africa's new clean operating enclosures. 1971, The Guthrie Clinic Bulletin 40:207-212.

Cowan David: The clean operating enclosure — its effect on the incidence of wound infection and its influence on the design of the operating department of a hospital. Stencil. Pretoria. January 1976, p 22-41.

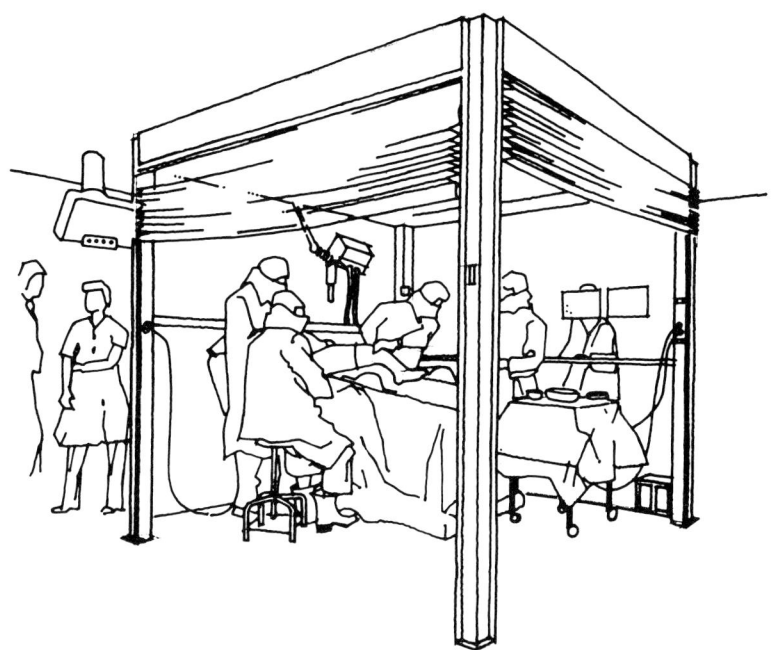

Pretoria enclosure with two curtains in the up position.

Air is delivered at a speed of 0.45 m/sec uniformly over the entire area of the enclosure. Because of the motors and fans, the generated noise is about 51 dB. This noise level could be reduced.

While it may be argued that filtering down to 0.3 microns is not required for the purpose of air cleanliness, in the Pretoria enclosure, HEPA filters are used which produce a unidirectional air flow pattern and filter air down to 0.3 microns at 99.97 per cent efficiency. Many HEPA filters have been found to leak after installation, therefore continuous tests are absolutely vital[70].

The operative staff has found that air movement speed, the temperature of 18°C, and relative humidity of 50 per cent are comfortable.

Generally, great reliance is placed on the enclosure. Persons wearing street clothes have been allowed to the area surrounding the enclosure.

70 personal communication 1975: David Cowan, Pretoria.

Allo pro enclosure

Also the Allo pro[71] enclosure in Switzerland was developed after the initial work of Charnley as an installable and adjustable unit for orthopaedic implantation surgery.

Protective clothing with ventilated helmets for the operating team is used.

The air is delivered in a down flow stream to be evacuated for refiltering and recirculation through low level slits and double glazed windows past the floodlights. 240 air changes per hour are provided[72].

The enclosure lighting is provided by 22 spotlights and a fibre-optic light unit.

At the Insel Hospital, Berne, the enclosure is 2.6 m wide and 5.2 m long with two operation tables in the enclosure[73].

The reason for making the enclosure to accommodate two tables was the chief surgeon's way to operate. While the assistants are finalizing the first patient, he would commence surgery on the second patient. Both patients are anaesthetized outside the enclosure. The users feel strongly that there is no possibility of airborne crossflow between the two operation tables within the enclosure.

The external access along three sides is approximately 1.2 m and on the anaesthesiologist's side approximately 2.5 m wide.

On the head side the glass panel reaches up to a height of 1.6 m above the floor. The anaesthesiologist and the heads of the patients are outside the enclosure.

The side partitions are fixed to the ceiling. The glass panels go down from the ceiling to 1.2 m above the floor. A good view for students and visitors is provided.

A LUWA clean room ceiling system is used, with the air-conditioning plant in an adjacent room. For sound attenuation neoprene fibre-glass is adapted in some of the ducts.

Fluorescent tubes provide the basic lighting. These lamps with a total capacity of 1,300 W are cooled by means of exhaust air extracted from the room. As operation lamps serve Chromophane Hanover lamps.

71 Die ultrasterile Operationsboxe der Orthopädischen Klinik des Kantonspitals St. Gallen. 1971, Veska 35:138–141.

72 Scheibe O: Laminarflow, nur in Grosskliniken? 1977, Der Chirurg 48:745–746.

73 personal communication 1975: David Cowan, Pretoria.

Lund enclosure

Also the Lund enclosure in Sweden has been inspired by the *Charnley* enclosure[74]. The enclosure can be erected in existing operation rooms.

Operation room air without any special cooling or heating is recirculated in the enclosure by two fans. Between 300 and 700 air changes per hour are provided in unidirectional down-flow. HEPA filters are used. The air escapes the enclosure through a space between the enclosure walls and the floor. Attention has been paid to level down the fan noise.

The operation lighting is placed outside the enclosure.

Some developments in the US

In the United States, considerable research work and practical experimentation to achieve contamination free environments according to room in room principle has been carried out at the Lovelace Clinic for Medical Education and Research in Albuquerque, New Mexico; the National Institute of Health, Cancer Research Division at Bethesda, Maryland; the Graduate Hospital in Philadelphia, Pennsylvania and at several other places.

In the early '70s unidirectional flow operation rooms were installed at the rate of 20 per month, mainly due to advanced salemanship from the manufacturers of unidirectional flow devices. New outlets for unidirectional flow devices after the contraction of their NASA space programme, NASA having been one of the main consumers of laminar flow systems, were sought, rather prematurely.

In the following years the high installation rates decreased.

Allander air curtain

The *Allander* air curtain unit is a ceiling mounted double air curtain down to the floor level to delineate an operation zone within the operation room[75]. The main distribution of air flow in the operation zone is through a perforated ceiling. The air flow to the curtains is about 15 per cent of the total air flow to the whole operation unit. Quantities of air are in the vicinity of 0.3 m^3/s. The air curtain has been capable of reducing the particle-sensitive area to one quarter as compared to a conventional ventilation system having the same capacity[76].

One difficulty experienced, particularly for the larger orthopaedic operations, is that the volume described by the air curtain is too small.

---

74 Strindehag Ove: Operationsbox för förbättrad operationsrumsstandard. 1975, Läkartidningen 72:4035-4036.

75 Allander Claës: Ventilation i rum med extrema renhetskrav. 1965, VVS: 183-193.

    Abel Enno och Allander Claës: Undersökning av nytt inblåsningssystem för rena rum. 1966, VVS:413-424.

76 Allander Claës and Abel Enno: Investigation of a New Ventilating System for Clean Rooms. 1968, Medical Research Engineering, 3rd quarter: 28-39.

Post-anaesthetic recovery area

The main objective of the post-anaesthetic recovery area is to ensure the safe recovery of all operated patients. The tendency to use the recovery area as an Intensive Care and Treatment Unit in those hospitals not adequately equipped for intensive care patients is unfortunate[1].

Philosophically and practically the post-anaesthetic recovery area could be considered as an extension of the operation room. Although the surgical procedure has been terminated, the awakening patient may be far from being stabilized. E g there may be concern with hypothermia, when the thermostatic regulating reflexes return and the patient experiences shivering. In some cases of intensive shivering, oxygen consumption might rise to 500 per cent of the normal level. It also contributes to an increased workload on the cardiovascular and respiratory systems[2].

Subtile, but important physiologic changes during that period can easily go unnoticed during the transition, and may present later as serious, even life threatening problems[3]. Therefore the post-operative patients have to be observed closely and treated until they are reasonably safe from untoward events. A patient should not leave the recovery area until his natural reflexes have returned, his blood pressure and respiration are stable, and he is out of danger for asphyxia, vomiting, schock, and complications which require circulatory or ventilatory resuscitation.

The routine nursing care in the recovery area includes washing of patients, treatment of pressure areas, and oral toilet.

Usually, the recovery room is a half-way house where the patient regains consciousness and reflexes. In his ward room he sleeps off the effects of depressant medication overnight or for days later[4].

The half-conscious patient is still under a physiologic stress in the recovery room. In addition to the derangement of physiological function imposed by general anaesthesia and surgery, there may be a profound disruption of mental functioning which can divulge a variety of memories associated with emotional states and perceptions which can resemble hallucinations, delusions, and other forms of irrational mental activity[5].

1   Kornfeld Donald S: Psychiatric aspects of patient care in the operating suite and special areas. in Modern Perspectives in the Psychiatric Aspects of Surgery. ed by John G Howells. Brunner/Mazel, Publishers. New York 1976, p 610.

2   Wanna Hanna T: Temperature Changes During Anesthesia and Surgery. 1978, Journal of the Iowa Medical Society 68:197–200.

3   Schowengerdt Carl G: The Recovery Room. in Monitoring in Anaesthesia. ed by William H L Dornette. F A Davis Company. Philadelphia 1973, p 364.

4   see also Epstein Burton S: Recovery from Anaesthesia. 1975, The Journal of Anesthesiology 43:285-287.

5   Gladstone Richard: Psychiatric aspects of general anesthesia. in Modern Perspectives in the Psychiatric Aspects of Surgery. ed by John G Howells. Brunner/Mazel, Publishers. New York 1976, p 573.

The types of anaesthetic agents and the particular practices of the anaesthesiologists influence greatly the duration of the patient's stay in the recovery area. In most cases the length of stay is less than two hours, the average length of stay being around one hour[6], but some patients, especially when major abdominal surgery is involved, have to be kept over night in the recovery room. 18 to 24 hours are regarded as a maximum length of stay[7].

The patient is returned to the regular ward first after the surgeon or the anaesthesiologist has given his permission. This should occur as soon as possible. A delayed departure for some administrative reason can be interpreted by the patient as a sign that something is surgically wrong[8].

Patients would request — when they can — return to rooms and areas which they pre-operatively identified as their territory. On return to their rooms, patients generally show a release of tension*.

U Hedstrand and *M H Holmdahl*[9] have calculated that 20 per cent of the post-operative patients are usually fit to return to their wards immediately. Of the remainder, 80 per cent can return after some time in the recovery room while 20 per cent need to go to the ICTU. There are exceptions from these estimates: the highly specialized units dealing with cardiac or neurological surgery. Their routine post-operative care and monitoring required is so demanding that patients have to be transferred immediately from operation room to an ICTU.

Before the patient leaves the recovery unit, his communication sheet is completed and conveys details of the operation, sutures, drains, treatment and drugs given in the recovery room, intravenous fluids, and any special instructions.

To reduce the time of transition, the post-anaesthetic recovery unit must be placed within the surgical department and on the same level as the operation unit. It is essential that an intensive care and therapy unit is not far from the recovery area.

6   Farman John V: The work of the recovery room. 1978, British Journal of Hospital Medicine 19:606-616.

7   see also Molnár István: Postoperative avdelinger. 1977, Tidsskrift for Den norske Laegeforening 97:730-732.

8   Kornfeld Donald S: Psychiatric aspects of patient care in the operating suite and special areas. in Modern Perspectives in the Psychiatric Aspects of Surgery. ed by John G Howells. Brunner/Mazel, Publishers. New York 1976, p 610.

*   Minckley Barbara: Space and place in patient care. 1968, American Journal of Nursing 68:510–516.

9   cited by Farman John V: The work of the recovery room. 1978, British Journal of Hospital Medicine 19:606-616.

The number of beds in the recovery unit depends on the turnover and organization of the surgical department. 1.5[10] to 3 beds[11] per operation room should be allowed for post-anaesthetic recovery.

To facilitate general supervision, the beds or bed-trolleys have usually been placed in one large room as sex differentation from the medical point is unnecessary. Therefore a post-anaesthetic recovery unit usually contains

> a multi-bed recovery room
> a multi-bed recovery room for children*
> (glassed-in) isolation rooms or a special recovery area
> a nurses' station
> a utility room
> stores for medicine, infusion fluids, instruments, catheters, apparatus, oxygen
>   tents, linen, etc
> staff changing rooms, lounge, toilets
> a family waiting room, toilet

In the multi-bed recovery area a distance of about 1.5 m between beds is required. The floor area per bed is estimated at 12 to 15 m². Washbasins should be provided.

The rather quick turnover of patients in a post-anaesthetic unit requires provision for ample circulation areas within the unit.

The patients should not be unnecessarily allowed to observe the terrific turmoil of recurring emergency activities[12], which may be for them frightening. Screens should be used.

Bed-head units have come to use. One design[13] consists of shelves at two levels: the upper at eye level to take monitoring equipment and the lower at waist height for the patient's notes, swabs, syringes and needles, mouth gags. The lower shelf is to carry oxygen outlets, suction bottles and suction catheter holders, sphygmomanometers, electric sockets, alarm calls, and data transmission sockets.

---

10 see also Farman John V: The work of the recovery room. 1978, British Journal of Hospital Medicine 19:606-616.

11 Atkinson R S and Rushman G B: A synopsis of anaesthesia. 8th revised edition. John Wright & Sons Ltd. Bristol 1977, p 915.

* A mother who wants to be with her child as the child wakes from an anaesthetic is expressing one of the most basic instinctive urges which humanity knows. Therefore proper arrangements for the parent participation have to be made (see also Young Children in Hospital. 1973, The Medical Journal of Australia 2:249).

The special paediatric recovery room should provide a group of nurses specially trained to deal with the specific problems of children, both psychological and physiological. These nurses develop an expertise in dealing with children which can be remarkably effective (Kornfeld Donald S: Psychiatric aspects of patient care in the operating suite and special areas. in Modern Perspectives in the Psychiatric Aspects of Surgery. ed by John G Howells. Brunner/Mazel, Publishers. New York 1976, p 609).

12 see also Badger Theodore L: The Physician — Patient in the Recovery and Intensive Care Units. 1974, Archives of Surgery 109:359-360.

13 Farman John V: The work of the recovery room. 1978, British Journal of Hospital Medicine 19:606-616.

Receiving bins for rubbish are to be placed in the recesses below the panels. Beneath the lower shelf open-fronted lockers are used to store intravenous solutions and drip sets. The disadvantage of the wall rail which requires every item of equipment to have a special bracket is avoided.

X rays are taken in the recovery room with a portable machine. These are usually either chest pictures for diagnostic purposes or displacement shots to record the position of radioactive implants.

Blood and other samples may be taken and sent to the clinical laboratories to control fluid, electrolyte, and acid-base disturbances.

Recovering patients may be monitored for ECG, respiration, blood pressure, blood gases, pulse-rate, and temperature. The multichannel monitor should be equipped with automatic run-off for abnormal ECG changes. The observation post is at the nurses' station.

Studies from a cardiac postoperative recovery unit indicate that patients admitted to the computerized cardiac postoperative recovery unit spend shorter periods in each phase of postoperative care than do patients admitted to the noncomputerized unit[14].

To warm the postoperative hypothermic patients heat lamps are frequently used, but they do not warm the patients any more rapidly than the blankets and they cannot be used on all patients[15]. Heat lamps make the usually crowded patient care environment even more crowded. It would seem that the use of cotton blankets should be preferred, at least for warming mildly hypothermic patients.

Individual cubicles for patients have been recommended to reduce the anxiety-provoking aspect of the recovery area[16]. As post-anaesthetic patients have an increased susceptibility to respiratory infection, separated glassed-in cubicles would cut down the potential of cross infection for all cases[17]. Individual cubicles may also obviate general contamination of the recovery area which has been shown to be effected by the volatile agents exhaled by recovering patients, unless it is relied upon intravenous anaesthesia agents[18]. About 16 m² should be allowed for an isolation room, each one equipped with a washbasin.

14 Tolbert Samuel H and Pertuz Alvaro E: Study shows how computerization affects nursing activities in ICU. 1977, Hospitals 51:17:79-82, 84.

15 Kucha Deloros H, Nichols Glennadee A, Christ Nancy M, Bynum Jessie W: The Warming of Postoperative Patients. 1974, Military Medicine 140:388−390.

16 Kornfeld Donald S: Psychiatric aspects of patient care in the operating suite and special areas. in Modern Perspectives in the Psychiatric Aspect of Surgery. ed by John G Howells. Brunner/Mazel, Publishers. New York 1976, p 608.

17 Laufman Harold: Surgical Hazard Control. 1973, Archives of Surgery 107:552-559.

18 Pollution in the Operating Theatre. 1973, The New Zealand Medical Journal 78:456.

For supervision of post-anaesthetic beds a *nurses' station* rather than a separate room has been preferred. It must be connected to the hospital intercom system. The connections with the head nurse of the operation department and the anaesthesia office are most important. A large post-anaesthetic unit might require several nurses' stations.

Some *storage* space should be provided close to the nurses' station. A room of about 5 m² is needed for pharmaceuticals, and another of about 12 m² for respiratories and other equipment, such as resuscitation boxes.

A blood refrigerator accessible from both within and outside the unit is needed[19].

A *utility room* contains trapped slop-sinks together with arrangements for the decontamination of bedpans or a destroyer for disposable bed-pans and urine bottles, a washbasin and an incinerator. In this room an allowance of about 10 m² floor

The changing rooms and toilets for staff should be sized for the ideal staff ratio: each patient should have a personal nurse, although this ratio is seldom achieved.

The recovery area staff shall have access to a tea or coffee lounge.

Ultraclean post-operative suite

For some transplantation patients an ultraclean postoperative isolation suite comprising bedrooms and bathrooms, and a facility for nursing and medical staff to scrub and change attire before entering the patient's room with a filtered positive pressure ventilation system has been suggested.

The importance of psychological elements in patient care in isolation cannot be overemphasized. The restricted environment, the constant attention, the knowledge of the dangers connected with transplantation surgery and fears for the future, all this puts an enormous stress on the morale of the patient. Support and encouragement from his medical advisers and a change of scene whenever possible go some way to lessen this burden[20].

19 Farman John V: The work of the recovery room. 1978, British Journal of Hospital Medicine 19:606-616.

20 see also MacArthur A M: Lung Transplantation. in Recent Advances in Surgery. Number Eight. ed by Selwyn Taylor. Churchill-Livingstone. Edinburgh and London 1973, p 126.

Radiology

Radiology for the operation department purposes comprises the pre-operative X ray examination, diagnostic radiology during operations and taking post-operative X-ray photos.

Operation room work which requires X ray staff is usually the responsibility of the hospital radiology department. It has been pointed out that the quality of surgical radiology is lagging behind in technical progress[1]. An X ray procedure performed in the same institution but in different locations — in the X ray department respective intraoperatively — often gives very different results.

When access to X ray is limited only to a few operation rooms the work in the operation department must be well organized. An operation list must clearly indicate which of the operations will require X ray examination.

X ray equipment comprises mobile X ray, tubes in the ceiling, possibly with a common control panel and transformer, X ray tubes in mobile frames with a common transformer for several tubes, and X ray apparatus including tube and transformer on wheels.

The operational performances of mobile (portable) X ray machines 220 to maximum 300 ma are considered to be limited and not optimal for the task at hand. If X ray tubes in the ceiling are not used, and only X ray apparatus on wheels is available, storage space for the X ray apparatus must be made available.

A considerable demand for X ray work in the operation room justifies the use of X ray tubes in the ceiling in preference to mobile apparatus.

One double-focus high-output 1,000 ma, three phase X ray generator can serve two adjacent operation rooms. A control console, requiring a space about 130 by 90 by 105 cm, can be located between them. Ceiling-suspended tubes should be installed so that the radiological procedures and the operation room illumination are not interfered. The ceiling must tolerate a weight of 400 kg.

Operation tables should have X ray cassette holders which eliminate the need for the staff to remain at the table during exposures.

If an operation room is used for orthopaedic surgery exclusively, an additional X-ray on a mobile cart or a second ceiling-suspended tube crane for the lateral tube is needed.

The control apparatus should, to protect the operation room staff, be placed in a separate control room or in the anaesthetic room.

---

1   see also Berci George and Steckel Richard: Modern Radiology in the Operating Room. 1973, Archives of Surgery 107:557-586.

As a trained radiographer is not always available in the operation room, it has proved of particular advantage to automate the setting on the control desk. The standardized exposure data can be selected via a relevant pushbutton.

In case the staff administering anaesthesia must remain at the operation table during exposure, the protection must be adequate. Lead-rubber aprons with an equivalence of 0.25 mm Pb are not very comfortable to wear, but they have been regarded as the most effective[2].

In an operation room there should be two TV monitors for displaying the fluoroscopic image — one for the surgeon, the second for the assistants — either fixed to the wall or suspended from the ceiling on movable fittings.

Operation rooms are usually equipped with one or two X ray film viewing screens or boxes. Bacteriological surveys have shown that a high degree of contamination occurs around the shelf where notes and patient's X ray films are laid out[3].

Currently in the surgical department a well ventilated processor room of about 8 to 10 m^2 size e g for a 90-second X ray film processor and storage space for cassettes and chemicals is needed.

If there is an X ray film transport system between the operation suite and the X ray department, TV monitors in the operation room display radiographs and their enlarged detail sections.

Laboratory services

Larger surgical departments must have access to clinical laboratory services on a 24 hour basis.

The services include

a *biochemistry* laboratory for maintaining a continuous check on procedures involved; acid-base determinations, metabolic balance and electrolyte values

a *histo-pathological* laboratory for quick diagnoses, including a space for frozen sections; initial preparation of surgical pathological material; two microscopes, a refrigerator, a washbasin, an island table, a stainless bench and cupboards. The frozen section room is equipped with two cryostats.

a laboratory for the preparation of *radioactive isotopes* to be administered in operation rooms, and for the preparation of measuring apparatus for operation room use, and for the measurement of sample tissues and fluids obtained in the operation room.

Each of these laboratories requires a floor area of about 15 m^2.

2   see also Mohr H: The design of X-ray equipment for use in operating rooms. 1973, Medical and Biological Engineering 11:396-402.

3   Helliwell P: Anaesthetic Rooms. in Operating Theatre and Ancillary Rooms. ed by T Cecil Gray and John Nunn. John Sherrat and Son. Altrincham 1964, p 75.

There have been objections against using subsidiary diagnostic laboratories instead of the main laboratories. A pneumatic tube connection between the laboratories and the surgical department has been recommended.

Concerning the frozen-section laboratory function, it has been pointed out[4] that an excellent colour audiovideo system is a good deal less expensive than building, equipping and maintaining that laboratory in or next to the surgical unit.

A *bacteriological* and general cleanliness study of every area of the surgical department should be a regularly scheduled part of the procedures.

4   Laufman Harold: Surgical Hazard Control. 1973, Archives of Surgery 107:552-559.

Facilities for sterilization, decontamination, maintenance, storage, disposal

The preparation of surgical department supplies which at the moment of their use have to have been sterilized, proceeds both in the sterile service area of the surgical unit and in the hospital's central supply department.

Operation room instruments and some anaesthetic equipment are preferably maintained and sterilized in the instrument service of the surgical department and not in the CSSD[1].

The central sterile supply department usually is remote from the surgical suite and requires some form of automatic delivery system. The most elaborate tote systems have not overcome loss or damage to expensive and delicate instruments, maldistribution of instruments, errors in makeup of surgical instrument trays, pilferage, and delays in obtaining emergency instruments. Often installed under the guise of economy, remote instrument processing has proved extremely costly in practice, necessitating the purchase of several times the number of surgical instruments ordinarily required in addition to the great installation cost of the tote system and additional area[2].

Although the amount of presterilized and disposable equipment has increased, there is a considerable residue of non-disposable items that require sterilization. Materials such as non-disposable syringes, tubes and rubber goods, are cleaned and sterilized in the central supply department of the hospital. This applies even to the items of stainless steel and plastics.

Alternatively, a special area within the sterile service of the surgical department is provided for these procedures.

Linen sets for the surgical department are sterilized in the central supply department or in the (central)laundry.

Sterile service area of the surgical unit

This service is responsible for cleaning, wrapping, sterilization, and storage of surgical instruments, single or in sets. Frequently eye surgery and microsurgery instruments are segregated.

Sterilized items delivered from the pharmacy and laundry are stored within the instrument service area.

---

1   see also Kure Ragna: Sterilsentraler. 1977, Tidsskrift for Den norske Laegeforening 97:722-723.

2   see also Laufman Harold: The control of operating room infection: discipline, defense mechanisms, drugs, design, and devices. 1978, Bulletin of the New York Academy of Medicine 54:472–483.

As soon as the operation list for a day is completed, a copy is delivered to the instrument service, where instruments are packed in sets or on trolley tops.

Instrument sets are marked with the patient's name, the type of operation, operation number and the operation room number. To the sets attached autoclave-proof listing tags facilitate the later instrument checking and re-checking.

The sterilized sets are stored in the designated operation room stores according to the operation schedule.

The instrument service must be prepared to deliver immediately additional instruments during an operation or sets for emergencies.

The used instrument are to be fetched by the instrument service either after the finished single operation or after the whole operation session. Prior cleaning, they would be stored in the area for non-sterile materials.

Cleaning efficiency varies with the kind of the instrument. Instruments with serrated surfaces, joints, or hinges are particularly difficult to clean. Polypropylene instruments are cleaned more easily than stainless-steel ones[3].

It may be that the overall instrument standard would be improved more by replacing substandard instruments than by installing a new and expensive washing machine[4].

Instruments for microsurgery are most easily damaged at the cleaning time. They should never be picked up by the fistful, all together, never clattered into a metal bowl, and never junked into a sink together with other, heavier instruments. Micro-instruments should be cleaned in their rack by immersion in hemolytic enzyme detergent and by subsequent rinsing in water[5].

It has been suggested that in order to protect the instrument service staff, used instruments, after immediate post-operative counting, should be decontaminated within the confines of the operation room. This should preferably be done in a washer-sterilizer or washer-deccntaminator. However, there has been no available evidence to the extent of that contamination risk[6].

The instrument service equipment may include

      a sink with drainer for used (and decontaminated) instruments
      a drainer with a fairly soft surface for washed instruments

3 Mostafa A B M G and Chackett K F: Cleaning of surgical instruments: a preliminary study. 1976, Medical & Biological Engineering 14:524-527.

4 ibid

5 Acland Robert D: Instrumentation for Microsurgery. 1977, The Orthopedic Clinics of North America 8:281-291.

6 Aseptic methods in the operating suite. 1968, The Lancet 1:763-768.

a washing machine and rinsing equipment for instruments
a work bench
a stacking rack
instrument inspection and wrapping benches, furnished with racks and drawers
a storage cupboard for wrapping materials
two automatic autoclaves, sized 41 by 60 cm* with a sterilization temperature variable between 134 and 143°C and with a prevacuum and postvacuum equivalent of 20 torr
storage cupboards for non-sterile instruments
a slop sink
intercom connections to all operation rooms
a gas sterilizer for some anaesthetic and similar equipment
wash basins.

Additionally, a system utilizing ultrasonic waves and chemical solutions to sterilize instruments and utensils may be found appropriate. The process operates at less than 80°C. Cleaning, sterilization, rinsing, drying and packaging is indicated to take about 30 minutes**.

Proper installation, inspection, and working precautions are necessary when dealing with ethylene oxide sterilizers. The sterilizers and aerators have to be placed in a separate room[7].

Maintenance of sterility of sterilized supplies depends on adequate wrapping of packs. Double wrapping prevents contamination during opening of packs. The packs must be protected against moisture[8].

Storage is frequently a neglected aspect in hospitals — uneconomic in space, labour and money terms[9].

Management and maintenance of anaesthetic equipment and other items

Basic hygienic management of anaesthesia machines will ensure safety from the standpoint of cross infection[10].

A wide variety of physical and chemical cleaning methods is available.

A frequently used method of cleaning is soaking manually in cold detergent and then cleaning under running water or in washing machines. Sometimes ultrasonic vibrators are used.

* If entire trolley tops for instruments, gloves etc are preferred, larger autoclaves are needed.

** Wave Energy Systems Inc. Newtown, Pa.

7 Runnells Glenn: Guidelines to assist hospitals in the use of ethylene oxyde. 1978, Hospitals 52:9:119-122.

8 see also Control of Hospital Infection. ed by E J L Lowbury, G A J Ayliffe, A M Geddes and J D Williams. Chapman and Hall. London 1975, p 145.

9 see also Allen S: Double Wrapping Necessary or Not? 1976, ASSA Journal 4:3:8-9.

10 du Moulin Gary C and Saubermann Albert J: The Anesthesia Machine and Circle System Are Not Likely to be Sources of Bacterial Contamination. 1977, The Journal of Anaesthesiology 47:353-358.

The circumstance that no generally accepted scheme exists for hygienic management of anaesthetic apparatus should be regarded as a commentary upon the difficulties involved.

The operation microscopes have been sterilized by gas* sterilizers. Damage to the waiting layer of the instrument and its optical system has been noticed[11]. To improve the sterilization procedure a 10-hour formaldehyde treatment in an airproof container has been introduced[12].

According to other experience ethylene oxide gas sterilization of the operation microscope is a feasible and desirable alternative to cumbersome draping techniques that have been employed[13].

A special hygienic management and maintenance room for anaesthesia equipment is often preferred to the services of the instrument unit.

This room could be used also to decontaminate operation table fittings. An anaesthesia equipment care centre[14] in a large operation unit may need an area of 35 to 40 m².

If *patient stretcher beds* are used in the surgical centre, a room of about 10 to 12 m² is needed for their decontamination and maintenance. It has been pointed out[15], that surgical infection has never been traced to a patient stretcher.

Repair and demonstration shop

The multiplicity and delicacy of modern equipment necessitates a quick repair service. A repair shop of 16 to 18 m² in area, with tool cupboards and work benches is required.

This room should be used also by visiting repair men and demonstrators of new apparatus.

---

* 85 per cent carbon dioxide and 15 per cent ethylene oxide.

11 Pia H W: Sterilization of the Operating Microscope. 1976, Acta Neurochirurgica 35:243-245.

12 ibid

13 Kurze Theodore, Apuzzo Michael L J, Weiss Martin H and Heiden James S: Experiences with sterilization of the operating microscope. 1977, Journal of Neurosurgery 47:861-863.

14 Ahnefeld F W, Kilian J, and Mehrkens H H: Das Anästhesie-geräte Pflegezentrum — Möglichkeiten zur methodischen Geräteaufbereitung in der Anästhesie und Intensivmedizin. 1977, Medizinal Markt — Acta Medicotechnica 25:388, 390-392.

15 Laufman Harold: The control of operating room infection: discipline, defense mechanisms, drugs, design, and devices. 1978, Bulletin of the New York Academy of Medicine 54:472-483.

The considerable lack of storage space in operation departments has often been pointed out, in spite of the fact that most of the supply requirements can be foreseen.

A storage for banked donor *blood* and *parenteral solutions* is required. A working space for crosstyping is needed.

Rotating cupboards and portable refrigerated carts for blood bottles maintaining a temperature of $4°C \pm 1°C$ are used. The loss of the opsonic activity in blood stored under standard banking conditions at $4°C$ has been pointed out[1].

Bank blood for transfusions is warmed to avoid lowering of body temperature, alterations in tissue perfusion, and untoward cardio-vascular effects.

As banked donor blood is expensive, can be wasted due to outdating, and is becoming a precious commodity due to increases in cardiac surgery, radical cancer surgery, and trauma, intraoperative respective preoperative autotransfusions — IAT resp PAT — may gain a wider adaption particularly in the surgery of the major blood vessels[2] and also become widely applied in general surgical procedures[3].

Recently hundreds of articles have appeared on many different aspects of autotransfusion. Almost all of these articles come to one conclusion: autotransfusion is both a life-saving and a blood-saving technique[4]. This would mean that the volume of blood stores might decrease.

On the other hand, autotransfusion requires extra effort by those involved in the care of the patient. Many are not willing to put forth this extra effort, thus limiting its application*.

Solutions for parenteral infusion are usually stored at room temperature in cupboards.

Supplies of sterile water for the operation room use, preferably in disposable plastic bottles, should be located adjacent to the store for blood. One and two litre bottles are used. Several bottles may be stored in a heated cupboard.

1   see also Alexander J Wesley: Emerging concepts in the control of surgical infection. 1974, Surgery 75:934-946.

2   Buth J, Rainesen J K and Darling R C: Autotransfusie, een oud concept opnieuv in de belangstelling. 1977, Nederlands Tijdschrift voor Geneeskunde 121:164-170.

3   Raines Jeff, Buth Jacob, Brewster David C and Darling R Clement: Intraoperative autotransfusion: equipment, protocols, and guidelines. 1976, The Journal of Trauma 16:616-621.

    McKenzie F N, Heimbecker R O, Wall W, Robert A, Black L and Barr R: Intraoperative autotransfusion in elective and emergency vascular surgery. 1978, Surgery 83:470-475.

4   Hauer Jerome M, Brawley Robert K: Introduction. 1978, Surgery 84:694.

*   Noon George P: Intraoperative autotransfusion. 1978, Surgery 84:719–721.

Medicine and *sera* should be stored in a separate room. Medicine cupboards or medicine carts in or near the operation rooms and anaesthetic rooms are required.

An *anaesthesiologists' storage* is required for apparatus and respirators, replacement materials, and infrequently used tubes of medical gas.

Large general hospitals should establish an *organ bank* for acquiring, preserving and dispensing transplantable tissues*. Organ banking would include preservation activities for blood, corneas, and kidneys. Because all severely burned patients require temporary coverage until autografting can be completed, a procedure and facility for obtaining and storing homograft or heterograft *skin* is necessary[5].

For *radium* and *other radioactive substances* a special room is needed.

The distribution of items from the central supply unit should be based on the storage cart system.

There should also be bulk stores evenly distributed within the operation department. Wire mesh shelves which cut down dust accumulation should be used, whenever possible.

General storage spaces are needed for surgical materials as well as for dressings and drapes, either factory manufactured and sterilized or processed in the hospital sterilization centre and for sterile linen produced in the hospital laundry or in an area laundry.

The basic Swedish operation textile package weighs about 6 kg and has following dimensions: length 52 to 55 cm, width 31 to 33 cm and height 16 to 18 cm[6].

Small disposable items — caps, masks, washcloths, wrappers, etc — are considered cost-effective. The use of large disposable items — gowns, sheets, drapes — is not considered economical. In the US their cost has exceeded the cost of using laundered goods by a ratio of ten to one[7]. More recent experience from the Federal Republic of Germany indicates that even the use of larger disposable drapes and sheets may be economical[8].

* Although the techniques of preserving each of these tissues share common foundation in biological principles, efforts for preservations are often inappropriately divided among several clinical services (Karow Armand M Jr: "Full service" organ banks. 1975, Southern Medical Journal 68:1324-1325).

5 Feller Irving and Crane Keith: Planning and Designing A Burn Care Facility. Institute for Burn Medicine. Ann Arbor, Michigan 1975, p 98.

6 Spri specifikation 46950. Stockholm 1.4.1975.

7 Badner Barry, Zelner Lawrence, Merchant Roland and Laufman Harold: Cost of linen versus disposable O.R. packs. 1973, Hospitals 47:23:76, 78, 80, 124.

8 see also Siefken Reinhold: Einweg-Operationswäsche, ein Beitrag zur Kostendämpfung? 1978, Krankenhaus-Umschau 47:684-686.

Working space for the preparation of special dressings should be provided in the operation department's dressings store.

Space is needed for storage carts carrying caps, gowns, masks, gloves, etc in the scrub-up room; for dressing trolleys in the anaesthetic room, and for sterile linen etc trolleys in the operation room store.

Storage space for splints etc is best located adjacent to the plaster room.

Storage space for apparatus and bulky equipment can be divided into units of about 9 m² each to serve about 4 operation rooms.

Operation room storage

Generally, storage should not be provided in the operation room. Only the requirements necessary for the actual operation should be there[9].

Limited storage space requiring more movement of operation room personnel between operations may influence the incidence of sepsis[10].

Carl Walter[11] has recommended open shelves in operation rooms with emphasis on frequent cleaning and rapid turnover of supplies. Swinging doors increase air currents. In sliding door tracks bacteria may be stored.

Pass-through cabinets that are stocked from outside have been found desirable, as they eliminate unwanted traffic through the operation room doors. Shelves on wheels or other supply distribution system elements can be used.

The pass-through cabinets could be replaced by a storage *room* of about 5 m² size adjacent to the operation room for the storage of sterilized instrument sets or trolley tops, emergency sets, syringes, operation linen and dressings in sets, surgical sutures, tissue adhesives, and also medicine and sterile water bottles.

In this room trolley-laying with sterile equipment could be carried out.

Storage space for clean beds

Emergency patients from the casualty department require clean beds or stretcher-beds after operation. A space of about 2.0 m² for each bed is needed. A stretcher-bed needs slightly less space.

9 see also 1977, Health and Social Service Journal 86:1473.

10 Fitzgerald Jr Robert H, Nolan Declan R, Ilstrup Duane M, van Scoy Robert E, Washington II John A and Coventry Mark B: Deep Wound Sepsis following Total Hip Arthroplasty. 1977, The Journal of Bone and Joint Surgery 59 A:847-855.

11 cited by Brand Lucy: A practical approach to infection surveillance in the intensive care unit. 1976, Heart and Lung 5:788-790.

Mortuary trolley parking

A space of about 4 m^2 is required for mortuary trolley parking.

Facilities for disposal, incineration

Disposal of used articles, empty containers and other rubbish, and possibly infected and fouled items, generates more of a problem than the supply of clean items[1].

Used instruments, linen, and materials can be removed from the operation room and conveyed to a collecting point in an appropriate container. Soiled linen should be checked for the loss of equipment, particularly instruments, to prevent cuts and other injuries to laundry workers.

Most used material from the operation room is not heavily contaminated[2].

When the operation table is stripped, linen should not touch the floor nor be tossed, thrown or shaken thus allowing micro-organisms to become airborne, but carried to the operation room disposal facility and there placed in a (disposable) bag.

Linen known to be contaminated with infectious microorganisms, should be handled with special care and clearly labelled. When carriers of hepatitis B antigen are operated, it is desirable for all linen, not only frankly bloodstained, to be destroyed[3].

Soiled linen and used operation room garments are collected in the operation room disposal room in disposable bags.

Waste products from the surgical department include body tissues, including amputations, soiled dressings, sponges, disposable needles and syringes, waste ampules, drapes, casts, disposable blood lancets, catheters, surgical gloves, underpads, pharmaceutical and solution bottles.

Also pathological preparations and excised tissues in closed containers may be temporarily stored in the disposal room.

The functions of the traditional central utility room ought to be divided between several rooms: an individual operation room disposal room, a central soiled linen room, and a central cleaners' or housekeepers' room.

A hand washing facility is a must in the disposal room.

---

1 see also Green John R B: Health service facilities planning and design. Part 1. School of Health Administration, University of New South Wales, Kensington, Australia. Stencil 1974, p 54.

2 Aseptic methods in the operating suite. 1968, The Lancet 1:834.

3 Waterson A P: Hepatitis B as a hazard in anaesthetic practice. 1976, British Journal of Anaesthesia 48:21-24.

Usually two disposal chutes with a diameter of 75 cm are provided — one for soiled linen and another for waste discharging. In hospitals with vacuum-driven disposal chutes the disposal rooms should be connected to the system. Experience from German Federal Republic indicates that while capital cost for vacuum-driven systems is high, the running cost is lower than with conventional collecting systems[4].

In case there is no central incineration installation, an *incineration room* in the operation department, where excised tissues and expendable materials may be disposed of, is strongly recommended.

The room — about 10 m^2 — should be provided with two incinerators, a bench, a sink, and a washbasin.

The capacity of incinerators is to be calculated in accordance with the requirements and work load of the particular surgical department.

4   Jaehn M: Müll- und Schmutzwäscheanlagen in Krankenhäusern. 1976, Das Krankenhaus 68:90-96.

DELIVERY (OBSTETRICS) DEPARTMENT

Currently the medicalization of childbirth is debated.

Within one paradigm, pregnancy and childbirth are regarded as states and processes akin to illness, relatively divorced from a social and psychological context. Consequently, it is seen as appropriate for the women to cede control over childbirth to medical experts, to adopt a relatively passive role of acquiescence in medical instructions, and to remain relatively ignorant of the basis of professional decisions. Childbearing is regarded as hazardous. Medical assistance and intervention are regarded uniformly necessary. The physical experiences of childbirth are perceived negatively and therefore to be alleviated, or removed from consciousness, when possible.

Within the second and probably dominating paradigm, pregnancy and childbirth are regarded as natural processes, embedded in social and psychological context, undergone by healthy women largely under their own control, and as positive and fulfilling experiences. Medical assistance is seen as an insurance against complications, and medical intervention as only necessary in the event of particular complications.

Unless such complications occur, the woman is not regarded as being in a sick or patient-role and her relationship with the medical profession is a relatively equalitarian one of active participation in, and full knowledge of the process of childbearing[1].

Some signs of turning away from hospitals have been observed. Practices, such as skin to skin contact between parents and child, choices of delivery position, closeness of the family unit surrounding the birth — generally not allowed in the hospital setting — have been demanded in several countries. E g in many areas of the US home birth has become increasingly prevalent in recent years[2].

New type maternity or childbearing centres* demonstrate that low-risk pregnancies and deliveries need not be managed in a traditional hospital setting.

The out-of-hospital alternative birth centre may include some or all the resources for prenatal care and education, labour and delivery care, immediate post-partal and neonatal care, and followup home visiting services. The centre under hospital administration and management may provide some postpartal examinations and health supervision. The centre may be adjacent to a hospital facility or a short distance from a hospital. Clearly understood arrangements for transfer to a hospital in the event of emergencies are important to ensure safety of the mother and infant. The economic feasibility of the out-of-hospital birth centre is dependent on a high volume service.

The in-hospital alternative birth centre usually consists of one or more labour/deliver rooms or a 2-bed postpartum room in the maternity unit, furnished in a home-

1 Macintyre Sally: The management of childbirth: a review of sociological research issues. 1977, Social science & medicine 11:477-484.

2 Mehl Lewis E: Delivery in the home. 1978, Comprehensive Therapy 4:3:18-26.

* e g Childbearing Center of the Maternity Center Association, Manhattan, New York City (Childbirth center responds to demands for more family participation. 1976, Hospitals 50:17:11-12).

like decor. Labour and delivery takes place in this room in a bed which may be specially designed to permit use of stirrups if desired or in an ordinary single or double bed. A couch or adjustable chair is provided for the father or family member supporting the mother. Usually the mother and the infant remain in this room until discharge. If a longer hospital stay is necessary, rooming-in care is provided. Sibling visiting and participation, as well as extended family members' involvement, is optional[3].

A combination of the security of home and safety of hospital is known as *6 hour discharge*[4]. Antenatal care is given as for home birth. The midwife is with the mother throughout the first stage of labour, whereafter the mother and her companions are transferred from home to hospital, where birth is given. If there should be difficulties then extra help is available, otherwise after six hours rest the mother goes back home again.

According to Swedish experience the distances up to 100 km to the full obstetrical service carry no rate of increased risk of birth during the transport[5]. Experience from Canada and Sweden indicates that in case of high-risk pregnancies, there is a better prognosis for the baby, if the baby is transported *in utero* to a complete delivery unit instead of being transported to a neonate unit in an incubator[6].

In the overwhelming majority of cases, birth is a happy event of considerable personal significance, traditionally a time for celebration. It is also a crisis period when new behaviour patterns, which will influence the family's welfare, are formed.

The birth entails an extensive adjustment process for the mother as it involves and reflects changes in not only her physical state but also in her ability to cope and adapt and in her self-concept as a woman, as a wife, and as a mother[7].

The growth of the family is to be regarded as a process which is based on the differentiated net work of conditions. The concentration of research on mother-child-contacts has to be rejected in the light of new findings as it can be considered as hostile against the family as a whole[*].

---

3   see also Gabel Harold D: Alternative Birth Centers: Fact or Fantasy? 1977, Virginia Medical 104:771-772.

4   see also Beels Christine: The Childbirth Book. Turnstone Books. London 1978, p 49.

5   cited by Hagenfeldt Kerstin and Rydbo Göran: Obstetrik och gynecologi. in Nytt från Läkarsällskapets Riksstämma 1975. Spri och Svenska Läkarsällskapet. S 25, Stockholm 1976, p 14.

6   personal communication: 1977, Allan Tamm, Boden, Sweden.

7   Mevs Lois: The Current Status of Cesarean Section and Today's Maternity Patient. 1977, JOGN Nursing 6:4:44-47.

*   Lehr Ursula: Eltern-Kind-Beziehung in der ersten Lebenszeit. 1978, Zeitschrift für Geburtshilfe und Perinatologie 182:317–330.

Childbirth should be a peak experience, a happening that units mother, father and infant psychologically into a caring, living, and involved family[8]. The first hour or two after delivery are considered very special from that point of view[9].

For the father's attachment to the infant, the quality of his experience of the actual labour and delivery is a most important predictor variable.[10]. The experience at childbirth may be intensely meaningful.

The presence of the husband during labour and delivery is a matter of growing popularity.

It is likely that many husbands would serve contributory roles but others might not. Enthusiastic but untutored, he can be easily demoralized by staff attitudes and labour-floor procedures. Some of them may faint, injure themselves or contaminate the area. However, most husbands can be very helpful in this psychologically trying situation[11]. He may be of considerable psychologic assistance to the mother. Also closer marital ties may be produced. This issue, however, is far from settled.

It is generally felt that the presence of the husband-father in the delivery room is a privilege to be granted and not a right to be demanded. The US Court of Appeals for the Seventh Circuit has said 1975 in its affirmation of a lower court ruling: The so-called right of marital privacy does not include the right of either spouse to have the husband present in the delivery room of a public hospital which, for medical reasons, has adopted a rule requiring his exclusion[12].

Birth ought to take place in an informal and relaxed atmosphere, not least because almost all obstetric patients are, more or less frightened[13].

Psychiatric disorders are common in connection with childbirth[14]. The risk of recurrence of puerperal psychosis in a subsequent pregnancy is approximately one in six[15]. Psychiatric morbidity in the puerperium is related to interpersonal and social stresses of various sorts and is not connected with obstetrical stresses[16].

---

8   see also Beck Joan: Childbirth: an experience to be shared. Chicago Tribune, June 20, 1972.

9   see also Rising Sharon Schindler: The Fourth Stage of Labor: Family Integration. 1974, American Journal of Nursing 74:870-874.

    Are fathers really necessary? 1973, The Medical Journal of Australia 1:920.

10 Mehl Lewis E: Delivery in the home. 1978, Comprehensive Therapy 4:3:18-26.

11 Greenhill J P and Friedman Emanuel A: Biological Principles and Modern Practice of Obstetrics. W B Saunders Company. Philadelphia, London, Toronto 1974, p 152.

12 1975, Hospitals 49:20:23.

13 personal communication: 1977, Allan Tamm, Boden, Sweden.

14 Martin Mary E: A maternity hospital study of psychiatric illness associated with childbirth. 1977, Irish Journal of Medical Science 146:239-244.

15 ibid

16 ibid

Deviations from normal physiological procedures may require immediate assistance. The rate of complications for mother and child is generally estimated to be about 10 to 20 per cent. 45 per cent of the infants born to them will require special on-going care[17].

Although about half of the complications are predictable, the other half is yet unpredictable[18]. Other authors state, that the vast majority of pregnancies at risk can now be predicted before birth and are amenable to intervention[19].

The time of maximum vulnerability in the life of an individual is during the transition from intrauterine to extrauterine life. This critical period and the first few minutes of life commands enlightened acute medical care.

Perinatal medicine has abolished the frontiers between the final stage of pregnancy, childbirth and the neonatal period. Obstetrics and paediatrics form one unit. It is important to have a neonatal unit adjacent to the delivery unit.

Asepsis in connection with deliveries consists mainly in the preservation of the patient's immunities[20]. This is reached by sustaining her strength, optimizing her general condition, and handling the tissues with utmost gentleness. The transfer of infective material to tissues higher up in the birth passage should be stringently prevented*.

After delivery, both mother and the newborn babies are susceptible to bacterial infections. The acquisition of organisms of any type by a newborn infant gives rise to changed circumstances but need not be harmful, and in certain situations may be beneficial. This is generally termed colonization and is superficial and confined to surfaces whether external, as on the skin, or internal, as in the gut. The immunological defences of the newborn against such invading organisms may be incomplete. Where the combination of number or virulence of invading organisms exceeds the infant's ability to limit the spread of those organisms, true infection will take place[21].

18 per cent of newborn infants have shown incidence of trivial infection and 5 per cent of them that of serious infection[22].

---

17 Segal Sydney: Perinatal intensive care: pediatric aspects. in Perinatal medicine. ed by James W Goodwin, John O Godden, and Graham W Chance. The Williams & Wilkins Co. Baltimore 1976, p 605.

18 Hagenfelt Kerstin and Rydbo Göran: Obstetrik och gynekologi. in Nytt från Läkarsällskapets Riksstämma 1975, Spri och Svenska Läkarsällskapet. S 25. Stockholm 1976, p 15.

19 Inwood Richard J and Hunt Carl E: The high-risk neonate. 1977, Comprehensive Therapy 3:9:8-17.

20 Greenhill J P and Friedman Emanuel A: Biological Principles and Modern Practice of Obstetrics. W B Saunders Company, Philadelphia, London, Toronto 1974, p 234.

* The incidence of postpartal infections after vaginal deliveries has been indicated to be between 1 and 8 per cent (Hirsch H A: Die geburtshilflichen Infektionen. 1976, Gynäkologische Rundschau 16: suppl 1:58–64).

21 Keay A J and Simpson R McD: Prevention of infection in nurseries for the newborn. 1977, Postgraduate Medical Journal 53:583-587.

22 Cockington R A and Drew J H: Neonatal Infection in a Maternity Hospital. 1977, Australian Paediatric Journal 13:105-109.

In 1971, The American College of Obstetricians and Gynecologists concluded in a White Paper* that full obstetrical services can be provided efficiently only when more than 1,500 births a year occur at a hospital. A Yale University study[23] has concluded that the best number is 3,000. It could be stated that about 2,000 deliveries a year are needed in order to maintain the quality of services in a maternity unit. Below this figure the number of parturitions and the fluctuations in daily census make that the personnel is used in multiple functions, which may lower the standards of patient care.

The *number of labour and delivery rooms* and obsterical beds in a hospital depends on the annual number of deliveries in the hospital's catchment area, the ward bed occupancy rate, the time to be spent in the delivery room, and the length of stay in the obstetrical ward.

Because of shorter length of stay of the post-partum patient, the tendency is towards an increased number of labour and delivery rooms.

In Poland[24] three labour beds are recommended per 1,000 annual deliveries. One labour bed for each 250 deliveries annually has been a rather general guide in the US[25].

A simple thumb-rule for determining the size of an obstetrical suite is two labour rooms and one delivery room per 20 post-partum beds. In many countries a combined labour-and-delivery room is used. In Sweden, there are three to four such rooms per 28 postpartum beds.

In the current medical practice the labour or first-stage-only room, the delivery room and the recovery area are arranged in sequence. There is now a rather general awareness that the normal duration of labour is substantially shorter than the median duration about 13 to 15 hours as quoted in most textbooks.

A use of combined labour-delivery rooms would minimize circulation of the patient during labour. However, they may need more space and the furnishing of a combined room is considerably less domestic than the labour room.

After having adapted a queuing theory model for the prediction of delivery room utilization, following room figures have been released[26]:

* National Needs in Obstetrics and Gynecology. White Paper. American College of Obstetricians and Gynecologists. Chicago 1971.

23 cited by Roeder James L: Building a system of larger and better obstetrical services. From the Desk of Dr. Rourke 3:3. No publishing year.

24 Jachowicz R: Dzialy zabigowe w szpitalu powiatowym. 1973, Szpitalnictwo Polskie 17:219-229.

25 see also Fleshin Frances: Designing an obstetrics department. 1975, Hospitals 49:75-79.

26 Milliken Ralph A, Rosenberg Lloyd and Milliken Gerry M: A queuing theory model for the prediction of delivery room utilization. 1972, American Journal of Obstetrics and Gynecology 114:691-699.

number of delivery rooms	vaginal delivery service only	complete delivery service, 12 per cent caesarean deliveries	US Public Health Service recommendations: vaginal delivery service only
1	1 — 90	1 — 80	1 — 1,220
2	90 — 1,350	80 — 1,200	1,221 — 1,950
3	1,350 — 4,000	1,200 — 3,600	1,950 — 2,680
4	4,000 — 7,700	3,600 — 7,000	2,681 — 3,410
4 — 5			3,411 — 4,140
5	7,700 — 9,000	7,000 — 9,000	4,141 — 5,000

The percentage of caesarean deliveries varies in different countries but is generally on increase. There has been a wider indication for it is in discussion, as some feel that caesarean section has changed from an operation of necessity to an operation of choice, with better maternal and fetal results[27].

In Sweden the caesarean section rate in one hospital rose from 2.0 to 7.8 per cent between 1966 and 1970[28]. In several hospitals the rate was in 1976 14 to 17* per cent[29]. In the US the incidence of mothers delivered by caesarean section grew from a 3 to 4 per cent rate to 10 to 15 per cent between 1969 and 1974, with reports of 30 per cent increase in some areas[30]. A survey of 12 teaching hospitals across Canada showed that in 1976 the proportion of caesarean section deliveries ranged from 9.8 per cent to 21.8 per cent, the average being 14.3 per cent[31].

There is now (1978) a growing unease among obstetricians as the increasing caesarean section rate is not accompanied by solid evidence that this improves perinatal results[32]. As it still represents a considerable risk for mothers[33], general caesarean section is not accepted[34].

It would appear that in the future 10 to 15 per cent of deliveries would require caesarean section. The section rates will obviously vary with the type of population served.

---

27 see also Jones O Hunter: Cesarean section in present-day obstetrics. 1976, American Journal of Obstetrics and Gynecology 126:521–530.

28 Johnell H E, Östberg H and Wåhlstrand T: Increasing caesarean section rate. 1976, Acta Obstetrica et Gynecologica Scandinavica 55:95–100.

* e g in Boden 16.4 per cent, in Uppsala 17 per cent.

29 personal communication: 1977, Allan Tamm, Boden, Sweden.

30 B Cochran cited by Mevs Lois: The Current Status of Cesarean Section and Today's Maternity Patient. 1977, JOGN Nursing 6:4:44-47.

31 Baskett T F: Cesarean section: what is an acceptable rate? 1978, Canadian Medical Association Journal 118:1019-1020.

32 ibid

33 see also Hochuli E: Infektionen in der Geburtshilfe und Gynäkologie. 1976, Gynäkologische Rundschau 16:suppl 1:52-57.

Riegel K, Elser H, Craffonara R, Schreiber M A and Messow K: Kaiserschnittkinder. 1977, Medizinische Klinik 72:1481-1486.

Baskett T F: Cesarean section: what is an acceptable rate? 1978, Canadian Medical Association Journal 118:1019-1020.

34 see also Seidenschnur G, Rissman M and Knaape H H: Pediatric neurologic morbidity in breech delivery. 5th European Congress of Perinatal Medicine. Uppsala, Sweden. June 1976.

A division of the maternity unit in an aseptic and a septic section is unusual and unnecessary. However, requirements in this direction have been made[35].

The delivery suite could take advantage of the administrative and mechanical features of the surgical department by being included in it. Increased staffing efficiency seems to be the principal operating cost saving attributed to this combination[36].

35 Grossman G and Liebtrau B: Hygienische Untersuchungen in geburtshilflichen Abteilungen. 1977, Zentralblatt für Gynäkologie 99:139-146.

36 see also Report to the Congress. Study of Health Facilities Construction Costs (B-164031 (3)) by the Comptroller General of United States. November 20 1972. US Government Printing Office 1973, p 64.

Spatial requirements

Family waiting room and early labour lounge

This facility should be available in or near the delivery department*. In the attractively furnished and decorated room patients in early labour could walk and visit with children, husbands, and others.

Telephone/intercom connections with the labour area and reading materials should be available. Access to light nourishment is an advantage.

Diagnostic-admitting room

In the admitting room, which must be easily accessible, the patient is prepared for the labour room. There should be an examination table with a stationary, an adjustable ceiling light fixture, a small laboratory unit for blood tests and urine–analysis[1], and a washbasin.

In this room women could be examined also to ascertain their status in labour without being formally admitted, if they are in early labour**.

The admitting room should have an area of about 17 m^2.

Facilities to shower the patient and to have an enema performed have to be included. In spite of the abandonment of the routine administration of a shower to all labour patients at the admission to the hospital, there still is a need for selected patients to be washed. Enemas are given to empty the lower bowel thoroughly. In some situations giving enema is to be avoided.

The standard practice of shaving the vulva and perineum — a degrading experience for the woman — is vanishing as its lack of benefit in preventing infection has been proved[2].

There should be a toilet with a wall-hung-wc-chair and an adjacent washbasin.

Equipment for emergency deliveries should be provided.

---

* The Development of Family-Centered Maternity/Newborn Care in Hospitals. 1978, JOGN Nursing 7:5:55–59.

1 Fleshin Frances: Designing an obstetrics department. 1975, Hospitals 49:9:75-79.

** The Development of Family-Centered Maternity/Newborn Care in Hospitals. 1978, JOGN Nursing 7:5:55–59.

2 see also Greenhill J P and Friedman Emanuel A: Biological Principles and Modern Practice of Obstetrics. W A Saunders Company. Philadelphia, London, Toronto 1974, p 243.

Observation room

It would be optimal to have an observation room, where patients in premature labour — six to eight months pregnant with labour pains — may be treated to slow or to stop the labour[3].

Labour room

The sense of isolation, particularly with the first baby, can be overwhelming[4] and the patient in labour can require the company of the husband. Some prefer privacy.

The support from the midwife should be readily available.

Labour or first-stage rooms should be for single-occupancy with a floor area of at least 12 m^2. They should be furnished with a homely touche, including radio and TV. Piped-in music may help to create a tranquil atmosphere.

A labour-delivery bed could be raised and lowered, it should be adjustable to semi-sitting position[*].

Labour rooms should be equipped with an oxygen source and a suction point for resuscitation.

Space is needed for resuscitation of the newborn and for a mobile anaesthesia trolley with a device for intermittent positive-pressure respiration, and an emergency cart.

A washbasin is needed.

Toilet and washroom facilities must be included. They should contain safety bars and emergency call bells.

Labour rooms should have temperature and humidity control.

Transmission of sound between labour rooms must be prevented.

Patients' lounge

It is important to have a lounge for the first stage of labour patients. The inability of the pregnant women to move about in the labour area is one of the most serious restrictions placed upon her. If the patient can be kept mobile as long as possible, a more normal and easy birth is made possible.

3   Fleshin Frances: Designing an obstetrics department. 1975, Hospitals 49:9:75-79.

4   Beels Christine: The Childbirth Book. Turnstone Books. London 1978, p 130.

*   The Development of Family-Centered Maternity/Newborn Care in Hospitals. 1978, JOGN Nursing 7:5:55–59

In the ambulant group the duration of labour has been shown significantly shorter, the need for analgesia significantly less, and the incidence of fetal heart abnormalities significantly smaller than in the recumbent group[5].

Allowing women in early labour to move around freely and socialize with others will help to minimize problems created by anxiety during labour[6].

The second stage of labour can last 1.5 to 2 hours particularly with a first birth[7].

The human female is quite adaptable to many physiological positions and cultural practices, the importance of which have not yet been entirely evaluated. The parturitional posture is not just an arbitrary position assumed by the mother while she is delivering, but instead, is an integral part of the culturally influenced birth process. Rather than have the delivery position dictated by culturally patterned behaviour or customs for something as important as the delivery of an infant, it should be chosen from a range of alternatives to suit the individual's physiological processes within the cultural setting[8].

If the mother chooses to be delivered in a hospital by an obstetrician, her delivery position choices are usually limited: the split delivery bed-table, designed so that one end may be dropped or retracted, allows the woman to be delivered either in the lithotomy position if one end is removed, or in the dorsal recumbent position if the lower end is not altered.

For normal deliveries, the usual position of the mother on the delivery table is the lithotomy position, with her buttocks at the edge or projecting over the edge of the table, and with her legs spread apart and in straight leg holders, knee rests, or stirrups. The woman's arms are not to stray into the sterile field. In some cases, the delivery table may have upright handles or hand grips against which the woman may pull in her bearing down efforts. The woman may have to lie flat on the delivery table, but some delivery tables have pillows for her head or for her back to give her a curved spine position. The woman may not have adequate foot support, though, because she has nothing to push against. She is then covered with sterile drapings, exposing only her perineum.

A recent innovation has been the adaptation of an adjustable back rest on to a standard delivery table[9]. The adjustable back rest lies under the delivery table mattress and the angle of elevation can be varied from about 15 degrees to about 55 degrees. Women appeared most comfortable with their backs raised at an angle of 30 to 45 degrees. The delivery table is equipped with stirrups and footplates, to be used during the second stage of labour in the lowered position so that there is no pressure under the knees, and is also equipped with handgrips, thus allowing the

5   Flynn A M, Kelly J, Hollins G, Lynch P F: Ambulation in labour. 1978, British Medical Journal 2:591-593.

6   Ascher Barbara H: Maternal Anxiety in Pregnancy and Fetal Homeostasis. 1978, JOGN Nursing 7:5:18-21.

7   Atwood Richard J: Parturitional Posture and Related Birth Behaviour. 1976, Acta Obstetricia et Gynecologica Scandinavica. Supplement 57.

8   ibid.

9   ibid.

mother either to push or to pull while bearing down. Another item is the pillow placed under the mother's head. Using this backrest, the mother assumes a modified sitting position: her back is curved and her head is flexed forward while her legs are bent.

For the mother, this position increases the efficiency of the expulsive effort by directing the force of the voluntary muscles towards the pelvis and by using the force of gravity on the weight of the baby and the abdominal contents. For the obstetrician, this position is compatible with modern methods of obstetric care and asepsis in procedures such as cleansing of the perineum, control of delivery, episiotomy, or the application of forceps. This propped, or semi-sitting, position has also been evaluated in terms of psychological and physical categories of information for both the mother and the baby. The results show no adverse effects while indicating increased comfort to the mother, greater efficiency of the expulsive efforts and considerable advantages in a programme of cooperative childbirth[10].

At each delivery bed there should be oxygen outlets, also for the babies, suction points, and wall-mounted sphygomomanometers. The access to gas supplies and suction points should be easy.

An overhead mirror should be available*.

As the importance of mother-baby attachment particularly during the first few minutes and hours has been shown and stressed as it facilitates optimal postpartum and extrauterine physiologic adaption[11], the opportunity for establishing contact between mother and baby in the delivery room should not be lost. This opportunity should be kept open also for potentially vulnerable preterm babies[12].

If the husband is allowed to be present, he should be given a seat at the head-end of the bed. Expectant husbands are usually banned from delivery department if caesarean-section deliveries are to be performed.

If the suggestions of *Frederick Leboyer***, who wants to make birth a more pleasant experience for the newborn, are to be followed, the delivery room requires a spotlight which is directed away from the perineum just before delivery of the infant's head — all other lights have to be extinguished —, a radiant heating element to be placed over the delivered baby on the mother's abdomen to prevent heat loss, and a (plastic) bassinet where the baby can be immersed to the face in a 36.5°C water bath until he appears relaxed and comfortable[13].

10 Atwood Richard J: Parturitional Posture and Related Birth Behaviour. 1976, Acta Obstetricia et Gynecologica Scandinavica. Supplementum 57.

* The Development of Family-Centered Maternity/Newborn Care in Hospitals. 1978, JOGN Nursing 7:5:55-59

11 see also Anderson Gene Cranston: The Mother and the Newborn: Mutual Caregivers. 1977, JOGN Nursing 6: sept-oct :50-57.

12 see also Karlberg P: Management of the preterm infant in the labour ward. in Perinatal Medicine. ed by Z K Stembera, K Polácek and V Sabata. Georg Thieme Publishers, Stuttgart and Aricenum, Prague 1975, p 222.

** Birth Without Violence. Alfred A Knopf. New York 1975. Loving Hands. Collins. London 1977.

13 Oliver Charlotte M, Oliver George M: Gentle Birth, 1978, JOGN Nursing 7:5:35-40.

The vast majority of babies are born normal and rigorous. However, a significant number will require resuscitation. Even though modern methods* have greatly improved the ability to predict depressed babies, no method is 100 per cent accurate. For that reason preparations should be made to resuscitate every baby[13].

The most dramatic changes and so also the most critical changes are related to the transfer from a transplacental gas exchange to a gas exchange via the lungs of a newborn infant[14].

The newborn does not tolerate even brief hypoxic episodes, so strict precautions for stabilization of the oxygen environment are mandatory. Oxygen warmed to 32 to 34°C with 60 to 80 per cent relative humidity is administered[15].

When a premature baby is anticipated, the delivery room temperature should be increased to 32°C or higher[16].

An incubator prewarmed to 35°C should be available in the delivery room. Infants not requiring resuscitation should be placed in this incubator as quickly as possible if a radiant heat source is not available[17].

For care of the depressed newborn infant is needed a table or bassinet with non-slippery surface on which to place the baby. The table should be tiltable to provide a head-down position. Radiant heaters will warm the surface on which the infant will be placed, as well as provide a radiant heat source for the infant if resuscitation is required.

Equipment for neo-natal resuscitation should be kept as simple as possible. It should include a resuscitator for pulmonary inflation, an oral suction device, oxygen supply, and an overhead radiant heater. When it is dealt with a patient weighing only 900 to 1300 g, the less equipment there is between the patient and the resuscitator the better the situation will be[18].

Hand washing facilities are needed.

Storage space must be available. Wall cabinets for resuscitation equipment — measured 65 by 60 by 22 cm — have been recommended.

---

* cardiotokography, blood gas analysis, fetal pH-analysis

13 see also DeVore Jay S: Resuscitation of the newborn. 1976, Clinical Obstetrics and Gynecology 19:3:607-617.

14 Karlberg P: Management of the preterm infant in the labour ward. in Perinatal Medicine. ed by Z K Štembera, K Poláček and V Šabata. Georg Thieme Publishers, Stuttgart and Aricenum, Prague 1975, p 218.

15 Schreiner Richard L, Ecobedo Marilyn B and Gresham Edwin L: Respiratory Problems in the Newborn. 1977, The Journal of the Indiana State Medical Association 70:239-243.

16 Schreiner Richard L, Ecobedo Marilyn B and Gresham Edwin L: Respiratory Problems in the Newborn. 1977, The Journal of the Indiana State Medical Association 70:239-243.

17 Kanto Jr William P and Calvert Lynette J: Thermoregulation of the Newborn. 1977, American Family Physician 16:157-163.

18 De Vore Jay S: Resuscitation of the newborn. 1976, Clinical Obstetrics and Gynecology 19:3:607-617.

A delivery room should have a floor area of about 30 m². For obstetrical or surgical lamps a ceiling height of at least 2.8 m is required. A doorwidth of 1.3 m allows the patients to be moved to the delivery room on a labour bed.

It is strongly felt that a delivery room must have a window.

Delivery rooms connected by doorways are believed to make it easier for one midwife to supervise two concurrent deliveries. Not all find this solution an advantage.

Transmission of sound between delivery rooms must be prevented.

If flammable anaesthesia is used, flooring must be conductive.

Sometimes a combination labour and delivery room for the patient and the husband during a normal labour and delivery, a so called birthing room, has been recommended.

Operation room

If the obstetric suite is a section of the surgical department, the occasional need for immediate surgical intervention is easily met. In an independent delivery suite an operation unit should be included as about 20 per cent of deliveries require a surgical intervention[19].

An operation table capable of both head-down and lateral tilt is frequently the first choice for caesarean sections.

Anaesthesia work-room

In obstetric units with more than 3,000 deliveries a year, anaesthesia work-rooms should be provided.

Basic equipment includes wall shelves, a work counter, a drainboard, and a sink for washing and checking accessoiries.

Recovery room

Immediately after delivery procedures are finished the mother should be assured rest even if a sedative has been used.

The maternity patient undergoing a caesarean section has had both abdominal surgery and a delivery, and one must consider the unique needs occuring during the

19 Jenssen Helge: Forløsningsavdelingers spesielle hygienekrav. 1977, Tidsskrift for Den norske laegeforening 97:735.

puerperal period which are engendered by the individual circumstances surrounding each procedure. As a planned physical assault on the body, the surgical experience becomes an intense event with physiological and psychosocial effects covering a wide range of reactions and behaviours[20].

For rest, observation, and care 12 m² recovery rooms are needed.

As an infant's first feeding may have an effect on his and his mother's later behaviour, breast feeding in the postpartum recovery room seems to be a positive factor and should be encouraged[21].

The husband should be allowed to visit the new mother and baby with some provision for privacy*.

The number of postpartum recovery rooms provided ought to be about a third of the number of labour rooms.

The recovery room should be placed adjacent to the delivery room and be equipped as a postanaesthetic recovery room. Oxygen and suction should be available. Easy movement of a bed or a stretcher and space for attending patients from either side of the bed should be provided for.

The recovery room windows should have shades.

Adjacent to the recovery room there should be a toilet.

Nursery for newborn

All infants to be sent to the normal newborn unit undergo an initial period of intensive observation and visual monitoring. The closer the infant is to term, the better are his adaptive processes.

Scales are needed in the examination area of the nursery.

About 3 m² should be allowed per bassinet.

After four to six hours, the newborn has usually made the initial adjustment necessary for extrauterine life and his vital signs and behaviour stabilize[22].

Several routine examinations suggest the neonate be unclothed during this postnatal period. An unclothed infant requires supplemental warming.

20 J J Bonica cited by Mevs Lois: The Current Status of Cesarean Section and Today's Maternity Patient. 1977, JOGN Nursing 6:4:44-47.

21 Cohen Mariam C: Factors Important to Continued, Successful Breast Feeding. 1978, The Guthrie Bulletin 48:1:15-26.

* The Development of Family-Centered Maternity/Newborn Care in Hospitals. 1978, JOGN Nursing 7:5:55–59.

22 Lubchenco Luisa O: The high risk infant. W B Saunders Company. Philadelphia, London, Toronto 1976, p 152.

It is of utmost importance to recognize that the normal full-term baby should not require the use of an incubator or other supplementary heating device to maintain his body temperature in an ordinarily adequately heated nursery — 25 to 27°C[23]. However, this temperature is not accepted by the majority of nurses.

Procedure room for newborn

A 12 m² procedure room is intended for exchange transfusion, not very complex diagnostic and therapeutic procedures and minor surgery of the newborn, as circumcision, or any other elective procedures.

Laboratory equipment, suction, an operation lamp and a washbasin are needed.

Special examination room

In teaching hospitals, a room of about 12 m² should be provided for maternal and neonatal examination.

Laboratory, Xray services

Access to laboratory services, blood bank and X ray and ultrasonic diagnostic services are necessary.

Sick newborn babies should be examined with minimal disruption of their environment. Equipment designed for paediatric use is available, but not essential. Neonates who are at risk e g, premature babies, babies born by caesarean section or after a prolonged labour, should have chest X rays as soon as possible after birth and again at 3, 6 and 24 hours, with subsequent films as indicated by the clinical picture[24].

Film developing facilities must be close at hand. An automatic film processor within the newborn unit may be justified.

Nurses' and midwives' station

The station should be centrally located within the maternity suite. It should contain desks, a table, shelves, a filing cabinet, bulletin boards, and a couch. The recommendable size of the nurses' and midwives' station is about 12 m².

Generally, at least two midwives per team are required. For 2,000 patients per annum three midwives are required, for 3,000 four, and for 3,500 five midwives[25].

23 Stern Leo: Thermoregulation in the newborn infant: physiologic and clinical considerations. 1977, Acta Paediatrica Belgica 30:3-14.

24 Murray J P: The chest in critical care. 1978, Radiography 44:173-178.

25 Socialstyrelsen redovisar Förlossningsvårdens organisation. Socialstyrelsen. Stockholm 1973, p 72.

Obstetrician's office

The doctor's office — about 12 m² — does not have to be centrally located within the obstetric suite.

Changing rooms, retirement room, staff lounge

Changing rooms for both female and male staff should be adjacent to the entrance to the delivery unit. Toilets and showers should be provided.

A small retirement room for every ten female employees is an asset. A washbasin is needed.

The needs for a staff lounge have too often been underestimated.

On-call rooms

Adjacent to the delivery section, there should be on-call accommodations for obstetricians, midwives and paediatricians.

Nourishment area, formula preparation

A kitchenette for patient catering is needed. It will have to rely on the hospital food distribution system. The required size is about 12 m².

An integrated formula preparation room for neonates offers advantages over the dependence on a centralized milk kitchen.

Cleaners' room

The number of cleaners' rooms — each of about 4 m² size — depends on the size of the obstetric department.

A bucket sink with hot and cold water, drainer, and space for cleaning utensils and mechanical cleaning equipment as well as housekeeping supplies and a cleaners' cart is needed.

Utility rooms, placenta disposal

Utility rooms, both clean and soiled, with deep double sinks are needed. There should be ample hampers for soiled linen, because maternity patients often need complete linen changes.

In the obstetric department the typical waste products include soiled dressings, sponges, disposable diapers and underpads, disposable gloves, waste ampules, needles and syringes, disposable masks, disposable catheters, disposable enema units, and disposable blood lancets.

There should be a provision for disposing placentas.

In large delivery units a room of about 8 m² area for examination and conservation of some placentas is needed.

A refrigerator, placenta disposal equipment and hand washing facilities are needed.

Washbasins should be included.

Storage facilities

Storage facilities are needed for linen, masks, dressings, underpads, drapes, sanitary napkins, sterilized instrument sets, anaesthetic drugs, medicaments, needles and syringes, and disposable gloves.

The use of disposables does not require increased storage space.

Gas storage rooms with conductive flooring and gravity ventilation should not be linked directly with the delivery rooms.

A space for a couple of stretchers is needed.

Area for relatives

A waiting room for relatives and friends near the admitting area should be provided. It should contain comfortable chairs, perhaps a TV set and a coffee machine.

A public telephone and a toilet should be available.

In the cases where husbands are allowed to be present during the delivery, changing rooms in principle like the staff changing rooms may be needed. For some husbands the stay overnight with the mothers should be provided.

Smoking room for patients

As long as mothers are not properly informed of the dangers of smoking and smoking is tolerated in hospitals, a well-ventilated smoking room should be provided within the delivery area.

AMBULATORY CARE FACILITIES

Background information, health centre – community centre

Because of the high costs involved in the complexity of in-patient care, international debate has emphasized the need of increasing the role of out-patient care and establishing of facilities which would give adequate treatment with less expense and disruption. These services should reduce the patient load of the hospitals by early diagnosis and treatment of the sick, and relieve the hospitals by taking care of the convalescent.

The term out-patient can primarily be applied on the patient who receives his treatment either in his home, in a doctor's consultation room or in a health centre. Out-patients do not need bed accommodation, except in the day-surgery section where the treatment may require a short stay recovery bed. There are no over-night stay provisions.

Out-patient service in an ambulatory care centre also called poly-clinic, health centre, walk-in-clinic, day hospital, dispensary, as a part of a hospital or standing free is substituted for in-patient medicine and on-going medical and para-medical care is provided also for not completely healed patients.

The out-patient departments have to provide to all members of a community the whole scope of services which are needed to keep them in good state of health, directly or by referral to more qualified institutions.

The economic importance of the role of out-patient care might be illustrated by the fact that e g in Sweden the cost for one million hospitalized short-term patients would correspond to the cost of 20 million visits in out-patient facilities.

It is expected that the out-patient care – private or community or state conducted – independent of larger hospitals will be the object of expansion.

The performances of all centres have to reflect the socioeconomic status of their target communities, the political philosophies and mission of the sponsoring body, the environmental conditions of the area, and the characteristic elements of the population which they serve.

The aim, objective and *modus operandi* of community health centres may vary considerably. Variations in types of health and sick care services between metropolitan areas, rural areas, and industrial districts are justified. In the absence of any unifying taxonomy, ultimate assessment of alternative models will be extremely difficult.

Administration must remain the servant of the health care and should not attempt to become its master. The community should have a voice in formulating the conclusion what kind of health service is to be provided and how it is to be provided. No matter what system is developed for the provision of health care, it must be acceptable to the health workers and in particular to the medical profession.

A health care and social welfare centre or super ambulatory care facility would be complete when the following units are included:

> medical and nursing care units
> on-call units
> dentistry service
> social welfare office
> work therapy and vocational training unit
> pharmacy for prompt prescription filling
> optician service
> chiropodist unit
> health insurance office
> health information office

A health centre should conduct ante- and post-natal as well as child welfare clinics. It is also the natural centre of prophylactic medicine for the community. As such it has to organize and conduct hygiene and nutrition education sessions and to follow the general health developments of the community inhabitants through health care visitors and district nurses.

The health care centre is only a part of community service centre. Following facilities in addition to the health centre would make a community centre complete:

> labour exchange
> community information centre
> library — books, newspapers, records, tapes
> exhibition hall with permanent and temporary exhibitions, art and educational
> premises for stage productions and movie showing
> premises for lecturing study circles and club meetings
> day centre for senior citizens
> adolescent recreational unit
> kindergarten
> infant care facilities
> clearing centre for domestic help
> clearing centre for flats and rooms
> equipment service for the handicapped
> restaurant — cafeteria

Ambulatory care department

It has been estimated that a population of 1,000 may have the need of 800 to 1,100 visits per year. About 3,000 inhabitants should be the maximum number to be taken care of by one general practitioner.

It would be most advantageous to have in a health centre at least two specialists in internal medicine, one in general minor surgery, one in gynaecology, one in paediatrics, one in oto-rhino-laryngology, one in ophthalmology and one in psychiatry. Through more intensive use of the facilities operating costs could be reduced.

In large health centres the services should include facilities for general medicine, internal medicine, minor general surgery, minor orthopedic surgery, paediatrics, gynaecology, ophthalmology, oto-rhino-laryngology, dermatology, adult psychiatry, child and adolescent psychiatry, dentistry, limited X ray diagnostics and pathological laboratory, and social welfare services.

Larger health centres — independent or hospital attached — with a highly differentiated out-patient care can have up to 20 physicians. 20 full-time year-around posts for physicians correspond to a total of 40,000 doctor-hours or a capacity of about 85,000 patient visits per year with some time to contribute to other primary communal health needs. For a population of about 30,000 people, such a health centre would provide 3 annual patient visits per inhabitant.

In an area with a concentrated population of 50,000 inhabitants, it may be appropriate to establish a central unit with about 20 doctors and additionally three health centres with 3 to 4 doctors each, rather than one health centre with 30 doctors. Specialists at the central unit have to act as consultants to the smaller health centres.

In the largest health-care centres following units might be included: specialized diagnostic and some therapeutic radiology; cystoscopy, pulmonary function laboratory; cardiography service; nuclear medicine; electroencephalography and electromyography, additional pathologic laboratories, and multiphasic testing. There may be provision for mother and child welfare; psychotherapy; observation playgroups for general community mental health service, and particularly for the child guidance service; facilities for the supply of welfare foods, issuing maternity packs, incontinence pads, contraceptives and lending and receiving back items for home care, such as walking aids, bedpans etc. Special activities, such as family planning, obesity, and anti-smoking and anti-alcoholic clinics, and geriatric screening can be included.

In all out-patient activities continuity in medical treatment should be maintained as much as possible between the patient and involved medical staff. Frequently, in such cases, a personal visit can be cancelled and replaced by a telephone call.

Each larger primary care area should have a health care information unit to assist uncertain patients and to avoid unnecessary patient visits. This information unit could be a part of an emergency unit or a medical on-duty unit.

There are three different types of out-patient: the booked out-patient, the unbooked out-patient, and the emergency patient.

The *booked out-patient* is given consultation or treatment only by appointment and only during clinic sessions. His visits may be repetetive.

It is possible to predict both the duration and the intensity of space use for a medical session. In Northern and Central Europe only about 5 per cent of the booked patients fail to show up. In other areas, e g in some African countries the percentage is much higher. In units with well-disciplined booked outpatients there is no uneffi- cient time for the medical staff between patients. Also the waiting time for patients is minimized and they are set at ease. The over-crowding and the risk of possible cross-infection in waiting areas is reduced.

There are three basic models of medical contacts applicable to booked out-patients: the personal care sequence, the group examination process, and the health educa- tion class.

The personal care encounters include examination and medical treatment, dressings, bandaging, and para-medical rehabilitation.

Group sessions cover sections of the population for routine tests and/or prophylac- tic care. The sessions include immunization, child health care, antenatal supervision, contraception advice, cytology. The intensity of space use is likely to vary unpre- dictably.

The so called pipeline process of the group sessions consists of a pre-determined programme of identical tests for a large number of patients carried out by a mixed medical team: a doctor, a nurse, and a midwife. Each member of the team performs one or several tests and sends thereafter the patient to a colleague for the next test.

There are always several patients simultaneously in the clinical pipeline. A number of waiting intervals is unevitable, because various tests take different lengths of time. Waiting patients may be only partially dressed.

A variant of the pipe-line process is the mode in which the medical staff, not the patients, is moving from room to room. There should be enough consulting rooms in conjunction with one another, so that patients can be allowed to dress in the same room where they had received professional attention.

Although each group session has its characteristic mode, the provision of separate accommodations for the exclusive use of each one is not motivated.

The group examination sessions as well as the classes are a matter of time-bound management policies.

The *unbooked out-patient* arrives unannounced and though he himself feels the need of immediate medical or surgical assistance, his case is not necessarily an emergency. Medical needs of this group are the same as the booked out-patients have.

The possibilities of admission to medical attention depend on the approach of the local community. There is experience from various areas outside Europe that for a rather large portion of the population a late afternoon/early evening unbooked out-patient department session is a desireable and practicable service.

Generally, in urban areas unbooked out-patients should not be encouraged. When the volume of unbooked patients is large, the examination becomes necessarily superficial. As many as possible should be referred to booked out-patients sessions. It will not be possible without an appointment system to select the necessary records before the session.

Emergency patients are the medical cases or injured needing immediate attention. This group forms a small percentage of the total out-patient visits. Because of their urgent needs and the priority given to their treatment, diagnostic and treatment facilities must be available round the clock.

General planning aspects

The main activities in an out-patient department are the reception of patients, consultation between doctor and patient, undressing, clinical examinations, diagnostic tests, minor procedures, dressing, giving of advice and instructions, dictation and/or writing.

An ambulatory care department organization aimed at the maximum number of patients being seen in a given time inevitably reduces the level of privacy and dignity of the patient. Consultation which is interrupted and divided between several patients is unsatisfactory both for patients and their companions.

The ambulatory care facilities must enable the clinical and non-clinical staff to give their best service and the patients to receive the services without surrender of personal dignity.

The main activity sequences are those where professional staff are involved with patients or with each other and with their supporting staff; and where the non-professional staff work with patients.

The facilities have to be planned so that

ease for access for ambulant patients or those arriving by public or private transport is ensured

the dignity and privacy of the patient is respected

a quiet orderly pattern of work is achieved

the requirements of handicapped visitors are wholly satisfied

some regrouping of functions within the centre is possible

an extension or expansion of the centre is possible without the need to re-arrange its basic circulation system

the building be of non-institutional character.

Designs characterized by simplicity can and ought to be produced.

An average total area of 250 m^2 per doctor ought to be sufficient for rather complex out-patient care. An out-patient department with, for example, six doctors, special quarters for child and maternity care, and for some other out-patient activities, can be estimated to have a total areal need of about 1,500 m^2.

In larger out-patient departments the accommodation for each separate and identifiable speciality or team should be closely associated with its own reception and waiting accommodations and visually recognizable.

No department should be boxed in.

611

Patients' routes within the building should cross staff's routes as little as possible and should never afford views into offices, stores, staff coffee or tea lounges, kitchens or nurses' service rooms. Documents for filing, blood and urine samples, instruments and sterilizers should remain concealed from the public view.

Even in complex out-patient departments coloured destination lines painted on floors may be confusing and abstruse and should therefore be avoided. Easily understandable signs should be used to identify destinations.

The grouping of all out-patient sections should preferably be at ground level to allow for future growth. If the building is multistoried, the out-patient facilities should be on the ground floor.

For occupational therapy and play-group sessions an out-door play area extension may be needed. It must be contiguous with in-door space.

Some deep plan buildings may be economical to erect but they do not create the non-institutional atmosphere which ought to be required. The out-patient departments should allow the majority of rooms the benefit of windows. Landscaped courtyards give frequently a pleasant touch to the building. Circulation routes along courtyards are attractive.

Generally, three functional zones in an out-patient department can be distinguished:

public zone	the entrance lobbies, waiting areas, public toilets, pram park
joint use zone	the reception areas, individual clinical rooms, seminar rooms
staff zone	the staff cloakrooms and toilets, workrooms, retirement rooms, communal rooms, stores

All separately operating functional entities should be approached by way of an administrative control centre.

The public entrance should be brought in near to the receptionist, so that she can handle the inquirers who need no other service.

The design of individual functional areas should not allow any extraneous traffic to penetrate any work area.

There may be separate entrances for staff and public, each giving access to the relevant zone.

If there are to be more than two joint use units, either the internal circulations must cross, bringing a risk of some confusion or there must be additional public entrances. The latter may be a preferable solution, when it is ensured that the patient need only use one entrance irrespective of the number of units he has to visit.

Circulation routes must not pass through waiting areas, which should be screened both visually and acoustically.

Waiting areas must relate closely to their associated group of clinical rooms so that verbal systems of patient call remain possible and walking distances short.

There should be a separation of incompatible types of patients, the noisy children from the anxious and infirm, pregnant women from coughing bronchitis, the sick from the fairly well. Provision for patient's companions is necessary.

Within the *joint use zone* standardized rooms should allow multifunctional usage and cater in detail for the needs of patients, their companions and the staff.

The seminar room has no direct relationship to other clinical rooms. It belongs to the joint use zone and relates to the public entrance.

Within the *staff zone* administrative patterns, role relationships and job description are frequently in a state of development and therefore room relationships must not impede development. Close grouping of rooms of similar type will permit easier changes in their use. However, the staff zone tends to be fragmented[1].

1 Cammock Ruth: Confidentiality in health centres and group practices: the implications for design. 1976, Journal of architectural research 4:5-17.

Spatial requirements

Entrance and parking

An approach road from the public transport with a wide footpath should lead to the entrance.

The space around the entrance has to be slip free and sized to allow the simultaneous setting down or picking up of infirm patients from two cars. Occasionally, a loading of a stretcher into an ambulance may occur.

The ambulance entrance should be separate and covered. It should be related to the admitting facilities used by the ambulatory patient.

It should be possible to *park* ambulances and the cars of staff and patients near the outpatient department entrance. The car park must include provisions for the vehicles of disabled staff and patients, and the private cars of the staff who are on-call. Part-time staff can share parking spaces.

A service area must be available for delivery vans at all times when the out-patient department is in a free-standing building. Delivery vehicles need ample space to turn.

Entrance lobby

On entering a large outpatient department — steps should be avoided — via a draught lobby, the visitor should find himself in an entrance hall faced by the inquiry desk, in a small outpatient department by the reception counter.

The entrance lobby must connect with public facilities. Entrance doors should be double doors with a width of 1.50 m. Floor covering must be slip free. Hand rails ought to be provided.

Wheelchairs should be readily available near the entrance for anyone requiring them for the duration of the visit. A wheelchair requires the space of 1.0 m^2.

A tea and refreshment bar or cafeteria should be provided in larger out-patient departments as well as at least one easily accessible public telephone box.

A space of about 10 m^2 adjacent to the entrance may be required for those patients waiting for ambulances or other transports.

A *store for about 12 prams*, — not less than 12 m^2 — is required.

614

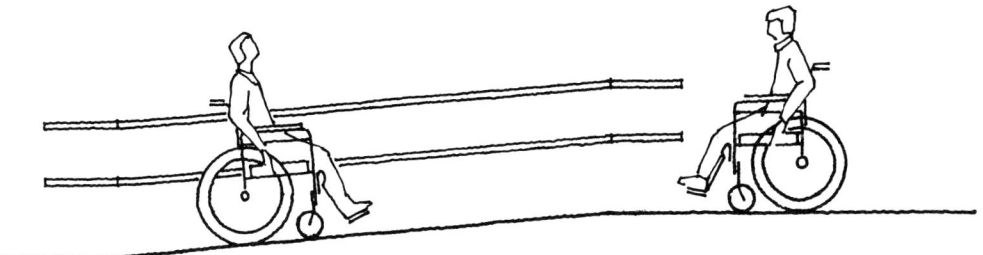

Ramps require double handrails. In the US a landing is required every 9 m, in Sweden every 6 m. For two meeting wheel chairs 1.7 m is needed.

Inquiry desk, reception stations

The workload at the inquiry desk, which should be given a prominent position, includes usually most of the following:

> receiving patients with appointments, and directing them to reception stations
>
> helping patients to complete forms
>
> explaining the implications of advice just received by confused patients and providing instructions to them
>
> making telephone appointments, unless a special telephone room is available
>
> receiving unbooked callers and making appointments for them
>
> supervising the entrance areas.

If the inquiry desk is part of a general hospital, the workload may include even the admitting service.

The needs of privacy and dignity of the patient must be recognized. Privacy implies also that the patient has control over the information about himself; he may want nobody except his doctors to know the nature of his illness.

The height of the counter should be adapted to the needs of wheel-chair patients.

In the immediate contiguity to the entrance lobby social service and cashier facilities should be provided. In these facilities confidential information is handled, both across the counter and on the receptionist's telephone. Callers should not have to talk loudly. External noise must be excluded.

615

The *receptionists* have to be located close to the particular medical team's accommodation. Each reception station should be distinct and separate.

The main activities in a reception station are:

receiving booked patients and directing them to subwaiting areas

helping patients to fill forms

producing out-patient identity cards

calling patients to consulting rooms

explaining the implications of advice just received by confused patients

supplying forms, letters to other health care facilities, reports to referring doctors

making appointments for further clinical sessions.

The amount of time spent by the receptionists on a patient varies mostly between 2 and 10 minutes. The activities may be partly confidential even embarrassing, and therefore all of them should be handled out of sight and hearing of other patients.

There may be good reasons for a patient not wanting his identity broadcast. In principle patients should not have to meet more of their acquaintances than unavoidable, and should have the opting of being addressed by number only.

Measures to meet this need involve the design of reception and waiting areas, of call systems and records filing systems.

To ensure privacy of discussion between patients and the reception staff it is desirable to subdivide the counter into individual positions.

Each receptionist requires 1.2 m length of counter with drawers, and shelving space. The counter should either be placed so that the individual positions are staggered or some screening provided to give privacy. The counter should be lowered to allow for sitting position for both staff and patient.

An area of 6 m^2 is the minimum working space for each receptionist. This area includes a circulation space behind the counter.

The reception areas should have direct communication with an office and the medical records area.

The noise level at the reception counter must permit confidential face-to-face communications from patients and clear reception of telephone messages. At least one enclosed telephone in or near the reception areas is needed for confidential calls. There must be also quiet office areas for work requiring more concentration.

The temperature and ventilation of the reception areas should maintain normal comfort levels and be controllable.

In small outpatient departments not only joint *registering* and *admitting facilities* should be provided, but cashiering or discharge facilities as well.

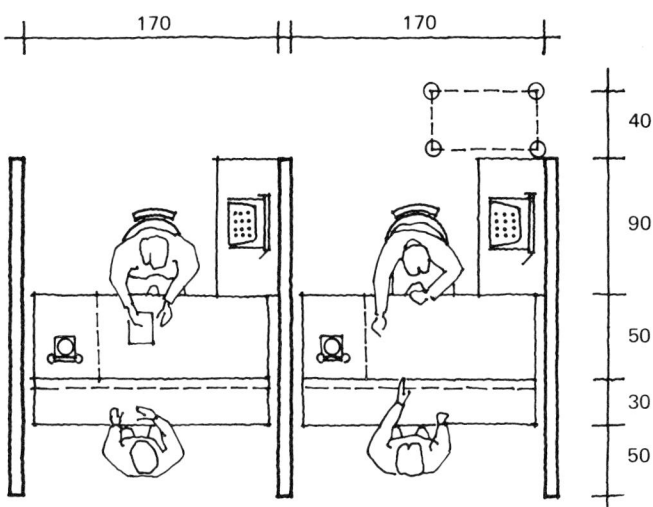

A comfortable two-receptionist station.

Waiting

Appointment systems may reduce the lines of waiting patients and the waiting areas. If no appointment system is used, the area required for waiting is about twice as great that that required with an appointment system.

Frequently shared waiting areas have been advocated for several lines of persons ready for the various consulting suites in simultaneous use. These lines may be differentiated by using colour schemes or distinct labelling of the chairs. Up to six consulting suites running individual type sessions — roughly 30 waiting patients — can share a single waiting area[2].

The patient calling system has to identify both the person and the room he is to go to. If the receptionist is to call in person, there is a limit to the distance across which she can be heard, even if silence on the waiting patients is enforced.

Some patients — as already indicated — prefer not to be identified by name to all their fellow patients. Instead, the patients could be given a number.

The walking distance from the shared waiting area to the consulting suites should be short, clearly marked, and unambiguous. The patient routes should not cross exclusive staff routes.

2   Cammock Ruth M: Health Centre Reception, Waiting and Patient Call. Her Majesty's Stationery Office. London 1973, p 27.

The shared waiting area is determined by adding to a basic size of about 7 m² for each participating doctor — internal medicine, ophthalmology, general practitioner, gynaecology, otorhinolaryngology — about 5 m². For surgery, orthopaedics and dermatology about 7 m², and for psychiatry 3 m² per doctor should be added.

In psychiatric consulting sections a special waiting room of a size of about 8 m² may be needed for emotionally disturbed patients.

The extra spatial needs of handicapped patients and accompanying relatives or friends should be observed.

Waiting area should be screened, visually and acoustically, from areas used for any other activities. The furniture grouping must relate to the type of call system. Informal furniture arrangement under the patients' control is desirable, but if visual signals are used this is not possible.

Some means of passing the time should be offered. Visual distractions need not to be elaborate. A view of movements in the outside world is a seldom exploited, but readily available and cheap distraction. The illumination must be sufficient also for elderly to read a book or magazine.

The advantages of a shared single area waiting have been assumed to include economy of space, ease of patient supervision, and maximum flexibility in use as peak loads of one consulting suite could spill over into the areas of a less hard-pressed suite.

As the user characteristics vary so much provision of more than one waiting area in a health centre seems to be more desirable than a shared waiting area. Pipeline clinic patients and participants to health education classes should not be accommodated in shared single area waiting. *Subwaiting* is essential. The term subwaiting or forward waiting is used when a patient leaves the main waiting area to a waiting space near his particular consultant's room until he can be received.

It is highly recommendable to provide a special waiting space for children. A crèche or play room for small children is desirable. Paediatric consulting requires segregated waiting for diagnosed or suspected infected patients. Also otorhinolaryngological and general medicine consulting units may require waiting rooms for infected patients.

An area of about 20 m² is required for a paediatrician acting. For each additional paediatrician 8 m² is needed.

A WC and a washbasin are needed as well as a room of about 4 m² for baby care.

Toilets

There must be an unobstrusive access to toilets.

The approximate provision is to allow a ratio of one WC and lavatory basin for every 20 patients attending a session.

Toilets must be close to waiting areas and all examination rooms, especially gynaecology, obstetrics, proctology, and radiology rooms.

At sessions like some contraceptive consultation, the female patients have to present themselves for examination with an empty bladder.

Generally, the patient and staff toilets are separated. Separation by sex is not considered necessary, if the single vestibule toilet system is adapted.

Toilet facilities, and the like must be designed with the comfort and convenience of the patient in mind.

Consultation rooms, examination rooms

As consultation and examination suites must allow for multi-functionality of use, some standardization of consulting and examination rooms has to be adopted. Tailored units should be provided only in exceptional circumstances e g for ent and eye examination.

In individual consultation rooms the patient is alone with his professional helper to explain his problem and receive advice, examination or treatment. He must not be overlooked or overheard by anyone else. On some occasions a third person is present, e g the mother of a child patient, a nurse during the gynaecological examination.

A consultation room of about 12 m^2 has proved adequate for most activities performed within the room. For developmental examination of children an area of about 14 m^2 is recommended. Every consultation room should have a door to the corridor.

A consultation room should be equipped with

a desk, 1.3 by 0.75 m, 0.8 high
a swivel chair for consultant
two chairs for visitors
about 4 m of bookshelves
an X ray viewing screen
a dictaphone
a desk telephone

Each combined consultation-examination room should have additionally an examination couch, a trolley for instruments, a washbasin, a soap dispenser, a paper towel dispenser and a container for used towels. The patient's undressing and dressing facility including clothes hooks and a mirror has to be screened off by a curtain.

For *examination only* a room of about 8 m² has proved adequate. The basic equipment would include

> a mirror
> clothes hooks
> curtains for the changing cubicle*
> an examination couch 1.9 by 1.6 m, 0.75 m high
> steps for examination couch
> an adjustable lamp over couch
> an instrument trolley 0.75 by 0.45 m, 0.85 m high
> scales
> an upright chair
> a writing pulpet 0.5 by 0.3 m
> an X ray viewing screen
> a washbasin
> a soap dispenser
> a paper towel dispenser
> a container for used towels

A left-handed doctor may have difficulties to use a room designed for right-hand use. The elements of an examination room have to permit a rearrangement of furniture by using loose furniture. In choosing lamps and sphygmomanometers, freestanding models or those which clip to couch are preferable to wall-fixed versions.

All examination rooms require daylight with visual privacy. Easily laundered textile curtains have been recommended.

Acoustic control is important. Penetration of external noise must be reduced to allow the use of headphones and stethoscopes. Conversation in consultation rooms must not be audible and overheard outside. The sound transmission rate should be no more than 55 decibels[4].

Local control of heating and ventilation to meet intermittently heavy demands is frequently essential.

The combination of two consultation rooms or one consultation and one examination room would be satisfactory for most practitioners. The advantage for the doc-

---

* In clinics where consultation and examination time is very short and a larger proportion of the patients than at the average clinic have to undress, changing cubicles outside the examination room may be required.

Where patients may require assistance in dressing and undressing a minimum area of 2 m² is recommended.

Provision should be made for safeguarding patients' belongings.

All patients must be enabled to make use of the clinical service without abandoning their personal dignity, therefore cubicles for undressing which can not be locked and provide no auditory privacy as well as public, partly dressed waiting with strangers should definitely be avoided.

4 Burgun J Armand: Construction Considerations for Ambulatory Care Facilities. 1976, Hospitals 50:3:79.

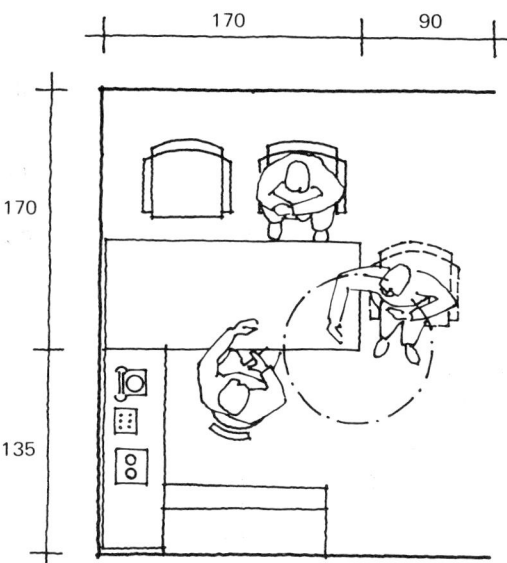

170   90

170

135

Spatial needs for a basic consultation unit.

tor in knowing that he has two rooms of his own, seems to make the provision worth while. If the consulting suites are designed in pairs this allows for a doctor-nurse team to have the use of four examination couches. Patients can in that case remain in the same room and need not move about while partially clad.

ENT and ophthalmic consultants need only one examination room per consultant. In psychiatric units one examination room can be shared by several doctors.

In paediatric examination rooms, where children are likely to be frightened, familiar toys, furniture, and decor can reassure the little patient. Coloured mobiles could be suspended over the examination table.

Each room should have one or two child-sized chairs and a small table for the child to work at[5].

When the diagnostic element has been chosen — e g two examination rooms and one consulting room — the number of diagnostic elements needed for each speciality — *N* — can be calculated:

$$N = \frac{P}{D \times H \times V}$$

P would mean the number of patient visits per year, *D* — the number of clinic days per year, *H* — the number of clinic hours per day and *V* — the number of visits per element per hour.

5   Heagarty Margaret C and Bond Deborah H: Pediatric Patients Need Diversion. 1974, Hospitals 48:9:50.

Per 100 inhabitants there are in the field of internal medicine about 35 estimated annual patient visits, in general surgery 30, in orthopaedics 15, in ENT 20, in ophthalmology 15, in dermato-venerology 5, in paediatrics 30, in gynaecology 15 and in psychiatry 10.

For a full time consultant it can be counted with 6 active consultation hours per day

The number of visits per element per hour is in the industrially developed countries as follows:

general practice	5 to 7
internal medicine	3 to 4
general surgery	7 to 8
paediatrics	3 to 5
orthopaedics	6 to 8
gynaecology	5 to 8
ophthalmology	4 to 6
ENT	6 to 8
dermatology	6 to 8
psychiatry	2 to 4

It could be assumed that when the quality of the medical service increases, the number of visits per element and per hour will be reduced.

Special diagnostic rooms

In internal medicine outpatient units with a considerable amount of cardiac patients an *ECG room* of about 20 m^2 is needed where the electro-cardiograph apparatus can be permanently housed. The room should have a couch and chair for the patient and a washbasin. A changing room and a shower for the patient are sometimes needed adjacent to the ECG room. Usually the ECG equipment is mobile and used in the examination rooms. There should be a room of about 10 m^2 for the technician for filing and temporary storing the cardiogram records, which later are kept in the central records department together with other records of the particular patient.

In *ophthalmic* outpatient units an additional examination room of 10 m^2 size is needed for perimeters, slit lamps and bjerrum, ness and less screens. Refractionists may wish to use the direct method of sight testing which will require a room with a length of 6.5 m. A room of approximately 25 m^2 would adequately serve two refractionists. An ophthalmic outpatient unit where frequent treatments are given, requires a *treatment room* for the exclusive use of the speciality.

For an *orthoptist* a room of approximately 12 m^2 equipped with desk, chairs, synoptophore test types, and less screens is required. As most of the patients attending orthoptic clinics are children, it is desirable to have a special sub-waiting space for children.

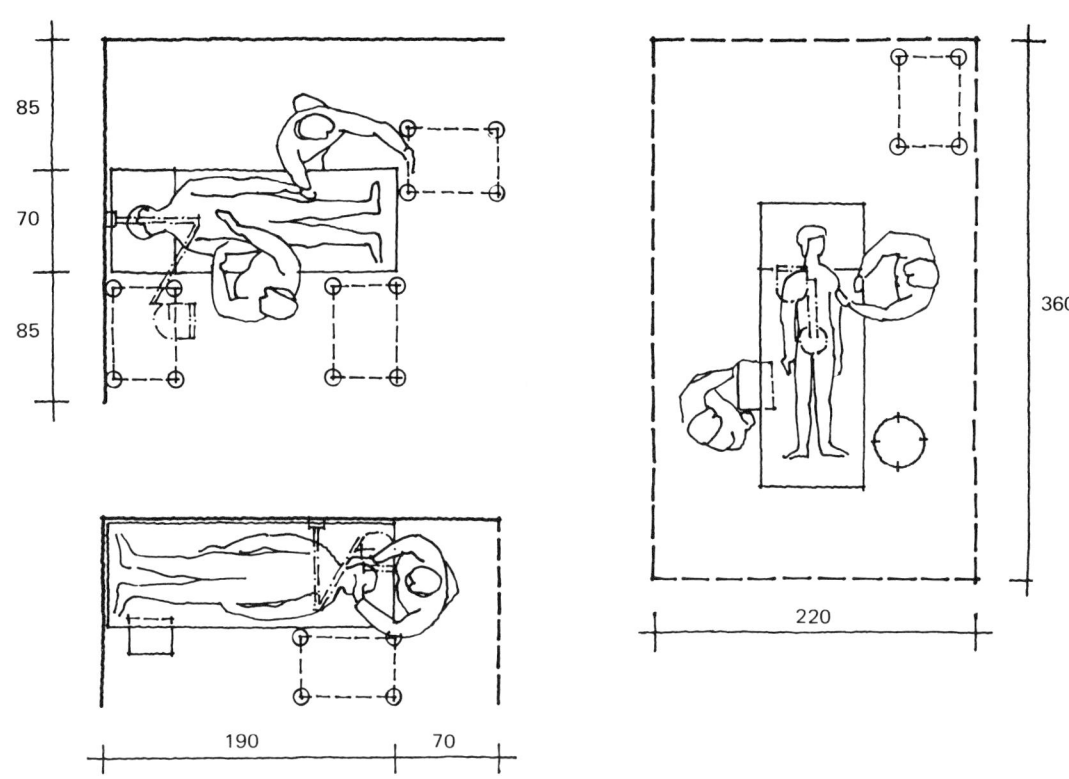

Some spatial needs in connection with assisted examinations.

In ENT outpatient units a sound insulated room of the size of about 6 m² is needed for *audiometry* tests, carried out by audiologists.

In *psychiatric* outpatient units a room of about 20 m² may be required for running the encephalogram apparatus. This room should contain a desk and chair for the technician. Adjacently there should be an examination room of about 8 m². A couch and a chair are required. A glass viewing panel should enable the technician to watch the patient under examination.

A *weighing* room, where patients can be weighed and measured without dressing, if not done in examination room, is of importance at *antenatal* clinics. For undressing a cubicle should be provided. The weighing room should have contact with waiting area and consultation and examination rooms.

For clinical chemistry purposes a *blood* and *urine testing room* is needed. Daylight is not required. General lighting of about 150 lux is recommended. The laboratory equipment includes a pair of scales and a wall desk at standing level with shelves for stationery.

623

Mostly it is relied on the central clinical chemistry laboratory. The average number of patient visits per doctor, the frequency of laboratory visits per out-patient visit and the frequency of analyses per visit in Sweden[6] was at the beginning of 70s

	Patients/ /day/doctor	Laboratory visits/doctor/visit	Laboratory analyses/ /doctor/visit
general practice	20	0.5	2.5
paediatrics	15	0.6	2.5
internal medicine	15	0.8	4.5
general surgery	40	0.2	0.8
orthopaedics	30	0.3	1.0
gynaecology	25	0.5	2.0
ophthalmology	20	0.1	0.3
ear-nose-throat	30	0.3	0.9
dermatology	30	0.3	1.5
psychiatry	10	0.2	0.6

One member of the laboratory staff can handle 9 to 11 patients an hour in a specimen and venipuncture room or cubicle.

Treatment rooms

Limited surgical treatment in shape of suture under local anaesthesia is carried out in a *surgical treatment room,* in case the outpatient department has no provision for day surgery. Patients generally remain lying for a short period or are moved to a *recovery* room.

In some cases, a *general purpose treatment* room may be needed for treatments such as orthopaedic manipulations, ENT, and some dermatological procedures which are carried out by doctors under aseptic conditions. The general purpose treatment room should be about 17 m² in size.

The equipment in a treatment room includes

curtains for an undressing cubicle
two clothes hooks
a mirror
an examination couch 1.9 by 0.6 m, 0.75 m high
steps for examination couch
an adjustable lamp over couch
oxygen and suction outlets 1 m above floor
a working top, length 1.2 m
an upright chair
an instrument trolley 0.75 by 0.45 m, 0.85 m high
containers for soiled linen and rubbish
a washbasin
a soap dispenser
a paper towel dispenser
a container for used towels

6 Öppen sjukvård — funktionskrav och resursbehov. Spri rapport 16/73, Stockholm 1973, p 26.

Clearcoloured general lighting of 120 lux, 250 lux at working area, should be provided.

For minor surgery on out-patient basis surgical day care facilities are provided.

One or more *patients' recovery rooms* may be required within an outpatient department. The minimum area for a room with two recovery couches is 8 m². Drinking water should be provided.

Clean and soiled *utility rooms* are needed.

Accommodation may be required for *dieticians, chiropodists, surgical appliance fitters* and similar staff. A general purpose consulting room is suitable for their needs but it may be preferable to provide one or more rooms of about 12 m².

Storage space for apparatus and furniture may be needed. In the chiropodist's, and surgical appliance fitter's room a washbasin is required.

Seminar room, antenatal exercise room

For groups to watch a health care demonstration, or to listen to a lecture a room of about 40 m² is needed. The seminar room is like a normal classroom, with facilities for projection and blackout. Loose furniture is preferred.

Different adjacent equipment storage(s) are needed.

Occasionally the outpatient seminar room can be used for emergency mass immunization sessions.

Location near the public entrance allows the use of these rooms out of regular outpatient hours without jeopardizing the security of the rest of the outpatient department.

For *antenatal* clinic programmes a well-ventilated and acoustically treated *exercise* room is needed. Its area ought to be large enough to make possible for a group of 12 antenatal patients in the relaxation class to lie on floor mattresses. Changing rooms and showers are needed.

This exercise facility can also be used for physiotherapeutic treatment.

Dental clinic

In all major out-patient departments a dental suite or clinic is required. Its main functions are emergency treatment for relief of pain and temporary fillings, prosthetic and orthodontic work and mouth treatment, and consultative advise to other ambulatory care sections.

For the first dental treatment room about 18 m² waiting space is needed, for each additional about 6 m². There should be toilet facilities.

Sometimes sub-waiting space is required for patients and their companions.

For pre-treatment tooth-brushing a room of 6 m² size is needed.

Some patients need access to this room after treatment.

Receptionist's space

In this room — size about 15 m² — also records are kept.

Dental treatment room — operatory

The operatory should be not less than 4.2 m wide (window wall) and at least 3.6 m deep to accommodate the equipment and to leave space for movement of staff. Although in Canada 10 m² is regarded as a minimum size for an operatory[7], 16 m² could be recommended as a fully satisfactory size for the dental treatment room[8]. It could accommodate both right-handed and left-handed dentists.

A north aspect is considered to provide the best natural light. The window head should be as near the ceiling as possible.

The general light should be about 150 lux and on working areas at least 400 lux.

The equipment of the operatory includes a dental chair, a dental unit with a mobile X ray unit attached, a cupboard for drugs, a washbasin, and a lock-up instrument cabinet. A mobile instrument cabinet is sometimes preferred.

A study has shown that the sitting height of a dental chair should be adjustable within the range of 37 to 75 cm in order to give all users an optimal working position. The front edges of the seats must be well rounded. Chairs with a seat depth of more than 35 cm must have the seat depth adjustable[9].

7   Cohen Hirsh J: The hospital dental unit, 1978, Dimensions in health service 55:7:21–23.

8   Distriktstandpolikliniker — planering, utformning. Spri råd 5.13. Stockholm 1972, p 12.

9   Arbetsstol för tandläkare och assistent. Spri rapport 10/77. Stockholm 1977, p 7.

Suction, hot and cold water are needed as well as sediment basins for plaster and wax.

The assistant should have a sink with a draining board, and a worktop with space for an instrument sterilizer.

A desk and chair are required.

Where there are two or more operatories, an X ray machine room of about 6 m² size is sometimes found. A dark room of 6 m² size is required. Special X ray needs should be satisfied by a central X ray department. Access to *panorex* and *cephalometric* units is needed.

Storage space need per dental treatment room is about 4 m². A centralized instrument sterilization and tray set up facility is sometimes preferred to the sterilizers in the operatories.

Recovery room

A recovery room can be shared between two dental treatment rooms and should have an area of about 7 m². Direct access from the dental treatment room has been found essential. Another door should be leading to the corridor.

There should be a couch, two chairs, a sink and rinsing bowls.

Work room, dental laboratory

A workroom mainly for adjusting and polishing of dentures should be equipped with a sink, worktop with fitted cupboards, and a point for an electric motor. A room of approximately 6 m² should be adequate for two operatories. If the dental clinic has several operatories, the area of the work room ought to be at least 12 m².

It is considered uneconomic to provide a dental laboratory in each dental suite and the tendency is to plan laboratories which will serve several dental departments.

If on premises, this laboratory should have a minimum area of 20 m². The size depends on the number of technicians employed. It should be equipped with a sink with special sediment basin for wax and plaster, work tops and storage cupboards.

Separate bays or rooms should be provided for plaster work and polishing work, to prevent the spreading of small particles of material. Where grinding machines are used, special suction ventilation is needed.

Dental office

A room of about 10 m² may be required as an office for the dental staff.

Outpatient clerical work and office, record stores

Although much clerical work of the outpatient department is done in consulting rooms, in the records store and at the reception counters, some *offices* — 12 m² each — are needed. They ought to be designed for natural lighting. General lighting should be about 150 lux, on working areas 250 lux. Non-institutional character can be achieved in spite of standardized furniture.

Typists require a room which should not be shared by more than two to contain the noise of their machines and to exclude distraction.

All clerical services mount up to about 8 minutes per patient visiting general practitioners and paediatric, internal medicine and psychiatric services. Surgical, orthopaedic, gynaecological and dermatological patients require about 6 minutes per visit, ophthalmological and otolaryngological patients about 4 minutes. These values are indicative for determing the number of the typists' rooms.

General equipment in the typists' offices includes

a L-shaped desk with double 0.4 by 0.5 m drawers
a filing cabinet
a book-shelf, length of shelves at least 4 m
an easy chair
upright chairs
a telephone outlet.

Nurses from the consultation units need access to an *office* of 12 m² for preparing reports and interviewing staff and relatives. Additional central offices may be required for nurses in charge of main divisions of the outpatient area.

A duty room or station similar to a general office — the size about 12 m² — may be needed as a general control point for administration. Equipment is as for typists' offices in general with following additional items

a medicine cupboard with lock-up section for habit forming drugs
a refrigerator
a lock-up keyboard and
a nurse-call board.

The records handling system should produce the records required immediately and ensure that their contents remain confidential in a for the patient apparent way. The total time for extracting the records from the files and refiling has been estimated to 3 minutes per patient visit.

According to Swedish experience[11] a doctor receiving 25 patients a day, 250 days a year needs 3.3 m length of shelving for his records.

11 Öppen sjukvård — funktionskrav och resursbehov. Spri rapport 16/73. Stockholm 1973, p 50.

Staff changing rooms, cloak rooms and toilets

Doctors and nurses ought not to hang outdoor clothes in the rooms where they attend to patients, unless the rooms are provided with cupboards.

A cupboard (0.3 by 0.55 by 1.8 m) in a cloakroom, which is not segregated by sex, is to be preferred. A lengthy mirror and at least one chair is needed.

When dimensioning the changing rooms, the supporting health care personnel is 1 to 1.5 per general practitioner, 1.5 to 2 in medical specialities, and 1.5 to 2.5 in surgical specialities. There is 0.5 to 1 receptionist per doctor.

If the employees have to change clothes for white or light blue coats or overalls the minimum space in the changing room from the cupboard to opposite wall is 1.4 and between cupboards 2.1 m. In the changing room a space of 0.6 m² is regarded as a minimum for a person.

At least one shower (1.8 m²) per 20 employees is needed.

Cloakroom will be needed also for the non-professional staff, until now, mostly women. Safe storage for coats, boots, umbrellas and shopping bags which possibly contain perishable food is needed. Each employee needs 0.25 m length of coatracks. Free space between the rack and opposite wall has to be at least 1.3 m, between two racks 1.9 m.

One or several *retirement rooms* for female staff may be needed.

When the staff toilet provision is calculated the peak loads in connection with the morning tea or coffee break and at lunchtime have to be observed. One WC per 12 persons is needed.

Separate vestibule WCs are recommended, all of them with washbasins. All WC compartments should be completely enclosed for auditory privacy and to allow separate ventilation. Mirrors, with shelves for handbags, should be outside the WC compartments and not over washbasins, as their users block the basin, and hair may block the drain.

Communal staff rooms

This room category includes the library, field work instructor's rooms, and the study. Generally they are furnished with tables and chairs, bookcases, bookshelves, etc.

These rooms provide for activities carried out by groups of staff e g whereever staff intend to discuss confidential matter, or in the context of individual or group study and investigation.

Even in a small outpatient department there should be the option of designating one *quiet* room as study and library. 1.3 m^2 per user is required.

With the development of integrated multi-professional health care teams each team may need a common room as its base. Such rooms are best grouped within the staff zone near to the records store and to the kitchen.

Catering facilities

Catering in the outpatient departments includes the preparation, serving and washing up for daily morning coffee and afternoon tea for all staff. The coffee break has to allow the staff to gather in professional rather than social groups. This is a break from seeing patients, not *for* meeting them.

The preferred pattern seems to be one of small groups succeeding each other.

The sale of cups of tea or coffee for up to about 25 patients could be a feature of the antenatal class, of child health care sessions and the classes of parenting and grandparenting.

The need for luncheon facilities has increased strongly. Also lunchtime meetings, with buffet or sandwiches and coffee are desirable. They may be possible only if they have been considered when the facility was being planned.

In the common luncheon room or cafeteria 1.2 m^2 is required per user.

About 8 m^2 is required for the smallest kitchen.

Supply

Provisions must be made within the ambulatory care department for the day to day stock of linen, blankets and disposable items.

Consulting suites and rooms for technical and auxiliary staff will require storage space for equipment, best planned in cupboards off the suites and rooms concerned.

Each 10 examination and treatment-rooms should be provided with a storage of about 9 m^2 size.

Maintenance of supplies is best carried out in the central supply facilities.

DAY CARE FACILITIES

Medical day-care has been defined as a setting where lengthy attendance — at least two hours — special equipment, rest or recovery, nursing services and the like can be conveniently scheduled for patients and staff.

The types of procedure are mainly time consuming investigations such as those which involve the collection of specimens for analysis over a period, of several hours. Patients may require some form of preparation.

The procedures may include blood transfusion and transfusion of special blood products, sigmoidoscopy, paracentesis, phlebotomy, taking of serial blood samples, and stimulation and tolerance tests[1].

In the rest and recovery section 10 beds could be regarded as a minimum unit, and about 20 a maximum. The accommodations would include two examination and treatment rooms, a day and dining space, a utility room, a kitchen, stores, a nurses' station, a janitor's closet, a telephone box, single or multiple patient rooms, female and male patient changing rooms, lavatories.

A *dermatology day care* unit for psoriasis treatment should include a therapeutic bath, whole body ultraviolet irradiation room and a room for application of tar.

There may be specialized day care facilities for *diabetic, rheumatic* and *pulmonary* patients.

The development of day care investigational and treatment facilities for *children* is in its infancy and making slow progress in spite of the obvious advantages to the child*.

Surgical day-care

In surgical day care or ambulatory surgical units, also called out-patient surgery units, in-and-out surgery, not-for-admission surgery, short stay surgery, one-day surgery, and come-and-go surgery, minor elective surgical operations and procedures are carried out on patients who are admitted and discharged on the day of operation. Required laboratory and X ray studies with the exception of preanaesthetic physical and laboratory evaluation, are performed in the 48 hours prior to admission.

Functioning hours vary, but do usually not exceed 7.00 o'clock to 20.30 o'clock in a five day week.

Operative procedures not exceeding 90 minutes in duration are best suited for out-patient anaesthesia, provided that they are associated with minimal bleeding and

---

1   Hart Peter F: Review of day care programs. 1974, Hospital Administration in Canada 16:2:43-44.

*   see also Deasy P F: The Special Needs of Children in Hospital. 1978, Irish Medical Journal 71:521–522.

only minor physiological derangement. The bulk of these operations are operations on superficial structures*.

It has been roughly estimated that 40 up to 60 per cent of operations now performed in general hospitals could be handled on out-patient basis. Particularly gynae-cological and urological procedures lend themselves to performance on outpatients. At any rate, the current variety of surgical out-patient procedures is expected to increase.

The hospitalization rates of surgical outpatient population have been reported to be between 0.5 and 7 per cent. The postoperative infections have been found to be less frequent at out-patient surgery than at inpatient surgery[2]. Until 1973 — the latest figures available — no deaths had been reported in any series of outpatient surgery[3].

A progressive increase in utilization of the ambulatory surgical unit seems not to be accompanied by a decrease in hospital admission[4].

Experience so far indicates that females outnumber the males as patients[5]. The pa-tient mix according to an American survey was about 60 per cent female and 40 per cent male. Patients aged 1 to 16 comprised 13 per cent of the total patient load; 17 to 29 years 42 per cent; 30 to 64 years 36 per cent; and patients aged 65 years and more 9 per cent of the patient load[6]. In connection with ambulatory inguinal hernia operations in Sweden, it was stated[7] that such treatment is suitable for adult patients below 65 years who have no co-existing psychic disorders or noteworthy somatic diseases.

The indications for outpatient surgery must be based on the skill of the surgeon, the complexity of the proposed operation, the conditions of the patient, the facili-ties available and the needs of the community[8]. The length of surgical procedures should not exceed 90 minutes and they should not require significant sedation or pain relief in the postoperative period[9].

*   see also Dechene Jean-Paul: Anaesthesia for ambulatory surgery. 1978, The Canadian Anaesthetists' Society Journal 25:512–515.

2   see also Georén Bengt: Postoperativa sårinfektioner vid poliklinisk och sluten vårdform i ortopedi. 1973, Läkartidningen 70:2954-2955.

3   see also Epstein Burton S, Cloakley Charles S and Levy Marie-Louise: Outpatient surgery. 1973, Hospitals 47:17:80-84.

4   see also Saltzstein Edward C, Sullivan Charles B, Patterson Elizabeth M and Hiller James A: Ambulatory Surgical Unit. 1974, Archives of Surgery 108:143-146.

5   see also Davis James E and Detmer Don E: The Ambulatory Surgical Unit. 1972, Annals of Surgery 175-857.

6   Nellis William L: Surgery in brief. 1972, Hospitals 46:13:136.

7   Andersson Åke, Larsson Åke, and Vallgren Sören: Poliklinisk operation av ljumskbråck. 1978, Läkartidningen 75:775-776.

8   see also Hill II George J: Outpatient surgery — what are the indications for it? 1975, Surgery 77:333-335.

9   Stehling Linda C and Zander Howard L: Outpatient surgery. 1974, Texas Medicine 70:61-64.

Surgical day-care units have good psychological effects for the patients, as their anxiety is alleviated. However, critics of the ambulatory surgery concept feel that a greater psychic trauma may be caused by some procedures carried out on an ambulatory basis. There is an unpleasantness for the patient when e g varicose vein ligation and stripping is done while the patient is under local anaesthesia[10].

The use of general anaesthesia for outpatients is much more feasible than ever before[11]. The number of out-patients receiving surgical treatment necessitating general anaesthesia has increased dramatically in the seventies[12].

About 3,500 anaesthesies[13] have to be performed per annum to motivate one anaesthesiologist and two anaesthesia nurses on the staff. It also means about 20 operations a day with two surgeons and two operation teams involved.

A programme of anaesthesia for outpatient surgery can be conducted without compromising patient safety. Patients are admitted about two hours preoperatively to perform the preanaesthetic physical and laboratory evaluation. To obtain these studies on the previous day is considered unnecessary. If there are symptoms of acute upper respiratory way or other infection, the operation is cancelled.

The literature related to the recovery period is confusing and contradictory[14]. Since the duration of sedative effect and physiological responses to sedation vary, no safe time can be given after which an individual can responsibly act for himself. The number of patients that exhibit slow recovery is small[15].

The duration of the return to preoperative mental status varies. After general anaesthesia about half of the patients take about five days before being able to carry out usual work[16].

A higher incidence of drowsiness, headache, nausea and dizziness occurs when the operation length exceeds 15 minutes[17]. Therefore before discharge in the afternoon, each patient must be examined by a surgeon or an anaesthesiologist. Patients should be accompanied by a responsible adult when they are permitted to leave the surgical day-care unit after sedation.

10 see also Egdahl Richard H: Ambulatory health-care delivery and the surgeon. 1973, Surgery 73:637-638.

11 Monheim Leonard M: Outpatient Procedures. in Monitoring in Anesthesia. ed by William H L Dornette. F A Davis Company. Philadelphia 1973, p 292.

12 see also Brindle G Fred and Soliman Magdi G: Anaesthetic complications in surgical out-patients. 1975, The Canadian Anaesthetists' Society Journal 22:613-619.

13 Spri rapport 16/73. Stockholm 1973, p 33.

14 Epstein Burton S: Recovery from Anaesthesia. 1975, The Journal of Anaesthesiology 43:285-287.

15 Enright A C and Pace-Florida A: Recovery from anaesthesia in outpatients: a comparison of narcotic and inhalation techniques. 1977, The Canadian Anaesthetists' Society Journal 24:618-622.

16 see also Brindle G Fred and Soliman Magdi G: Anaesthetic complications in surgical out-patients. 1975, The Canadian Anaesthetists' Society Journal 22:613-619.

17 Ogg T W: An Assessment of Postoperative Outpatient Cases. 1972, British Medical Journal 4:573-576.

A German investigation indicates that despite the high incidence of complaints — 88 per cent — of patients who in day surgery had received halothane or enflurane anaesthesia, 75 per cent of them would have chosen day-stay care and 77 per cent of them general anaesthesia again[18].

The fact that the patient leaves the surgical day care unit before being completely recovered and is away from professional observation requires that the patient's condition during and immediately following the anaesthesia and operation be satisfactory before dismissal. Monitoring gains importance in that situation as the physiologic state could be assessed to make known physiologic deviations which would prevent or retard dismissals.

Arrangements must be made for about 10 per cent of the patients[19] to spend the night after the operation under medical supervision. A collaboration with the admission unit of the hospital seems to be a good solution.

Concerning *infants* and *children*, the principal advantage of out-patient surgery is the elimination of the inconveniences connected with hospitalization.

The ratio of paediatric day patients to paediatric inpatients is frequently estimated to 1:1.

It has been found[20] that paediatric out-patient surgery can be safer, more convenient, and more economical than conventional management on inpatient basis. In the day-care units emotional trauma, fear and anxiety of the children is minimal[21]. The children are happier, less frightened, and therefore seem to recover more smoothly. The maximum emotional disturbance occurs in children under five years of age — i e the age-group accounting for 50 per cent of the cases qualifying for day surgery[22].

The parents may be anxious about the care of their child postoperatively, but much of this can be avoided[23].

18 Kreienbühl G: Subjektive Beschwerden nach Halothan- und nach Enflurananaesthesie bei ambulanten (Tagesklinik-)Patienten. 1978, Der Anaesthesist 27:533-537.

19 see also Andersson Åke, Larsson Åke, and Vallgren Sören: Poliklinisk operation av ljumskbråck. 1978, Läkartidningen 75:775-776.

20 Morse Thomas S: Pediatric Outpatient Surgery. 1972, Journal of Pediatric Surgery 7:283-286.

21 see also Gien I: Outpatient Surgery in Day Clinics. 1971, South African Medical Journal 45:1395-1397.

Cloud Daniel T, Reed Wallace A, Ford John L, Linkner Laurence M, Trump David S and Dorman George W: The Surgicenter: A Fresh Concept in Outpatient Pediatric Surgery. 1972, Journal of Pediatric Surgery 7:206-212.

22 Armitage E N, Howat J M and Long F W: A day-surgery programme for children incorporating anaesthetic out-patient clinic. 1975, The Lancet 2:21—23.

23 Atwell J D: Changing patterns in paediatric surgical care. 1978, Annals of the Royal College of Surgeons of England 60:375-383.

Most operations in children, especially those in the younger age-groups, require general anaesthesia with its attendant need for thorough preoperative assessment. It is in this respect that day surgery, as it is generally practiced, is most likely to be unsatisfactory[24].

Children selected for out-patient surgery have generally been younger than 18 months[25]. Surgeons are not in agreement on using day-care for neonates and infants under 6 months.

Although it has been felt[26] that day-care surgical units should be small and widely dispersed to be of most value to the public and to maintain a friendly and concerned atmosphere, hospital attached units are to be preferred[27] not least because of the security of the back-up facilities provided by a general hospital[28]. However, the day care surgical unit should be distinctly segregated from the rest of the hospital.

Out-patient surgery has to be provided in facilities which are designed for that purpose only and not in the operation department, although the latter alternative has been required[29].

Emergency cases are not to be handled in the surgical day-care units. However, the facilities could be used for acute care in case of a community disaster.

The approximate space requirements for an ambulatory surgical unit elements are:

a receptionist's unit	15 m^2
a waiting area for the patients	25 m^2
a waiting area for relatives and friends	25 m^2
a light refreshments service	15 m^2
patients lavatories	3 m^2
a nurses' office-desk	16 m^2
a clerical office	12 m^2

24 see also Armitage E N, Howat J M and Long F W: A day-surgery programme for children incorporating anaesthetic out-patient clinic. 1975, The Lancet 2:21-23.

25 Cloud Daniel T, Reed Wallace A, Ford John L, Linkner Laurence M, Trump David S and Dorman George W: The Surgicenter: A Fresh Concept in Outpatient Pediatric Surgery. 1972, Journal of Pediatric Surgery 7:206-212.

26 see also Davenport Harold T, Shah Chandrakant P and Robinson Geoffrey C: Day surgery for children. 1971, Canadian Medical Association Journal 105:500.

Crouch Boyden L, Ford John L and Reed Wallace A: The surgical center: concept care, cost in freestanding facility. 1971, Hospital Topics 49:12:72.

27 see also Davis James E: Ambulatory surgical care: Basic concept and review of 1,000 patients. 1973, Surgery 73:483-485.

28 see also Saltzstein Edward C, Sullivan Charles B, Pattersson Elizabeth M and Hiller James A: Ambulatory Surgical Unit. 1974, Archives of Surgery 108:143-146.

29 Victor Vogt: Operationsavdelningar förr och nu. at the symposion Planering av operationsavdelningar. ISIMA 78. Malmö, april 1978.

two changing rooms with lockers and rest cubicles	16 m^2
an anaesthetic room	15 m^2
an operation room	28 m^2
a plaster room	22 m^2
a scrub-up	6 m^2
a recovery area with bed bays *	50 m^2
an instrument room	10 m^2
stores	25 m^2
a utility room	8 m^2
a disposal room	8 m^2
a laboratory	10 m^2
an X ray apparatus room	6 m^2
two staff changing rooms	12 m^2
a staff lounge	12 m^2
a doctors' office	12 m^2
a consultation room	12 m^2
a cleaners' room	4 m^2

At least two operation rooms and one endoscopy room are needed.

The number of operation rooms R is

$$\frac{A \times T}{D \times M \times Q}$$

The number of out-patient operation rooms R depends on the number of annual operations A, the time in minutes under which the operation room is disposed per operation T, the number of annual working days D, the time in minutes during which the operation room is available M, and on the realistic usage quote Q, which varies between 0.55 to 0.8.

The frequency of operations in the main specialities per 100 out-patients is estimated to be in surgery-orthopaedics 2.5, in gynaecology 4.0, in ENT 2.0 and in ophthalmology 0.8.

The length of ambulatory operation time, which includes preparation and postoperative rearranging of the operation room is about 30 minutes for surgery-orthopaedics, 25 minutes for gynaecology, 40 minutes for ENT, and 25 minutes for ophthalmology.

---

* There should be one isolation bed to eight recovery beds (Bregande Barbara J: Modular units offer design flexibility. 1975, Hospitals 49:19:66-69).

The modern operation room suite is designed for major surgical procedures. The large rooms, conductive flooring and extensive anaesthesia equipment far exceed the requirements for same day programmes[30]. Therefore a simplification and reduction of ambulatory surgery rooms must be achieved.

30 see also Bregande Barbara: Major Issues of Construction and Design. in Ambulatory Surgical Centers. ed by Thomas R O'Donovan. Aspen Systems Corporation. Germantown, Maryland 1976, p 50.

The emergency patient is considered or considers himself to need immediate medical, surgical or psychiatric care. A high percentage of the latter category may be non-emergency cases. To avoid an overrun of the emergency department, the regular out-patient services must be well developed.

One of the most important periods affecting a patient's survival and the degree of his disability is the time immediately after the injury. Genuine emergency patients have to be examined and treated without delay. An uncomfortable and apprehensive patient is not prepared for the delays in treatment and for the impersonal attitude sometimes evident in busy emergency rooms[1]. Consequently, the emergency department must be operational 24 hours a day and is expected to deal immediately with a wide variety of complex problems.

Surgical and traumatic patients represent between 35 to 70 per cent of emergency cases. Less than 5 per cent of ED visits are with lifethreatening conditions[2].

In some areas genuine emergencies represent only one third to one half of the patients who use the emergency services.

The solution, where emergency services are physically and administratively separated from other services in a hospital set up, has been found to be the most practical.

Larger emergency departments can be divided according to specialities into five major areas: surgery, medicine, obstetrics-gynaecology, paediatrics, and psychiatry[3]. Some of them can be subdivided.

The emergency department should have ready access to the operation department, X ray, blood bank, laboratories, intensive care and treatment unit, obstetrical unit, record department and morgue.

Layout and work flow in emergency departments have been notoriously poor in the past[4]. Frequently the lack of clear planning principles has impaired the standards of performance.

Emergency departments must be designed to handle peak loads.

1   see also Beal John M: Emergency Room Physicians. 1976, The American Journal of Surgery 132:297-298.

2   Safar Peter, Benson Don M, Esposito Gerald, Grenvik Åke and Sands Patricia A: Emergency and Critical Care Medicine: Local Implementation of National Recommendations. in Public Health Aspects of Critical Care Medicine and Anaesthesiology. ed by Peter Safar. F A Davis Company. Philadelphia 1974, p 66-135.

3   see also Thal Erwin R and Shires G Tom: Emergency Assessment and Management. in Anesthesia for the Surgery of Trauma. ed by A H Giesecke Jr. F A Davis Company. Philadelphia 1976, p 8.

4   see also Beattie Alan: Layout in the accident and emergency department. An Interim Research Report. Stencil. Medical Architecture Research Unit. The Polytechnic of North London 1972.

McCabe Elizabeth: The human aspect of treatment in emergency departments and outpatient clinics. Canadian Hospital Association. — Association des Hospitaux de la Province de Quebec. 1975 (?), p 48.

There is a frequently used thumb rule for the total spatial needs[5] — a daily patient load of 100 patients requires about 1,000 m^2.

Access to emergency department

The emergency department should be easily accessible to pedestrians and vehicular traffic.

More people come to the EDs between 17 o'clock and 21 o'clock than any other time. The second time period of higher frequencies is between 21 o'clock and 1 o'clock[*].

The directional signs to the ED should be unmistakably marked and clearly visible, day and night. Weatherproof fittings and accessoires should be used in all external situations.

Differences in entrance levels should be bridged by ramps.

The ambulance port should be of drive-through type, covered and enclosed to protect the patients from the weather as they are transferred from the ambulance or car into the emergency department. There should be no backing into the doorway and no interference with following ambulances. Relatives' cars, police cars, press cars, and even ambulances must not clutter up the ambulance port.

Per 10,000 annual visits about 6 parking spaces should be provided in a nearby parking lot.

Entrances

The emergency department entrances — one for ambulant patients and the other for patients on stretchers — should be slip-proof and at grade level and separated from other entrances.

For the entrances two-way doors with glass panel at eye height and springs to keep the door in open position are recommended. A door width of 1.6 m should allow the attendants to walk on either side of a stretcher or trolley as the patient is taken in.

Porters' room

This room should be near the entrances for both non-ambulant and ambulant patients.

---

5   see also Rutherford Robert B: Organization, Design, Function and Operation of Outpatient Clinics and Emergency Rooms. in Outpatient Surgery. ed by George J Hill II. W B Saunders Company. Philadelphia, London, Toronto 1973, p 9.

*   see also Parker Susanna: Emergency room utilization at Hermann Hospital. 1978, Texas Medicine 74:10:62–70.

Stretcher, trolley, wheelchair store

A trolley, stretcher, and wheelchair store or bay should be located immediately adjacent to the entrance. Usually a wheelchair per about 800 annual visits is needed.

An additional room may be needed for cleaning the stretchers, which have become soiled.

Ambulance attendants', police, mass media room

The needs of ambulance attendants, police and mass media are served by a room of about 10 m² near the entrance hall equipped with a desk, chairs and telephones. Access to a toilet is necessary.

Waiting area for ED patients

The main function of the waiting area — one or several rooms — is to be the passageway to the patient examination and treatment area. Exceptionally this area is used as a triage area. It should be easily accessible from the entrances.

As to the feelings of embarrassment, fear and anxiety, the main cause is the presence of seriously injured persons. Therefore the seriously injured should wait — if no treatment or examination room is vacant — in separate waiting rooms.

Seriously disturbed psychotic patients should not be kept in waiting rooms together with other patients.

A sub-division of the main waiting area depends on the organization of the ED.

Clearly marked telephone booths should be located adjacent to the waiting area to secure privacy to their users.

A coffee-tea bar or vending machine is required.

Readily supervised *sub-waiting areas* will be required for those patients who have to wait for e g operation room, plaster room, laboratory and X ray reports.

Waiting area for relatives

Patients' relatives and friends* should not be allowed in the work areas of the emergency department. A comfortable, well appointed waiting room should be provided

* in the US only about 25 per cent of patients are unaccompanied, 50 per cent of patients have one companion, the rest two or more (Davis Ella H: Study shows who comes to the emergency room and what happens to them after they get there. 1973, Modern Hospital 120:6:84-87).

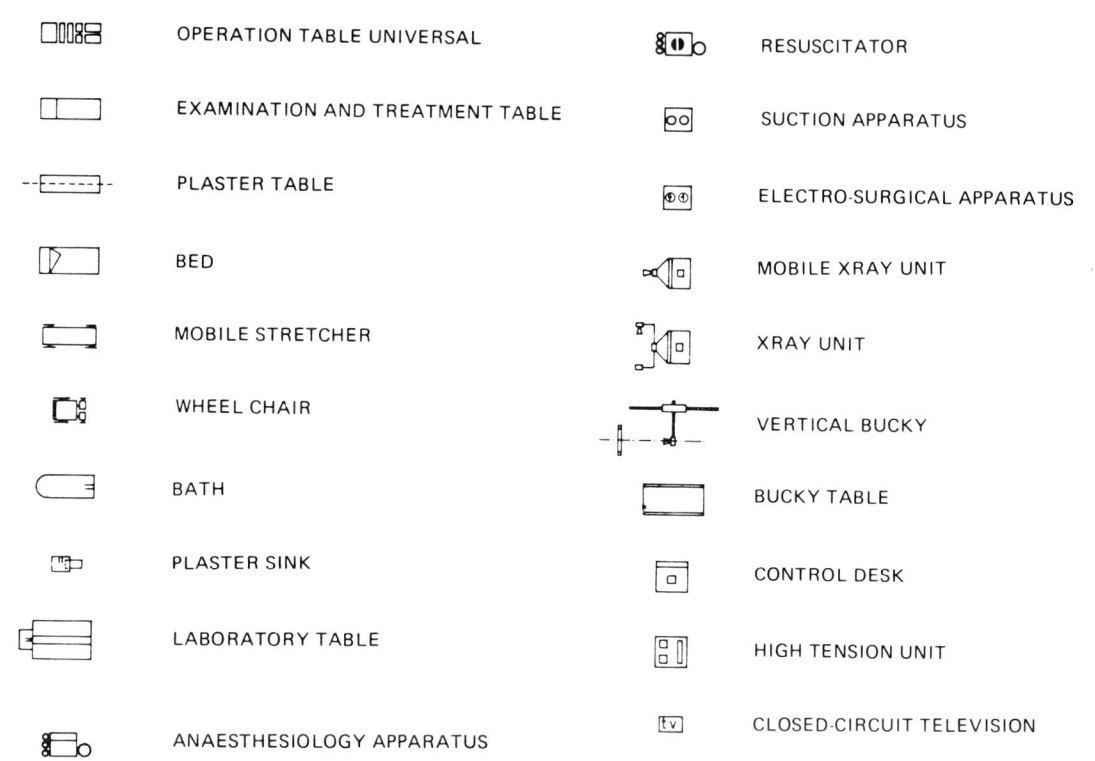

OPERATION TABLE UNIVERSAL		RESUSCITATOR	
EXAMINATION AND TREATMENT TABLE		SUCTION APPARATUS	
PLASTER TABLE		ELECTRO-SURGICAL APPARATUS	
BED		MOBILE XRAY UNIT	
MOBILE STRETCHER		XRAY UNIT	
WHEEL CHAIR		VERTICAL BUCKY	
BATH		BUCKY TABLE	
PLASTER SINK		CONTROL DESK	
LABORATORY TABLE		HIGH TENSION UNIT	
ANAESTHESIOLOGY APPARATUS		CLOSED-CIRCUIT TELEVISION	

Symbols of equipment for emergency department designed by Netherlands Hospital Planning Consultants.

for them. There should be shelves for literature describing the functions and the rules of the department as well as other well-chosen current reading material. A TV set may be an asset.

Access to a tea or coffee bar or vending machines is valuable. The relatives and/or friends who come with the patient are themselves sometimes in a state of shock. A hot drink can prove extremely benefical.

For accompanying children a separate waiting area should be provided. A pram bay of about 6 m² is needed.

Visitors' toilets

643

Clearly marked visitors' toilets should be provided near the main waiting space. They should be large enough for those who need assistance.

Administration office

Admissions, discharges, future appointments, record keeping, and care of patients' valuables are carried out in a reception and registration room of about 15 m² size, located immediately adjacent to the entrance.

This office has to be manned on a 24-hour basis. Nurses trained in emergency care serve as triage officers.

Nurses' station

The nurses' station should be adjacent to the admission office. The room should be glass enclosed above the counter level to give visual access to the emergency area.

A counter, a bulletin board with rosters of doctor-on-call and directives pertaining to the emergency department are needed. Procedure manuals, requisitions for diagnostic procedures and basic reference books should be kept here.

Multiple telephones are essential.

Because of frequent heavy traffic doors could be omitted.

Nurses' work room

The nurses' station should be adjoined by a work room. There should be counter space with cabinets below and above for the storage of drugs, intravenous fluids, and other medical materials. A refrigerator is needed for biologicals and specimens.

All cabinet and shelves must be clearly marked to show their contents. A key plan must be clearly visible at entrance to the work room.

Interview room

An interview room is required in larger emergency departments for interviewing patients' escorts or the police.

Examination and treatment area

644

The emergency examination and treatment area must be ready at all times for the reception of seriously injured or acutely ill patients.

For patients who on arrival need to be cleaned and washed before the treatment can be started, a shower-bath room with floor drains of about 13 m² size is needed.

A washbasin for head cleaning is an advantage.

The area could consist of a large room and a number of separate smaller examining and treatment rooms.

The emergency room is for the patient a particularly sensitive area in hospitals. Often this is the patient's first contact with medical care, a contact that may occur under unfavourable circumstances.

Application of oxygen mask, introduction of intravenous lines, nasogastric intubation, tracheal aspiration, or urinary bladder catheterization, are all important therapeutic measures, but they also tend to increase the emotional stress. This is because the patient does not fully understand the situation, which is seldom sufficiently explained by the medical staff[6].

The extent of examinations and treatments to be carried out in the separate rooms is determined by the policies of the individual hospitals and local circumstances.

The most important feature of this area is the urgency of diagnosis and treatment, and not the social considerations[7].

A large unobstructed well-illuminated space is mostly advantageous[8], particularly when several injured or critically ill patients are received at the same time and constant observation is required. Stretchers, beds, and equipment should be moved about easily.

There must be space around the stretchers to permit undisturbed use of portable X ray, electrocardiograph, and similar equipment.

Space for instrument tables, traction equipment and resuscitation or gas machines is needed. Several persons* may have to attend the patient and work simultaneously. Access to the patient must be possible from all sides. In other situations several seriously injured individual may need to be handled by a very small number of personnel at one time.

---

6   see also Weisz George M: Psychiatry and the management of an accident service. in Modern Perspectives in the Psychiatric Aspects of Surgery. Brunner/Mazel, Publishers. New York 1976, p 534.

7   Spencer James H: The Hospital Emergency Department. Charles C Thomas Publisher. Springfield, Ill. 1972, p 38.

8   ibid, p 37.

*   The initial management of the critically injured patient can not be performed adequately by teams of specialists. Invariably during the all-vital resuscitative phase, a unification of direction and effort goes astray and the worst aspects of committee medicine emerge. The patient and his life-threatening condition is lost amidst the conflict of speciality interests and the indecision regarding priorities (Gill William: Multiple trauma: the wind of change. 1975, Journal of the Royal College of Surgeons of Edinburgh 20:151-162).

On the wall at each stretcher space electric outlets, sphygmomanometers, oxygen, suction, running water and intercom equipment is needed. All stretchers in the emergency reception area should be alike and should conform to design mobility, durability, easy operation, and versatility. With proper type of stretchers in the emergency area the need for operation tables is greatly reduced.

The open emergency treatment room should not be smaller than 7.0 by 13.5 m. To provide at least semiprivacy the area should be partitioned in non-permanent booths.

Curtains, being at least soundproof, invite invasion of privacy. Rigid partitions and doors reduce the adaptability of the room to various procedures. Sliding doors save space but may create problems of cleaning.

The doors should be at least 1.30 m wide.

A *separate examining and treatment room* in this area should contain a portable examining stretcher, a stool, a chair, a small desk for stationery, a Mayo stand, an intravenous pole, and a gooseneck lamp. Multiple outlets, wall oxygen, wall suction and running water are needed.

The separate examining rooms should be about 3.3 by 4.5 m in size.

One room should have equipment for gynaecological examinations.

Another examination room should have a chair suitable for eye, ear, nose and throat, and dental examinations and treatment. The room should be equipped with a slit lamp and arranged for complete darkening.

Resuscitation room

The patient is to be stabilized in the resuscitation room.

In the resuscitation room immediate attention is given also to patients who need opening or cleaning of the air passages and restoring the blood volume of the body.

It has been found preferable to provide good resuscitative facilities within the emergency department rather than to refer the patient directly to the coronary intensive care unit[9].

Relatively inexpensive effective emergency resuscitation can often prevent the need for expensive intensive care.

All the equipment including ECG and medications for comprehensive cardiac care should be kept in this room so that the procedure could be immediately started. All the shelves, drawers, and cabinets should be clearly labelled.

9   see also Pentecost B L: A critical appraisal of the success of coronary care units in the United Kingdom. in Progress in Cardiology. ed by Paul N Yu and John F Goodwin. Lea & Febiger. Philadelphia 1976, p 352.

The equipment includes a treatment table or a patient's trolley, an oxygen outlet and a suction point, adjustable lamps, one of them for performing minor surgical procedures, a lock-up cupboard for respiratory equipment, an X ray viewing screen, shelves, even for liquids and drugs, a refrigerator for blood, a working top, shelves for blankets, a washbasin, a soap dispenser, a paper towel container and a container for used towels.

Easy access to IV solutions is needed.

An area of about 30 m^2 is needed.

There should be protection from electrical hazards. The resuscitation room must be connected to the emergency electrical supply system.

From resuscitation room the patient is moved either to a treatment room, or a recovery room, an intensive care unit, or transported to a nursing unit.

Operation room

In the emergency department proper only patients who do not need admission to hospital — superficial wounds, fractures, etc — and those with very serious injuries, who are critically ill and who require tracheotomy, cardiac massage, etc should be treated. Other emergency patients should be transferred to regular operation rooms in the surgical department into the hands of the surgeons on-duty, who can follow the patients up until recovery.

Operation rooms which serve emergencies and no other purposes have been suggested[10]. The emergency department operation room should be selfcontained. Operation lighting should be similar to that used in a regular operation room.

It is advisable that general anaesthesia be given only in the regular operation rooms. Since exceptions occur, it might be proper to provide the ED operation room with conductive flooring.

Wall suction and oxygen are indisposable.

If the operation room has windows, they must have obscure glass.

The operation room must be connected to the emergency electrical supply system.

Fracture room

Any emergency department with an annual number of patient visits in excess of 15,000 should have a separate fracture room. This room is primarily for the treat-

10 see also Gill William: Multiple trauma: the wind of change. 1975, Journal of the Royal College of Surgeons of Edinburgh 20:151-162.

ment of fresh, closed fractures, but may by prearrangement be employed for change of plaster.

Only a stable stretcher is needed for emergency work. If the field is widened, a fracture table and overhead and wall hooks may be required. Reduction of a fracture should be started here only if the complete procedure can be carried out under local anaesthesia.

In general, the fracture room should be equipped in the same way as the operation room. Additional items are an orthopaedic table, a traction apparatus, splints, plaster, electric cast cutters, crutches, felt, sheet wadding, dressings, a large sink equipped with a plaster trap, and wallhung X ray view boxes. There should be space for a portable X ray machine.

The fracture room may serve as a second operation room. In institutions with a small patient load, the surgery and fracture room may be physically the same unit, or one examining room may be supplied with a plaster sink etc.

Plaster room

For the treatment of some fractures and the application of plaster, a separate room is needed. The room should be provided with traction equipment and a sink.

Care of burns

In larger EDs a room of about 20 m² should be reserved for the immediate care of burn patients.

Epidemiological disease and poison-control room

Patients suspected of having an epidemiologic disease should be diagnosed in a for this purpose designated easily decontaminable room.

The room should be equipped with wall cabinets for storage of supplies.

The room for diagnosis of epidemiologic diseases is, as a rule, not used frequently. Therefore, it could be given also the function of a *poison-control* unit. A poison treatment media cabinet must be provided.

Psychiatric examination room

It is desirable to have a soundproof examination room for handling of noisy, disturbed and dangerous psychiatric emergency patients, who may require overnight observation and rest or arrangements for transfer to another facility.

Space should be provided for the presence of patient's family members. While an occasional psychiatric patient prefers to be apart from his family, more are comforted and supported by the presence of familiar people[11].

Even patients suffering from *alcoholic poison* can be accommodated and treated in this room.

To reduce the emotional shock and the implication of rejection and punishment, the room should be well lighted. Light fixture should be recessed into the walls or ceiling and protected by non-breakable material.

Inventious use of decor could make the room attractive. The use of bars must be strictly avoided[12].

The equipment should be limited to a bed or stretcher and chairs. There are suggestions to reduce the furniture to a mattress on the floor.

There should be no projections from the walls, not even a doorknob and radiator. The room should be soundproof so that other patients can not become disturbed or upset. If constant attendance is impossible, a large oneway window of unbreakable glass would simplify the observation of the patient.

The room must be well ventilated.

Toilet facilities should be adjacent the isolation room and not included in it.

The water temperature in the washbasin taps should be kept below 42°C.

Radiology unit

About one quarter of the emergency room patients have roentgenograms of some type taken, therefore a diagnostic radiological unit as a part of emergency services is considered to be essential.

Badly injured patients should be accommodated in an enclosed area so that other waiting patients are not emotionally disturbed. Attention before and after examination should be given to serious cases.

The mixing of emergency patients with other patients has usually resulted in diminution of efficiency. It is better to provide diagnostic rooms for the handling of emergency patients in reasonable proportion to their expected presence. The overflow from emergency work can be accommodated in the regular X ray rooms as the demand arises[13].

---

11 see also Worthylake Ralph D and Branch C H Hardin: The psychiatric patient in the emergency department. in The Hospital Emergency Department. James H Spencer. Charles C Thomas Publisher. Springfield. III. 1972, p 277.

12 ibid, p 278.

13 see also MacEwan Douglas W: Editorial. 1977, The Journal of The Canadian Association of Radiologists 28:94.

An emergency department diagnostic X ray unit would have two or three diagnostic rooms, a dark room, and a dry film room. The usual ancillary services include a reporting room for the radiologist, a radiographer's room, a reception and record office, store rooms, toilet facilities and waiting areas.

A larger X ray room, may be divided by partition into two or three bays, each large enough to carry out an X ray examination of a patient on a stretcher. The partition walls should not be more than 1.5 m high, so that an overhead mounted X ray tube assembly with telescopic column can be passed over and be used in each bay.

The operator must be able to see into each bay from the control cubicle.

Sometimes angiography capabilities are included[14].

Automatic processing is of greatest advantage even in cases when the number of roentgenograms taken per hour in itself might be insufficient to justify the capital outlay.

Many patients involved in motor-car accidents are found to be suffering from deep seated vascular damage caused by the seat belt. Traumatologists are now asking for immediate X ray examinations to indicate the degree of such injuries and the demands of surgery. Such studies call for highly sophisticated X ray facilities. To cater for this growing demand, the accident X ray department becomes a fairly sophisticated special procedure suite, with its attendant ancillary activities[15].

The reliability of the CT in detecting traumatic intracranial haematoma offers a solution to one of the major problems in assessing the head-injured patient. Its value demands a fresh approach to the management of patients with traumatic head injuries[16].

It is believed that computer-assisted axial tomography will eventually be used much more freely, for head injury, trauma and coma examinations in emergency department settings[17].

High-resolution ultrasonography tests should be performed in the evaluation of acute surgical emergencies. In many conditions this completely atraumatic and highly accurate procedure may spare the patient other diagnostic procedures that are time-consuming and potentially hazardous[18].

14 Bailey Judith A: Development of a Regional Trauma Center. 1978, The Nursing Clinics of North America 13:2:255-265.

15 Terry William G: Pre-planning considerations. A paper prepared for the International Symposium on the Planning of Departments of Radiology and Imaging Sciences. Lisbon, May 1978.

16 see also Galbraith Sam, Teasdale Graham and Blaiklock Christopher: Computerised tomography of acute traumatic intracranial haematoma: reliability of neurosurgeon's interpretations. 1976, British Medical Journal 2:1371-1373.

Bull James: The EMI brain scanner and its value in cerebrovascular accidents. 1978, The Chest, Heart and Stroke Journal 3:2:4-9.

17 Phillips Donald F and Lillé Kenneth: Putting the leash on 'Cat'. 1976, Hospitals 50:13:45-49.

18 Hassani Sam N and Bard Robert: Ultrasonography of Acute Surgical Emergency. 1978, New York State Journal of Medicine 78:738-741.

The ED radiology unit has to be connected to the emergency electrical system.

Clinical laboratory

Frequently there is a need for emergency laboratory tests such as blood typing and cross-matching, and identification of poison.

An emergency department laboratory staff should be capable to perform the following tests: hemaglobin, haematocrit, blood count, blood smear, Gram stain, and routine urine examination, including microscopic examination.

Microscopes, centrifuges and a Bunsen burner are needed.

Photography room

In a large ED a room of 10 m² size is reserved for photographic recording.

Observation or admission ward

In resolving cases, when the question arises whether the patient may be safely sent home or not, a ward of about 6 to 8 beds managed by emergency-area nursing personnel and with a regulary assigned nurse, is most helpful. The need of one observation or admission bed per 100 inpatient beds in the catchment area has been indicated[19].

The time a patient may stay in the observation ward should be strictly controlled. The patient may be detained overnight, but the limit for occupancy should be less than 24 hours. It is a great advantage when the observation ward can be closed for a few hours a day to ease the housekeeping procedures.

The need for an adequate storage space in the admission ward has been stressed.

The observation ward could be used as an acute treatment facility in times of mass casualities or when the patient load is exceptional.

Patients' clothes room

To safeguard the patients' clothing and valuables a room of about 6 m² size would be needed.

19 see also Rutherford Robert B: Organization — Design, Function and Operation of Outpatient Clinics and Emergency Rooms. in Outpatient Surgery. ed by George J Hill II. W B Saunders Company. Philadelphia, London, Toronto 1973, p 19.

Isolation room

When clinically indicated, privacy should be provided above all for obstetric and paediatric patients, or patients who are moribund.

A room of about 10 m² is needed.

Disaster area

A disaster can be defined as an event which produces more casualities than can be dealt with by the services immediately available. The term disaster may cover anything from a bad traffic accident and a bomb explosion to an earthquake.

In the United Kingdom most disasters have produced between 15 and 50 casualities[20]

A large — about 90 m² — well-lighted open space close the entrance with little fixed furniture and adequate storage spaces, is more useful than the ordinary emergency department in case of mass casualties[21].

The arrangement where patients enter by one entrance only and can leave by another route is frequently preferred.

There should be an easy access from the disaster area to the admission ward of the hospital to which patients can be admitted without disrupting the working of the rest of the hospital. Here the patients on stretchers are classed first according to the severity of their injuries. Triage may include the necessity for deciding which patients, though still alive, do not warrant treatment because the severity of their injuries is such that they are unlikely to survive[22]. Also for diagnostic radiology a rigid sorting of priorities has to be carried out[23]. The third triage is in arranging priorities for the operations.

The occurence of large numbers of *burns* in major disasters requires special consideration[24]. When burn casualities occur in tens and hundreds a rapid initial sorting is important.

The following patient groups are recognized:

> patients with burns less than 15 per cent surface area who can be immediately transferred to a distance

20 Moles T M: Planning for major disasters. 1977, British Journal of Anaesthesia 49:643-649.

21 see also Mackay Iain: The management of mass casualties. 1975, Dimensions in Health Service 52:2:19-20.

22 see also Irving Miles: Major disasters: hospital admission procedures. 1976, The British Journal of Surgery 63:731-734.

23 Moles T M: Planning for major disasters. 1977, British Journal of Anaesthesia 49:643-649.

patients with burns of 15 per cent or more surface area who need transfusion

patients with respiratory burns who need a tracheotomy.

For all those, who suffer from *emotional schock* but have no injuries, there should be a separate, larger room, where treatment, comfort and help could be given and documentation carried out[25].

Special areas for waiting relatives and mass media have to be provided.

Room for deceased

A room is needed for patients who are dead on arrival* or die in the ED.

Nourishment room

Patients under observation may require hot or cold fluids. A pantry of the size of about 7 m^2 would be sufficinet.

Storage

Storage space must be provided for

intravenous solutions, narcotics, and other pharmaceuticals

clean linen

instruments

plaster

larger mobile equipment such as portable X ray machines, electrocardiographs, resuscitators, orthopaedic equipment and appliances

wheelchairs and stretchers.

Life saving equipment, such as cardiac arrest trays and tracheotomy sets, should be clearly marked for instant identification.

The location of all items should be unmistakably marked and registred in an index at the nurses' station or in the emergency department manual.

The lack of storage space may seriously interfere with the efficiency of the emergency department service.

25 Rutherford William H: Traumatic Surgery. 1975, Progress in Surgery 14:121-135.

* In Sweden about 2 per cent of the emergency patients are dead on arrival.

Utility and soiled linen room

Utility room for the emptying, cleaning and storing of bed-pans should be equipped with a bedpan washer-disinfector and cupboards.

Sometimes the utility room is used for urine testing. Additional equipment includes in that case a worktop, a laboratory sink and cupboards or shelves.

In the utility room soiled instruments and containers are rinsed and soiled linen stored. The number of these rooms depends on the size of the department.

Each room should have the size of about 7 m^2. The equipment should include a worktop, shelving, a draining board, containers for disposable items, stands for soiled linen and rubbish bags, a sink, and a hand washing facility.

Cleaners' room

A bucket sink with hot and cold water, drainer and space for mechanical cleaning equipment, cleaning utensils, cleaners' cart, and housekeeping supplies are required.

About 4 m^2 are needed per unit. One unit would cover about 750 m^2 of surface to be cleaned.

Staff changing, lounge, conference room

Changing rooms for female and male staff should include lavatories, showers, and lockers for personal possessions.

There should be a retirement room.

A lounge with pantry should be found for the staff's recreation, and tea or coffee breaks.

Physicians and other ED personnel may need a neutral room, where they can confer with relatives and others concerned about patients.

A reference library — size about 8 m^2 — is desirable.

On-call rooms

Comfortable quarters for slack periods are needed for doctors and nurses on-duty.

An on-call room of about 9 m^2 should be furnished with a bed, a chair, a desk, a shelf for reference books, a telephone, a TV, closets or lockers, a toilet, and a shower.

MORTUARY

A mortuary is required so that the pathologist may investigate the causes of death and make other scientific investigations; bodies may be viewed or identified by relatives and friends, and bodies may be kept until burial can be arranged.

The status of the autopsy is the subject of much debate, and its turbulence is documented in the medical literature[1].

The mortuary should be near the pathology department and easily accessible from the wards, emergency department, and operation department.

A hearse approach, screened from the view of patients and public roads, is essential. A covered area of about 18 m^2 for vehicles should be provided at the entrance to the body store as a protection in wet weather and as a screen from adjoining areas. An exit to a subsidiary road, and nearby car parking space, are considered desirable[2].

Morgue

Bodies are kept in the refrigerated body store and examined in the post-mortem room. They usually remain in the mortuary for a very limited time. The period is longer if complicated investigations have to be carried out or if the next-of-kin are difficult to trace.

The number of refrigerated places needed in the *body store* will depend on the number of deaths per day, with some allowance for week-end accidents, epidemics and the possibility of major accidents. As a general rule, four mortuary places for each hundred beds is satisfactory excluding any provision in the isolation section.

The bodies are brought to the morgue on stretchers and left on stretchers in the cold room until the autopsy is performed. Then the stretcher is wheeled into the autopsy room and the body slid off the stretcher onto the autopsy table.

A depth of about 5.4 m for the body store is usually satisfactory[3]. A body on a loose tray or stretcher may require the space of about 3 m^2 in the cold chamber.

Space is needed in front of the cold chambers for the withdrawal of trays. Clean shrouds, drapes, towels and other linen; also toilet articles that may be required in the viewing room should be available. Additional space should be considered for decomposed bodies or for those being stored for forensic purposes at 6.5°C[4].

1 Williams Majorie J and Peery Thomas M: The Autopsy, A Beginning, Not an End. 1978, American Journal of Clinical Pathology 69:2 (supplement):215-216.

2 Mortuary & Post-mortem Room. Hospital Building Note 20. Department of Health and Social Security. Welsh Office. 1970, p 1.

3 ibid, p 4.

4 Pierson Paul S: Morgue construction guidelines. 1973, Hospitals 47:24:12.

The *refrigerating plant* should be immediately adjacent to the cold chamber. The main electrical intake and switch board may be sited here. Access for maintenance and servicing should be arranged externally so that it is unnecessary to enter the department.

When the initial temperature of the chamber, before loading, is 5.5°C the temperature of the chambers and contents should be reduced to 3.5°C in 10 hours from loading with bodies at a temperature of 37°C[5]. Thermostatic control will be required for each chamber. Facilities should be provided to enable the chambers not in use to be switched off.

A bay of at least 6 m^2 is required for the mortuary trolleys.

Autopsy area

The *post-mortem* or *autopsy room* should be either adjacent to the morbid anatomy section of the pathology department or have direct vertical communication with it.

At autopsy the organs are removed from the body and dissected. Specimens for morphological, micro-biological and chemical examinations are removed. Frequently photography is used as a means of recording the gross findings.

The dead body, whether previously infected or not, may be a source of infection. When a post-mortem examination is being made the infection risk increases by contaminated aerosols released through squeezing sponges, sawing bones and cutting tissues.

The room should have two or more post-mortem or autopsy tables.

Up to 400 beds require 2 tables[6], each additional 200 beds another table. A two-tabled room needs about 40 m^2. About 15 m^2 of space will be needed for each additional table.

There should be sufficient room for physicians, medical students and nurses to observe the autopsy[7].

The tables are of porcelain, fireclay, or stainless steel. Stainless steel is favoured.

A loose hardwood or cork dissecting board or platform will normally be wanted on each table as well as an rinsing sink incorporated at the foot. It is important to have a water hose as well as a saline wash readily available because water will hemolyze red cells and cause staining and discolouration of specimens[8].

5   Mortuary & Post-mortem Room. Hospital Building Note 20. Department of Health and Social Security. Welsh office 1970, p 7.

6   Mortuary & Post-mortem Room. Hospital Building Note 20. Department of Health and Social Security. Welsh office 1970, p 4.

7   see also Manual for laboratory planning and design. College of American Pathologists. Skokie III 1977, p 19.

8   ibid, p 18.

Individual water hoses should be supplied with water from a thermostatically controlled mixing valve. Water suction pumps should not be used. Floor service ducts should be avoided.

A cool spotlight should be available for use, for example, in removing the brain[9].

A dissection worktop will be needed for selective dissecting and the cleansing and weighing of organs. The surface of the worktop should be of impermeable material, preferably of stainless steel.

Two large sinks with hot and cold water should be adjacent to the worktop — one for clean, and one for unclean work. A flushing sluice and a washbasin are needed.

Gas could be used for a Bunsen burner in the post-mortem room; alternatively a methylated spirit burner or an electric Bunsen burner may be used[10].

There should be a writing top or wallboard for notes. A wallmounted X ray viewing box is needed.

The telephone should be arranged so that the prosector can use it, if necessary, without contaminating it. The hospital paging system should operate in the autopsy room[11].

A small sterilizer should be available[12].

A recess shelf or wall cupboard should be provided for formalin, saline and other solutions.

Instruments and equipment store should hold the reserve stock instruments, specimen containers, chemical solutions, the electric reciprocating saw etc. A glass-fronted instrument cupboard is desirable.

Post-mortem room must be kept scrupulously clean. Impermeable and easily washable floor and wall surfaces are required, and a hose point should be available. Surface pipes and conduits should be avoided.

Specimens are as a rule sent for examination to the pathology department, where also the files are kept. Sometimes it may be convenient to keep organs and body tissues for further study temporarily in the mortuary. Shelves of impervious material will be required for containers of varying sizes, and floor space or skirting high benching for formalin tanks[13]. The room must be well ventilated. About 5 m^2 will be needed.

---

9 see also Manual for laboratory planning and design. College of American Pathologists. Skokie III 1977, p 18.

10 Mortuary & Post-mortem Room. Hospital Building Note 20. Department of Health and Social Security. Welsh Office 1970, p 7.

11 Manual for laboratory planning and design. College of American Pathologists. Skokie III 1977, p 19.

12 Mortuary & Post-mortem Room. Hospital Building Note 20. Department of Health and Social Security. Welsh Office 1970, p 3.

13 ibid, p 6.

Occasionally a so called *foul room* is provided in which a temperature of 10°C is maintained for autopsy procedures involving decomposed bodies[14].

A *sluice room* of about 8 m² in size should open directly off the autopsy room. A sink and a fireclay slab will be required for the washing and disinfecting of bowls and instruments. Waterproof aprons are washed and dried here.

Space will be required for the soiled linen trolley, a small instrument steriliser, and specimens in containers awaiting removal to the laboratory. Cleaning equipment for the post-mortem room and the body store could be kept in the sluice room.

An incineration for disposal of unwanted organs etc, is useful but not essential[15].

Changing rooms are required for the pathologists and clinical staff. There should be separate lockers for personal clothes and for autopsy room gowns, aprons and boots.

A storage space for clean gowns, aprons, boots, gloves, towels is needed. One WC, one lavatory basin and a shower cubicle are needed per changing room.

A small room is needed for discarding soiled garments and boots before the pathologists return to the changing room.

A *pathologist's office* of about 12 m² size is required for dictating or writing reports. It may also be used for discussions with members of the clinical staff.

For *attendants,* who will attend on staff bringing visitors to the mortuary, arrange the viewing room and assist in the autopsy room, a room of about 10 m² size is needed. The attendants' room should be readily accessible from the visitors' waiting-room, the body store, and the autopsy room.

A writing top will be required for records of admissions and removals of bodies, viewing periods, etc. A small stationery store will be needed. A WC and washbasin will be necessary, together with a shower cubicle and a clothes cupboard.

A *cleaners' room* is for the cleaning materials for all rooms except the autopsy room and body store. A bucket sink with hot and cold water, drainer and space for mechanical cleaning equipment, cleaning utensils, etc., will be required.

Viewing and religious service

Visitors will wait in a waiting-room of 12 to 15 m² size before going into the viewing room. It should be pleasantly furnished.

A lavatory with a basin and WC is required. A drinking water point should be provided.

14 Pierson Paul S: Morgue construction guidelines. 1973, Hospitals 47:24:12.

15 Manual for laboratory planning and design. College of American Pathologists. Skokie III 1977, p 19.

A viewing room of about 20 m² size is to enable bodies to be viewed by relatives and friends. The room should be attractively decorated and subdued lighting is recommended. It should be treated so that it can be used by all religions and denominations.

A draped trolley is regarded as more hygienic and practical for viewing purposes than a fixed bier[16].

A 12 m² room for the priest may be an asset.

A working space of about 15 to 18 m² size for the undertakers' assistants should be provided and could contain a table.

Isolation section

A separate isolation section of the mortuary will be needed for the storage and viewing of bodies of persons who have died from an infectious disease.

A 6 m² bier room is needed. It should be free of hangings and drapes and the finishes should be capable of being easily cleaned and disinfected. Visitors will not be allowed in this room. Therefore a viewing room must be provided between the bier room and the waiting room. The separating fixed glazed viewing window should have a curtain on the viewing side.

16 Mortuary & Post-Mortem Room. Hospital Building Note 20. Department of Health and Social Security. Welsh Office 1970, p 5.

ANIMAL FACILITIES

Animals are needed for diagnostic and research purposes. Diagnostic laboratories in support of the animal facilities may include capability for microbiology, haematology, blood and urine chemistries and preparation of histologic slides, both normal and pathologic.

Commonly used animals kept for stock do not require very special and very closely controlled conditions. Where breeding is concerned, the requirements may be more stringent. Highest requirements are adapted when germ-free animals are involved.

Whenever possible animal quarters should occupy the ground floor of a building to keep the labour required to handle incoming animals, their feed, bedding, cages and refuse to a minimum.

Animals quarters should be easily identified. They should be designed with the animal's physical comfort as a primary consideration.

All laboratory animals, unless on diet, should have daily access to feed and water.

The environmental requirements of animal accommodations vary according to the species of animals and the purpose for which they are kept.

They must be dry and easy to clean. Most of the animal attendance should be carried out from the outside. Excreta ought to be collected without disturbing the animals. Paper inserts could be used.

Good housekeeping procedures are of prime importance for limiting or preventing the exposure of personnel and experimental animals to hazardous conditions.

Animal rooms should be, to prevent cross-infection, isolated from one another. No connecting openings are allowed. Storage of infected animals in individually ventilated cages has also been recommended[1].

Animal rooms

Animal rooms should not be overcrowded. Particularly stock rooms are heavily utilized and there is a considerable heat gain from the animals. In a plastic enclosure the temperature may be 3 to 4°C higher than in the surrounding room.

Animal caging arrangements must be examined for the possibility that the cross infection between animal species will occur. This depends upon agent, animal and experimentation[3].

---

1 see also Sansone Eric B and Slein Milton W: Application of the microbiological safety experience to work with chemical carcinogens. 1976, American Industrial Hygiene Association Journal 37:711-720.

3 Manual for laboratory planning and design. College of American Pathologists. Skokie III 1977, p 17.

In the US[2] following cage spaces have been recommended:

Species	weight	floor area cm²/animal	free height in cm
mouse	up to 10 g	39	13
	10 to 15 g	52	13
	16 to 25 g	77	13
	over 25 g	97	13
rat	up to 100 g	110	18
	101 to 200 g	148	18
	201 to 300 g	187	18
	over 300 g	258	18
hamster	up to 60 g	65	15
	61 to 80 g	84	15
	81 to 100 g	103	15
	over 100 g	123	15
guinea pig	up to 250 g	277	18
	251 to 350 g	374	18
	over 350 g	652	18
rabbit*	up to 2 kg	1400	36
	2 to 4 kg	2800	36
	over 4 kg	3700	36
cat**	up to 4 kg	2800	61
	over 4 kg	3700	61

Germ-free animals are kept either in stainless or other heat resistant containers of plastic or nylon which can be sterilized in an autoclave or in plastic containers which are not heat resistant and are sterilized by ethylene oxide[4].

Food, water and bedding to be delivered to these containers must be sterile.

Doors should be about 1.15 wide and 2.15 high, and the corridors 2.2 m wide to allow easy passage.

There should be easy access to washbasins in each room. The faucet should be of screw-type to attach a hose when needed.

---

2 Guide for the Care and Use of Laboratory Animals. U.S. Department of Health, Education, and Welfare. Public Health Service. National Institutes of Health. Washington DC. 1972, p 25.

* in Sweden separate cages of at least 0.3 m² size have been recommended.

** in Sweden standardized cages (90 by 60 cm, height 70 cm) have been recommended.

4 Falkmer Sture and Waller Tage: Försöksdjurskunskap. Allmänna Förlaget. Stockholm 1972, p 37.

The floors should be nonslip, wear resistant, smooth and resistant to solvents, acids, and chemical substances present in animal urine.

Terazzo, cupric oxychloride cement, smooth hardsurfaced concrete, neoprene terrazzo, hardened rubber-base aggregates and some synthetic products have proven satisfactory. A continuous waterproof membrane may be needed[5]. In some animal rooms squared-off vitrified ceramic tiles may be used[6].

Large animals rooms should have floor drains fitted with hair traps and washdown facilities. The drainpipes should not be less than 10 cm in diameter.

There should be curved junctions between floors, walls and ceilings. Recesses and cracks should be avoided. Durable, waterproof, fire-resistant, seamless materials are most desirable. Paints and glazes should, in addition to being highly resistant to chemical solvents, cleaning agents, and scrubbing, also be highly resistant to high-pressure sprays[7].

Windows are not necessary in a facility for acute animal experiments[8]. They should be omitted where there is a risk for solar heat gain. In many cases cooling will be necessary to avoid the occurence of temperatures, which can give rise to sickness and death amongst the stock as well as uncomfortable conditions for the attendants and technicians.

Lighting should be uniformly diffused throughout the animal area.

It is important that in windowless animal facilities a time-controlled lighting system provides regular diurnal lighting cycles.

Independent control of temperature in each room, in some cases in each enclosure, should be provided. Ideally, a system should permit individual adjustments within $\pm 1^{\circ}C$ for any temperature within a range of 18° to $29^{\circ}C$ and the relative humidity should be maintained through the year within a range of 30 to 70 per cent according to the needs of the species being maintained[9].

5   Guide for the Care and Use of Laboratory Animals. U.S. Department of Health, Education, and Welfare. Public Health Service. National Institutes of Health. Washington DC 1972, p 24.

6   see also Everett K and Hughes D: A Guide to Laboratory Design. Butterworths. London and Boston 1975, p 14.

7   Guide for the Care and Use of Laboratory Animals. U.S. Department of Health, Education, and Welfare. Public Health Service. National Institutes of Health. Washington DC 1972, p 23.

8   Harrell George T: Planning Medical Center Facilities. The Pennsylvania State University Press. University Park and London 1974, p 81.

9   Guide for the Care and Use of Laboratory Animals. U.S. Department of Health, Education, and Welfare. Public Health Service. National Institutes of Health. Washington DC 1972, p 37.

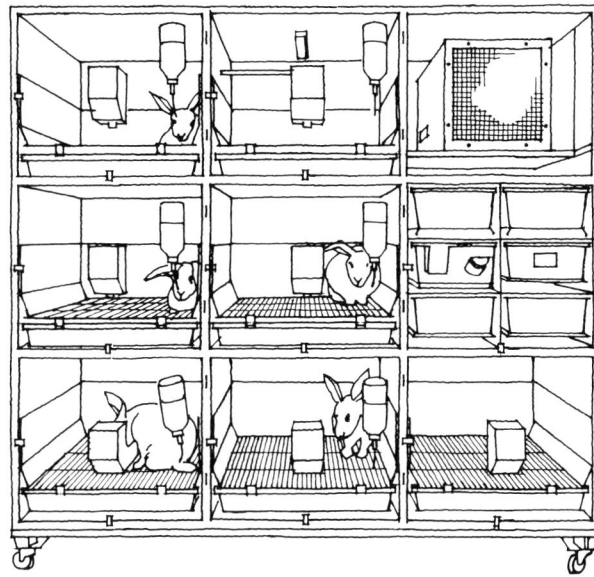

GETINGE environmental control cage rack for normal, infected, or quarantine laboratory animals.

The climatological needs of some species are:
mice — 12°C[10], rats — 21° to 23°C and 50 to 60 per cent relative humidity[11], hamsters — max 23°C[12], guinea pigs — min 16°C and 40 to 60 per cent humidity[13], rabbits — 16° to 20°C and 40 to 60 per cent humidity[14], and cats — about 20°C[15].

About 15 to 20 changes of air per hour have been required[16]. Recirculation of air is not adviseable[17].

Air from the intake to germfree animal area must be sterilized.

Infected animals kept for laboratory use may be a source of airborne contamination, frequently of the Gram-negative microorganisms[18]. Therefore the infected animal room should be under negative air pressure. An instrument measuring the ventilation pressure condition inside the infected animal room should be located on the clean side of the access door to enable staff to check the system without entering the room.

---

10 Falkmer Sture and Waller Tage: Försöksdjurskunskap. Allmänna Förlaget. Stockholm 1972, p 70.

11 ibid, p 48

12 ibid, p 91

13 ibid, p 103

14 ibid, p 129

15 ibid, p 167

16 see also Lokaler för försöksdjur. Byggnadsstyrelsen. KBS-Rapport 34 Stockholm 1969, p 59.

Harrell George T: Planning Medical Center Facilities. The Pennsylvania State University Press. University Park and London 1974, p 81.

17 Manual for laboratory planning and design. College of American Pathologists. Skokie III 1977, p 17.

18 Infection Control in the Hospital. American Hospital Association. Chicago 1974, p 79.

Access to the infected animal suite should be through an airlock lobby.

In order to control cross-infections, the rooms should be arranged — as far as possible — on a clean-soiled cycle with no retrograde traffic[19].

Where rooms are pressurized there is a possibility of unwelcome diffusion of animal room odours to other areas.

Emergency power for light and ventilation in the event of a power failure is necessary

Background and animal-care operational noises may be an environmental factor in the control of animal experiments when they exceed 40 dB[20] and should be considered in the design of animal facilities.

Working area

A room with *diagnostic X ray* machine, fluoroscope and film developer should be provided as well as an *operation unit* with movable animal operation table when large animals are involved[21].

There should be facilities for feed and bedding *supplies.* Refrigerated storage is needed for perishable items such as fresh vegetables and meat. Food storage areas should be physically separated from refuse areas.

Before re-use cages are decontaminated, disinfected, or sterilized. The equipment used to house infected animals should be steam sterilized. Provision should be made for a separate room for *cage washing and sterilization.*

Cage cleaning is commonly carried out by a washing machine, utilizing 83°C water[22] under pressure to remove the fouling. Tunnel washers which can be loaded on the soiled side and which extend through a wall into a clean storage room have been recommended[23].

The processes of cleaning and sterilizing release heat and vapour. A good standard of ventilation is necessary in the cage washing room.

There should be a facility for minor *repairs.*

19 Harrell George T: Planning Medical Center Facilities. The Pennsylvania State University Press. University Park and London 1974, p 82.

20 Lokaler för försöksdjur. Byggnadsstyrelsen. KBS-Rapport 34. Stockholm 1969, p 61.

21 see also Harrell George T: Planning Medical Center Facilities. The Pennsylvania State University Press. University Park and London 1974, p 85.

22 Guide for the Care and Use of Laboratory Animals. US Department of Health, Education, and Welfare. Public Health Service. National Institutes of Health. Washington DC 1972, p 7.

23 Harrell George T: Planning Medical Center Facilities. The Pennsylvania State University Press. University Park and London 1974, p 83.

Dead animals

After examination and autopsy, dead animals are held in the refrigerator until incinerated.

A freezer will be needed for storage of dead animals injected with radioactive isotopes and their bedding until the radioactivity has decayed to a safe level before the animals can be autopsied and disposed of[24].

Waste disposal

Animal waste comprises primarily bedding and carcasses. Both may be infected. It is undesirable, even unsafe, to transport the waste and refuse elsewhere for disposal. Local incineration is necessary, also for dead animals.

The incinerator may also handle combustible trash. Its size and design depends on the local building codes, the largest expected cadaver, and the amount of plastics to be burned[25].

To avoid nuisance, attention must be paid to the location of incinerators, to the prevention of undue heat transmission to surrounding areas, to the provision of a satisfactory combustion air supply and to the location of the fuel outlet.

A special corridor may only be recommended to permit the removal of unprotected contaminated material for disinfection or disposal.

Staff rooms

Attendants should change clothes and shoes before entering the animal area. Provision must be made for staff *changing rooms* with lockers, showers and toilet facilities.

Attendants to germfree animals have to pass a special room after a bath, scrubbing of hands, and complete changing of clothes[26].

As smoking by personnel must be forbidden within animal rooms, a separate well ventilated area is recommended for this purpose. This room, provided with a pantry, could be used also for the staff tea or coffee breaks.

---

24 Harrell George T: Planning Medical Center Facilities. The Pennsylvania State University Press. University Park and London 1974, p 83.

25 see also Manual for laboratory planning and design. College of American Pathologists. Skokie III 1977, p 18.

26 Falkmer Sture and Waller Tage: Försöksdjurskunskap. Allmänna Förlaget. Stockholm 1972, p 39.

Administration

Facilities for administration, supervision, and direction of the animal quarters should be physically separated from the animal area.

INDEXES

Bibliographic index

About the author

Ervin Pütsep is a hospital architect, planner and advisor in private practice in Stockholm. He is a member of the Public Health Group of the International Union of Architects and a lecturer at the Nordic School of Public Health, Gothenburg.

He holds the B Arch and M Tech degrees from the Royal Institute of Technology, Stockholm and a D Tech degree from the University of Lund.

He has studied British hospitals as a British Council Fellow and North American hospitals as a World Health Organization Fellow.

Ervin Pütsep has been with the Swedish Central Board of Hospital Planning. He has been director of planning for the Karolinska Teaching Hospital, Stockholm and a member of a working party of the Royal Swedish Medical Board for hospital hygiene.

In his practice hospitals, totalling more than 7,000 beds, have been designed. They include the 1,100 bed Sundsvall hospital, the avant project for the Algiers University Medical Centre, in collaboration with SEC, and a major hospital in Iran.

Ervin Pütsep has lectured in Europe, Africa, and Asia and contributed to national and international hospital publications.

He is the author of the following books

PLANNING OF SURGICAL CENTERS
NATUR OCH KULTUR, STOCKHOLM 1969

CERRAHI MERKEZLERIN PLÂNLANMASI
MIMARLAR ODASI YAYINLARI, ISTANBUL 1971

ΜΕΛΕΤΗ ΚΑΙ ΔΙΑΜΟΡΦΩΣΗ ΧΕΙΡΟΨΓΙΚΩΝ ΚΕΝΤΡΩΝ
ΕΚΔΟΤΙΚΟΣ ΟΙΚΟΣ ΜΙΧ. ΤΡΙΑΝΤΑΦΥΛΛΟΥ ΥΙΟΙ, ΘΕΣΣΑΛΟΝΙΚΗ, 1973

PLANNING OF SURGICAL CENTRES
LLOYD-LUKE (MEDICAL BOOKS) LTD, LONDON 1973

手術センターの計画
相模書房 SAGAMI SHOBO, TOKYO 1976

The poem No one called me by name by professor
Harold Rodgers is reprinted by the courtesy of the
author and Proceedings of the Royal Society of
Medicine.

LAY OUT BY ERVIN PÜTSEP
ILLUSTRATIONS DRAWN BY KURT GÖRBLICH
JACKET BY OTTO PAJU AND ERVIN PÜTSEP
JACKET PHOTOGRAPH BY LÜFTI ÖZKÖK
PRINTED BY REPRO PRINT STOCKHOLM 1981